Also in the Variorum Collected Studies Series:

JERZY TOPOLSKI
L'Essor des grandes domaines en Europe Centrale et Orientale
Origines et conséquences économiques

JERZY KŁOCZOWSKI
La Pologne dans l'Eglise médiévale

ALAIN DUCELLIER
L'Albanie entre Byzance et Venise (Xe-XVe s.)

DIMITRI OBOLENSKY
The Byzantine Inheritance of Eastern Europe

SAMUEL H. BARON
Explorations in Muscovite History

ERIK FÜGEDI
Kings, Bishops, Nobles and Burghers in Medieval Hungary

WLADIMIR VODOFF
Princes et principautés russes, Xe-XVIIe siècles

GUSTAV ALEF
Rulers and Nobles in 15th-Century Muscovy

BRIAN PULLEN
Poverty and Charity
Europe, Italy, Venice, 1400-1700

HARRY A. MISKIMIN
Cash, Credit and Crisis in Europe, 1300-1600

VESELIN BEŠEVLIEV
Bulgarish-Byzantinische Aufsätze

ADRIAAN VERHULST
Rural and Urban Aspects of Early Medieval Northwest Europe

ANDRÉ-E. SAYOUS
Structure et évolution du capitalisme européen XVIe-XVIIe siècles

FRANK PERLIN
The Invisible City
Monetary, Administrative and Popular Infrastructures in Asia and Europe, 1500-1900

COLLECTED STUDIES SERIES

Studies on East-Central Europe 1500–1900
General Editor: Ivan T. Berend

Hungary and the European Economy in Early Modern Times

Zsigmond Pál Pach

Hungary and the European Economy in Early Modern Times

Routledge
Taylor & Francis Group
LONDON AND NEW YORK
1994

First published 1994 by Variorum, Ashgate Publishing

Published 2017 by Routledge
2 Park Square, Milton Park, Abingdon, Oxon OX14 4RN
52 Vanderbilt Avenue, New York, NY 10017

Routledge is an imprint of the Taylor & Francis Group, an informa business

British Library CIP Data
Pach, Zsigmond Pál.
Hungary and the European Economy in Early Modern Times.
(Variorum Collected Studies Series; CS 469)
I. Title II. Series
330. 943904

US Library of Congress CIP Data
Pach, Zsigmond Pál.
Hungary and the European Economy in Early Modern Times / Zsigmond Pál Pach; with Forword by Ivan T Berend.
p. cm. -- (Collected Studies Series; CS469)
Reprint articles originally published between 1960-1970.
ISBN 0-86078-462-2 (acid-free paper)
1. Hungary--Economic conditions. 2. Europe, Eastern--Economic conditions. I. Title. II. Series: Collected Studies; CS469.
HC300. 26. P33 1994 94-21507
330. 9439' 04--dc20 CIP

ISBN 13: 978-0-86078-462-3 (hbk)

COLLECTED STUDIES SERIES CS469

CONTENTS

This volume contains xii + 338 pages

PUBLISHER'S NOTE

The articles in this volume, as in all others in the Collected Studies Series, have not been given a new, continuous pagination. In order to avoid confusion, and to facilitate their use where these same studies have been referred to elsewhere, the original pagination has been maintained wherever possible.

Each article has been given a Roman number in order of appearance, as listed in the Contents. This number is repeated on each page and quoted in the index entries.

FOREWORD

Variorum begins a new series on early modern East-Central European economic and social history with this volume. What an appropriate and symbolic act to open the series with the reprint volume of Professor Paul Siegmund Pach (b. October 4th, 1919), the 'Grand Old Man' of early modern East-Central European economic history, and scholar of the highest international stature. Professor Pach was one of the founders and former president of the International Economic History Association. He is now serving as Honorary President.

As this volume convincingly illustrates, Paul Siegmund Pach was one of the pioneers of comparative studies on the role of the East-Central European region as one of the peripheries in the emerging modern world system. His research, though focused on early modern times, strongly enriches our knowledge and has added to our understanding of the region's stormy modern history, the desperate attempts at modernization in order to break from the peripheral backwardness, and the ensuing failures of modernization.

Paul Siegmund Pach, who established a chair and a school of economic history in Budapest, taught generations of Hungarian economists. The department of Economic History at the Budapest University of Economics, which he chaired for two decades, and the Institute of History at the Hungarian Academy of Sciences, which he directed for more than another two decades, played important roles in the rise of modern historiography in Hungary. His school and his students have become internationally known and recognized.

Variorum and the international scholarly community are celebrating Paul Siegmund Pach's 75th birthday with this impressive volume.

IVAN T. BEREND

UCLA
March 1994

PREFACE

Many historians were inclined to consider backwardness as a permanent feature of Eastern Europe's position compared to the West. One of the founders of modern history writing, Leopold von Ranke, believed that the Roman and German peoples in the West had undergone 'a common and homogeneous development' from the beginning, while the Slav and other peoples in the East 'exerted no influence of their own', and were only affected by 'the waves of general development which ran over them from time to time'.[1]

As a matter of fact, historiography has preserved some elements of this concept until quite recently. In the preface to their new-style presentation of general economic history, entitled *The Rise of the Western World*, D.C. North and R.P. Thomas wrote as follows: 'The affluence of Western man is a new and unique phenomenon. In the past several centuries he has broken loose from the shackles of a world bound by object poverty and recurring famine and has realized a quality of life which is made possible only by relative abundance. This book explains that unique historical achievement, the rise of the Western World'.[2] Accordingly, the authors consider the superiority of Western Europe (and North America) as given from the beginning and thus set themselves only the task of explaining the denouement of this inherent quality.

Other scholars—mainly old-style economic historians—preferred to regard the 16th and 17th centuries as the crucial period for Eastern Europe's lagging behind the West. As advance in Western Europe coincided in time and was obviously connected with the overseas discoveries and colonization, most economic historians focused their attention on these developments, on the intercontinental trade with America and the Far East, on the colonial sources of West European economic growth. 'The new overseas undertakings acted as yeast—Herbert Heaton argued in his *Economic History of Europe*—, they leavened a lot of bread in the West, but their influence did not extend to the whole of Europe'.[3] Moreover, the East European countries (which had but little access to the

[1] *L. Ranke*, Geschichten der romanischen und germanischen Völker von 1494 bis 1514, Berlin, 1824. Third edition, Leipzig, 1885, pp. V–VI, XV–XIX.

[2] *D.C. North and R.P. Thomas*, The Rise of the Western World. A New Economic History, Cambridge, 1973, p. 1.

[3] *H. Heaton*, Economic History of Europe. Revised edition, New York–Evanston, 1948, p. 229.

centres of the new Atlantic trade) also lost their role in the traditional Levantine trade with Asia. Consequently, the Eastern part of Europe failed to join in the process of economic transformation in early modern times.

In the light of recent research the above explanation needs supplementing. Some studies posed the question whether there was a *direct* connection between West European growth and East European lag in the 16th–17th centuries. It has been shown that in the age of overseas colonization and rise of *inter*continental trade, Western Europe's *intra*-continental trade with Eastern Europe—more correctly: with *East-Central Europe*[4]—did not diminish either, but considerably increased in both quantity and significance. Commercial relations *within* Europe also became a substantial factor in the emerging system of world economy. They promoted the industrial/agricultural division of labour between West and East and contributed to the restrengthening and survival of feudal conditions in the agriculture eastwards of the river Elbe for a long time. Thus, East-Central Europe itself became a *hinterland*, a periphery, a reserve in several respects for the economic growth of the West European *centre* that, at the same time, exploited overseas territories as *colonies*.

Let us add, however, right now: it would be a mistake to disregard the noticeable differences between the position of the East-Central European region and that of the overseas colonies in the framework of the nascent modern world economy. This must be stressed all the more as there occurred such interpretations of the process in question that had nearly placed a sign of equality between the two relations, and tried to define also the position of Eastern Europe by applying to it the term of *colonial* dependence (as has been done e.g. by Gunder Frank).[5] On the other hand, some scholars seem inclined to judge both relations by the same standard, and consider the East-Central European countries and the Hispano-American colonies alike as *peripheries* versus the West European centre in the 16th and 17th centuries (as has been suggested by Immanuel Wallerstein).[6] Yet, it was not only the political conditions of the long-distance trade that obviously differed in the East-Central

[4]By the term *East-Central Europe* the following countries are understood: Poland, Bohemia, Hungary and Croatia. 'East-Eastern Europe' (Russia) and South-Eastern Europe (the Turkish-occupied Balkans) were not yet integrated into the nascent modern world economy during the 16th–17th centuries; cf. *F. Braudel*, Civilisation matérielle, économie et capitalisme, XVe–XVIIIe siècle, III, Le temps du monde, Paris, 1979, pp. 380–416.

[5]*A. Gunder Frank*, L'accumulation mondiale 1500–1800, Paris, 1977, *passim*.

[6]*I. Wallerstein*, The Modern World-System. Capitalist Agriculture and the Origins of the European World-Economy in the 16th Century, New York–London, 1974, pp. 91, 100, 103; II. Mercantilism and the Consolidation of the European World-Economy 1600–1750, New York–London, 1980, pp. 131, 144, 147.

European states from the trading by force of arms in the overseas colonies, but the economic roles they played in the rise of world economy also were unlike. The difference resulted mainly from the fact that the demands and aspirations on behalf of Western Europe, the 'Western challenge' found and affected the countries of East-Central Europe not in a state of stagnancy at the end of the Middle Ages, but on the way to the gaining ground of market economy.

Thus, the 15th–17th centuries may be regarded, indeed, as a crucial period for the 'economic destiny' of the East-Central European region. The papers collected in this volume try to outline some problems of and to draw some lessons from the economic history of the region in the given period, with special respect to Hungary. We mean the territory of the medieval Kingdom of Hungary which displayed a certain unity even after the battle of Mohács (1526) and the occupation by the Turks of its capital Buda (1541), that is during the time of its partition between Habsburg, Turkish and Transylvanian rulers up to the late 17th century.

Papers I–V (Part One) are concerned with issues of the rural economy, in papers VI–XI (Part Two) issues of commercial relations have been discussed. The final writing (XII) is something like recapitulation and outlook.

All the papers (first published, for the most part, in the 1960s–1970s) have Addenda, giving some information on later research and debates.

ZSIGMOND PÁL PACH

Budapest
December 1993

ACKNOWLEDGEMENTS

I am grateful to the following publishers and institutions for their permission to reproduce the papers included in this volume: Basil Blackwell Ltd, Oxford (for paper I); Akadémiai Kiadó és Nyomda, Budapest (II, IV, V, VI, VII, IX, X, XII); Routledge and Kegan Paul, London (III); Österreichisches Staatsarchiv, Vienna (VIII); Franz Steiner Verlag Wiesbaden GmbH, Stuttgart (XI).

I

The Development of Feudal Rent in Hungary in the Fifteenth Century

I

Hungary in the fifteenth century was a country of large feudal estates (manors). Around 1440 the Barons, the sixty biggest landlords, owned, on a rough estimate, about 40 per cent of all villages; [1] even foreigners visiting Hungary were impressed by the large area of the private estates: they travelled for days on end on the domain of one and the same landlord.[2] However, the overwhelming part of the land owned by a lord was occupied and used by his dependent tenants. Since the beginning of the fourteenth century, it is true, strips belonging *ad proprium aratrum* (to the lord's own plough), i.e. demesne fields, were mentioned time and again.[3] Later, in the first decades of the fifteenth century in several manors, for instance in those of the Szentgyörgyis[4], the Kanizsais [5] and the Garais, [6] demesne farms are found around the domanial centre or among the strips of the dependent holdings[7]. Some data concerning home farms have also survived from the second half of the fifteenth century; later the low Latin term *allodium* was in current use and became, so to say,

[1] E. Molnár, *A magyar társadalom története az Árpád-kortól Mohácsig* (History of Hungarian Society from the Age of the Árpáds till the Rout at Mohács) (Budapest, 1949) p. 264.

[2] G. Wenzel, *Magyarország mezőgazdaságának története* (The History of Hungary's Agriculture) (Budapest, 1887), p. 258.

[3] *Tanulmányok a parasztság történetéhez Magyarországon a XIV. században* (Studies on the History of the Hungarian Peasantry in the Fourteenth Century), ed. Gy. Székely (Budapest, 1953), p. 103; M. Belényesy, 'A földművelés fejlődésének alapvető kérdései a XIV. században' (Fundamental Questions of the Development of the Agriculture in the Fourteenth Century), *Etnographia* (1955), p. 77.

[4] B. Ila, *A Szentgyörgyi és Bazini grófok birtokainak kialakulása* (The Formation of the Manors of Szentgyörgy and Bazin) (Budapest, 1927), pp. 13–14.

[5] *Sopron vármegye oklevéltára* (Records of the County of Sopron) (Sopron, 1891), II, 55.

[6] I. Sinkovics, *A magyar nagybirtok élete a XV. század elején* (The Life of the Hungarian Manor at the Beginning of the Fifteenth Century) (Budapest, 1933), p. 65.

[7] It also occurred that tenant holdings were added to the demesne: 'unam sessionem pro allodio . . . conservarent' (*Hazai okmánytár* (Hungarian Records) (Győr, 1866), III, 301).

generally accepted for the designation of demesne.[1] Among the ecclesiastical landlords the Pauline friars of Gönc at Telkibánya in the county of Abauj,[2] the Benedictines of Szekszárd at Földvár in the county of Baranya,[3] the chapter of Pécs in the same county at Keményfalva,[4] the convent of Óbuda at Szempte in the county of Pilis,[5] the nuns of St Margaret Island at Jenő [6] alongside the Danube and at Csaba in the county of Pilis,[7] the chapter of Esztergom between Buda and Nyék [8] had retained home farms in their own occupation. As for the lay landowners, we may mention for example the demesne fields of the family of Töttős at Asszonyfalva in the county of Bodrog [9] and at Szentlőrinctelke in the county of Fejér,[10] those of the Darócis at Daróc in the county of Bereg,[11] the Vetésis at Vetés in the county of Szatmár,[12] the Kenderesis near Szemeréd in the county of Hont,[13] the Szaláncis in the village of Jéke in the county of Szabolcs,[14] the Mátéfis at Otrokocs in the county of Gömör,[15] the Tárnokis at the village Csipcs in the county of Bodrog,[16] etc. As a matter of course, the demesne farms consisted not only of ploughlands, but also of meadows,[17]

[1] In the fifteenth century the terminology of this subject is rather varied. So, e.g. *sessio nobilitaris* (*A zichi és vásonkeői gróf Zichy-család idösb ágának okmánytára* (Records of the senior line of the Count Zichys of Zichi and Vásonkeő, subsequently referred to as *Zichy okmt.*) (Budapest, 1915), XI, 504 (1489)); *curia seu sessio nobilitaris* (*A nagykárolyi gróf Károlyi-család oklevéltára* (Records the of Count Károlyis of Nagykároly, subsequently referred to as *Károlyi oklt.*) (Budapest, 1883), II, 474 (1478)); *sessio propria* (*A sárvár-felsővidéki gróf Széchényi-család oklevéltára* (Records of the Count Széchényis of Sárvár-Felsővidék, subsequently referred to as *Széchenyi oklt.*) (Budapest, 1911, I, 545–6 (1425); *Zichy okmt.* XI, 33(1469)); *curia propria* (*Zichy okmt.* XI, 202–3 (1477)); *propria terra* (*Károlyi oklt.* II, 131 (1431); *Zichy okmt.* XI, 413 (1485)); *terra ad domum seu curiam applicata* (*Károlyi oklt.* II, 251 (1446)); *terrae arabiles ad proprium domum seu fundum pertinentes* (*Zichy okmt.* IX, 203 (1448)); sometimes only: *terra arabilis*, by indicating its size or by setting it against the tenant holdings (*Károlyi oklt.* II, 312 (1456); R. Békefi, *A pilisi apátság története. Oklevéltár* (Records of the History of the Abbey of Pilis (Pécs, 1891), I, 441 (1478); *Zichy okmt.* XI, 409 (1485)). – At that time the term *allodium* points rather to the manor-house or farm-buildings. So, e.g. *domus allodialis* (*Országos Levéltár* (National Archives, subsequently referred to as O.L.), Collection of Documents dating from before 1526 (subsequently referred to as DIG.),17,474 (1473)); *domus et curia allodialis* (*Károlyi oklt.* II, 528, 529–30 (1487)); *stabulum seu allodium* (*ibid.* II, 496 (1481)). – The demesne is designated by the following phrases: *terrae ad curiam allodialem* or *ad propriam curiam pertinentes* (*Zichy okmt.* X, 169 (1461)); *terrae arabiles circa allodium habitae* (*Pest megye történetnek okleveles emlékei* (Documentary Relics of the History of the County of Pest, subsequently referred to as *Pest m. okl.*) (Budapest, 1938), p. 209 (1455)); *praedium seu allodium cum terris et pratis* (*ibid.* p. 280 (around 1480)). – The Hungarian expression *várfölde* (boardland) figures too (e.g. *Károlyi oklt.* II, 465 (1477), O.L. Dl. 36, 996 (1492)).

[2] E. Kisbán, *A magyar pálosrend története* (History of the Order of St Paul in Hungary) (Budapest, 1938), I, 119. (At the middle of the fifteenth century.)

[3] *Zichy okmt.* X, 169 (1461).

[4] *Ibid.* X, 246 (1463).

[5] O.L. Dl. 16,518 (1467).

[6] O.L. Dl. 17,474 (1473).

[7] Békefi, *op. cit.* I, 438–9 (1477).

[8] *Pest m. okl.* pp. 187, 209, 231, 279, 289, 300, 302 (from 1462 on).

[9] *Zichy okmt.* IX, 450 (1454).

[10] *Ibid.* X, 66–67 (1459).

[11] *Ibid.* XI, 164 (1473).

[12] *Ibid.* XI, 202–203 (1477).

[13] *Károlyi oklt.* II, 465 (1477).

[14] *Zichy okmt.* XI, 409 (1485).

[15] *Ibid.* XI, 413 (1485).

[16] *Ibid.* XI, 516 (1489).

[17] E.g. *magnam quantitatem fenilis, quam semper ad curiam nostram allodialem usi fuimus* (*Zichy okmt.* X, 169 (1461)); *quoddam pratum ipsius domini* (*ibid.* XI, 255 (1479)).

sometimes vineyards [1] and gardens,[2] also fishponds,[3] and even stud-farms.[4]

However, the great number of similar cases should not mislead us, not only because they often point explicitly to the small size of the home farms,[5] but mainly because isolated instances of this kind mean only that at the places in question there was some kind of demesne. They do not throw light upon the weight and proportion of the *allodia* within the feudal manor and upon their role in the economic structure of the country. Only documents which directly reveal the economic arrangements of entire manorial estates – rather than touching indirectly on one particular village – can illuminate the real situation for us. For this purpose we can use manorial surveys (*urbaria*), manorial accounts, and some other indirect sources.

Despite the scarcity of this kind of documentary evidence in relation to the fifteenth century, the conclusions which may be drawn are fairly clear. In 1448, for example, the demesne of the estate of Szarvkő, which consisted of five villages, comprised only 12 Hungarian acres (*jugera*).[6] In 1476, on the manor of Atya (15 villages) in the county of Valkó, there was no home farm at all,[7] and about 1484 there was none on the estate of Csente (five villages) in the county of Bodrog either.[8] In the years 1470–80 *allodia* were held only in three villages of the manor of Kisvárda, which consisted of one borough (*oppidum*) and 15 villages in the county of Szabolcs.[9] The rentals of the bishopric of Eger mentioned, in 1476, only three small demesne plots, though this estate included one borough and 55 villages.[10] Out of 12 villages of the counties of Hont, Bars and Fejér only one could have been home farmed in 1486.[11] The survey dating from 1492 of the Sárvár-Kapuvár manor, which consisted of five boroughs and 34 villages, already mentioned 'boardlands', i.e. demesne strips, in relation to seven villages; on the other hand, however, it testified that in eight villages the 'boardlands' were let out to tenants, mainly for payment

[1] E.g. *vinea propria prope curiam habita* (*Széchényi oklt.* I, 546 (1425)); *vineas tam proprias, quam jobagionum suorum in promontoriis ubique habitas* (*Zichy okmt.* X, 248 (1463)).

[2] E.g. *ortum ipsius proprium fructiferum* (*Zichy okmt.* IX, 187 (1447)); *ex proprio orto penes domum habito* (*Károlyi oklt.* II, 528, 530 (1487)).

[3] E.g. *piscina sua propria, recia domini* (*Zichy okmt.* IX, 379 (1453)); *piscina ac terrae et particulae silvae ad eandem piscinam adiacentes* (*ibid.* IX, 445 (1454)).

[4] e.g. *conservatorium equaciarum suarum* (*Zichy okmt.* IX, 177 (1477)); *equaciales domini* (*ibid.* XII, 325 (1486)); *agazones domini, qui cum equis juvenibus procurant – excipere equos juvenes de medio equariciarum* (*Bakócs-codex. Adatok az egri egyházmegye történelméhez* (Codex Bakócs, Data for the History of the Episcopate of Eger), ed. Kandra Kabos (Eger, 1887), II, 407, 423 (1495)).

[5] E.g. *quattuor jugera terrarum arabilia* (*Zichy okmt.* XI, 38 (1469)); *quandam particulam terrarum ad sex jugera se extendentem* (*ibid.* XI, 632 (1483)). For the size of *jugerum* (Hungarian acre, *hold*) of the age, see page 5. Later, 1 *hold* = 1.42 English acres. Sometimes larger areas are also mentioned: 40 *jugera* of demesne (*ibid.* XI, 409 (1485)), double the extent of a virgate (K. Tagányi, *A földközösség története Magyarországon* (History of the Rural Community in Hungary, Budapest, n.d. 2nd ed.), p. 58 (1487)), etc.

[6] *Magyar Gazdaságtörténelmi Szemle* (Hungarian Economic History Review, subsequently referred to as *M.Gt.Sz.*) (1895), pp. 211–15.

[7] O.L. Dl. 36,993.

[8] *Zichy okmt.* XII, 315–19.

[9] *Ibid.* XI, 74, 85, 99; XII, 325.

[10] E.g. *Dominus Episcopus potest habere aratra duo vel tria.* The grasslands, belonging to the Bishop's demesne, were of greater importance (O.L. Dl. 37,008).

[11] *Zichy okmt.* XI, 431–2; cf. *ibid.* pp. 428–9.

in kind.[1] At the same time in the neighbouring estate of Léka, consisting of one borough and ten villages, only such 'boardlands' were mentioned as were farmed by tenants.[2]

Thus, it can be stated that in the second half of the fifteenth century the demesne fields retained in the lords' occupation were very small in proportion to the vast mass of the holdings of tenants, and the latter, besides their tenure proper (*sessio colonicalis*, i.e. yardland), shared with the lord the use of the common fields – waste, pastures, forests and fishing grounds – too.[3]

In the fifteenth century in Hungary as well as in the countries of western Europe the predominant feature of the agrarian system was the overwhelming preponderance of the dependent tenant holdings, predominantly in the form of yardlands, within the feudal estate.[4] Like the contemporary English *manor*, French *seigneurie* and German *Grundherrschaft* the Hungarian big estate was not a large-scale farm, but in the prevailing majority of cases, sometimes even entirely, a conglomerate of numerous small tenements, an organization with the function of collecting the dues and contributions of dependent tenants over an immense area, so to say, a network of feudal rents.

II

As for the various forms of rent, let us look in the first place at the labour dues (*servitium*, *labor*) which may be considered as the most simple and brutal form of feudal rent. In this respect the evidence concerning liability for predial services is of particular interest. At the beginning of the century the dependent tenants of Rácsa in the county of Tolna were compelled to till the soil, sow, harvest and gather in the crop of the landlord for two days annually for every plough.[5] At Bozók, on the estate of the Order of the Premonstratensians, the

[1] Sometimes it occurred that the yardland of the tenant was carved out of the lord's demesne (O.L. Dl. 36,992).

[2] O.L. Dl. 36,996.

[3] In section IV of this paper we shall see that in the course of the fifteenth century the landlords began to claim extra services against the use of the common fields. As yet it was not usual, though there were precedents for this too, for tenants to be prohibited to use the common forests and pastures, in such a way that these became appurtenances of the lord's demesne, e.g. *silvas nostras custodire* (*Zichy okmt.* XI, 543 (1457)); *ab usu silvarum glandinosarum inhibuissent* (*ibid.* XI, 253–4 (1463)); *custos silvarum* (*ibid.* XI, 330–1 (1483)). Cf. the terms *silva communis seu usualis* or *silva permissionalis* with *silva sub custodia deputata* or *silva custodiae tradita* (*Zichy okmt.* XI, 339–41 (1483)).

[4] On the main features of the agrarian system in western Europe in the thirteenth-fifteenth centuries see, e.g. M. M. Postan, *The economic base of medieval society* (IXe Congrès International des Sciences Historiques, Paris, 1950, I), p. 226 *et seq.*; G. Duby, *L'économie rurale et la vie des campagnes dans l'occident médiéval* (Paris, 1962), II, 581–92, 600–1, 767 *et seq.*; W. J. Ashley, *Englische Wirtschaftsgeschichte* (Leipzig, 1896), I, 25–7; G. Brodnitz, *Englische Wirtschaftsgeschichte* (Jena, 1918), I, 63, 81–2, 95–6; E. Lipson, *The Economic History of England* (9th ed. London, 1947), I, 118–21; F. R. H. Du Boulay, 'Who were Farming the English Demesnes at the End of the Middle Ages?', *Economic History Review*, 2nd ser. XVII (1965), 443–5; H. Sée, *Französische Wirtschaftsgeschichte* (Jena, 1930), I, 38–9; G. Duby, *Le grand domaine de la fin du moyen âge en France* (Première Conference Internationale d'Histoire Économique, Stockholm, 1960), pp. 335, 377; W. Wittich, *Die Grundherrschaft in Nordwestdeutschland* (Leipzig, 1896), p. 317 *et seq*; Th. Mayer, *Deutsche Wirtschaftsgeschichte des Mittelalters* (Leipzig, 1928), p. 109 *et seq.*; F. Lütge, *Deutsche Sozial- und Wirtschaftsgeschichte* (Berlin, 1952), p. 98 *et seq.*; H. Mottek, *Wirtschaftsgeschichte Deutschlands* (Berlin, 1957), I, 133 *et seq.*

[5] In addition to haymaking, gathering and conveying hay 'in due time' (Wenzel, *op. cit.* p. 289 (1403)).

virgaters had to plough in spring one Hungarian acre (*jugerum*) and in autumn two acres of the landlord's demesne.[1] In the middle of the century, in 1459, the inhabitants of the Monyorós estate of the Pauline friars were burdened with a predial service, including the cultivation of the vineyards, on two days every year.[2] In 1476, on the estate of Eger, the tenants were required to mow the bishop's meadow on one day yearly and, in some of the villages, to plough and harvest two acres (*iugera*) of the demesne.[3] All these data are, by and large, concordant since the square measure *jugerum* was originally equal to the area which could be ploughed in the course of one day with the heavy plough used in those days.[4]

Similar evidence is available from the last decades of the fifteenth century too. Around 1483 the population of Karakó was obliged to mow the grassland of the St Paul's Order in the Bakony hills and to gather in the hay.[5] In 1492, in some communities of the Sárvár-Kapuvár manor, the semi-virgaters were to plough one acre of the demesne in autumn and one in spring [6] and in 1493, in some villages of the estate of Kanizsa, which included 35 villages and three boroughs in the counties of Somogy and Zala, the tenants were required to perform the same predial service, in addition to some mowing and vineyard works.[7]

In this connexion, another type of data must also be taken into consideration. Thus, for instance, in 1465, a landowner in the county of Pozsony discharged his tenants in five villages of every kind of labour dues – ploughing, mowing gathering in, etc. – and imposed a money payment upon them.[8] About 1490, on the estate of the bishopric of Eger, the area of demesne was expanded to a certain extent and *pro nova allodiatione*, i.e. for the purpose of the new home farm, hired labour was applied instead of increasing the labour services.[9]

In our endeavour to estimate the weight of labour rent in the Hungarian rural economy of the fifteenth century the fact, however, should not be disregarded that the annual liability to plough two-three acres or to till the soil on two-three days meant, in practice, more days because in most instances the tenants were responsible for the subsequent agricultural operations too.[10] Neither can the fact be left out of consideration that, apart from ploughing, mowing and various kinds of agricultural work in the demesne fields, other sorts of labour service were also in use. So, for example, the tenants of Zalavár, exempt from all other kinds of '*servitus*', had to keep up the bridge leading to

[1] Sinkovics, *op. cit.* p. 50 (1406).
[2] O.L. Dl. 15,416.
[3] O.L. Dl. 37,008.
[4] M. Belényesi, 'A földművelés Magyarországon a XIV. században' (Agriculture in Hungary in the Fourteenth Century), *Századok* (Centuries) (1956), p. 222.
[5] O.L. Dl. 20,902.
[6] O.L. Dl. 36,992.
[7] O.L. Dl. 36,997.
[8] I. Acsády, *A magyar jobbágyság története* (History of the Hungarian Peasantry) (3rd ed. Budapest, 1948), p. 136.
[9] *Codex Bakócs*, p. 356
[10] Cf. Molnár, *op. cit.* pp. 213–14.

the monastery.[1] The inhabitants of the manor of Kisvárda in the county of Szabolcs, and those of the estate of the archbishopric of Kalocsa were required to contribute to the fortification of the castle.[2] On the estate of the bishopric of Eger some groups of the population were obliged to carry wine and timber, to work at the mill, to be on duty as night watchmen in the castle.[3] The tenants of Karakó had to convey the returns in kind of the mill to the monastery, those of the Kanizsai manors were obliged to carry out labour service in the castle. On the other hand, however, it deserves attention too that, according to the evidence of the manorial documents, the various kinds of labour dues briefly described above did not affect all the manorial tenants but only a minority of them. Thus, about 1480, the landlord of Sempte imposed an agricultural service only upon two communities of the manor, which comprised five boroughs and 16 villages.[4] About 1484, as the manorial rolls testify, not a single village of the estate Csente in the county of Bodrog was charged with labour duties.[5] In 1492 the manorial survey of Sárvár-Kapuvár recorded labour rent in 18 per cent of the communities while that of the manor of Léka[6] did not mention this kind of obligation in any of the villages,[7] etc.

Considering these and other manorial documents, it can be laid down as a fact that the importance of labour rent in general and that of predial service, the agricultural work in the demesne fields, in particular was usually very limited in Hungary in the second half of the fifteenth century. This form of feudal rent was, so to say, petering out not only in the boroughs but also in a great number of the villages.[8] Such a turn of things had, of course, a close connexion with the features of the agrarian system outlined above in Section I.

[1] *Zala vármegye oklevéltára* (Records of County Zala) (Budapest, 1890), II, 390–2. The document dates from 1413, and was confirmed in 1424 and 1474.

[2] *Zichy okmt.* XII, 256 (1458); *ibid.* X, 128 (1460); *ibid.* X, 447 (1468).

[3] On this special kind of labour service (sentry-duty) see also O.L. Dl. 15,488 (1460).

[4] O.L. Dl. 36,995.

[5] *Zichy okmt.* XII, 315–18.

[6] O.L. Dl. 36,992, 36,996.

[7] F. Graus, analysing the manorial surveys of Bohemian estates dating from the period before the Hussite movement, observed that sometimes the labour dues were omitted from these documents, though the landowner demanded extra services for special purposes. (*Dějiny venkovského lidu v Čechách v době předhusitské* (Prague, 1957), II, 322.) In his opinion, from the fact that, in relation to certain villages, the surveys do not mention any labour duty, it cannot yet be concluded undoubtedly that the tenants of the village in question did not actually perform such service; consequently, the surveys should be compared, if possible, with other manorial documents. ('Vývoj feudální rentý v Čechách v 14 a 15. stoletì', *Československý Časopis Historický* (1959), pp. 302–3.) This critical point of view may be applied also to the Hungarian sources dating from the fifteenth century. The contribution to the fortification of the castle of Kisvárda, for instance, was obviously an extra service (*Zichy okmt.* X, 447 (1468)) and it had not been recorded in the manorial surveys. At the same time, however, it should be noted that if the possibility arises of comparing various types of documentary evidence relating to one and the same estate as, for example, the rentals of the bishopric of Eger from 1476 (O.L. Dl. 37,008) with the dominial accounts from 1493 (*Codex Bakócs*, p. 345 *et seq.*), the statement made on the very limited role of the labour rent proves to be confirmed.

[8] Evidence from 1432 discloses that the tenants of the Pauline friars at Streza in County Körös were required to perform labour service on four or five days in a week. This, however, must be regarded as an exception and no kind of general conclusion for the fifteenth century may be drawn from this local custom (E. Mályusz, 'Az 1514. évi jobbágyháború okai' (Causes of the Peasant Revolt in 1514), *Társadalomtudomány* (Social Science) (1926), pp. 373–4).

III

The second form of feudal rent, i.e. *rent in kind* (produce rent), which appeared in a rich variety, was of far greater importance. In the first decades [1] and also in the second half of the century food rents and animal contributions were still in current use. These can be grouped under the *first* head of produce rents and are known as 'gifts' (*munera, muneralia*). In the overwhelming majority of the villages the household of the landlord or often that of the manorial officials were to be supplied from two to five times yearly with bread, cheese, butter, eggs, poultry, now and then with bacon, roast meat, sheep, goats and so on. In 1459, on the feast of the Holy Cross, the Pauline friars at Bodrogsziget claimed from their dependents *duas tortas seu circulos panis* (two round loaves of bread) and one chicken and at Easter one round loaf and ten eggs.[2] In 1476, on the estate of the Marótis, at Easter, six eggs and three loaves, at All Saints' Day and at Christmas three loaves of bread and one chicken were due to the officials, per virgate.[3] Around 1483, on St Mauritius Day the tenants of Karakó had to give *unam tortam et unam assaturam de carnibus*, at Christmas one loaf and, per two virgates, one capon, at Easter one loaf and seven eggs.[4] About the same time the people of Csente and the neighbouring villages contributed to the household of the landlord at Whitsuntide and at Michaelmas one chicken and at Christmas one capon as well as to the household of the officials, in some communities, two loaves of bread and four eggs, three times yearly.[5] In 1492 the inhabitants of the villages Zoltán and Nyőgér of the manor of Sárvár-Kapuvár were liable to pay per virgate at Emeric's Day one chicken and two loaves, at Christmas per virgate one capon and per quarter of a virgate two loaves of bread, at Lent jointly one quarter of butter and per quarter of a virgate one egg, at Easter jointly one capon, per quarter of a virgate one cheese, two loaves and one egg, and in addition, per quarter of a virgate yearly four chickens, one fine cheese (*formagium*), one quarter of butter and per semi-virgate one goose. The tenants of the village of Család had to supply the landlord at Christmas per semi-virgate with one chicken, one loaf of bread, a half bacon, at Easter per virgate eight eggs, one cheese, one loaf of bread and in addition annually per semi-virgate five chickens, one cheese and per virgate one goose and a quarter of butter.[6]

[1] E.g. in 1403 the tenants of Rácsa owed gifts three times a year: three loaves of bread, one cheese and ten eggs at Easter, one capon at Nicholas Day and one at Christmas, each time per virgate (Wenzel, *op. cit.* p. 289). In 1430 the inhabitants of Ógalgóc provided at Christmas and at Michaelmas *dona consueta*, and at Easter one cheese, eight eggs per virgate and three lambs jointly (Wenzel, *op. cit.* p. 285; Sinkovics, *op. cit.* p. 50). In 1438 the Easter and Christmas *munera* of the tenants of Pécsvárad consisted of ten eggs and two loaves per virgate, and 24 pigs and 42 goats jointly (J. Koller, *Historia Episcopatus Quinqueecclesiarum* (Pozsony, 1784), III, 374–5).

[2] O.L. Dl. 15,416.

[3] O.L. Dl. 36,993.

[4] O.L. Dl. 20,902.

[5] *Zichy okmt.* XII, 315–17.

[6] O.L. Dl. 36,992. The examples cited above go to show that the 'gifts' can be grouped according to whether the delivery took place per virgate (part of a virgate, per household), or jointly by the village, and whether at a fixed date or at a not precisely prescribed point of time, in the course of the year.

As for the *second* group of produce rents, even this kind of manorial service often weighed heavily on the tenants, though it was not so normal as the contribution of 'gifts'. This group of burdens included the *corn tax* to be paid in kind to the landlord for the yield of the tenant land and the *wine tax*, due from the tenants' vintage. In this respect it is noteworthy that the delivery of the ninth part of the corn and wine produce (*nona*), which was enacted by the law of 1351 (art. 6), was not in general use [1] either in the boroughs or in the villages. We come across a corn ninth, e.g., in 1438 on the estates of the abbey of Pécsvárad,[2] in 1451 in the borough of Belényes of the bishopric of Várad,[3] in 1465 at the village of Köszvényes in the county of Tolna,[4] in 1481 at Károly in the county of Szatmár,[5] in 1483 at Lippó in the county of Baranya,[6] and wine ninth, e.g., in 1453 at the vineyards of Németi of the chapter of Esztergom,[7] in 1476 in some villages of the manor of the Marótis,[8] about 1480 in two boroughs of the estate of Sempte,[9] in 1490 at Pásztó in the county of Heves,[10] in the seventies to the nineties of the century in the royal borough of Miskolc,[11] etc. Corn tax, payable in kind, figures more frequently as a fixed quantity, not in proportion to the yield, usually imposed upon the tenants per virgate, sometimes upon the community as a whole in one item, and this applies with equal force to the wine tax too. ('Butt-corn', 'butt-wine' = *cubuli*, *aconalia*.) [12] Thus, the people of Zalavár gave for each virgate one butt of cereals not only at the beginning [13] but also at the middle of the century.[14] About 1460 the tenants of the royal domain of Komárom [15] as well as the inhabitants of the manor of Bátmonostor in the county of Bodrog and those of 21 villages of the Töttős estates in Baranya delivered corn and oats in a fixed quantity and not as *nona* of the yield, if any obligation of this kind was imposed on them.[16] The population of the manor of the Marótis were required to pay, in the villages which were burdened with corn rent at all, per four tenant holdings three butts of corn and three of oats.[17] The tax on the inhabitants of Karakó came to one butt of corn,

[1] A researcher on the first decades of the fifteenth century also pointed out that 'the concept of the ninth of the law 1351 seems . . . not to have been effected in practice everywhere' (Sinkovics, *op. cit.* p. 49).
[2] Koller, *op. cit.* III, 374.
[3] Acsády, *op. cit.* p. 131.
[4] *Zichy okmt.* X, 342–3.
[5] *Károlyi oklt.* II, 495–6.
[6] *Zichy okmt.* XI, 362.
[7] *M.Gt.Sz.* (1904), p. 352.
[8] O.L. Dl. 36,993.
[9] O.L. Dl. 36,995.
[10] R. Békefi, *A pásztói apátság története, Oklevéltár* (Records for the History of the Abbey of Pásztó) (Budapest, 1898), I, 442.
[11] J. Szendrei, *Oklevéltár Miskolc város történetéhez* (Records for the History of the Borough of Miskolc) (Miskolc, 1890), pp. 105–6, 111, 125.
[12] The *cubulus* (in Hungarian *köböl*) and the *akó* are old measures of capacity of fluctuating value (from 45 to 124 litres, i.e. 9·9 – 27·3 gallons).
[13] Cf. with the levy of the tenants of Bozók amounting to one butt of oats and half a butt of rye per virgate (Sinkovics, *op. cit.* pp. 49–50 (1406)).
[14] See footnote 1, p. 6.
[15] *Zichy okmt.* X, 413–14 (1466).
[16] Corn returns were collected from 15 out of 21 villages, under the title of *acones* (*Zichy okmt.* XII, 287–9 (1469–1470)).
[17] O.L. Dl. 36,993.

one of rye and one of oats *per capita.*[1] In the seventies and eighties of the century, the corn and oats tax was levied on the estate of Sempte in a fixed quantity per village.[2] From among the five communities of the manor of Csente only two were burdened with corn rent, for one of them the tax being settled as a ninth, for the other in the form of two or three butts of corn.[3] At the beginning of the nineties the *aconalia* to be delivered for each virgate to the landlord of Sárvár-Kapuvár amounted to one butt of corn, rye or oats, while for the vineyards mostly a common 'mountain tax' (*ius montanum*) was to be paid by the whole community; *nona* was mentioned in only one of the villages but, as a matter of fact, a fixed quantity was delivered there, too.[4] In the estate of Kanizsa the ninth appears more often, though from among 39 villages only 11 were burdened with a corn ninth and just three with a wine ninth, while on the majority of the communities the tax was imposed in *cubulis* or *aconibus.*[5] In the estate of Léka the *nona* is not mentioned at all, both the corn and the wine tax being settled in fixed quantities.[6]

Thus, on the strength of the documentary evidence it can be stated that the manorial services, grouped under the *second* head of the produce rent, i.e. the corn tax, payable in kind for the arable land of the holdings, and the wine tax, payable in kind for the vintage of the tenants, including the ninth as well as the levies in fixed quantities, though frequently employed, were not in general use in fifteenth-century Hungary. They did not find such widespread acceptance as the food rents and animal contributions, pertaining to the first group of rent in kind ('gifts') and did not reach by far the importance of the *third* form of feudal rent, i.e. money rent.

IV

In the second half of the fifteenth century, in the feudal rural economy of Hungary, *money rent* played an at least equal, in a great number of places, however, an even more important role than the rent in kind. This applies, first of all, to cases where virgin soil was settled or deserted land re-occupied, i.e. to the villages of settlers (*hospites*) as well as to the so-called boroughs (*oppida*)[7] which were more densely populated settlements with a market of their own and artisans among the inhabitants. The fact that the boroughs were responsible, mainly or exclusively, for money payments, what is more for a money rent payable often not per head but in a global sum unrelated to the number of

[1] O.L. Dl. 20,902.
[2] O.L. Dl. 36,995.
[3] *Zichy okmt.* XII, 315–16.
[4] O.L. Dl. 36,992.
[5] O.L. Dl. 36,997. On the estate of the bishopric of Eger the corn ninth and wine ninth are in different proportions because from among 56 villages eight delivered *nona* of wine and only four *nona* of corn (O.L. Dl. 37,008). Cf. with the data quoted above of the manor of the Marótis and the estate of Sempte where only ninth of wine figures, but that of corn cannot be met with.
[6] O.L. Dl. 36,996.
[7] See Wenzel, *op. cit.* pp. 291–2; Acsády, *op. cit.* pp. 119–21; Sinkovics, *op. cit.* pp. 57–8; *Studies on the History of the Peasantry in Hungary in the Fourteenth Century*, p. 213 *et seq.*

the population, is strongly emphasized by Hungarian historians.[1] We want, however, to emphasize that money rents were imposed on simple villages of the general type too and were scarcely ever absent from the liabilities of a manorial tenant. The manorial surveys usually start the enumeration of services by mentioning in the first place the money payments, and a special stress is laid on them in other manorial documents too.[2] In the course of the fifteenth century the amount of money rent increased steadily and it came more and more to the fore among the various forms of feudal rent.

The money taxes exacted by the landlord under various legal and illegal titles and denominations came already in the first decades of the century, to about one florin [3] per virgate, and in some cases came close to one and a half florins.[4] However, in the second half of the century the, so to say, 'legalized' main type of money rents, i.e. the manorial *census*, which had to be paid in two to five annual instalments, not only reached but sometimes even surpassed this level.[5] We can illustrate this fact by the example among others of the estate of Kisvárda, the tenants of which were burdened about 1450 with a money tax according to their livestock. From among 23 inhabitants of one village only seven paid less than one florin, four of them paid one florin, six of them two florins, five paid three florins and one tenant even four florins.[6] In 1476, on the estate of the bishopric of Eger, not taking into account the villages which owed a global sum and those which were exempt from the regular money payments, the latter were below one florin in only nine of the villages, while in 21 villages the *census* amounted to one to one and a half florins, and in one village even to two florins *per capita*.[7] In the same year the population of ten communities [8] belonging to the domain of the Marótis had to pay yearly one and a half florins per virgate. A few years later the tenants of the Pauline

[1] Mályusz, *op. cit.* pp. 375–6; I. Szabó, 'Hanyatló jobbágyság a középkor végén' (Decline of Tenantry at the End of the Middle Ages), *Századok* (1938), pp. 42–5; Molnár, *op. cit.* pp. 229–30, 239; etc.

[2] *Károlyi oklt.* II, 336 (1461); *Zichy okmt.* XI, 197 (1477); *ibid.* XII, 287–9 (1469–1470); etc.

[3] The florin (*florenus*, in Hungarian *forint*) as a monetary unit had been introduced in Hungary by the Angevin King Charles about 1330. In the fifteenth century one golden florin = 100 silver *d.* (*denarii*, in Hungarian *dénár*).

[4] Gy. Székely, 'A huszitizmus és a magyar nép' (The Hussite Movement and the Hungarian People), *Századok* (1956), pp. 334–5.

[5] In this paper we are treating only the rents exacted by the landlord. It should be mentioned, however, that at the same time, the pecuniary obligations of the tenants were considerably increased by the State and the Church too. An extraordinary war tax of one florin has been turned into a fixed payment for the public purse (see, e.g. I. Jánossy, *A magyar jobbágyság Mátyás korában* (The Hungarian Peasantry at the Age of King Matthias) (Komárom, 1914), pp. 22–32), and the corn and wine tithe (*decima*) was often exacted in money by the Church (see, e.g. J. Holub, *Zala megye története a középkorban* (History of the County of Zala in the Middle Ages) (Pécs, 1929), I, 368–70, 419).

[6] *Zichy okmt.* IX, 340–1. This is not a striking example because in other villages of the same manor there were tenants who owed even five or six florins (*ibid.* IX, 399–402, 410–11, and XII, 218–19). It should be noted that the payment in question was termed a *census*; however, it is possible it had the sense of a *taxa extraordinaria* (cf. with footnote 6, p. 11).

[7] The value of exemption from *census* is rather problematical. The tenants of Pusztaszikszó, e.g. *non habent censum alium, nisi quis eis imponat*; those of Halásztelek *de censu nihil habent, quando vult, Dominus Episcopus imponit super eos taxam* (O.L. Dl. 37,008).

[8] These ten villages were not burdened with corn tax in kind. The villages liable to a corn tax paid only half a florin per virgate (O.L. Dl. 36,993). Consequently, a payment of one florin was substituted for the contribution in kind.

friars at Nagyvázsony were charged one florin and 77*d.*,[1] those of Csente and of the neighbouring villages one florin and 16–34*d.* per virgate.[2] A *census annualis* of one florin per virgate was often considered as a favour; such a favour was granted by King Matthias to the *oppidum* Neszmély [3] and to the communities Nagymegyer and Izsép of the royal manor of Komárom; [4] such a reduction was requested of the landlord of Kisvárda by his manorial tenants.[5]

On the other hand, it should not be disregarded that feudal landowners continued in the second half of the fifteenth century to exact 'irregular' money payments, without any legal title but purely and simply by open force. Such payments are mostly mentioned in contemporary documents as *taxa extraordinaria* or simply as *taxa*.[6] At the mid-century, for example, a landlord by name Szécsi, used violence against the 54 tenants of another lord, Csapi by name, and exacted not only a *census* but also a *taxa* of one to two and a half florins from them.[7] A few years later, the Garais squeezed out of the inhabitants of some villages held in pledge by them more than 2,000 florins *minus iuste et indebite*, that is apart from the *census ordinarius*.[8] In the eighties, the tenants of an estate of László Károlyi were assessed at an irregular tax by acts of force.[9] When János Váradi was put in possession of a part of the Töttős heritage and the Palatine admonished him not to impose any extraordinary tax on the manorial population, this warning turned out to be fully justified because, about the same time, the same landlord celebrated the seizure of a part of the manor of Kisvárda by exacting a *taxa extraordinaria et superflua* of one and a half florins from the tenants per head.[10]

Finally it should be pointed out that apart from the *census* there were also other sorts of 'regular' money payments which were registered in the manorial surveys. The latter kinds of money rent weighed particularly heavily on the tenants in the case of a relatively low *census*, i.e. if it did not reach the sum of one florin. Though the *census* imposed on the boroughs and villages of the estate of Sempte about 1480 did not exceed a half florin per head, various extra rents were added to this sum, especially for the use of the common fields; thus, the amount of the extras came close to and sometimes even surpassed the basic

[1] The tenants there paid 22*d.* at Michaelmas, half a florin at Martinmas, 33*d.* at Christmas and 22*d.* and half a florin at St George's day (O.L. Dl. 20,902).

[2] *Zichy okmt.* XII, 315–17.

[3] *Ibid.* XI, 89–90 (1471).

[4] *Ibid.* X, 413–14 (1466).

[5] '. . . . *petitioni ipsorum* . . . , *ut de cetero de singulis portis solvant per unum florenum* . . . .' (*ibid.* X, 463–4 (1468)).

[6] The *census* proper is often mentioned under the denomination *taxa* too, e.g. *taxa seu census* (J. Károly, *Fejér vármegye története. Oklevéltár* (Records of the History of the County of Fejér) (Székesfehérvár, 1899), III, 528–9 (1476)); *taxa seu terragium* (*Zichy okmt.* XII, 317 (about 1481)); *taxa ordinaria* (*Codex Bakócs*, p. 345 (1493)); *taxa* (*ibid.* p. 394 (1495)); etc. However, the term *taxa extraordinaria* denotes in each case, and often even the word *taxa* without any attribute, an additional assessment apart from the *census*.

[7] *Zichy okmt.* XII, 201–8 (1443). On the extraordinary *taxa*, in the thirties to the fifties of the century, see also E. Mályusz, 'A magyar rendi állam Hunyadi korában' (The Hungarian Estates in the Age of Hunyadi), *Századok* (1957), pp. 105–7.

[8] *Sopron vármegye oklevéltára*, II, 462 (1469).

[9] *Károlyi oklt.* II, 495 (1481).

[10] *Zichy okmt.* XI, 429, 438–9 (1486).

payment. In a small village of this estate, for instance, the global sum of the *census* of 11 tenants came to six florins and 60*d.* per year, while for the use of the wood, the meadow and the fishing ground they had to pay seven florins and 90*d.*[1] On the manor of Sárvár-Kapuvár in 1492, the census exacted from the boroughs as well as from the villages amounted to an average of about 70*d.* per semi-virgate; however, the greater part of the villages was also burdened with an extra rent of half a florin or 200*d.*, the latter being payable instead of some contributions in kind (*pro pecude mactabili* and *pro porco seu lardo*). In addition to all these, nine villages were also responsible for other payments – for pasturing cattle in the woods, for fishing and catching crabs, etc.[2] At about the same time, on the estate of Kanizsa, the pecuniary *census* was lower, while the cattle and pig contributions were usually to be discharged by a payment of 400*d.* or ten florins per village.[3]

The data mentioned above already reveal the two different kinds of 'regular' money rents which were exacted apart from the *census.*[4] On the one hand, contrary to the old practice, extra rents were levied on the tenants for the share they had in the use of the common fields,[5] which was a way of increasing the degree of exploitation. On the other hand, we can observe the commutation of certain services and contributions in kind for money rents. Both processes had already started earlier. Such an origin for the *census* itself, i.e. the commutation of the services for a money rent, can seldom be illustrated by direct evidence,[6] but we have data enough to indicate that many *extra payments* resulted from a substitution of this kind. Already in 1413 the tenants of Zalavár discharged their pig contribution by a payment of 100*d.*[7] In 1438 the inhabitants of Pécsvárad commuted the same obligation for one florin and the goat contribution for 5*d.* by the piece.[8] In 1448 the tenants of Szarvkő either delivered one calf at Easter and one at Michaelmas or substituted for this service a payment of 60*d.* each time. The population of Büdöskut, of the same manor, gave 316*d.* instead of food gifts, 316*d.* and 375*d.* instead of wine and corn contribution.[9] In 1477 the 'butt'-tax, to be paid in wine by the inhabitants of Szeged for their vintage, was commuted into '*pecuniae tinales*' (i.e. 'butt-money').[10] Manorial surveys dating from the last decades of the century evaluated certain kinds of '*munera*',[11] and what is more, they assessed some

[1] O.L. Dl. 36,995.
[2] O.L. Dl. 36,992.
[3] O.L. Dl. 36,997.
[4] In the fifteenth century the Hungarian landlords drew in many places, in addition to *census*, *taxa* and extra rents, also other money incomes from the tenants, e.g. fines and tolls, multure payments and tavern revenues. The latter kinds of payments we do not treat in this paper, because they became important at about the end of the fifteenth century.
[5] Cf. with footnote 3, p. 4, above.
[6] See footnotes 8, p. 5 and 8, p. 10, above.
[7] *Zala vármegye oklevéltára*, II, 391.
[8] Koller, *op. cit.* III, 374–5.
[9] *M.Gt.Sz.* (1895), pp. 211–15.
[10] J. Reizner, *Szeged története. Oklevéltár* (Records for the History of Szeged) (Szeged, 1900), IV, 75–8.
[11] E.g. '*assaturam in valore unius d.*' (O.L. Dl. 36,997); '*unum pullum et d. quattuor, ova duo et d. unum*' (O.L. Dl. 36,992).

gifts and even entire groups of '*muneralia*' immediately in money.[1] Occasionally – though more rarely than in the case of the substitution of money payments for contributions in kind – we can observe cases of commutation of labour services into money rents. So, for instance, some villages of the Sárvár-Kapuvár manor paid half a florin as 'cart rent' and half a florin as 'scythe money' instead of carriage duties and mowing labour.[2]

Both facts, namely that new services were mainly assessed in the form of money payments and, particularly, that services in kind, various sorts of labour and produce rents, were more and more frequently commuted into money rents, confirm us in our conclusion about the ever-increasing, in a great number of places even primary, role of money rent in the rural economy of Hungary and in the feudal exploitation of Hungarian tenants in the second half of the fifteenth century.

All this goes to show that in the second half of the fifteenth century the development of the feudal agrarian system had in Hungary too reached the level where labour dues played a merely subsidiary role; moreover, feudal rent assessed in money came more and more to the fore and even had, sometimes, preponderance over rents in kind (produce rents), though the latter continued to be of great importance. This points to the fact that in Hungary, until the end of the fifteenth century, the trend of development of medieval rural economy [3] was fundamentally concordant with that of the west European countries, and what is more, at about this time it came near to the level of the agrarian arrangements of the west, at least in certain highly important respects.[4] In western Europe too it was in the course of the thirteenth to fifteenth centuries that the development of the feudal economy resulted in the advance of money rents; in fact, money payments became decidedly and generally predominant in England and Flanders only, while in France and Germany the rents in kind continued to be important.[5]

[1] E.g. '*officiali hoc ordine solvere muneralia tenentur . . . circa festum beati Georgii martiris tenentur dare singulos decem denarios. In festo autem beati Michaelis archangeli similiter . . . singulos decem denarios . . .*' (*Zichy okmt.* XII, 317).

[2] O.L. Dl. 36,992.

[3] Similar results were obtained in relation to Bohemia and Poland. It was found that in Bohemia, already prior to the Hussite movement, money payments were preponderating (Graus, *op. cit.* II, 159–93; R. Novy, 'Struktura feudální rentý v předhusitských Čechách', *Československý Časopis Historický* (1961), p. 63). In Poland the fourteenth century is regarded as the starting period for the advance of money rent and a further development of it is observed in the fifteenth century (M. Małowist, 'Die Problematik der sozial-wirtschaftlichen Geschichte Polens vom 15. bis zum 17. Jahrhundert', *Renaissance und Reformation in Polen und in Ungarn* (Studia Historica Acad. Sci. Hung. 53. Budapest, 1963), p. 11 *et seq.*).

[4] Namely, from the aspect of the development of feudal rent. In our study, *Das Entwicklungsniveau der feudalen Agrarverhältnisse in Ungarn in der zweiten Hälfte des XV. Jahrhunderts* (Studia Historica Acad. Sci. Hung. 46. Budapest, 1960), we try to cover other aspects of this subject.

[5] J. Kulischer, *Allgemeine Wirtschaftsgeschichte des Mittelalters und der Neuzeit* (München-Berlin, 1928), I, 119–20; Ashley, *op. cit.* I, 27–30; Lipson, *op. cit.* I, 89 *et seq*;. E. A. Kosminsky, 'Evolutsia form feodalnoy renty v Angly v XI-XV vekach', *Voprosy Istory* (1955), no. 2. p. 44 *et seq.*; M. Bloch, *Les caractères originaux de l'histoire rurale française* (2nd ed. Paris, 1955) p. 95 *et seq.*; G. Sicard, *Le métayage dans le Midi toulousain à la fin du Moyen Âge* (Toulouse, 1957); Duby, *op. cit.* II, 593–9, 772 *et seq.*; G. Below, *Probleme der Wirtschaftsgeschichte* (2nd ed. Tübingen, 1926), pp. 45–49, 56; W. Abel, *Die Wüstungen des ausgehenden Mittelalters* (2nd ed. Stuttgart, 1955), p. 199 *et seq.*; F. Lütge, *Geschichte der deutschen Agrarverfassung vom frühen Mittelalter bis zum 19. Jahrhundert* (Stuttgart, 1963), p. 71 *et seq.*

What we have said underlines the negative role of the subsequent historical process which started at about the turn of the fifteenth to the sixteenth century and took a decided shape in the seventeenth century. Because of this process, the agrarian development of Hungary deviated and diverged from that of the west European countries and the feudal regime was extended for several centuries.[1]

[1] On the subsequent process, see Zs. P. Pach, *Die ungarische Agrarentwicklung im 16–17. Jahrhundert. Abbiegung vom westeuropäischen Entwicklungsgang* (Studia Historica Acad. Sci. Hung. 54. Budapest, 1964).

ADDENDA

THE DEVELOPMENT OF FEUDAL RENT IN HUNGARY IN THE FIFTEENTH CENTURY

Page 2, Note 1:

Previously another Latin term: *praedium* had been in use for the designation of the demesne fields that had played a far greater role in the agrarian structure of Hungary at the earlier stage of feudalization. However, from the 13th century onwards there commenced, in this country too, the process of contraction of the home farms and the letting out of demesne plots to the peasants, under the conditions of yardland–tenement or leasehold, along with the commutation of labour services. — For the early period see *I. Szabó*, The praedium. Studies on the Economic History and the History of Settlement of Early Hungary, Agrártörténeti Szemle (=AtSz, Review of Agricultural History), 1963. Supplement. — For the developments during the 13th century: *J. Szűcs*, Megosztott parasztság — egységesülő jobbágyság (Divided peasantry — unified dependent tenantry), Századok (Centuries), 1981; *I. Bolla*, A jogilag egységes jobbágyosztály kialakulása Magyarországon (The Formation of a Legally Unified Dependent Tenant Class in Hungary), Budapest, 1983.

Page 4, Note 4:

"In the 15th century agriculture was, in most cases, no longer conducted by the masters, but rather by the peasantry" — this was *G. Duby*'s conclusion to his analysis of the decay of the demesne–based manorial economy in the Late Middle Ages (op. cit. Eng. transl. by C. Postan), Rural Economy and Country Life in Medieval West, London, 1968, p. 331. — Similar statements may be found in any recent major work on the topic, e. g. Handbuch der europäischen Wirtschafts– und Sozialgeschichte. Hg. von H. Kellenbenz, II, Stuttgart, 1980, pp. 113, 238, 316, 542–544. — For a dissenting (but not persuasive) voice: *M. Toch*, Lords and Peasants. A Reappraisal of Medieval Economic Relationships, The Journal of European Economic History, XV, 1 (1986), p. 163 et seq.

Page 13, Note 4:

An overall picture of the agrarian system of late–medieval Hungary has been drawn by *I. Szabó*, Ungarns Landwirtschaft von der Mitte des XIV. Jahrhunderts bis zu den 1530-er Jahren, AtSz, 1966. Supplement; conf. *F. Maksay*, A magyar falu középkori településrendje (The Medieval Order of Settlement in the Hungarian Village), Budapest, 1971, esp. p. 133 et seq.

II

DER BAUERNAUFSTAND VOM JAHRE 1514 UND DIE "ZWEITE LEIBEIGENSCHAFT"

Der Titel des Vortrags verweist auf die historische Verbindung zwischen dem Bauernaufstand und der sogenannten zweiten Leibeigenschaft. Breiter ließe sich das folgendermaßen formulieren: welche Bedeutung hatte der ungarische Bauernaufstand von 1514 im Entstehungsprozeß der sogenannten zweiten Leibeigenschaft? Die weitere Aufgliederung des Themas ist folgende: inwiefern trugen die auf die zweite Leibeigenschaft hindeutenden Tendenzen zu der Vorgeschichte des Bauernkrieges bei bzw. konnten sie überhaupt dazu beitragen? Das ist die eine Frage. Die andere Frage lautet: welche Rolle spielten *die Folgen* des Bauernaufstandes bzw. seiner Niederschlagung bei der Entstehung der zweiten Leibeigenschaft, bei der Entstehung der ungarischen Variante dieses Systems, der sogenannten perpetua rusticitas (erbliche Untertänigkeit)?

Die flüchtige Skizzierung des Themas genügt, um zu erkennen, daß wir nicht nur vor einem entscheidenden Problem unserer Wirtschafts- und Gesellschaftsgeschichte (ja breiter gesehen, der Wirtschafts- und Gesellschaftsgeschichte Ostmitteleuropas) stehen, sondern zugleich auch an einem neuralgischen Punkt unserer Geschichtswissenschaft, an dem sich ungelöste Fragen, wesentlich voneinander abweichende – aber nicht entsprechend konfrontierte – Anschauungen treffen. Natürlich dürfen wir nicht hoffen, sie jetzt bei dieser Gelegenheit lösen zu können. Ein bescheidener Vortrag kann dergleichen Ansprüche noch weniger erheben. Dennoch glaube ich, daß wir den Anlaß der Fünfhundertjahrfeier und der internationalen wissenschaftlichen Konferenz zumindest dazu nützen müssen, einige Diskussionsfragen aufzuwerfen und damit die Voraussetzungen zu ihrer Klärung zu schaffen.

1 Schon im Hinblick auf die *Vorgeschichte, auf die Vorereignisse* von 1514 sind die Anschauungen sehr unterschiedlich. Nicht selten treffen wir auf die Ansicht – zuletzt bei der Diskussion zur Vorbereitung der Thesen zum Jubiläum – die bezweifelt, daß sich die zur „zweiten Leibeigenschaft" hinweisenden Momente schon vor 1514 gezeigt hätten. So wird der Einfluß der beginnenden Abweichung von der westeuropäischen Agrarentwicklung aus den Gründen und Vorereignissen des Bauernaufstandes ausgeklammert, die Möglichkeit eines Zusammenhangs lediglich auf die *Folgen* des Mißlingens und der Vergeltung des Aufstandes durch harte Bestimmungen beschränkt.

Aber auch der Gegenpol dieser Ansicht ist mehrfach in unserer Geschichtsliteratur dargelegt worden. „Das in den Gesetzen des Jahres 1514 formulierte System der erblichen Untertänigkeit ist nicht allein als Folge der fehlgeschlagenen Revolution, ohne jede vorherige Entwicklung entstanden", hat István Szabó, gestützt auf seine früheren Forschungen, in seinem vor einem Vierteljahrhundert veröffentlichten wertvollen Studienband festgestellt. Dieser Prozeß hat bereits um die Mitte des 15. Jahrhunderts begonnen, um dann „mit dem durch die Revolution des Jahres 1514 ausgelösten Dammbruch der Vergeltung auf einmal am *Schlußpunkt* anzugelangen". „Die mit der Vergeltung des Jahres 1514 entstandene Bindung an die Scholle ist keiner theoretischen Konstruktion entsprungen, die in der Gesellschaft wirkenden Kräfte hatten die ungarische Entwicklung schon vorher auf diese Ebene gelenkt."/1/

Im wesentlichen den gleichen Standpunkt in *dieser* Frage vertritt János Vargas vor kaum drei Jahren erschienene, umfangreiche Monographie über das System der bäuerlichen Verhältnisse im spätfeudalen Ungarn. Nachdem sich der Autor zuvor der Ansicht angeschlossen hat, die die erbliche Untertänigkeit (perpetua rusticitas) als ungarische Form der „zweiten Leibeigenschaft" anerkennt, bringt er an anderen Stellen seiner Arbeit ebenfalls die Meinung zum Ausdruck: „die auf den Dózsa-Aufstand folgenden Dekrete . . ., die zum Teil der rechtlichen Fixierung des einmal entstandenen Zustandes, zum Teil aber der Vereinheitlichung des in seinen Umrissen bereits herausgebildeten Systems und der Ausfüllung seiner Lücken dienten, waren nicht Anfang oder Ausgangspunkt, sondern vielmehr Ergebnis und *erster Höhepunkt* jenes Prozesses, den wir als Entstehung der Erbuntertänigkeit zu bezeichnen pflegen . . . 1514 ist Vorwand und Gelegenheit, das System der erblichen Untertänigkeit rechtlich zu kodifizieren."/2/

Ähnlich scharfe Divergenzen zeigen sich auch in der Beurteilung der *Folgen* von 1514, in der Bewertung des Charakters der Agrarentwicklung des 16. Jahrhunderts. Nach der zuletzt erwähnten Monographie hat die Gesetzgebung von 1514 die „*klassische*" Form der erblichen Untertänigkeit kodifiziert, die zwar um die Mitte des 16. Jahrhunderts „. . . durch die Gesetze des Jahres 1556 eine Modifizierung erfuhr, das System der erblichen Untertänigkeit selbst hörte jedoch nicht auf". Ja, „. . . nach vorübergehender und teilweiser Lockerung stabilisierte sich in der ersten Hälfte des 17. Jahrhunderts wieder die Variante, die die Gesetzgebung von 1514 und das daran anknüpfende Tripartitum kodifiziert hatte. Die Entwicklungskurve verlief also wieder zu jener Ebene zurück, die sie zuerst im Jahre 1514 erreicht hatte."/3/

Das andere Extrem der Ansichten in dieser Frage vertritt István Kiss' Quellenbearbeitung über die Zehntverzeichnisse des 16. Jahrhunderts, der wir das reiche Material über die Weiterentwicklung der bäuerlichen Warenproduktion in fünf Komitaten an der oberen Theiß verdanken. „Die politische Anarchie um die Wende vom 15. zum 16. Jahrhundert, nach der Katastrophe bei Mohács, war (zwar) für die bäuerliche Entwicklung nicht günstig" – der Ausbruch der Ereignisse von 1514 und ihre Unterdrückung werden hier im Entwicklungsverlauf nicht berücksichtigt – „dennoch beweist das Bild, das uns die Angaben um die Mitte des 16. Jahrhunderts zeigen," zieht der Autor die Schlußfolgerung, „daß die Lage und die Bestrebungen der Bauern, besonders aber der wohlhabenderen Bauern, bereits über das feudale System hinausweisen . . . die Tatsache der (bäuerlichen) Fluktuation, ihr Ausmaß und ihr Tempo, zählen zu den stärksten *Gegenbeweisen und Entkräftigungen* der Theorie von der Entstehung der Leibeigenschaft im 16. Jahrhundert."/4/

Für die krassen Unterschiede in den Auffassungen ist nichts bezeichnender als die Tatsache, daß der Verfasser der Monographie über die spätfeudalen gutsherrlich-bäuerlichen Verhältnisse – wie wir bereits erwähnten – in den Jahrzehnten nach 1514 die *„klassische Form" der erblichen Untertänigkeit* Gestalt annehmen sieht; in der Bearbeitung der Zehntverzeichnisse der fünf Komitate jedoch glaubte einer der Rezensenten gerade den Beweis dafür zu erblicken, daß „der zugleich *klassische Abschnitt der bäuerlich-bürgerlichen Entwicklung,* die Blütezeit der bäuerlichen Warenproduktion" auf das 16. Jahrhundert, auf die Jahre zwischen 1550 und 1600 gefallen sei./5/

Vollkommen wird schließlich das Spektrum der unterschiedlichen Meinungen dadurch, daß einige Autoren – worauf wir bereits verwiesen – in Zweifel zogen, die auf die zweite Leibeigenschaft, bzw. auf die erbliche Untertänigkeit hindeutenden Momente wären schon vor 1514 aufgetreten und zur Geltung gekommen, andere wieder setzten sie auf die Jahrzehnte nach 1514, und schließlich fehlt auch die Ansicht nicht, die ganz allgemein für das 16.–18. Jahrhundert leugnet, daß die „zweite Ausgabe der Leibeigenschaft" sich auf dem damaligen Gebiet Ungarns herausgebildet habe. Es genügt, hier auf die Studien unseres scharfsinnigen Kollegen Anton Špiesz aus Bratislava zu verweisen. „Unsere Entwicklung", hat der slowakische Historiker seinen Standpunkt zusammengefaßt, „hatte einen ganz anderen Charakter als das, was man zweite Leibeigenschaft bzw. Gutsherrschaft nennt" und wollte anerkannt wissen, daß sich „in Böhmen, Mähren und in der Slowakei in der Neuzeit" – darunter versteht er das 16.–18. Jahrhundert – „. . . eigentlich eine Entwicklung westeuropäischen Typs abgespielt hat . . . und auch weiterhin Grundherrschaft bzw. Wirtschaftsherrschaft" bestanden hat./6/

Wenn wir nach dem Grund dafür fragen, daß in unserer neuesten Geschichtsliteratur – schließlich haben wir ja unsere historiographischen Beispiele vorwiegend aus den letzten Jahren genommen – zu unserem Thema so wesentlich voneinander abweichende Meinungen aufgetreten sind, so werden wir bei unserer Antwort vermutlich auf eine ganze Reihe von Gründen stoßen. Auf die Unterschiede zwischen den im Vordergrund der Aufmerksamkeit der Forscher stehenden Regionen und dem unterschiedlichen Charakter der erforschten Quellengruppen ebenso wie auf die wesentlichen Unterschiede in der Auslegung der Quellenbelege, selbst bei einer Übereinstimmung in den allgemeinsten theoretisch-methodologischen Grundsätzen. Es muß uns auch ins Auge fallen, wie große Unterschiede sich bei unseren Historikern in der Verwendung des *Begriffs* zweite Leibeigenschaft bzw. Erbuntertänigkeit zeigen. Mit dieser Frage – auf die ich im Schlußteil meines Vortrages noch zurückkommen werde – hängt in vieler Hinsicht ein anderer Unterschied in der Betrachtungsweise zusammen. In unterschiedlichem Maße waren die Historiker bemüht, die Entwicklung der Agrarverhältnisse der Epoche in der Einheit und im Gegensatz der Richtungen der bäuerlichen Warenproduktion und der gutsherrlichen Warenproduktion, weiter gefaßt: in der Einheit und im Gegensatz der *bäuerlichen und gutsherrlichen Tendenzen* der feudalen Agrarentwicklung, in ihrer Gesamtheit und in ihrem Kampf darzustellen – wobei diese Tendenzen nicht nur die verschiedenen Wege und Möglichkeiten der Entwicklung der feudalen *Wirtschaft* vertreten, sondern (und 1514 enthüllt dies in aller Schärfe) gegensätzliche *soziale* Inhalte, gegensätzliche Klassenkräfte verkörpern.

Dies vor Augen, wollen wir eine kurze Analyse der ungarischen Agrarentwicklung in den Jahrzehnten vor 1514 unternehmen, nicht zuletzt eine Antwort auf die Frage suchend, ob die in die Richtung der zweiten Leibeigenschaft weisenden Erscheinungen eine Rolle in der Vorgeschichte des Bauernaufstandes gespielt haben.

2 Im 14.–15. Jahrhundert nahm in Ungarn nicht nur die bebaute Bodenfläche wesentlich zu, sondern auch die Produktivität der bäuerlichen Arbeit stieg durch die Entwicklung der landwirtschaftlichen Technik und die Umgestaltung des Anbausystems./7/ Ein Teil der Bauernfamilien begann außer dem Produkt für den Eigenbedarf und dem vom Grundherrn angeeigneten Mehrprodukt, der Grundrente, mehr oder weniger auch systematisch weitere Überschüsse zu produzieren. Die landwirtschaftliche Warenproduktion begann sich also allmählich auszudehnen, dazu noch in der Form bäuerlicher Warenproduktion. Das heißt, sofern zwischen Stadt und Dorf auf dem Produktenmarkt Verbindungen entstanden, lagen sie vornehmlich in den Händen der unmittelbaren Produzenten, in den Händen der Bauern.

Um die Mitte und in der zweiten Hälfte des 15. Jahrhunderts zeigt sich uns in den Quellen bereits ein reiches und buntes Bild der bäuerlichen Warenproduktion und Handelstätigkeit. Im Zusammenhang mit Gewalttätigkeiten und gewaltsamen Zolleintreibungen treffen wir oft auf Bauern, die Waren verschiedener Art und in verschiedenen Mengen auf den Markt brachten. So führten die Grundsassen, von György Rozgonyi aus Csallóköz (Schütt) 200 Ochsen, 6 Pferde und anderes Vieh sowie sonstige Waren im Werte von mehr als 200 Gulden auf den Markt,/8/ der Bauer János Gáspár aus Szatmár ebenfalls Ochsen, Pferde und andere Waren,/9/ Márton Megyerics und andere aus dem Komitat Zágráb Wein und Ochsen,/10/ Weinbauern aus Károly und Vada im Komitat Szatmár hatten auf neun von 58 Ochsen gezogenen Fuhrwerken 22 Faß Wein geladen,/11/ Gál Szabó, ein Großbauer aus Mindszent im Komitat Zala, beförderte auf achtzehn von 40 Ochsen und 20 Pferden gezogenen Fuhrwerken Getreide,/12/ die Untersassen der Töttös im Komitat Bodrog brachten Körnerfrucht im Werte von 54 Gulden auf den Markt,/13/ ein Grundsasse aus Eszeny Salz und andere Waren,/14/ Ferenc Sebestyén und Domonkos Magas, Einwohner von Várda allerlei Waren im Werte von 100 Gulden, usw./15/ Die angeführten Beispiele beleuchten auch, welche Agrarprodukte bei der Markttätigkeit der Bauern im Vordergrund standen. Den wichtigsten Platz nahm das Lebendvieh (Rinder) ein, danach folgte der Wein, aber auch Getreide kam bereits regelmäßig in den Handelsverkehr, abgesehen von anderen, kleineren Lebensmitteln.

Andererseits werfen größtenteils königliche Urkunden, die gerade Schutz gegen die Anarchie gewähren wollten bzw. Zollvergünstigungen gewährten, Licht auf die zunehmende Bedeutung der Markttätigkeit von *Bauern der Marktflecken (oppida) und Dörfer* in der zweiten Hälfte des 15. Jahrhunderts. Sehr bezeichnend ist, daß neben den Kaufleuten der königlichen Freistädte nicht nur die Bewohner der königlichen Marktflecken wie Szeged/16/, Gyula/17/ oder Miskolc/18/ als „pro acquirendis victuum eorum necessariis, cum ipsorum rebus venalibus proficiscentes" (zum Zweck des Lebensunterhalts, berufsmäßig mit Warenartikeln herumreisen) bzw. „de quibuscumque mercibus venalibus" (nach Waren jeder Art) allgemeine oder lokale Zollvergünstigungen genießen, sondern zum Beispiel auch die Grundsassen von Boldogasszonyfalva im Komitat Bihar/19/, die aus den Gemeinden Get und Lak im Komitat Bács/20/, aus Szentgyörgy im Komitat Szabolcs/21/, aus dem Marktflecken Károly und den Gemeinden Fény, Vada und Kaplony im Komitat Szatmár/22/, die Bauern von Nagykőrös/23/ und Ráckeve/24/ im Komitat Pest und die aus Gárdony im Komitat Fejér,/25/ auch Einwohner von Dörfern und kleineren Märkten, also ebenfalls „pro victuum suorum necessaria acquisitione diversas partes regni nostri perlustrantes/26/ (verschiedene Teile unseres Landes für ihren Lebensunterhalt aufsuchend), „cum rebus et bonis ipsorum venalibus et mercimonialibus" (mit zum Verkauf bestimmten Gütern und Waren) –natürlich überwiegend oder geradezu ausschließlich mit Agrarprodukten – „ire, stare, morare, pausare et negotiari" (sich zu bewegen, aufzuhalten, zu verweilen, den Weg zu unterbrechen und Handel zu betreiben), „forisari" (auf den Märkten tätig zu sein) pflegten und im Zusammenhang damit Zollvergünstigungen oder Schutzbriefe erhalten.

In dieser lebhaften, sich auf verschiedene Landesteile erstreckenden Handelstätigkeit der Bauern hat – wie auch die weiter oben angeführten Beispiele zeigen – der *Rinderhandel* eine besonders wichtige Rolle gespielt. Das hing vor allem mit der Viehzucht in den Marktflecken in der Tiefebene zusammen, zum Teil gerade jener, die dann 1514 den Weg von Dózsas Heer, die lokalen Herde des Aufstandes anzeigen werden (Cegléd, Tiszavarsány, Mezőtúr, Békés, Gyula, Lippa, Simánd usw.). Die wohlhabenden Viehzüchter und Händler bäuerlicher Abstammung, die ihre verarmten Klassengenossen in großer Zahl als Hirten und Heiducken angestellt hatten,/27/ ließen riesige Viehherden auf Pußtaflächen, die sie in Gebrauch genommen oder gepachtet hatten, weiden./28/ Sie trieben ihre Herden auf die Großmärkte von Debrecen, Szeged, Kecskemét oder Pest,/29/ ja, durch Vermittlung von Stadtbürgern oder auch selbst noch weiter, an die Westgrenze des Landes und auf Märkte im Ausland. Viele Anzeichen sprechen dafür, daß der nach dem Westen und Südwesten gerichtete Rinderhandel gerade in der zweiten Hälfte des 15. Jahrhunderts einen Aufschwung nahm, wodurch Ungarns in westlicher Richtung ehemals defizitäre Handelsbilanz aktiv wurde./30/

Die ansteigende landwirtschaftliche Produktion, die Entstehung und Verbreitung der Marktverbindungen der Bauern entgingen natürlich nicht der Aufmerksamkeit der Grundherren. Sehr bald zeigte sich ihr Bestreben, sich selbst die Früchte der steigenden Produktivität der bäuerlichen Arbeit zu sichern, diese ebenfalls in ihre Grundrente einzubeziehen, das heißt die Ausbeutung ihrer Grundsassen zu steigern.

Der auf der bäuerlichen Wirtschaft basierenden Warenproduktion die auf dem grundherrlichen Boden basierende Warenproduktion entgegenzustellen, den Anteil des eigenbewirtschafteten Grundbesitzes zu vergrößern, die Eigenbetriebe zu Marktzwecken auszubauen – dieser Weg wurde im 15. Jahrhundert noch *kaum* beschritten. Der bäuerlichen Warenproduktion den herrschaftlichen Warenhandel gegenüberzustellen, das heißt die in den Bauernwirtschaften erzeugten und von den Grundherren angeeigneten Produkte selbst auf den Markt zu bringen, dazu entschieden sich vor dem Ende des Jahrhunderts nur *wenige*./31/ Einstweilen wandten die Grundherren die für sie bequemste, einfachste Methode an, nämlich an dem entstandenen Mechanismus der Produktion und des Absatzes nicht zu rühren, sondern – gestützt auf ihre feudale Macht – die Entwicklung der Waren-Geldverhältnisse *von außen* zu nutzen: sie versuchten, sich die Früchte der Warenproduktion der *Bauern unmittelbar in Geldform* anzueignen.

Das bedeutet gleichzeitig, daß die feudale Grundrente in der zweiten Hälfte des 15. Jahrhunderts in Ungarn ein Niveau erreichte, auf welchem die Arbeitsrente, die Fron nur mehr eine geringe Rolle spielte, ja daß die Geldform der feudalen Rente auch mit der Produktenrente zumindest gleichrangig war, vielerorts sogar schon eine wichtigere Rolle spielte. Dies ist nicht nur im Zusammenhang mit der Besiedlung jener Gebiete zu beobachten, die neu oder aber wieder genutzt wurden, nämlich in Siedlerdörfern, in Hospes-Gemeinden, wo die Grundherren schon früher vornehmlich oder geradezu ausschließlich Geldleistungen eingetrieben hatten./32/ Und nicht nur bei den Marktflecken (oppida), diesen dichter bevölkerten Siedlungen, in denen auch Gewerbetreibende lebten und die in der landwirtschaftlichen Warenproduktion und im Warenaustausch an der Spitze standen. (Die ungarische Fachliteratur hat nämlich mit nachdrücklicher Betonung darauf hingewiesen, daß dort Geldrente geleistet wurde, noch dazu oft nicht pro Kopf, sondern in einem von der Anzahl der Bewohner unabhängigen Pauschalbetrag.)/33/ Dies gilt auch für die ungarischen Dörfer allgemein. Die Geldrente fehlt auch bei den Lasten der einfachen Dorfbauern nur sehr selten. Die Urbarien beginnen gewöhnlich die Aufzählungen der Leistungen damit und auch andere Quellen weisen mit besonderem Nachdruck darauf hin./34/ Insgesamt wird sie im Verlaufe des 15. Jahrhunderts, in der zweiten Hälfte immer schwerer. Innerhalb der Struktur der feudalen Rente treten die verschiedenen Geldrenten immer mehr in den Vordergrund: der urbarial festgelegte Zensus (oder Terragium), die außerordentliche Taxe und die Sonderrenten für die gemeinsamen Nutznießungen (Weide, Wald, Fischereigewässer)./35/

In vielen Fällen ist aus den Quellen auch unmittelbar der Prozeß der Kommutation, der Umwandlung der Naturalleistungen in *Geldleistungen* ersichtlich. Die Bauern von Pécsvárad konnten im Jahre 1438 statt eines Mastschweines 1 Gulden, statt einer Ziege 5 Denar bezahlen./36/ Die Grundsassen von Szarvkő gaben im Jahre 1448 zu Ostern und zu Michaeli je ein Kalb oder konnten je ein Kalb mit 60 Denar ablösen. Die Einwohner der Gemeinde Büdöskút in derselben Domäne entrichteten statt kleinerer Lebensmittelgeschenke 316 Denar, statt Wein- und Getreideabgaben 316 bzw. 375 Denar./37/ Die Weineimerleistung, die die Bewohner des Marktfleckens Szeged nach ihren Weingärten entrichteten, erscheint 1477 in der Form von „pecuniae tinales seu chibryonales"./38/ In den aus den letzten Jahrzehnten des Jahrhunderts stammenden Urbarien werden gewisse „munera" – teils mit Wertbezeichnung – angeführt, ein anderes Mal wurden kleinere Geschenke,/39/ ja manchmal sogar ganze Muneraliengruppen unmittelbar in Geld bemessen./40/ Im Quellenmaterial aus der zweiten Hälfte des 15. Jahrhunderts ist auch die Umwandlung nicht nur der Produktenrente, sondern auch gewisser Arbeitsleistungen in Geldrente zu beobachten. Ein Grundbesitzer im Komitat Pozsony erließ seinen Grundsassen in fünf Gemeinden jedwedes „servitium" (Pflügen, Mähen, Einbringen der Ernte) und forderte von ihnen statt dessen pro Kopf 1 Gulden „terragium"./41/ In der Domäne Sárvár-Kapuvár wurde in einzelnen Ortschaften im Jahre 1492 statt Fuhren- und Mähfron pro Gemeinde je ein halber Gulden gezahlt usw./42/

II

Eine auf den ersten Blick überraschende, jedoch eigentlich natürliche, ja notgedrungene Folge der Kommutation der Naturalrenten in Geldleistungen ist die Tatsache, daß um die Mitte und in der zweiten Hälfte des 15. Jahrhunderts neben dem Lebensmittelbedarf der ***Städte*** nunmehr auch von seiten der Grundherren (Kirchengüter, Magnatenhöfe) auf den Märkten eine bedeutende Nachfrage nach landwirtschaftlichen Produkten, nach Lebensmitteln auftrat. In der Abtei von Pécsvárad betrug 1438 – über die Verwendung der Naturalleistungen der Bauern hinaus – die Küchenrechnung des Abtes und seiner Familiaren wöchentlich 6 Gulden und die der Mönche 150 Denar./43/ In der Domäne Kisvárda kam es in den Jahren 1450–1470 nicht selten vor, daß der Hofrichter auch gewöhnliche Lebensmittel für Bargeld kaufte: Getreide, Hülsenfrüchte, Kraut, Wein, Fische, Speck, Fleisch, auch Hafer und Heu./44/ Auch für die Hofhaltung des Erzbischofs von Esztergom (Gran) wurden Ende der 1480er Jahre – mit Ausnahme von Heu – ebenfalls sozusagen alle benötigten Agrarprodukte für Geld gekauft: abgesehen von importierten Gewürzen und Südfrüchten, Wein, Brennholz usw. Letztere wurden zum großen Teil in dem gegenüber von Esztergom, am linken Ufer der Donau gelegenen Marktflecken Kakat beschafft./45/ Der Hof des Bischofs von Eger (Erlau) kaufte 1493–1495 an landwirtschaftlichen Produkten nicht nur orientalische Gewürze (Pfeffer, Ingwer, Gewürznelken) auf dem Markt – hauptsächlich in Pest –, sondern auch große Mengen Weizen, Weizenmehl, Hirse, Erbsen, Linsen, Obst, Zwiebeln, Kraut, Wein, Fische, Geflügel, Hasen, Schweine, Speck, Schlachtvieh und Kälber (für den Eigenbedarf und teilweise zur Entlohnung von Gewerbetreibenden und Arbeitern), außerdem Hafer und andere Futtermittel, Getreide- und Gemüsesaatgut, Latten, Schindeln usw. Dies alles wurde überwiegend in Eger selbst und auf anderen Märkten des Besitzkomplexes beschafft, also von den warenproduzierenden Bauern der eigenen Grundherrschaft gekauft./46/

Wir sehen also, daß zwischen der Entwicklung der bäuerlichen Warenproduktion und der Entwicklung der Geldrente auf mehreren Ebenen Wechselbeziehungen bestehen. Einerseits (und grundlegend) entsteht die Geldrente auf dem Boden der bäuerlichen Warenproduktion; der Grundherr kann sich die Geldrente nur auf der Grundlage der Produktion der Bauern für den Markt – für den städtischen Markt – aneignen. Andererseits schafft das Vordringen der Geldrente, das Zurücktreten der naturalen Rentenformen auf dem Gebiet der Agrarprodukte auch eine Nachfrage seitens der Herrenklasse, wodurch wiederum die Ausweitung der bäuerlichen Warenproduktion gefördert wird. Weiterhin: die Geldrente kommt auf dem Boden der Produktion des Bauern für den Markt auf, der Grundherr ***kann*** sich nur auf dieser Grundlage systematisch Geldleistungen vom Bauern aneignen; andererseits ***zwingt*** die steigende Geldrentenforderung des Grundherrn den Bauern zunehmend auf dem Markt zu verkaufen. Nicht nur dann, wenn er über eine ausreichende Menge von Mehrprodukten verfügt, sondern auch dann, wenn er dazu die zum Unterhalt seiner Familie notwendigen Produkte angreifen muß. Nicht nur dann, wenn er für seine Produkte gute Preise erzielen kann, sondern auch im entgegengesetzten Fall, ***bei ungünstiger Preisgestaltung.***

Offensichtlich war letzterer Fall im damaligen Ungarn häufiger, natürlich nicht überall und nicht immer, sondern was die „longue durée“, die Richtung der Entwicklung auf lange Sicht anbetrifft. Die preisgeschichtlichen Forschungen zeigen – die vor einigen Jahren erschienene zweite Auflage von Wilhelm Abels „Agrarkrisen" hat die entsprechenden Ergebnisse veranschaulicht und verallgemeinert/47/ –, daß in mehreren west- und mitteleuropäischen Ländern von der zweiten Hälfte des 14. Jahrhunderts an die Preise für landwirtschaftliche Produkte eine *sinkende*, die der Industrieartikel hingegen eine *steigende* Tendenz aufwiesen – oder zumindest weniger sanken als die der landwirtschaftlichen Erzeugnisse. Dieses Wechselverhältnis der Preise, das die Industrieartikel begünstigte und die der landwirtschaftlichen Produkte – vor allem den Getreidepreis – drückte, diese „Agrarschere" war im 15. Jahrhundert zum größten Teil grundlegend und in vielen Teilen Europas anzutreffen, wenn auch mit mehr oder weniger großen Abweichungen in den einzelnen Ländern, ja auch Städten. Sie kam – wenn auch nicht in so scharfer Form – sicher auch in Ungarn zur Geltung, wie Vera Zimányi in ihrer preisgeschichtlichen Studie dargelegt hat./48/

Und wenn dem so ist, dann können diese Preisverhältnisse zur Erklärung und zum Verständnis zahlreicher angeführter Erscheinungen beitragen. Daß die Grundherrn vor dem Ende des 15. Jahrhunderts nur sehr selten begannen, Eigenwirtschaften auszubauen und sich auch in den Handel mit Agrarprodukten nur vereinzelt einschalteten, geschah nicht nur, weil für sie das Eintreiben der Geldrente bequemer und einfacher war, sondern auch, weil die niedrigen Produktenpreise sie nicht zur landwirtschaftlichen Produktion und Handelstätigkeit hinzogen. Das überließen sie getrost ihren Bauern.

Die Tatsache, daß die Umwandlung der naturalen Rentenformen in Geldabgaben im Verlaufe des 15. Jahrhunderts im großen Umfange fortschritt, bezeichnet nicht nur den Erfolg der entsprechenden Bestrebungen der *Bauern*, – für die dadurch die Ausweitung ihrer Warenproduktion, gelindere Formen der feudalen Abhängigkeit ermöglicht wurden –, sondern fiel auch mit den Interessen der *Grundherren* zusammen, die durch die Preisverhältnisse zur Kommutation angeregt wurden, verzichteten sie doch für gutes Geld (Goldgulden, Silberdenar) auf Produkte von rückgängigem Preis.

Daß der Prozeß der Kommutation vielerorts eine Stufe erreichte, auf der kirchliche und weltliche Großgrundherren ihren Eigenbedarf an gewöhnlichen Lebensmitteln größtenteils auf dem Markt deckten, kann nicht nur ihrer großzügigen Lebensweise (oder aber den finanziellen Methoden ihrer an ausländische Verhältnisse gewöhnten Gutsverwalter) zugeschrieben werden, sondern auch dem Umstand, daß es – bei niedrigen Preisen – vorteilhafter war, die Agrarprodukte für die Hofhaltung auf dem Markt zu besorgen und die Naturalabgaben der Grundsassen in Geld umzuwandeln.

Ziehen wir dies alles in Betracht, so ist das Vordringen der Geldrente unter den Formen der feudalen Renten eine komplizierte, aus mehreren Komponenten zusammengesetzte, *widerspruchsvolle* Erscheinung. Wenn sie der Ausdruck dessen ist, daß der Bauer zum Warenproduzenten geworden war, daß er sich der drückendsten Formen der persönlichen Abhängigkeit entledigt hatte, nicht selten direkt und bewußt danach strebte und daß sie die Möglichkeit zum Emporsteigen einer wohlhabenden Bauernschicht, die Möglichkeit zu einer bäuerlich-bürgerlichen Entwicklung gab, so eröffnete sie gleichzeitig den Weg einer gesteigerten feudalen Ausbeutung. Sie verschärfte den Kampf um die Verteilung des bäuerlichen Mehrprodukts, förderte die Verwirklichung der grundherrlichen Bestrebungen zur Erhöhung der Rente, förderte die Verarmung breiter Bauernschichten. Die Entwicklung der Warenproduktion, das Vordringen der

Geldrente erweiterten so den Hauptgegensatz der feudalen Ordnung, den Gegensatz zwischen Grundherrn und Bauern um zahlreiche neue Momente. Sie verschärften *den Klassenkampf zwischen ihnen, hoben ihn auf eine höhere Stufe.*

Die Atmosphäre des feudalen Dorfes war also spannungsgeladen. In solcher Atmosphäre brachen die westeuropäischen Bauernaufstände des 14.–15. Jahrhunderts aus; zum Teil aus solchen wirtschaftlichen Antezedenzen resultierte auch der ungarische Bauernaufstand des Jahres 1514.

3 Denn am Ende des 15. und zu Beginn des 16. Jahrhunderts setzten sich jene Erscheinungen, die wir bisher beobachten konnten, fort, ja wurden stärker und nahmen noch schärfere Formen an.

Der Zusammenbruch der staatlichen Zentralisation bot den Grundherren nach 1490 weitere Möglichkeiten, den Nutzen der bäuerlichen (und bürgerlichen) Warenproduktion in Geldform an sich zu reißen. Kirchliche und weltliche Herren, althergekommene Barone und „Emporgekommene", sich hocharbeitende Gemeinadlige stürzten sich – von des Zügeln der Zentralmacht befreit – vor allem auf die königlichen Güter und andere Staatseinnahmen (Dreißigst, Bergwerkseinkünfte) und veränderten die Verteilung der „zentralisierten Rente" radikal, gemessen an der Zeit König Matthias' zum Nachteil der königlichen Schatzkammer./49/ Gleichzeitig waren sie bestrebt, die grundlegenden Verteilungsverhältnisse auf Kosten ihrer Grundsassen weiter abzuändern und ihre Renten als private Grundbesitzer zu vermehren, was sie – ähnlich den bisherigen Gepflogenheiten – tailweise durch Steigerung der Geldrenten verwirklichten. Manchmal wurde auch der Zensus erhöht: die Pauliner von Nagyvázsony erhoben z.B. von ihren Bauern in Karakó um das Jahr 1483 einen Gulden und 77 Wiener Denar, 1506 nach einer ganzen Session bereits 2 Gulden./50/ Häufiger ist die Ausnutzung der außerordentlichen Taxe, die Steigerung der Sonderrenten für die gemeinsamen Nutznießungen (Waldabgabe, Wiesenabgabe usw.), die Erhöhung der Ablöse für die Naturalleistungen. So wurden zum Beispiel in der Domäne Sempte, wo die Geldeinnahmen nach dem Urbarium vom Beginn des 16. Jahrhunderts jährlich 214 Gulden betrugen, vom Grundherrn als Taxa ordinaria zu Michaeli im Jahre 1500 sogar 900 Gulden und im Jahre 1501 nach den Fischereigewässern bereits 370 Gulden eingetrieben./51/

In dieselbe Linie fiel die Vermehrung der Mautstellen im Lande. Daß dieses ebenfalls auf eine lange Vergangenheit zurückblickende grundherrliche Vorgehen in den Jahrzehnten unmittelbar vor 1514 besonders wucherte und entartete, das beleuchtet unter anderem eine Reihe damaliger Gesetze./52/ Es braucht wohl nicht im einzelnen ausgeführt zu werden, welche Schikanen, welche empfindliche Schäden dies für jene Bauern der Marktflecken und Dörfer bedeutete, die – wie wir weiter oben angeführt haben – durch die verschiedenen Teile des Landes zogen, um ihre Waren auf den Markt zu bringen, die besonders lange Strecken zurücklegten und so auf viele Mautstellen stießen, wenn sie ihre Rinderherden auf den Markt trieben. So zum Beispiel auch Lőrinc und Domonkos Kis, Einwohner von Battonya im Komitat Zaránd, die in den ersten Jahren nach 1510 Ochsen im Werte von 300 Gulden nach Pest trieben „quaestus causa". Unterwegs aber griff sie ihr ehemaliger Grundherr (von dessen Grundherrschaft sie Jahre zuvor nach Zahlung des Terragiums weggezogen waren) an, nahm ihnen ihr Vieh weg und setzte sie selbst gefangen./53/ Zu ihnen gehörte auch Péter Rewdy aus Boncida im Komitat Doboka an, der mit den Ochsen seines Grundherrn Ferenc Bánffy zusammen auch sein eigenes Vieh „vendendi gratia ad civitatem Pestiensem“ zum Verkauf trieb und unterwegs von Imre Tordai überfallen und ausgeraubt wurde./54/

Die Beschwerden der Bauern und die Schikanen widerspiegelten sich auch in den Ereignissen wie in der Ideologie von 1514. Der Befehl des Erzbischofs Tamás Bakócz vom 15. Mai 1514, mit dem er die Anwerbung für das Kreuzheer aussetzte, berief sich unter anderem darauf, daß die unberufenen Verkünder des Kreuzzuges das Volk aufriefen, „den weltlichen Herren den ordentlichen Zensus und die der königlichen Majestät gebührende Dica sowie die anderen berechtigten und üblichen Abgaben zu verweigern“ und dazu aufstachelten, die Zensus- und Dicaeintreiber zu töten und zu steinigen./55/ Die bei den humanistischen Historikern nachzulesende sogenannte Cegléder Rede György Dózsas drückte über das allgemeine Bestreben zur Befreiung von den feudalen Lasten hinausgehend – hier sei auf die Darlegung unseres Kollegen György Székely verwiesen – den Protest der warenproduzierenden Bauern gegen die Enteignung der Früchte ihrer Arbeit aus, gegen die Wegnahme ihres Geldes, indem sie das ganze Gewirr der Geldrenteneinrichtung aufdeckte./56/ Auch die Briefe der in der Umgebung von Kassa wirkenden Hauptleute des Kreuzheeres, Lőrinc Mészáros aus Megyaszó und Tamás Kecskés aus Aszaló, enthielten den Aufruf, nicht zuzulassen, daß von jenen, die sich zum Kreuzheer meldeten oder ihnen behilflich waren, *Geld* erpreßt wurde oder von jenen, die dem Heer folgend Lebensmittel und Ausrüstung lieferten, Mautgebühren erhoben wurden./57/ So wie auch das von Cegléd in südöstlicher Richtung ziehende Bauernheer unterwegs gegen Steuereinnehmer (Geldeintreiber) und Mauteinnehmer (Mautstellen) auftrat./58/

Es steht also außer Zweifel, daß die Geldlasten und die Binnenzölle unter jenen Faktoren, die den Bauernkrieg in Ungarn auslösten, mit großem Gewicht in die Waagschale fielen. Die Tätigkeit der Feudalherren war in beiden Beziehungen im Grunde genommen ähnlich: sie wollten den Nutzen aus der Ausweitung der Waren – Geldverhältnisse, aus der Entwicklung der bäuerlich-bürgerlichen Warenproduktion möglichst *von außen* abschöpfen, indem sie sich zunehmend in die Geldwirtschaft einschalteten, sich jedoch mit dem Warenhandel und vor allem der Warenproduktion kaum befaßten.

Beachtung verdienen gleichzeitige Maßnahmen anderen Charakters, die ebenfalls zur Verschärfung der Ausbeutung der Bauernschaft beitrugen: die Gesetzesartikel von 1492, 1498, 1500 und aus noch weiteren Jahren/59/, die – den Artikel 6 des Dekrets vom Jahre 1351 erneuernd – die Grundsassen der Marktflecken und Dörfer nach ihrem Acker- und Weinbau zu bedeutenderen *Produkten*abgaben verpflichteten, zum Neuntel oder zu Eimern in bestimmter Menge. Diese Vorschrift wurde auch auf die gepachteten Äcker und Weingärten der Bauern, ja sogar der städtischen Bürger ausgedehnt. Schließlich wurde noch erklärt, sie hätten dieser Pflicht nicht in einer im voraus bestimmten Menge, sondern mit dem Neuntel der Ernte nachzukommen.

Die Bedeutung dieser Gesetzesartikel hat als erster Elemér Mályusz in seinen beiden vor vier Jahrzehnten erschienenen Studien aufgedeckt./60/ Seine Auffassung, die seither in unserer Geschichtsliteratur ziemlich allgemeingültig geworden ist, möchten wir lediglich dadurch ergänzen, daß wir die Vorschrift über das Getreide- und Weinneuntel als eine Verfügung betrachten, die eine Verschärfung der Lasten nicht nur der *Marktflecken* (und im Falle der Weingartenpacht auch der Stadtbürger), sondern auch zahlreicher Bauerndörfer zum Ziel hatte. Dies um so mehr, als unsere Forschungsergebnisse zeigen, daß das Produktenneuntel in der zweiten Hälfte des 15. Jahrhunderts auch im Hinblick auf die einfachen Dorfbauern bei weitem nicht allgemein verbreitet war./61/ Bezeichnenderweise wurde die Wein- und Getreideabgabe von den Gesetzesartikeln 47/48 vom Jahre 1492 noch in *alternativer* Form bemessen „nonam partem . . . aut acones consuetos" (die mengenmäßige Festlegung war nämlich bis dahin auch bei den Dörfern relativ mehr verbreitet). Einen weiteren Schritt tat dann der Gesetzesartikel 27 vom Jahre 1500, der schon *ausschließlich* das Neuntel – „non acones, prout certis in locis solebant, sed nonam partem" – vorschrieb, also die härtere Form der Abgabe zur allgemeinen Praxis machen wollte.

Wenn wir dem noch die, mit dem damaligen Pachtsystem verbundenen – ähnliche Lehren bietenden, sich nicht nur auf die Marktflecken, sondern auf eine ganze Reihe von Bauerndörfern beziehenden – Angaben hinzufügen/62/, müssen wir jene Auslegungen als zu eingeengt betrachten, die die Spitze dieser Gesetzesartikel auf „*Marktfleckenfeindlichkeit*" beschränken und in ihnen die Kodifizierung der Interessen und Ansprüche des (auf die Marktflecken des Königs und der Aristokratie eifersüchtigen) *Kleinadels* sehen; oder wie es eine neuere Studie über dieses Thema formulierte, darin eine Aktion der Schicht des kleineren und mittleren Adels erkennen wollen, der die auf dem Landtag eine entscheidende Kraft repräsentierende Aristokratie nur aus taktischen Gründen freien Lauf ließ./63/

Unmittelbar daran knüpft sich die Frage, wieweit die Kodifizierung dieser Maßnahmen bereits mit der Hinwendung einzelner Herrenschichten zum *Warenhandel* in Verbindung steht/64/ (was, vom Bisherigen abweichend, nunmehr einen Eingriff in den einmal entstandenen Mechanismus der Marktverhältnisse bedeuten könnte). Daß Ende des 15. Jahrhunderts bereits einzelne Elemente oder Gruppen der herrschenden Klasse begannen, sich nicht nur von *außen* her für den Handel mit landwirtschaftlichen Produkten zu interessieren, sondern sich selbst in diesen einschalteten, wird durch zahlreiche Tatsachen wahrscheinlich. Diese Grundherren – und zwar nicht nur die mittleren oder kleineren Adligen – interessierten die Binnenzölle nicht mehr bzw. nicht *nur* vom Gesichtspunkt der Möglichkeit, die Markttätigkeit *der Bauern* abzuschöpfen, sondern um ihrer *eigenen* Handelstätigkeit – ähnlich den Bürgern der königlichen Städte – die innere Zollfreiheit im ganzen Lande zu sichern./65/ Von seiten dieser Grundherren dürfte also – der Gesetzesartikel 35 vom Jahre 1498 bediente sich dabei des Ausdrucks „nobiles istius regni, tam scilicet *potiores,* quam *minores*" – in diesem Zusammenhang bereits bei den Vorschriften für die Erhebung des Neuntels die Absicht mitgespielt haben, auf solche Weise an *Wein* oder *Getreide* heranzukommen, das auf den Markt gebracht werden konnte. Wie mit Recht auch angenommen werden kann, daß jene gleichzeitigen Gesetzesartikel, die die Viehausfuhr beschränkten oder geradezu verboten,/66/ die Bestrebungen jener Herren zum Ausdruck brachten, die sich mit Viehhandel befaßten und sich ihrer Konkurrenten entledigen wollten./67/ So zum Beispiel der Judex curiae Péter Geréb, der sich im

Jahre 1497 die Genehmigung der dreißigstfreien (zollfreien) Ausfuhr von 600 Ochsen erwirkt hatte./68/ So der ebenfalls zum Hochadel gehörende Ambrus Sárkány, der spätere Judex curiae, von dem die Partei des Kleinadels am Vorabend der Schlacht von Mohács sagen wird: „Du betriebst Wein- und Viehhandel, schikaniertest das arme Volk, während wir die Grenzen verteidigten."/69/

Diese Folgerungen werden auch durch die Tatsache unterstützt, daß gerade in den letzten Jahrzehnten des 15. und den ersten Jahrzehnten des 16. Jahrhunderts – natürlich in den einzelnen Ländern nicht vollkommen zum gleichen Zeitpunkt – in zahlreichen europäischen Ländern die langfristige Tendenz der Preisgestaltung eine Wende nahm. Die Getreidepreise begannen – nach jahrhundertelangem Rückgang bzw. Stagnieren – anzusteigen, in ihrem Gefolge auch die Preise der übrigen Lebensmittel. Die Preise der Industrieartikel hingegen blieben bei geringem Ansteigen immer hinter diesen zurück. Während also in der zweiten Hälfte des 14. Jahrhunderts und im überwiegenden Teil des 15. Jahrhunderts die Preisrelationen zwischen Agrarprodukten und Industrieartikeln für letztere günstig gewesen waren, zeigte sich im wechselseitigen Verhältnis zwischen landwirtschaftlichen und industriellen Preisen jetzt eine Richtung, die sich im Verlaufe einiger Jahrzehnte beschleunigend, die „Preisschere" nunmehr für die Agrarprodukte öffnete./70/ Alle Anzeichen sprechen dafür, daß diese Veränderung, die sich um die Mitte des 16. Jahrhunderts auch in Ungarn in verschärfter Form vollzog, hier an der Wende vom 15. zum 16. Jahrhundert ihren Anfang genommen hat./71/

Und wenn dem so ist, dann konnten die Grundherren auf den beginnenden Anstieg der Preise für landwirtschaftliche Produkte auf zweierlei Art reagieren. Einerseits konnten sie den Betrag der Geldablöse der Produktenabgaben erhöhen. Und die zeitgenössichen Urbarien enthalten in der Tat zahlreiche Angaben für dieses Vorgehen. So bezahlten zum Beispiel die Gemeinden Babót und Ordód in der Domäne Kapuvár zusammen „pro pecude mactabili" (statt Schlachtvieh) im Jahre 1492 noch 200 Wiener Denar, 1507 bereits 400 Wiener Denar und Babót im Jahre 1519 allein 800 Wiener Denar./72/ Der Vergleich der Urbarien der Grundherrschaft Sárvár aus den Jahren 1492 und 1518/19,/73/ jener der Burgherrschaft Kanizsa aus den Jahren 1493, 1512, 1519/74/ zeigen, daß die Ablöse, die für Schlachtvieh und Mastschweine gezahlt werden mußte, auf das 2- bis 8fache angestiegen war, daß an mehreren Orten (darunter auch Marktflecken) „ad rationem victualium" (als Ablöse von Geschenken in Form von Lebensmitteln) neue Geldleistungen eingeführt wurden.

Die zweite Art der Reaktion der Grundherren konnte sein, daß sie danach strebten, sich den im Preis ansteigenden Wein und das ebenfalls im Preis steigende Getreide von ihren Grundsassen *in natura* anzueignen. Das hätte sie anregen können, auch das Getreide und Weinneuntel einzuführen.

Eine gesonderte Frage ist natürlich, wieweit die entsprechenden Gesetzesartikel in den folgenden Jahrzehnten auch durchgeführt wurden. Die zeitgenössischen Urbarien zeigen, daß selbst in den Bauerndörfern die Neuntelverpflichtung nicht lückenlos erfüllt wurde. So entrichteten die Dörfer der Grundherrschaft Léka im Jahre 1519 ebenso wie 1492 kein Neuntel.Das Urbarium einiger Gemeinden des Komitats Vas schrieb um 1500 auch weiterhin die festgelegte Getreideabgabe vor./75/ Die Bauern von Polgárdi und Battyán mußten 1502 sowohl von Getreide wie von Wein ein

Neuntel,/76/ die Dörfer der Burgherrschaft Torna 1497 ein Zehntel abliefern,/77/ Kövesd, Bajta und einige zu anderen kirchlichen Gütern gehörende Gemeinden des Komitats Hont mußten dem Grundherrn zu Beginn des 16. Jahrhunderts das Neuntel und den Zehnten entrichten./78/ Gleichzeitig wurde die Verschärfung der Getreideabgabe auch in einzelnen Marktflecken durchgeführt, hauptsächlich durch Anheben der mengenmäßigen Belastung. Der Marktflecken Szil der Domäne Kapuvár zum Beispiel leistete 1492 an Weizen 15 Scheffel, an Hafer 8 Scheffel, im Jahre 1507 bereits 30 Scheffel Weizen und 15 Scheffel Hafer, 1518 jedoch 60 Scheffel Weizen und 30 Scheffel Hafer./79/

Es muß aber darauf hingewiesen werden, daß die in den angeführten Gesetzesartikeln enthaltenen Verfügungen – unabhängig davon, in welchem Umfange sie in den folgenden Jahrzehnten verwirklicht wurden – Bestrebungen der Grundherren widerspiegeln, die neben der *Geldrente* auch auf eine stärkere Ausnutzung der *Produktenform* der feudalen Rente (genauer der Getreide- und Weinabgabe) gerichtet waren. Auf diese Weise waren in diesen Artikeln – zusammen mit den, die sozial-rechtliche Lage der Bauern berührenden, besonders den die Freizügigkeit einschränkenden zeitgenössischen Gesetzesartikeln/80/ – bereits dem bisherigen Entwicklungsgang entgegengesetzte Momente enthalten. Sie waren nicht mehr darauf gerichtet, den Nutzen der bäuerlichen Warenproduktion *von außen* abzuschöpfen, sondern sie stellten einen *Eingriff* in den einmal entstandenen Mechanismus der Markttätigkeit des Bauern dar. Die Erhöhung der Produktenrente verminderte nämlich einerseits jene Produktenmenge, die der Bauer über die Sicherung des Lebensunterhalts seiner Familie hinaus auf den Markt werfen konnte und beschränkte andererseits die Marktchancen der bäuerlichen Wirtschaft. Und nicht nur, wenn der Grundherr sich selbst als Konkurrent in den Warenhandel einschaltete und die von den Bauern als Abgabe aneigneten Produkte auf den Markt brachte, sondern auch dann – und das sollte besonders beachtet werden – wenn er diese selbst für sich und sein Haus in Anspruch nahm. Im letzteren Falle verminderte sich nämlich *die Nachfrage der Herren* nach den auf den Markt gebrachten Lebensmitteln, worin wir ja vorhin einen wichtigen Faktor des Marktsektors der bäuerlichen Warenproduktion erkannt haben.

Die Beschwerden der Bauern über die Geldlasten und die Schikanen bei der Zollerhebung – worüber wir weiter oben bereits gesprochen haben – widerspiegelten sich auch in den Ereignissen und in der Ideologie des Bauernkriegs von 1514. Die andersartigen Ausbeutungs- und Unterdrückungsbestrebungen der Grundherren – die wir jetzt erörtern – kommen nicht so sehr in den Dokumenten des *Aufstandes* selbst, als vielmehr durch die Maßnahmen zu seiner *Vergeltung* augenfällig zum Ausdruck. Auf dem Landtag nach der blutigen Niederwerfung des Bauernkrieges begnügten sich nämlich die Grundherren – nachdem sie über die von den Bauern zu leistenden persönlichen und materiellen Entschädigungen schwerwiegende Maßnahmen beschlossen hatten – nicht mehr mit der Möglichkeit, sich neben der *Geld*rente die Produktenrente in größerem Umfange anzueignen, sondern nahmen in das Gesetz auch das Recht auf, ihre Grund- und Untersassen in den Dörfern und Marktflecken in *allen drei Formen* der Feudalrente, im Zensus (bzw. anderen Geldlasten), im Neuntel (und Geschenken in natura) und außerdem auch in der Form der *Arbeitsrente* (wöchentlich 1 Tag Fron) ausbeuten zu können./81/ Wenn wir in Betracht ziehen, daß nach unseren

Forschungen in den Jahrzehnten vor 1514 nicht nur in den Marktflecken, sondern auch in einer ganzen Reihe von Dörfern allenfalls einige Tage Fron *jährlich* geleistet werden mußte,/82/ dann bedeutet der *wöchentlich* eine Tag eine wesentliche Erschwerung. In der stickigen Atmosphäre im Herbst 1514 begnügte sich der Landtag auch nicht mehr mit der ***Beschränkung***, der Erschwerung der Freizügigkeit der Bauern, sondern beschloß die ***Abschaffung*** derselben, die Bindung der Bauern in den Dörfern und in den Marktflecken an die Scholle./83/ Das zur gleichen Zeit, da dieses Gesetz verkündet wurde, vom König bestätigte Tripartitum macht nicht beim Entzug der Freizügigkeit, der Erklärung des „vollkommenen und erblichen Bauerntums" halt/84/, sondern dehnte die Strafmaßnahmen auch auf das andere Hauptmerkmal der sozialrechtlichen Lage der unmittelbaren Produzenten aus, auf ihr Recht der Bodenbenutzung und Bodenbesitzung. Werbőczis berüchtigte Satzung/85/ formulierte das feudale Monopol des herrschaftlichen Grundeigentums derart, daß darin nicht einmal der erbliche Anspruch des Bauern auf seine Hufe anerkannt wurde.

Das Vergeltungsdekret des Jahres 1514 und das Tripartitum – diese beiden organisch zusammenhängenden Gesetzeswerke – legten durch die Kodifizierung der Verschärfung der grundherrlichen Rechte, durch die Aufhebung der Freizügigkeit und durch Einschränkung der Hufenbesitzung und Bodennutzung für Jahrhunderte die rechtlichen Rahmen und die Grundlagen der ungarischen Variante der „zweiten Leibeigenschaft", des Systems der erblichen Untertänigkeit. Die Kunde von dieser Rechtsgebung hallte sogar in den in Venedig im Jahre 1516 erschienenen „Antiken Vorträgen" des italienischen Humanisten Coelius Rodiginus wider, in denen die elende Lage der Heloten von Sparta gerade mit jener der ungarischen Leibeigenen in Parallele gesetzt wurde. Der humanistische Autor erwähnt die Redensart: „Wer in Sparta ein freier Mann ist, der ist wirklich frei, wer aber in Sparta Knecht ist, nur der ist wirklich Knecht" und fügt hinzu: „Ich höre, daß dies jetzt in Pannonien oder wie man jetzt sagt in Ungarn, besser als irgendwo beobachtet werden kann; deshalb sagt man bei ihnen, daß man woanders gar nicht wirklich von Knechten sprechen kann '. . . non recte dici servitutem, nisi un Pannonia'."/86/

4 Natürlich ist es wieder eine andere Frage, wieweit die Beschlüsse von 1514 in den unmittelbar folgenden Jahren und Jahrzehnten tatsächlich zur Praxis wurden. Wir wollen hier weder vom Verlauf, den Wenden und einzelnen Stufen der Durchführung dieser Verordnungen sprechen, die die Sicherheit der bäuerlichen Bodennutzung beeinträchtigten, noch von jenen, die seine Freizügigkeit aufhoben, sondern nur einige Worte über die Entwicklung der feudalen Leistungen nach 1514 sagen.

Ebenso wie die Gesetze aus den zwei Jahrzehnten vor dem Bauernkrieg, gingen – natürlich – auch die entsprechenden Artikel des Dekrets von 1514 nicht sofort in die Praxis über. Dieser Feststellung müssen wir jedoch auch hinzufügen, daß die tatsächliche Richtung der Entwicklung der bäuerlichen Leistungen – natürlich mit wesentlichen Abweichungen in den einzelnen Gegenden, Grundherrschaften, ja manchmal sogar Ortschaften – einige Zeit noch langsam, dann in immer beschleunigterem Tempo im allgemeinen mit der sich in den Gesetzen der Jahre 1492–1514 abzeichnenden Tendenz zusammenfiel.

Das Urbarium der Domäne Léka erwähnte im Jahre 1519 weder das Neuntel noch die Fron./87/ In der Domäne Kisvárda war das Wein- und Getreideneuntel im Jahre 1521 schon ziemlich häufig, die Fron jedoch überstieg kaum das vor der Jahrhundertwende übliche Ausmaß./88/ Das Urbarium der Burgherrschaft von Kanizsa aus dem Jahre 1519 zeugt hingegen sowohl vom Ansteigen der zum Neuntel verpflichteten Ortschaften wie der Ausbreitung der Arbeitsrente. Die hier (und im Urbarium der Domäne Sárvár aus dem Jahre 1518) erscheinende neue Belastung, der Frondienst für viele Ortschaften zum Weintransport, läßt darauf schließen, daß die Grundherren begannen, sich in den Weinhandel einzuschalten. Daneben verschärfte sich zwischen 1512 und 1519 in einzelnen Ortschaften der Grundherrschaft auch die im eigentlichen Sinne genommene landwirtschaftliche Fron. Die Grundsassen von Mikefalva und Szentgyörgy waren bereits verpflichtet, nach jedem Pflug 7 1/2 Joch grundherrliches Ackerland zu bestellen (die Urbarien aus dem 15. Jahrhundert schrieben meist noch 2 Tage bzw. 2 Joch Fron je Pflug vor).Die Bewohner von Bankfalva, Iharos und anderer Dörfer waren „verpflichtet, zu ernten, bis die Ernte beendet ist" und die Ernte einzubringen. Inzwischen war nämlich in Szepetnek ein neues Allodium entstanden und in Gelse zwei grundherrliche Weingärten; letztere wurden ebenfalls in Fronarbeit bestellt./89/

An dieser Stelle soll noch das Beispiel der Domäne des Markgrafen Georg von Brandenburg in Gyula erwähnt werden, das – wie wir wissen – in den heißen Monaten des Jahres 1514 in sehr exponierter Lage war. Hier kam es – von der Bemessung der Schadenersatzsumme und die mehrfache Eintreibung der Staatssteuern durch den Grundherrn abgesehen – in der Zeit nach der Niederwerfung des Bauernaufstandes zuerst zu einer Steigerung der in *Geld* vorgenommenen Ausbeutung der Bauern. Die Verrechnungen der Grundherrschaft vom Jahre 1519 wiesen den Zensus mit 737 Gulden, die außerordentliche herrschaftliche Taxe hingegen mit 1 100 Gulden aus; das Urbarium aus dem Jahre 1525 besagte, daß der Grundherr außer dem Zensus „Taxe auswerfen und verordnen kann, so oft es ihm beliebt". Andererseits verbreitete sich in der Grundherrschaft auch die Neuntel-Form der *Produkten*rente immer mehr, und zwar zu Handelszwecken: in den Verrechnungen des Jahres 1519 werden Einnahmeposten erwähnt, die ausdrücklich aus dem Verkauf von Neuntelgetreide bzw. aus dem Verkauf und Ausschank von Neuntelwein stammten./90/ Besonderes Interesse verdient dann die wirtschaftliche Anordnung, die Georg von Brandenburg 1520 an die Burghauptleute und den Hofrichter von Gyula erließ, und die nunmehr bereits zur Eigenwirtschaft ansporn te und dafür zwei Beweggründe beleuchtet: „. . . der neue Hofrichter widme der Ackerwirtschaft erhöhte Aufmerksamkeit und ordne mehr Aussaat an als bisher . . . er verbessere das Allodium, sichere den Ackerbau und die Viehwirtschaft, damit nicht immerfort für Bargeld gekauft werden müsse, sondern damit wir verkaufen und daraus Gewinn ziehen können . . ."/91/ Die Ausbreitung der Allodialwirtschaft war daher nicht nur im Interesse der Entwicklung der *Handels*tätigkeit der Burgherrschaft erwünscht, sondern auch an sich zur Selbstversorgung, „damit nicht immerfort für Bargeld gekauft werden müsse". Die möglichst direkte Befriedigung des Bedarfs der Hofhaltung und der Lebensmittelversorgung der Soldaten der Burg ohne Einkauf auf dem Markt, damit die Ausschaltung eines wichtigen Marktsektors der bäuerlichen Warenproduktion – um erneut auf diesen wichtigen

Gesichtspunkt hinzuweisen – fielen zu einer Zeit, da die Agrarpreise im Steigen begriffen waren (und das Land in einen Kriegsschauplatz verwandelt wurde), mit besonderem Gewicht in die Waagschale.

Das Ansteigen der Preise für Agrarprodukte, das um die Wende vom 15. zum 16. Jahrhundert einsetzte, wurde in den folgenden Jahren immer schneller, um die Mitte des Jahrhunderts bereits stürmisch und gab dem grundherrlichen Warenhandel und der grundherrlichen Warenproduktion immer stärkeren Antrieb.

Dies widerspiegelten auch die Verhältnisse in der Burgherrschaft von Gyula, obwohl diese nach der Schlacht bei Mohács den Besitzer wechselte und in den folgenden Jahrzehnten oft Kriegschauplatz war./92/ Das Einkommen der Domäne aus dem Getreideverkauf betrug im Jahre 1519 insgesamt 225 Gulden, 1527 schon 627 Gulden, im Jahre 1557 aber bereits 2808 Gulden. Und wenn im Jahre 1519 der ertragreiche Getreidehandel „venditio frugum nonalium", das heißt die Verwertung des Getreideneuntels bedeutete, so ist im Jahre 1557 „de venditione frugum, quae ex agricultura, nonis et molendinis provenire solent" etwa das Dreizehnfache dieses Betrages durch den Verkauf von Getreide aus der Allodialwirtschaft, aus dem Neuntel und aus dem Mühleneinkommen eingeflossen./93/ Parallel zum Ansteigen der Produktenpreise wurde also auch das Allodium der Domäne Gyula ausgebaut. Es kann uns daher nicht überraschen, daß nach dem Text des Urbariums aus den Jahren 1559 und 1561 die Leibeigenen zu fast „allen Arbeiten und Dienstleistungen verpflichtet" sind, „pflügen, säen und andere Leistungen zu erbringen haben", während das Urbarium aus dem Jahre 1525 neben der Ausdehnung des Getreide- und des Weinneuntels lediglich 2 Tage Mäh- und 1 Tag Erntefron vorschrieb./94/

Bis zur Mitte des Jahrhunderts wurden also die *rechtlichen Rahmen* des Systems der erblichen Untertänigkeit in zahlreichen Gegenden des Landes immer mehr mit schwer drückendem *tatsächlichem Inhalt* ausgefüllt, um dann bis zur Jahrhundertwende den letzten Abschnitt des Entwicklungsprozesses zu erreichen.

5 Den Prozeß im 16.–17. Jahrhundert, die Phasen der Herausbildung der zweiten Leibeigenschaft in den Jahren nach 1514, können wir natürlich im Rahmen dieses Vortrags nicht verfolgen. Ausweichen können wir jedoch nicht jener – zu Beginn unserer Darlegungen übernommenen – Aufgabe, zum Schluß noch einige Worte über den unterschiedlichen Gebrauch des Begriffs „zweite Leibeigenschaft" (bzw. perpetua rusticitas) zu sagen. Denn gerade die unterschiedliche Auslegung des Begriffes ist auch eine der Quellen der verschiedenen Ansichten, die sich in unserer Fachliteratur im Hinblick auf die wirtschafts- und gesellschaftsgeschichtliche Stellung des Bauernaufstandes von 1514 ergeben haben. Vielleicht irren wir uns nicht, wenn wir in unserer neueren Literatur drei Hauptvarianten zu entdecken glauben: eine enge, eine breitere und eine ausgebreitete Auslegung.

Die enge Auslegung des Begriffs geht von der sozial-rechtlichen Lage der Untertanen aus, konzentriert sich auf die Rechtsverhältnisse der unmittelbar Produzenten (und auf ihre Rechte der Bodennutzung und der Bodenbesitzung). Diese Annäherung findet sich – um bei dieser Gelegenheit nicht auf frühere historiographische Vorläufer zurückzugreifen – in der 1948 veröffentlichten Studie des vor wenigen Jahren verstorbenen, verdienstvollen ungarischen Agrarhistorikers István Szabó.

Zwei Hauptmomente sind für seine Auffassung bezeichnend. Einmal, daß bei ihm die perpetua rusticitas mit der ewig *an die Scholle gebundenen* Leibeigenschaft, mit dem „System der *ewigen Bindung an die Scholle*“ gleichbedeutend ist, wobei „die ewige Bindung des Grundsassen an die Scholle. . . bedeutete, daß die Bindung zwischen Bauern und Bauernhufe im Prinzip unauflösbar wurde.“/95/

Der andere Hauptzug ist jedoch, daß „das neuzeitliche System der perpetua rusticitas nicht identisch war mit dem mittelalterlichen System der Leibeigenschaft“. Der mittelalterliche Begriff von servilis conditio oder Leibeigenschaft bedeutet nämlich, daß „der Leibeigene in Wirklichkeit nicht an die Scholle gebunden war, sondern an die persönliche Gewalt seines Herrn, was damit einherging, daß der Herr den Leibeigenen jederzeit seine Hufe wegnehmen, unabhängig von seiner Hufe auch veräußern, kaufen und verkaufen, tauschen konnte, ja das konnte der Grundherr auch mit den Familienangehörigen seiner Leibeigenen tun.“ „Der ungarische Untertan war an die Scholle und an die Gewalt seines Herrn gebunden, aber wurde kein Leibeigener, seine Person kam nicht in den Verkehr, noch weniger die einzelnen Mitglieder seiner Familie . . . Der ungarische Untertan war untrennbar von seinem Boden, er war wirklich an die Scholle gebunden.“ Er selbst habe „keine Angaben dafür gefunden, wo ausgesprochen und klar vom Verkauf der Person des Untertanen die Rede sei“, betonte István Szabó mehrfach, sich mit Acsády auseinandersetzend./96/

In Ungarn entwickelte sich also im 16.–17. Jahrhundert das System der erblichen Untertänigkeit, was aber nicht als „zweite Ausgabe“ der frühmittelalterlichen Leibeigenschaft und in diesem Sinne als „zweite Leibeigenschaft“ angesehen werden kann – dahingehend können wir István Szabós Auslegung zusammenfassen.

Von der Veröffentlichung dieser Studie vergingen mehr als zwei Jahrzehnte, bis János Varga sich in seiner Monographie dem Problem der perpetua rusticitas auf ähnliche Weise annäherte: von der sozial-rechtlichen Lage der unmittelbaren Produzenten her, im engeren Sinne genommen, vom gesellschaftsgeschichtlichen bzw. rechtsgeschichtlichen Aspekt her. Von ähnlichem Aspekt her, aber mit wesentlich abweichendem Ergebnis. Nach Vargas Auslegung nämlich ist das Hauptmerkmal der ungarischen perpetua rusticitas nicht *die Bindung an die Scholle*, sondern die Bindung an die Person, das Eigentum am Menschen:„. . . in dem Verhältnis ist das persönliche Moment das bestimmende Element: der Untertan ist, als die den Besitzgegenstand darstellende Person, dem Grundherrn, als der den Besitzer darstellenden Person, untergeben“. Die Schollengebundenheit jedoch ist, „da das Recht der Freizügigkeit fehlt, nicht allgemein für das Wesen des Systems bestimmend . . . sondern lediglich Kennzeichen und Charakteristikum einer – der verbreitetsten und strengsten – Variante des Systems der erblichen Untertänigkeit“, während sich seine niedrigere Stufe, die Vorstufe der „klassischen“ Variante, mit der sich innerhalb der festgesetzten Rahmen der Freizügigkeit bewegenden Form vereinbaren läßt./97/ Varga führt zugleich reiches Material für die schwerste Form der persönlichen Abhängigkeit an: wie Eigentum wurden die Grundsassen von den Grundherren getauscht, verpfändet, verschenkt, gekauft und verkauft, in den meisten Fällen zusammen mit ihrer Hufe, aber auch ohne dieselbe. Der Untertan konnte auch getrennt von seinem Boden, ja auch getrennt von seiner Familie, allein, nur seine Person Gegenstand von Verpfändung, Tausch, Kauf und Verkauf und auch zeitweiliges Geschenk sein./98/

II

Wenn dem so ist – können wir die Schlußfolgerung aus Vargas Darlegungen ziehen – dann zeigte das ungarische System der perpetua rusticitas sehr wohl die rechtlichen Kennzeichen, Kriterien der frühmittelalterlichen Bauern von servilis conditio, der Leibeigenschaft, ist also bei engster und strengster Auslegung als „zweite Ausgabe" der Leibeigenschaft, kurz als „zweite Leibeigenschaft" zu bezeichnen.

Ganz gleich um welche wesentlichen Faktoren und Unterschiede der sozialrechtlichen Lage der unmittelbaren Produzenten es sich auch in der Alternative von Bindung an die *Scholle* oder Bindung an die *Person* handelt, so kann dies unserer Meinung nach die Frage dennoch nicht entscheiden, ob wir die Institution der spätfeudalen erblichen Untertänigkeit als „mutatis mutandis" „zweite Ausgabe" des frühmittelalterlichen Leibeigenensystems betrachten können, selbst im engsten, rechtlichen Sinne.

Wir würden uns nämlich irren, wenn wir glaubten, daß die besonders schwerwiegenden Formen der bäuerlichen Abhängigkeit, die im frühen Mittelalter zur Geltung kamen, unbedingt und ausschließlich die Bindung an die *Person* des Herrn bedeuteten. Wenn wir die westeuropäische Entwicklung betrachten – wo wir die frühmittelalterlichen Agrarverhältnisse am klarsten studieren können – dann stellt sich heraus, daß das Bauernvolk auf der frühfeudalen Grundherrschaft in viele Gruppen zerfiel, mit zahlreichen Übergangsformen – und diese Unterschiede ergeben sich unter anderem daraus, ob die unmittelbaren Produzenten aufgrund des von ihnen genutzten Bodens vom Grundherrn abhingen, ob sie *an die Scholle* gebunden waren, oder auch *persönlich* abhängig, an den Herrn gebunden waren. Letztere nannte man in England villain, in Frankreich serf, in Deutschland Leibeigener – auf erstere dürfte sich der französische Ausdruck vilain und das deutsche hörig (grundhörig) beziehen – wobei diese Kategorien nicht selten ineinander übergingen./99/ Die Bindung an die Scholle (Hörigkeit, Grundhörigkeit) und die Bindung an die Person des Herrn (Leibeigenschaft) erweisen sich schon unter den westeuropäischen frühfeudalen Verhältnissen als oft verschmelzende Variationen ein und derselben schwerwiegenden Abhängigkeit./100/ Zum Begriff der Erneuerung des frühmittelalterlichen Leibeigenensystems, seiner zweiten Ausgabe, gehört also nicht nur die zweite „*Bindung an die Person*", die „zweite Leibeigenschaft" – die auch in der Neuzeit im Deutschen „Leibeigenschaft" genannt wurde – sondern auch die zweite „*Bindung an die Scholle*", wenn ich es so nennen darf, die „zweite Hörigkeit" (Grundhörigkeit), die die deutsche Terminologie des 17.–18. Jahrhunderts etwa als „erbliche Untertänigkeit" oder „Erbuntertänigkeit" bezeichnet. Charakteristisch ist im übrigen, daß der Wortgebrauch auch in der Neuzeit nicht konsequent war: die Ausdrücke „Leibeigenschaft" bzw. „erbliche Untertänigkeit" wurden oft als Synonyma gebraucht – worauf Josef Kočí für Böhmen verwiesen hat./101/

In den letzten Jahrzehnten jedoch hat die ungarische Forschung das Wesen der zweiten Leibeigenschaft weniger vom Gesichtspunkt der *rechtlichen* Lage untersucht, vielmehr im breiteren Sinne: sie hat sich ihm vom *wirtschafts*geschichtlichen Gesichtspunkt genähert. Im Vordergrund der Aufmerksamkeit stand also: welchen wirtschaftlichen Bedingungen entsprachen, aus welchen *Agrarverhältnissen* resultierten die persönlichen Beziehungen der unmittelbaren Produzenten, die in der rechtlichen Form der erblichen Untertänigkeit verkörpert wurden? So gingen vornehmlich László

Makkai, István Sinkovics und andere Forscher vor,/102/ die die Entwicklung der sozial-rechtlichen Lage der Leibeigenen vor allem als Begleiterscheinung und Folge der wirtschaftlichen Prozesse behandelt haben.

Diese Forschungen haben, was das Wesen betrifft, zu ähnlichen Ergebnissen geführt wie in Polen oder in den ostdeutschen Gebieten. Die besonders schwerwiegenden Formen der Abhängigkeit der Leibeigenen waren auch in Ungarn mit Ausbeutungsverhältnissen verbunden, gekennzeichnet durch die wichtige, ja gerade durch die dominierende Rolle der Arbeitsrente, als nämlich ein großer Teil der Bauernfron zur Bewirtschaftung der gutsherrlichen Eigenbetriebe (Allodium, folwark, Vorwerk, gutsherrliche Eigenwirtschaft) erzwungen wurde. Wenn wir jetzt in Betracht ziehen, daß auch die frühfeudale Leibeigenschaft mit drückenden Fronverpflichtungen und mit dem ansehnlichen Gewicht der grundherrlichen Eigenwirtschaft (terra dominicalis, terra salica, demesne, Salland, Hofland) zusammenhing,/103/ so bieten die erwähnten Forschungsergebnisse für das 16.–17. Jahrhundert die Grundlage dafür, daß wir die spätfeudale Leibeigenschaft auch vom wirtschaftsgeschichtlichen Gesichtspunkt als „zweite Leibeigenschaft" betrachten, als „zweite Ausgabe" des frühmittelalterlichen Leibeigenensystems qualifizieren.

Hier müssen wir wiederum kurz auf die Frage eingehen, wann wir vom „ansehnlichen Gewicht" der gutsherrlichen Eigenwirtschaft innerhalb der Struktur des feudalen Grundeigentums als grundlegendem, in die Richtung der Leibeigenschaft weisenden Faktor sprechen können. Wir müssen darauf auch unter anderem deshalb eingehen, da einige Historiker, so auch unser schon an anderer Stelle erwähnter slowakischer Kollege Anton Špiesz, das Gewicht der ungarischen (slowakischen) Allodialwirtschaft im 16.–17. Jahrhundert nicht für ausreichend halten, um sie als eine Variante der osteuropäischen Gutswirtschaft zu betrachten; gerade auf dieser Grundlage hat er das Vorhandensein des Systems der zweiten Leibeigenschaft auf dem Boden des ehemaligen Ungarn in Zweifel gezogen./104/ Nun also berechtigen die bisherigen Forschungen zu der Feststellung, daß das gutsherrliche Ackerland in der ersten Hälfte und um die Mitte des 17. Jahrhunderts im königlichen Ungarn bereits vielerorts 15–30% der in bäuerlicher Hand befindlichen Saatfläche erreicht hatte (von der Entwicklung im 18. Jahrhundert gar nicht zu sprechen)./105/ Dieses Verhältnis bedeutet aber nicht wesentlich weniger als das, welches die zeitgenössischen Angaben über die zweite Leibeigenschaft in den, wenn ich den – hier paradoxen – Ausdruck verwenden darf, „klassischen" Ländern zeigen. In Estland wurde das Verhältnis von gutsherrlicher Saatfläche zu Bauernland in der ersten Hälfte des 17. Jahrhunderts auf 1:4, Ende des Jahrhunderts auf 1:3 geschätzt./106/ In Mecklenburg gehörte unmittelbar vor dem 30jährigen Krieg auf den Rittergütern halb soviel eigenbewirtschaftetes Ackerland zu den Herrenhöfen, als zu den Bauernhufen./107/ Ja noch ein Jahrhundert später, zu Beginn des 18. Jahrhunderts war der Umfang des Bauernlandes größer als jener der ritterlichen Eigenbetriebe. (Erst um die Mitte des 18. Jahrhunderts senkte sich die Waage zugunsten der letzteren.)/108/ Und fügen wir noch hinzu: der oben erwähnte Anteil in Ungarn zeigte, selbst gemessen an der westeuropäischen Grundeigentumsstruktur die mit der mittelalterlichen „ersten Leibeigenschaft" verbunden war, keinen grundlegenden Unterschied. Wenn sich die Saatfläche des Klosters Saint Germain des Près bei Paris zu Beginn des 9. Jahrhunderts zu ungefähr gleichen Teilen zwischen dem grundherrschaftlichen Eigenbetrieb und den Leibeigenenhufen aufteilte,/109/ so machte in England nach der Eroberung durch die Normannen die *demesne* fast 1/3,1/5 des gesamten Ackerlandes des *manor* aus./110/ In Deutschland jedoch war die Eigenbetriebswirtschaft in den frühen Jahrhunderten des Mittelalters zumeist noch weniger entwickelt./111/

Dieser allgemein aufgezeigte Zusammenhang zwischen feudalem Grundeigentum und der Struktur der Grundrente einerseits und der sozial-rechtlichen Lage der Leibeigenen andererseits bedeutet natürlich nicht, daß die schwerwiegendsten Formen der bäuerlichen Untertänigkeit historisch jederzeit und ausschließlich unter den vorher skizzierten Agrarverhältnissen auftreten konnten bzw. auftraten. Unter keinen Umständen können wir zum Beispiel die Variante außer acht lassen, die der Entwicklungsprozeß in Rußland zeigt, darauf hinweisend, daß das System der Leibeigenschaft auch ohne „ansehnliches Gewicht" der Selbstwirtschaft entstehen konnte./112/

Diese Erscheinung hat die mehrfach zitierte Monographie über das spätfeudale System der perpetua rusticitas in Ungarn mit der *geringen Bevölkerung*, mit dem Rückgang der Zahl der Leibeigenen erklärt. In diesem Zusammenhang zog sie die verallgemeinernde Schlußfolgerung, daß „zur Bindung der Bauern an die Scholle, zur Einführung des Leibeigenensystems nicht nur der aus gutsherrlichen Eigenbetriebsform resultierende Arbeitskräftebedarf den entscheidenden Anstoß geben kann, sondern die derart starke Abnahme der Rentenpflichtigen die dazu führen kann, daß die Ausbeutung unter das bereits erreichte Niveau sinkt". Oder knapper ausgedrückt: „Die Leibeigenschaft kann sich auch ohne gutsherrliche Warenproduktion entwickeln, wenn die Zahl der Renten-Leistenden relativ niedrig ist."/113/

Ohne unsererseits an dieser Stelle Anspruch auf die Deutung der Motive der russischen крепостничество zu erheben, fügen wir an die zitierte verallgemeinernde Schlußfolgerung lediglich die Bemerkung, daß wir die dünne Bevölkerung die geringe Anzahl oder den Rückgang der Zahl der rentenpflichtigen Bauern – um wie wichtige Momente es sich dabei auch handeln mag – *an sich* schwerlich als *ausreichenden* Grund für eine erbliche Bindung ansehen können. Denn Wirtschafts- und Gesellschaftsgeschichte bieten zahlreiche Beispiele dafür, daß *die gleiche* Tatsache: geringe Bevölkerungsdichte, Rückgang der Zahl der *unmittelbar Produzenten* durch Krieg oder Epidemien gerade zum Hebel für die Entstehung freier bäuerlicher Verhältnisse und nicht der erblichen Bindung an die Scholle geworden sind – um nur an die Auswirkungen des Rückgangs der landwirtschaftlichen Bevölkerung durch den um die Mitte des 14. Jahrhunderts große Teile Europas verheerenden „schwarzen Tod" oder weiter gefaßt,an den demographischen Rückgang in Westeuropa im 14. und 15. Jahrhundert zu erinnern./114/ Die zahlenmäßige Entwicklung der zur Rentenleistung verpflichteten Bevölkerung müssen wir meiner Meinung nach in einen breiteren Rahmen fassen, in das komplizierte Gewebe der wirtschaflichen Bedingungen der jeweiligen Epoche einfügen und im Zusammenhang mit dem Entwicklungsprozeß der *gesellschaftlichen Arbeitsteilung* bewerten.

Der auf die Ebene der Agrarverhältnisse projizierte Index dieses Zusammenhangs ist die Form und Zusammensetzung der feudalen Rente. Dabei ist historisch nicht ausgeschlossen – auch die ungarische Schollengebundenheit hat solche Fälle hervorgebracht –, daß bei den gutsherrlichen Abgaben der Leibeigenen vorübergehend die

Bargeldleistung vorherrschend wurde./115/ Was jedoch die *Hauptlinie* der Entwicklung betrifft, so stehen die milderen Formen der Abhängigkeit, die freieren bäuerlichen Verhältnisse mit der *Geld*form der feudalen Rente, die schwerwiegendere Abhängigkeit der Leibeigenen jedoch mit den *Naturalformen* der feudalen Rente in gesetzmäßiger Verbindung/116/: mit der *Arbeits*rente *und* der Produktenrente, wo es keine gutsherrliche Eigenwirtschaft größeren Umfanges gibt – wie Ende des 16. und zu Beginn des 17. Jahrhunderts in Rußland – dort *vor allem* mit der Produktenrente. Die Varianten der „zweiten Leibeigenschaft" (der erblichen Untertänigkeit) konnten nur dort und nur unter Verhältnissen und zu einer Zeit entstehen, wo die (um einen Ausdruck von Marx zu gebrauchen) „. . . auf . . . nationalem Maßstab vor sich gehende Verwandlung der Produktenrente", der Naturalformen der feudalen Rente „in Geldrente"/117/ auf Hindernisse stößt.

Das bedeutet zugleich, daß neben der seit Georg Friedrich Knapp üblichen Alternative Grundherrschaft – Gutsherrschaft bzw. neben dem entsprechenden Verhältnis in Bezug auf die Rente: (Geld + Produkt) zu Fronarbeit ähnlich wichtig auch die Untersuchung des Verhältnisses ist, welches einerseits die *Geld*leistungen, andererseits die naturalen Rentenformen (Produkt + Fron) bilden. Das bedeutet weiterhin, daß die schwerwiegenden sozialrechtlichen Bindungen der zweiten Leibeigenschaft nicht nur mit der Agrarstruktur der *Guts*herrschaft (gutsherrliche Eigenwirtschaft) verbunden sein können, sondern auch mit einer Struktur vom Charakter der *Grund*herrschaft, in der aber nicht die Geldverhältnisse, sondern die Naturalleistungen dominieren./118/

Das alles führt bereits zur Interpretation im breitesten Sinne hinüber. In umfassender Auslegung betrachten wir die zweite Leibeigenschaft nicht nur als einen, die *rechtliche Abhängigkeit* der unmittelbar Produzenten ausdrückenden bzw. einen bestimmten Typus der feudalen Agrarverhältnisse bestimmenden Begriff, sondern als *komplexe wirtschaftlich-gesellschaftliche Kategorie;* wir verstehen sie als bestimmte Form der feudalen Ordnung, als eine historische Epoche der ostmitteleuropäischen Entwicklung. Charakteristisch für diese Epoche, dieses System war neben der schwerwiegenden persönlichen Abhängigkeit des Leibeigenen die hervorragende Rolle der naturalen Rentenformen, der Arbeits- und Produktenleistungen und meist, aber nicht immer, das ansehnliche Gewicht der gutsherrlichen Eigenbetriebe. Grundlegend und am allgemeinsten aber die Beschränktheit, die Schwäche der bürgerlichen Entwicklung sowohl auf dem *Dorf* wie auch in der *Stadt*, die außergewöhnlich ungünstigen Kräfteverhältnisse der Klassen vom Gesichtspunkt der Aussichten für die Kapitalisierung.

Denn die „auf ... nationalem Maßstabe vor sich gehende Verwandlung der Produktenrente in Geldrente", um wieder auf die Analyse von Marx zu verweisen, „setzt eine schon bedeutendere Entwicklung des Handels, der städtischen Industrie, der Warenproduktion überhaupt und damit der Geldzirkulation voraus . . . eine Verwendung, die überhaupt nur bei schon gegebener relativer Entwicklungshöhe des Weltmarktes, des Handels und der Manufaktur möglich ist. . ."/119/ Das Fehlen dieser Voraussetzungen, ihre negative Wirkung bzw. Schwäche rief notwendigerweise das Stocken, den Rückfall des „klassischen" Verlaufs des Formwandels der feudalen Rente, die Wiederbelebung der naturalen Rentenformen hervor.

Gerade das Stagnieren der industriellen Entwicklung unserer Städte, das Ersticken der modernen, auf den allgemeinen Konsum gerichteten Tendenzen des Gewerbes, solche Kräfteverhältnisse der Handel treibenden Patrizier und der Handwerk ausübenden Bürger in den Städten, die für die letzteren ungünstig waren – was zugleich die Schwäche oder das Fehlen des städtischen Klassenverbündeten im antifeudalen Kampf des Bauerntums bedeutete, ja dazu führte, daß manche Städte dem Gegenlager verbunden waren wie Kassa oder Brassó im Jahre 1514 –, das ebenfalls hieraus resultierende politische und wirtschaftliche Übergewicht der adligen Grundherren, diese Klassenverhältnisse ermöglichten statt der Auflösung der feudalen Ordnung ihre neuerliche Stabilisierung in Ungarn (und in anderen ostmitteleuropäischen Ländern). Sie waren die Hauptvoraussetzungen für die Herausbildung der zweiten Leibeigenschaft.

In diesem weitesten Sinn bedeutet also die „zweite Ausgabe" der Leibeigenschaft nichts anderes als eine Neuausgabe des *Feudalismus*. Bedeutet sie nichts anderes als die Prolongierung der *mittelalterlichen* Verhältnisse in der *Neuzeit*. Bedeutet sie nichts anderes als den Einschub der – im „klassischen" westeuropäischen Entwicklungsprozeß nicht vorhandenen, Mittel- und Osteuropa eigenen – *Spät*epoche des Feudalismus zwischen seine Blütezeit und seine Verfallsperiode.

In dieser umfassendsten Auslegung hebt sich die Bedeutung des Jahres 1514 im Gesamtprozeß unserer Geschichte mit besonderer Schärfe ab.

Des Jahres 1514, das leuchtender Höhepunkt der antifeudalen Kämpfe des ungarischen Mittelalters und zugleich in seinen Konsequenzen tragischer Wendepunkt unserer feudalen Gesellschaftsentwicklung war. Des Jahres 1514, dessen heißer Sommer und schwüler Herbst als Symbol des historischen Epochewechsels zwischen der reifen und der späten Periode des Feudalismus zu betrachten ist.

Anmerkungen

/1/ Szabó, I., Tanulmányok a magyar parasztság történetéből (Studien aus der Geschichte der ungarischen Bauernschaft). Budapest 1948, 71–72. 77.

/2/ Varga, J., Jobbágyrendszer a magyar feudalizmus kései századaiban 1556–1767 (System der erblichen Untertänigkeit in den späten Jahrhunderten des ungarischen Feudalismus 1556–1767). Budapest 1969, 15, 183–184.

/3/ Ebenda, 95, 183.

/4/ N.Kiss, I., 16. századi dézsmajegyzékek. Borsod, Heves, Bereg, Bihar és Közép-Szolnok megyék (Zehntverzeichnisse aus dem 16. Jahrhundert. Aus den Komitaten Borsod, Heves, Bereg, Bihar und Mittel-Szolnok). Budapest 1960. Zusammenfassung 1079–1080, 1024.

/5/ Zimányi, V., Rezension zu dem Buch von I.N. Kiss. Agrártörténeti Szemle 3, 1961. 133–136.

/6/ Špiesz, A., Vývoj agrárnych pomerov v strednej a východnej Európe v novoveku a problém existencie druhého nevol'níctva na našom území (Die Entwicklung der Agrarverhältnisse in Mittel- und Osteuropa in der Neuzeit und das Problem der Existenz der zweiten Leibeigenschaft auf unserem Gebiet). Historický časopis, 15, 1967. 539–558; Ders., Slovensko v procese refeudalizácie v 16.–18. storočí. (Die Slowakei im Prozesse der Refeudalisation im 16.–18. Jahrhundert). Historické štúdie 17, 1972. 47 ff. – Vgl. auch Historický časopis, 19, 1971, 310–312.

/7/ Belényessi, M., A földművelés fejlődésének alapvető kérdései a XIV. században (Grundlegende Fragen der Entwicklung des Ackerbaus im 14. Jahrhundert.) Ethnographia 65, 1954. 387–415 und 66, 1955, 57–98, Dies., Viehzucht und Hirtenwesen in Ungarn im 14. und 15. Jahrhundert. In: Viehzucht und Hirtenleben in Ostmitteleuropa. Budapest 1961, 13 ff. – Bersényi, I., A mezőgazdasági termelés néhány kérdéséhez a XIV–XV. században (Zu einigen Fragen der landwirtschaftlichen Produktion im 14.–15. Jahrhundert). Agrártörténeti Szemle

4, 1962. 569 ff.– Szabó, I., Ungarns Landwirtschaft von der Mitte des 14. Jahrhunderts bis zu den 1530er Jahren. Agrártörténeti Szemle 8, 1966, Supplementum 1 ff.

/8/ Bártfai Szabó, L., A sárvár-felsővidéki gróf Széchenyi-család története (Geschichte der Familie Graf Széchenyi von Sárvár-Felsővidék). Budapest 1911, (Im weiteren: Széchenyi-Urkundenbuch,) 555, (1444).

/9/ Kammerer, E., A zichi és vásonkeői gróf Zichy-család idősb ágának okmánytára (Urkundenbuch des älteren Zweiges der Familie Graf Zichy von Zich und Vásonkeő). Budapest 1907, X, 131 (1460). Im weiteren: Zichy-Urkundenbuch.

/10/ Zichy-Urkundenbuch, X, 396–397 (1466).

/11/ Géresi, K., A nagykárolyi gróf Károlyi-család oklevéltára (Urkundenbuch der Familie Graf Károlyi von Nagykároly). Budapest 1883, II, 450 (1476). Im weiteren: Károlyi-Urkundenbuch.

/12/ Nagy, I. – Véghelyi, D. – Nagy, Gy., Zala vármegye története. Oklevéltár. (Geschichte des Komitats Zala. Urkundenbuch.) Budapest 1890, II, 526–527 (1445).

/13/ Zichy-Urkundenbuch, IX, 437, 443 (1454).

/14/ Ebenda, XII, 209 (1444).

/15/ Ebenda, X. 145 (1461).

/16/ Reizner, J., Szeged története. IV. Oklevéltár. (Geschichte Szegeds. IV. Urkundenbuch.) Szeged 1900. 25–44 (1415–1438), 58 (1464), 87–88 (1498). Im weiteren: Szeged. Urkundenbuch. Szeged wurde übrigens im Jahre 1498 zur königlichen Freistadt erhoben.

/17/ Veress, E., Gyula város oklevéltára. 1313–1800 (Urkundenbuch der Stadt Gyula. 1313–1800). Budapest 1938, 22–23 (1476). Im weiteren: Stadt Gyula, Urkundenbuch.

/18/ Szendrei, J., Oklevéltár Miskolc város történetéhez (Urkundenbuch zur Geschichte der Stadt Miskolc). Miskolc 1890, 103–104 (1467).

/19/ Zichy-Urkundenbuch, IX, 108 (1446).

/20/ Ebenda, IX, 439–440 (1454), 516 (1456).

/21/ Ebenda, X, 105–106 (1460), 217 (1462), 296–301 (1464).

/22/ Károlyi-Urkundenbuch, III. 11–12 (1492).

/23/ Zichy-Urkundenbuch, XI. 130 (1473).

/24/ Magdics, I., Ráckevei okmánytár (Ráckeve-Urkundenbuch). Székesfehérvár 1888, 38 (1458), 48 (1475), 51–53 (1489).

/25/ Zichy-Urkundenbuch, XI, 40 (1469).

/26/ Vgl. Gesetzesartikel 29 v.J. 1486; „mercatores et negotiatores caeterique pauperes, qui aut quaestus gratia, aut pro necessaria victuum acquisitione, vel etiam pro aliis ipsorum rebus, per regnum hinc inde proficisci habent".

/27/ Szabó, I., A hajdúk 1514-ben (Die Heiducken im Jahre 1514). Századok 84, 1950, 189–194.

/28/ Zichy-Urkundenbuch, IX, 332, 353 (1452–1453).– Szeged, Urkundenbuch, 57–58, 63, 67–69, 72, 89 (1462, 1465, 1469, 1473, 1499).– Zsilinszky, M., Csongrád vármegye története (Geschichte des Komitats Csongrád). Budapest 1897, I, 133. Zoltai, L., Ismeretlen részletek Debrecen múltjából (Unbekannte Einzelheiten aus der Vergangenheit von Debrecen). Debrecen 1936, 100–101.

/29/ Zichy-Urkundenbuch, X, 105–106, 217, 296–301 (1460, 1462, 1464),– Hornyik, J., Kecskemét története (Geschichte Kecskeméts). Kecskemét 1860, I. 209–213 (1458).– Kubinyi, A., Die Städte Ofen und Pest und der Fernhandel am Ende des 15. und am Anfang des 16. Jahrhunderts. In: Der Außenhandel Ostmitteleuropas 1450–1650. Hrsg.v.I.Bog. Köln–Wien 1971, 355–357.

/30/ Pach,Zs.P., The Role of East-Central Europe in International Trade (16th and 17th centuries). In: Études Historiques 1970. Budapest 1970, 242–244.

/31/ Daß die Warenverkaufstätigkeit der Grundherren – worunter der Vorkauf sowohl der in den Allodien produzierten wie der als Rente aneigneten Produkte oder die Weiterveräußerung der auf dem Markt gekauften Waren usw. zu verstehen ist – zu Beginn des Jahrhunderts im allgemeinen nicht bedeutend war, ist natürlich nicht dahingehend auszulegen, daß dies auf einzelnen Gütern bzw. in bestimmten Formen nicht regelmäßig vorgekommen sei. Von der Grundherrschaft Kisvárda z.B. berichten einzelne Belege über den Verkauf von Wein, Getreide, Schweinen und Salz, von der erzbischöflichen Grundherrschaft Eger über den Verkauf von Wein, Honig, von Lämmern und Salz. Zichy-Urkundenbuch XII, 221 (1449), IX, 542, 558 (1457), XI, 67–75, (1470–1471), 93–94 (um 1471). – Kandra, K., Bakócs-codex vagy Bakócs Tamás egri püspök udvartartási számadó könyve 1493–1496. évekről (Der Bakócs-Kodex oder das Hofhaltungs-Rechnungsbuch des Bischofs von Erlau, Tamás Bakócs, aus den Jahren 1493–1496). Adatok az egri egyházmegye történelméhez (Beiträge zur Geschichte der Diözese Erlau). Eger 1887, II, 345, 346, 364, 370, 377, 380, 393, 412, 414, 427,– Aber die aktive Markttätigkeit der Grundherren war auch so verschwindend im Vergleich zu jener der Bauern, ihre Geldeinnahme aus dem Verkauf gering, gemessen an ihrer Einnahme aus der Geldrente.

/32/ Wenzel, G., Magyarország mezőgazdaságának története (Geschichte der Landwirtschaft Ungarns). Budapest 1887, 291–292.– Acsády, I., A magyar jobbágyság története (Geschichte des ungarischen Bauerntums). Budapest[3], 1948, 119–121.– Sinkovics, I., A magyar nagybirtok élete a XV. század elején (Das Leben des ungarischen Großgrundbesitzes zu Beginn des 15. Jahrhunderts). Budapest 1933, 57–58,– Székely, Gy. (Red.), Tanulmányok a parasztság történetéhez Magyarországon a XIV. században (Studien zur Geschichte der Bauernschaft in Ungarn im 14. Jahrhundert). Budapest 1953, 213 ff.

/33/ Mályusz, E., Az 1514. évi jobbágyháború okai (Die Ursachen des Bauernkrieges im Jahre 1514). Társadalomtudomány 6, 1926, 375–376.– Szabó, I., Hanyatló jobbágyság a középkor végén (Rückgängiges Bauerntum am Ende des Mittelalters). Századok 72, 1938, 42–45.– Molnár, E., A magyar társadalom története az Árpád-kortól Mohácsig (Die Geschichte der ungarischen Gesellschaft von der Arpadenzeit bis Mohács). Budapest 1949, 229–230, 239.– Vgl. noch Bácskai, V., Magyar mezővárosok a XV. században (Ungarische Marktflecken im 15. Jahrhundert). Budapest 1965, 103.

/34/ Zum Beispiel Bodenschenkungen: „in omnibus parere et obedire, universos ... census et proventus ... solvere"; Károlyi-Urkundenbuch, II, 336 (1461); „cum omnibus fructibus, scilicet censibus, redditibus et proventibus": Zichy-Urkundenbuch, XI, 197 (1477); bei der Summierung der grundherrlichen Einnahmen steht an erster Stelle–summa florenorum, dann – summa tritici, danach – summa avene. Ebenda, XII, 287–289 (1469–1470).

/35/ Ausführlich siehe: Pach, Zs.P., Nyugat-európai és magyarországi agrárfejlődés a XV–XVII. században (Westeuropäische und ungarische Agrarentwicklung im 15.–17. Jahrhundert). Budapest 1963, 52–54, 82–84.

/36/ Koller, J., Historia Episcopatus Quinqueecclesiarum. Pozsony 1784, III, 374–375.

/37/ Tagányi, K., Szarvkő várának bevételei és kiadásai 1448–ból (Einnahmen und Ausgaben der Burg Hornstein im Jahre 1448). Magyar Gazdaságtörténelmi Szemle 2, 1895. 211–215, – Vgl. Mohl, A., Szarvkő és urai (Hornstein und seine Herren). Századok 37, 1903, 627–628.

/38/ Szeged, Urkundenbuch, 75–78.

/39/ In vielen Gemeinden der Burgherrschaft Kanizsa: assaturam in valore unius denarii Wiennensis; in einzelnen Ortschaften der Domäne Sárvár–Kapuvár: unum pullum et Wienn. quattuor, ova duo et den.W.unum. Országos Levéltár (Ungarisches Staatsarchiv, im weiteren: OL), Sammlung der Urkunden aus der Zeit vor 1526 (im weiteren: Dl), 36 997, 36 992.

/40/ Zum Beispiel in Tótfalu im Komitat Bodrog; officiali hoc ordine solvere muneralia tenentur ... circa festum beati Georgii martyris tenentur dare singulos decem denarios. In festo autem beati Michaelis archangeli similiter... singulos decem denarios ... Zichy-Urkundenbuch, XII, 317.

/41/ Acsády, op.cit., 136.

/42/ OL Dl 36 992.

/43/ Koller, op.cit., III, 375.

/44/ Zichy-Urkundenbuch, IX, 317–318 (1452), 477 (1454); XII, 268 (1460); XI, 70–79 (1470–1471).

/45/ Fügedi, E., Az esztergomi érsekség gazdálkodása a XV. század végén (Die Wirtschaft des Erzbistums von Gran am Ende des 15. Jahrhunderts). Századok 94, 1960, 506–507, 525.

/46/ Kandra, op. cit., 353, 361, 363, 372, 374, 375, 376, 408, 409, 415 usw.

/47/ Abel, W., Agrarkrisen und Agrarkonjunktur. Eine Geschichte der Land- und Ernährungswirtschaft Mitteleuropas seit dem hohen Mittelalter. Hamburg–Berlin² 1966, 57–58.– Siehe auch: Ders., Die Wüstungen des ausgehenden Mittelalters. Stuttgart² 1955, 100–104, 174–175.– Vgl. Kuczynski, J., Einige Überlegungen über die Rolle der Natur in der Gesellschaft anläßlich der Lektüre von Abels Buch über Wüstungen. Jahrbuch für Wirtschaftsgeschichte. Berlin 1963, III, 295–297.

/48/ Zimányi, V., A magyarországi ármozgások helye az európai fejlődésben (Die Stellung der ungarischen Preisbewegungen in der europäischen Entwicklung), Történelmi Szemle 15, 1972. 378–412.

/49/ Siehe die Rechnungsbücher des königlichen Schatzmeisters Zsigmond Ernuszt, Bischof von Pécs, für die Jahre 1494–1495: Engel, J.Chr. von, Geschichte des ungrischen Reichs und seiner Nebenländer. Halle 1797, I, 17–81.– Vgl. Fejérpataky, L., II. Ulászló jövedelmeinek jegyzéke (Verzeichnis von Wladislaus' II. Einkommen). Történelmi Tár 1880, 167–170 und besonders: Fógel, J., II. Ulászló udvartartása. 1490–1516 (Die Hofhaltung Wladislaus' II, 1490–1516). Budapest 1913, 13–28.

/50/ OL Dl 20 902, 21 571.

/51/ OL Dl 37 002, 34 994, – Vgl. OL Dl 24 619.

/52/ G.A. 86–88 v.J. 1492, G.A. 74 v.J. 1498, G.A. 40–42 v.J. 1500. Vgl. G.A. 12 v.J. 1518, G.A. 6 v.J. 1519.

/53/ OL Dl 37 986.– Vgl. Márki, S., Dósa György (György Dósa). Budapest 1913, 223, 270.

/54/ Károlyi-Urkundenbuch, III, 88–89 (1513 – Der Vorfall hat sich zwei Jahre früher ereignet).

/55/ Márki, op.cit., 104, 157, 194, 198–199.– Den authentischen Text stellten mir die Redakteure des in Vorbereitung befindlichen Dózsa-Urkundenbuches zur Verfügung.

/56/ Székely, Gy., A Dózsa-parasztháború ideológiájához (Zur Ideologie des Dózsa-Bauernkrieges). Századok 95, 1961, 477, 480.

/57/ Frankl, V., Adalékok az 1514-dik évi pórlázadás történetéhez (Beiträge zur Geschichte der Bauernrebellion von 1514). Századok 6, 1872, 440.

/58/ Márki, op.cit., 203., Székely, op.cit. 481, 484–485.

/59/ G.A. 47–48 v.J. 1492, G.A. 49 v.J. 1492 und G.A. 41 v.J. 1498, G.A. 27 v.J. 1500.- Vgl. noch G.A. 58 v.J. 1514, G.A. II/27 v.J. 1518, G.A. 25 v.J. 1519.

/60/ Mályusz, op.cit., 374.ff, Ders., Az 1498. évi 41. törvénycikk (Der Gesetzesartikel 41 aus dem Jahre 1498). Századok 63–64, 1929–1930, 809 ff.

/61/ Pach, op.cit., (s.Anm.35.) 50–52, 81–82.

/62/ Ebenda, 68–70, 92–93.

/63/ Barta, G.–Szakály, F., Dózsa népe és a magyar társadalom (Dózsas Volk und die ungarische Gesellschaft). Társadalmi Szemle 27, 1972: 6, 77.

/64/ Zum ersten Mal zu dieser Frage: Molnár, op.cit. 239.

/65/ G.A. 35 v.J. 1498, G.A. 41–42 v.J. 1500. Vgl. OL Dl 104 071 (1498–1499).– Károlyi-Urkundenbuch, III, 44 (1500).– Die Adelsgemeinschaft des Komitats Pest bestätigt, daß Mihály Kenderesi ein zu ihnen gehörender echter Adliger ist, also ein „qui iuxta contenta novi decreti et ipsius articulorum pridie in campo Rákos per regiam maiestatem ac universos dominos praelatos et barones ac nobiles et proceres huius regni editi (verweist offensichtlich auf G.A. 41–42 v.J. 1500) de . . . personis et rebus ac bonis suis ubique intra ambitum regni Hungariae nullum tenetur solvere tributum. . ."

/66/ G.A. 27 v.J. 1495, G.A. 31 v.J. 1498, G.A. 28 v.J. 1504, G.A. 10 v.J. 1507. Vgl. G.A. 66 v.J. 1514, G.A. 34 v.J. 1518, G.A. 12 v.J. 1522.

/67/ Szabó, op.cit. (s.Anm.27.) 194–196.

/68/ OL Dl 25 383. – Über Péter Vingárti Geréb, der im Jahre 1500 Palatin wurde, siehe Fógel, op.cit. 59–60.

/69/ Fraknói, V., Magyarország a mohácsi vész előtt a pápai követek jelentései alapján (Ungarn vor der Niederlage bei Mohács aufgrund der Berichte der päpstlichen Legaten). Budapest 1884, 147.– Zur Tätigkeit von Ambrus Sárkány vor 1514, der im zweiten Jahrzehnt des 16. Jahrhunderts als Obergespan von Pozsony den Dreißigst von Pozsony und dann von Buda in Pfandbesitz hatte, siehe: Fógel, op. cit., 18, 25, 53, 117, 120, 123.

/70/ Abel, op.cit., 113–120. – Braudel, F.P. – Spooner, F., Prices in Europe from 1450 to 1750.

The Cambridge Economic History of Europe. Vol.IV. The Economy of Expanding Europe in the 16th and 17th centuries. Cambridge 1967, 417, 421, 464, 470–475. – Hoszowski, S., The Revolution of Prices in Poland in the 16th and 17th centuries. Acta Poloniae Historica,II, 1959, 7–12; The Price Revolution in Sexteenth-Century England. Ed. with an introduction by P.S. Ramsey. London 1971, 63–68.

/71/ Zimányi, op.cit. Vgl. Braudel-Spooner, op.cit., 401–404.

/72/ OL Dl 36 992, 36 983, 36 994, 37 007.– Vgl. Károlyi-Urkundenbuch,III, 40: Der Woiwode von Siebenbürgen, Péter Szentgyörgyi, untersagte in seiner Verordnung an das Komitat Doboka die Rinder- und Pferdeausfuhr in einem Werte von über 6 Gulden und führte als Grund dafür die „non parvam caristiam . . . in animalibus, videlicet bobus et equis" an.

/73/ OL Dl 36 992, 37 007.

/74/ OL Dl 36 997, 36 998, 37 007.

/75/ OL Dl 104 622.

/76/ OL Dl 104 125.

/77/ OL Dl 37 169.

/78/ OL Dl 48 305.

/79/ OL Dl 36 992, 36 983, 37 007.

/80/ G.A. 93–94 v.J. 1492, G.A. 18, 22 v.J. 1495, G.A. 47 v.J. 1498, G.A. 16 v.J. 1504.– Vgl. Károlyi-Urkundenbuch,III, 27–30 (1498), 34–36 (1449) usw.

/81/ G.A. 15–20, 22–23 v.J. 1514.

/82/ Pach, op.cit., (s. Anm. 35.), 48–49. 79–80.

/83/ G.A. 14 v.J. 1514; vgl. auch G.A. 25–30, 44–45 v.J. 1514.

/84/ Partis III, Tit. 26, § 2.

/85/ Partis III, Tit. 30, § 7.

/86/ Waldapfel, I., Két közmondás Mohács Magyarországáról (Zwei Redensarten über das Ungarn von Mohács), Magyarságtudomány 2, 1943, 215–216.

/87/ OL Dl 37 007.

/88/ Zichy-Urkundenbuch, XII, 343–364.

/89/ OL Dl 36 998, 37 007.

/90/ Stadt Gyula, Urkundenbuch, 74–75, 90.

/91/ Ebenda, 77–79.

/92/ Maksay, F.,Urbáriumok. XVI–XVII. század (Urbarien.16.–17. Jahrhundert). Budapest 1959, 785.

/93/ Stadt Gyula, Urkundenbuch, 74, 99, 383.

/94/ Ebenda, 88, 289, 348.

/95/ Szabó op.cit. (s. Anm. 1.) 65, 69–71.

/96/ Ebenda, 75, 150–153.

/97/ Varga, op.cit. 94–96.

/98/ Ebenda, 169–182.

/99/ Pirenne, H., Sozial- und Wirtschaftsgeschichte Europas im Mittelalter. Bern (1946), 62–69.– Kötzschke, R., Allgemeine Wirtschaftsgeschichte des Mittelalters. Jena 1924, 235–238, 372.– Lütge, F., Die Agrarverfassung des frühen Mittelalters. Jena 1937, 191.- Kosminski, E.A.- Skaskin, C. D. (E. A.| Косминский—С. Д. Сказкин), История средних веков. I. Moskau 1952, 137–138, 151, 165, 363.- Brentano,L., Eine Geschichte der wirtschaftlichen Entwicklung Englands. Jena 1927, I, 346. Sée,H., Französische Wirtschaftsgeschichte. Jena 1930,I, 4,6. Mottek, H., Wirtschaftsgeschichte Deutschlands. Berlin 1957, I. 87. Perrin, Ch. E. Le servage en France et en Allemagne. X. Congresso Internazionale di Scienze Storiche. Roma 1955. Relazioni III, 213–246.

/100/ Vgl. Pach, op.cit. (s. Anm. 35.) 19–21, 256.

/101/ Kočí, J., Problém druhého nevolnictví v českých zemích v období pozdního feudalismu (Das Problem der zweiten Leibeigenschaft in den böhmischen Ländern in der Periode des Spätfeudalismus.) Historické štúdie 17, 1972. 63 ff.

/102/ Makkai, L., I. Rákóczi György birtokainak gazdasági iratai. 1631–1648 (Wirtschaftsakten der Güter György Rákóczis I. 1631–1648). Budapest 1954.- Maksay, F., Parasztság és majorgazdálkodás a XVI. századi Magyarországon (Bauernschaft und Allodialwirtschaft in Ungarn im 16. Jahrhundert). Budapest 1958.- Pach, Zs.P., Nyugat-európai és magyarországi agrárfejlődés a XV–XVII. században (Westeuropäische und ungarische Agrarentwicklung im 15.–17. Jahrhundert). Budapest 1963. – Sinkovics, I., Le servage héréditaire en Hongrie aux 16–17e siècles. In: La Renaissance et la Réformation en Pologne et en Hongrie (1450–1650). Budapest 1963, 47–89. – Zimányi, V., A rohonc-szalonaki uradalom és jobbágysága a XVI–XVII. században (Der Bauernstand der Herrschaft Rechnitz-Schlaining im 16.–17. Jahrhundert). Budapest 1968.

/103/ Vgl.: Slicher van Bath, B.H., The Agrarian History of Western Europe a.D. 500–1850. London 1963. 40–53.

/104/ S. Anm. 6.

/105/ Makkai, op.cit., Einleitung, 69–70. – Maksay, op.cit. (s. Anm. 92.) Einleitung,30, 47. - Pach op.cit. (s. Anm. 35.) 206, 265.

/106/ Soom, A., Der Herrenhof in Estland im 17. Jahrhundert. Lund 1954, 56.

/107/ Tessin, G., Wert und Größe mecklenburgischer Rittergüter zu Beginn des Dreißigjährigen Krieges. Zeitschrift für Agrargeschichte und Agrarsoziologie 3, 1955. 155.

/108/ Heitz, G., Zum Charakter der „zweiten Leibeigenschaft". Zeitschrift für Geschichtswissenschaft 20, 1972, 31.

/109/ Kulischer, J., Allgemeine Wirtschaftsgeschichte des Mittelalters und der Neuzeit. München–Berlin 1928, I, 53–54.- Grazianski, N.P. (Грациянский, Н. П.), Крепостное крестьянство на поместьях аббатства св. Германа в начале IX столетия. Из социально-экономической истории западноевропейского средневековья. Moskau, 1960, 110 ff.

/110/ Ashley, W.J., Englische Wirtschaftsgeschichte. Leipzig 1896, I, 5–9; II, 283. – Brodnitz, G., Englische Wirtschaftsgeschichte. Jena 1918,I, 27–39.– Lipson, E., The Economic History of England. London[9] 1947, I. 33–41. – Kosminski, E.A. ;(Косминский, Е. А.), Эволюция форм феодальной ренты в Англии в XI—XV веках. Вопросы Истории 1955. Nr. 2, 47.
– Barg, M.A. (Барг, М. А.), Нормандское завоевание и становление крепостничества в Англии. Вопросы Истории 1957, Nr. 7, 92, 95.

/111/ Lamprecht, K., Deutsches Wirtschaftsleben im Mittelalter. Leipzig 1886, I/2, 745–746.– Below, G., Probleme der Wirtschaftsgeschichte. Tübingen[2] 1926, 33–34.– Kötzschke, R., Studien zur Verwaltungsgeschichte der Großgrundherrschaft Werden. Leipzig 1901, 7 ff.; ders., Salhof und Siedelhof im älteren deutschen Agrarwesen. Aus dem Nachlaß hrsg. v.H. Helbig. Berlin 1953.

/112/ Grekov, B.D. Az orosz parasztság története a legrégibb időktől a XVII. századig (Geschichte des russischen Bauerntums von den ältesten Zeiten bis ins 17. Jahrhundert). Budapest 1957, II, 254.ff.

/113/ Varga, op.cit., 548, 12.

/114/ Kulischer, op.cit., I, 126–135.– Pirenne, op.cit., 69–81.– Postan, M.H., Revisions in Economic History: the Fifteenth Century. The Economic History Review. IX, 1939, 160 ff.– Abel, op.cit., (1955) 159–161.– Vgl.: Slicher van Bath, B.H., Vrijheid en lijfeigenschap in agrarisch Europa (16e–18e eeuw). A.A.G. Bijdragen, 15. Wageningen 1970, 94–95, 103.

/115/ Pach, op.cit. (s. Anm. 35.), 213–214 - Varga, op.cit. 474–475.

/116/ Marx, K., Das Kapital. Berlin 1964, III, 806.

/117/ Ebenda, 805.

/118/ Ähnlich neuerdings Heitz, op.cit. 26.

/119/ Marx, op.cit. 805, 807.

ADDENDA

DER BAUERNAUFSTAND VOM JAHRE 1514 UND DIE „ZWEITE LEIBEIGENSCHAFT"

(The Peasant Revolt of the Year 1514 and the „Second Serfdom" in Hungary)
Lecture delivered at the International Conference of Historians, held on the Quincentenary of the birth of the peasant leader György Dózsa. (Budapest, September 12, 1972)

Page 227, Note 6:

The concept of *Wirtschaftsherrschaft* — as a third type of estate management, transitional between *Grundherrschaft* and *Gutsherrschaft* — has been created by the Austrian scholar *A. Hoffmann* to denote a kind of rural economy in which the landlord used the peasants' labour services for domanial husbandry only in a relatively small measure, but mainly exploited his monopolistic rights on the domain (tavern, mill, slaughterhouse) and also engaged in commercial ventures on his own to increase his income: Die Grundherrschaft als Unternehmen, Zeitschrift für Agrargeschichte und Agrarsoziologie, VI (1958). — Hoffmann suggested applying the term chiefly to estates in Upper Austria of the 16th–18th centuries, but the Slovak historian *A. Špiesz* attempted to assign to this type the lands of the Czech Crown (Bohemia, Moravia and Silesia) as well as Slovakia, then a part of the Hungarian Kingdom: Czechoslovakia's Place in the Agrarian Development of Middle and East Europe of Modern Times, Studia Historica Slovaca, VI (1969). — The resulting debate proved, first of all, that it was impossible to deal with Slovakia without seeing it as an integral part of the agrarian conditions prevalent in the then Hungary. Moreover, some disputers found out the problematical points of the concept of *Wirtschaftsherrschaft* itself, referring (among others) to the seignorial monopolies (inn–keeping, above all) that constituted a major source of domanial revenues in Poland, too, which country certainly belonged to the region of *Gutsherrschaft*. For the debate see the special issue of Historické Študie, XVII (1972). — Quite recently, the question has been raised again by the Austrian historian *H. Knittler*, considering that the main characteristics of "second serfdom" and *Gutsherrschaft* did not apply to the regions of present day Austria. On the other hand, the management of estates in Lower and Upper Austrian districts differed so significantly from the "ideal type" of *Grundherrschaft* that the introduction of a transitional category seems to be justified: Zwischen Ost und West. Niederösterreichs adelige Grundherrschaft 1550–1750, Österreichische Zeitschrift für Geschichtswissenschaften, IV, 2 (1993), pp. 191–217.

Page 280, Note 35:

See the paper *The Feudal Rent in Hungary in the Fifteenth Century* in this volume.

Page 282, Notes 47-48:

For the mutual relation of agricultural and industrial prices also see from the present writer: Die Stellung des ungarischen Bauernkrieges von 1514 in der Agrargeschichte. In: Wirtschaftliche und soziale Strukturen im saekularen Wandel. Festschrift für W. Abel zum 70.Geburtstag. Hg. von I. Bog *et al.*, Hannover, 1974, I, pp. 199–211.

Page 284, Note 55:

The collection of sources concerning the peasant revolt of 1514 has been published in the meantime: Monumenta rusticorum in Hungaria rebellium anno MDXIV. Maiorem partem collegit A. Fekete Nagy. Ediderunt V. Kenéz et L. Solymosi atque in volumen redegit G. Érszegi. Budapestini, 1979. — The quotation: "... census dominorum temporalium ordinarios dicasque regiae maiestatis debitas ac alia iustissima et consueta debita... denegare praesumunt eosque insuper, qui huius modi census ordinarios et dicas regias... exigerent, occidendos esse... docent": p. 73.

Page 286, Note 71:

The domanial accounts of the bishopric of Eger from the years 1500–1508 explicitly referred to the rise in prices (*magna caristia rerum*) more than once: Estei Hippolit püspök egri számadáskönyvei (The Account Books of Eger of Bishop Hippolit of Este) 1500–1508. Ed. by P. E. Kovács, Eger, 1992, pp. 221, 316, 324. — The rise of agricultural prices might have induced the estate's manager to get up the dues payable by the peasants in cash instead of certain "gifts" in kind. The villagers were obliged to pay 1 florin 32 d. for pig contribution (*pro uno porco*) in 1501 and 1502, but 1 florin 50 d. in 1503: pp. 64, 168–169.

Pages 288-290:

For more detailed information on the further developments in the Hungarian rural economy see the paper *Sixteenth–century Hungary: Commercial Activity and Market Production by the Nobles* in this volume.

Page 293, Note 106:

In Poland, a typical country of second serfdom, the size of arable land retained in the lord's own occupation varied appreciably according to time and place (just as in Hungary). Generally speaking, the acreage of the Polish demesnes amounted to 16–50 per cent of the total area of peasant holdings: *L. Żytkowicz*, Les transformations du paysage agraire polonais avant le XIXe siècle. In: Agricoltura e trasformazione dell'ambiente secoli XIII–XVIII. Atti della undicesima settimana di studio (Prato, 1979), Firenze, 1984, p. 169.

Page 295, Notes 117-118:

In his recent papers on *Gutsherrschaft*, the German historian *H. Harnisch* rightly considered the predominance of labour rent (the labour services of the peasants) to be the main criterion of that type of estate management; accordingly, he carefully examined, in several instances, the ratio between the amount of the labour rent on the one hand, and the rents in kind + cash, on the other: Die Gutsherrschaft. In: Jahrbuch für Geschichte des Feudalismus (=JGF), Berlin, IX (1985); Probleme einer Periodisierung und regionalen Typisierung der Gutsherrschaft im mitteleuropäischen Raum. In: JGF, X (1986.) — At the same time he failed to pay a similar attention to the ratio between the rent in cash on the one hand, and the rents in kind + labour, on the other. However, the latter ratio is no less significant because, firstly, it sheds light on the general level of market economy under feudal conditions; secondly, serfdom could be attached historically not only to the overwhelming role of labour services, but also to the preponderance of rents in kind (as has been suggested in the text).

III

Sixteenth-century Hungary: Commercial Activity and Market Production by the Nobles

About the middle of the fifteenth century agriculture in Hungary was beginning to catch up with that of western countries. What then were the salient features of Hungarian farming at that time?

The feudal system of land ownership was characterized by the predominance of peasant tenure in relation to seignorial demesnes. The large seignorial estate rested on a foundation of feudal revenues rather than a system of large-scale directly-managed farming. Of the two forms of feudal rent not paid in money—corvee and tithes—it was the latter which was still widespread, while the corvee had become much less usual. The cash payment of rent had developed considerably not only in small towns, which had become more densely populated and were generally further advanced, but also in small villages. As for the peasant, although he had already managed to obtain partial freedom from serfdom and the far heavier impositions and bondage that weighed upon him in the early days of feudalism, he was still obliged to pay dues and still laboured under the lord's yoke; but within the limits of feudal laws and discretionary powers he enjoyed freedom of movement and relative security of tenure.

Following the normal pattern, trade in agricultural produce developed alongside the social division of labour, and in fact this trade lay largely in the hands of the producers themselves. Thus the key figures in the expanding trade in agricultural produce were the peasants of the small market towns and villages, especially the cattle breeders and cereal- and wine-producers. With the growth of the market the peasantry became a less homogeneous class, and the first signs of capitalist farming thus appeared in the midst of the feudal system, e.g. paid employment of the poorer villagers and of day-labourers, especially on lands owned or rented by wealthy peasants.[1]

But towards the end of the fifteenth century there began in Hungary, as in several other countries in central and eastern Europe, a trend that counteracted both the natural tendency of the peasantry to develop into small-scale bourgeois landowners and the expansion of their market production. This new trend in Hungary may be summed up in economic terms as the growing participation of the nobility in commerce and, subsequently, in the actual production of commercial goods.

There were three successive stages in the process by which the nobles reached this position. First, they exploited their privileged right to sell wine. Second, they took an increasingly active part (especially the big landowners and the lesser nobility) in trade in livestock. Third, they developed their trade in wheat and even their own wheat production.

Let us now consider the first factor in the development of such commercial activity on the part of the nobles: the use they made of their privilege for the sale of wine (*educillatio*). Exercise of this privilege spread increasingly and was bound up with seignorial monopolies. This privilege was not unknown previously, but in the sixteenth century it became a legally recognized source of seignorial revenue throughout the country, and the lords took full advantage of it.

In 1570, a trade decree by the Chamber of Szepes laid down the following: 'passim toto regno [educillatio] receptissima habetur et genus censetur ordinarii proventus.'[2] The law laid down the nobles' exclusive right to sell wine; for those whose estates did not include any vineyards, this right extended from Christmas to Michaelmas (29 September); for those whose estates did include vineyards, from St George's day to Michaelmas, with the right to extend the period.[3] The exercise of this right was generally left to the lord's discretion or to the bailiff of his domain: 'vinorum educillatio fit et exercetur pro arbitrio domini terrestris', as can be found in numerous land registers.[4]

In the exercise of this privilege in selling wines, production by the lord himself was not the dominant financial factor. The lords therefore did their best to increase the quantity of wine available to them for sale. They increased the revenues paid to them in kind, especially those coming from wine-growing peasants. They sought to seize every advantage and to transform vineyard rents that might be paid in cash into rents payable only in kind.[5] For the same reason they tried, in cases where revenues in the form of wine were set at a fixed amount (*jus montium*), to change this fixed amount into a ninth-part tithe (*nona*) on the peasant's entire wine harvest, at any rate when the change was to their advantage.[6] Quite often they also added to their seignorial dues the ecclesiastical tithe on wine (*decima*) which was farmed out to them, and even insisted on their prerogative in the collection of such tithes on their own lands[7] (although they were later forced to recognize the higher claim of the Royal Chamber in districts such as the fortress regions on the borders of the country).[8] Thus they received the tenth (tithe)[9] as well as fixed revenues in kind, or, putting the tenth and the ninth together, they took a *quinta* of the wine produced on peasant vineyards.[10]

Not content with this, the lords also exercised the right of pre-emption on the wine offered by their serfs for sale—that is, on what was left after deduction of the tenth, the ninth, and sometimes fines also paid in wine.[11] Thus wine sales cannot be said to have taken place on an open market; what we have are, rather, forced sales (at very low prices, perhaps paid for in wheat or not paid for at all), and 'seizure of wine', according to the expression which we find in commercial decrees, land registers and laws passed by the Diet, etc. . . .[12]

Thus increases in wine sales by the nobles meant encroachment upon the peasant wine trade and led to a monopoly of the market. The lord, by taking advantage of provisions stipulating that only his wine could be sold on his domains throughout the greater part of the year, deprived the serf wine-growers of the means of selling their product. The lord further robbed the serfs by requiring payment of revenues in kind, and by demanding wine in payment of other dues, and thus took from them a large portion of their market yield; it all amounted to a constantly increasing seizure of peasant produce. As a result, wine consumers in the villages might find themselves buying at high prices in the lord's wine shops the very wine which their lord had got from them at no cost, in the form of revenues paid in kind, or bought from them at a minimal price or even taken from them by force. This first form of trade on the part of the lords severely reduced peasant market production in one of the most important branches of agriculture.

The second phase in the development of the nobles' commercial activity consisted in active participation by the large landowners and the middle nobility in the livestock trade. This activity, which for the nobles was a new one, had started early in the sixteenth century,[13] but did not become important until after the battle of Mohács (1526). In contrast to the village wine and livestock trade, where sales outside the area and exports (for instance to Moravia or Poland)[14] played only a minor role (though a sizeable one even so), the nobility's participation in the livestock trade in the sixteenth century grew chiefly through exports—to Vienna, the towns of the German Empire (Augsburg, Nuremburg), Moravia, Venice and other towns of northern Italy. This large-scale export trade on the part of the nobles, involving some tens of thousands of animals sold to western countries, represented the major part of Hungary's total annual exports. These first two phases in the development of the nobles' trade—in livestock and in wine—depended only to a very small extent on the produce of their own lands. The majority of the herds of oxen taken to the markets came from peasant farms. But with oxen there was the difference that the lords of the western region of the country, which was under Hapsburg rule, did not trade in animals obtained from their serfs (as they did with wine) but were generally content to take an active part in the extensive cattle trade stemming from the large *puszta* around the towns of the great Hungarian plain in the lands that had fallen to the Turks. Livestock changed hands on the great markets of the western provinces and elsewhere. Exporters then sent the herds on to Austria and Moravia.[15]

In these western regions of Hungary under Hapsburg domination the great lords were, in ever-growing numbers, engaging in wholesale and export trade in livestock with the help of agents (*factores mercenarii*), and this activity developed alongside and at the expense of that of the stock-raisers of the Great Plain and the large-scale traders, who had risen principally from the ranks of the prosperous peasants and bourgeoisie. In the 1520s, György of Brandenburg, the owner of the domain of Gyula, several times bought cattle from the peasant breeders of the village of Gyula for export to Silesia. Pál Bakits, a great landowner in the county of Pozsony, passed the customs barrier at Esztergom in 1535 with 2,000 oxen. According to the registers recording payment of the *traite* (thirtieth), established in 1542, about 12 per cent of the export trade in oxen was conducted by the following lords: Ferenc Nyáry, Imre Balassa, Sebestyén Thököly, Ferenc Révay, Anna Pekry. About the middle of the century István Dobó, Ferenc Zay and Sebestyén Bornemissza, all bearers of illustrious names, went into partnership to trade in oxen, selling them in Hungary and exporting them to Vienna. In 1544 Gáspár Serédi and in 1563 Menyhért Balassa obtained licences for the duty-free export of 1,000 oxen each; in 1580 Gábor Kendi, Péter Krusith and his heirs, Gyula Salm and others obtained export licences for large consignments exempt from the *traite*. The Palatine, Támas Nádasdy and the supreme captain of Gyula, László Kerechényi, often bought up beef stock to resell it at a profit or export it to Austria. About the end of the century, the Zrinyi were delivering oxen to Venice. But the great lords were not alone in this trade; large numbers of the middle and lesser nobility also took part.[16]

Naturally the lords and nobles used their privileges to gain every advantage over their peasant and bourgeois competitors. They not only obtained regular renewal of their exemptions from inland duty,[17] in particular on 'oxen being transported from one place to another within the country',[18] but also gained exemption from customs charges on exports, at least 'for animals reared on their own seignorial farms'.[19] They then took steps to include in this category oxen that they had bought for export without payment of the *traite*.[20] Although the law expressly charged dues (*traite*) on goods purchased for commerce and subsequently exported,[21] and furthermore laid down that export of *propri allodiatura* (produce from the demesne) required a licence,[22] these obstacles were freely circumvented: 'Die hungarischen Herrn ... schreiben Mautbrief, dass mann frei passieren soll lassen', reported the captain in charge of the mining region as early as the middle of the century.[23]

As participation by lords and nobles in the livestock trade increased, so the activity of peasant and bourgeois traders was considerably reduced. It is no surprise, therefore, to learn that in 1574 'the citizens of the free and mining towns' presented a petition to the Diet asking that 'lords and nobles should not be allowed to trade in leather, horses, livestock and similar goods'. There is hardly any need to add that the Estates, far from approving this petition, decided that 'the great lords, and the nobles as well, might freely engage in trade in any types of goods'.[24] Thus peasant trade was progressively eliminated in this field too.

The third stage in the development of trade on the part of the lords was wheat marketing. In 1542 a certain great Hungarian lord wrote: 'Est mihi animus, ut emam unam navem, quae mille metretas ordei et tritici ferre potest. Ordeum, farinam et alia victualia mecum ducam.'[25] Such ideas were put into practice. As early as the middle of the sixteenth century a large number of seignorial domains were producing wheat for the market: among them the estates of Nádasdy, Dobó, Forgách, Drugeth, Perényi, Choron and others. Revenue for the estates of the fortress of Gyula from the sale of wheat rose from 225 florins in 1519, to 627 in 1527 and 2,808 in 1557.

Export of wheat did not take place on a very large scale;[26] nor did enforced sales to villagers constitute an important factor, although certain instances are related of the lord using undisguised force to sell the wheat from his domains—and spoiled wheat at that—to his own serfs.[27] Such compulsory sales were less extensively made in respect of wheat than wine. We must point out in this connection a related problem, which, it is true, is of a different kind, but still of great interest: it concerns the heavy demand for agricultural produce on the part of impoverished peasants and manual workers without tenure; the degree to which the well-to-do peasants profited by unloading surplus produce on this extending sector of the home market, and the part played by seignorial produce in the same market.[28] The question requires more research but in any case there is evidence that impoverished serfs bought wheat and other produce from their own lords.[29]

In the wheat sector as in the two others, research done shows that seignorial trade could make progress in town markets only at the expense of peasant producers. We may note for instance that in the 1570s the wheat suppliers to the town of Selmecbánya were István Dobó, Imre Forgách, Gábor Dóczy and Zsigmond Pándi, all four great feudal landowners.[30] In this, as in the two other sectors, the nobles made full use of their privileges to gain commercial advantage. Nothing could be easier for them than to evade payment of duties on wheat grown for the most part on their own demesnes and brought into towns near their estates. They took over the supply of wheat and fodder to the armies, in particular the armies of mercenaries billeted on the country, and the frontier fortresses. Through their sales to the national exchequer during the favourable market conditions in the wars with the Turks, which had become more or less permanent, an important new commercial outlet was opened for them, and if we bear in mind the rise in prices throughout Europe we can easily understand how great landowners, especially those with influential connections, made vast profits as they rose to high positions in politics or the army.[31]

In fact the wheat which the nobles brought on to the market came from the same source as the wine they sold: a rising proportion of the peasants' harvest was taken by the nobles for this purpose, either in the form of revenues paid in kind ('ninths' of the wheat yield and other revenues), or by means of bulk purchase. In order to increase revenues payable by serfs in the form of wheat, the great landowners adopted a wide variety of methods. Sometimes they would raise the rate of fixed annual revenues (*aconalia*), sometimes they would replace them by the *nona* (ninths)—which was the most widespread method—or, when the peasant had previously bought the right to pay the ninth in cash, the lord forced him once more to pay in kind (*in specie*).[32] Payment in ninths became even more widespread in respect to the wheat yield than for wine;[33] it was often joined to the tenth and the two together made up the tax, farmed out by the church, known as the *quinta*.[34] Another means of increasing revenues paid in wheat, although less widespread, achieved the same result: the serfs were deprived of their tenure and compensated with small strips of land of a few acres, paid for by rent consisting of a quarter or a fifth of the harvest.[35] Apart from these measures, although the lords did not enjoy the right of pre-emption, as they did for wine, they still often 'bought' or 'borrowed' wheat from their peasants by force, paying much less than the current price; and it is clear that their purpose was to resell at a profit.[36]

The measures described above had the same effects as in the wine and cattle trades. The peasants' share of the market contracted, and eventually production on their land was permanently reduced. The nobles' requirements in wheat marketing affected the whole structure of feudal revenues: rent paid in kind took on a new importance in relation to cash rents. On an estate such as that of the Archbishopric of Esztergom, for instance, where at the close of the previous century rent in cash had been preferred to rent in kind,[37] we note that in the years 1568–70 and 1581–4 income from revenues paid in the form of wheat (i.e. the ninth and the tenth) equalled income from revenues previously paid in cash—which included income from farming the demesne.[38] In 1575 in the Tokaj district the value of revenues in kind was several times greater than the cash payments received;[39] and we could cite other examples. . . . From this trend, i.e. the return to payment in kind, we can conclude that payments in the form of wheat and wine, taken as a proportion of the harvest, had gradually become the main forms of feudal dues paid by the serfs of Hungary.[40]

But the nobles' growing participation in the wheat trade was a severer blow to market production by the peasants than the expansion of the nobles' trade in wine and livestock, for it was as a result of this activity that the lords turned their attention more and more to the cultivation of their own lands, to the cost of their serfs. This third type of commercial activity, wheat marketing, proved to be one of the chief stimuli to the expansion of the demesnes and of direct farming undertaken with the aim of increasing yields. In contrast to developments in the wine and cattle trade, sales of wheat produced on the demesnes were in several regions soon able to gain ground not only over the produce of peasant tenures, but also over that of the rapidly growing *terra indominicata*. The estate of Gyula is a highly characteristic example of this: in 1519 wheat sales brought in 225 florins and this figure represented only sales of wheat levied as payment of the ninth; in 1557 income was over twelve times as great, and this considerable sum was essentially the result of farming of the demesne.[41]

The excellent opportunities offered by trade and commerce, and the increased food requirements of the courts of the great lords and the rich, also stimulated the development of farming on the demesnes whether they were in private or royal possession. Food for private armies and the king's mercenary troops had to be supplied directly, without actual purchase, and the same held for supplies to the courts of the nobles, and for the lords' domestic requirements, which were constantly on the increase. This factor in the development of farming, which was no less important, is brought out by an instruction from Munkács, issued in 1570, according to which farming of the demesne 'was to take precedence over all else' and was necessary for the following reasons: 'ex ea potissimum loci sustentatio pendeat et alimenta praesidii reponi soleant.'[42] Direct supplies to the courts, the troops and the border fortresses meant that in many cases the major part of the produce paid by serfs in dues or harvested on the seignorial demesnes was allocated automatically.[43] We must stress that besides actual commerce on the part of the nobles, consumption on the seignorial estates also impeded market production by the peasantry. When we find in the detailed accounts for the Nádasdy estates almost only special commodities (spices, citrus fruits), 'wine and victuals always being at hand',[44] and since the instruction from Munkács mentioned above provided for the rearing of cows and poultry and the growing of fruit on estates in order to ensure supplies of dairy produce, eggs, vegetables and so on 'without need to purchase', or to 'avoid superfluous expenditure',[45] we must recognize this to be evidence of efforts to stifle the peasant market, which had previously enjoyed a measure of prosperity as a result of demand on the part of the estates at the time when they received revenues most in cash.

From the 1530s and 1540s onwards the *allodia*—a Latin term used generally in Hungary to designate farmed demesnes—had appeared in considerable numbers, especially in the western regions under Hapsburg rule: the part of Transdanubia not occupied by the Turks, the western and central regions of north Hungary (Slovakia), and especially the domains of the great lords and the royal estates and even the estates of the lesser nobility. By the middle of the century there were few regions in the 'royal' Hungary of the Hapsburgs without seignorial demesnes. About the middle of the century a great landowner such as Tamás Nádasdy possessed more than a dozen farms which were exploited directly, quite apart from his own estate at Sárvár-Kapuvár;[46] there was also his property at Léka where, in 1549 and in 1557, two new demesnes were created;[47] and also his property at Kanizsa where, in 1564, despite the constant threat of Turkish attack, seven direct farming enterprises continued to operate.[48] From 1532 onwards the county of Pozsony (Bratislava) saw the appearance of demesnes[49] on the properties of Gáspár Serédi, Pál Bakits and Elek Thurzó; and in the county of Szepes the land register, drawn up in 1564–5 on the estates of the Thurzó family, refers to two of these: 'the old' and 'the new'. In 1570 the land register of the Szendrő district mentioned wheat-fields farmed directly[50] in fourteen villages, and that of Sárospatak mentioned the same in seven villages.

In contrast with the earlier practice of keeping relatively small areas of land for seignorial farming,[51] expansion of the system of direct management began with the cultivation of the fallow land of the villages and of land not being used for agricultural purposes; it then progressed by means of forest clearance and reclamation of pasture and grazing land. This sort of expansion thus went on at the expense of the serfs, depriving them of their rights to common use of the forest and their common grazing rights. Land-holdings left by serfs were taken over,[52] and even tillage forming part of inhabited holdings was incorporated into the demesnes or otherwise annexed to the seignorial reserve. In some cases we meet direct seizure of the land or total or partial expropriation of peasant tenures.[53] The land register for the Csejte domain, dating from 1568, mentions serfs 'quorum terrae coluntur domino terrestri', and who for this reason were excused payment of rent. The document dealing with direct farming of the cameral domain of Szatmár, drawn up in 1572 for the Chamber of Szepes, states that all the demesnes had been created on land taken from the serfs 'cum injuria eorum'.[54] On the domain of Kapuvár, in the 1580s, the serf lived as a labourer without land (*inquilinus*), his holding being worked by the lord's plough and treated as belonging to the demesne.[55] It is indicative of this situation that from the middle of the century onwards the law made a distinction between 'land belonging directly to the nearby estate' and that which 'was taken from the serfs and recently appropriated for the purpose of farming as part of the demesne'.[56]

The demesnes (for the most part arable land, grazing land, vineyards, fish ponds), the area of which continued to increase as a result of the methods we have already mentioned, were farmed partly by means of the corvee (*servitium*, *labor*) performed by the serfs who worked with their own tools and their own beasts of burden. Thus, this method of direct farming yielded an income additional to produce revenues, and led in the end to the extension of the other natural form of feudal revenue, rent paid in labour. Whereas in the years 1510–20, one day of compulsory labour was the rule, according to the laws of 1514[57] (at least on the large seignorial properties), and this in fact was often not enforced,[58] by the middle of the century the situation was very different. This change finds expression in the provisions of the law of 1548, defining the corvee to be carried out on demesnes for the five following types of work: ploughing, sowing, haymaking, harvesting, wine-growing, to which must be added haulage of wine and other produce—and already authorizing the lord to demand two days of corvee in the wine-growing, hay harvest and harvest seasons.[59] The ever-mounting burden of the corvee is also described in a number of sources. The land register for the domain of Gyula (1525) required only two days of labour for scything and one day at harvest-time; but in the same book, entries for 1559 and 1561 tell of serfs being generally required 'to carry out all the work and services', 'to plough, sow and attend to other tasks as well'.[60] Whereas in 1530 the land register for the domain of Kanizsa mentions a relatively slight corvee, letters written by serfs in the 1550s complain of the unbearable increase in the corvee, quite apart from the frequent illegal seizures of land.[61] The workers on the estate of Pozsony, previously required to work seven days of corvee per year, were in 1574 forced to work a total corvee of 60 days.[62] At Krasznahorka in 1578 the lord 'cogit eos toties, quoties opus est'.[63] In 1570 the villages belonging to the domain of Szendrö unanimously complained of 'intolerable servitude'; they were so burdened by the corvee that they had no time left for cultivation of their own vineyards and fields; the same is true of the domain of Tokaj where, according to the 1581 land register, the serfs were often required to carry out domanial corvee without any free days for two or three weeks on end.

In another respect, the development of commerce based on the farming of demesnes went hand-in-hand with the utilization, on a fairly large scale, of domanial equipment and paid labour, where servants, farm lads, gardeners, shepherds, harvesters and day-labourers were partly recruited from the impoverished and expropriated peasantry.

There had already been some mention of servants and farm lads ('mercenarii et alii servitores nobilium, qui proprio victu et amictu dominorum suorum utuntur') in the laws and estate documents dating from before the Mohács disaster.[64] In the following decades we come across them frequently in accounts, land registers and instructions under various titles—*allodiator, allodiatrix, mercenarii et servitores allodiorum, pastores in allodiis, hortulanus*, etc. . . .[65] They are mostly mentioned together with certain pieces of equipment on the demesne, for instance 'farm hands with plough'.[66] Some other examples: in 1572 the steward of the cameral estate of Szatmár proposed that the Chamber of Szepes should, for the four farms being directly farmed, in addition to a higher rate of corvee, provide four ploughs with eight oxen and three farm servants, who were probably not all adults, for we read 'there are some men with two or three children in their care who can be taken on'.[67] The landowners also called upon seasonal workers in addition to their regular hands ('diversos laboratores tam vinearum dominii, quam agriculturae allodiorum'),[68] day-labourers for the harvest and for reaping, harvesters and reapers paid in kind, hoers and vine-workers, etc. . . .[69]

This practice is explained by the fact that previous trends could not immediately be reversed; the corvee which had, in the previous century, played a very limited role, could not suddenly be greatly increased to the new requirements of direct farming, and, at least for a time, the lords were forced to employ some paid labour.[70]

This phenomenon can be seen in certain mixed forms of working relationships: the same serfs carried out certain forms of work sometimes free and sometimes for payment; they were sometimes paid (in cash or in kind) for the work done as corvee, sometimes paid only for that part of the work done in addition to the corvee; sometimes the lord's oxen were used in the corvee; sometimes a serf with tenure was made to work as a farm-hand, and so on. The land register of Gyula, drawn up in 1525, laid down that workers from the town were to thresh the wheat from the demesne in fulfilment of the corvee due from them, but guaranteed them a tenth part of the threshed wheat. The land register for Világosvár in the same year laid down special dues to be paid in money to cover the cost of wages paid to the farm lads who had been recruited by the captain from among the 'good serfs', that is those with tenure. According to the land registers of Esztergom, drawn up in 1527 and 1553, all reaping, hay-harvesting and harvesting required of serfs in the form of corvee were to be paid in wages.[71] When in 1554 the land register of Hédervár laid down that rent was to be paid in labour instead of in money, and was to become due on St George's day and at Michaelmas, it stated that any agricultural work which could not be carried out as corvee was to be carried out by the serfs 'for money paid by the lord'. The land register of Eger, drawn up in 1558, laid down the general obligation that work should be carried out free, but it nevertheless provided for any work carried out in addition to the corvee (reaping, for example) to be paid in wages (allowed on rent due at Michaelmas), and finally, in exchange for certain forms of work (for instance, work carried out within the fortress), it provided for payment of a daily wage, in cash or in the form of goods. In 1562, the serfs of Komárom received a cube of salt per day for their corvee, done in the form of reaping; reapers carrying out the corvee in the domain of Nagybánya received foodstuffs as payment for their work in 1566 and for work carried out in addition to the corvee they received wages (although this was still a sum well below the wages of a day-worker). The land register of Szendrő, drawn up in 1570, tells us that about the middle of the century farm-hands received wages paid in money and that the sum used to meet these costs represented dues paid in cash by the serfs. According to the land register of Pozsony (1574), certain villages were required to provide reapers for the demesne as well as harvesters to whom daily wages were paid (although such wages were below the usual rate); labourers who had previously benefited from a food allowance granted during the period of the corvee continued to do so but received wages in the form of money for work done in the vineyards. If we may accept the evidence of the land register of the domain of Tokaj, drawn up in 1581, only a certain number of the vineyards of the demesne were cultivated by means of the corvee; on the rest, work was carried out in return for cash wages. In some cases, the steward had substituted work in the vineyards for payment of rent at Martinmas.[72] Paid work was combined with the corvee but it was none the less always in the grip of the feudal system and exacted under duress.

Thus the new trends in Hungarian agriculture in the sixteenth century are extension of the demesne at the expense of peasant holdings, extension of seignorial commercial production and an increase in the use of paid forms of labour.

The development of trade and market production on the part of the Hungarian nobles in the sixteenth century differs sharply from what happened in the countries of western Europe (France in particular).[73] However, this divergence of Hungarian development will not seem unique in all respects if it is compared with English developments in the same period, which followed a similar path. We refer to the 'new nobility', the English 'gentry', which received rent due as feudal revenue largely in the form of cash. This class engaged in trade in wool, wheat and other goods, and after expropriating the peasants and small-scale farmers, undertook direct farming of its own lands, as was typical of capitalist economy, and progressively took on bourgeois characteristics.[74]

The Hungarian lords of the sixteenth century, as we read in a document from the year 1550, 'devoted themselves to trade, engaging merchants and dealers in livestock, cloth, lead, copper and all manner of things';[75] as we learn from another source for that period, they 'built up large stocks of wine, wheat, meat and other foodstuffs, waiting for prices to rise in order to sell them at four times their value';[76] as we have seen, they enlarged their demesnes by seizing peasant holdings if need be, and making use of paid labour on their domains. Thus these Hungarian lords of the sixteenth century, from many points of view, showed bourgeois characteristics similar to those of the English gentry.

However, there was still a marked feudal aspect to the Hungarian trader-cum-farmer lord of the sixteenth century. As a trader, he took advantage of his feudal prerogatives and the pressure he could apply outside the economic sphere; in order to ensure commercial success he created a forced market (let us simply mention in this connection the sale of seignorial wine to local customers and the seizure of the wine trade in villages); he employed his privileges as a nobleman (in the wheat and livestock trade) against his peasant and bourgeois competitors, and, by means of the 'ninth' on wheat and wine and other dues paid in kind, derived ever-increasing profit from feudal rent. As a producer he made a rising profit from that other form of feudal income, the forced labour of his serfs. This second characteristic of the Hungarian lord distinguishes him from his English counterpart and brings out the essential nature of the conditions prevailing in central and eastern regions of Europe (German territories east of the Elbe, Bohemia,

Poland) where the type of agriculture known as *Gutsherr* farming developed.[77]

These features become increasingly important during the last decades of the sixteenth century. In the first half of the seventeenth, *Gutswirtschaft*, based on the corvee, became the main system of farming, and the divorce between Hungarian agricultural development and that of western Europe was complete.[78]

Notes

1 For more detailed information, see Z. P. Pach, 'Das Entwicklungsniveau der feudalen Agrarverhältnisse in Ungarn in der zweiten Hälfte des XV. Jahrhunderts', *Studia Historica Acad. Sci. Hung.*, vol. 46, Budapest, 1960.

2 *Magyar Gazdaságtörténeti Szemle* (*M.Gt.Sz.*) (*Hungarian Economic History Review*), 1896, p. 70. The land registers of the Kapuvár district, about the end of the 15th and the beginning of the 16th century; *Országos Levéltár* (OL) (*National Archives*), *Collection of Documents before 1526* (Dl.): 36 992; 36 983; 37 007 do not mention this; however the selling of seignorial wine is mentioned in the document for 1584 as an 'old custom'. (OL) '*Urbaria et Conscriptiones*' (*U. et C.*) 56:33.

3 Article 36 of the law of 1550. Cf. OL, *U. et C.*, 26:67.

4 For example, Szendrő: 1570; Tokaj: 1581. See: *Urbáriumok XVI–XVII század* (16th- and 17th- Century Land Registers), ed. E. Maksay, Budapest, 1959. All land registers which are referred to without reference number are to be found in this work.

5 See for example the complaint made by the serfs of Iharos to their lord in 1551: 'It used to be customary on our vineyard for us to pay our tithe in money; but after the last two wine harvests it was taken in the form of wine.' *Magyar Müvelödéstörténet* (*History of Hungarian Civilization*), vol. III, Budapest (no date), pp. 116–17. A similar complaint was made in the same year by the inhabitants of the market town of Somogycsicsó against the taking of the wine tithe in kind instead of cash: *Jobbágylevelek* (*Serfs' Letters*), ed. E. H. Balazs, Budapest, 1951, pp. 21–2. The land register for the Vöröskö district for 1543 records that money-rents paid for vineyards and fixed-amount payments in kind were changed into ninth-part tithes. *Urbáre feudálnych panstiev na Slovensku. XVI storocie*, R. Marsina and M. Kusik, vol. I, Bratislava, 1959, pp. 69 et seq.

6 Regarding the ninth-part wine tithe, cf. for example the land registers of the Léva district, 1554 (OL, *U. et C.*, 16:5); the Palota district, 1578; the

estates of the nuns of Somlóvásárhely, 1593 (transcribed text), *Történelmi Tár* (*T. T.*) (*Historical Journal*), 1903, pp. 414–19.

7 Article 35 of the law of 1547; article 61 of the law of 1548; article 43 of the law of 1556.

8 Article 68 of the law of 1563; article 27 of the law of 1569; article 22 of the law of 1574.

9 See, for example, the decree for the Kanizsa and Sztenyicsnyák districts of 1564, *M. Gt. Sz.*, 1896, pp. 67–8, 72–3.

10 See, for example, the land registers of the Csábrág and Eger districts, 1558; the Vác district, 1578; Tokaj, 1581; or the tithes (tenths and ninths) taken on wine in 1561 by the fortress of Gyula. The latter in *Gyula város oklevelt ára* (*Archives of the Town of Gyula*), Budapest, 1938, p. 353. Other examples of the compounding of the ninth and the tenth taken on wine by nobles at the beginning of the 16th century: OL, Dl. 37 007, 104 125.

11 Article 36 of the law of 1550.

12 Cf., for example, the decree of the Munkács district of 1570: *M. Gt. Sz.*, 1896, p. 70; land register for Szendrő of the same year; article 21 of the law of 1574.

13 It will be rightly assumed that the restrictive laws on livestock trade, issued by the Diets of the time, reflected the efforts of the nobles who engaged in livestock trade and tried to get rid of their competitors (Cf. I. Szabó, 'A hajduk 1514-ben' ('The Hajduks in 1514'), *Századok* (*Centuries*), 1950, pp. 194–6). Thus the lesser nobility said of Ambrus Sárkány, Grand Judge, in 1525: 'You were trading in wine and livestock, you were oppressing the poor, while we protected the frontiers'; V. Fraknói, *Magyarország a mohácsi vész előtt a pápai követek jelentései alapján* (*Hungary before the Disaster of Mohács in the Light of Reports by Papal Nuncios*), Budapest, 1884, p. 147.

14 *M. Gt. Sz.*, 1894, pp. 108–9, etc. Cf. article 38 of the law of 1567; article 35 of the law of 1595.

15 For the chief features of the livestock trade see: S. Takáts, *Rajzok a török világból* (*Sketches from the Time of the Turkish Occupation*), vol. III, Budapest, 1917, pp. 8 et seq.; for its extent: Gy. Ember, 'Külkereskedelmünk történetéhez a XVI. században' ('Data on the History of our Foreign Trade in the 16th Century'), published in *A Magyar Tudományos Akadémia Társadalmi-Történeti Tudományok Osztályának Közleményei*, vol. 8, no. 4, Budapest, 1958, pp. 335–8. According to this work, in 1542—if we are to accept the evidence of accounts registers for the 'thirtieth' (customs dues)—with the exception of copper and precious metals, which represented $\frac{4}{5}$ of the total volume, 93·4% of the total volume of Hungarian exports to the west consisted of cattle, mainly oxen. In 1542, 27,529 oxen were exported to Austria and Moravia. The total volume of cattle exports appears to have increased subsequently. In the period 1549–51 the Hungarian traders sold

128

more than 180,000 oxen on the markets held weekly in Vienna: S. Takáts, *Szegény magyarok* (*Poor Hungarians*), Budapest (no date), p. 135. In 1588 more than 84,000 oxen passed over the bridge of Érsekujvár (*M. Gt. Sz.*, 1897, p. 194). Cf. *Budai török számadáskönyvek* (*Turkish Accounts Registers*), *1550–1580*, published by L. Fekete and Gy. Kaldy-Nagy, Budapest, 1962, p. 588 et seq.

16 *Archives of the Town of Gyula*, pp. 77–9, 84, 101–2, 126, 152; J. Hornyik, *Kecskemét város története* (*History of the Town of Kecskemét*), vol. I, Kecskemét, 1860, p. 235; *M. Gt. Sz.*, 1898, p. 422, and 1899, pp. 250–1; I. Acsády, *Közgazdasági állapotaink a XVI. és XVII. században* (*Economic Situation of Hungary in the 16th and 17th Centuries*), Budapest, 1899, pp. 62–3; S. Takáts, op.cit. (*Poor Hungarians*), pp. 143–4; Gy. Komoróczy, *Nádasdy Tamás és a XVI. századi magyar nagybirtok gazdálkodása* (*Tamás Nádasdy and Large-scale Estate Management in the 16th Century in Hungary*), Budapest, 1932, p. 106; Gy. Ember, *Magyarország XVI. századi külkereskedelmének történetéhez* (*Contributions to the History of the Export Trade of Hungary in the 16th Century*), Századok, 1961, no. 1, p. 40, etc.

17 Article 26 of the law of 1543; article 55 of the law of 1548, etc.

18 Article 18 of the law of 1553; article 16 of the law of 1557.

19 Article 36 of the law of 1567; article 17 of the law of 1569; article 25 of the law of 1574, etc.

20 The frauds committed by the lords and nobles engaged in this commerce in evading the *traite* were described in detail in article 44 of the law of 1559—among such frauds was that of marketing large numbers of animals that had been purchased but which were presented as stock reared on the seignorial reserve. Cf. *M. Gt. Sz.*, 1896, p. 73.

21 Article 37 of the law of 1574.

22 Article 34 of the law of 1599.

23 Takats, op.cit. (*Poor Hungarians*), p. 143.

24 Article 24 of the law of 1574.

25 *Archives of the Hédervár y Family* (*Hédervár y oklt.*), vol. II, Budapest, 1922, p. 122.

26 Komoróczy, op.cit., pp. 102–6; J. Belitzky, *A magyar gabonakivitel története* (*History of Wheat Exporting in Hungary*), Budapest, 1932, p. 27; *Archives of the Town of Gyula*, pp. 74, 99, 383.

27 For exportation of wheat to Austria, see *M. Gt. Sz.*, 1900, pp. 242, 252; for exportation to Venice, *M. Gt. Sz.*, 1899, pp. 241–2. At all events wheat exports from Hungary were still not very great in the 16th century. Wine exports were far more extensive (especially to the north) but were far from being as extensive as livestock exports, which were considerable.

28 Cf. *M. Gt. Sz.*, 1896, p. 70; *Archives of the Town of Gyula*, pp. 301, 387. Cf. I. Szabó, *Tanulmányok a magyar parasztság történetéből* (*Studies in the History of the Hungarian Peasantry*), Budapest, 1948, p. 188.

29 *Archives of the Town of Gyula*, p. 299; L. Ruzsás, *Az egri vár gazdálkodása a XVI. században* (*Management of the Fortress of Eger in the 16th Century*), Budapest, 1939, pp. 35, 39.

30 J. Sobó, *Selmecbánya sz. kir. város társadalma, ipara és kereskedelme a XVI. század második felében* (*Society, Industry and Commerce in the Royal Free Town of Selmecbánya in the Second Half of the 16th Century*), Budapest, 1910, pp. 31–6.

31 Concerning the business transactions of one of the greatest military suppliers, who was a noble, see P. Jedlicska, *Adatok erdődi báró Pálffy Miklós, a győri hősnek életrajza—és korához 1552–1590* (*Facts concerning the Life and Times of Miklós Pálffy, Baron of Erdőd, the Hero of Győr*), Eger, 1897, pp. 116, 184, 298, 614, etc. The importance of the economic factors resulting from the wars and the armies' requirements in foodstuffs has already been brought out in previous research, but the view taken of the relationship between the political and economic role of the great lords of the 16th century is open to criticism. G. F. Knapp's theory (*Die Bauernbefreiung und der Ursprung der Landarbeiter in den älteren Teilen Preussens*, vol. I, 2nd ed., Munich-Leipzig, 1927, p. 37), emphasizing the progressive decline of the military role played by the great landowning knights and attributing the development of the lords' economic role to their exclusion from 'national affairs' and public life by the central authority, has been supported by some historians; cf. I. Wellmann, 'Mezőrógazdaságtörténetünk uj utja' ('New views on the history of Hungarian agriculture'), in *Domanovszky emlékkönyv*, Budapest, 1937, pp. 684–6. But this conception has proved to be untenable.

32 For increase in fixed revenues, see Léka and Sárvár (OL, Dl., 37 007 (1519)); for replacement of fixed revenues by the ninth, see the Komárom domain (OL, *U. et C.*, 4:45 (1592)); for suppression of the right to buy back for cash, cf. land register for Pilis Abbey (OL, *U. et C.*, 62:32 (1578)).

33 See, for example, the land registers of the domain of Kanizsa (1530), Gyula (1560), of the provost's domain of Lelesz (1566) (OL, *U. et C.*, 18:15), the domain of Sztropkó (1569), in *Urbáre feudálnych panstiev na Slovensku*, vol. I, pp. 239–40.

34 See respectively Murány (1573), Csábrág (1558), Munkács (1570) (*M. Gt. Sz.*, 1896, p. 69), Krasznahorka (1570) (OL, *U. et C.*, 2:22).

35 *Magyar Országgyulési Emlékek* (*Documents from the Hungarian Diets*), vol. V, Budapest, 1877, p. 432 (1572).

36 Article 44 of the law of 1559: *Magyar Országgyulési Emlékek*, vol. IV, Budapest, 1877, p. 563 (1563); *M. Gt. Sz.*, 1900, p. 252 (1570).

37 E. Fügedi, *Az esztergomi érsekség gazdálkodása a XV. század végén* (*Finances of the Archbishopric of Esztergom at the close of the 15th Century*), *Századok*, 1960, nos. 1–3, pp. 90 et seq.

38 *M. Gt. Sz.*, 1905, p. 175, and 1894, pp. 35–6. See *Urbáre feudálnych*

panstiev na Slovensku, vol. I, pp. 278 et seq., also OL, *U. et C.*, 45:28 (1571 and 1597).

39 As has been shown by I. Acsády, *M. Gt. Sz.*, 1895, p. 135. See I. N. Kiss, 'Uradalmi gazdálkodás Sárospatakon és Tokajban a XVI. század második felében' ('Seignorial management at Sárospatak and Tokaj in the Second Half of the 16th Century'), in *Történelmi Szemle* (*Historical Journal*), 1960, no. 1, pp. 22–4.

40 See Z. P. Pach, 'Neuvième et dixième prélevés par les seigneurs au XVIIe siècle', in *Nouvelles Études historiques publiés par la Commission Nationale des Historiens Hongrois*, Budapest, 1965, pp. 417 et seq.

41 *Archives of the Town of Gyula*, pp. 74, 383.

42 *M. Gt. Sz.*, 1896, pp. 67, 70.

43 See, for example, J. Holub, *Egy dunántuli egyházi nagybirtok élete a középkor végén* (*A Large Ecclesiastical Estate in Transdanubia at the End of the Middle Ages*), Pécs, 1943, pp. 39–40; F. Maksay, *Parasztság és majorgazdálkodás a XVI. századi Magyarországon* (*The Peasantry and Demesne Farming on the Part of the Nobles in Hungary in the 16th Century*), Budapest, 1958, pp. 18–19, 22.

44 Komoróczy, op.cit., p. 109.

45 *M. Gt. Sz.*, 1896, pp. 68, 75. Cf. '. . . to ensure that the desmesne is farmed and beasts reared there, so that we are not forced to pay cash the whole time, but in a position to sell and derive profit from so doing. . . ' (*Archives of the Town of Gyula*, pp. 77–9).

46 Komoróczy, op.cit., p. 62; J. Tholt, *A sárvári uradalom majorgazdálkodasa a XVII. század első felében* (*Farming of the Demesne at Sárvár in the First Half of the 17th Century*), Budapest, 1934, pp. 13–18.

47 *Levéltári Közlemények* (*Archives Bulletin*), 1929, p. 234; *T.T.*, 1911, pp. 448–9.

48 *M. Gt. Sz.*, 1894, p. 71.

49 Maksay, op.cit., pp. 25–9.

50 The land registers for Szepesvár and Szendrő for 1570 were recently published in the work quoted above; the land register for the Sárospatak estate for the same year: OL, *U. et C.*, 95:22.

51 K. Tagányi, *A földközösség története Magyarországon* (*The History of Community Ownership of Land in Hungary*), 2nd ed., Budapest (no date), pp. 58–9.

52 See the land registers for Nagytapolcsány (1570) (OL, *U. et C.*, 60:70) and Szepesvár (1596) (OL, *U. et C.*, 49:17). This does not mean that seizure of abandoned peasant holdings was general practice.

53 The case, which is in fact fairly frequent, of the lord joining to his estate a holding 'freely' given up by an impoverished serf forms a transition between the two methods of seizure: annexation of a vacant holding and occupation of an inhabited holding.

54 OL, *Városi és Kamarai Iratok (Municipal and Cameral Documents)*, Fol. lat. 913. Cf. 'Agoston, the Provost, arranged for a large arable field to be occupied by force.' OL, *U. et C.*, 8:15 (1566): 'Ferenc Bebek occupied the best land, which had formerly been part of peasant holdings, in order to join it to his nearby estate, leaving them [i.e. the serfs of Krasznahorkaváral ja] tenures only of inferior quality.' OL, *U. et C.*, 2:22 (1570); the same document gives information on the seizure of vineyards and grazing land

55 OL, *U. et C.*, 56:33 (1584). The same land register relates the following facts concerning one of the villages (Pordány): 'Before the conquest of Buda (1541), the serfs possessed a whole holding there. But after direct seignorial farming had been introduced there and fields and pastures used for this purpose, the serfs were reduced to possession of half a holding.'

56 Article 70 of the law of 1563.

57 These laws formed part of the repressive measures taken as a result of the peasants' revolt of 1514. Services rendered by serfs, including the corvee, which was established at one day per week, were controlled by articles 15–20 of the law of 1514.

58 See, for example, Léka: 1519 (OL, Dl., 37 007); Kisvárda: 1521, *A zichi és vásonkeői gróf Zichy-család idősb ágának okmánytára (Archives of the Line of the Eldest Sons of the Zichy Family, from Zichy and Vásonkeő)*, vol. XII, Budapest, 1931, pp. 343–64; Világosvár: 1525 (OL, Dl., 37 000).

59 Articles 33–8 of the law of 1548; cf. articles 10–12 of the law of 1553.

60 *Archives of the Town of Gyula*, pp. 88, 289, 348.

61 OL, *U. et C.*, 27:55; *Serf Letters*, pp. 25–31.

62 OL, *U. et C.*, 34:74.

63 OL, *U. et C.*, 82:89.See Tapolca (1570), OL, *U. et C.*, 61:71; Léva (1589), OL, *U. et C.*, 16:5; Szepesvár (1596), OL, *U. et C.*, 49:17.

64 Article 1 of the law of 1522; article 24 of the law of 1523; *Archives of the Town of Gyula*, p. 86; OL, Dl., 37 000.

65 *Kulturtörténeti szemelvények a Nádasdyak 1540–1550-ös számadásaiból (Texts for the Study of the History of Civilization, Selected from the Accounts Books of the Nádasdy Family for the Years 1540–1550)*, vol. II, Budapest, 1959, pp. 11, 14, 31, 36, 196; Kanizsa (1563), OL, *U. et C.*, 101:19; Munkács (1570), *M. Gt. Sz.*, 1896, p. 79; Kapuvár (1584), OL, *U. et C.*, 56:33, etc.

66 For example, *aratra sex cum bobis arabilibus 48, item bigis, iugis, vomeribus et omnibus instrumentis ad ea attinentibus, quibus exercuerunt allodiaturam additis mercenariis idoneis pretio conductis* (Szendrő (1570); but refers back to the middle of the century).

67 OL, *Documents municipaux et caméraux*, Fol. Lat. 913.

68 *Kulturtörténeti szemelvények...*, vol. II, pp. 20, 25.

69 Kanizsa (1564), *M. Gt. Sz.*, p. 68; Esztergom (1580), Acsády, op.cit.,

pp. 125, 142; Cegléd (1584), *M. Gt. Sz.*, 1898, p. 345; Tihany (1588), *ibid.*, 1905, pp. 199–200, etc.

70 To take one example, the land register of Vöröskő (1543), which illustrates the same period. In it references are made to the need to employ, quite apart from the corvee, paid labour for most of the work (ploughing, harvest, threshing, gathering of crops, wine-growing, reaping). Anything 'outside custom' must be paid, it states. *Urbáre feudálnych panstiev na Slovensku*, vol. I, pp. 10, 152–5. The decree of Munkács (1570) requires the steward to have the estate vineyards cultivated '*partim subditorum gratuita opera, partim vero mercede operariis conductis*' (*M. Gt. Sz.*, 1896, p. 68).

71 For the land register of Gyula, see *Archives of the Town of Gyula*, pp. 87–90; for that of Világosvár: OL, Dl., 37 000; the information on Esztergom is given by Fügedi, *Századok*, 1960, nos. 1–3, pp. 97–8.

72 For the land register of Hédervár, see *Héderváryoklt*, vol. II, pp. 185–6. The information on Komárom in *M. Gt. Sz.*, 1897, pp. 492 (cf. OL, *U. et C.*, 4:45); the rest in the published texts quoted, *Urbáriumok, XVI-XVII. század.*

73 See, for example, H. Sée, *Histoire économique de la France*, vol. I, Paris, 1948, pp. 125 et seq.; M. Bloch, *Les Caractères originaux de l'histoire rurale française*, new edition, Paris, 1960, vol. I, pp. 105 et seq.; J. Meuvret, 'Domaines ou ensembles territoriaux? Quelques exemples de l'implication du régime de la propriété et de la structure sociale dans la France du XVIIe et du XVIIIe siècle', in *Première Conférence Internationale d'Histoire Économique*, Stockholm, 1960 (ed. F. Braudel, M. M. Postan, E. Söderlund), Paris-The Hague, 1960, pp. 343 et seq.; G. Duby, *L'économie rurale et la vie des campagnes dans l'occident médiéval*, Paris, 1962, vol. II, pp. 599 et seq.

74 See, for example, R. H. Tawney, 'The rise of the gentry 1558–1640', *Economic History Review*, 1940; E. Lipson, *The Economic History of England*, vol. I, 9th edn, London, 1947, pp. 133 et seq.; H. R. Trevor-Roper, 'The gentry, 1540–1640', *Economic History Review*, 1953, Supplement 1; L. Stone, 'The Nobility in Business, 1540–1640', in *The Entrepreneur*: Papers presented at the Annual Conference of the Economic History Society at Cambridge, England, April 1957, pp. 14–21; J. Cornwall, 'The Early Tudor Gentry', *Economic History Review*, 1965.

75 Quoted by Takáts, op.cit. (*Poor Hungarians*), p. 143.

76 *Bornemissza Péter válogatott irásai* (*Selected Writings of Péter Bornemissza*), *1553–1584*, Budapest, 1955, p. 229.

77 Cf., for example, H. Mottek, *Wirtschaftsgeschichte Deutschlands*, vol. I, Berlin, 1957, pp. 333 et seq.; F. Luetge, *Geschichte der deutschen Agrarverfassung vom frühen Mittelalter bis zum 19. Jahrhundert*, Stuttgart, 1963, pp. 101 et seq.; W. Rusiński, 'Hauptprobleme der Fronwirtschaft im XVI. bis zum XVIII. Jahrhundert in Polen und den Nachbarländern', *Première Conférence Internationale d'Histoire Économique*, Stockholm, 1960, pp. 418

et seq.; J. Valka, 'La structure économique de la seigneurie tchèque au XVIe siècle', *Deuxième Conférence Internationale d'Histoire Économique*, Aix-en-Provence, 1962, Paris-The Hague, 1965, pp. 211 et seq.

78 Cf. Z. P. Pach, 'Über einige Probleme der Gutswirtschaft in Ungarn in der ersten Hälfte des XVII. Jahrhunderts', *Deuxième Conférence Internationale d'Histoire Économique*, Aix-en-Provence, 1962, pp. 223 et seq.

ADDENDA

SIXTEENTH–CENTURY HUNGARY: COMMERCIAL ACTIVITY AND MARKET PRODUCTION BY THE NOBLES

Page 113:

In this paper the term *tithes* has been used to denote all sorts of feudal rent paid by the peasants in grain and wine, either in a fixed quantity (*cubuli, aconalia*) or in proportion to the actual yield. The latter sorts were the ninth part (*nona*) and the tenth part (*decima*), due from the tenant's harvest to the landlord and the church, respectively.

Page 114:

St George's day: 24 April; Michaelmas: 29 September; Martinmas (page 124): 11 November.

Page 114, Note 4:

Conf. the developments in Poland where the landlords, from the late 16th century onwards, concentrated increasingly on brewing and on the compulsory selling of beer (later also of spirits). Particularly in those districts where the marketing of grain was difficult the *propinatio* (= *educillatio*, that is the retail of beer and spirits to the peasants) became the main source of the nobles' income: *J. Leskiewicz*, Sur le niveau et les composantes du revenue foncier en Pologne du XVIe siècle au XVIIIe siècle. In: Première Conférence Internationale d'Histoire Économique (Stockholm, 1960), Paris–La Haye, 1960, pp. 409–414.

Page 116:

For more detailed information on Hungary's cattle and wine exports, see the paper *The Role of East–Central Europe in International Trade (16th and 17th Centuries)* in this volume.

Page 117, Note 24:

Similar views were expressed by Polish landlords of those days: the peasant's contact with the market should be strictly limited and permitted only as far as to enable him to pay his money rents. Quoted by *A. Mączak*, Agricultural and Livestock Production in Poland: Internal and Foreign Markets, The Journal of European Economic History (=JEEH), I, 3 (1972), p. 671.

Page 118, Note 29:

During the 17th century the big landowners made many sophisticated attempts at creating closed markets inside their estates. The landlord became a buyer and also a seller of wine, wheat and other agricultural produce, and the supplier of various indispensable industrial goods (hardware etc.). See from the present writer: Die ungarische Agrarentwicklung im 16–17. Jahrhundert. Abbiegung vom westeuropäischen Entwicklungsgang, Budapest, 1964, pp. 82–83, 155–156.

Page 120:

Instead of "to gain ground... terra indominicata" (lines 3–5) read: "to gain ground over the produce of peasant tenures, marketed by the landlords".

Page 121, Note 53:

The occupation of fallow lands and vacant holdings (*sessiones desertae*) and the curtailment of inhabited holdings *(sessiones populosae)* for the purpose of direct seignorial farming occurred more frequently than the total incorporation of inhabited holdings into the demesne. The reason for this was that the landlords were interested, at the same time, in keeping the majority of the villagers on their plots in order to retain their payments and labour services. It was this two-sided interest that motivated the seemingly contradictory measures of depriving the peasants of their land while tying them to it. — For similar conditions in Poland, see *L. Żytkowicz,* The Peasant's Farm and the Landlord's Farm in Poland from the 16th to the Middle of the 18th Century, JEEH, I, 1 (1972), pp. 138–139.

IV

CORVÉES ET TRAVAIL SALARIÉ DANS LES EXPLOITATIONS SEIGNEURIALES DE LA HONGRIE DES XVIe ET XVIIe SIÈCLES

Tout comme celle des pays de l'Europe Occidentale, la structure agraire de la féodalité hongroise du XVe siècle était caractérisée par l'énorme majorité des exploitations paysannes, essentiellement sous forme des manses serviles. Semblable en cela au manor anglais, à la seigneurie française, ou bien au Grundherrschaft allemand de la même époque, la grande propriété terrienne hongroise n'était pas, elle non plus, une grande entreprise agricole, mais surtout, ou dans sa totalité, le conglomérat d'un grand nombre de petites exploitations paysannes, ainsi qu'une organisation constituée en vue de faire rentrer et exécuter les prestations serviles sur une étendue considérable. Pendant la seconde moitié du XVe siècle encore, les réserves seigneuriales étaient, pour ainsi dire, noyées parmi la masse des tenures serviles (1).

En ce qui concerne les domaines hongrois du XVIe et du XVIIe siècle, on y observe en revanche - contrairement à l'évolution qui a lieu en Europe Occidentale - un accroissement sensible du nombre et de l'étendue des réserves seigneuriales.

Nous nous proposons d'étudier le caractère des conditions du travail dans les réserves seigneuriales de la Hongrie des XVIe et XVIIe siècles.

I

1. La première vague de l'expansion des réserves seigneuriales atteignit la Hongrie entre 1530 et 1540 (2).

Sans cesse plus étendues, les terres de cette catégorie étaient cultivées en partie au moyen de corvées, fournies par des serfs employant leur propre outillage et leurs bêtes de somme; il en résulta une aggravation constante des prestations serviles. Parachevant la sanglante répression qui avait mis fin au grand soulèvement paysan de 1514, la Diète avait décrété une journée de corvées obligatoires par semaine et si, au lendemain de ces événements, la plupart des seigneurs (3) n'usaient pas encore de cette ressource supplémentaire, la situation se modifia progressivement vers le milieu du siècle. L'aggravation se traduit notamment par la loi de 1548, qui étend l'obligation des corvées à cinq sortes de travaux, à savoir les labours, les semailles, la fenaison, la moisson, les soins des vignes, sans compter le charroi des vins et des victuailles; la même loi autorise les seigneurs à s'arroger, au moment des soins des vignobles, de la fenaison et de la moisson, deux journées de corvées par semaine (le total ne devant toutefois pas excéder 52 journées par an) (4), le fait est attesté par nombre d'informations de détail. Le terrier de 1525 du domaine de Gyula ne prévoit encore que 2 journées de corvées pour la fenaison et 1 pour la moisson, mais selon les formules employées par le même document en 1559 et en 1561, les serfs sont pratiquement "tenus de fournir tous travaux et services", comme "labours, semailles et autres travaux" (5). Le terrier de 1530 du château de Kanizsa fait état de corvées relativement limitées encore, à savoir des labours de 2 jougs de terres en automne et d'un joug au printemps par charrue, ainsi qu'une ou deux journées de fauchage par tenure (bien que, dans plusieurs endroits déjà tenentur metere pro officialis voluntate; aux environs de 1550, les lettres de serfs de cette région se plaignent déjà autant des nombreuses appropriations de terres que de l'intolérable accroissement des corvées (6). Contre 7 journées annuelles de corvées fournies auparavant, les serfs du domaine de Pozsony en fournissaient 60, en 1574 (7). Aucune corvée ne figurait encore au terrier du domaine de Kapuvár, à la fin du XVe siècle; en 1507, on n'y trouve encore que l'obligation du charroi des vins. En 1518-19, des corvées de fauchage et d'entretien des ponts y apparaissent déjà. Le même terrier, en 1584, prescrit déjà "pour la vallée du Raab et pour plusieurs domaines de Sa Grandeur mon maître" des corvée trihebdomadaires et bihebdomadaires, ces dernières devant avoir lieu entre la Saint-Jean et la Nativité. A ces corvées il fallait ajouter trois semaines annuelles à consacrer à l'entretien des ponts et des forteresses (8).

L'essor de l'exploitation allodiale allait par ailleurs de pair avec un emploi assez étendu des outillages appartenant au domaine. Le travail salarié était largement admis, la main-d'oeuvre se recrutant parmi les serfs du domaine.

Des textes de lois et divers autres documents antérieurs à la défaite de Mohács (1526) font déjà état de valets de ferme et de travailleurs domaniaux salariés (mercenarii et alii servitores nobilium, qui proprio victu et amictu dominorum suorum utuntur) (9). On les rencontre souvent, pendant les décennies suivantes, sous diverses dénominations telles que allodiator, allodiatrix, mercenarii et servitores allodiorum, pastores in allodiis, hortulanus etc., dans des livres de compte, comme par exemple dans ceux de 1540-1550 des domaines de la famille Nádasdy, dans des terriers et des instructions domaniales, où ils figurent aux côtés du cheptel mort et des "charrues louées" (10). En 1572, le proviseur du domaine du Trésor de Szatmár proposait à la Chambre du comitat de Szepes de faire cultiver les quatre alleux du domaine au moyen de fortes corvées et de 4 charrues avec 8 boeufs et 3 domestiques agricoles, qui ne devront pas être tous des adultes, "car on trouve des gens avec deux ou trois enfants qu'on peut embaucher" (11). En dehors de leurs domestiques permanents, les seigneurs employaient dans leurs réserves des ouvriers saisonniers et d'occasion (diversos laboratores tam vinearum dominii, quam agriculturae allodiorum); c'étaient des journaliers pour la moisson et pour la fenaison, des moissonneurs et des batteurs partiaires, des ouvriers pour la culture des vignobles (12). Le binage devra être fait en partie par des journaliers et en partie par des corvées, lit-on dans les instructions de 1564 du seigneur de Kanizsa; le régisseur doit faire cultiver les vignobles du domaine "partim subditorum gratuita opera ... partim vero mercede ... operariis conductis", disent les instructions de 1570 du domaine de la Marche de Munkács (13).

L'usage mentionné voulait que le même seigneur employât des corvées et des travaux payés; nous allons parler à présent des cas où les mêmes serfs accomplissaient certains travaux à titre de corvées gratuites et d'autres, en échange d'un paiement. Nombreuses étaient les formes de transition entre ces deux types de travail à certains endroits, les corvées obligatoires elles-mêmes étaient payées, tandis qu'ailleurs seuls les travaux excédant les corvées prescrites recevaient un salaire, soit en espèces soit en nature, mais d'un montant également règlementé; parfois la corvée pouvait être effectuée au moyen de l'outillage et du cheptel appartenant au seigneur, des serfs à tenure étaient parfois désignés à des emplois payés etc. Le terrier de Gyula de 1525 imposait aux serfs la corvée du battage des biés de la ville, tout en leur garantissant le versement d'un dixième (14). Selon le terrier de Világosvár, de la même année, le capitaine du château fort désignait certains "bons serfs" à des emplois payés (15). Le terrier d'Esztergom de 1527 et de 1553 stipule le versement d'un salaire en espèces pour les travaux de fauchage, de fenaison et de moisson, exigés par ailleurs à titre de corvées obligatoires (16). Tout en exigeant "en sus du travail hebdomadaire" des corvées gratuites en remplacement du cens de la Saint-Georges et de la Saint-Michel, le terrier de Hédervár de 1554 accordait aux serfs "le denier du maître", en paiement de certains travaux agricoles non compris dans "les corvées écrites" (17). Le terrier d'Eger de 1558 prescrivait nombre de corvées gratuites, tout en précisant que les travaux accomplis en excédent de ces dernières seraient rétribués (notamment dans le cas des corvées de fauchage) et que le salaire serait défalqué du cens de la Saint-Michel; certains autres travaux (notamment des charrois et des services de piéton au château fort) recevaient un salaire journalier en espèces ou en nature. En 1562, les serfs de Komárom touchaient un cube de sel par journée de corvée de fauchage. En 1566, les serfs du domaine de Nagybánya astreints à la corvée de fauchage étaient parfois nourris et, pour les travaux excédentaires, ils recevaient un salaire en espèces, encore qu'inférieur à celui des journaliers embauchés. Le terrier de Pozsony de 1574 atteste que certaines communes étaient tenues de fournir des faucheurs et des faneurs touchant un salaire journalier, qui était toutefois inférieur aux salaires courants (18).

Le travail salarié subissait parfois des contraintes extra-économiques, la corvée féodale, le cas échéant, présentait déjà certains éléments du salariat.

2. Ce n'est pas la propagation du travail salarié qui accompagnera, pendant la première moitié du XVIIe siècle (19), la seconde poussée de l'expansion des réserves seigneuriales, mais bien l'accroissement démesuré des corvées et des autres prestations serviles.

La constante aggravation des corvées balaya les survivances de l'état de choses antérieur, qui avait caractérisé la seconde moitié du XVe siècle, où les redevances sous forme de travaux jouaient un rôle relativement réduit et, ou bien ne figuraient pas du tout parmi les obligations serviles, ou bien y étaient définies à des taux relativement bas (20). Elle excédait désormais de loin même la mesure fortement rechaussée – une journée hebdomadaire – par la loi répressive de 1514, atteignant deux, voire trois journées par semaine et tendant de plus en plus à généraliser la pratique d'un recours quasi illimité au travail gratuit et obligatoire (21). A cette époque, les serfs "ne sont plus astreints à aucune corvée déterminée, mais ils sont tenus de fournir leurs travaux au gré du seigneur" (22).

Il convient cependant de préciser que les corvées sans limites, exécutées à la discrétion du seigneur, ne découlaient pas de la nouvelle poussée de l'extension des réserves seigneuriales au XVIIe siècle, mais avaient déjà fait leur apparition, à bien des endroits, dès les années 70 du XVIe siècle. Le terrier de 1570 de l'abbaye de Tapolca décrétait déjà que les serfs ad omnia servitia pro libitu domini compellantur et dès 1578, le seigneur de Krasznahorka cogit eos toties, quoties opus est (23). En 1589, les sujets du domaine de la Marche de Léva iuxta arbitrium domini magnifici debent subire omnes labores necessarios; ceux du domaine d'Erdőd-Szatmár, en 1592, serviunt ad libitum capitaneorum et provisorum ... sine ulla discretione, en 1596, les habitants des villages relevant du château fort et du domaine de Szepesvár tenentur omnes labores... quando illis iniungetur, praestare (24).

Au cours du XVIIe siècle, les cas de ce genre se multiplieront sans nombre. Il suffit d'évoquer, sur ce point, le témoignage des terriers de Mada (1601), de Csábrágszitnya (1602), de Sárvár-Kapuvár (1608), d'Adorjánvár (1625), de Derencsény (1632), de Csetnek (1636), de Serke (1643), de Murány (1672), de Nagybánya (1688), de Sárospatak, daté de 1689, mais résumant l'état de choses qui prévalait au milieu du siècle, ou encore celui de Szendrő, de 1690 (25). Ajoutons d'ailleurs que, même dans les cas où le terrier déterminait la mesure des corvées, selon la durée ou selon le rendement, le seigneur et le régisseur avaient toute liberté de faire comme ils voulaient. Les jugements de tribunaux seigneuriaux déclarent plus d'une fois rondement qu'aucun usage ni règlement ne saurait limiter les droits du seigneur, en ce qui concerne les corvées à imposer à ses serfs de toute catégorie (26).

Au cours du XVIIe siècle, les réserves seigneuriales cultivées au moyen de corvées, continuent à offrir les diverses formes du travail salarié ou représentant une transition vers ce dernier, tels que l'emploi de domestiques de ferme avec contrat annuel et usage du cheptel du domaine, aussi bien dans les travaux champêtres que dans l'élevage, ou encore l'embauchage d'ouvriers saisonniers, à la journée ou autrement, pour la culture des vignes, la moisson et la fenaison (27). Mais l'importance de toutes ces formes du travail salarié diminue considérablement dans les réserves seigneuriales de la Hongrie du XVIIe siècle, en comparaison non seulement à celle des corvées gratuites considérablement accrues, mais aussi à celle que le travail salarié avait atteinte auparavant, vers le milieu du siècle précédent. A plusieurs endroits, on constate une rechute très nette des conditions qui caractérisent la production dans les réserves seigneuriales: ce qui y était fait jusqu'alors partiellement ou totalement par des travailleurs salariés, l'est désormais par des serfs astreints à des corvées gratuites. Là où, auparavant, les paysans accomplissant leur corvée touchaient soit leur nourriture, soit une gratification en argent, les seigneurs adoptent l'usage des corvées parfaitement gratuites. Les seigneurs qui, auparavant, payaient les travaux faits en excédent sur les corvées définies, abandonnent cet usage et exigent désormais à titre gratuit la totalité des services. Bien des domaines qui employaient des journaliers et d'autres ouvriers salariés pour les labours, pour le charroi du bois ou pour la culture des vignes, finissent par assignes ces travaux à leurs serfs corvéables (28).

Il convient de souligner, une fois de plus, que la régression du travail salarié dans les fermes et les réserves seigneuriales est loin d'être l'apanage exclusif du XVIIe siècle, mais s'observe déjà depuis les environs de 1570. Au cours du XVIIe siècle, cette régression continuera de gagner du terrain, au premier chef dans les labours, secteur principal de l'agriculture allodiale, mais même dans la viticulture des réserves, où la supériorité de la productivité et de la qualité du travail salarié sur la corvée gratuite et obligatoire se manifestait pourtant on ne peut plus nettement (29). Dans les domaines de György Rákóczi Ier, la situation était encore relativement plus favorable, puisqu'une partie considérable de ses immenses vignobles de Hegyalja continuait d'être cultivée par une main-d'oeuvre salariée (30), mais les symptômes de la régression s'y faisaient sentir tout autant, notamment par la réduction considérable des paiements en nature (1632), versés sous le seigneur précédent aux travailleurs des vignobles (31). Dans les villages du comitat de Bihar, sujets du fief d'Adorján, on ne trouve plus, à la même époque, que très peu de vignes "cultivées contre salaire" et le terrier de 1625 présente, vignoble par vignoble, pour ainsi dire, l'évolution rétrograde par laquelle le seigneur achevait de transformer les travaux auparavant salariés, par la reconversion des cens de la Saint-Georges et de la Saint-Martin, en corvées gratuitement et obligatoirement fournies par les serfs (32). Les vignobles de Pereszleg, relevant du domaine de Sárvár-Kapuvár, étaient de ceux, très rares désormais, que l'on faisait cultiver pour de l'argent, parce que beaucoup de serfs du village avaient péri dans la guerre; c'était un cas unique dans ce domaine (33). La corvée des vignes se répand. Elle devient prépondérante, voire exclusive dans des cas sans cesse plus nombreux, notamment à Dávidcenk, dans le comitat de Sopron (34), à Kisbaráti, dans celui de Győr (35), chez Zsigmond Kapy, dans la vallée du Hernád (36), chez Pál Rákóczi, à Mád (37), ainsi que dans les vignobles de Misztótfalu (38) relevant du domaine d'Ecsed, et dans ceux de Podhering, sujets de la châtellenie de Szentmiklós (39).

3. L'apparition assez fréquente de diverses formes du travail salarié dans les réserves seigneuriales de la Hongrie du XVIe siècle, puis leur régression sans cesse plus accentuée à partir des dernières décennies du siècle sont des faits indiscutables.

Des faits semblables, un progrès, puis une régression analogues dans l'ensemble s'observent en Pologne et en Bohème aussi. Dans l'évolution de l'économie folwark, les historiens distinguent la période du XVIe siècle, caractérisée par la présence, dans certaines réserves et dans différentes régions du pays, d'un travail salarié assez largement répandu, coexistant avec les corvées serviles. Au cours de la période suivante, par contre, la plupart des réserves seigneuriales se fondaient presque exclusivement sur les corvées (40). En Bohème et en Moravie, abstraction faite des fermes piscicoles, les réserves seigneuriales étaient encore, pendant la première moitié du XVIe siècle, à un niveau de production assez bas. Le fardeau des corvées pesaient donc relativement peu sur les serfs, d'autant plus que, le cas échéant, les seigneurs recouraient volontiers à une main-d'oeuvre salariée. Les recherches relatives à la seconde moitié du XVIe et au commencement du XVIIe siecle font par contre état de l'expansion considérable des cultures céréalières dans les réserves seigneuriales des différentes régions du pays, se fondant en partie sur des corvées constamment aggravées et, en partie encore sur une main-d'oeuvre salariée (41).

Voilà pour les faits. Quant à leur interprétation, les avis sont fort différents les uns des autres.

Certains auteurs rappellent – à juste titre d'ailleurs – que le travail salarié se retrouve – à titre secondaire et complémentaire – dans toutes les périodes et tout au long de l'histoire de la féodalité; telle était donc la situation dans les réserves seigneuriales du XVIe siècle (42). – Nous sommes pourtant d'avis que le problème ne saurait se réduire à cette formule générale, mais qu'il s'agit essentiellement d'examiner les conditions dans lesquelles le travail salarié surgit au cours des différentes périodes historiques, ainsi que le climat économique qui lui donne naissance et les fonctions qui lui sont assignées. On comprendra alors que, dans la période que nous étudions, il s'agit d'une conséquence nécessaire de la propagation des redevances en espèces. (Voir plus loin II. 1.) Il devient évident que la fonction, assez importante au XVIe siècle, des travaux d'un caractère salarial dans les réserves seigneuriales de Hongrie, de Bohème et de Pologne ne doivent nullement se confondre avec leurs apparitions bien plus restreintes au cours des siècles précédents de la féodalité (quand les rentes féodales en espèces ne prévalaient pas encore sur les prestations en nature), ni même avec le rôle considérablement diminué, que devait leur réserver le XVIIe siècle (quand les redevances en espèces perdaient déjà du terrain contre les redevances en nature et les corvées et que la lente transformation de l'économie domaniale fondée sur la corvée – le développement agraire capitaliste selon le modèle dit prussien – n'avait pas encore commencé).

D'autres auteurs soulignent que les seigneurs avaient recours à une contrainte extra-économique, même dans les cas où ils versaient un salaire, en espèces ou en nature, à leurs serfs exécutant une corvée; il s'agirait donc, même dans les cas de ce genre, de rentes féodales obtenues par contrainte (43). - Nous ne saurions partager cette opinion, qui tend également à minimiser les faits cités plus haut.

Il est vrai que l'on a pu voir, dans les réserves seigneuriales de Hongrie, les seigneurs verser un salaire pour les corvées elles-mêmes, employant ainsi une contrainte extra-économique, pour obliger leurs propres serfs à fournir un travail salarié. Sans parler des autres formes de travail salarié citées plus haut, on conviendra pourtant aisément que la différence était considérable, au point de vue des serfs, entre la corvée faite gratuitement et celle qui leur valait une rétribution, même si dans ce dernier cas, le seigneur imposait un tarif inférieur à celui des journaliers libres! Ce n'est pas sans raison que, par la suite, les serfs se plaignirent de la suppression de ces paiements. N'est-il pas évident que ce n'est nullement par hasard que, précisément à cette époque, les seigneurs avaient recours à des procédés de ce genre. En effet, ce n'est pas par caprice qu'ils extorquaient à leurs serfs des corvées payées, mais bien parce qu'ils y étaient contraints eux-mêmes par les circonstances. Aussi, par la suite, au fur et à mesure que celles-ci changeaient, abandonnaient-ils ces usages.

Jugeant les faits selon leur importance effective, certains expliquent enfin la propagation des modalités salariées, en affirmant que les seigneurs "reconnaissaient de plus en plus clairement" que ces dernières étaient d'une productivité supérieure à celle des corvées obtenus gratuitement et par contrainte. Par la suite cependant, la penurie de la monnaie les aurait obligés a revenir aux corvées gratuites (44). Pour clair qu'il soit, ce raisonnement ne nous paraît pourtant pas absolument convaincant, pour un certain nombre de raisons sur lesquelles nous reviendrons par la suite, quand il s'agira d'interpréter les faits.

II

1. Notre interprétation se fondera sur le niveau d'évolution atteint par les conditions de la production agricole en Hongrie, au cours de la seconde moitié du XVe siècle; il s'agit essentiellement des structures de la propriété et de la rente foncières propres à la féodalité.

Ainsi que nous l'avons indiqué au commencement de la présente étude, les réserves seigneuriales étaient, à l'époque, d'une étendue généralement réduite, la structure agraire se caractérisait essentiellement par la prédominance décisive des exploitations paysannes. En ce qui concerne les redevances féodales, les corvées jouaient un rôle très limité, celui des redevances en produits restait toujours assez important, tandis que les redevances en espèces ne cessaient de gagner du terrain (45).

A ce degré d'évolution – caractérisé par l'essor de la propagation des redevances en espèces – l'apparition de certaines formes de travail agricole salarié était déterminée par la nécessité. La loi qui détermine cette corrélation entre la propagation des redevances en espèces et l'apparition du travail salarié a été analysée par Marx à propos des économies de paysans aisés (46), elle s'applique cependant parfaitement aux réserves seigneuriales aussi. Dans les sources datées de la seconde moitié du XVe siècle, on trouve déjà de nombreuses indications concernant les charrues et les chariots du seigneur, ainsi que leur attelage bovin, ou les valets ou journaliers travaillant aux labours avec l'outillage et les bêtes du seigneur (47).

Les livres de compte conservés dans certains domaines révèlent aussi des faits plus étendus, en ce qui concerne les origines du travail salarié dans les réserves seigneuriales. En 1453, les fermes du domaine de Kisvárda engagèrent cinq pâtres et journaliers, contre un salaire en partie en especes et en partie en nature; en 1471, on y trouve un certain nombre de travailleurs agricoles - dont cinq laboureurs travaillant avec l'outillage et les bêtes du seigneur - ainsi que deux porchers et plusieurs vignerons, qui avaient tous droit, pro mercede annuali, à une rétribution en espèces et en produits; il y avait aussi, dans ces mêmes fermes, des moissonneurs, des vignerons et des journaliers pour divers travaux autour de la maison, tous salariés; le cas échéant, des salaires y étaient payés pour le fauchage et pour le charroi des vins (48). Dans le domaine appartenant à l'évêché d'Eger - dont les revenus étaient constitués surtout par des redevances en espèces - on décida, en 1493-1495, de donner une certaine extension (49) aux réserves seigneuriales. Lors de la prise, ou la reprise, en culture de labours, de jardins, de vignes et d'étangs à poisson (non seulement au centre du domaine, mais aussi à Pusztaszikszó, à Sajóhidvég, à Gyöngyöspüspöki, à Polgári) il était tout naturel que, pro nova allodiatone, on eût surtout recours au travail salarié, au lieu d'accroître les corvées des serfs. Le nouvel administrateur du domaine loua des gens ayant leurs chariots et leurs boeufs, enbaucha des valets et des journaliers - dans une ferme, notamment, 8 valets pour 4 couples de boeufs et, dans une autre, 4 valets pour 2 couples - et il payait des salaires en espèces aux bineurs et aux faucheurs - à ces derniers parfois seulement ultra gratam falcaturam - de même qu'aux ouvriers des vignes et aux moissonneurs. Le débit du bois de chauffage, le charroi des porcs, des vins et du sel étaient également rétribués en espèces. Les femmes chargées de monder des graines, les enfants travaillant dans les potagers recevaient, de même, des gratifications en espèces (50). Ainsi que l'attestent ses comptes de 1502, le régisseur du domaine de Battyán du seigneur Boldizsár Batthyány avait des valets de ferme et des gardiens de chevaux embauchés à titre permanent et il payait souvent des salaires à la journée à des faucheurs (falcatores appreciati), faneurs, metteurs en meules, javeleurs, moissonneurs, vignerons, de même qu'aux gens chargés du charroi des vins et d'autres produits. Il n'était pourtant pas facile de trouver des journaliers en pleine saison d'été; le régisseur se rendit de Battyán à Fehérvár, pour y "recruter des moissonneurs à la criée"; il alla aussi à Lepsény, "pour trouver et embaucher des batteurs de blé", sans y parvenir pendant plusieurs jours (51).

La corrélation entre les redevances en argent et le travail salarié dans les réserves devient évidente et directe dans les cas où les redevances en espèces versées par les serfs servaient au seigneur à s'acquitter des salaires qu'il devait à ses ouvriers. C'était le cas, notamment, du domaine de Világosvár où, selon le témoignage du terrier de 1525, le versement d'une redevance spéciale en espèces (le denier de l'ouvrier) était imposé aux serfs, afin de servir au paiement des mercenarii (52). Il en était de même dans le domaine de Szendrő, dont le terrier de 1570 relate que les valets de ferme étaient payés auparavant avec l'argent de la redevance spéciale en espèces, imposée aux serfs en sus du cens (53).

A ce degré du développement de l'agriculture féodale, les revenus du seigneur se composaient surtout de recettes en espèces; la main-d'oeuvre salariée que le seigneur employait était financée, directement ou indirectement, sur ces fonds. Bien entendu, l'emploi du travail salarié restait fort limité dans les réserves seigneuriales, tant que celles-ci restaient relativement peu étendues.

2. L'apparition nécessaire, mais limitée, du travail salarié dans les réserves seigneuriales n'accèdera à une importance supérieure qu'au moment où, à ce même degré d'évolution, les seigneurs (certains groupes de la classe seigneuriale) se trouveront en présence de circonstances qui les pousseront à étendre les réserves seigneuriales. Et encore faudra-t-il que les seigneurs soient en mesure de réaliser cette ambition.

Les circonstances auxquelles nous faisons allusion devaient se produire, à partir de 1530-40, surtout en Pologne, mais aussi en Hongrie. La Pologne, on le sait, fut de plus en plus vigoureusement encouragée dans ce sens par ses exportations de blé toujours plus considérables, à destination de l'Europe Occidentale et, surtout, des Pays-Bas. Les transports se faisaient par la Vistule jusqu'à Gdansk, puis par la mer Baltique et celle du Nord jusqu'au port d'Amsterdam (54). A défaut de voies de transport fluviales susceptibles de lui garantir une liaison adéquate avec l'Ouest, la Hongrie ne pouvait alors prendre part au commerce international des céréales. Mais la conjoncture suscitée par les guerres pour ainsi dire permanentes contre les Turcs, avec les énormes commandes de céréales et de fourrages du Trésor, destinées au ravitaillement des armées mercenaires, y exerçaient des effets plus ou moins semblables (55). L'extension des débouchés entraîna, aussi bien en Pologne qu'en Hongrie, la hausse des prix. Ce furent les débuts de ce qu'il est convenu d'appeler la révolution des prix, qui se traduisit essentiellement par la hausse du prix des produits agricoles, bien plus que par celle du prix des articles industriels (56).

Outre cette évolution propice des possibilités d'écoulement de leurs produits, il y avait encore un autre mobile qui poussait les seigneurs féodaux hongrois à agrandir leurs réserves. C'était notamment, l'accroissement des besoins de victuailles qui se manifestait autant dans les cours seigneuriales que dans les forteresses – aussi bien les forteresses privées que celles gérées par le Trésor – en raison de l'état de guerre. L'extension des réserves seigneuriales devait, en effet, permettre directement et sans le recours au marché, la couverture des besoins de la cour seigneuriale, de ceux d'une domesticité de plus en plus nombreuse, ainsi que de ceux des gens d'armes au service du seigneur et des mercenaires qui formaient la garnison de la forteresse. A l'époque où les prix des produits agricoles augmentaient sans interruption, c'était là une considération particulièrement importante.

Les différents motifs encourageant l'extension des réserves seigneuriales transparaissent dans l'instruction donnée par Georges de Brandebourg en 1520, c'est-à-dire aux débuts de cette période, aux majordomes et au régisseur de Gyula, document qui va, pour ainsi dire, inaugurer la série des instructions d'exploitation détaillées, qui caractérisent le XVIe siècle: "... le nouveau régisseur devra consacrer une attention accrue aux labours et accroître les emblaves... il devra améliorer les fermes, leur culture et leur élevage, pour nous éviter de faire constamment des achats pour de l'argent comptant et pour nous permettre plutöt de vendre et de nous procurer ainsi des bénéfices... il faudra qu'il y ait toujours à la forteresse des réserves de vivres pour l'année" (57). Le seigneur Tamás Nádasdy, au milieu du siècle, forçait en premier lieu la vente, au point d'en oublier parfois les nécessités de la garnison (58); le domaine de Munkács, géré par le Trésor, s'attachait, par contre, à des principes autarciques, ainsi qu'en fait foi l'instruction publiée en 1570 par son régisseur. Ce document place l'agriculture des réserves "par-dessus tout", déclarant que "c'est ce dont dépend au premier chef le ravitaillement de la place et qui permet de pourvoir aux besoins de la garnison" (59).

3. A partir des années 30-40 du XVIe siècle, les circonstances évoluent donc de plus en plus dans un sens propre à encourager matériellement les seigneurs hongrois à accroître leurs réserves domaniales. Comment expliquer, dans ces conditions, que seule une partie des besoins accrus de main-d'oeuvre des fermes seigneuriales était, à cette époque, couverte par le recours à l'aggravation des corvées, tandis que le reste l'était par l'emploi d'une main-d'oeuvre salariée et de types intermédiaires?

Pour certains historiens, ainsi que nous l'avons indiqué plus haut, l'explication en réside dans le fait que les seigneurs reconnaissaient de plus en plus nettement la productivité supérieure du travail salarié par rapport à celle de la corvée gratuite (60).

Nous disposons, en effet, de sources attestant que les seigneurs - certains seigneurs du moins, ou, plus exactement, leurs intendents intelligents - étaient plus ou moins conscients des avantages du travail salarié. Citons, dans cet ordre d'idées, Ferenc Medvei, proviseur du domaine de la Marche de Szatmár, ou Dániel Jobbágy, régisseur du domaine Batthyány de Rohonc-Szalonak, qui eurent, le premier en 1572, le second au milieu du siècle suivant, le bon sens de favoriser l'embauchage de travailleurs avec contrat annuel. Citons aussi le seigneur Imre Thököly, dont l'instruction de 1684 souligne: "L'attelage payé convient souvent mieux aux travaux urgents et difficiles" (61). Il existe donc des documents de ce genre, aussi bien du XVIe que du XVIIe siècle, quoique, vers la fin de cette période, les formes salariées du travail aient déjà perdu du terrain. Or, voici la conclusion qui s'en dégage pour nous: même en admettant que des milieux assez larges reconnaissaient la supériorité du travail salarié, il y avait d'autres éléments, a savoir des conditions objectives qui incitaient les seigneurs d'y recourir, ou bien de le refuser.

Il est donc possible que certains seigneurs embauchaient la main-d'oeuvre salariée de propos délibéré, parce qu'ils étaient conscients de ses avantages. Il est par contre certain que, dans les conditions historiques qui leur étaient faites, la plupart étaient contraints d'agir ainsi, et ne pouvaient éviter d'employer des travailleurs salariés, et des corvées rétribuées.

Force était aux seigneurs de se rendre à l'évidence que les corvées – qui avaient joué un rôle, en général, très limité au cours du siècle précédent et au début du XVIe – ne pouvaient être augmentées (62) du jour au lendemain, dans une mesure assez considérable pour suffire aux besoins accrus par l'extension des réserves. Le grand soulèvement paysan de 1514 était encore bien vivant dans leur mémoire; ils ne pouvaient risquer de multiplier brusquement le fardeau des corvées, sous peine de se heurter, une fois de plus, à la vive résistance de leurs serfs. Il était impossible, en effet, de faire brusquement machine arrière, en transformant radicalement et d'un jour à l'autre le système traditionnel des obligations imposées à la paysannerie.

Nous ne pouvons donc guère partager les vues de ceux qui affirment que les réserves seigneuriales, au XVIe siècle, n'avaient pratiquement pas besoin de main-d'oeuvre salariée (63). Ainsi par exemple, le terrier de Vöröskő de 1543 – fort révélateur, précisément pour cette période d'extension des réserves seigneuriales – prend bien soin de spécifier, au regard de presque tous les travaux (labours, moisson, battage, engrangement, vignes, fauchage) qu'en sus des corvées, le travail salarié est indispensable. Il y ajoute des observations de ce genre: ce qui excède "la coutume admise" doit être payé; l'herbage appartient au seigneur qui, "n'ayant pas de corvées, doit recourir à l'argent" (64) etc.

Au cours de la première période d'extension des réserves, les seigneurs ne pouvaient donc couvrir leurs besoins sans cesse accrus de main-d'oeuvre que par un recours toujours plus étendu à une main-d'oeuvre de type salarié ou assimilable; l'accroissement des corvées ne pouvait y répondre que pour une petite part. Il est à noter, par exemple, que le terrier de 1524 du domaine de Szenyér (comitat de Somogy) prescrit expressément des corvées qui sont à exécuter sine solutione et que, pendant un certain temps, on procédait à l'augmentation des corvées en rétribuant le travail supplémentaire. Une instruction, datée du milieu du XVIe siècle, concernant l'exploitation du domaine capitulaire d'Eger précise qu'en ce qui concerne le fauchage et le charroi, "il faut convenir d'une rétribution en espèces" avec les serfs (65).

Dans certaines régions, l'évolution de la situation militaire agissait également dans ce sens. Au domaine de Kanizsa – où en 1534, malgré la menace turque directe, sept fermes subsistaient toujours – la châtelaine, qui était la veuve du palatin Tamás Nádasdy, décréta la diminution des corvées serviles, qui ne devaient plus dépasser les limites fixées en 1530. Les travaux en sus devaient être exécutés par des valets de ferme et des journaliers payés; les serfs astreints à la corvée du binage recevaient "le boire et le manger" (66).

4. La nouvelle vague d'extension des réserves seigneuriales survint pendant la première moitié du XVIIe siècle, mais le recul des types rétribués du travail s'observe, dans les économies domaniales de Hongrie, depuis les environs de 1570. Cela est attesté, ainsi que nous l'avons indiqué plus haut, non seulement par l'apparition et la propagation des corvées illimitées, à la discrétion du seigneur, mais aussi par de nombreux documents relatant la suppression des rétributions et gratifications auparavant admises, ou l'exécution de travaux auparavant payés par des serfs astreints à la corvée gratuite. C'est ainsi qu'on lit dans le terrier de Szendrő, de 1570, que dans les endroits ou, une vingtaine d'années auparavant, vers le milieu du siècle encore, les travaux étaient faits par des ouvriers payés travaillant avec le cheptel du seigneur quibus exercuerunt allodiaturam, additis mercenariis idoneis pretio conductis, les serfs sont à présent accablés par un intolerabilis servitus; on leur impose, en effet, tant de corvées qu'ils n'ont plus le moyen de cultiver leurs propres terres et vignes. Le livre dit de saint-Albert de l'archevêché d'Esztergom (1571) fait état de rétributions en espèces, pratiquées auparavant. Le terrier de Pozsony de 1574 relate que jadis les tenanciers de Váralja étaient nourris pendant le temps des corvées, mais que cet usage a disparu. Il apparaît du terrier de Tokaj de 1581 qu'auparavant seule une partie des vignes domaniales était cultivée en corvée gratuite, tandis que l'autre partie l'était aux frais du seigneur, nunc vero absque pecuniis laborare coguntur, quod ipsis valde onerosum est. Le terrier de 1592 du domaine d'Erdőd-Szatmár cite des vignes seigneuriales que gratuito labore colonorum modo colitur, olim tamen pro pecuniis colebatur, ainsi que des labours allodiaux ad quorum culturam intertenebantur aratra duo cum bobus, nunc autem cum bobus incolarum ... excolere faciunt etc. (67).

Cette évolution rétrograde peut-elle vraiment s'expliquer par le manque d'argent des seigneurs? Nous avons cité plus haut l'opinion qui explique la propagation du travail salarié dans les réserves seigneuriales par le fait que les seigneurs avaient reconnu que sa productivité était supérieure à celle de la corvée; cette même opinion explique ainsi la régression ultérieure et le retour aux corvées: "... les avantages du travail salarié eurent beau être reconnus à temps par nombre de seigneurs en train d'accroître leurs réserves; ceux-ci tentèrent en vain, vers le milieu du XVIe siècle, d'adopter le salariat" (68), le manque d'argent comptant devait les empêcher de persévérer dans cette voie.

Nous ne saurions faire nôtre ce raisonnement. On sait, en effet, que ce fut précisément aux environs de 1570 – au moment donc où cette tendance rétrograde devenait sensible – que la "révolution des prix" se déploya pleinement en Hongrie. Les produits agricoles atteignirent des prix sans précédent; l'écart entre les prix agricoles et les prix industriels fut plus large que jamais, au bénéfice des premiers. La révolution des prix fit, en effet, monter les prix des produits agricoles à un niveau plusieurs fois plus haut que ceux des articles industriels; il en fut ainsi aussi bien dans les pays d'Europe Occidentale que dans ceux d'Europe Centrale et Orientale, donc en Hongrie (69). Les seigneurs hongrois, qui faisaient, depuis des dizaines d'années, un commerce très actif de leurs produits agricoles trouvèrent donc là une abondante source de profits très élevés, mettant parfaitement à leur portée les moyens monétaires nécessaires à l'organisation et à l'extension du salariat (70). Ce qui plus est, la révolution des prix avait bien de quoi rendre le travail salarié très souhaitable aux yeux des seigneurs, puisqu'elle accroissait l'écart non seulement entre les prix agraires et les prix industriels, mais aussi entre les prix et les salaires. Il était, en effet, évident que les salaires n'emboîteraient jamais le pas à la montée des prix (71).

Il n'en est pas moins aisé de déceler une relation directe de cause à effet entre le changement survenu dans les méthodes de culture des réserves seigneuriales et la révolution des prix ..., seulement ce changement ne se situe pas sur le plan des salaires et des bénéfices, mais sur celui de l'évolution de la rente foncière. Les progrès de la révolution des prix et la détérioration considérable de la monnaie, qui ne tarda pas à s'étendre à la Hongrie aussi, réduisirent, en effet, sensiblement et très rapidement la valeur des redevances paysannes en espèces, qui représentaient naguère la forme prédominante de la rente féodale (72). Or, il n'était, bien entendu, pas question pour les seigneurs de majorer périodiquement le montant des redevances en espèces, proportionnellement à sa dévalorisation (73), adoptant ainsi une sorte d' "échelle mobile" de la rente foncière. Pour faire contrepoids à cette réduction de leurs revenus, il était tout naturel pour eux d'avoir désormais recours, au détriment des redevances en espèces, aux formes en nature des redevances féodales, exploitant le plus énergiquement possible les redevances en produits, ainsi que celles versées sous forme de travail. Ils entendaient se dédommager ainsi de la constante dévalorisation de leurs recettes en espèces.

Cette corrélation ressort notamment du terrier de 1602 du domaine de Csábrág-Szitnya, qui établit les cens à un niveau relativement bas, n'excédant pas celui de 1558, mais abolit toute limitation des corvées et étend considérablement les redevances en produits (74). Des dispositions sensiblement analogues se retrouvent dans les sources concernant les domaines des Thurzó, en ce qui concerne surtout les villages relevant des châteaux forts de Sempte, de Galgóc et de Temetvény (75): maintien des redevances en espèces à des niveaux tres bas par rapport aux prix du premier tiers du XVIIe siècle – pratiquement sans majoration par rapport aux redevances en usage à la fin du XVe et au commencement du XVIe siècle – mais augmentant sans mesure les corvées et les prestations en produits. Le terrier du domaine de Tokaj, celui de 1581, comme celui de 1640, relate que les habitants de Rakamaz, ainsi que ceux de Tokaj étaient auparavant soumis au cens, mais que celui fut supprimé par le seigneur, en échange des soins de ses vignes (76). Le terrier de 1625 des biens de Bihar relevant du château fort d'Adorján, que nous avons déjà cité plus haut, souligne à plusieurs reprises que les serfs – étant par ailleurs redevables de "tous services" – "ne payent rien", mais qu'ils doivent "à titre de rachat de leur cens" (parfois expressément pour celui du cens de la Saint-Martin et de la Saint-Georges) "cultiver les vignes et fournir les tuteurs" (77).

La révolution des prix fut favorable à l'emploi de la main-d'oeuvre salariée dans les entreprises des fermiers, entrepreneurs capitalistes de l'agriculture. Ce fut le cas en Angleterre, où "la constante détérioration de la valeur de la monnaie portait des fruits dorés au fermier", qui payait aussi bien le salaire de ses ouvriers que le fermage de son propriétaire en une monnaie qui se dépréciait de jour en jour. Il "s'enrichissait donc aussi bien sur le dos de ses ouvriers que sur celui de son propriétaire" (78).

La révolution des prix fut défavorable à l'emploi de la main-d'oeuvre salariée dans les réserves seigneuriales de Hongrie – et de toute l'Europe Centrale et Orientale – car les seigneurs de ces pays étaient tout au plus des "capitalistes débutants". En réalité, ils n'étaient que des rentiers féodaux. Dans les conditions économiques créées par la détérioration de la monnaie, le salariat leur aurait rapporté des bénéfices, tandis que les redevances en espèces leur infligeaient des pertes. Or, ils ne pensaient pas en salaires et en profits, mais en rentes foncières.

Tout en exerçant donc une influence analogue dans toute l'Europe sur l'évolution des rapports entre les prix, ainsi que sur ceux entre les prix et les salaires, la révolution des prix fut loin d'avoir les mêmes effets sur l'évolution des conditions de la production en Europe Occidentale et en Europe Orientale.

5. Orientés par la détérioration constante de la monnaie vers les redevances féodales dites naturelles – et surtout vers les prestations revêtant la forme du travail – les seigneurs eurent désormais la possibilité d'obtenir ce qu'ils voulaient.

Par rapport à celles qui avaient prévalu pendant la première période d'extension des réserves seigneuriales (1530–40), les conditions socio-économiques et politiques s'étaient, en effet, profondément modifiées. A l'époque, il eût été impossible d'accroître rapidement et de beaucoup les corvées imposées aux serfs, qui avaient d'ailleurs subi des limitations considérables au cours du XVe siècle. Mais depuis cette époque, les redevances en travail ne faisaient qu'augmenter et l'usage des corvées à merci se répandait de plus en plus. Depuis cette époque, l'appareil de coercition des classes dirigeantes s'était consolidé dans la Hongrie royale. Le grand soulèvement paysan de 1514 ne put se rééditer; les petites révoltes paysannes d'ordre local – celle de la région de Debrecen, ou encore celle de Slavonie – purent être écrasées, précisément au commencement des années 1570. Dans ces conditions qui modifiaient sensiblement les rapports de force entre les classes de la société, les seigneurs n'avaient plus besoin de recourir, dans une mesure tant soit peu importante, à l'emploi d'une main-d'oeuvre salariée, car il leur était désormais possible de charger des serfs corvéables de la plupart des travaux dans leurs réserves.

La cause essentielle de la régression du salariat et des formes de travail assimilées doit donc être recherchée d'une part dans les conséquences de la révolution des prix et, d'autre part, dans le fait que le developpement des réserves seigneuriales à la fin du XVIe et au commencement du XVIIe siècle fut étroitement rattaché à la consolidation totale du système de la servitude perpétuelle, variante hongroise de la "deuxième édition du servage". C'était là une force diamétralement opposée à l'adoption et à la propagation du travail salarié; par la confirmation de l'attachement à la glèbe et par la possibilité d'obtenir des corvées à la discrétion du seigneur, elle devait aboutir à la disparition des formes d'un caractère capitaliste ou de transition qui existaient déjà, mais qui furent englouties par les formes féodales (79).

Il convient d'ailleurs de préciser, dans cet ordre d'idées, que les formes de travail jusqu'alors atteintes par l'évolution n'étaient pas, dans la plupart des cas, des formes capitalistes pures; tout comme au cours du XVIe siècle, ou plus encore, le salariat ne portait guère sur une main-d'oeuvre libre "dans les deux sens du mot" (80). Les cas où l'ouvrier va trouver un emploi en dehors du domaine dont il relève restent extrêmement rares (81); fût-ce contre un salaire journalier, une part des produits ou un salaire à l'année, le seigneur recourait, au premier chef, à ses propres serfs et colons. Les batteurs de blé partiaires du domaine de Makovica étaient recrutés parmi les serfs sans tenure du domaine; à Csejte, les journaliers chargés du fauchage et de la fenaison étaient aussi des gens "qui ne surgissaient qu'au moment des travaux des vignes, de la moisson et de la fenaison" (82), mais qui relevaient du domaine.

Cela vaut encore davantage pour les valets de ferme et autres travailleurs embauchés à titre permanent, qui se recrutaient en majorité parmi les serfs et les colons du domaine et qui bénéficiaient d'une exemption de leurs redevances serviles pendant la durée de leur emploi dans les réserves seigneuriales. En 1608, dans le domaine de Kapuvár, à Pordány, il y avait des serfs comme journaliers, des colons à manse comme bouviers, un colon à demi-manse comme jardinier du seigneur. En 1625, à Szalárd, dans le comitat de Bihar, le bouvier était un "serf sans boeufs". En 1631, un colon sans manse, mais ayant sa maison à Zboro servait comme valet de ferme à Upor (donc dans une autre propriété de la famille Rákóczi). Le terrier d'Ecsed de 1648 cite des colons qui servaient soit dans le même village, soit dans des fermes du même domaine, mais situées dans d'autres villages de la région, comme valets, jardiniers, gardiens de chevaux ou bouviers (83). La châtelaine de Kapuvár estimait que la pratique du travail salarié n'était pas souhaitable, car elle diminuait "le nombre de nos serfs corvéables", "... ne faites pas de nos serfs des fermiers, des valets ni des laboureurs", enjoint-elle à son régisseur. "Prenez-les parmi les colons sans emploi ... et non parmi les serfs", lit-on dans l'instruction du régisseur de Szendrő (84).

La consolidation du servage, du régime des corvées et de l'attachement à la glèbe endigua donc la propagation du travail salarié, étouffant dans l'oeuf, pour ainsi dire, toute initiative dans le sens de la formation d'un marché libre de la main-d'oeuvre.

6. Cette régression fut en quelque sorte parachevée – mais non provoquée – par l'extinction de la révolution des prix, par l'arrivée de la "dépression agraire", qui s'était manifestée par de nombreux signes avant-coureurs dès la première moitié du XVIIe siècle, pour se faire sentir de tout son poids à partir du milieu du siècle (85). Dans les conditions créées par l'instabilité, la stagnation, puis la

baisse des prix des produits agricoles, il pouvait désormais effectivement arriver à des seigneurs de se trouver accablés de difficultés financières (86). Quoi qu'il en fût, ils ne se privaient pas de s'en plaindre et de le prouver, le cas échéant, en retenant jusque sur leur lit de mort le salaire en espèces qu'ils devaient à leur personnel domestique et à leurs travailleurs agricoles de tout rang (87). Ils n'en dépensaient pas moins avec libéralité, parfois des sommes considérables, pour des buts de caractère féodal: acquisition de nouvelles terres, pierres précieuses et objets en or, vêtements somptueux, armes, dot de leur fille etc. Ils amassaient souvent de véritables fortunes sous forme de bijoux, de perles, de pierres précieuses (88). Mais pour les dépenses d'un caractère capitaliste, l'argent leur faisait défaut, essentiellement parce que les conditions socio-économiques, qui n'étaient plus les mêmes que jadis, ne les y obligeaient plus, ni même ne les y encourageaient.

Voilà pourquoi le régisseur de Sárvár se vit semoncer pour avoir engagé des coupeurs de choux "pour de l'argent", alors que "nous avons assez de serfs qui eussent pu le faire" (89); voilà pourquoi fut supprimé le salaire des serfs astreints à des travaux pénibles à l'atelier de monnayage de Nagybánya, travaux qui ne tardèrent pas à être convertis en corvées gratuites (90); voilà encore pourquoi les seigneurs s'efforçaient non seulement de maintenir entre des limites strictes le nombre des valets, domestiques, journaliers etc. de leurs fermes, mais encore de le réduire. "Ne garde pas de domestiques nombreux et inutiles dans les fermes", dit l'instruction de Csicsavár de 1636, "mais seulement ceux qui y sont utiles et nécessaires". Celle de Szendrő (1652) ordonne: "... ne payez pas pour rien les valets, domestiques et journaliers de nos fermes !" Celle de Holics (1660) dit: "Ne conservez dans les fermes pas plus de domestiques que ce qui est nécessaire". Et d'ajouter: "Et que ceux que vous y garderez soient des gens connus et de bonne mentalité". L'instruction de Szentmiklós (1698) en dit autant, tout en insistant sur la nécessité d'économiser sur les dépenses (91). Il va de soi que cet appel à des considérations d'économie n'est pas l'argumentation de quelque capitaliste agraire désireux de comprimer ses frais de revient, mais un ordre de seigneur féodal disposant d'une quantité illimitée de main-d'oeuvre servile et gratuite. Pour lui "les ouvriers ne méritent pas même ce qu'ils mangent, de sorte qu'ils sont payés beaucoup, pour ne rien faire" (92), car il compare le salaire au travail servile gratuit et dans cet ordre d'idées, toute considération de productivité paraît négligeable.

NOTES

1. Pour l'ensemble de la question voir ZS. P. PACH, Nyugat-európai és magyarországi agrárfejlődés a XV–XVII. században (Développement de l'agriculture en Europe Occidentale et en Hongrie aux XVe–XVIIe siècles), Budapest 1963, p. 45 et suiv.

2. F. MAKSAY, Parasztság és majorgazdálkodás a XVI. századi Magyarországon (Paysannerie et économie allodiale dans la Hongrie du XVIe siècle), Budapest 1958, p. 17 et suiv.; PACH, op. cit., p. 152 et suiv.
3. Voir par exemple les terriers des châteaux de Léka et de Kanizsa de 1519, celui d'un domaine féodal du comitat de Turóc de 1520, ainsi que celui de Kisvárda de 1521. - Archives Nationales, Dl. 37007; Archives de la branche aînée de la famille des comtes Zichy de Zichi et Vásonkeő (= Zichy-okmt.). T. XII., Budapest 1931, pp. 343–364; Arch. Nat. Convent de Garamszentbenedek. Protocollum B. fol. 7.
4. Articles 33–38 de la loi de 1548; 10–12 de la loi de 1553.
5. Archives de la ville de Gyula 1313–1800, Budapest 1938, pp. 88, 289, 348.
6. Terriers XVIe–XVIIe siècles, Dir F. MAKSAY, Budapest 1959, pp. 133–142; Lettres de serfs, Dir. É. H. BALÁZS, Budapest 1951, pp. 25–31.
7. Terriers, p. 194.
8. Arch. Nat. Dl 36992, 36994, 37007; U et C 56: 33.
9. Articles 1 de la loi de 1522, 24 de la loi de 1523; 1524; Archives de la ville de Gyula, p. 86; etc.
10. Par ex.: Morceaux choisis des relevés de comptes de la famille Nádasdy entre 1540 et 1550, T. II, Budapest 1959, pp. 11, 14, 31, 36, 196; Alsószeleste, 1555–1580: Agrártörténeti Szemle, 1961, N°s 3–4, pp. 447–49; Kapuvár, 1584: Arch. Nat. U et C. 56: 33. - Il ressort de ce dernier que les valets de ferme et les pâtres, les jardiniers et les vignerons des réserves seigneuriales sortaient généralement des rangs des serfs appauvris: il y eut parmi eux des serfs à tenure entière qui, laissant leur session en friche, s'engageaient comme valet de ferme dans un autre village, mais aussi de tels qui gardaient leur tenure entière ou leur demi-charrue et de ce fait étaient exempts pendant la durée de leur service des redevances seigneuriales et devenaient culverts.
11. Arch. Nat. documents municipaux et de la chambre. Fol. Lat. 913.
12. I. ACSÁDY, Közgazdasági állapotaink a XVI. és XVII. században (Les conditions économiques en Hongrie au XVIe et au XVIIe siècle), Budapest 1889, pp. 125, 142; Morceaux choisis, T. II, pp. 20, 25; Magyar Gazdaságtörténelmi Szemle, 1896, p. 108; 1898, p. 345; 1905, pp. 199–200.
13. Magyar Gazdaságtörténelmi Szemle, 1894, p. 68; 1896, p. 68.
14. Archives de la ville de Gyula, pp. 87–90.
15. Arch. Nat. Dl. 37000.
16. Cf. E. FÜGEDI, Az esztergomi érsekség gazdálkodása a XV. század végén (Economie de l'archevéché d'Esztergom à la fin du XVe siècle), Századok, 1960, N°s 1–3, pp. 97–98.
17. Archives de la famille Hédervάry (= Hédervάry oklt.), T. II, Budapest 1922, pp. 185–86.
18. Pour la donnée de Komárom voir Magyar Gazdaságtörténelmi Szemle 1897, p. 492 (cf. Arch. Nat. U et C 4: 45); pour les autres: Terriers, pp. 179–180, 621, 624, 695, 697–99, 704–5, 711.

19. En face de la théorie du déclin de l'exploitation allodiale notre historiographie a généralement adopté celle du progrès de l'expansion des alleux dans la première moitié du XVIIe siècle. – Cf. Agrártörténeti Szemle, 1961, N° 1, p. 137.
20. PACH, op. cit., pp. 48-49, 1970, 215.
21. Pour la corvée de deux jours par semaine voir par ex. le terrier de 1648 et de 1672 du domaine d'Ecsed, pour la combinaison des systèmes de deux et de trois jours par semaine, ceux de 1586 et de 1597 du domaine de Sárvár-Kapuvár; le terrier de Csejte de 1641 parle d'une corvée de trois jours par semaine, ceux des domaines Ibrányi dans le comitat de Szabolcs-Szatmár (1656) de 4 jours de service, en précisant souvent que "lors de la moisson on exige des corvées non pas selon les systèmes hebdomadaires, mais conformément aux ordres des régisseurs". Archives de la famille des comtes Károlyi de Nagykároly (= Károlyi-oklt.), T. IV, Budapest 1887, pp. 304, 310, 330.; Arch. Nat. U et C 108:9, 69:82, 12:42/2, 119:8; G. WENZEL, Magyarország mezőgazdaságának története (Histoire de l'agriculture en Hongrie), Budapest 1887, p. 363.
22. C'est ainsi que l'avocat des domaines Batthyány de Szalonak formule le point de vue de la classe dirigeante dans le procès intenté en 1651 aux serfs de Balf (comitat de Vas) accusés d'avoir manqué à la corvée. – Justice seigneuriale. Textes de procès des XVIe–XVIIe siècles, publiés par E. VARGA, Budapest 1958, p. 176.
23. Arch. Nat. U et C 61:71, 82:29.
24. Arch. Nat. U et C 16:5, 49:17, Károlyi oklt., T. III, pp. 501–502.
25. Arch. Nat. U et C 37:56, 102:24, Irregestrata, Fasc. 7; Archives des comtes Csáky (=Csáky-oklt.), T. I. 2, Budapest 1919, p. 629; I. Rákóczi György birtokainak gazdasági iratai, 1631–1648 (Documents économiques des domaines de György Rákóczi Ier), publiés par L. MAKKAI, Budapest 1954, pp. 150-51, 153-55, 163–65.; Terriers, pp. 289, 294, 333, 337, 627, 633, 797.
26. VARGA, op. cit., Introduction, p. 23.
27. Salaire en espèces des domestiques de ferme du château fort de Galgóc en 1614: Arch. Nat. Thurzó-lt, Irregestrata. Fasc. 13. fol. 50: Registres des salaires en espèces et en nature de l'année 1628 à Sárvár-Felsővidék, de l'année 1631 à Szerencs; Comptabilité des années 1645–46 de Kálló: Arch. Nat. Nádasdy-lt. Comptes. Fasc. H. fol. 47–55; Documents économiques des domaines Rákóczi, pp. 85-86, 402–3; Soldats des places fortes des confins comme moissonneurs partiaires en 1645, 1648: S. TAKÁTS, Rajzok a török világból (Scènes de la vie hongroise pendant la domination ottomane), Budapest 1917, T. III, pp. 215–216; "Journaliers" dans les vignes de Hegyalja confisquées par le trésor en 1675–1689: Magyar Gazdaságtörténelmi Szemle, 1900, pp. 3, 13, 16–17 etc.
28. MAKSAY, op. cit (1958), pp. 84–85; Terriers, XVIe-XVIIe siècles. Introduction, p. 30; I. SINKOVICS, Magyarország története. A késői feuda-

lizmus korszaka (Histoire de Hongrie 1526–1790. La fin de l'époque féodale), Budapest 1962, p. 92; PACH, op. cit., p. 235.

29 Il ressort par exemple des inventaires de 1635 et de 1634 de Szerencs que les vignes cultivées pour une rétribution en espèces réussissaient bien, tandis que celles entretenues en corvée se trouvaient dans un mauvais état. – Documents économiques des domaines Rákóczi, pp. 89–90, 94.

30. MAKSAY, op. cit., Introduction, p. 62.

31. En même temps on refusa de nourrir les paysans accomplissant leur corvée pendant la moisson dans le domaine de Bors. – Documents économiques des domaines Rákóczi, p. 219.

32. Les vignes de Ders, Szente, Meszes et les vignes "plantées" sont cultivées en corvée, "comme redevances à leur seigneur", "ils fournissent gratuitement les tuteurs"; "quatre parties en sont cultivées pour de l'argent", mais "pour le reste ils ne touchent rien", et de plus, "ce sont eux qui fournissent les tuteurs". – Csáky-oklt., I. 2., pp. 629-646.

33. Arch. Nat. U et C 37:56 (1608); cf. J. THOLT, A sárvári uradalom majorgazdálkodása a XVII. század első felében (L'exploitation des réserves seigneuriales du domaine de Sárvár dans la première moitié du XVIIe siecle), Budapest 1934, p. 24.

34. Magyar Gazdaságtörténelmi Szemle, 1899, p. 276 (1608).

35. Hédervár y-oklt. T. II, p. 293 (1655).

36. Magyar Gazdaságtörténelmi Szemle, 1895, p. 198 (1620).

37. Les serfs de Mád sont tenus d'effectuer gratuitement chaque année "tous les travaux sans faute" de cinq vignes dominiales; de plus, le seigneur désire qu'ils récoltent, décantent et transportent le vin aussi dans "les vignes cultivées pour de l'argent". Magyar Gazdaságtörténelmi Szemle, 1903, pp. 463-464 (1635).

38. Les vignes allodiales de la région sont cultivées par les serfs de l'oppidum et des deux villages voisins qui "effectuent tous les travaux"; de plus, on y a engagé un vigneron et quatre gardiens contre convention. – Károlyi-oklt., T. IV. pp. 341–342 (1648).

39. "Tous les travaux annuels (de deux vignes seigneuriales) doivent être effectués par les paysans de Podhering". – Terriers, p. 558 (1699).

40. J. RUTKOWSKI, Pańszczyzna i praca najemna w organizacji folwarków królewskich w Prusach Królewskich za Zygmunta Augusta. Roczniki Historyczne, T. 4., Poznań 1928; A. WYCZAŃSKI, O folwarku szlacheckim w Polsce XVI. stulecia, Kwartalnik Historyczny, 1954, N° 4, pp. 183-188; J. TOPOLSKI, Islédovania po agrarnoï istorii v narodno-democratitcheskoï Polche, Moscou 1961, p.426,

41. A. MÍKA, Problém počátků nevolnictví v Čechách, Československý Časopis Historický, 1957, pp. 226-248; K otázce počátků původní akumuláce kapitálu v Čechách, Ibid., pp. 632-634, F. MATĚJEK, Z feudální problematiký moravské předbělohorského období, Časopis Matice Moravské, 1954, pp.

220-251, J. RADIMSKÝ, Produkce obilí na Moravě na sklonku XVI. století. Ibid., 1956, pp. 153–193.

42. D. POHILEVICS, Labyrinthes "capitalistes" dans l'histoire des domaines féodaux, Agrártörténeti Szemle, 1962, N°s 1–2, p. 1 et suiv.
43. J. VÁLKA, Některé otázky vývoje feudálniho pozemkového vlastnictví na Moravě v obdobi rozvinutého a pozdniho feudalismu, Časopis Matice Moravské, 1956, p. 339 et suiv.
44. C'est l'avis de MAKSAY qui a attiré le premier l'attention sur le rôle du travail salarié dans les réserves seigneuriales en Hongrie au milieu du XVIe siècle et sur son déclin à partir des dernières décennies du siècle. – Op. cit., (1958) p. 38, Terriers, XVIe-XVIIe siècles, Introduction, p. 30.
45. Voir PACH, op. cit., p. 45 et suiv.
46. K. MARX, A tőke (Le capital), T. III. Budapest 1951, p. 866.
47. Zichy-okmt., T. X, pp. 366-367 (1466); T. XI, p. 158 (1475); F. BALÁZSY Heves vármegye története (Histoire du comitat de Heves), T. I, Eger 1897, p. 287 (1474); R. BÉKEFI, A pilisi apátság története (Histoire de l'abbaye de Pilis), T. I, Pécs 1891, p. 438 (1477); Károlyi-oklt., T. II, p. 491 (1490).
48. Zichy-okmt., T. XII, p. 221 (1453); T. XII, pp. 292-294 (1470); T. XI, pp. 67-79 (1470-1471); T. XII. p. 325 (1486) etc.
49. FÜGEDI, op. cit., p. 90 et suiv.
50. Bakócz-codex vagy Bakócz Tamás egri püspök udvartartási számadó könyve 1493–1496. évekről. Adatok az egri egyházmegye történelméhez (Codex Bakócz ou livre des comptes de la maison de Tamás Bakócz éveque d'Eger dans les années 1493–1496. Contribution à l'histoire de la diocèse d'Eger), Dir. K. KANDRA, T. II, 3., Eger 1887, pp. 355, 362, 368–71, 373, 375, 378–79, 381, 405–7, 409, 413, 416–17, 424, 430.
51. Arch. Nat. Dl. 104125.
52. Les valets de ferme furent recrutés ici parmi les "bons serfs" (serfs à tenure). – Arch. Nat. Dl. 37000.
53. Terriers, pp. 450, 452-453.
54. J. RUTKOWSKI, La genèse du régime de la corvée dans l'Europe Centrale depuis la fin du Moyen-Age (La Pologne au VIe Congrès International des Sciences Historiques), Varsovie 1930: M. MAŁOWIST, Le commerce de la Baltique et le problème des luttes sociales en Pologne aux XVe et XVIe siècles (La Pologne au Xe Congrès International des Sciences Historiques), Varsovie 1955; Z. zagadnień popytu na produkty krajów nadbałtyckich w Europie zachodniej w XVI wieku, Przegląd Historiczny, 1959, N° 4, pp. 720-752.
55. GY. SZEKFŰ, Magyar történet^2 (Histoire de Hongrie), T. III, Budapest 1935, p. 198 et suiv.; PACH, op. cit., p. 149 et suiv.
56. Voir note 69.
57. Archives de la ville de Gyula, pp. 77–79.

58. GY. KOMORÓCZY, Nádasdy Tamás és a XVI. századi magyar nagybirtok gazdálkodása (Tamás Nádasdy et l'exploitation de la grande propriété hongroise au XVIe siècle), Budapest 1932, p. 102.
59. L'éventuel surplus devra être vendu ou affecté à l'approvisionnement des autres garnisons, en particulier lorsque le prix du blé est élevé et en cas de disette. – L'instruction prescrit l'élevage de vaches, de volaille et le jardinage dans les réserves seigneuriales également, afin d'assurer les produits de laiterie, les oeufs, les légumes etc. "gratuitement", sans "achats superflus". – Magyar Gazdaságtörténelmi Szemle, 1896, pp. 67–68, 70, 75.
60. Voir note 44.
61. Arch. Nat. Documents municipaux et de la chambre, Fol. Lat. 913; V. ZIMÁNYI, Majorsági gazdálkodás a rohonc-szalonaki társuradalomban a XVII. század derekán (Exploitation des alleux dans le domaine de Rohonc-Szalonak au milieu du XVIIe siècle), Agrártörténeti Szemle, 1962, pp. 321-322; Magyar Gazdaságtörténelmi Szemle, 1894, pp. 155, 245.
62. Voir notes 3 et 20.
63. N. KISS, 16. századi dézsmajegyzékek (Registres de dîmes du XVIe siècle), Budapest 1960, pp. 1049, 1066, 1072, 1077.
64. Urbáre feudálnych panstiev na Slovensku. XVI. storočie, publié par R. MARSINA–M. KUŠÍK, T. I, Bratislava 1959, pp. 101, 152-155.
65. Agrártörténeti Szemle, 1957, N°s 1–2, pp. 30–35; Contribution à l'histoire de la diocèse d'Eger, T. I, Eger 1885, p. 430. – Cf. le terrier de 1558 du domaine d'Eger qui prescrit un salaire à la journée pour la fenaison effectuée en sus du travail gratuit obligatoire et le registre des prestations de cette même année qui mentionne les récriminations des communes Mezőhidvég et Sarud à cause de la suppression de cette rétribution. – Terriers, pp. 697–698, 704-705, 723-724.
66. Magyar Gazdaságtörténelmi Szemle, 1894, pp. 66, 68, 71.
67. La donnée d'Erdőd-Szatmár: Károlyi-oklt., T. III, pp. 501, 543: celle d'Esztergom: Urbáre feudálnych panstiev na Slovensku, T. I, pp. 288, 294–96, les autres: Terriers, pp. 194, 450–52, 455–58, 461, 740, 744, 748.
68. Voir note 44.
69. F. P.BRAUDEL–F. SPOONER, Prices in Europe from 1450 to 1750. The Cambridge Economic History of Europe. Vol. IV. The Economy of Expanding Europe in the Sixteenth and Seventeenth Centuries, Cambridge 1967, p. 391 et suiv.; S. HOSZOWSKI, The Revolution of Prices in Poland in the 16th and 17th Centuries, Acta Poloniae Historica, 1959, T. 2, p. 3 et suiv.; V. ZIMÁNYI, A magyarországi ármozgások helye az európai fejlődésben (Mouvements des prix en Hongrie à la lumière de l'évolution européenne), Manuscrit.
70. PACH, op. cit., p.145 et suiv.
71. BRAUDEL–SPOONER, op. cit., pp. 425–30, 482–83; ZIMÁNYI, ms. cit.
72. Une tentative de résoudre la question a été faite par T. WITTMAN, Az "árforradalom" és a világpiaci kapcsolatok kezdeti mozzanatai 1566–1618 (La

"révolution des prix" et les débuts du développement du marché mondial), Budapest 1957, pp. 53-56;MAKSAY, op. cit., 68, 84; Terriers, XVIe-XVIIe siècles, Introduction, p. 30.

73. T. HORVÁTH, A magyar aranyforint értékváltozása 1490–1700 (Changements de la valeur du florin d'or hongrois 1490–1700), Numizmatikai Közlöny, 1959–1960, pp. 33–50. – Dès la fin des années 1550 on voit surgir des plaintes telles que: "pour l'argent en cours ... on ne peut plus rien acheter". – Történelmi Tár, 1889, p. 781.
74. Terriers, pp. 281-299.
75. J. BERLÁSZ, A Thurzó-birtokok a XVII. század első harmadában, különös tekintettel a jobbágyság helyzetére (Les domaines des Thurzó dans le premier tiers du XVIIe siècle, compte tenu en particulier de la situation des serfs), Budapest 1936, pp. 54–56. – Cf. les salaires en espèces du domaine de Sempte à la fin du XVe et au début du XVIe siècle: Arch. Nat. Dl 36995, 37002.
76. Terriers, p. 755: Documents économiques des domaines Rákóczi, pp. 375-376. – Pour des cas semblables de recommutation voir PACH,op. cit., pp. 229–30, 290–91.
77. Csáky-oklt., T. 2, pp. 629, 633–34; cf. Arch. Nat. U et C 12:32.
78. K. MARX, A tőke (Le capital), T. I, Budapest 1948, p. 804.
79. PACH, op. cit., pp. 158, 237.
80. Voir notes 10 et 52.
81. Comme il ressort des relevés des impôts d'Etat, au début du XVIIe siècle les serfs de la région du Vág se rendaient régulièrement dans la Grande Plaine pour battre le blé ou pour exécuter d'autres travaux agricoles. A la fin du siècles le terrier du domaine de Szentmiklós (comitat de Bereg) note à propos de certains fragments de tenure abandonnés que les fils des serfs décédés étaient descendus servir dans le Nyirség. – L. JUHÁSZ, A porta története 1526-1648 (Histoire de maisons 1526–1648), Budapest 1936, p. 23; Terriers, pp. 559, 561, 565, 569.
82. Documents économiques des domaines Rákóczi, p. 100 (1631); Terriers, pp. 257-258 (1695).
83. Arch. Nat. U et C 37:56; Terriers, p. 92; Csáky-oklt., I. 2, p. 630; Documents économiques ..., p. 100; Károlyi-oklt. T. IV, pp. 302, 305, 316, 320, 328, 330.
84. Magyar Gazdaságtörténelmi Szemle, 1905, p. 282 (1633); 1901, pp. 120, 123 (1652).
85. B. H. SLICHER van BATH, The Agrarian History of Eastern Europe A. D. 500-1850, London 1963, p. 206 et suiv.; W. ABEL, Agrarkrisen und Agrarkonjunktur. Eine Geschichte der Land- und Ernährungswirtschaft Mitteleuropas seit dem hohen Mittelalter[2], Hamburg–Berlin 1966, p. 145 et suiv.; ZIMÁNYI, ms. cité.

86. Cf. I. OROSZ, A hegyaljai mezővárosok társadalma a XVII. században, különös tekintettel a szőlőbirtok hatására (La société des bourgades de Hegyalja au XVIIe siècle, eu égard en particulier à l'influence des exploitations viticoles), Agrártörténeti tanulmányok, Dir. I. SZABÓ, Budapest 1960, pp. 47, 52, 55.
87. Károlyi-oklt., T. IV, p. 214 (1626); Héderváry-oklt., T. II, p. 320 (1681).
88. P. JEDLICSKA, Eredeti részletek gróf Pálffy-család okmánytárához (Sur quelques documents des archives de la famille des comtes Pálffy), Budapest 1910, pp. 34, 37 (1621); Károlyi-oklt., T. IV, pp. 263–73, 416–23, 459–64 (1643, 1641, 1666); Csáky-oklt., T. I, 2, pp. 717–20, 751–58 (1646, 1675); Héderváry-oklt., T. II, pp. 260, 312–13 (1642, 1681).
89. THOLT, op. cit., p. 60.
90. Terriers, p. 626.
91. Magyar Gazdaságtörténelmi Szemle, 1895, p. 305 ; 1897, pp. 341, 470; 1901, p. 119.
92. Cité par THOLT, op. cit., p. 25.

ADDENDA

CORVÉES ET TRAVAIL SALARIÉ DANS LES EXPLOITATIONS SEIGNEURIALES DE LA HONGRIE DES XVIe ET XVIIe SIÈCLES

(Serf Labour and Wage Labour on the Hungarian Landlords' Demesnes in the 16th and 17th Centuries)

Page 78:
One day of compulsory labour service (*robot* =corvée) per week had been imposed upon the Hungarian peasants by the law of 1514. However, from the 1570s onwards, the landlords made light of this legal rule. The main types of their increased claims were these: a) the performance of labour services every third week or two days' service per week; b) the system of alternate weeks or three days' labour a week; c) the lord or his bailiff demanded labour services whenever he pleased. Labour dues of more than one day per week were usual, at that time, also in Mecklenburg, Brandenburg and Poland, later on in the lands of the Czech Crown, too. Conf.*J. Varga,* Jobbágyrendszer a magyarországi feudalizmus kései századaiban (The Serf System in the Late Centuries of Hungarian Feudalism) 1556–1767, Budapest, 1969, pp. 541–544; *B. H. Slicher van Bath,* Serfdom in Central and Eastern Europe. In: The Cambridge Economic History of Europe, V. Edited by E.E. Rich and C. H. Wilson, Cambridge, 1977, pp. 113–123; *H. Rebel,* Frondienst und Mehrwert in der preussischen Gutswirtschaft, Österreichische Zeitschrift für Geschichtswissenschaften, IV, 2 (1993), pp. 254–258.

Page 80, Note 40:
As for Poland, seignorial farms employing paid labour developed mainly on the fertile lands of Malbork and in the surroundings of Poznań (and some other towns), as a result of favourable market conditions: *J. Rutkowski,* Ze studiow nad polozeniem czeladzi fołwarcznej w dawnej Polsce. In: Studia z dziejów wsi polskiej XVI–XVIII w., Warszawa, 1956, pp. 127–142; *J. Majewski,* Gospodarstwo fołwarczne we wsiach miasta Poznania w l. 1582–1644, Poznań, 1957, pp. 154–195. — For the employment of paid labour, in addition to the predominant compulsory services, on Estonian demesnes: *H. M. Ligi,* O razvitii myzno–barshciznogo hoziaistva v Estonii v seredine 16 v. In: Ezhegodnik po agrarnoi istorii Vostocnoi Evropy, Moskva, 1961, pp. 83–85.

Page 80, Note 41:
It was the Thirty Years' War that played a crucial part in the development of rural economy in Bohemia. From the mid–17th century onwards, the number of seignorial demesnes greatly increased all over the country. It went together with the consolidation of serfdom and with the growing exploitation of the peasants' labour services, but without

employment of hired labour. According to the *Robotpatent* (Labour Services Decree) of 1680, a serf was obliged to perform three *robot*-days per week, but at haymaking and harvest time the number of days could be increased by the lord "at will": *A. Klíma*, Agrarian Class Structure and Economic Development in Pre–Industrial Bohemia, Past and Present, LXXXV (1979), pp. 49–57; *J. Macek*, The Emergence of Serfdom in the Czech Lands. In: East-Central Europe, IX (1982), pp. 7–23.

Page 82, Note 50:
A similar mode of farming prevailed on the estate of the bishopric of Eger also at the beginning of the 16th century, the demesnes having been tilled by hired farm–hands and with the help of domanial equipment. Labour services were only required for the reaping of the bishop's meadows, and even this compulsory sort of labour was remunerated for by a reduction in the money rent of the tenants. For instance, the village Nagytálya "solvit florenos 15, debuissent esse fl. 22, sed relaxavimus pro falcatione feni fl. 7": Estei Hippolit püspök egri számadáskönyvei (The Account Books of Eger of Bishop Hippolit of Este) 1500–1508. Ed. by P. E. Kovács, Eger, 1992, p. 62 (1501); similarly pp. 10, 168, 236, 300 (1500, 1503, 1507, 1508). — But during the 16th century the labour conditions on the estate changed for the worse. While the manorial records of the year 1558, though prescribing mainly unpaid services, still recalled the practice of reapers being granted some monetary payment or allowance, the list of "ordinary, extraordinary and prejudicial services" dating from the same year remarked of certain villages that "when the peasant did reaping here for the bishop, each was paid ten d. a day, but they are given nothing now": Urbáriumok. XVI–XVII. század (Manorial Records. 16th and 17th Centuries). Edited by F. Maksay, Budapest, 1959, pp. 697–699, 704–705, 711, 723–724. — Conf. Adatok az egri egyházmegye történelméhez (Contributions to the History of the Diocese of Eger), I. Edited by K. Kandra, Eger, 1885, p. 430.

Page 86, Note 69:
The paper of *V. Zimányi* has been published in the meantime: Mouvements des prix hongrois et l'évolution européenne (XVIe–XVIIIe siècles), Acta Historica Acad. Sci. Hung., XIX (1973), pp. 305–333. — See also *Št. Kazimír*, Adalék a XVI. és XVII. századbeli árak és bérek fejlődéséhez (A Contribution to the Development of Prices and Wages in the 16th and 17th Centuries), Történelmi Szemle (Historical Review), XIX, 1–2 (1976), pp. 167–210.

Page 90, Note 92:
The Polish landlords were conducted by similar considerations. "Large investments of capital would have been necessary to base production on paid labour. The landlord would have been compelled to buy and maintain beasts of burden and tools and to build and provide for the upkeep of buildings and installations. Serfdom system placed all or almost all of the expenses for stocks and movable equipment on the peasants, thus reducing the landowner's expenses to a minimum. The serf–labourer worked on the *fołwark* (=demesne) with his own tools and beasts of burden and the farm installations could be built and repaired without spending any money": *L. Żytkowicz*, The Peasant's Farm and the Landlord's Farm in Poland from the 16th to the Middle of the 18th Century, The Journal of European Economic History, I, 1 (1972), p. 140. — See also *W. Kula*, Teoria ekonomiczna ustroju feudalnego, Warszawa, 1962, pp. 57–58.

V

NEUVIÈME ET DÎME SEIGNEURIALE AU XVIIe SIÈCLE EN HONGRIE

1.

L'histoire du neuvième* *avant la défaite de Mohács* a amplement préoccupé les recherches historiques hongroises. Les recherches et les débats au sujet de cette période se rapportent principalement à deux problèmes: d'une part à l'article de loi de l'époque de la dynastie des Anjou qui le mit en vigueur, ou plutôt le codifia pour la première fois, d'autre part aux articles de l'époque Jagellon, renforçant et remettant en vigueur l'obligation du neuvième. Laissant de côté la première question — celle des préliminaires, de la naissance, du caractère, de l'efficacité pratique de l'article de loi 6 de 1351.[1] — nous ne désirons nous consacrer dans une certaine mesure qu'aux problèmes de la fin du XVe et du début du XVIe siècle. Les décrets datant de 1492, 1498, 1500 et quelques autres renouvelant le règlement de l'année 1351, exigeaient des paysans des bourgades et des villages un terrage en nature sur leurs récoltes de labours et de vignobles sous forme de neuvième ou d'un certain nombre fixe de «muid» (partie fixée du vin recueilli par les paysans); cette obligation fut étendue aux vignobles et aux labours cultivés affermés par les paysans et même les bourgeois des villes; finalement ceux-ci décretaient que cette redevance devait être accomplie sous forme de neuvième de la récolte et non pas selon une quantité prescrite à l'avance.[2]

Elemér Mályusz, vers 1920, fut le premier à attirer l'attention sur l'importance de ces articles dans ses études d'histoire sociale. Il soulignait, entre autres, le caractère de la législation de 1492 qui était dirigée contre les bourgades. Le but de cette loi était de rabaisser celles-ci au niveau des villages de paysans, les différenciant nettement des villes royales; car jusqu'à cette époque c'était l'obligation ou la non-obligation du neuvième qui était l'un

* Le neuvième était une redevance seigneuriale, semblable à la dîme, dans l'origine la neuvième partie de la récolte que les serfs étaient obligés de payer à leur seigneur.

[1] Au sujet de cette discussion cf. I. Acsády: *A magyar jobbágyság története* (Histoire de la paysannerie hongroise). 3e éd. Bp. 1948. pp. 107—108; B. Hóman—Gy. Szekfű: *Magyar történet* (Histoire hongroise). T. II. 3e éd. Bp. 1936, pp. 280—281, p. 628; I. Szabó: *Hanyatló jobbágyság a középkor végén* (Le dépérissement de la paysannerie à la fin du Moyen-Âge). Századok 1938, pp. 31—34; E. Molnár: *A magyar társadalom története az Árpád- kortól Mohácsig* (Histoire de la société hongroise de l'époque des Árpád à Mohács). Bp. 1949 p. 213; Gy.Székely: *A jobbágyság földesúri terheinek növelése és az erőszak- apparátus további kiépítése* (Accroissement des charges féodales des serfs et extension de l'appareil d'oppression). *Tanulmányok a parasztság történetéhez Magyarországon* (Études concernant l'histoire de la paysannerie au XIVe siècle en Hongrie). Bp. 1953 p. 276 et suiv., I. Szabó: *Az 1351. évi jobbágytörvények* (Lois de 1351 sur les serfs). Századok 1955. p. 497 et suiv.

[2] Article 47—48 de la loi de 1492, art. 49 de 1492 et 41 de 1498; art. 27 de la loi de 1500 — Cf. aussi art. 58 de la loi de 1514, 27(II) de 1518, art. 25 de la loi de 1519.

des critères de la différence entre villages et villes.[3] L'opinion de Mályusz s'est assez généralisée dans la littérature historique hongroise. Cette opinion a été également soutenue par István Szabó, dans son étude consacrée au «dépérissement de la paysannerie» ainsi que dans ses écrits ultérieurs.[4] Ce point de vue a été développé ensuite, par Erik Molnár, dans son œuvre d'histoire sociale, en l'associant à plusieurs importantes opinions nouvelles: surtout concernant le problème de la production de marchandises de paysans des bourgades, à laquelle s'opposait l' activité commerciale seigneuriale à ses débuts (chez lui: production marchande de la noblesse moyenne).[5] La tendance de ces prescriptions mentionnées, limitant les droits des bourgades, est soulignée dans plusieurs publications récentes, telle l'étude de György Székely parue dernièrement et consacrée à l'examen des branches de la production paysanne de l'époque.[6]

Cette opinion — qui attire l'attention sur des connexions importantes — peut être surtout complétée, son appréciation peut être élargie par le fait que les prescriptions de neuvième en céréales et en vin doivent être considérées comme une augmentation des charges féodales, un accroissement de l'exploitation seigneuriale non seulement des *bourgades* (et en cas de location de vignobles de la bourgeoisie des villes), mais aussi des nombreux *villages de paysans* — car cette obligation spécifique concernant la récolte, n'était pas entièrement généralisée au XVe siècle, même pas pour les paysans *des villages*. En ce qui concerne les premières décades du XVe siècle, István Sinkovics, dans une rédaction contenue, a déjà montré précédemment «. . . la conception de la loi de 1351 concernant le neuvième, semble-t-il . . . n'a pas reçu d'application généralisée».[7] Pour la seconde partie du siècle, c'est-à-dire pour les décades précédant directement les articles discutés, nous avons conclu dans une étude récemment publiée que «le neuvième de céréales et de vin, est loin d'être généralisé dans les bourgades ou *dans les villages de paysans*»; que «la redevance préscrite dans une certaine quantité, en muid ou en banneau (non pas en proportion de la récolte), généralement fixée pour le nombre de tenures (ou d'âmes), parfois fixée pour l'ensemble du village selon une quantité globale, tout comme la prestation de vin indépendamment de la quantité de la récolte, sont beacoup plus répandus». Cette redevance même «en comprenant dès maintenant le neuvième *et* le terrage fixe — malgré sa fréquence — ne peut être considérée comme généralisée dans la seconde partie du XVe siècle, en Hongrie; il n'apas la fréquence de cet autre — ou plutôt du premier — groupe de redevances en produits, comprenant les *munera*, la redevance en vivres et en animaux, ou encore moins celle *en argent.*»[8] Cette situation est aussi reflétée par le texte de

[3] E. Mályusz: *Az 1514. évi jobbágyháború okai* (Les causes de la jacquerie de 1514). Társadalomtudomány, 1926. p. 374 et suiv.; Az 1498. évi 41. törvénycikk (Art. 41 de la loi de 1498). Századok, 1929—30, p. 809 et suiv.

[4] Szabó: op. cit. (1938) p. 56, etc.

[5] Molnár: op. cit. pp. 239, 351, 360.

[6] Gy. Székely: *Vidéki termelőágak és az árukereskedelem Magyarországon a XV—XVI. században* (Les branches de production en province et le commerce en Hongrie aux XVe et XVIe siècles). Agrártörténeti Szemle, 1961 No 3—4. pp. 333, 335.

[7] I. Sinkovics: *A magyar nagybirtok élete a XV. század elején* (Le régime de la propriété foncière en Hongrie au début du XVe siècle). Bp. 1933. p. 49.

[8] Zs. P. Pach: *Das Entwicklungsniveau der feudalen Agrarverhältnisse in Ungarn in der zweiten Hälfte des XV. Jahrhunderts.* (Studia Historica Academiae Scientiarum Hungariae. 46.) Bp. 1960, pp. 14—15.

la loi: la prestation sur la récolte de labours et de vignobles est fixée de manière encore alternative dans le décret de 1492 (parfois cité avec inexactitude) — «nonam partem . . . aut acones consuetos» — (l'introduction même d'une redevance fixée aurait signifié en maints endroits en effet, l'élargissement des charges féodales). La diète de l'année 1500 poursuivant cette voie, prescrit exclusivement le neuvième — «non acones (prout certis in locis solebant), sed nonam partem» — voulant ainsi généraliser la forme de redevance plus lourde.[9]

L'autre aspect du problème de l'époque des Jagellon (sans nous occuper dans cette étude de la question du commerce seigneurial qui en est le troisième aspect) réside dans le fait que les articles touchant le neuvième — appelons-les ainsi pour plus de simplicité — dans quelle mesure ont-ils été appliqués durant les décades suivantes, c'est-à-dire à la fin du XVe siècle et au début du XVIe siècle. A l'opposé de Mályusz, qui estime que l'article 47 de la loi de 1492 fut immédiatement «mis en application» concernant *les bourgades*,[10] István Szabó estime que les seigneurs «n'atteignirent . . . certainement pas ce but (c. à. d. le payement du neuvième des bourgades) . . . au cours des 20 à 30 années qui suivirent la mort du roi Mathias . . .»[11] — Naturellement nous ne pouvons pas entrer ici dans les détails de cette question; nous voudrions signaler seulement que nos recherches ont renforcé la constatation faite par Erik Fügedi dans son étude analysant l'économie de l'archevêché d'Esztergom de la fin du XVe siècle.[12] En effet, nous avons constaté que les livres terriers de l'époque ne prouvent pas de manière percutante la réalisation de l'obligation du neuvième dans les *villages de paysans*, par contre les prestations en produits deviennent plus lourdes dans certains *bourgades* aussi, principalement par l'augmentation des redevances fixes. Dans le domaine seigneurial de Léka, par exemple, en 1519, tout comme en 1492, les villages non plus ne payent pas de neuvième, mais une quantité de blé, de seigle et d'orge fixée à l'avance.[13] Dans le domaine seigneurial de Sárvár et Kapuvár aussi, la livraison de céréales était fixée en une quantité préscrite à l'avance — bien que cette quantité augmente aussi dans des bourgades entre 1492, 1507 et 1518—1519;[14] par contre dans le domaine de Kanizsa, où le neuvième n'était pas rare dès les années 1490, la série des villages imposées de cette redevance s'étend en 1512, puis en 1519.[15] Les livres terriers de quelques localités du comitat de Vas, vers 1500, prescrivent la prestation fixée en céréale;[16] par contre les paysans de Polgárdi et de Battyán, en 1502, payent uniformément en neuvième leurredevance en céréales et en vin,[17] les villages du domaine de Torna, en 1497 payent la dîme.[18] Kövesd, Bajta et

[9] Art. 47 de la loi de 1492. §. 1.; Art. 27 de la loi de 1500. §. 1.

[10] E. Mályusz: op. cit. (1926) p. 378.

[11] Szabó: op. cit. (1938) p. 56.

[12] E. Fügedi: *Az esztergomi érsekség gazdálkodása a XV. század végén* (Économie de l'archevêché d'Esztergom à la fin du XVe siècle). Századok. 1960. No. 1—3. p. 99—101.

[13] Országos Levéltár (Archives Nationales = O. L.). Collection de chartes d'avant 1526 (= Dl.) 36.996; 37.007.

[14] O. L. Dl. 36.992; 37.007.

[15] O. L. DL. 36.997; 37.007.

[16] O. L. DL. 104.622.

[17] O. L. DL. 104.125.

[18] O. L. Dl. 37.169.

quelques autres communes du comitat de Hont, propriétés de l'église, au début du XVIe siècle, sont redevables à leur seigneur du neuvième et de la dîme.[19]

A cette période, l'obligation du neuvième se généralisait encore moins pour les champs que les paysans travaillaient ou louaient en plus de leur tenure, our les vignobles qu'ils cultivaient en qualité d'*«extranei»* dans d'autres villages ou vignobles seigneuriaux. En 1492, comme en 1519, dans les domaines seigneuriaux de Léka, Sárvár, Kapuvár, le terrage par acre était un muid de céréales pour les terres désertes, défrichées ou les réserves seigneuriales (terra domini, terra pertinens ad allodium domini, terra arabilis propria) travaillées par les paysans.[20] Dans le comitat de Hont, à Bajta la redevance en céréales des terres désertes était fixée par «setiers»,[21] par contre dans le domaine de Torna, le terrage était exigé en neuvième ou en dîme.[22] Dans le domaine seigneurial de Kanizsa, ceux qui utilisaient les terres désertes et défrichées, devaient s'acquitter d'une demi-moyette de céréales par acre (ou bien par endroit de 2 à 4 deniers), tandis que les personnes domiciliées ailleurs, les «extranei» étaient astreintes à la dîme. De même, on prescrivait aux paysans vignerons, originaires d'autres localités, des muids de vin et 1 denier; pour certains vignobles du domaine seigneurial de Világosvár, un cens en argent et les *munera* en nature étaient exigés.[23] — Finalement il faut noter que les seigneurs exigeaient régulièrement une redevance en argent pour l'utilisation des prés et des pâturages déserts de leurs domaines. Selon le livre terrier datant de 1522 du domaine de Beckó, par exemple, l'un des herbages du domaine fut loué aux habitants du village voisin *«in feudum»* pour une somme de 12 florins,[24] tandis qu'il prescrivait le blé, le seigle, l'orge, l'avoine fixés en muids, par tenure, et le tiers des moyettes récoltées ou deux muids, par acre des champs déserts.

2.

Quelle a été ensuite l'évolution du neuvième et en général des terrages en céréales et en vin, au cours *des XVIe et XVIIe siècles?* Le dessein des seigneurs féodaux visant à l'imposition en neuvième, était-il uniquement un stade *intermédiaire* qui devait être remplacé à partir des années 30 et 40 du XVIe siècle, par des tentatives nouvelles «plus modernes», lorsque les seigneurs ne se contentaient plus d'exiger les prestations en produits, mais tentaient plutôt de développer leur propre production agricole sur leur réserve seigneuriale et par suite d'imposer aux paysans *la corvée?* C'est ainsi que voit le problème Sándor Domanovszky, dans son résumé historique de la «Gutsherrschaft» hongroise, englobant les résultats d'importantes thèses élaborées par ses disciples, et qui soulève en même temps de nombreuses questions nouvelles; il qualifie d'arriérés les seigneurs qui, à la fin du XVe

[19] O. L. Dl. 48.305.
[20] O. L. Dl. 36.992; 36.996; 37.007.
[21] O. L. DL. 48.305.
[22] O. L. Dl. 37.169.
[23] O. L. Dl. 37.007; 37.000.
[24] *Urbáre feudálnych panstiev na Slovensku. XVI. storočie* (Livres terriers des domaines féodaux en Slovaquie. XVIe siècle). (Réd. R. Marsina—M. Kušik.) T. I. Bratislava 1959. pp. 41—68.

siècle, exigèrent la généralisation du neuvième, et de modernes ceux qui quelques décennies plus tard incitèrent à l'exploitation de la réserve seigneuriale.[25]

Ou bien s'agit-il d'une tendance continue *progressiste* et non provisoire, bien que cette évolution n'ait pas suivi une ligne droite? S'agit-il du renforcement de la rente en produits dont la forme principale antérieure était les *munera?* Cette rente en produits qui au cours du XVe siècle — *parallèlement à l'évolution constatée en Europe occidentale* — commençait à perdre de son importance et regressait par rapport à l'imposition en argent, est-ce qu'elle semble reprendre force sous forme du neuvième en céréales et en vin, constituant, en quelque sorte, une «seconde édition» de la rente féodale en produits? Il semble donc que le problème s'élargisse ainsi par rapport à sa première apparition; il ne s'agit pas d'une chose moindre que du changement des formes de la rente foncière féodale en Hongrie, d'une évolution hongroise de la structure de la rente seigneuriale, avec toutes ses conséquences économiques et sociales; c'est-à-dire qú'il s'agit de la proportion respective de la corvée, du terrage en produits et du cens en argent.

Le problème des formes de la redevance seigneuriale, des différentes impositions, aux XVIe et XVIIe siècles, s'est déjà posé chez Ignác Acsády. Étudiant le fond du sujet il exposa déjà l'intensification de la corvée et les différents exemples de corvée illimitée; cependant il se trompa en constatant à cette période «une tendance primordiale croissante de l'imposition du cens» en argent.[26] Plus tard, — justement à la suite des travaux de l'école Domanovszky — la reconnaissance du développement de l'exploitation des réserves seigneuriales a attiré l'attention des chercheurs — pour citer un élève de Domanovszky — sur le fait que «le seigneur exploitant sa réserve avait plus besoin du travail de son serf que du cens. Il estime que le cens a moins d'importance et exige plutôt la corvée».[27]

Les recherches de l'histoire économique d'avant la seconde guerre en étaient arrivées essentiellement à ce stade dans l'examen des problèmes des XVIe et XVIIe siècles. De nouveaux progrès n'ont pu être faits que par la réalisation conjointe de deux conditions: d'une part par un travail important d'édition de sources de cette époque — mentionnons ici les publications des documents dues à László Makkai, Ferenc Maksay, Endre Varga, István N. Kiss, les statistiques historiques de Bálint Ila et d'autres auteurs qui commencent à faire disparaître les lacunes criantes existant précédemment au sujet des sources de l'époque; d'autre part, grâce à la méthodologie historique marxiste (dans ce cadre la méthode et les resultats de l'analyse de la rente foncière faite par Marx), grâce à son application dans notre science historique — sans que, bien entendu, ce progrès puisse être considéré comme terminé dans un sens comme dans un autre.

Grâce aux recherches étendues des sources de cette époque, récemment, Ferenc Maksay a pris position dans une étude, qui a éclairé de nombreux phénomènes concernant l'évolution des formes de la rente seigneuriale au

[25] A. Domanovszky: *Zur Geschichte der Gutsherrschaft in Ungarn.* Festschrift Dopsch. Baden bei Wien. 1938. pp. 458, 463.

[26] Acsády: op. cit. p. 226.

[27] L. Juhász: *A porta története* 1526—1648 (Histoire de la porte [ménage, unité de l'imposition] 1526—1648). Bp. 1936. p. 45.

XVIe siècle en Hongrie. Selon l'opinion de Maksay, tandis qu'à *la fin du XVe siècle*, dans les «livres terriers, les redevances en produits occupent une position déterminante par rapport aux cens et à la corvée», tandis qu'«à la fin du XVe siècle, parmi les trois groupes d'impositions: en argent, en nature, en travail, il est significatif que ce soit le deuxième groupe qui occupe une place prépondérante», (cette constatation de l'auteur est basée principalement sur l'analyse quelque peu rapide du livre terrier du domaine seigneurial de Sárvár-Kapuvár, datant de 1492) — au cours du *XVIe siècle* dans les domaines, dans lesquels l'exploitation de la réserve seigneuriale n'était pas développée, le cens était augmenté, dans les domaines où cette exploitation était poursuivie, la corvée augmentait; par contre «dans la majorité des domaines les terrages en produits étaient réduits» en même temps.[28] On peut donc constater que l'importance des terrages en produits, au XVIe siècle, *par rapport* à leur rôle — soi-disant — dominant de la fin du XVe siècle semble moindre, plus limité; mais si nous les comparons aux conditions *réelles* de la seconde partie et de la fin du XVe siècle — constatées par l'analyse détaillée des livres terriers de Sárvár-Kapuvár et d'autres sources — dont nous avons déjà fait mention: avance du cens en argent, désavantage du neuvième en céréales et en vin —, dans ce cas l'aspect de la tendance du XVIe siècle change immédiatement et nous ne pouvons plus guère faire mention de l'amoindrissement des redevances en produits. Ici donc, c'est le manque d'une base solide de comparaison, qui a empêché l'éclaircissement des tendances d'évolution.

Le spécialiste des recherches sur l'exploitation du domaine des Rákóczi prend une position semblable à celle de Maksay, au sujet du XVIIe siècle, pour les années 1630 à 1640. László Makkai en offrant de riches documents et une analyse convaincante sur l'importance de la *corvée*, a également conclu à l'éclipse simultanée des redevances en *produits* et en *argent :* «Dans les domaines de Rákóczi (et probablement dans l'ensemble du pays) le cens et les terrages sont d'une bonne part remplacés par la corvée et par l'utilisation des droits régaliens.»[29] Mais — pourrait-on dire — le droit régalien le plus important du seigneur est précisément le droit de débit de vin; et la majorité du vin vendu aux serfs, même dans les domaines de Rákóczi, qui cultivaient relativement de nombreux vignobles de la réserve seigneuriale, provenait justement du terrage en vin des serfs. Il semble donc dans l'analyse mentionnée qu'à côté de l'imposition brutale et radicale de la corvée, le poids des redevances en produits croissant lentement, et pesant avec moins d'acuité sur les serfs, paraît être réduit à l'arrière-plan.

Ici nous devons parler d'un élément théorique aussi, qui, à notre avis, limitait dans une certaine mesure la juste exposition de l'évolution. A ce sujet, notre littérature consacrée à l'histoire économique — fidèle à l'alternative «Grundherrschaft-Gutsherrschaft» traditionnelle depuis G. F. Knapp[30]

[28] F. Maksay: *Parasztság és majorgazdálkodás a XVI. századi Magyarországon* (Paysannerie et exploitation des réserves seigneuriales en Hongrie, au XVIe siècle). Bp. 1958, pp. 9, 43—44.

[29] L. Makkai: *I. Rákóczi György birtokainak gazdasági iratai. 1631—1648.* (Comptabilité des propriétés de György I. Rákóczi. 1631—1648). Bp. 1954. Introduction, p. 69.

[30] G. F. Knapp: *Die Bauernbefreiung und der Ursprung der Landarbeiter in den älteren Teilen Preussens.* T. I. 2e éd. (Iére éd. 1887). München—Leipzig. 1927; p. 27 et suiv.;

— généralement compare l'exploitation du domaine par la voie de la réserve seigneuriale, par la corvée, à «l'ancien type d'exploitation basée sur le cens», à «l'ancien type de redevance en argent et en produits».[31] Une semblable opinion est exposée par quelques chercheurs marxistes, tel A. Míka, un des meilleurs spécialistes de ce problème concernant la situation en Bohême à la même époque. Lorsqu'il souligne avec justesse que le critère *fondamental* de la naissance du *novolnictví* (variante tchèque de la «deuxième édition du servage») doit être cherché non pas dans la situation juridique, mais sur le plan des rentes foncières — il ne voit de changement radical dans le processus historique que lorsque la *corvée* devint prépondérante dans l'exploitation du serf, par opposition aux «deux formes de rente plus évoluées»: c'est-à-dire en opposition aux redevances en *produits* et en *argent.*[32] Cette proportion — proportion de la corvée par rapport aux redevances en argent et en produits — est naturellement très significative quant à l'évolution de la structure agraire. Mais il est également important d'examiner la proportion du *cens en argent* par rapport aux redevances *en nature :* terrage et corvée. Cette dernière proportion, dans une certaine mesure, reflète encore plus fidèlement les conditions de l'évolution en Bohême ou en Hongrie, par rapport à celle de l'Europe occidentale. L'évolution de l'Europe occidentale, dont la tendance principale avait justement été marquée par l'avance de la rente en argent, par son progrès, même par endroit par sa généralisation par rapport aux formes de rente en nature, se manifeste le plus nettement en Angleterre, aux Pays-Bas aussi d'une manière prononcée, de manière relativement moins marquée en France, où pourtant elle est à constater en ce qui concerne la censive.[33]

Où en est cette question en Hongrie? Nous sommes arrivés dans notre résumé au XVIIe siècle, et il nous semble que le problème n'est toujours pas résolu. Arrétons-nous donc à cette époque et considérons — dans le cadre étroit de cette étude — le rôle de la rente en produits, son importance parmi les dfférentes formes de la rente seigneuriale, la dynamique de son évolution, sa tendance dans la Hongrie du XVIIe siècle — en utilisant les documents cités,* tout comme d'autres documents publiés ou non, tels des ordonnances économiques et de dîme, des comptes et spécialement des livres terriers.

[31] Maksay: op. cit. p. 110.; *Urbáriumok. XVI—XVII. század* (Livres terriers. XVIe—XVIIe siècles). Bp. 1959. Introduction, p. 48.

[32] A. Míka: *Problém počátků nevolnictví v Čechách* (Le problème des débuts du «nevolnictví» en Bohème). Ceskoslovenský Časopis Historický 1957. No 2. pp. 226 et suiv.

[33] V. par ex. E. Lipson: *The Economic History of England.* T. I. 9e éd. London. 1947 p. 152 et suiv.; B. H. Slicher van Bath: *Agriculture in the Law Countries* (cca 1600—1800). (Relazioni del X. Congresso Internazionale di Scienze Storiche. IV.) Roma, 1955. p. 169 et suiv.; J. Meuvret: *Domaines ou ensembles territoriaux?* Quelques exemples de l'implication du régime de la propriété et de la structure sociale dans la France du XVIIe et du XVIIIe siècles (Première Conférence Internationale d'Histoire Économique). Stockholm 1960. pp. 343 et suiv. — Cf. Zs. P. Pach: *A tőkés földjáradék keletkezése a nyugat-európai agrárfejlődésben* (Origine de la rente foncière capitaliste dans le développement agraire de l'Europe Occidentale). Közgazdasági Szemle, 1958 No 12 pp. 1217 et suiv.; T. Wittman: *A flamand posztóipar tőkés lehetőségei a manufaktúrakorszak küszöbén* (Possibilités capitalistes de la draperie flamande au seuil de l'époque des manufacture). Századok, 1961. No 2—3. pp. 271 et suiv.

*Nous ne communiquons que la cote d'archives des documents qui n'ont pas été publiés; pour les documents qui ont été publiés ces dernières années nous ne men-

3.

Le *premier* groupe des redevances en produits: les *munera*, c'est-à-dire «cadeaux» de quelques vivres ou animaux, est en effet en régression; par-ci par-là, il disparaît dans l'économie seigneuriale de la Hongrie du XVIIe siècle. Bien que les seigneurs, en maints endroits, exigent encore les «munera» — comme par exemple György Drugeth, dans le domaine de Homonna, Pál Révai dans le domaine de Ráró[34] —; il est assez fréquent toutefois qu'ils exigent une somme en espèces «pro annualibus victualibus» — par famille ou par village — comme le prouvent les livres terriers en 1614 à Bajmóc, en 1636 à Rihnó, en 1670 à Léka, en 1672 à Murány ou en 1686 à Szendrő.[35] Le stade intermédiaire se manifeste dans le livre terrier de László Iványi Fekete, datant de 1668. Selon celui-ci, par exemple, les serfs du comitat de Hont sont imposés de «deux pintes de beurre, s'il ne peut donner du beurre, qu'il paye 24 deniers par pinte; deux oies, sinon qu'il donne pour chaque oie 18 deniers, quatre poules, sinon qu'il paye pour chaque poule 12 deniers[36]» etc. Il est également possible de payer en espèces par ailleurs aussi: le livre terrier de Rozgony, datant de 1636, par exemple, énumère les «cadeaux», mais l'intendant du domaine reçoit en même temps l'ordre «de fixer en argent les prestations en vivres et de les exiger des serfs en argent». De même les instructions de Csicsvavár de cette même année fixent: «Ceux qui selon le terrier, sont redevables en poules, oies et autres produits semblables, doivent en donner la contrepartie en argent» par le somme qu'ils en payent sur le marché».[37]

La diminution de l'importance des «cadeaux» est liée en partie à l'extension de l'exploitation des réserves seigneuriales: les seigneurs qui poursuivent cette exploitation veulent pourvoir leur table en produits de leurs fermes *(allodia)* beurre, fromage, œufs, volailles et autres[38] et même ils veulent en faire commerce — comme différentes ordonnances économiques de cette époque nous le prouvent. «L'intendant doit exiger de l'argent de ceux qui nous sont redevables en poules, oies et œufs» décrète György I Rákóczi. «Les besoins de notre maison doivent être assurés par nos fermes *allodiales* et non pas de ces redevances. Il faut même que les différentes fermes qui pourvoient notre table, soient aussi capables de produire pour de l'argent».[39]

---

tionnons que la publication — même si nous l'avons utilisé antérieurement. — Nous remercions ici aussi Madame László Muzsnai, collaboratrice des Archives Nationales, qui nous a assuré par son aide précieuse la copie de documents.

[34] O. L. Urbaria et Conscriptiones (= U. et C.) 109: 2 (1612); Magyar Gazdaságtörténeti Szemle (= M. Gt. Sz.) (Revue hongroise d'histoire économique). 1905. pp. 273 et suiv. (1624)

[35] Urbáre feudálnych panstiev na Slovensku. XVII. storočie. T. II. pp. 40—57; J. Berlász: *A Thurzó birtokok a XVII. század első harmadában* (Les domaines des Thurzó dans le premier tiers du XVIIe siècle). Bp. 1936. pp. 64, 68; Urbáriumok. XVI—XVII. század. pp. 122, 333, 485.

[36] Történelmi Tár (= T. T.) (Archives historiques). 1898. pp. 471—472.

[37] M. Gt. Sz. 1894. pp. 266, 271; 1897. p. 335.

[38] Cf. *Oklevéltár a gróf Csáky-család történetéhez* (= Csáky-oklt.) (Recueil de chartes pour servir à l'histoire de la famille comte Csáky). T. I/2. Bp. 1919. p. 686.

[39] M. Gt. Sz. 1894. p. 322. (1634); cf. ibid. 1897. p. 518. (1616); 1897. p. 332. (1636); 1895. p. 305. (1698); etc. — On doit noter que le recul des munera ne signifiait nullement le désistement des redevances extraordinaires en vivres (extraordinariae imposi-

Il en est tout autrement pour le *second* groupe des redevances en produits: redevances provenant des labours et des vignobles. Nous ne trouvons que très peu de traces de la commutation de ces redevances en argent, ou concernant leur absence. Pour le neuvième également, est en vigueur le principe défini par le domaine de Galgóc en 1607, concernant la dîme provenant du blé, du seigle, de l'orge, de l'avoine, de l'épeautre «que la dîme ne soit pas perçue en argent . . . que les pauvres donnent la dîme *sub poena* et non pas en argent».[40] Les livres terriers qui prescrivent alternativement la corvée et le cens prouvent une stabilité de la redevance en céréales.[41] C'est un cas rare, que celui des habitants de Lózs: en plus de la corvée domaniale, ils ne sont pas astreints à donner à «leur seigneur le neuvième . . . uniquement la dîme, selon la coutume ancienne, et même celle-ci en espèces»,[42] tout comme les paysans des 11 bourgades du comitat de Szepes qui sont astreints à la dîme au lieu de la corvée domaniale.[43] — Il est rare de rencontrer la commutation en espèces ou l'absence des prestations, énumérées dans le second groupe des rentes en produits, tout comme il est rare de rencontrer des terrages prescrits en quantités fixées à l'avance, tout particulièrement pour les différentes céréales — par exemple en 1628, dans le domaine de Felsőlendva—Muraszombat, et durant les années 1630—40 dans le domaine de Pokorád.[44] Par contre, nous voyons de plus en plus souvent l'imposition *proportionnelle* de la récolte, principalement le *neuvième*, quelquefois au lieu de l'imposition fixée à l'avance en muid ou autre unité.

Le livre terrier de l'année 1602 du domaine de Csábrág, confisqué de István Illésházy, prescrit le neuvième de la récolte et des vignes.[45] Le terrier de 1625 du domaine d'Adorjánvár de Csáky le prescrit pour les céréales.[46] Les terriers de 1631 du domaine de Felsővadász et de Makovica et de 1632 de Serke appartenant à György I Rákóczi[47] en fait autant. On mentionne dans le domaine de Sennyei—Károlyi dans le comitat de Bihar en 1622 le neuvième en vin et en céréales, tout comme l'ordonnance de Sempte de 1641 du palatin Miklós Eszterházy, qui oppose le «neuvième en céréale»

tiones) que le seigneur exigeait des paysans lors des festins de noces, de baptêmes, de repas de funérailles, de la diète ou autres. A ce sujet voir O. L. U. et C. 37:56 (1608); M. Gt. Sz. 1901. p. 165 (1635); *Csáky-oklt.* T. I/2, p. 728. (1662); *Urbáriumok. XVI—XVII. század.* p. 122. (1670); etc. — Au sujet de la dîme seigneuriale en moutons, abeilles, porcs, etc. voir la 4e partie de l'étude.

[40] M. Gt. Sz. 1897. pp. 124—125.

[41] Par exemple dans de nombreuses localités des domaines de Somoskő, Szécsény et Gács (O. L. U. et C. 11: 50 — 1596), à Guta et Szklabonya du comitat de Nógrád (*Urbáriumok. XVI—XVII. század.* pp. 306—307. — 1673), dans plusieurs localités des domaines de Szendrő, Csetnek et Derencsény (ibid. p. 483 et suiv — 1686., ou O. L. U. et C. 102:24 — 1690).

[42] M. Gt. Sz. 1901. 164 (1635). — Cf. *Úriszék. XVI—XVII. századi perszövegek.* (Justice seigneuriale. Documents de procès du XVI—XVIIe siècles.) (Réd. E. Varga) Bp. 1958. pp. 393 et suiv.

[43] O. L. U. et C. 49:17 (1956).

[44] *Urbáriumok. XVI—XVII. század.* pp. 61., 69., 71.; *I. Rákóczi György birtokainak gazdasági iratai. pp.* 151, 156, 163; etc.

[45] Cf. avec le texte de 1558: l'obligation du neuvième est élargie entretemps. — *Urbániumok. XVI—XVII. század.* pp. 296—298, 281—287.

[46] *Csáky-oklt.* T. I/2. pp. 629, 634.

[47] *I. Rákóczi György birtokainak gazdasági iratai.* pp. 78—79, 108, 122, 133, 148—149.

à celui de «notre propre domaine».[48] Les domaines du comitat de Heves confisqués aux propriétaires moyens à la suite de la conjuration de Wesselényi, vers 1670 «donnent le neuvième en vin, en blé, en céréale de printemps»,[49] tout comme les nouveaux colons de Balassagyarmat, après un laps de trois années[50] etc.

Les seigneurs cependant exigeaient le neuvième de leurs serfs, ou des quantités de céréales et de vin correspondant au neuvième, non seulement où les sources prescrivent expressément le neuvième. En cas de recette en premier lieu de la dîme ecclésiastique, le neuvième seigneurial, comme on le sait, correspondait au neuvième dixième de la récolte; c'est pourquoi souvent l'imposition *seigneuriale* était aussi qualifiée de *dîme* (dixième, decima). Ainsi les termes de «neuvième» et de «dîme» sont utilisés indifféremment comme des synonymes, indépedamment de l'ordre dans lequel ceux-ci sont exigés (ce qui a donné lieu à de nombreuses chicanes).[51] Certainement c'est le cas de la bourgade de Belényes, où les livres terriers plus anciens prescrivent le *neuvième*, tandis que celui de 1600 prescrit «frugum et vini *decimas*».[52] Selon le texte du livre terrier de 1578 du domaine de Palota «*nonam* dant de seminaturis», tandis que celui de 1617 parle «de omnibus segetibus solvunt *decimam*».[53] Le texte des livres terriers du domaine de Serke est encore plus explicite, si le texte de 1632 — comme il en a déjà été fait mention — prescrit «le neuvième pour tous les labours», celui de 1636 prescrit soit le neuvième, soit la dîme et celui de 1643 désigne par dîme cette imposition manifestement identique.[54] Les biens conjoints du domaine de Serke confirment cette constatation: le livre terrier de 1632 de Derencsény prescrit la dîme en vin et autres récoltes, celui de Csetnek de 1643, prescrit dans certaines communes le neuvième, mais plus souvent la dîme.[55] La locution consacrée au neuvième en céréales «dîme en blé» existant dans de nombreux documents fait disparaître toute incertitude,[56] ou encore l'expression «seconde dîme» pour l'imposition destinée au seigneur féodal,[57] éventuellement celle-ci est qualifiée de «dîme neuvième»[58]. Par conséquent, les sources mentionnant non seulement le neuvième, mais

[48] *A nagykárolyi gróf Károlyi-család oklevéltára* (Recueil de chartes de la famille comte Károlyi de Nagykároly). (= Károlyi-oklt.) T.IV. Bp. 1887. pp. 185, 187; M. Gt. Sz. 1904. p. 143.

[49] Par ex. dans la bourgade de Pásztó et le village de Hasznos. — *Urbáriumok. XVI—XVII. század.* p. 304.

[50] M. Gt. Sz. 1897. pp. 530—531.

[51] Au sujet de l'ordre des réquisitions (et différentes autres questions concernant la perception de la dîme) cf. B. Ila: *A dézsmajegyzékek mint a történeti statisztika forrásai* (Les régistres de la dîme, comme sources de la statistique historique). *A történeti statisztika forrásai* (Les sources de la statistique historique). (Réd. J. Kovacsics.) Bp. 1957, pp. 82. et suiv. — Selon ses constatations le neuvième était perçu au préalable à cette époque.

[52] O. L. U. et C. 17:6 — Cf. O. L. DL. 36.982 (1491)

[53] *Urbáriumok. XVI—XVII. század.* pp. 151 et suiv.; p. 172.

[54] *I. Rákóczi György birtokainak gazdasági iratai.* pp. 148—149, 157—158, 163—165.

[55] Ibid. pp. 150—151, 159—161.

[56] Tel par ex. l'inventaire de l'année 1641 de la propriété de Felsővadász. — Ibid. pp. 79—83.

[57] Par ex. le livre terrier du domaine de Sárospatak — Ibid. p. 219.

[58] O. L. U. et C. 59:14 (1601); T. T. 1898. pp. 472—479. (1668—1669); *Urbáriumok. XVI—XVII. század.* p. 303. (1670); etc.

encore souvent la dîme, se rapportent à la *redevance seigneuriale proportionnelle* à la récolte en céréales et en vin.

Toutefois, la dîme due au seigneur ne correspondait pas seulement au neuvième, mais aussi à la dîme ecclésiastique, c'est-à-dire dîme originelle, par suite de l'affermage de celle-ci de la part du seigneur ou du trésor, éventuellement à la suite de saisie ou de sécularisation.[59] Le livre terrier de la région du château d'Ecsed en 1648, qui n'emploie point le mot de neuvième, prescrit la dîme pour les céréales d'automne et de printemps de presque toutes les localités, et pour le vin des communes productrices de vigne, désignant sans doute la dîme *seigneuriale*, car par endroit le terrier affirme que les paysans «doivent donner la dîme . . . au *dominus terrestris*, en sus de la dîme redevable au *prêtre*»; puis il souligne que les localités qui jusque là n'avaient jamais donné la dîme de céréales, «la payent depuis trois ans»: il est clair que cette mesure correspond en fait à l'introduction du *neuvième* seigneurial.[60] Le livre terrier de Pozsony (Bratislava), datant presque de cette même, époque prescrit la dîme de blé, de méteil, d'avoine. Cette redevance semble avoir pour origine la dîme *ecclésiastique*, car celle-ci, en sa majorité, est perçue par le seigneur féodal, mais en quelques endroits celle-ci est réservée à l'archevêque d'Esztergom. Là, où la redevance est perçue par le domaine seigneurial, l'archevêque reçoit une certaine quantité de blé, fixée en muids en guise de compensation. Ici donc la perception seigneuriale de la dîme ecclésiastique remplaçait à peu près l'imposition du neuvième seigneurial.[61] Le livre terrier de Tokaj, datant de 1640. donne de semblables informations concernant la rente en céréales: le seigneur a droit au neuvième de la récolte, l'évêché d'Eger à la dîme, mais le neuvième fut supprimé par le seigneur précédent, et la dîme est partout perçue par le domaine «iuxta inscriptionem»[62]. Par ailleurs, souvent il est clair qu'il s'agit de ce dernier cas de la perception seigneuriale de la dîme ecclésiastique, de son bail, comme dans le domaine de Galgóc, où «la dîme a un prix élevé»[63]. Le domaine de Csicsva ordonne également à l'intendant «de percevoir dans tous les cas la dîme ecclésiastique selon l'affermage»[64]; le domaine de Murány loue pour 1000 thalers par an, la dîme en céréale de 5 districts ecclésiastiques[65].

Finalement, nous devons signaler l'origine dela dîme seigneuriale, provenant de la dîme ecclésiastique louée ou sécularisée par le trésor, donc perçue par le fisc — qui parfois à cause de cela s'appelait «*royale*» ou «princière»

[59] Au sujet des précédents du louage de la dîme ecclésiastique cf. E. MÁLYUSZ: *Az egyházi tizedkizsákmányolás* (L'exploitation par la dîme ecclésiastique). *Tanulmányok a parasztság történetéhez Magyarországon a 14. században* (Études sur l'histoire de la paysannerie en Hongrie au XIVe siècle). Bp., 1953, pp. 326—327; au sujet des baux par seigneurs féodaux et par le trésor au XVIe siècle: art. 35. de la loi de 1547, 61 de 1548, 43 de 1556., 68 de 1563. 27 de 1569, 22 de 1574; pour la saisie, la sécularisation O. L. U. et C. 2:22 (1570); L. RUZSÁS: *Az egri vár gazdálkodása a XVI. században* (Économie du château d'Eger au XVIe siècle). Bp. 1939. pp. 37 et suiv.; etc.

[60] *Károlyi-oklt*. T. IV. pp. 326—327, pp. 340—341. — Cf. O. L. U. et C. 4:45 (1592); U. et C. 11:50 (1596).

[61] *Urbáriumok. XVI—XVII. század*. pp. 216 et suiv.

[62] *I. Rákóczi György birtokainak gazdasági iratai*. p. 375.

[63] M. Gt. Sz. 1897. p. 124 (1607).

[64] M. Gt. Sz. 1897. p. 341 (1636).

[65] *Urbáriumok. XVI—XVII. század*. p. 331.

(ce dernier dans les régions de la Hongrie, jointes à la principauté de Transylvanie, comme dans les domaines du comitat de Bihar, attenant au château fort d'Adorján, par contre sous la dénomination *decima regia*), par exemple dans les domaines de Serke ou de Derencsény.[66] Celles-ci sont passées parfois aux mains des seigneurs féodaux, par suite de la location par le trésor ou de le donation royale. Ainsi, l'archiduc Ernest, gouverneur royal vers les années 1580, donnait en location à Miklós Pálffy la majorité des dîmes du domaine de Vöröskő, dont disposait la chambre royale; à cette époque, ce dernier acquit également le domaine même.[67] Le prince Gábor Bethlen, en 1614, donna en bénéfice à Mihály Károlyi, toutes les dîmes de certains villages du comitat de Bihar — «universas et quaslibet decimas . . . hactenus in rationem fisci nostri accumulari solitas» — il lui donna, en 1626, également le bénéfice de la dîme de vin de Nagymuzsaj du comitat de Bereg —«nobis et successoribus nostris quotannis pendi solitam»—; en même temps Mihály Károlyi était propriétaire de ces domaines et percevait donc le neuvième (dîme seigneuriale) en provenant.[68] Au sujet du conflit en connexe avec la possession des villages mentionnés du comitat de Bihar, nous pouvons lire la phrase caractéristique: «. . . il n'a pas été permis de saisir ni le neuvième, ni la dîme. Sa Majesté (le prince Gábor Bethlen) a la libre disposition de la dîme, car c'est lui qui l'a donnée.»[69] Une semblable évolution est reflétée par les documents selon lesquels en 1648, le roi Ferdinand III fit don des propriétés des comitats de Bars et de Nyitra des Dóczy aux Hédervváry, puis après l'extinction de la branche masculine de cette dernière famille, Léopold I, en 1658, fit don de domaines des comitats de Győr et de Nyitra à la branche féminine de la famille, «y compris . . . les neuvièmes et les dîmes».[70]

[66] *Csáky-oklt.* T. I/2, pp. 629, 634. (1625); *Urbáriumok XVI—XVII. század,* pp. 502, 506.

[67] Cf. aussi avec les autres baux de Miklós Pálffy. — P. JEDLICSKA: *Adatok erdődi báró Pálffy Miklós a győri hősnek életrajza és korához. 1552—1600.* (Matériaux concernant la biographie et l'époque du baron Miklós Pálffy de Erdőd, héros de Győr) 1552—1600.) Eger, 1897. pp. 86, 107, 145, 148, 151.

[68] *Károlyi oklt.* T. IV. p. 88—89. Le capitaine de Várad est aussi informé de la donation: certainement parce que jusqu'à cette époque, les «dîmes princières» de ces villages étaient perçues par le château — Ibid. de Várad. — Cf. encore ibid. T. IV.p. 37. (1609), p. 61. (1610) et pp. 95—99 (1614). T. IV. pp. 201—202. La chambre de Kassa est aussi informée de cette donation.

[69] *Károlyi oklt.* T. IV. p. 175. (1622) — La dîme ecclésiastique en Transylvanie par suite de la sécularisation se transforme en principe en perception du trésor: en dîme princière. Donc les seigneurs féodaux de Transylvanie s'efforçaient d'obtenir du prince la dîme de leurs domaines par location, en gage ou par donation: périodiquement le prince s'efforçait de les récupérer. Par ex. Gábor Bethlen écrit à Árpád Illésházy, en 1621: «Laissez percevoir nos dîmes par les décimateurs des dits lieux . . . Et même rendez ceux qui ont été imposé à la dîme, car . . . nous n'avons pas besoin de l'argent de l'affermage, mais de la dîme.» — *Magyar Történelmi Tár* (Archives historiques hongrois). T. XXVII. Bp. 1915, p. 42. — Cependant les conditions existant en Transylvanie sont caractérisées par le fait qu'au XVIIe siècle la majorité de la dîme est devenue seigneuriale et même elle est devenue presque une des principales sources de revenus des seigneurs féodaux. (M. SZENTGYÖRGYI: *Jobbágyterhek a XVI—XVII. századi Erdélyben* (Charges des serfs en Transylvanie aux XVIe—XVIIe siècles). Bp. 1962, pp. 31 et suiv.).

[70] *A Hédervváry-család oklevéltára* (Recueil de chartes de la famille Hédervváry). (= Hédervváry oklt.) T. II. Bp. 1922. pp. 273, 300.

Ainsi, la perception par le seigneur féodal d'un *double* impôt en céréales et en vin, tant dans les domaines privés que royaux, devint de plus en plus fréquente. Les sources l'expriment en partie par les termes techniques originaux et prescrivent le *neuvième* et la *dîme* seigneuriale.[71] Tel le livre terrier datant de 1636, de Rozgony,qui prescrit dans certains villages la dîme et dans d'autres le neuvième, mais plus généralement «le neuvième et la dîme pour toutes les récoltes»;[72] l'ordonnance de Sempte datant de 1641, qui mentionne en outre du neuvième de céréales des dîmes aussi et fait percevoir tous les deux par les décimateurs;[73] ou encore l'ordonnance de Munkács ultérieure de quatre années, qui mentionne ensemble *pro decimatoribus et nonatoribus*, «partout où le neuvième et la dîme en blé, orge et avoine doivent être perçus . . . pour notre maître».[74] En 1668, dans les domaines des comitats de Gömör, Nógrád, Hont et Heves de László Iványi Fekete, dans quelques villages, le neuvième est exigé en blé des labours de printemps et, par exception, en vin, de quelques vignobles, mais pour la plupart des villages «le neuvième et la dîme sont exigés pour toutes les récoltes et pour le vin».[75] La situation est semblable, quelques années plus tard, dans le domaine confisqué de la femme de János Gesztelyi, du comitat de Nógrád, où face au revenu provenant «ex allodiali frumento» sont les revenus du «decimalis frumenti» et de la «nonae frumenti»;[76] tout comme les serfs des domaines de Szendrő et de Serke confisqués par le trésor sont imposés des «decima regia et nona» ou «pendunt et nonam et decimam» sur les récoltes d'automne et de printemps au bénéfice du seigneur féodal.[77]

Dans d'autres cas par contre, les sources décrivent cette exploitation par le droit du seigneur aux *«deux dîmes»*, ou plus simplement à la dîme qui n'est ni la *decima*, ni la *nona*, mais les deux *ensemble*. Selon la conscription datant de 1609 du château fort de Tihany, «toutes les *deux dîmes*» de Tósok doivent être livrées au château (tandis que Szőlős doit la dîme au capitaine de Veszprém et le neuvième au château de Tihany);[78] les vignes d'Aszaló

[71] Le neuvième et la dîme figurent souvent ensemble dans la liste habituelle des redevances seigneuriales. V. par ex. *Károlyi-oklt.* T. IV. p. 401 (1614) — Au sujet de l'obligation de la dîme et du neuvième seigneurial des villages dépendant de Debrecen à partir de la fin du XVIe siècle v. M. Szűcs: *Debrecen mezőgazdasági története* (Histoire agricole de Debrecen). M. Gt. Sz. 1894, p. 291.

[72] M. Gt. Sz. 1894. pp. 266—269.

[73] M. Gt. Sz. 1904. p. 143. — L'ordonnance de cinq années antérieures de deux districts du domaine (Szempc et Cseklész) nous apprend qu'il s'agit de la location de la dîme ecclésiastique: «nous achetons à prix élevé la dîme annuellement». (M. Gt. Sz. 1903. p. 161) — Ces documents échappèrent à Berlász, qui dans le domaine de Sempte n'a observé que la prestation du vin et non pas le terrage en céréales (op. cit. pp. 63—64).

[74] M. Gt. Sz. 1905, pp. 38—39.

[75] T. T. 1898, pp. 468—473.

[76] *Urbáriumok. XVI—XVII. század.* p. 308.

[77] Au sujet des «domaines associés» également confisqués, le domaine de Derencsény prescrit en même temps la «decima regia», celui de Csetnek prescrit le neuvième au seigneur (ce dernier de plus, ou plutôt à sa place prescrit la dîme de céréales pour l'église). — *Urbáriumok. XVI—XVII. század.* pp. 487, 493, 499, 503, 506.

[78] Les dîmes des environs étaient louées par la chambre de Pozsony au chapitre de Veszprém, ou plutôt à l'archiabbaye de Pannonhalma pour les comptes du château de Tihany. Dans quelques villages appartenant à Tihany les seigneurs hongrois et turcs se partageaient «les deux dîmes». Voir L. Erdélyi: *Pisky István tihanyi*

(comitat de Borsod) des bourgeois de Kassa (Košice) sont redevables «de *deux dîmes*, soit de la dîme et du neuvième».[79] Selon les prescriptions du domaine de Hernád de Zsigmond Kapy, par contre, «percevez la *dîme* de telle sorte que ceux de Kétely et de Fancsal payent le *sixième* . . . ceux de Sáp une dîme».[80] Gábor Bethlen aussi, en tant que propriétaire du vignoble du nom de Páli de Munkács (Mukatchevo), en 1625, diminue les impôts des vignerons en fixant la «*dîme* du vignoble à un dixième, c'est-à-dire à neuvième, afin qu'ils soient libres du dixième».[81] György Rákóczi, en 1632, à Sárospatak, cède la moitié de la *dîme* dénommée «première dîme» et le quart de «la seconde dîme, c'est-à-dire du neuvième» au prêtre réformé.[82] L'ordonnance de Murány, datant de 1662, mentionne la rentrée, le battage des récoltes de blé de «la réserve seigneuriale et de la *dîme*»; mais le livre terrier de 1672 nous apprend qu'en plus de la *dîme* de blé (louée), le seigneur perçoit également le neuvième.[83] Le terrier du domaine de Serke, datant de 1686, décrit parfois la perception conjointe du neuvième et de la dîme ainsi: «*Decimam* praestant in *nona* et *decima* regia»[84].

La mention de telles et de semblables sources témoigne du fait que sous le nom de dîme les deux différentes redevances, «les deux dîmes» se confondent, ainsi donc l'expression «dîme» signifie non seulement le neuvième seigneurial: «la seconde dîme», ou la dîme ecclésiastique perçue par le seigneur féodal: «la première dîme», mais parfois les «deux dîmes» ensemble. La description de mode de perception de la dîme de vin de Tokaj confirme ce fait de façon frappante: selon celle-ci «la *dîme* en vin des vignobles entourant le château, dès le début était *unique*, comme aujourd'hui, indifféremment, pour tout le monde: habitants, extraneis . . ., ils sont redevables au seigneur du *cinquième*», c'est-à-dire ils doivent «remettre au seigneur chaque *cinquième* baquet ou muid». Comment faut-il donc, dans ce cas, comprendre «*une*» dîme? La suite de l'explication nous éclaire: «Ici *la dîme royale* n'était pas exigée ab antiquo».[85] La dîme était exigée

---

kapitány számadáskönyve (Livre de compte d' István Piski capitaine du château de Tihany). M. Gt. Sz. 1905. pp. 205—206. — Au sujet de la perception de la dîme par les Turcs cf. *Gyula város oklevéltára 1313—1800* (Recueil de chartes de la ville de Gyula 1313—1800.). (Réd. E. Veress) Bp. 1938. pp. 365., 416; *Hivatalos nyomozások a török adó s hódítások körül Borsodban a XVII. sz. első felében* (Recherches officielles concernant l'impôt et les conquètes des Turcs dans le comitat de Borsod, dans la première partie du XVIIe siècle). Magyar Történelmi Tár. T. VI. Pest, 1859. pp. 120—121, 154, 159, 162—163.; O. L. U. et C. 30:20; etc.

[79] M. Gt. Sz. 1904. p. 296.

[80] M. Gt. Sz. 1895. p. 196.

[81] M. Gt. Sz. 1895. p. 362.

[82] *I. Rákóczi György birtokainak gazdasági iratai.* p. 219. — En outre dans le domaine de Sárospatak — selon les livres terriers des années 1631, 1632 et 1648 — étaient perçus la dîme, mais en plusieurs endroits la dîme et le neuvième pour les céréales, la dîme et le neuvième en général pour le vin; la majorité des dîmes étaient perçus par le seigneur et la partie moindre par le prêtre réformé. (Ibid. pp. 175, 189, 193, 267.)

[83] M. Gt. Sz. 1901. pp. 272—273; *Urbáriumok. XVI—XVII. század.* pp. 333. et suiv.

[84] *Urbáriumok. XVI—XVII. század.* p. 502.

[85] M. Gt. Sz. 1897. p. 525. — Nous pouvons franchement utiliser ce document datant de 1700 pour caractériser la situation du milieu du XVIIe siècle, parce que nous nous basons également sur le livre terrier datant de 1640, selon lequel le neuvième + la dîme étaient exigés pour la vigne de la bourgade de Tokaj, c'est-à-dire le cinquième. (V. *I. Rákóczi György birtokainak gazdasági iratai.* p. 375.)

uniquement par le seigneur; mais cette «dîme *unique*» était composée dans l'origine par «*deux* dîmes» — et cette dîme correspondait au cinquième de la récolte.

Nous pouvons constater donc le rôle important et croissant du deuxième groupe des rentes en produits, c'est-à-dire l'imposition *proportionnelle* des céréales et des vins, dans la Hongrie du XVIIe siècle. Nous pouvons dire que les efforts des seigneurs féodaux pour l'augmentation des redevances de céréales et de vin, fixées dans les décrets de la fin du XVe et du début du XVIe siècle — sous l'influence de l'expansion du système des réserves seigneuriales (allodia) — non seulement n'a pas diminué, sinon, parallèlement à l'exploitation des réserves domaniales,[86] elle est devenue une pratique répandue justement à cette époque. Elle s'est répandue non pas sous forme de neuvième, mais sous sa forme double: imposition unifiée du neuvième et de la dîme, des «deux dîmes», parfois expressément du «cinquième».[87] Souvent il arrive que les sources mentionnant simplement la perception seigneuriale de la *dîme*, en fait, fixent la redevance des seigneurs à 20% de la récolte des serfs (sans compter les excès et les abus dans la perception de la dîme, assez fréquents d'ailleurs)[88], diminuant ainsi de façon importante, ou supprimant totalement la possibilité des paysans de produire pour le marché.

4.

L'unification, la fonte du neuvième et de la dîme — comme nous l'avons constaté plus haut — est sans doute en rapport étroit avec la propagation de la pratique, selon laquelle, le neuvième ou la dîme seigneuriale étaient perçus non seulement sur les céréales et sur le vin, mais aussi sur tous les produits et animaux qui étaient frappés par la dîme — ecclésiastique à l'origine.[89] Dans les sources contemporaines, un point revient fréquemment: «Ab universis segetibus suis decimari solitis . . . dant nonam pro domino terrestri, ita et ab agnellis ac apibus»; «du vin, des céréales, des moutons, dont on donnait la dîme, ils donneront dorénavant le neuvième»[90]; etc. A ceci s'ajoute la dîme de porc — qui originairement était due pour les

[86] Au sujet de l'élargissement au XVIIe siècle de la culture des réserves seigneuriales, dans notre conférence faite à l'Académie Hongroise, en 1951 nous avons exposé cette question: *A majorsági gazdálkodás és a parasztság kisajátítása a XVII. századi Magyarországon* (L'exploitation de la réserve seigneuriale et l'expropriation de la paysannerie en Hongrie au XVIIe siècle). A Magyar Tudományos Akadémia II. Osztályának Közleményei. (Communications de la IIe section de l'Académie des Sciences de Hongrie) 1952. pp. 39 et suiv.) Notre hypothèse par laquelle nous avons lié les faits en question à l'accumulation primitive a été à l'origine d'un vif débat; par contre notre constatation faite au sujet de l'expansion de l'exploitation des réserves seigneuriales au XVIIe siècle a été renforcée en pleine mesure par les recherches postérieures: celle-ci est devenue une opinion courante de notre science historique par opposition aux opinions anciennes. (V. par ex. Agrártörténeti Szemle (Revue d'histoire agraire), 1961. No 1. p. 137. §)

[87] Le livre terrier datant de 1631 du domaine de Sárospatak mentionne par endroits expressément le cinquième (cinquième de vin). *I. Rákóczi György birtokainak gazdasági iratai.* p. 175.; celui du domaine d'Ecsed, en 1648, aussi (*Károlyi oklt.* T. IV. p. 229.); etc.

[88] V. par ex. ILA: op. cit. pp. 84—85.

[89] Au sujet de l'étendue des dîmes ecclésiastiques v. MÁLYUSZ: op. cit. (1953.) p. 320.; FÜGEDI: op. cit. pp. 105—106.; ILA: op. cit. pp. 82—83.

[90] *Urbáriumok, XVI—XVII. század.* p. 333.; M. Gt. Sz. 1897. pp. 530—531; etc.

porcs nourris des glands des forêts ou paissant dans les prés, — habitude qui en Hongrie, semble-t-il, est d'origine seigneuriale et non pas ecclésiastique.[91]

Le livre terrier des domaines du château d'Adorján, de l'année 1625, prescrit par exemple la dîme de porc. De même le terrier du domaine de Rozgony, de l'année 1631[92] tandis que le livre terrier de Pozsony pour 1646 prescrit la dîme de moutons et d'abeilles, et celui de 1672 de Murány (dans certains villages)[93] prescrit le neuvième en moutons et en abeilles. En plus de la dîme en céréales et en vin, leterrier d'Ecsed, datant de 1648, exige également la dîme de porc pour la patûre et les glands, ainsi que pour les moutons et les abeilles;[94] cette même année, les serfs de Szentmiklós «bien que n'ayant pas de dette de céréale d'autumne et de printemps» sont redevables au seigneur de la dîme pour les porcs et les abeilles, à laquelle s'ajoute en 1699 la dîme en moutons («stronga», au fait le vingtième).[95] Dans ce cas aussi, nous avons affaire à la perception unifiée des «deux dîmes». En 1668, dans le domaine de László Iványi Fekete, à côté de la redevance sur les céréales et les vins, existe ici la dîme de porc et d'agneau, là la «dîme neuvième» des moutons et des essaims d'abeilles, ou bien les serfs sont redevables *de neuvième et de dîme* de leurs agneaux et leurs abeilles.[96] L'ordonnance de Miskolc, datée de 1686, élargit singulièrement les obligations: «j'exige la dîme des moutons, des abeilles, des agneaux, des chèvres, des porcs et de tous biens quels qu'ils soient.»[97]

Ces faits mettent en relief l'importance de la rente en produits, du terrage *proportionnel* dans la structure de la rente féodale au XVIIe siècle en Hongrie — d'autant plus, que l'expansion de cette dernière forme de la perception, c'est-à-dire les différentes formes de réquisition du bétail des serfs, contrebalançaient, dans une certaine mesure, l'amoindrissement — mentionné précédemment — du premier groupe des prestations en produits, des *munera*, car il est notoire que les «cadeaux» en nature s'étendaient non seulement aux vivres, mais aussi aux animaux. Ainsi, l'extension de la perception de la dîme — à côté de l'expansion de l'exploitation de la réserve seigneuriale — peut être considérée comme un autre facteur de l'affaiblissement de l'importance des cadeaux.

Mentionnons ici également: le changement sémantique du mot «dîme» se manifeste aussi si l'on prend en considération la perception de la dîme en animaux qui ne signifie plus strictement le dixième. En effet, du point de vue sémantique, il faut examiner non seulement les cas déjà mentionnés,

[91] En 1463 déjà, le seigneur du domaine de Munkács percevait la dîme de porc en contre-partie du glandage. Voir: *A zichi és vásonkeői Zichy-család idősb ágának okmánytára.* (Recueil de chartes de la branche aînée de la famille du comte Zichy de Zichi et Vásonkeő). T. X. Bp. 1907. p. 254. — Dans la propriété de Belényes la dîme ecclésiastique de porc apparaît tôt. (O. L. Dl 36.892. — 1491)

[92] *Csáky-oklt.* T. I/2. pp. 629., 634; M. Gt. Sz. 1894. p. 266.

[93] *Urbáriumok. XVI—XVII. század.* pp. 218, 333.

[94] *Károlyi oklt.* T. IV. pp. 282—346.

[95] A ce sujet les remarques des livres terriers de 1648 et 1699 du domaine de Szentmiklós *(Urbáriumok. XVI—XVII. század.* pp. 522, 527, 551, 558, 567) cf. avec le livre terrier de Zsigmond Lipcsey, datant de 1648, contenant des directives pour les serfs ukrainiens de Verhovina. (M. Gt. Sz. 1894. pp. 331—343.)

[96] T. T. 1898. pp. 467—476.

[97] M. Gt. Sz. 1899. pp. 83—84.

c'est-à-dire la dîme qui correspond au cinquième ou au sixième, ou la «dîme neuvième», mais aussi des expressions telles que «chaque vingtième mouton doit être pris pour la dîme», «la dîme doit être acquittée par un dixième»[98], «la dîme doit être remise au seigneur *per decimam*», «la dîme est due . . . *per vigesimationem*»[99], etc. Donc le mot dîme ou dixième se rapporte à une proportion allant du vingtième au cinquième — mais de toute manière il signifie une imposition *proportionnelle* à la récolte ou au troupeau.

La vaste littérature linguistique hongroise concernant le mot dîme ne s'occupe que de l'origine du mot: son attention est attirée par l'évolution du mot latin «*decima*» qui est devenu en hongrois «*dézma*» ou «*dézsma*», à ce sujet elle propose plusieurs conjectures du vieux provençal au slave.[100] La linguistique ne s'occupe guère du changement sémantique du mot hongrois. Ainsi, les explications données peuvent également avoir un certain intérêt au point de vue linguistique.

5.

Pour en revenir au neuvième ou à la dîme seigneuriale, perçus sur les champs et les vignobles des serfs, il faut constater que la redevance fixe du vin, *indépendante de la récolte* (impôt sur les vignobles, muid de vin, ius montanum, Bergrecht) a fait preuve d'une plus grande solidité et persiste comparativement en plus d'endroits que la redevance fixe de céréales (muid ou mine de céréal, aconalia), bien qu'à cette époque, la perception *proportionnelle* du vin ait pris également une grande importance. A ce sujet nous avons mentionné déjà de nombreux faits, et il en existe encore bien d'autres.

Les vignobles de Tállya, au début du XVIIe siècle, étaient grevés d'impôts, bien que ces impôts aient été payés par le neuvième, ou le neuvième auquel s'ajoutaient 2 muids.[101] A cette même époque, les habitants et les *extranei* du domaine de Galgóc, possession de la famille Thurzó, devaient payer le muid de vin. Parmi les bourgades du domaine de Sempte, à Sempte par exemple, l'impôt sur les vignobles était obligatoire, tandis qu'à Szempc et à Cseklész, la redevance était exigée en neuvième de vin.[102] En 1643,

[98] M. Gt. Sz. 1894, pp. 335, 341 (1646).

[99] *Urbáriumok. XVI—XVII. század.* pp. 567, 572 (1699).

[100] G. Szarvas—Zs. Simonyi: *Magyar Nyelvtörténeti Szótár* (Dictionnaire linguistique hongrois). T. I. Bp. 1890, 500e colonne; I. Szamota—Gy. Zolnai: *Magyar Oklevél Szótár* (Dictionnaire des chartes hongrois). Bp. 1902—1906. 151e colonne; Z. Gombocz—J. Melich: *Magyar Etymologiai Szótár* (Dictionnaire étymologique hongrois). Bp. 1927. 1344—1346e colonne; J. Melich: *Szláv jövevényszavaink* (Mots d'emprunt slave dans le hongrois). Nyelvtudományi Közlemények. 1904. T. XXXIV. pp. 201—203.; G. Bárczi: *Óprovençal jövevényszavak a magyarban* (Mots d'emprunt du vieux provençal dans le hongrois). Nyelvtudományi Közlemények 1936. T. L. pp. 19—20.; G. Bárczi: *Magyar Szófejtő Szótár* (Dictionnaire étymologique hongrois). Bp. 1941, p. 51.; I. Kniezsa: *A magyar nyelv szláv jövevényszavai* (Les mots d'emprunt slave dans la langue hongroise). T. I/2. Bp. 1955, pp. 622 et suiv. — Szarvas—Simonyi (op. cit.) communiquent un exemple historique concernant le vingtième en tant que «genre de dîme»; Czuczor—Fogarasi sans mentionner de rapport historiques, ni de changement sémantique, notent que «le peuple nomme dîme le neuvième et le septième aussi» (*A magyar nyelv szótára.* [Dictionnaire de la langue hongroise]. T. I. Pest 1862, 1216e colonne.)

[101] M. Gt. Sz. 1901, pp. 143—144.

[102] Berlász: op. cit. pp. 59—64.

les vignobles des bourgades de Szentgyörgy et de Guar, du littoral du Balaton, payent l'impôt,[103] une dizaine d'années plus tard, les vignobles de Diars et de Vonyárcs du comitat de Zala doivent payer en partie l'impôt sur les vignobles et en partie le neuvième[104], etc.

La raison de la plus grande «persistance» de l'imposition fixe en vin est due certainement aux grandes variations de la récolte des vignes et à ce que le traditionnel muid ou mine de céréales était plus petit que le neuvième (ou la dîme) de la récolte, tandis que, comme le vin était une denrée recherchée, et une grande quantité de vin était nécessitée par les débits de boisson des seigneurs, la quantité de l'impôt sur les vignobles était fixée à plusieurs endroits très haut, dépassant le neuvième de la récolte.[105] Dans ce cas, le seigneur n'avait pas intérêt à abandonner l'impôt sur les vignobles pour le simple neuvième ou la dîme, mais il s'efforçait d'obtenir, en plus de l'impôt fixé ou du neuvième, *aussi la dîme*. Ainsi, l'augmentation des prestations en vin résultait soit de l'imposition double (neuvième et dîme), c'est-à-dire des «deux dîmes», ou à l'impôt s'ajoutait encore la dîme en vin.

Nous constatons souvent que le seigneur perçoit la dîme de vin, ainsi p. ex. dans le domaine de Belényes appartenant au trésor,[106] dans le domaine de Lánzsér de Miklós Eszterházy,[107] dans certaines communes du domaine de Rozgony,[108] dans la propriété de Kisbarát des Héderváry,[109] par les seigneurs de Nagyszőllős,[110] etc. S'agit-il dans ces cas du synonyme du neuvième, ou de dîme ecclésiastique, perçue par les seigneurs, ou éventuellement de sa signification plus large des «deux dîmes», il n'est possible de l'établir qu'en possession d'autres données y relatives. Il existe cependant certaines informations qui mentionnent sans aucun doute la perception de neuvième + dîme ou de l'impôt fixé + dîme. Mentionnons ici outre les cas de neuvième + dîme, avancés déjà auparavant, l'exemple des domaines des Thurzó de Galgóc et Sempte, où selon les comptes de 1614, en plus de neuvième *ou* de l'impôt fixé, le seigneur perçoit aussi le *vinum decimale* pour chaque vignoble (sur la base du bail);[111] mentionnons le domaine de Rohonc-Szalonak des Batthyány, où à cette époque la dîme de vin louée s'ajoute au *ius montanum*;[112] la bourgade de Lózs dont le contrat terrier de 1635 exige «selon l'ancienne coutume des vignobles la redevance fixe et la dîme affermée en argent»;[113] tout comme les vignobles de Sümeg pour lesquels le préfet István Sennyei, en 1680, exige «*la dîme et le ius montanum*»,[114] etc.

[103] M. Gt. Sz. 1899. pp. 467—471.
[104] M. Gt. Sz. 1894. pp. 32—33.
[105] Cf. Berlász: op. cit. p. 92.
[106] O. L. U. et C. 17:6 (1600).
[107] M. Gt. Sz. 1903, pp. 456—457 (1615).
[108] M. Gt. Sz. 1894, p. 267 (1636).
[109] *Héderváry-oklt.* T. II. pp. 292—293 (1655).
[110] M. Gt. Sz. 1895, p. 180 (1674).
[111] O. L. Archives Thurzó Irregestrata. Fasc. 13.
[112] V. Zimányi: *Majorsági gazdálkodás a rohonc-szalonaki társuradalomban a XVII. század derekán* (Exploitation des réserves seigneuriales dans le domaine jumelé de Rohonc-Szalonak, au milieu du XVIIe siècle). Agrártörténeti Szemle. 1962. No. 1—2. pp. 36—46.
[113] M. Gt. Sz. 1901, p. 164.
[114] M. Gt. Sz. 1905. p. 307. — Nous rencontrons d'autres méthodes de l'augmentation de la redevance en vin aussi. Il y a des cas lorsque les serfs payent la dîme pour *deux* suzerains, et le seigneur, malgré tout, perçoit une part plus grande que le neuvième. Dans les vignobles de Szőlősardó dépendant du domaine de Szendrő par exemple.

Il est intéressant de noter ici le livre terrier du domaine de Léka-Borsmonostor, datant de 1608, qui comprend de semblables mesures non seulement au sujet de l'imposition en vin, mais aussi en céréales. Dans ce cas «l'impôt sur les vignobles *et* la dîme sont exigés d'après les vignobles, *in specie*»; de plus en dehors du muid de céréales (de l'impôt fixé en blé), «il est perçu une dîme *in specie* pour toutes les récoltes des semailles d'automne et de printemps» — même là «où auparavant la dîme n'était pas perçue. . . depuis quelques années celle-ci était de nouveau exigée».[115] Cette imposition fut exigée, ajoutons-le, sans que celle-ci ait été louée à l'église; donc, en plus de l'imposition *fixe* en céréales, l'imposition *proportionnelle* fut également exigée. Une telle mesure n'était pas rare dans l'imposition en céréales non plus. Nous constatons une évolution — si l'on veut: un tournant — semblable dans les documents du domaine voisin de Sárvár-Kapuvár de cette même époque, non pas sous la forme d'une mention directe de l'imposition de la dîme, mais sur la base du collationnement des sources. Ici, les livres terriers du XVIe siècle ne mentionnent pas l'imposition proportionnelle, ni au début du siècle, ni en 1584 — il n'est uniquement fait mention que de muid ou de mine. Par contre, le texte datant de 1608, mentionne la dîme seigneuriale, pour les céréales d'automne et de printemps (tout comme pour les abeilles, agneaux, chevrettes);[116] les comptes ultérieurs du domaine (p. ex. ceux datant de 1628 ou 1640) énumèrent régulièrement en plus de l'impôt sur les vignobles, du muid ou l'impôt en céréales les recettes provenant de la dîme due au seigneur.[117] — Par ailleurs, dans le domaine de Terebes du comitat de Zemplén, une évolution semblable est signée directement par le livre terrier de l'année 1601, qui note «de terris arabilibus sessionum colonicalium antea nunquam exactae sunt *decimae nonales* pro domino terrestri, sed nisi a triennio iam relicta magnifici domini Georgii Homonnay exigere curavit»; par endroit même, deux dîmes étaient perçues.[118] Mentionnons encore le livre terrier de Homonna datant de 1612, de ce même seigneur: prescrivant une imposition fixe en muids de blé, seigle, avoine, orge, houblon et aussi «la dîme en blé et la dîme des semailles de printemps des paysans» (celles-ci ne peuvent être payées en argent que par les maires des villages) — et bien entendu la dîme en porc, mouton, agneau et chèvre (ces dernières parfois correspondaient au vingtième).[119]

Conformément aux faits énumérés, la persistance en certains endroits du terrage fixe reçoit un sens différent de celui constaté par la littérature

---

la dîme est due à l'église et le septième au seigneur. (M. Gt. Sz. 1894, p. 174. — 1617-1694) — Lorsqu'à la suite de la conjuration de Wesselényi le trésor en 1675 établit l'inventaire des vignes confisquées de la région de Tokaj, une ordonnance fut promulgée pour examiner «comment ces vignes étaient exploitées, au tiers, au quart ou autrement». Les vignobles du fisc, les années suivantes n'étaient exploitées que partiellement par celui-ci, une certaine partie était attribuée pour exploitation «au tiers, au quart ou au cinquième, selon la qualité». (J. Illésy: *A kincstár hegyaljai szőlőgazdálkodása a XVII. század második felében* (Exploitation des vignes de Tokaj par le trésor, durant la seconde partie du XVIIe siècle). M. Gt. Sz. 1900, pp. 3—5, 15. Ainsi la redevance en vin perçue par le seigneur (le trésor) dépassait le cinquième — pour les vignobles des réserves seigneuriales, données en location aux paysans.

115 *Urbáriumok. XVI—XVII. század.* pp. 93—94, 103—104.

116 O. L. Dl. 36.992, 36.994, 36.983, 37.007; U. et C. 56: 33; U. et C. 37:56

117 O. L. Archives Nádasdy. Comptabilité. Fasc. H. fol. 555—584; fol. 799—830.

118 O. L. U. et C. 59: 14.

119 O. L. U. et C. 109: 2.

historique précédente.[120] Dans de nombreux cas, on peut en effet affirmer que l'impôt sur les vignobles ou le muid de céréales indépendant de la quantité de la récolte ne constituaient qu'*une* partie de la *redevance* du serf au *seigneur*, à ceux-ci *s'ajoutaient* l'imposition proportionnelle, la dîme de vin ou de céréales. Par endroit, le seigneur introduisait simplement par son autorité seigneuriale le terrage proportionnel, auprès des prestations en muids, sans l'avoir loué de l'église. L'examen de la structure de la rente seigneuriale et dans ce cadre, du poids, de l'importance du second groupe des redevances en produits, dans la Hongrie du XVIIe siècle, ne peut être limitée à la question du neuvième et du muid: il faut l'étendre à la dîme perçue par le seigneur, c'est-à-dire aux nombreux cas de la perception de terrage en vin et en céréales *sous dénomination de dîme*.

6.

Les constatations précédentes sont renforcées encore par l'examen bref des rentes perçues pour les labours *hors* des tenures, de cas où soit les serfs du village en question, soit des personnes domiciliées ailleurs (*extranei*) utilisaient et louaient des terres désertes (*praedia*), des réserves domaniales (*allodia*), ou des terres défrichées. Le livre terrier du domaine de Csábrág-Szitnya, datant de 1602, par exemple, exige de l'argent pour la location des *prés* des terres désertes, et fixe par contre en *neuvième* la redevance du serf pour les *champs* du *praedium* ou de la *sessio deserta*.[121] Dans le domaine de Sempte le neuvième était exigé par les percepteurs pour les terres désertes, en 1636;[122] dans le domaine de Nagytapolcsány également, le neuvième était dû pour les terres appelées en slovaque *kopanica* (terres défrichées, qui n'étaient pas cultivées pour les besoins du seigneur);[123] tout comme dans certaines localités du domaine d'Ecsed, pour les labours des *extranei* en 1648.[124]

Le neuvième est souvent remplacé dans ce cas aussi par la *dîme*. Les serfs des domaines de Léka-Borsmonostor et de Sárvár-Kapuvár, tout comme les *extranei*, en 1608 devaient payer la dîme pour les terres défrichées et les terres désertes qu'ils cultivaient;[125] le livre terrier de Csetnek et l'inventaire de Felsővadász durant les années 1630–1640 exigeaient soit le neuvième, soit la dîme pour les terres désertes.[126] Le terrier de Derencsény, au milieu du siècle, exigeait la dîme pour les locations des terres désertes et en 1686, exigeait le neuvième;[127] l'ordonnance de Miskolc à cette même date, exigeait la dîme pour les terres des réserves qui n'étaient pas cultivées pour le seigneur.[128] Cette même année, les serfs du domaine de Szendrő qui avaient souffert des dévastations de la guerre louaient des terres de la réserve seigneuriale,

[120] Berlász: op. cit. p. 69.; Maksay: *Urbáriumok. XVI–XVII. század.* Introduction. p. 41.
[121] *Urbáriumok. XVI–XVII. század.* pp. 289, 297–298.
[122] M. Gt. Sz. 1903, p. 161.
[123] M. Gt. Sz. 1906, p. 85 et suiv.
[124] *Károlyi-oklt.* T. IV. p. 334.
[125] *Urbáriumok. XVI–XVII. század.* pp. 97, 100; O. L. U. et C. 37:56.
[126] *I. Rákóczi György birtokainak gazdasági iratai.* pp. 81–82, 153–155.
[127] Ibid. pp. 150–151; *Urbáriumok. XVI–XVII. század.* p. 505.
[128] M. Gt. Sz. 1899, pp. 83–84.

«unde dant nonam domino terrestri»; dans le «caput bonorum» les réserves sont remises aux paysans provisoirement «pro decimis inseminandi».[129]

Pour les labours, hors des tenures, on constate également la perception *conjointe* des *deux* impositions proportionnelles dues au seigneur. En 1620, les *extranei* du domaine de Zsigmond Kapy, qu'ils travaillent les terres seigneuriales ou les terres désertes, «que ce soit dans mes terres ou dans les terres de mes serfs», doivent remettre «deux dîmes»;[130] dans certaines communes du domaine de Sárospatak, en 1632, les serfs doivent remettre «la dîme et le neuvième» pour les terres désertes qu'ils cultivaient;[131] le livre terrier du domaine de Rozgony, datant de 1636, mentionne que certaines terres désertes cultivées sont redevables «de toutes les deux dîmes au seigneur ... aussi bien de la part des extranei ... que des natifs» (et le texte poursuit de manière significative — «ils ne donnent rien à l'empereur»);[132] le seigneur de Serke, à cette même époque, perçoit le neuvième pour les défrichements (puis le septième[133]); pour la location de terres désertes et des réserves seigneuriales, par contre, il perçoit le cinquième de la récolte, ou bien un loyer de 1 florin + le neuvième qui souvent porte le nom de dîme.[134]

Nous pouvons même presque dire que lors de l'utilisation par les paysans de labours hors des tenures l'obligation de payement proportionnel est encore plus sévère et plus complète que pour les tenures. Ceci se manifeste en partie par la perception des «deux dîmes» — comme dans le domaine de Pozsony ou dans certaines communes du domaine de Munkács, où «ex desertarum sessionum terris percipitur tam nona, quam decima de omnibus frugibus domino terrestri»[135] ou encore «les extranei doivent remettre deux dîmes selon l'ancienne coutume»,[136] tandis que les tenures des paysans de ces domaines n'étaient redevables que d'une seule dîme. L'obligation plus sévère se manifeste aussi dans les localités où l'imposition seigneuriale était *fixée* pour les *tenures*, par contre les *autres* champs cultivés par les serfs ne pouvaient éviter l'imposition *proportionnelle*. Ce dernier cas est illustré au début du XVIIe siècle par l'exemple du domaine de Galgóc et de celui de Temetvény: tandis que les tenures des serfs — en plus de la dîme louée à l'église, comme il en a déjà été fait mention — étaient imposées du terrage fixe (*aconalia*), les défrichements et les champs des réserves seigneuriales utilisées par les paysans étaient redevables du neuvième ou de la dîme, les terres désertes du septième ou

[129] *Urbáriumok. XVI–XVII. század.* p. 487.; O. L. U. et C. 44:24 — Lorsque dans le domaine de Sárospatak la veuve de György I. Rákóczi ordonna le «transfert de l'exploitation et des bâtiments seigneuriaux de Gáva à Vencsellő ... elle prescrivit la dîme pour ces terres». (O. L. U. et C. 58:17; cf. Irreg. 7.)

[130] M. Gt. Sz. 1895, p. 197.

[131] *I. Rákóczi György birtokainak gazdasági iratai.* p. 226.

[132] M. Gt. Sz. 1894. p. 266.

[133] «... ex liberis agris, dictis kopane, praestant septimam» — pouvons nous lire près d'un demi-siècle plus tard dans le livre terrier de Serke, datant de 1686. (*Urbáriumok. XVI–XVII. század.* p. 502.)

[134] *I. Rákóczi György birtokainak gazdasági iratai.* pp. 148–149, 157–158.

[135] *Urbáriumok. XVI–XVII. század* p. 218 (1646). — Le livre terrier de Terebes, datant de 1601, remarque également du sujet de promulgation de la dîme seigneuriale des terres des tenures que «deux dîmes, c'est-à-dire le neuvième et la dîme sont perçus par le seigneur des terres désertes». (O. L. U. et C. 59:14)

[136] M. Gt. Sz. 1897, p. 517 (1616).

du cinquième.[137] A la fin du siècle, dans le domaine de Szentmiklós, on constate la même situation. Même le livre terrier de 1699 maintenait l'usage «ab antiquo», selon lequel si «quelqu'un dans sa tenure effectue les semailles de printemps ou d'automne, il n'est pas tenu à la dîme» (uniquement quelques redevances fixes en muid); par contre il est prescrit: «si quelqu'un ensemence les terres des domaines ou désertes au printemps ou en automne, il est redevable de la dîme au seigneur. . .» Pareillement, les semailles des *extranei* sont imposées du neuvième ou la dîme; les habitants originaux sont aussi imposés si les semailles ne sont pas faites «dans la vallée ou dans la plaine», mais sur les montagnes, c'est-à-dire dans les terres défrichées.[138] Finalement nous pouvons considérer comme une expression de la perception plus sévère du neuvième et de la dîme, la pratique que nous rencontrons lors de l'établissement de nouveaux habitants à Balassagyarmat, en 1671: le seigneur n'exige de neuvième qu'après un délai de trois années pour les tenures du village, par contre pour les «praedia» d'Illés et de Szob il l'exige immédiatement «a dato praesentium».[139] La dîme exigée par les seigneurs pour les terres hors des tenures signifie donc le début de l'imposition de tous les labours cultivés par les serfs.

Ainsi, si le paiement en muid ou en argent ne disparaît pas en tant que bail, surtout pour les prés et les pâturages et non pas pour les labours,[140]

[137] BERLÁSZ: op. cit. pp. 59—62. — Remarquons que l'auteur néglige non seulement la location par le seigneur de la dîme en céréale de l'église — bien que ceci est prouvé aussi bien dans le domaine de Sempte que dans celui de Galgóc (M. Gt. Sz. 1897, pp. 124—125. — 1607) — mais aussi il néglige d'autres faits établis dans d'autres domaines des Thurzó se rapportant à la prestation en produits pour les terres hors de tenures, pensant qu'il s'agit dans ce cas «d'une particularité du domaine de Galgóc» (op. cit. p. 69) — Dans le domaine de Nagytapolcsány, les tenures sont frappées de rédevances fixes, au milieu du XVIIe siècle encore, par contre «pour les terres désertes ils sont redevables du quatrième et pour les terres défrichées du neuvième» (M. Gt. Sz. 1906. p. 88. — Cf. O. L. U. et C. 60:70.)

[138] *Urbáriumok. XVI—XVII. század.* pp. 558, 567, 572, 614. — L'exemption de la dîme des labours des tenures du domaine de Szentmiklós «ab antiquo» provient certainement de ce que dans leur majorité, les serfs dépendant de l'église orientale ne payaient pas de dîme *ecclésiastique.* (Cf.: «Nonam et decimam de hiemalibus et vernalibus solvunt Hungari, sed non Valachi» — O. L. U. et C. 2:22; Domaine de Krasznahorka, 1570. — «Decimas frugum nullas dant eo quod sunt Rutheni.» — O. L. U. et C. 59:14; domaine de Terebes, 1601.) Ainsi les serfs ukrainiens de la Ruthénie Subcarpatique et les Roumains ne commencent à payer la *dîme* en produits qu'à la suite de la généralisation de la dîme *seigneuriale.*

[139] M. Gt. Sz. 1897, pp. 530—531.

[140] Nous avons déjà mentionné de tels cas dans le texte: dans les livres terriers du domaine de Csábrág-Szitnya, de 1602, du domaine de Serke de 1632 et 1636, et naturellement d'autres exemples encore peuvent être cités. Le livre terrier de Sárvár de 1608 prescrit 20 deniers par acre en *plus* de la dîme perçue «in specie» pour certaines terres hors des tenures ou pour des défrichements (O. L. U. et C. 37:56). — Il faut noter: le loyer exprimé proportionnellement à la récolte en céréales se rapportait naturellement à des terres de *labour* et ne pouvait se rapporter à des *prés* ou des *pâturages* appartenant à la réserve seigneuriale ou à des terres désertes, cultivées par les paysans. Par exemple, les terres désertes du domaine des Lorántffy de la région de la Mátra, en 1642, étaient imposées du neuvième (ou du quinzième) des labours, par contre, le pâturage et les prés devaient être payés en argent; une année plus tard le domaine de Derencsény percevait la dîme pour les labours des terres désertes, et un fermage en argent devait être payé pour les pâturages — si les paysans du village les fauchaient. (*I. Rákóczi György birtokainak gazdasági iratai.* pp. 161, 167—168.) En 1673 dans les domaines confisqués du comitat de Nógrád de la femme de János

il est possible de dire qu'à cette époque devient réalité cette pratique, cet effort des seigneurs, qui apparaît dans les lois de la fin du XVe siècle, tendant à imposer le neuvième aussi pour les labours hors de tenures, quasi sous bail. Cet effort devient réalité par la perception seigneuriale non pas simplement du neuvième ou de la dîme, mais d'une quote-part bien plus importante: souvent du cinquième, pour des terres qui jouent un rôle tout particulier dans la production de marchandises des paysans.

En plus de la corvée, l'imposition proportionnelle en nature des terres des tenures et hors des tenures devient ainsi l'autre lourde charge des serfs de Hongrie, limitant sensiblement leur production de marchandises; la corvée et le neuvième que nous pouvons nommer «*corvée et dîme*», deviennent les impositions seigneuriales caractéristiques des serfs hongrois, qui subsistent tant qu'en Hongrie existe le système féodal, «l'édition tardive» de ce système limitant sévèrement le développement de la production marchande de la paysannerie, donnant une acuité plus grande à l'antagonisme fondamental des classes féodales.

C'est ainsi que prit forme avec netteté la *divergence du développement agraire de l'Europe occidentale*, dans la transformation de la structure de la rente foncière féodale, dans le renforcement des formes de rente en nature, délaissant les formes en argent, pour la rente du travail et les redevances en produits.

Voilà les prémisses d'une situation, qui plusieurs siècles plus tard, furent la cause du désespoir des théoriciens économiques hongrois de «l'époque des réformes», principalement d'István Széchenyi, qui mentionne la corvée et la dîme comme des facteurs inutiles, qui «désarment le fermier, réduisant tous ses efforts»; en dehors de la corvée, il lui fallait s'attaquer à la dîme seigneuriale, «car il est difficile de trouver un moyen plus apte à avilir l'économie agricole». Il attirait justement l'attention de ses concitoyens sur les succès de l'évolution dont le régime agraire en Hongrie s'était éloigné au cours des derniers siècles du féodalisme, sur l'état des terres affranchies de dîme de la Grande-Bretagne et de la France, préconisé comme exemple à suivre.[141]

Gesztelyi, certains prés et certaines terres désertes utilisés comme pâturage étaient loués pour de l'argent chaque année par les serfs («vendere», «appretiare»). (*Urbáriumok. XVI–XVII. század.* pp. 306–309.)

[141] Comte ISTVÁN SZÉCHENYI: *Hitel* (Crédit). Pest 1830, pp. 83, 104.

ADDENDA

NEUVIÈME ET DÎME SEIGNEURIALE AU XVIIe SIÈCLE EN HONGRIE

(The Ninth Part Delivery and the Seignorial Tithe in Hungary in the 17th Century)

Page 271, Note 61:

On the West–Hungarian estate Rohonc–Szalonak (County of Vas) the delivery of the ninth part (*nona*) of the produce was not customary even in the 16th and 17th centuries, the grain tax being still imposed upon the tenants as a fixed quantity (*in cubulis*). At the same time, however, the collection of the ecclesiastical tithe (*decima*) of grain and wine was the landlord's right: *V. Zimányi*, A rohonc–szalonaki uradalom és jobbágysága a XVI–XVII. században (The Estate of Rohonc–Szalonak and its Peasantry in the 16th–17th Centuries), Budapest, 1968, pp. 67–68, 124. — The usufruct of the ecclesiastical tithe was a bone of contention between the nobles and the clergy in Poland, too. For a remarkable phase of the conflict: *H. Kowalska*, Walka o dziesieciny na sejmach egzekucyjnich w l. 1562–1565. In: Reformacja i Odrodzenie w Polsce, Warszawa, 1956, I, pp. 71–101.

Page 275, Note 86:

The conclusions arrived at in the text have been corroborated by further research. "It is beyond doubt that from among the various forms of feudal prestations to be delivered by the peasants it was the rent in kind that took the first place in Hungary throughout the 17th century." Grain contributions were in any case required of the peasants to complement the produce of seignorial demesnes: *J. Varga*, Jobbágyrendszer a magyarországi feudalizmus kései századaiban (The Serf System in the Late Centuries of Hungarian Feudalism) 1556–1767, Budapest, 1969, pp. 451–452. — For some international comparison: *E. Le Roy Ladurie–J. Goy*, Prestations paysannes, dîmes et mouvements de la production agricoles dans le sociétes pre–industrielles. In: Proceedings of the Seventh International Economic History Congress. Edited by M. W. Flinn, Edinburgh, 1978, I, pp. 113–125.

VI

LEVANTINE TRADE AND HUNGARY IN THE MIDDLE AGES (THESES, CONTROVERSIES, ARGUMENTS)

In a paper published recently, Professor Ashtor gave a valuable survey of "Recent Research on Levantine Trade", and discussed some of the much debated questions of the topic.[1] But I was sorry to see that he omitted a question which belongs undoubtedly to these hotly debated ones – what is more: a question which has been debated in historiography for nearly two centuries. The present paper is focused on this question.

The fact is that from the beginning and during the greater part of the 19th century the thesis that Levantine goods had been transported to Central and even to Western Europe through Hungary and Transylvania in the Middle Ages, was almost generally accepted by international history writing.

The other fact is, in turn, that roughly since the end of the 19th century this very thesis has been almost generally rejected by historians, I mean, by historians who paid special attention to the transport routes of medieval Levantine trade.

And the third fact is that in textbooks and in general presentations of international economic history of the Middle Ages, we can observe, even now, a sort of confusion concerning the routes of medieval Levantine trade in general and concerning the so-called Hungarian route of medieval Levantine trade in particular. This also refers, to some degree, to the Cambridge Economic History, volume II, i.e., the interesting chapter on Mediterranean and Levantine trade, written by Professor Lopez.[2]

According to these three facts, I should like to discuss three points in the present paper.

Point one:	How and where did the thesis of the medieval Levantine trade-route passing through Hungary and Transylvania emerge in historiography in the beginning of the 19th century?
Point two:	How and why has this thesis been rejected and refuted by historians roughly from the end of the 19th century on?
Point three:	Is it possible for us to join either the adherents or the refuters of this thesis, in the light of recent research?

[1] E. Ashtor: "*Recent Research on Levantine Trade*". The Journal of European Economic History, Vol. 2, No. 1, 1973, pp. 187–206.

[2] R. S. Lopez: "*The Trade of Medieval Europe: the South*". The Cambridge Economic History of Europe, II, Cambridge, 1952, pp. 272, 292, 319.

1

Let us now come to point one: How and where did the idea of the medieval Levantine trade-route passing across Hungary and Transylvania appear in historiography?

The decline of the Ottoman Empire revived interest in eastern commercial and territorial expansion also in the "Danube Monarchy" of the Habsburgs.[3] Endeavours to participate in Levantine trade grew strong especially after the peace of Kutsuk–Kainardzi (1774), when the so-called Eastern Question had come into the lime-light of world politics.[4] It was in this connection that as early as in the 1780's the Austrian Emperor Joseph the Second's Chancellor, Duke Kaunitz, commissioned the Hungarian historian György Pray to demonstrate the "historical title" of the Hungarian Crown to the domains stretching from Dalmatia to the Roumanian principalities on the Danube and the Black Sea.[5]

Projects of this kind,[6] stimulated by the developments of the Eastern Question, were adapted to the peculiar conditions of the Napoleonic Era and treated from perspectives of the world trade by Gergely Berzeviczy, a Hungarian economist of wide political scope. He argued in his work of 1808, *Ansicht des asiatisch–europäischen Welthandels* (and later, too, in several writings), in favour of using an overland route for intercontinental trade between Asia and Europe under the prevailing circumstances of the continental blockade and sea blockade, carried out by Napoleon and the British government respectively. Trying to substantiate his proposal historically, the Hungarian economist explained that in the Middle Ages, before the circumnavigation of Africa, intercontinental trade had been transacted by

[3] F. M. Mayer: *Die Anfänge des Handels und der Industrie in Österreich und die orientalische Kompagnie*, Innsbruck, 1882; J. Dullinger, *Die Handelskompagnien Österreichs nach dem Orient und nach Ostindien.* Zeitschrift für Sozial- und Wirtschaftsgeschichte, 7, 1899, p. 44 et seq.; S. Takáts: *A dunai hajózás a XVI. és XVII. században* (The Danube shipping in the 16th and 17th centuries). Magyar Gazdaságtörténelmi Szemle (Hungarian Economic History Review), 1900, pp. 182–176, 193–206; H. v. Srbik: *Der staatliche Exporthandel Österreichs von Leopold I. bis Maria Theresia. Untersuchungen zur Wirtschaftsgeschichte Österreichs im Zeitalter des Merkantilismus,* Wien–Leipzig, 1907, pp. 68–70, 298–299; K. Fajkmajer: *Zur Geschichte der ersten orientalischen Kompagnie.* Mitteilungen des Instituts für österreichische Geschichtsforschung, 30, 1909, p. 634 et seq.; H. Hassinger: *Die erste Wiener orientalische Handelskompagnie 1667–1683.* Vierteljahrschrift für Sozial- und Wirtschaftsgeschichte, 35, 1942, pp. 1–53; H. Halm: *Habsburgs Osthandel im 18. Jahrhundert,* München, 1954.

[4] M. Herzfeld: *Zur Orienthandelspolitik Österreichs unter Maria Theresia in der Zeit 1740–1771.* Archiv für Österreichische Geschichte, 108, Wien, 1919; A. Beer: *Die orientalische Politik Österreichs seit 1774,* Prag–Leipzig, 1883; H. Marczali: *II. József első terjeszkedési tervei* (The first expansionist plans of Joseph II). Századok (Centuries), Budapest, 1880, p. 194 et seq.

[5] For the motives and circumstances of the commission (1784–1787): L. Thallóczy: *Pray György s a magyar korona melléktartományai* (G. Pray and the dominions of the Hungarian Crown). Századok, 1888, pp. 523–532. — Pray's manuscript, which emphasized the importance of the Danube-line for Levantine and Asian commerce, became known to the public before long; but it was printed only a few decades later: G. Pray–G. Fejér: *Commentarii historici de Bosniae, Serviae ac Bulgariae, tum Valachiae, Moldaviae ac Bessarabiae, cum Regno Hungariae statu.* Budae, 1837.

[6] For similar proposals, drafted by commercial experts in Vienna (1799, 1804), with the aim to promote the Danube–Levantine traffic: A. Beer: *Die österreichische Handelspolitik im neunzehnten Jahrhundert,* Wien, 1891, pp. 37–38, 434–435.

overland routes; moreover, he added, supplies of oriental goods, coming from the region of the Black Sea, had been transported through Transylvania and Hungary.[7] This historical picture — one of the first to formulate the thesis in question — was evoked by the Hungarian economist in connection with his actual commercial proposals and he may have felt his historical outlook supported by contemporary developments. I mean, in the years following 1806, eastern trade was in fact compelled to avail itself of overland routes, owing to the continental and sea blockade; and the Habsburg Monarchy,[8] Hungary and Austria really did join in this Levantine traffic rather eagerly.

Similar views were put forward simultaneously in German historiography. (I would like to stress, *simultaneously*, exactly at the same time.) Contrary to previously prevalent attitudes,[9] the Göttingen professor Arnold Ludwig Heeren, in his work *Versuch einer Entwicklung der Folgen der Kreuzzüge für Europa*, written for the competition of the Institut de France and published first in French under the title *Essai sur l'influence des croisades* (translated by Charles Villers) and his younger colleague, Karl Dietrich Hüllmann, in his famous book *Geschichte des byzantischen Handels bis zum Ende der Kreuzzüge*, written for the competition of the Göttingen Societät der Wissenschaften, both stated the opinion that not later than from the 8th century up to the middle of the 13th century the main route of Levantine trade from Constantinople to South German towns passed through Hungary (along the Danube or on the river itself).[10] As it has already been suggested by the eminent medievalist, Franz Bastian,[11] we can take it for granted that both to Heeren and to Hüllmann — whose works were published in the same year, 1808 — it was Napoleon's eastern policy, so frequently alluded to between 1806 and 1808 as purporting to establish an overland connection with the Levant, what is more, with India, through Constantinople and

[7] G. v. Berzevitzy: *Ansicht des asiatisch-europäischen Welthandels nach dem jetzigen Zeitbedürfnis betrachtet.* Pest, 1808, pp. 43–54; *Über die Beförderung des ungarischen Commerzes. Ein gedrängter deutscher Auszug aus der ungedruckten lateinischen, im November 1809 geschriebenen Abhandlung.* Archiv für Geographie, Historie, Staats und Kriegskunst, 8, Wien, 1817, pp. 185–186; *Die Erweiterung des nordischen Handels, dem hohen Wiener-Congress unterthänigst dargestellt.* Wien, 1814, pp. 5–12; etc.

[8] Mémoire sur le commerce de l'Illyrie avec le Levant (1810), Magyar Gazdaságtörténelmi Szemle (Hungarian Economic History Review), 1899, pp. 173–177; S. G. Meisner: *Statistische Darstellung des Breslauischen Handels im ganzen Umfange,* Breslau, 1807, pp. 141–143; M. Schwartner: *Statistik des Königreichs Ungern,* 2. ed., Ofen, 1809, I, pp. 137–138. — Cf. L. Ungár: *Szempontok a magyar polgári osztály kialakulásának vizsgálatához* (The rise of the bourgeoisie in Hungary. Research contributions). Századok, 1942, pp. 315–318; A. Fugier: *La révolution française et l'empire napoléonien.* Histoire des relations internationales publiées sous la direction de P. Renouvin, IV. Paris, 1954. p. 235.

[9] Summed up for instance by J. v. Hormayr: *Historische Bruchstücke über das tyrolische Strassenwesen und den Transitohandel dieses Landes.* Historisch-statistisches Archiv für Süddeutschland, 4, Frankfurt–Leipzig, 1807, pp. 226–227. — Cf. A. Robert: *L'Idée nationale autrichienne et les guerres de Napoléon. L'Apostolat du baron Hormayr et le salon de Caroline Pickler,* Paris, 1933.

[10] A. H. L. Heeren: *Versuch einer Entwicklung der Folgen der Kreuzzüge für Europa,* Göttingen, 1808. pp. 309, 312, 322, 337, 386, 389; K. D. Hüllmann: *Geschichte des byzantischen Handels bis zum Ende der Kreuzzüge,* Frankfurt an der Oder, 1808, pp. 73–99, 105–106.

[11] F. Bastian: *Die Legende vom Donauhandel im Frühmittelalter.* Vierteljahrschrift für Sozial- und Wirtschaftsgeschichte, 22, 1929, p. 301.

Persia as against British naval power,[12] it was Napoleon's eastern policy which served as a contemporary parallel and incentive in shaping their conception of the overland route of medieval eastern commerce *along the river Danube*. All the more so as after the Peace of Tilsit Göttingen became part of the Kingdom of Westphalen founded for Jerome by the Emperor, and the university professors have rather quickly conformed to the new political conditions.[13] So, that is the *first* source of the idea, and that is one variant of the thesis in question.

But there is *another* source and another variant as well. According to this other variant, in the 14th and 15th centuries Levantine trade forwarded merchandise to Central Europe *through Transylvania*. Remarkably enough, this other variant also derives chiefly from Göttingen University scholarship, but in another context of historical and political conditions. This theory, based partly on source references given by Transylvanian German (Saxon) historians,[14] was formulated first by the Göttingen Professor August Ludwig Schlözer, a historian of Europe-wide renown, in his book *Kritische Sammlungen zur Geschichte der Deutschen in Siebenbürgen* published as early as 1795–97, with an aim to demonstrate the historical title of the Germans (Saxons) to maintain their autonomous community within Transylvania.[15] Although this work churned up a violent storm as regards political and national problems,[16] his commercial idea concerning the outstanding role of Transylvanian Germans (Saxons) in medieval Levant trade seemed to be acceptable. It was taken over and elaborated further by Johann Christian Engel, a German-speaking Hungarian historian, in his works published in 1804, 1805 and 1813.[17]

[12] Cf. P. Bertrand: *M. de Talleyrand, l'Autriche et la question d'Orient en 1805*. Revue historique, XIV, 39, 1889, pp. 63–75; É. Driault: *La politique orientale de Napoléon. Sébastiani et Gardane 1806–1808*, Paris, 1904, pp. 20, 56–68, 181–184, 207–213, 242–256, 310.

[13] The political attitudes of the Göttingen University's professors in those days were sharply characterized in the letters of the famous Göttingen classical philologist C. G. Heyne, partly published by L. Thallóczy: *Johann Christian von Engel und seine Korrespondenz 1770–1814*, München–Leipzig, 1915, pp. 39, 85–94, 101–116. — Cf. G. v. Selle: *Die Georg-August-Universität zu Göttingen 1737–1937*, Göttingen, 1937, pp. 142, 210–220, 370.

[14] J. C. Eder: *De initiis juribusque primaevis Saxonum Transsilvanorum commentatio*, Viennae, 1792, p. 139; G. Herrmann: *Die Grundverfassungen der Sachsen in Siebenbürgen und ihre Schicksale. Ein Beitrag zur Geschichte der Deutschen ausser Deutschland*, Offenbach, 1792, pp. 50–52.

[15] A. L. Schlözer: *Kritische Sammlungen zur Geschichte der Deutschen in Siebenbürgen*, Göttingen, 1797, III, pp. 678–682. For the story of the work's creation: Fr. Teutsch: *A. L. Schlözers Kritische Sammlungen zur Geschichte der Deutschen in Siebenbürgen* — J. Bedeus v. Scharberg: *Briefwechsel über Entstehung und Herausgabe der Kritischen Sammlungen*. Archiv des Vereines für siebenbürgische Landeskunde, NF XXVII, Hermannstadt, 1897, pp. 263–330; cf. Gy. Szekfű: *Az erdélyi szász történetírás* (The historiography of the Transylvanian Saxons). Magyarságtudomány (Hungarology), 2, 1943, pp. 329–339.

[16] See Gy. Aranka's criticism in Allgemeine Literatur-Zeitung, I, Jena–Leipzig, 1798. col. 417–440; J. C. Eder: *Gebührliche Notwehr gegen die Ausfälle des Recensenten in der Jenaer Allgemeinen Literatur-Zeitung*. Siebenbürgische Quartal-Schrift, VI, Hermannstadt, 1798, p. 359 et seq.; E. Jancsó: *Gyarmathi Sámuel levelei* (The letters of S. Gyarmathi). Magyar Nyelv (Hungarian Language), 1944, pp. 222, 361–362; 1950, p. 156.

[17] J. Ch. v. Engel: *Geschichte des Ungrischen Reichs und seiner Nebenländer*, IV, *Geschichte der Moldau und Walachey*, Halle, 1804, p. 127; Vorrede zur D. Cornides' Bruchstücke zur Geschichte der städtischen Cultur und des Gewerbefleisses in Ungern, *Beiträge zur Topographie des Königreichs Ungern*, IV, Wien, 1805, p. 5; *Geschichte des Ungrischen Reichs*, II, Wien, 1813, pp. 149–151.

The first thesis of the early- and high-medieval *Danube* traffic of oriental commodities and the second idea of the late-medieval *Transylvanian* route of Levant trade were connected then by historians in the 1830's and 40's. That is to say, amalgamation of the two variants of the thesis in question was fulfilled partly by the Hungarian Mihály Horváth, in his book on Hungary's medieval industry and commerce, written for the competition in 1835 of the Hungarian Academy of Sciences and partly by the paper of Friedrich Hann, a Transylvanian Saxon, published under the title *Zur Geschichte des siebenbürgischen Handels* in the year 1848.[18] Both authors made references mostly to Heeren, Hüllmann, Schlözer and Engel. In addition, they quoted other German writers, G. Gülich and J. Hormayr who, in turn, relied on Hüllmann as their main source as well.[19]

Hormayr, Hann and Horváth alike believed that after the impending transformation of the East, following the collapse of the Ottoman Empire, world trade between Asia and Europe would again be transacted overland rather than by sea, in a similar way as it happened in the Middle Ages prior to the fall of Constantinople, or prior to the discovery of the Cape-route to India. Their aim was undoubtedly and expressively to substantiate historically the contemporary claims and aspirations, from the German, Transylvanian Saxon and Hungarian sides respectively, to play the greatest role possible in the international traffic to be renewed in the Levant.[20]

This is how the views of historians on medieval eastern trade came to be influenced by contemporary conditions, by the developments, requirements and hopes of the Eastern Question, in the Napoleonic Era as well as around the middle of the 19th century.

[18] M. Horváth: *Az ipar és kereskedés története Magyarországban a XVI. század elejéig* (The history of industry and commerce in Hungary up to the beginning of the 16th century), Buda, 1842, second edition: Pest, 1868, pp. 4–24, 41–46, 77–82, 128, 153.; (Fr. Hann): *Zur Geschichte des siebenbürgischen Handels vom Jahre 972 bis 1845.* Archiv des Vereines für siebenbürgische Landeskunde, III, Hermannstadt, 1848, pp. 140–145, 154–159, 168–169, 267–268.

[19] G. v. Gülich: *Geschichtliche Darstellung des Handels, der Gewerbe und des Ackerbaus der bedeutendsten handeltreibenden Staaten unsrer Zeit,* IV, Jena, 1844, pp. 143–148, 167, 528–529 (728–729); J. v. Hormayr: *Der Deutsche Handel nach dem Morgenlande und die freie Donau.* Taschenbuch für die väterländische Geschichte, XXX (NF XVII), Berlin, 1846, pp. 262–263. — Similarly Hüllmann's work was referred to in this question by the contemporary French expert of Levantine trade, while arguing: "Depuis les croisades Constantinople fut l'entrepôt des marchandises de l'Orient et de l'Occident. — Il paraît qu'une partie de ces denrées orientales s'écoulait par le Danube en Allemagne . . . Les Hongrois livraient aux Grecs, en échange de ces denrées, des ouvrages en bois et en fer, des armes, de la sellerie." — G. B. Depping: *Histoire du commerce entre le Levant et l'Europe depuis les croisades jusqu'à la fondation des colonies d'Amérique*, I, Paris, 1830, pp. 117–118; cf. pp. 194–200.

[20] Hormayr: *op. cit.*, pp. 258–261, 267, 272, Hann: *op. cit.*, 281–282, 316–319, 333–335; M. Horváth: *Az ipar és kereskedés története Magyarországban a három utolsó század alatt* (The history of industry and commerce in Hungary during the last three centuries), Buda, 1840, second edition: Pest, 1868, pp. 231–244, 356–359. — Cf. L. Szabó v. Bártfa: *Der Briefwechsel des Freiherrn Joseph Hormayr mit dem Grafen Stephan Széchenyi.* Ungarische Jahrbücher, XIII. Berlin–Leipzig, 1933, pp. 139–146.

2

Similar opinions were represented by German, Austrian, Hungarian, and Transylvanian Saxon historians from the 1850's to the 70's.[21]

However, by the last decades of the 19th century there came a turning-point in the historiographic "destiny" of the thesis in question. The change in international scholarship was started by the comprehensive work of Wilhelm Heyd on medieval Levantine trade[22] (1879), but statements of this kind soon appeared in Hungarian literature as well. Dezső Csánki expressed the opinion (in the year 1880) that Hungary's traffic with the East was carried on via the Dalmatian towns of the Adriatic shores in the time of Louis of Anjou, who was king of Hungary from 1342 to 1382. Hungarian and Transylvanian merchants, Csánki suggested, had often visited Dalmatia and brought back eastern produce as well as manufactured goods from Northern Italy. Thus, contrary to former views, Hungary, he emphasized, "obtained oriental commodities not through Transylvania, but from the shores of the Adriatic."[23]

Heyd's standard work, Csánki's study, and the famous paper of another German author, Jastrow, *Über Welthandelsstrassen in der Geschichte des Abendlandes*[24] accomplished the turn-about in the historiographic "destiny" of the thesis of Levantine trade having passed through medieval Hungary. Former approval now lost ground and met with a flat refusal. The number of historians increased to declare unanimously that Levantine goods and oriental spices had reached medieval Hungary and South Germany not by an overland route from the Black Sea region or the shores of the Eastern Mediterranean, but exclusively from the shores of the Adriatic, to where they had been transported by Mediterranean sea-borne trade.[25]

[21] J. Falke: *Die Geschichte des deutschen Handels im Mittelalter*. Leipzig, 1859, I, pp. 65, 78, 106, 131; W. Kiesselbach: *Der Gang des Welthandels. Entwicklung des europäischen Völkerlebens im Mittelalter*, Stuttgart, 1860, pp. 36–38; A. Beer: *Allgemeine Geschichte des Welthandels*, Wien, 1860, I, pp. 171–172; G. D. Teutsch: *Geschichte der Siebenbürger Sachsen für das sächsische Volk*, second edition, Leipzig, 1874, I, pp. 129–130; C. J. Jireček: *Die Heerstrasse von Belgrad nach Constantinopel und die Balkanpässe*, Prag, 1877, pp. III, 103; I. Hajnik: *Adalékok a magyar kereskedelem történetéhez a vegyes házakbeli királyok alatt* (Contributions to the history of the Hungarian commerce under the kings from "different dynasties"). Századok, 1868, p. 148; L. Thallóczy: *Utazás a Levantéban. A keleti kereskedelem története Magyarországon* (A travel to the Levant. The history of oriental trade in Hungary), Budapest, 1882, pp. 82–85; F. Salamon: *Budapest története* (The history of Budapest), Budapest, 1885, II, pp. 148, 331, 418–426, III. p. 209.

[22] W. Heyd: *Geschichte des Levantehandels im Mittelalter*, I–II, Stuttgart, 1879. — Its augmented French translation was published a few years later: *Histoire du commerce du Levant au Moyen Age*, I–II, Leipzig, 1885–1886.

[23] D. Csánki: *Hazánk kereskedelmi viszonyai I. Lajos korában* (Hungary's trade relations in the time of Louis I), Budapest, 1880, pp. 31–40.

[24] J. Jastrow: *Über Welthandelsstrassen in der Geschichte des Abendlandes*. Volkswirtschaftliche Zeitfragen, 63–64, Berlin, 1887, pp. 17–23.

[25] For similar views as early as in the 1880's: K. W. Nitzsch: *Geschichte des deutschen Volkes*, Leipzig, 1883, II. p. 165; W. Götz: *Die Verkehrswege im Dienste des Welthandels. Eine historisch-geographische Untersuchung*, Stuttgart, 1888. p. 592. — The former "Danube-theory" was presented, in turn, even in the 1890's by A. Luschin v. Ebengreuth: *Die Handelspolitik der österreichischen Herrscher im Mittelalter*. Almanach der kaiserlichen Akademie der Wissenschaften in Wien, 1893, pp. 4, 8; G. v. Below, *Das ältere deutsche Städtewesen und Bürgertum*, Bielefeld–Leipzig, 1898, pp. 8, 11. — It is worth mentioning, however, that in the second edition of Below's study this reference was already left out, obviously under the influence of Heyd; cf. Bastian: *op. cit.*, p. 300.

When the factors and motives lying *outside* scientific research are examined for their bearing on this turn-about in historiography, it seems highly probable that a role may have been played in this change of opinions by the building and opening of the Suez Canal (1869), a momentous event in the development of world economy, followed by a rapid expansion of international trade. By the last decades of the 19th century it became evident that the hopes attached in the first half of the century to the predominance of overland world trade routes to be renewed parallel to the decline of the Turkish Empire had been exaggerated. This change of understanding is obvious from the paper of Jastrow who stressed that under recent conditions of international commerce main routes of world trade could not be referred to any longer in the old sense of the term, since the whole globe had been covered with a compact network of trade routes. If, nevertheless, some sort of analogy to earlier main routes is sought under contemporary circumstances, Jastrow added, this was not to be found in any overland route, but rather in the sea-route from England to East India, over the Mediterranean and the Suez Canal.[26]

This understanding of economic changes may have been accompanied (as for Austria and Hungary) by the realization of some political changes. I mean that the decisions of the Congress of Berlin (1878) concerning the Eastern Question, the subsequent occupation of Bosnia-Hercegovina and further political developments shifted orientation of the Austro-Hungarian Monarchy from the eastern to the western parts of the Balkan Peninsula, from the Black Sea region to the Adriatic, in contrast to earlier intentions of Habsburg foreign policy.[27] And the Austrian and Hungarian historians somewhat conformed to the political trends as well.

As regards the *scientific* argumentation of the historians of the new trend, they referred, generally speaking, to similar issues. On the one hand they drew attention to the obvious exaggerations of the earlier theory and pointed to the weak foundations of the belief that the main route of medieval trade between the Orient and the Occident might have led through Transylvania, and that Transylvanian Saxon merchants might have maintained direct relations with commercial centres in the eastern region of the Mediterranean, such as Smyrna or Alexandria.[28]

[26] Jastrow,: *op. cit.*, pp. 1–2, 52–59. — A similar point of view was taken by a Hungarian expert on communication and transport problems as early as around the mid-1860's. Though adopting the thesis of the medieval long-haul trade having passed through Hungary, he pointed out that "the Danube route had lost its one-time importance in world trade"; "Great Britain and the western nations would not communicate with Asiatic territories via Hungary, albeit the shortest way from London to India is that leading through this country"; "the trade with Arabia, Persia and India would be transacted via the Suez Canal". — J. Hunfalvy: *Hazánk közlekedési eszközeiről* (On the transportation facilities of Hungary), Budapest, 1867, pp. 2–3, 17–19, 25–29, 50–51. — Cf. H. L. Hoskins: *British Routes to India*, London, 1928; A. T. Wilson: *The Suez Canal. Its Past, Present and Future*, Oxford, 1939, pp. 31–42.

[27] Beer: *op. cit.* (1883), pp. 56, 65, 92, 261, 383–385, 560, 573, 751–752; P. Hanák- I. Diószegi: *Magyarország története 1849–1918* (The history of Hungary, 1849–1918), Budapest, 1972, pp. 205–216; E. Palotás: *A Balkán-kérdés az osztrák-magyar és az orosz diplomáciában a XIX. század végén* (The Balkan Question in Austro-Hungarian and Russian diplomacy at the end of the 19th century), Budapest, 1972, pp. 9–10, 127–132, 226–233; B. Jelavich: *The Ottoman Empire, the Great Powers, and the Straits Question 1870–1887*, Bloomington, 1973. pp. 57–77.

[28] O. Meltzl: *Az erdélyi szászok ipara és kereskedelme a XIV. és XV. században* (Industry and commerce of the Transylvanian Saxons in the 14th and 15th centuries). Századok,

This argument has to be regarded as justified, but by no means as conclusive. From the fact that Transylvanian Saxons did not maintain direct connections with commercial centres of the Eastern Mediterranean, it does not follow that business could not have been transacted with Balkan-Levantine merchants acting as intermediaries. Moreover, the lack of direct relations with Mediterranean ports does not preclude commercial connections with the region of the Black Sea. Finally, the assertion that this route was not the *main* line of oriental trade, does not disprove the possibility of *one* branch of Levant trade having still passed through the Roumanian principality Wallachia to Transylvania and Hungary (even if Levantine merchandise was not forwarded further to West-Central Europe from Transylvania and Hungary).

On the other hand, all the adherents of the new theory made reference to Wilhelm Heyd and quoted his authority as against the former view. For instance, the Transylvanian Saxon historian Oscar Meltzl in his paper published in the early 1890's lost no time in emphasizing his "full agreement" with the latest results of German scientific research concerned with the history of medieval Levant trade and in quoting Heyd.[29] However, let us look more closely into Heyd's view on the subject.

"There is not much ground to support the widely accepted hypothesis", wrote the eminent German scholar, "that until the early 13th century oriental spices were transported to Germany from Constantinople and up the Danube and that it was only after the conquest of Constantinople by the Latins [that is after the fourth Crusade, 1204] that Italy became the source of spices for Germany." In this connection, he argued, "little attention was paid to the unfriendly and turbulent conditions prevailing even in the 12th century in the countries situated between the Greek Empire and Hungary. Armies of crusaders," Heyd stressed, "may have fought their way through these parts, but regular caravan trade could hardly have developed there."[30]

Thus Heyd's attitude is perfectly clear: he refused — and with good reason — the thesis of early-medieval transit trade on (or along) the Danube, but he did not touch at all the late-medieval Transylvanian route of Levant transports. However, to those who referred to him, his criticism of the "first variant" of the thesis served as an incentive to refuse the "second variant" as well.[31]

1892, p. 721; O. Fr. Jickeli: *Der Handel der Siebenbürger Sachsen in seiner geschichtlichen Entwicklung*. Archiv des Vereines für siebenbürgische Landeskunde, NF XXXIX, Hermannstadt, 1913, pp. 41–49; B. Borcsiczky: *A politikai változások befolyása Magyarország kereskedelmi útjaira a XIV–XV. században* (The influence of political changes on the trade routes of Hungary in the 14th and 15th centuries), Budapest, 1914, pp. 3–8.

[29] O. Meltzl: *Über Gewerbe und Handel der Sachsen im XIV. und XV. Jahrhundert*, Hermannstadt, 1892, p. 33.

[30] Heyd: *op. cit.*, I, pp. 94–95, II, 717–718.

[31] There were, nevertheless, two Hungarian economic historians in the early 20th century who interpreted Heyd's view correctly, and refused, in accordance with him, anything else than the theory of the medieval *Danube* route of oriental goods. Regrettably enough, these historians were not concerned with the problem of the *Transylvanian* route of Levant trade: S. Takáts: *A dunai hajózás a XVI. és XVII. században* (The Danube shipping in the 16th and 17th centuries). Magyar Gazdaságtörténelmi Szemle (Hungarian Economic History Review), Budapest, 1900, p. 170; F. Kováts: *Adalékok a dunai hajózás és a dunai vámok történetéhez az Anjouk korában* (Contributions to the history of Danube shipping and Danube tolls in the time of the Anjous). Magyar Gazdaságtörténelmi Szemle, 1901, pp. 433–434.

It was up to further arguments, therefore, to bridge this obvious gap. And the adherents of the new trend brought forward further arguments, indeed. They claimed there was no reliable documentary evidence to confirm the role of Transylvanian towns in supplying oriental spices from the eastern direction, from the Black Sea region. What is more, they referred to charters of King Louis of Anjou which, in their opinion, were to be interpreted as practically precluding the possibility of spices having been imported by the Transylvanian route.

What sort of charters are meant here? Royal charters which favoured journeys of merchants from Transylvanian Saxon towns to Dalmatia, notably Zara (Jadra, Zadar), with a stereotyped motivation: "in order that the Realm of Hungary should abound in goods supplied by maritime trade" *(ideo, ut regnum Hungariae rebus et bonis maritimis locupletetur)*.[32]

Csánki and Meltzl alike were of the opinion that two charters of King Louis threw clear light on the place from where Transylvanian Saxons purchased pepper and other oriental spices. "King Louis had declared in the charters of 1367 and 1370," these historians asserted, "that maritime goods should be imported to Hungary from the Adriatic-Dalmatian town Zara by the Transylvanian Saxons ... This fact proves," they concluded, "the untenableness of the idea of Levantine commodities having passed from the Black Sea through Transylvania and Hungary."[33]

And this pattern of argumentation as against the *second* variant of the thesis recurred from time to time in the historiography of the subsequent decades: in works published before the First World War[34] as well as in monographs of the interwar period.[35]

As concerns the *first* variant of the thesis, in turn, there have been made attempts at its rehabilitation in historiography now and again. These attempts, prior to and mainly at the time of the First World War, were closely connected with the claims and endeavours of German imperialism to establish an overland route and outlet for expansion to the Middle East along the Danube and through Turkey, challenging English naval power and sea blockade — somewhat similarly to Napoleon's eastern policy a hundred or so years ago.[36] The actual aspirations of politicians and economists — the "Berlin–Baghdad Railway Project", the so-called "Mitteleuropa-Plan," etc. — found, this time again, an echo in historical writings which resuscitated the century-old idea of the Constantinople–Danube route of medieval "Asiatic–European

[32] See f. e. G. Wenzel: *Budai regesták* (Digests of charters concerning Buda). Magyar Történelmi Tár (Hungarian Historical Archive), IV, Pest, 1857, p. 149.

[33] Csánki: *op. cit.*, pp. 34–36; Meltzl: *op. cit.*, pp. 731–732.

[34] See above Footnote 28.

[35] See below Footnotes 44–45.

[36] Driault: *op. cit.*, p. 7; Fr. Naumann: *Mitteleuropa*, Berlin, 1915; M. Jastrow: *The War and the Bagdad Railway. The Story of Asia Minor and its Relation to the Present Conflict*, Philadelphia–London, 1917, p. 100; E. M. Earle: *Turkey, the Great Powers and the Baghdad Railway. A Study in Imperialism*, New York, 1923, pp. 1–8 (Chapter I: *An Ancient Trade Route is Revived*), p. 33; F. H. Bode: *Der Kampf um die Bagdadbahn 1903–1914. Ein Beitrag zur Geschichte der deutsch-englischen Beziehungen*, Breslau, 1941, pp. VI, 11; K. Irinyi: *A Naumann-féle "Mitteleuropa"-tervezet és a magyar politikai közvélemény* (The "Mitteleuropa"-Plan of Naumann and the Hungarian political public opinion), Budapest, 1963, pp. 13–14, 42–53, 73–93, 110–112; Iu. A. Pissariev: *Germano-avstriskie plany na Balkanach v gody pervoi mirovoi voiny*. Novaia i noveishaia istoria, Moskva, 1973, No. 2, pp. 79–82.

world trade".[37] However, these attempts at the historical rehabilitation of the Danube-route soon came to be antiquated by subsequent political developments and soon came to be discredited by erudite scholars:[38] by the Hungarian historian Sándor Domanovszky (1918),[39] and by the German medievalist Franz Bastian (1929) who expanded and completed Heyd's argumentation convincingly.[40]

This is why the great Belgian historian Henri Pirenne who, in the 1920's, explained his famous thesis of Mediterranean sea-borne trade having died out between the Orient and the Occident owing to the Islamic expansion from the 8th up to the 11th century,[41] deemed it necessary to add to his presentation: "One could suggest, and it has been suggested now and then, that the Danube Valley had replaced the Mediterranean as the big transport route between the Orient and the Occident. This case would have ensued, indeed, if the Danube had not been blocked up at first by the Avars, and shortly afterwards by the Hungarians."[42] True enough, his motivation was far from perfect, but the important thing in this context was that the "Pirenne thesis",[43] too, did exclude the "Danube-thesis", i.e., the *first* variant of the theory of oriental goods having been transported to Central Europe through medieval Hungary.

At the same time the *second* variant of this concept, i.e., the Black Sea route of Levantine trade to Transylvania was rejected, as mentioned above, by the followers of Csánki's and Meltzl's argumentation quite flatly, and the Adriatic–Dalmatian route was declared to have been the only and sole commercial line to procure Levant goods for late-medieval Hungary.

[37] H. Zimmerer: *Orienthandel und Donauschiffahrt*, 1914; H. Wendt: *Schlesien und der Orient. Ein geschichtlicher Rückblick*, Breslau, 1916, pp. 52, 55, 191, 209; C. V. Suppan: *Die Donau und ihre Schiffahrt*, Wien, 1917; H. Grothe: *Die Donaustrasse in ihrer wirtschaftsgeschichtlichen Bedeutung*. Die freie Donau, 1918, pp. 189, 221. — Cf. Bastian, *op. cit.*, 300.

[38] A Hungarian scholar, though accepting this main overland route as for the Middle Ages, argued as early as in the depth of the war that the renewal of this line was absurd in the 20th century, just as (or still more than) it had proved unattainable in Napoleonic times: E. Czóbel: *Berzeviczy Gergely javaslata a kontinens vámuniójáról. Közép-európai törekvések a 19. század elején* (G. Berzeviczy's proposal of the continental customs union. Middle-European projects in the early 19th century). Huszadik Század (Twentieth Century), Budapest, 1916, pp. 209–221, 391–411.

[39] S. Domanovszky: *Die Vergangenheit der ungarischen Donau-Handelsschiffahrt*. Ungarische Jahrbücher, II, Berlin–Leipzig, 1922, pp. 161–187. (Hungarian edition four years earlier).

[40] Bastian: *op. cit.*, pp. 289–330.

[41] H. Pirenne: *Mahomet et Charlemagne*. Revue belge de philologie et d'histoire. I, 1922, pp. 77–86; *Une contraste économique: Mérovingiens et Carolingiens*. Revue belge de philologie et d'histoire. II, 1923, pp. 223–235; *Les villes du Moyen Age*, Bruxelles, 1927, p. 7. et seq.

[42] H. Pirenne: *La civilisation occidentale au Moyen Age du XIe au milieu du XVe siècle*, Histoire générale, VIII, Paris 1933, p. 11. — Further motivation in obvious concordance with Heyd, but for the 13th century: p. 131: "Le magnifique débouché que le Danube ouvre sur la mer Noire demeure inutilisé . . . Le faible développement de la Hongrie et au-delà les troubles incessants des régions balkaniques interdisent tout trafic sur son cours inférieur".

[43] For the debate on the Pirenne thesis — which goes beyond the framework of the present paper — see H. Laurent: *Les travaux de M. Henri Pirenne sur la fin du monde antique et les débuts du Moyen Age*. Byzantion, VII, 1932; A. Riising: *The Fate of Henri Pirenne's Thesis on the Consequences of Islamic Expansion*. Classica et Medievalia, XIII, 1952; Ashtor: *op. cit.*, pp. 187–190.

Moreover, from the latter attitude there sprang the bold idea — which, paradoxically, was not far short of the exaggerations of Hüllmann's or Schlözer's theory — ascribing to 14th century-Hungary a Europe-wide significance in Levantine trade, yet not on the Danube-line or the Black Sea–Transylvanian route, but on the Adriatic–Dalmatian one.[44] "The Peace of Zara (1358) liberated Dalmatian towns from the overlordship of Venice," explained the Hungarian historian Fekete Nagy. "King Louis saw to it," he continued, quoting the royal charters mentioned above, "that the oriental commodities should be forwarded by Saxon merchants, to reach not only Transylvania and Hungary but also other countries . . . , Polish, Bohemian and German markets." This was the excessive conclusion of the new concept on the "Hungarian world trade" in the 14th century.[45]

Some obvious exaggerations of this "Dalmatian hypothesis" were already pointed out in the early 1940's;[46] yet, up to the present, the arguments used since Csánki and Meltzl have not been critically analyzed so far, more precisely: there has been no analysis of *all* the charters granted by King Louis of Anjou to promote *Dalmatian* trade; nor has the question been discussed in the light of documentary evidence whether or not oriental goods had reached Transylvania from the eastern direction, i. e. from the *Black Sea* region.

3.1

It must be admitted that, at first sight, the arguments advanced in favour of the Dalmatian route seem to be convincing. If Transylvanian Saxon merchants, those of Nagyszeben (Hermannstadt, Sibiu), and Brassó (Kronstadt, Braşov), actually had to travel west as far as Dalmatia, especially Zara (Zadar), to buy "sea-borne goods", there is hardly any likelihood that they might have acquired them nearer, from the eastern direction, from the Black Sea region.

However, upon thorough insight into the sources, the weak points of this argumentation become more and more conspicuous.

First of all it is noted that after the Peace of Zara (1358), in which Venice was obliged to renounce the Dalmatian towns on behalf of the Hungarian kingdom, King Louis of Anjou granted charters, favouring the trade with Dalmatia, not only to Transylvanian Saxon burghers, but also to other, Hungarian merchants. Moreover, charters of this kind went in chronological order first not to the Transylvanian southern-border town of Szeben (Sibiu), but to the Hungarian western-border town of Pozsony (Bratislava). This very

[44] A. Pleidell: *A nyugatra irányuló magyar külkereskedelem a középkorban* (Hungary's foreign trade with the West in the Middle Ages), Budapest, 1925, pp. 53–56, 60.

[45] A. Fekete Nagy: *A magyar–dalmát kereskedelem* (The Hungarian–Dalmatian Trade), Budapest, 1926, pp. 35–64. — As a matter of fact, not even the Danube-thesis entirely disappeared from historiography of the interwar period. Further efforts to preserve this route of "world trade" in favour of the medieval (11th and 12th centuries) Hungary and Germany: K. Weller: *Die Hauptverkehrsstrasse zwischen dem westlichen und südöstlichen Europa.* Württembergische Vergangenheit, Stuttgart, 1932, pp. 89–128; L. Glaser: *Der Levantehandel über Ungarn im 11. und 12. Jahrhundert.* Ungarische Jahrbücher, XIII, Berlin-Leipzig, 1933, pp. 356–363; Gy. Komoróczy: *A kereskedelem és ipar Szent István korában* (Trade and industry in the time of King St. Stephen), Budapest, 1938, pp. 22, 29–33, 49.

[46] D. Huszti: *Olasz-magyar kereskedelmi kapcsolatok a középkorban* (Commercial relations between Italy and Hungary in the Middle Ages), Budapest, 1941, pp. 10–17, 74–77.

charter dating from 1361 is the first to formulate the stereotype motivation: "*ideo, ut regnum nostrum Hungariae diversarum rerum maritimarum ubertate et affluentia locupletetur.*"[47] At this point, however, it is obvious that Pozsony merchants could also cover their needs for sea-borne goods, among them oriental spices, on a market lying much nearer than Dalmatia, namely in Vienna which had been maintaining lively commercial relations with Venice for a long time, using mainly the famous Semmering–Judenburg–Villach–Tarvisio–Pontebba route.[48]

Actually, import of spices from Vienna to Pozsony was common in the second half of the 14th century, too. As a matter of fact, the embargo introduced against Austrian commerce in 1324 by King Louis's father and predecessor, Charles Robert, in retribution to the "Stapelrecht" of Vienna, was repealed by Louis in 1346, permitting Austrian merchants to sell their goods in Hungary. In the following decades trade with Vienna began to flourish again, bringing supplies to the Hungarian border towns of Sopron and —chiefly — Pozsony, and, from here, on the Danube waterway, to Buda.[49]

Information about merchandise imported from Vienna to Hungary also came down to us in the charters issued by King Louis and Queen Elizabeth in 1366, 1380, and 1381, protecting Austrian merchants from the payment of excessive customs duties on the goods they usually brought to Hungary, notably pepper, wool fabrics, hardware and so on.[50] Hence we may draw the lesson that after the Peace of Zara, King Louis bestowed favours, in the form of Dalmatian imports, upon those Hungarian towns, too, which could and did purchase Levant commodities, among them spices from other (western) markets as well.[51] Favours of this kind extended to Transylvanian Saxon towns, therefore, by no means preclude the possibility that Transylvanian merchants may also have acquired supplies of spices from other (eastern) markets, too.

Indeed, several charters of King Louis furnish further information in this respect. They say that Dalmatia, having been wrested from the "tyrannous hands of our rival, the usurper" (that is, Venice), "*universis mercatoribus regni nostri aditus pateat mercantias faciendi*", access to the Dalmatian coast should be opened to every single merchant of the Kingdom, as formulated now

[47] G. Fejér: *Codex diplomaticus Hungariae ecclesiasticus ac civilis*, IX, 7, Budae, 1842, pp. 198–199. — Five years later (1366) the burghers of Pozsony were given another charter, exempting them from customs duties, "*quotiens . . . aliquas res mercimoniales partis maritimae de Dalmatia et de Jadra versus dictam nostram civitatem* [sc. Budam] *deferre et importare voluerint*": Fejér: *Codex diplomaticus*, IX, 3, Budae, 1834, pp. 552–553.

[48] H. Simonsfeld: *Der Fondaco dei Tedeschi in Venedig und die deutsch-venetianischen Handelsbeziehungen*, Stuttgart, 1887, II, pp. 50, 98; Th. Mayer: *Der auswärtige Handel des Herzogtums Österreich im Mittelalter*, Innsbruck, 1909, p. 32; C. Schalk: *Rapporti commerciali tra Venezia e Vienna*. Nuovo Archivio Veneto, NS 23, 1912, pp. 52 et seq.

[49] Pleidell: *op. cit.*, pp. 34–35, 53, 58. — Cf. Kováts: *op. cit.*, pp. 438, 444, 461, 468; T. Smičiklas: *Codex diplomaticus regni Croatiae, Dalmatiae et Sclavoniae*, XII, Zagrabiae, 1914, pp. 588–589.

[50] Fejér: *Codex diplomaticus*, IX, 3, p. 526; IX, 5, Budae, 1834, pp. 384–386, 487–489.

[51] As for the quantity of spice imports from the western direction, relevant data are available only later, about the middle of the 15th century. According to the customs books of Pozsony in the fiscal year 1457–58 (that is from April 1457 to April 1458) 166 2/3 hundredweight of pepper was imported from Vienna to Pozsony, in a value of roundly 5000 Hungarian golden florins: F. Kováts: *Nyugat-Magyarország áruforgalma a XV. században a pozsonyi harmincadkönyv alapján* (The trade of West Hungary in the 15th century on the basis of the Pozsony customs books), Budapest, 1902, pp. 72–81.

and again, first in the above-quoted charter of Pozsony in 1361.[52] Because, as explained more clearly in the royal charter granted to Nagyszeben in 1370, "*hitherto* Saxon merchants have been unable to visit Dalmatian areas of our realm and *did not use to travel there*... owing to the despotic harshness of our rivals [that is Venice] from whose clutches we retrieved these parts with God's help and by a no slight war effort."[53]

In the charter granted to the other Saxon town Brassó in the same year, the object was defined in unmistakable terms, notably that merchants should get used to trips to Dalmatia: "*quod iidem in ipsa via Jadrensi procedere assuescant*" and hereby Hungary should abound in sea-borne commodities.[54]

The situation, then, is perfectly clear: after having taken possession of Dalmatia, King Louis strove to establish economic relations with the coastal towns and intended to shift the source of supply in Adriatic "maritime goods" from Venice to Dalmatian ports, chiefly Zara.[55] To promote this scheme he insisted on a trade route which had been *unfamiliar*, not in use so far. Indeed, the trade and communication of Hungary with Venice was not being transacted by this route, but partly by sea from Venice to Zengg (Senj), and from here by land to Zagreb and Buda,[56] partly by the overland route Görz (Gorizia)–Laibach (Ljubljana)–Pettau (Ptuj)–Muraszombat (Murska Sobota).[57] Now, however, "all merchants," Transylvanian Saxons and

[52] Fejér: *Codex diplomaticus*, IX, 7, pp. 198–199.

[53] Fejér: *Codex diplomaticus*, IX, 7, pp. 297–299; Wenzel: *op. cit.*, p. 148; Fr. Zimmermann–C. Werner–G. Müller: *Urkundenbuch zur Geschichte der Deutschen in Siebenbürgen*, II, Hermannstadt, 1897, pp. 337–339.

[54] Fejér: *Codex diplomaticus*, IX, 4, Budae, 1834, pp. 227–229; Wenzel: *op. cit.*, p. 149; Zimmermann–Werner–Müller: *Urkundenbuch*, II, pp. 354–355.

[55] It is to be noted that King Louis had already laid a special stress upon the possession of Zara during the negotiations preceding the conclusion of peace in 1358: S. Ljubič: *Listine o odnošajih izmedju južnoga slavenstva i mletačke republike*, I, (Monumenta spectantia historiam Slavorum meridionalium, I) U Zagrebu, 1868; III, U Zagrebu, 1872, pp. 361–368; V, U Zagrebu, 1875, pp. 279–289, 324–326. — Cf. R. Cessi: *La repubblica di Venezia e il problema adriatico*, Napoli, 1953, pp. 98–99.

[56] J. B. Tkalčić: *Monumenta historica liberae regiae civitatis Zagrabiae metropolis regni Dalmatiae, Croatiae et Slavoniae*, Zagrabiae, 1889, I, pp. 159–161, 165–169, 180–183, 444–445, (1335, 1343, 1346); Smičiklas: *Codex diplomaticus*, XI, Zagrabiae, 1913, pp. 344–345 (1347); Ljubić: *Listine*, III, pp. 84–86 (1348), p. 316 (1356); IV, U Zagrebu, 1874, pp. 23, 73, 90, 99, 108, 173, (1360, 1364, 1367, 1372, 1374, 1381); G. Wenzel: *Magyar diplomáciai emlékek az Anjou-korból* (Hungarian diplomatic records from the times of the Anjous), III, Budapest, 1876, pp. 70–71, 95, 154 (1374, 1377). — The existence of spice imports via Zengg and Zagreb is evident from these sources, but it cannot be grasped quantitatively. — For the Zengg route in the subsequent century: Zs. Teke: *La politica economica Adriatica di Venezia nel secolo XV e i conti Frangipane*. Venezia e Ungheria nel rinascimento, Firenze, 1973, pp. 119–134.

[57] L. Glaser: *Dunántúl középkori úthálózata* (The road-system of Transdanubia in the Middle Ages), Századok, Budapest, 1929, pp. 141–144; Simonsfeld: *op. cit.*, II, p. 98; Huszti: *op. cit.*, pp. 98–100. — For the "Laibacher Strasse" in the 15th and 16th centuries: K. Tagányi: *Marhakivitelünk Velencébe 1514-ben* (The Hungarian cattle exports to Venice in the year 1514). Magyar Gazdaságtörténelmi Szemle (Hungarian Economic History Review), 1899, pp. 147–149; T. Kardos: *Velencei vonatkozású gazdaságtörténelmi adatok a Jagelló-korból, 1502–1518* (Economic-historical data from the times of the Jagellonians, 1502–1518). Századok, 1951, pp. 437–442; O. Pickl: *Die Auswirkungen der Türkenkriege auf den Handel zwischen Ungarn und Italien im 16. Jahrhundert*. Die wirtschaftlichen Auswirkungen der Türkenkriege, Graz, 1972, pp. 73–74. — About the two routes from Venice to Buda, "*unam videlicet per viam terrae, aliam vero per viam maris de Segna*" (Zengg): Ljubić: *Listine*, IV, pp. 23–26 (1360). — Another overland route from Venice to Buda via Sacile, Splimbergo, Villach, Vörösvár, Óvár: Ljubić: *Listine*, V, pp. 337–346 (1379).

Hungarians alike, were encouraged by the king to do business in Dalmatia, and to make use of the route to Zara.[58] Moreover, not only all merchants of his own realm were stimulated by him to do so, but also his allies, the chief enemies of Venice, the Genoese. In a charter given to the Genoese in the year 1379 the king provided for free entry and exit as well as exemption from customs duties to all Genoese merchants whether they come to Hungary *from the eastern or from the western direction*; in the latter case "*de regno nostro Dalmatiae, tam per mare nostrum* [that is via Zengg], *quam per viam Jadrensem,*" that is by the Zara route.[59]

Thus, the arguments used since Csánki and Meltzl may be dropped. The charters of King Louis favouring the Transylvanian Saxons in trade with Dalmatia are not to be interpreted as precluding the possibility of Transylvanian merchants having obtained Levant articles from the eastern direction as well. And the charter of the Genoese explicitly covered both directions.

The charters, analyzed before, only bear witness to the king's *aspirations* and ambitions to establish the traffic on the Zara route, on a route which had not at all been in use so far, but these charters do not prove that the king succeeded in putting his ambitions into *practice*, as against the hegemony of Venice in Adriatic trade.

As a matter of fact, doubts may arise on the score whether or not "plenty of sea-borne goods" could be obtained through Dalmatian towns, notably Zara, in spite of the city of lagoons, i.e. independently of Venetian trade. One of the main motives of Venetian policy concerning Dalmatia was at all times to prevent Levantine goods from reaching Dalmatian towns directly, and to make these commodities available only through Venetian merchants.[60] Characteristic enough, a commercial treaty between Venice and Zara in 1347 included such a disposition "*de aromatibus, seta vel alio havere subtile, quod non possint deferri Jadram vel districtum aliunde, quam de Venetiis.*"[61] And now, after the Peace of Zara, after the loss of Dalmatia, Venice insisted on continuing this policy in a still more severe form: she restricted even this source of supply to the Dalmatian towns while under Hungarian supremacy. In the same years when Louis of Anjou issued the afore-mentioned charters encouraging Dalmatian trade in "maritime goods", Venice did not

[58] The charter of Nagyszeben (1370) repeated that to the Dalmatian coasts "*omnibus mercatoribus regni nostri libera via pateat et secura, regnumque nostrum Hungariae rebus maritimis et Dalmatiae locupletetur et exuberetur*": Fejér: *Codex diplomaticus,* IX, 4, pp. 234–235; Wenzel: *op. cit.*, 149; Zimmermann–Werner–Müller: *Urkundenbuch,* II, pp. 361–362.

[59] *Historiae patriae monumenta edita iussu regis Caroli Alberti, Liber iurium reipublicae Genuensis,* II, Taurini, 1857, pp. 854–858. — Cf. G. Wenzel: *Magyar diplomáciai emlékek* (Hungarian diplomatic records), III, Budapest, 1876, pp. 131–132; G. Wenzel: *Magyarország bányászatának kritikai története* (A critical history of mining in Hungary), Budapest, 1880, p. 158.

[60] Cessi: *op. cit.*, pp. 60–83; G. Luzzato: *Storia economica di Venezia dall'XI al XVI secolo,* Venezia, 1961, pp. 122–127; L. Szabó: *Városi élet a középkori Dalmáciában* (Town life in medieval Dalmatia), Budapest, 1917, p. 53; Huszti, *op. cit.*, p. 11.

[61] "*. . . et si portabitur aliunde quam de Venetiis* — the text goes on — *et discaricabitur in Jadra vel districtu, incurrant contrafacientes de quinquaginta pro centenario* [!] *de toto eo, quod discaricatum esset contra praedicta*". This is obviously a very heavy duty; any other merchandise but Levantine goods — the treaty prescribed — "*quae conducentur Jadram et districtum aliunde quam de Venetiis, . . . solvant duas pro centenario*". — Ljubić: *Listine* III, pp. 1–3.

hesitate to introduce effective counter-measures. In 1359 a ban on export of any goods from Venetian territory by merchants of Zara was put into force;[62] at the same time a long controversy started between the city of St. Marcus and Ragusa (Dubrovnik),[63] which eventually resulted in a general prohibition of Venetian trade with Ragusa in 1372–1373[64] and was followed by a commercial prohibition against Cattaro (Kotor) in 1372–1374,[65] and against the whole of Dalmatia in 1378.[66] Though temporarily weakened and defeated, Venice still remained a formidable adversary on the Adriatic when it came to defending her commercial interests. This is why it seems scarcely credible that Zara and other Dalmatian towns (whether by their own trade activities, or through Transylvanian and Hungarian merchants acting as intermediaries) would have been able to provide Hungary with "*abundantia rerum maritimarum*" independently of Venice, defying Venice, as intended by King Louis of Anjou.

If some traffic of Levantine commodities did actually start towards Hungary and Transylvania "*in ipsa via Jadrensi*," that is from Zara (Zadar) to Bihać, Topusko, Petrinja and Zagreb[67] (which Louis so much wanted his subjects to get used to), it cannot have been else than a short-term affair of minor significance[68] which did not last even as long as the Hungarian king's supremacy over Dalmatia. The Peace of Torino concluded between Hungary and Venice in the year 1381 still upheld and prolonged the title of the Hungarian Crown to Dalmatia;[69] after the death of King Louis, how-

[62] "... *per officiales vestros* [that is, of Venice] *suis* [that is, to the burghers of Zara] *non datur licentia et facultas pro sua pecunia extrahendi de civitate et aliis locis vestrae dominationi subditis ... quamplurima suo usui necessaria*", — Miklós Szécsi, the Hungarian *Bán* (= Duke) of Dalmatia complained in his letter addressed to the Venetian Council in December 1359. Venice, in her answer of March 1360, had virtually kept up the prohibition: Ljubić: *Listine*, IV, pp. 15, 26–27; Wenzel: *Magyar diplomáciai emlékek*, II, Budapest, 1875, pp. 553–554. — Cf. Cessi: *op. cit.*, p. 111 (with a sort of bias).

[63] J Gelcich–L. Thallóczy: *Raguza és Magyarország összeköttetéseinek oklevéltára* — Diplomatarium relationum reipublicae Ragusanae cum regno Hungariae, Budapest, 1887, pp. 7, 21–22, 61–73; Smičiklas: *Codex diplomaticus*, XII, pp. 480–484, 617–618; Ljubić: *Listine*, IV, pp. 38–40, 93.

[64] In December 1372 the Council of Venice ordered that "*elapso mense Januarii proximo aliquis Raguseus non audeat nec possit extrahere de Venetiis aliquas mercationes*", and added to this in April 1373 that "*de cetero aliquis noster civis ... non audeat, possit vel praesumat ... conducere seu conduci facere aliquod havere, res, pannos vel mercationes de Venetiis, vel de aliqua alia parte, ad partes Ragusii, nec ad aliquas alias partes intra Culphum, unde possint conduci Ragusium*": Ljubić: *Listine*, IV, pp. 104–105; Wenzel: *Magyar diplomáciai emlékek*, III, pp. 47, 51–52.

[65] Ljubić: *Listine*, IV. pp. 102–103, 107; Wenzel: *Magyar diplomáciai emlékek*, III, pp. 73, 94.

[66] Wenzel: *Magyar diplomáciai emlékek*, III, p. 155. — Cf. Pleidell: *op. cit.*, p. 54.

[67] Smičiklas: *Codex diplomaticus*, XII, pp. 665–671. — The Zara route is presumably identical with the old military road, made use of by King Ladislaus and Coloman when conquering Croatia and Dalmatia: Gy. Pauler: *Horvát-Dalmátország elfoglalásáról, 1091–1111* (On taking possession of Croatia and Dalmatia, 1091–1111). Századok, 1888, pp. 212–213. — Other suggestions about the running of this route: Csánki: *op. cit.*, p. 32; Borcsiczky: *op. cit*, pp. 16–17.

[68] The sources have preserved not more than one single datum to make it likely that a travel to Dalmatia had actually been carried out by three Brassó merchants who, mentioned by name, were exempted from the customs duties on the road to Zara in 1370; Fejér: *Codex diplomaticus*, IX, 4, p. 228; Zimmermann–Werner–Müller: *Urkundenbuch*, II, p. 354.

[69] Ljubić: *Listine*, IV, pp. 119, 126–128; Wenzel: *Magyar diplomáciai emlékek*, III, pp. 434, 439–441.

ever, from the mid-1380's on, this supremacy became in reality always more vague,[70] amidst disorders in the southern parts of the kingdom and ceaseless struggles with the rulers of Bosnia and the House of Naples. These conditions, ultimately, made it possible for Venice to take possession of the coastal region in 1408–1409 again.[71] The campaign, launched in 1411 by Sigismund of Luxembourg, king of Hungary (1387–1437), failed to prevent her from asserting her claims, and in the armistice of 1413 the Hungarian king was obliged to give up his title to a part of Dalmatia, in 1420 and 1437 to the whole of it. But, characteristic enough, the royal intentions to establish the traffic of Levantine commodities on the Zara route towards Hungary and Transylvania were dropped long before. The charters of King Louis favouring the Dalmatian trade of Brassó and Nagyszeben merchants were renewed by King Sigismund in 1395 and 1406 for the last time[72] and never again.

3.2

Finally, the last and most important argument of the adherents of the Dalmatian theory has to be discussed: whether or not the allegation of oriental spices having reached Transylvania from the eastern direction, from the Black Sea region, can be proved by documentary evidence. In this respect, we now confine the discussion to trade relations between the Roumanian principality Wallachia and the Transylvanian town of Brassó.

The burghers of *Civitas Coronae* (Brassó) were favoured in the so-called "transalpine trade", that is, in the trans-Carpathian trade as early as the year 1358 by Hungary, 1368 by Roumania (Wallachia). King Louis of Anjou gave them permission for free crossing to Wallachia between the rivers Bodza and Prahova, and for going on there as far as to the Danube-mouths of the rivers Iălomiţa and Sereth;[73] it is on this strip of land stretching in the south-eastern, eastern direction — with the town Brăila as their chief destination — that Brassó merchants were the most frequently encountered afterwards, too. In a charter dated ten years later, Ladislaus, Voivod of

[70] Wenzel: *Magyar diplomáciai emlékek*, III, pp. 619, 628–632; Ljubić: *Listine*, IV, pp. 231-239, 413, 473, 477; V, pp. 348–361.

[71] Gelcich-Thallóczy: *Raguza és Magyarország*, pp. 188–189; Ljubić: *Listine*, V, pp. 177 et seq.; Cessi: *op. cit.*, pp. 126–131.

[72] Fejér: *Codex diplomaticus*, X, 2, Budae, 1834, pp. 308–309; Zimmermann-Werner-Müller: *Urkundenbuch*, III, Hermannstadt, 1902, pp. 128–129, 388. — It is characteristic, too, that the charters given by King Sigismund to the merchants of five West- and North-Hungarian towns: Sopron, Pozsony (Bratislava), Nagyszombat (Trnava), Bártfa (Bardejov) and Lőcse (Levoča) in 1402, do not refer to the Zara route any more, but to the road "*ad Segniam*" (to Zengg) and the charter of the Transylvanian town Kolozsvár (Cluj) from the year 1404 already refers to the direction "*versus Venetias*": Fejér: *Codex diplomaticus*, X, 4, Budae, 1841, pp. 108–116, 121–124; B. Iványi: *Bártfa szabad királyi város levéltára* (Records of the royal free town Bártfa), I, Budapest, 1910, p. 8; J. Házi: *Sopron szabad királyi város története* (A history of the royal free town Sopron), I, 1, Sopron, 1921, pp. 267–269; E. Jakab: *Oklevéltár Kolozsvár történetéhez* (Records on the history of Kolozsvár), I, Buda, 1870, pp. 117–118; Zimmermann-Werner-Müller: *Urkundenbuch*, III, pp. 323–325; E. Mályusz: *Zsigmondkori oklevéltár* (Records on the times of Sigismund), II, 1, Budapest, 1956, pp. 167–170.

[73] Fejér: *Codex diplomaticus*, IX, 2, Budae, 1833, p. 688. — Cf. R. Manolescu: *Comerţul Ţării Romîneşti şi Moldovei cu Braşovul (secolele XIV–XVI)*, Bucureşti, 1965, pp. 5–14.

Wallachia, called the liberties of Brassó merchants in Brăila as rights "of long standing". In the same charter he ordered that they should pay just a simple duty in *Longo campo* (Cîmpulung) on their sales and purchases made within the territory of Wallachia, but crossing Wallachia and going on to foreign countries, they should pay the "thirtieth", too (that is the thirtieth part of their invoice value). More precisely, when crossing via Brăila, they had to pay only one "thirtieth"; on their return, in Cîmpulung, however, when going on another road *(per quamlibet viam terrae nostrae Transalpinae excepta via Braylam ad regna extranea transeuntes)*, they had to discharge two "thirtieths": one on the way out in Cîmpulung, the other on their return at the Danube.[74] The route through Brăila must have led to the coastal region of the Black Sea, the Danube estuary, the later Kilia, in which district some Genoese settled down about the year 1370, after having established their colony at Caffa about a century before.[75] The other route may have led to Balkan regions lying south of the Danube; as a matter of fact, Stracimir, the tsar of the Vidin-Bulgaria, had about the same time also permitted the Brassó burghers "to do business in his country to their liking."[76]

The list of commodities of Brassó–Wallachian trade is found in sources from the early 15th century. One of them is a charter of Stibor, Voivod of Transylvania, from 1412, laying down the customs duties to be paid by Brassó merchants on goods exported to and imported from Wallachia. The main exports supplied from Transylvania to Wallachia were West-European cloths: fabrics of the Netherlands (Ypres and Louvain), of Germany (Cologne), and of Silesia, customs duties depending on quality. Imports to Transylvania consisted partly of Wallachian agrarian produce (fish, cattle, hides, wax, etc.), partly — and here we have the indisputable documentary evidence — of *pepper, spices and other oriental goods* with a duty of the "thirtieth".[77]

In the following year (1413) a similar customs tariff was issued, concerning the trans-Carpathian trade of Brassó burghers, by Mircea Voivod of Wallachia, too.[78] According to this document, Transylvanian merchants had to pay fixed duties on the way out at the Wallachian customs stations *Ruffa arbor* (Rucăr) and Dîmboviţa, on the way back at Brăila, *Novum forum* (Tîrguşor), Tîrgovişte, and again at Dîmboviţa; those, in turn, who travelled farther

[74] Fejér: *Codex diplomaticus*, IX, 4, pp. 148–150.

[75] Heyd: *op. cit.*, I, p. 583, II, p. 165.

[76] G. Tocilescu: *534 documente istorice slavo-române din Ţăra Românească şi Moldova privitoare la legăturile cu Ardealul 1346–1603*, Viena–Bucureşti, 1931. p. 3.

[77] Zimmermann–Werner–Müller: *Urkundenbuch*, III, pp. 544–547.

[78] J. Bogdan: *Documente şi regeste privitoare la relatiile Ţării Rumîneşti cu Braşovul şi Ungaria in secolul XV şi XVI*, Bucureşti, 1902, pp. 3–5; G. Gündisch: *Urkundenbuch zur Geschichte der Deutschen in Siebenbürgen*, IV, Hermannstadt, 1937, pp. 425–426. — The issue of both customs tariffs is in obvious connection with the commercial plans of King Sigismund who, frustrated in the Dalmatian area, shifted the focus of his anti-Venetian Levant policy to the Black Sea region. For the oriental policy of Sigismund — the discussion of which goes beyond the framework of this paper and will be presented separately — see Simonsfeld: *op. cit.*, II, pp. 44–46; A. Schulte: *Geschichte des mittelalterlichen Handels und Verkehrs zwischen Westdeutschland und Italien mit Ausschluss von Venedig*, I, Leipzig, 1900, p. 513; H. Heimpel: *Zur Handelspolitik Kaiser Sigismunds*, Vierteljahrschrift für Sozial- und Wirtschaftsgeschichte, 23, 1930. pp. 135–156; and recently W. v. Stromer: *König Siegmunds Gesandte in den Orient*. Festschrift für H. Heimpel, II, Göttingen, 1972, pp. 501–609, and *Die Kontinentalsperre Kaiser Sigismunds gegen Venedig 1412–1433 und die Verlagerung der interkontinentalen Transportwege*, Prato, 1973, pp. 1–6 (with exaggerations).

than Wallachia had to pay first before crossing the Danube, the second time when returning from the sea coast region or from parts beyond the Danube *(venientes de marinis partibus seu trans Danubium)*, at the rate of "three per hundred", that is roughly the "thirtieth". Their exports consisted of the above-mentioned West-European woollen fabrics and of hardware (arms, knives); their imports again comprised partly Wallachian agricultural produce, partly pepper, spices and other oriental commodities. To make matters perfectly clear, this fact is expressed in the charter of 1412 as follows: "*De pipere, croco, sinsibero, cariofolis et de crinibus caprarum, bombasio et de omnibus rebus mercimonialibus, quae per Sarracenos asportantur, habetur tricesimum.*"[79] And the Slavonic variant of the charter from the year 1413 says (I give the translation) " . . . on pepper, saffron, cotton, camel's hair, goat's hair, hides and other goods *from overseas* three per hundred" are to be paid.[80] Hence, the spices and oriental wares, imported by Brassó merchants from Wallachia to Transylvania, had come from the Black-Sea region, and had been brought to the Black Sea region by Saracen (Islamic) traders.

These, then, were the real "*res maritimae*" in Transylvanian Saxon towns; however, not from the Dalmatian coasts, as suggested by historians adherent to the Dalmatian–Adriatic theory, but from the coasts of the Black Sea.

From the subsequent decades, there are offered a great number of similar evidence by Hungarian and Roumanian documents alike. In the year 1419 and later, in 1428, Sigismund of Luxembourg, king of Hungary, granted new charters to the Saxons of Transylvania, favouring their trade with Wallachia over the Pass of Törcsvár (Bran);[81] moreover, protection against misuse by customs officers at Törcsvár was extended already in 1426 to Wallachian merchants, too, coming to Brassó from "transalpine regions" and returning to their country.[82] This draws attention to the important fact that not only Brassó merchants visited trans-Carpathian lands, but Wallachian traders also brought their goods, including oriental spices, to Transylvanian markets.

On the Roumanian part, customs tariffs laid down by Mircea in 1413 were renewed after his death (1418) by all his successors in due order. Thus, in the year 1421, Voivod Radul II Praznaglava gave a new, detailed wording to the favours enjoyed by Brassó burghers in Wallachia, particularly on the "Brassó route to Brăila", via Dîmboviţa, Tîrgovişte and Tîrguşor. Among the exports, woollens (from Ypres, Louvain, Cologne and Silesia) again were at the head of the list; as regards imports, among others, the typical phrase was repeated: "on pepper, saffron, cotton, camel's hair, goat's hair, hides, and other goods *from overseas* three per hundred" are to be paid.[83] The charter granted by the next voivod, Dan II, to Brassó merchants in 1422 contains a similar formula concerning pepper and other sea-borne goods, and so do instructions sent by Dan to his customs officers of Dîmboviţa, Rucăr and Prahova, as well as his Latin and Slavonic charters from the year 1424.[84]

In the second period of Dan II's rule, 1429, probably in connection with

[79] Zimmermann–Werner–Müller: *Urkundenbuch,* III, p. 546.
[80] Bogdan: *Documente şi regeste,* p. 4.
[81] Gündisch: *Urkundenbuch,* IV, pp. 102–103, 365–367.
[82] Gündisch: *Urkundenbuch,* IV, pp. 248–249.
[83] Bogdan: *Documente şi regeste,* pp. 9–10; Gündisch: *Urkundenbuch,* IV, pp. 149–151.
[84] Bogdan: *Documente şi regeste,* pp. 12–18; Gündisch: *Urkundenbuch,* IV, pp. 168, 170–173, 222–228.

a peace-treaty concluded with the Turks, the voivod called upon Brassó burghers to come and practice free trade again "*right down to the Sea*".[85] In 1431 he repeated that merchants of Brassó might pursue trade "from the Iron Gate" (that is what has been called the Porta Hungarica) "*to the Great Sea*" (that is the Black Sea). Obviously this implied the eastward route from Brăila to the sea-coast, to Kilia, too (in which direction the Saxons had to pay one "thirtieth" according to the former tariff). However, when going in another direction, that is southwards — "whether they crossed the Danube with their wares at Durostor [Silistra], Giurgiu or Nicopol" — they had to pay two "thirtieths": one on the way out at the Danube ferry, the other on their return at Rucăr.[86]

Even in the subsequent troublous years, before and after the Turkish irruption to South Transylvania (June 1432), the connections were maintained between Brassó and Dan's successor, Alexandru Aldea. And when a new voivod, Vlad Dracul came into power, soon a new agreement was reached with *Civitas Coronae* (1436),[87] and the customs tariff was renewed again (1437), with the usual phrases referring to "the Brassó route to Brăila" and to pepper, saffron, cotton, camel's hair, goat's hair and all goods coming "*from overseas*".[88]

So, the last argument of the historians who claim imports of spices to have come to medieval Hungary exclusively from the *Adriatic*, that is, in the final analysis from the Mediterranean sea-borne trade, must be dropped as well. On the contrary: the sources, both Transylvanian and Roumanian, both Latin and Slavonic, provide indisputable documentary evidence of pepper, spices, and other oriental commodities having been imported regularly from the *Black Sea* coasts through Wallachia to Transylvania and Hungary, that is from the Black Sea coasts by an overland route to Hungary — somewhat similarly to the overland route of Levantine trade to Poland (Caffa, Lwów, Cracow).[89]

Sure enough, the Black Sea–Transylvanian route was by no means a *main* line of Levantine trade during the 14th and 15th centuries; but, no doubt, *it existed*[90] and supplied oriental spices to Transylvania and Hungary.[91]

[85] Bogdan: *Documente şi regeste*, p. 19; Gündisch: *Urkundenbuch*, IV, pp. 373–374.

[86] Bogdan: *Documente şi regeste*, pp. 20–23; Gündisch: *Urkundenbuch*, IV. pp. 426–429.

[87] Gündisch: *Urkundenbuch*, IV, pp. 609–619.

[88] Bogdan: *Documente şi regeste*, pp. 49–50; Gündisch: *Urkundenbuch*, IV, pp. 626–628.

[89] St. Kutrzeba: *Handel Krakowa w wiekach średnich*, Kraków, 1902, pp. 12–14, 109–113; Wendt: *op. cit.*, pp. 16–38; P. P. Panaitescu: *La route commerciale de Pologne à la Mer Noire au Moyen Age*. Revista Istorică Română, III, 1933, pp. 172–193; M. Małowist: *Les routes du commerce et les marchandises du Levant dans la vie de la Pologne au Bas Moyen Age et au début de l'époque moderne*. Mediterraneo e Oceano Indiano, Firenze, 1970, pp. 157–175.

[90] As concerns the quantity of spice imports from the eastern direction, relevant data are available only later, from the first years of the 16th century. According to the customs books of Nagyszeben from the year 1500 and of Brassó from the year 1503, the annual pepper imports of these two Transylvanian customs stations amounted to 825 hundredweight, in a value of roundly 36 000 Hungarian golden florins. It is to be noted that this quantity is nearly five times as much as the above mentioned pepper imports of the Hungarian west-border town Pozsony from the western direction around the middle of the 15th century. — For the details see S. P. Pach: *La route du poivre vers la Hongrie médiévale* (Contribution à l'histoire du commerce méditerranéen au XVe siècle). Mélanges en l'honneur de Fernand Braudel, Toulouse, 1973, II, pp. 449–458.

[91] The further route of the pepper imports of Brassó, can be traced as far as Nagyvárad (Oradea) and Kassa (Košice) in the first years of the 16th century. — See Footnote 90.

The monopoly of the Mediterranean route of Levantine trade was challenged — to a certain degree, of course,[92] — by the Black Sea route, leading not only to Poland, but also to Transylvania and Hungary in the 14th and 15th centuries.

[92] As it appears, among others, from a comparison of the data given in Footnote 90 with those concerning the quantity of the Venetian spice imports from Beirut and Alexandria in the years 1497, 1498 and 1501: F. C. Lane: *Venetian Shipping during the Commercial Revolution*. American Historical Review, 38, 1933, and *The Mediterranean Spice Trade: Further Evidence of its Revival in the Sixteenth Century*. American Historical Review, 45, 1940, reprinted in: *Crisis and Change in the Venetian Economy in the Sixteenth and Seventeenth Centuries*, edited by B. Pullan, London, 1968, pp. 33, 47. — Cf. F. Braudel: *La Méditerranée et le monde méditerranéen à l'époque de Philippe II*, 2. ed., Paris, 1966, I. p. 500.

ADDENDA

LEVANTINE TRADE AND HUNGARY IN THE MIDDLE AGES (THESES, CONTROVERSIES, ARGUMENTS)

Page 5, Note 1:

In the continuation of his scholarly report *E. Ashtor* already included the issue of the Hungarian route of Levantine trade, reviewing several papers of the present author on this topic: Recent Research on Levantine Trade, The Journal of European Economic History, XIV, 2 (1985), pp. 382–383.

Page 7, Note 10:

For the weak points in the argumentation of Hüllmann (and other adherents of the "Danube–thesis") and further details of the controversy, see from the present writer: Levantine Trade Routes and Eastern Europe in the Middle Ages. In: XVe Congrès International des Sciences Historiques. Rapports, II, Bucarest, 1980, pp. 222–230.

Page 21, Note 75:

For the Genoese colonies on the Black Sea coasts see recently: *L. Balletto*, Genova, Mediterraneo, Mar Nero (sec. XII–XV), Genova, 1976; Colloquio romeno–italiano: I Genovesi nel Mar Nero durante i secoli XIII e XIV, Bucarest, 1977; *M. Balard,* La Romanie génoise, Genoa, 1978.

Page 21, Note 78:

The oriental policy of Emperor Sigismund has been treated (and compared with that of King Louis) by the present writer in a separate study: Die Verkehrsroute des Levantehandels nach Siebenbürgen und Ungarn zur Zeit der Könige Ludwig von Anjou und Sigismund von Luxemburg. In: Europäische Stadtgeschichte in Mittelalter und früher Neuzeit. Hg. von W. Mägdefrau, Weimar, 1979, pp. 60–91. — Conf.Ş. *Papacostea,* Kilia et la politique orientale de Sigismond de Luxembourg, Revue Roumaine d'Histoire, XV (1976), pp. 421–436.

VII

THE TRANSYLVANIAN ROUTE OF LEVANTINE TRADE AT THE TURN OF THE 15TH AND 16TH CENTURIES

Certain results of our research on the Hungarian aspects of medieval Levantine trade have already been published. In the first volume of *Études Historiques Hongroises* (1975), we analyzed the sources which prove incontrovertibly that from the direction of the Black Sea in the 15th century oriental spices, chiefly pepper, were imported regularly through Wallachia (Ţara Romînească) to Transylvania, notably to the South-Transylvanian Saxon towns, to Brassó (Kronstadt, Braşov) and Nagyszeben (Hermannstadt, Sibiu).[1]

Three questions need be answered then:

1. *How large* was this import of spices?
2. *Who* acted as middlemen in the import of spices?
3. What was the *further* route of the imported spices? (In case they prove to have been of quantities which make it improbable that the whole import should have found consumers in the South-Transylvanian Saxon towns.)

In the present paper an attempt is made to answer these questions.

1

What quantity did this import of spices reach then? Did these consignments arriving from the region of the Black Sea move volumes of merchandise which contributed considerably to covering the spice demand of the country and were of decisive importance on the Transylvanian or Hungarian pepper market? How large was this import compared to supplies coming from the south-west or west, from Venice or Vienna?[2]

We are in the fortunate position of being able to give a fairly accurate reply—at least as regards the gist of the question—concerning the turn of the 15th and 16th centuries. Two precious sources are at our disposal on this issue, notably the customs (twentieth,

[1] Levantine Trade and Hungary in the Middle Ages (Theses, Controversies, Arguments), in: *Études Historiques Hongroises 1975 publiées à l'occasion du XIVe Congrès International des Sciences Historiques par la Commission Nationale des Historiens Hongrois* (hereafter: *Études Historiques Hongroises*), Budapest, 1975, I, pp. 283–307.

[2] Cf. Le route du poivre vers la Hongrie médiévale, in: *Mélanges en l'honneur de Fernand Braudel*, Toulouse, 1973, I (hereafter: *Mélanges*), pp. 449–458. Le commerce du Levant et la Hongrie au Moyen Age, *Annales ESC*, Paris, 1976, No. 6, pp. 1176–1194.

vicesima) register of Nagyszeben for the year 1500,[3] furthermore the twentieth register of Brassó for the year 1503;[4] these offer data suitable for detailed, quantitative elaboration of the export and import turnover passing through the customs stations of the southern border of Transylvania, including spice imports from Wallachia.

The survival of the most precious sources of medieval foreign trade of *Western* Hungary, the customs (thirtieth, *tricesima*) registers of Pozsony (Pressburg, Bratislava) for the years 1457–58 and the similarly instructive thirtieth registers of Sopron (Ödenburg) for the years 1483–89 is due to the fact that these western border towns of the country rented for a certain period of time the royal thirtieth offices active within their respective boundaries and during the time of their lease they collected the thirtieth (wholly or partly) on their own account.[5] Registers of some years of the towns' thirtieth revenues were, therefore, preserved by the municipal archives—unlike the registers kept by royal thirtieth managements, the medieval documents of which have been destroyed in the subsequent centuries.[6]

Highly valuable late-medieval sources on *eastern* foreign trade of the country have come down to us for similar reasons and in like manner. In the year 1491 Nagyszeben acquired a lease for the collection of twentieth revenues, and so did Brassó for the years 1493–94 and 1496; from 1497–98 Nagyszeben, the seven Saxon quarters, Brassó, Barcaság (Burzenland, Tara Bîrsei) and Besztercebánya (Nösen, Bistrița) acquired a joint lease–paying a yearly rent of 7,000 florins[7]–for the collection of Transylvanian customs duties, that is the twentieth revenues of the customs stations of

[3] *Quellen zur Geschichte Siebenbürgens aus sächsischen Archiven*, I. Abteilung, Rechnungen aus dem Archiv der Stadt Hermannstadt und der sächsischen Nation, I, Hermannstadt, 1880, pp. 270–307.

[4] *Quellen zur Geschichte der Stadt Kronstadt in Siebenbürgen*, I, Rechnungen aus dem Archiv der Stadt Kronstadt, I, Kronstadt, 1886, pp. 1-81.

[5] For lease of the thirtieth revenue of the town Pozsony see: F. Kováts: *Nyugat-Magyarország áruforgalma a XV. században a pozsonyi harmincadkönyv alapján* (The Trade of Western Hungary in the 15th Century on the Basis of the Customs Registers of Pozsony), Budapest, 1902, IV–V, pp. 3–4. For (partial) lease of the thirtieth revenue of the town Sopron see: J. Házi: *Sopron szabad királyi város története* (The History of the Royal Free Town Sopron), Vol. II, 4, Sopron, 1936, pp. 317–318.

[6] Cf. Gy. Ember: Külkereskedelmünk történetéhez a XVI. században (Contribution to the History of Hungarian Foreign Trade in the 16th Century), *A Magyar Tudományos Akadémia Társadalmi–Történeti Tudományok Osztályának Közleményei* (Communications of the Department of Social and Historical Sciences of the Hungarian Academy of Sciences), Vol. VIII. No. 4, 1958, p. 310.

[7] A report by Osvald (= Laki Thuz Osvát), Bishop of Zagreb, royal treasurer, from the early 1490s on the king's revenues put the yearly proceeds of Transylvanian customs (twentieth, vicesima) at 6,000 florins: "Ibidem [sc. in Transylvania] vicesima seu vectigal de rebus mercimonialibus in tribus locis, puta: Cibinio, Brassovia et Bistricia exigitur, quae facit usque florenos VI milia", see: L. Fejérpataky: II. Ulászló jövedelmeinek jegyzéke (Record of the Revenues of Wladislas II), *Történelmi Tár* (Historical Magazine), 1880, pp. 167–170. Cf. J. Fógel: *II. Ulászló udvartartása* (The Household of Wladislas II), Budapest, 1913, p. 54. Here we have to thank Professor E. Mályusz for drawing our attention to two items of the royal account book for the years 1494–95, dealing with the lease of customs revenue by Transylvanian Saxons, see: J. Chr. Engel: *Geschichte des Ungrischen Reichs und seiner Nebenländer*, I, Halle, 1797, p. 19.

Szeben, Brassó and Beszterce[8] This was the situation in 1500 and 1503, too. (Foreign trade customs duty, previously–and in Hungary subsequently as well–named thirtieth (tricesima), was at the time already termed twentieth (vicesima, vigesima) in Transylvania.)

Customs registers of Szeben and Brassó–which have survived from several other years of the 16th century, too, and have partly been published[9]–have, of course, not escaped the attention of research. Relevant studies, particularly the significant works of *Radu Manolescu,*[10] exempt us from the task of going into the general discussion of the structure of trade entered in the registers in question. Hence, we confine ourselves to remarking that the list of goods in the years 1500 and 1503 largely recall the picture presented by the Transylvanian and Wallachian customs tariffs between the years 1412 and 1437.[11] Western cloths (Flemish, North-Italian, South-German, Silesian sorts) continued to figure as important items of export to Wallachia, considerably exceeded, however, in ratio by hardware–"Styrian" and other knives. Widely varying imports included Wallachian livestock and fish, far surpassed, however, in value by oriental textiles, evidently brought chiefly from several parts of the Ottoman Empire. The first place among imported goods was nevertheless occupied, as found at the turn of the 15th and 16th centuries, by oriental spices, mainly by pepper. In fact, closer study of this import of spices is indispensable in the present paper, considering the lack of quantitative evaluation in this area.[12]

[8] *Quellen zur Geschichte Siebenbürgens aus sächsischen Archiven,* I, Einleitung, pp. XIII–XIV.

[9] Fragmentary edition of the customs book of Nagyszeben for January, 1501, *Quellen zur Geschichte Siebenbürgens aus sächsischen Archiven,* I, pp. 308–309. Abridged edition of surviving customs registers of Brassó for the years between 1529 and 1550: *Quellen zur Geschichte der Stadt Kronstadt in Siebenbürgen, I, Rechnungen aus dem Archiv der Stadt Kronstadt,* II, Kronstadt, 1889, pp. 171–175, 215–234; III, Kronstadt, 1896, pp. 185–215, 229–246, 291–306, 364–368, 424–428, 464–465, 530–532, 584–589. Further customs registers have come down of Brassó for the years 1551 and 1554, of Nagyszeben for the years 1537, 1540, 1542, 1543, 1546, 1550, 1553, 1554, 1559, 1578, 1579, 1583, 1585, 1587, 1588, 1591, 1593, 1596, 1597 and 1600. Finally it must be mentioned that the above quoted editions of Nagyszeben and Brassó sources also give quite a few accounts of customs (vicesima) from 1500–1509 and 1515–1516 respectively, etc. The latter are not customs (vicesima) *registers,* but *accounts* of the use of these revenues.

[10] H. Wendt: *Schlesien und der Orient.* Ein geschichtlicher Rückblick, Breslau, 1916, pp. 63–64. R. Manolescu: Schimbul de mărfuri dintre Ţara Romîneasca şi Braşov în primă jumatate a secolului al XVI-lea, *Studii şi materiale de istorie medie* (hereafter: *Studii*), II, Bucuresti, 1957, p. 147. et seq. S. Goldenberg: Der Südhandel in der Zollrechnungen von Sibiu (Hermannstadt) im 16. Jahrhundert, *Revue des études sud-est européennes* (hereafter: *Revue*), II, Bucarest, 1964, p. 385. et seq. Manolescu: *Comerţul Ţării Romîneşti şi Moldovei cu Braşovul* (secolele XIV–XVI), Bucureşti, 1965. E. Fügedi: Magyarország külkereskedelme a XVI. század elején (Hungarian Foreign Trade in the Early 16th Century), *Agrártörténeti Szemle* (Review of Agrarian History), 1969, p. 6.

[11] For the structure of trade in these years see: Levantine Trade and Hungary in the Middle Ages, *Études Historiques Hongroises, 1975,* I, pp. 301–303.

[12] Manolescu, who dealt the most thoroughly with the history of foreign trade transacted through Brassó in the 14th to 16th centuries, calculated the amounts of customs values of oriental or "Turkish wares" *(res turcales)* per year–regarded as transit goods by the Rumanian principalities – in one sum, i.e. not distinguishing between customs duty on oriental *textiles* and on oriental *spices; op. cit.,* 1965, pp. 172–173. Fügedi did calculate the percentual share of various commodities, including the spices, within imports, but made no attempt to determine the *absolute* quantity of imported

The entries referring to the import of spices in the customs registers of Nagyszeben and Brassó have been grouped in ten tables.

1. Pepper import according to the twentieth register of Nagyszeben for the year 1500.
2. Import of other spices according to the twentieth register of Nagyszeben for the year 1500.
3. Pepper import according to the twentieth register of Brassó for the year 1503 (Transylvanian merchants).
4. Pepper import according to the twentieth register of Brassó for the year 1503 (Wallachian merchants).
5. Pepper import according to the twentieth register of Brassó for the year 1503 (Moldavian merchants).
6. Pepper import according to the twentieth register for the year 1503 (merchants of unspecified Rumanian Principality).
7. Ginger import according to the twentieth register of Brassó for the year 1503 (Transylvanian merchants).
8. Ginger import according to the twentieth register of Brassó for the year 1503 (merchants of Rumanian Principalities).
9. Clove import according to the twentieth register of Brassó for the year 1503.
10. Import of other spices according to the twentieth register of Brassó for the year 1503.

These tables have been published in the Hungarian periodical *Századok* (Centuries), 1978;[13] here we present only two tables, summing up the particulars. (See pp. 9–10)

Detailed statistical elaboration of the items in the twentieth registers of Nagyszeben and Brassó for the years of 1500 and 1503, respectively, has actually made it possible to give an account of the volume of spice imports to the South-Transylvanian Saxon towns at the turn of the 15th and 16th centuries. The total data presented in Tables I and II have permitted an attempt at answering the *first* question posed in the introduction: of what magnitude were the spice imports coming from the region of the Black Sea; what role did they play in covering the spice demand of the country; what was their quantitative ratio in relation to imports from Venice, was it high or low?

There is no documentary evidence to go by concerning the quantity of the spices brought in directly from Venice over Zagreb or Pettau. A number of sources permit the inference that in the 15th century the route Zengg (Senj)–Zagreb may be supposed to have played just a modest role in forwarding "maritime goods" into the *interior* of the country.[14] On the Görz (Gorizia)–Laibach (Ljubljana)–Pettau (Ptuj) route traffic

---

spices; *op. cit.*, p. 6. M. Dan and S. Goldenberg: Le commerce balkano-levantin de la Transylvanie au cours de la seconde moitié du XVIe siècle et au début du XVIIe siècle, *Revue,* V, Bucarest, 1967, p. 88. Note 3 of their text provides some summary data on pepper imports by wholesale dealers of Brassó in the year 1503, but obviously these figures were derived by way of an inadequate interpretation of the source; see below, Notes 25 and 100.

[13] A Levante-kereskedelem erdélyi útvonala a 15–16. század fordulóján (The Transylvanian Route of Levantine Trade at the Turn of the 15th Centuries), *Századok,* 1978, No. 6, pp. 1055–1104.

[14] Zs. Teke: *Velencei–magyar kereskedelmi kapcsolatok a XIII–XV. században* (Venetian–Hungarian Commercial Relations in the 13th–15th Centuries), Budapest, 1979, pp. 39–40, 55–56.

Table I

Total Import of Spices According to the Twentieth Register of Nagyszeben for the Year 1500

No.	Kind of imported spice	Nationality of importers	Imported spice		Imported spice	
			quantity (quintals)	per cent	customs value (florins)	per cent
1	Pepper	Transylvanians	–	–	–	–
		Wallachians	105 3/4	100	4120 1/2	100
		Moldavians	–	–	–	–
		Total	105 3/4	100	4120 1/2	100
2	Ginger	Transylvanians	–	–	–	–
		Wallachians	3	100	90	100
		Moldavians	–	–	–	–
		Total	3	100	90	100
3	Clove	Transylvanians	–	–	–	–
		Wallachians	2	100	160	100
		Moldavians	–	–	–	–
		Total	2	100	160	100
4	Incense	Transylvanians	–	–	–	–
		Wallachians	3	100	63	100
		Moldavians	–	–	–	–
		Total	3	100	63	100
5	Saffron	Transylvanians	–	–	–	–
		Wallachians	3 pounds	100	4	100
		Moldavians	–	–	–	–
		Total	3 pounds	100	4	100
1–5	All kinds of spices	Transylvanians	–	–	–	–
		Wallachians	113 3/4 3 pounds	100	4437 1/2	100
		Moldavians	–	–	–	–
		Total	113 3/4 3 pounds	100	4437 1/2	100

Table II

Total Import of Spices According to the Twentieth Register of Brassó for the Year 1503

No.	Kind of imported spice	Nationality of importer	Imported spice: quantity (quintals)	(pounds)	per cent	Imported spice: customs value (florins)	(aspers)	per cent
1	Pepper	Transylvanians	98 3/4		13.73	4,043 2/3		12.58
		Wallachians	593	43 1/2	82.55	26,720	40 1/2	83.29
		Moldavians	26	47	3.72	1,320	17	3.13
		Total	719	15 1/2	100.00	32.084	40 5/6	100.00
2	Ginger	Transylvanians	6	3 1/2	14.3	182 1/2		14.11
		Wallachians	34	1/2	80.29	1,037 3/4		80.24
		Moldavians	2	17 1/2	5.41	73		5.65
		Total	42	21 1/2	100.00	1,293 1/4		100.00
3	Clove	Transylvanians	–		–	–		–
		Wallachians	8	26 1/2	92.77	683 1/2		93.7
		Moldavians		39 1/2	7.23	46		6.3
		Total	9	6	100.00	729 1/2		100.00
4	Incense	Transylvanians	8	9	27.86	171	7 1/2	27.86
		Wallachians	21	6	72.14	443	5	72.14
		Moldavians	–		–	–		–
		Total	29	15	100.00	614	12 1/2	100.00
5	Saffron	Transylvanians	–		–	–		–
		Wallachians		4 1/2	100.00	6		100.00
		Moldavians	–		–	–		–
		Total		4 1/2	100.00	6		100.00
6	Cinnamon	Transylvanians	–		–	–		–
		Wallachians	–		–	–		–
		Moldavians		22	100.00	14	30	100.00
		Total		22	100.00	14	30	100.00
7	Nutmeg-flower	Transylvanians	–		–	–		–
		Wallachians	–		–	–		–
		Moldavians		12	100.00	8		100.00
		Total		12	100.00	8		100.00
1–7	All kinds of spices	Transylvanians	112	57 1/2	14.11	4,396	32 1/2	12.65
		Wallachians	657	21	82.11	28,891	8	83.14
		Moldavians	30	18	3.78	1,461	47	4.21
		Total	800	36 1/2	100.00	34,749	37 1/2	100.00

became livelier as a result of increased cattle- (and hide) export from Hungary to Venice, but its counterpart on the import side may be assumed to have consisted much rather of Western European and Italian textiles.[15] From Adriatic *spice* imports Hungary obtained its share chiefly indirectly,[16] by the "Venezianerstrasse", from commodities which travelled along the Tarvisio–Judenburg–Semmering–Vienna route.[17] From Vienna the bulk of consignments reached Hungary after having passed Pozsony, the commercial centre and principal customs station of the western border region.

Regarding the customs office of Pozsony, two sources have survived from the 15th century which provide numerical particulars not only about the volume, but also the structure, of trade: thirtieth registers (as mentioned before) of the fiscal year 1457–58, and those of the fiscal years 1496–97 and 1497–98. However, the latter[18] do not contribute to answering our question, because they only contain the lots imported and exported by merchants of Pozsony, although it may be taken for granted that, similarly to the mid-century years[19], the bulk of trade in spices in the

[15] O. Pickl: Die Auswirkungen der Türkenkriege auf den Handel zwischen Ungarn und Italien im 16. Jahrhundert, in: *Die wirtschaftlichen Auswirkungen der Türkenkriege*, Graz, 1971, pp. 74–77.

[16] Of course, it cannot be ruled out that spices may have been brought to Hungary from Venice through Zagreb, or Pettau. This is suggested by the tricesima tariff of Buda for the year 1436 compiled by Johannes Siebenlinder, the ex-magistrate of Buda, castellan of Óbuda and toll collector of Queen Barbara at the time. After putting down the duty to be paid on various spices (in kind or in money), he also dealt separately with duty on pepper and imposed 40 good groats "de uno *karig* piperis", see: G. Fejér: *Codex diplomaticus Hungariae ecclesiasticus ac civilis*, X, 8, Budae, 1843, pp. 662–669. Kováts: *op. cit.*, pp. 211–213. The word *karig* (karg) was identified by Kováts with the Italian term *cargo*: *op. cit.* p. 78. It may be added that in Venice *cargo* (carico) was one of the usual units of measurement actually used for consignments of pepper, see: F. C. Lane: Pepper Prices before Da Gama, *The Journal of Economic History*, 28, New York, 1968, No. 4. pp. 592, 594–599. The famous passage in the diary of the Venetian merchant Girolamo Priuli from 1501 is also worthy of mention owing to the following comment on the appearance of the Portuguese in India: ". . . *Hungarians*, Germans, Flemish, French people, and in general Transalpine denizens *who up to the present brought their money to Venice* to purchase goods, will henceforward prefer to go to Lisbon. . ." The continuation of the sentence: "it being nearer to all other countries" is, however, untrue, see: G. Priuli: I Diarii, Rerum Italicarum Sciptores, T. XXIV/III, p. 423, referred to in J. Sz. Jónás (ed.): *Egyetemes történeti szöveggyűjtemény. Középkor.* (Collection of Historical Texts. Middle Ages), Vol. I, 1, Budapest, 1971, pp. 416–419.

[17] H. Simonsfeld: *Der Fondaco dei Tedeschi in Venedig und die deutsch-venetianischen Handelsbeziehungen*, Stuttgart, 1887, II, pp. 58, 98. Th. Mayer: *Der auswärtige Handel des Herzogtums Österreich im Mittelalter*, Innsbruck, 1909, p. 32. C. Schalk: Rapporti commerciali tra Venezia e Vienna, *Nuovo Archivio Veneto*, NS 23, 1912, p. 52 et seq. Fr. Engel-Jánosi: Zur Geschichte der Wiener Kaufmannschaft von der Mitte des 15. bis zur Mitte des 16. Jahrhunderts, in: *Mitteilungen des Vereines für Geschichte der Stadt Wien*, VI, Wien, 1926, p. 41.

[18] Országos Levéltár, Filmtár (National Archives, Film Collection), X 4755, Box No. C 488, Title 13.

[19] In the fiscal year 1457–58, on imports of pepper and other spices foreigners paid 201.73 florins customs duty, 115.05 florins of which was levied on pepper; inhabitants of Pozsony, however, paid only 53.84 florins, including 51.63 florins on pepper. Accordingly–since customs duty on pepper was 1 florin per quintal–in 1457–58 foreign merchants brought 115.05 quintals of pepper to Pozsony, inhabitants of the town only 51.63 quintals, see: Kováts: *op. cit.*, p. 77.

Table III

Spice Imports of Pozsony According to the Thirtieth Register for the Fiscal Year 1457–58

No.	Kind of imported spice	Imported spice		Remark
		quantity (pounds)	customs value (florins)	
1	Pepper	166.68 quintals	2,833.56	According to another estimate, customs value was 5,004 florins
2	Saffron	573 11/12	1,147.50	
3	Clove	130	78.00	
4	Ginger	268	67.00	
5	Mixed spices		218.5	Items where several kinds of above-mentioned spices as well as additional ones, nutmeg, etc. are treated as one lot
1–5	All kinds of spices		4,344.56	

nineties was also transacted by foreigners, i.e. not by merchants of Pozsony.[20] Thus only the thirtieth register of Pozsony for the fiscal year 1457–58–from the end of April, 1457, to the end of April, 1458–can be used for comparison. In this year–when in Western Hungary foreign trade was at the height of prosperity–F. Kováts, the meritorious statistician of the thirtieth register, having gone into establishing the amount of the imported spice supplies to Pozsony, came to the results presented in Table III.[21]

As shown in Table III, the principal item of spice imports to Pozsony: pepper, amounted to about 166 2/3 quintals *(centners)*, representing a customs value of 2,833 1/2 (according to another estimate 5,004) florins. Since most probably spice goods were weighed in Buda quintals (of 120 pounds) which correspond to 58.8

[20] Statistical calculation of the customs (tricesima) register of Pozsony for April 27, 1496 to April 19, 1498, has nevertheless been done, separating the items of the fiscal years 1496–1497 and 1497–1498. These are to be dealt with in detail elsewhere, here only a part result is presented. Merchants of Pozsony imported 22 1/2 quintals and 8 pounds of pepper in 1496–97, 29 quintals and 16 pounds in 1497–98, the total of two years amounting approximately to as much as that of one year in 1457–58. In all probability, therefore, the total pepper import of Pozsony was smaller at the end than in the middle of the century.

[21] Kováts: *op. cit.*, p. 81.

kilograms,[22] in the fiscal year 1457–58 *pepper imports of Pozsony*, amounted to *about 98 metric quintals*, as calculated by Kováts.[23]

Let us now draw a parallel between these figures and the respective data of the South-Transylvanian customs records tabulated by the present author. As evidenced by Table I, in the year 1500, 105 3/4 quintals *(kanthners)* of pepper were imported to Nagyszeben in the customs value of 4,120 1/2 florins. However, this quantity is dwarfed by the imports of Brassó. Here, as shown in Table II, in the year 1503 imports of pepper amounted to 719 1/4 quintals, of 32,084 4/5 florins customs value. In view of the fact that the proportions of the twentieth revenues of Nagyszeben and Brassó underwent little change in the years in question,[24] it seems permissible to totalize imports to Nagyszeben in 1500 and imports to Brassó in 1503. So in the opening years of the 16th century pepper imports streaming from Wallachia to Transylvania through these two stations amounted to yearly 825 quintals altogether and represented a customs value of over 36,200 florins. Since the weight of the quintal *(kanthner)* in use here presumably corresponded to 56,144–56,716 kilograms,[25] *the total yearly pepper import of Brassó and Nagyszeben* in the opening years of the 16th century may be put at *463.188–467.907 metric quintals.*

Thus the quantity of pepper imported from the direction of the Black Sea—more accurately: the annual quantity reaching Transylvania by the main route of the eastern import at the turn of the 15th and 16th centuries—was *nearly five times*[26] as much as the yearly volume of pepper coming from the direction of the Adriatic, more precisely: forwarded to Hungary along the principal route of the western import in the mid- 15th century. In this sense the quantity of spice imports coming from the region of the Black Sea was *"large"*: they contributed in a very significant degree to supplying the Transylvanian and Hungarian markets.

This statement applies in the first place to the most important kind of spice, to pepper, but it may be extended to other oriental spices, too. As shown by Tables I and

[22] The term *centn, centner* used in 15th-century Pozsony, found also in customs registers, stood for four kinds of quintal: that of Vienna weighing 100 or 120 pounds, and that of Buda weighing 100 or 120 pounds. The 100-pound quintal of Buda weighed 49 kilograms, the 120-pound quintal weighed 58.8 kilograms; the 100-pound quintal of Vienna weighed 56 kilograms, the 120-pound quintal weighed 67.2 kg. Of the four units of weight to be considered Kováts thought the use of the 120-pound Buda quintal the most likely; *op. cit.*, pp. 78–79, and Kováts: Pénzértékviszonyok Pozsonyban 1435–60 között (Monetary Value Relations in Pozsony between 1435 and 1460), *Magyar Gazdaságtörténelmi Szemle* (Hungarian Economic History Review; hereafter MGSZ), 1900, p. 386. Cf. B. Hóman's assertion that the 120-pound Hungarian quintal weighed 58.92906–59.86445 kilograms, while the 100-pound Vienna quintal corresponded to 56.1229 kilograms; see: *Magyar pénztörténet 1000–1325* (Monetary History of Hungary, 1000–1325), Budapest, 1916, pp. 118, 122: A 15–19. századi magyar súlymértékekről (Hungarian weights in the 15th–19th centuries).

[23] Kováts: *op. cit.*, 1902, p. 79.

[24] Cf. e.g. *Quellen zur Geschichte Siebenbürgens aus sächsischen Archiven*, I, pp. 311–312.

[25] See Appendix

[26] 4.726- to 4.775-fold.

II, at the turn of the 15th and 16th centuries, the ginger imports of Nagyszeben and Brassó totalled 45 quintals and 1/2 pound, of 1.383 1/4 florins customs value, while those of Pozsony amounted at the middle of the 15th century only to 268 pounds (calculated in 120-pound Buda quintals 2 quintals and 28 pounds) of 67 florins customs value; clove import of the South-Transylvanian towns was 11 quintals and 6 pounds of 889 1/2 florins customs value, that of Pozsony only 130 pounds (calculated in 120-pound Buda quintals 1 quintal and 10 pounds) of 78 florins customs value; the proportions emerging from these volumes are but slightly "improved", bringing them nearer to the above-mentioned ratio of pepper imports, when "mixed spices" figuring in Pozsony imports with 218 1/2 florins customs value are also taken into consideration. It was in saffron alone that imports of Pozsony considerably surpassed those of Transylvania. However, saffron did not belong to the group of spices of exclusively oriental origin, since it had also been produced in European countries, including Hungary.[27]

Another single feature of the comparison between the items of Pozsony in the fiscal year 1457-58 and those of Nagyszeben and Brassó in the years 1500 and 1503, respectively, has to be emphasized, too, notably the price of pepper (or its customs value or assessed value). Regarding the mid-15th century Pozsony F. Kováts has given two estimated values: in accordance with his statistical methods,[28] the customs value of 1 quintal pepper he counted in 17 florins, its market price in 30 florins, with reference to a deal transacted in Buda in the year 1438.[29] On the other hand, as shown above, the customs value of a (slightly lighter) quintal of pepper was registered in 1500 at Nagyszeben as 40-44 florins (averaging 41.33 florins), in 1503 at Brassó as 40-55 florins (averaging 44.6 florins). Obviously enough, between the two points of time there was a steep rise in the price of pepper; it is, however, questionable whether the price increase came about in the years between 1460 and 1490 or set in as a new development at the turn of the century. Concerning the main Mediterranean route of Levantine trade *Frederic C. Lane*,[30] and *Eliahu Ashtor*[31] have lately come to the

[27] For saffron production in Hungary see, e.g., the records of the estates of Léka and Csejte; see: F. Maksay: *Urbáriumok, 16-17. század* (Manorial Records, 16th-17th Centuries), Budapest, 1959, pp. 104, 244, 247, 249-251, 254, 256, 259-262, 264, 266-268, 272, 273-276. "Saffron ... became acclimatized all over Europe ... So people of the West did not have to turn to the Orient in order to obtain this favoured merchandise. Notwithstanding its own saffron production, Europe nevertheless continued to show a demand for oriental produce of superior quality"; see: W. Heyd: *Die Geschichte des Levantehandels im Mittelalter,* Stuttgart, 1879, II. 645-646. It must be remarked that later, for instance in 1540, besides pepper, considerable lots of saffron were brought to Szeben; see: Goldenberg: *op. cit.*, pp. 398-399.

[28] Kováts regarded the use of a certain principle of imposing customs duty—rendered very probable from numerous aspects—as the pillar of his statistical method, according to which "1 florin customs duty (tricesima) was to be paid per 17 florins assessed value; thus the assessed value (customs value) amounted to 17 times the customs duty imposed on the goods". As a matter of fact, "1 golden florin was to be paid as duty on 1 quintal of pepper." See *op. cit.*, pp. 19, 78.

[29] Kováts: *op. cit.*, pp. 21, 79.

[30] Lane: *op. cit.*, New York, 1968, pp. 590-597.

[31] E. Ashtor: La découverte de la voie maritime aux Indes et les prix des épices, in: *Mélanges,* I, pp. 31-38.

conclusion that, contrary to the traditional concept which had assumed an increase in the price of oriental spices during the century prior to the geographical discoveries, stimulating ocean-wide enterprises, the price of spices at Alexandria and Venice actually declined considerably in the course of the 15th century, and it was only after 1498 that a rise of prices—lasting several decades—ensued (not only in Venetian but also in Portuguese relations). The curve of changes in pepper prices may have been similar on the trade route studied in the present paper, too. Contrary to the above quoted prices of *40–44* florins of Nagyszeben in 1500 and *40–55* florins of Brassó in 1503–and the list could be completed in a large number of cases by prices varying between 36 and 54 florins, in most instances 40–42 florins for the years 1502–1509[32]–on the strength of an account of Szeben from the year 1495, only *22* (!) florins were paid for a quintal of pepper.[33] However, since only this single record of South-Transylvanian pepper prices is known from the decade *preceding* the year 1500, it may be interpreted solely as a *possibility* of the price curve of the Wallachian–Transylvanian spice trade having developed in the direction as indicated in the Venetian commerce.

In effect this brings us back to our original question concerning the order of magnitude of imports—to another, wider aspect of the issue, namely the quantitative proportion of spice import through the overland route from the Black Sea region in relation to the traffic on the *main* route of Levantine trade, that is the sea-borne spice import transacted by *Venice.*

According to the data and estimates of Frederic C. Lane,[34] regarded by *Fernand Braudel* too as a starting-point,[35] completed by Eliahu Ashtor's further contributions,[36] at the close of the 15th century and at the very beginning of the 16th (before the Portuguese opened up the direct maritime route to India, or the effect of this event came to be felt in the spice trade) Venetian galleys brought home from their principal Levantine supply port, *Alexandria,* a yearly average of approximately 1,150,000 English lbs of pepper, i.e. about 5,215.25 metric quintals. At the same time pepper imports of *Brassó and Nagyszeben* from the region of the Black Sea may be estimated to have totalled—as shown before—463.2–467.9 metric quintals. Thus South-Transylvanian imports amounted to *8.89–8.98 per cent,* to nearly the eleventh part of Venetian imports shipped at Alexandria.

If beside *Alexandria* the other important source of spice supplies, *Beirut,* is also taken into consideration, average yearly pepper imports of Venice, also according to

[32] *Quellen zur Geschichte Siebenbürgens aus sächsischen Archiven,* I, pp. 313–314, 318, 332–335.

[33] *Ibid,* p. 196.

[34] Lane: Venetian Shipping during the Commercial Revolution, *American Historical Review,* 38, 1933, and Lane: The Mediterranean Spice Trade: Further Evidence of its Revival in the Sixteenth Century, *American Historical Review,* 45, 1940; reprinted in: B. Pullan (ed.): *Crisis and Change in the Venetian Economy in the Sixteenth and Seventeenth Centuries,* London, 1968, pp. 33, 35, 47, 54; and Lane: *Venice and History,* Baltimore, 1966, pp. 13, 25.

[35] F. Braudel: *La Méditerranée et le monde méditerranéen à l'époque de Philippe II,* 2nd ed., Paris, 1966, I, p. 500.

[36] Ashtor: *op. cit.* I, pp. 38–41 and The Volume of Levantine Trade in the Later Middle Ages (1370–1498), *The Journal of European Economic History,* 4, Rome, 1975, No. 3, pp. 607–609.

Lane,[37] may at the time have increased to about 1,400,000 to 1,750,000 English lbs, i.e. to *6,349 to 7,936 metric quintals.* Compared to these figures the volume of merchandise travelling along the overland route was only *5.84–7.38 per cent:* so the City of Saint Mark handled more than thirteenfold or even seventeenfold volumes of the pepper supplies forwarded from the region of the Black Sea to Transylvania. Of course, at the time the city state was *already* and *still* a virtually monopolist supplier of Western European and West-Central European markets in oriental spices and in Levantine articles,[38] by running a service of 9–10 galleys annually to the eastern basin of the Mediterranean. Viewed in *this* aspect, the pepper import of Brassó–Nagyszeben was *"small".* More precisely, its volume makes clear numerically the place and role of the Wallachian–Transylvanian route in the whole route system of late medieval Levantine trade.

2

Table I and Table II shed light not only on the order of magnitude of South-Transylvanian spice imports and the sorts of goods involved, but also illustrate the distribution of imports among various groups of merchants, thus providing an answer to the *second* question posed in the introduction: who acted as middlemen of spice imports. In the picture presented, the *predominant participation of Wallachian merchants* is a striking feature. In the year 1500 the whole of spice imports to Nagyszeben and in 1503, 82.11 per cent (according to customs value 83.14 per cent) of the spice imports to Brassó, including 82.55 per cent import of pepper (83.29 per cent of customs value), were transacted by Wallachians.

In the case of Nagyszeben this is hardly astonishing. The charter of King Louis of Anjou from as far back as 1382–quoted so often in historical literature[39]–bears witness to the reluctance of many a burgher of Szeben to take the risks of going in for active trading in areas south of the Carpathians; they kept all the more jealously

[37] See Note 34. According to the sources and assessments of Ashtor, at the end of the 15th century the Venetians imported from Egypt (Alexandria), and Syria (Beirut and Damascus) altogether 2,500–3,000 *sportas* of pepper yearly; see: Ashtor: *op. cit.*, 1973, I, pp. 39–40 and Ashtor, *op. cit.* 1975, p. 607. This is slightly below the calculation of Lane, because 1,400,000–1,750,000 English lbs correspond to about 2,800–3,500 sportas. Hence, preferably, South-Transylvanian imports have been calculated with the lower value, Venetian imports with the higher. For conversion of the *sporta*, see Lane: *op. cit.*, 1968, pp. 591–592; Ashtor: *op. cit.*, 1973, I, p. 46 and 1975, p. 576. According to Schaube: *op. cit.*, p. 814, the *sporta* unit used in Alexandria weighed 217.5 kilograms, the *cargo* usual in Venice (see Note 16), corresponding to 400 *libbre sottili,* weighed 121 kilograms.

[38] Cf. Ashtor: The Venetian Supremacy in Levantine Trade: Monopoly or Pre-Colonialism? *The Journal of European Economic History*, 3, Rome, 1974, No. 1, p. 5 et seq.

[39] G. Pray: *Specimen hierarchiae Hungaricae complectens seriem chronologicam archiepiscoporum et episcoporum Hungariae*, II, Posonii et Cassoviae, 1779, pp. 261–262. St. Katona: *Historia critica regum Hungariae stirpis mixtae, ex fide domesticorum et exterorum scriptorum concinnata,* tomulus III, ordine X, Budae 1790, pp. 713–714. Fejér: *Codex diplomaticus Hungariae ecclesiasticus ac civilis*, IX, 5, Budae, 1834, pp. 517–573. Fr. Zimmermann, C. Werner and G. Müller: *Urkundenbuch zur Geschichte der Deutschen in Siebenbürgen*, II, Hermannstadt, 1897, p. 555.

watchful eyes on preventing Balkan merchants, crossing from Wallachia over Vöröstorony (Rotenturm, Turnu Roşu) Pass to enter Transylvania, from travelling *beyond* Szeben, in order to secure for themselves the profits deriving from *further* mediation (and detail sales in the town).[40] The fact that the nature of their activities did not undergo any change later either is revealed not only by the twentieth registers, but also by other sources, e.g. the documents of a litigation in the year 1500, of legal proceedings of a merchant of Tîrgovişte against the widow of a burgher of Szeben.[41] In the case of *Brassó*, on the other hand, the prominent role of Wallachian importers in the early 16th century indicates a *change* compared to conditions which prevailed under Louis of Anjou and Sigismund of Luxemburg, when spice consignments to Brassó from the region of the Black Sea were an *active* branch of commerce pursued by Brassó townsmen, who, in possession of their privileges, acquired both from the Hungarian and the Rumanian sides, were free to trade "along the Brassó route as far as Brăila", even farther "up to the Great Sea".[42]

The roots of the change may be traced as far back as the first half of the 15th century. It should be kept in mind that King Sigismund, who granted charters, among others in 1419 and 1428, to the Transylvanian Saxons for their journeys to Wallachia over the Törcsvár (Törzburg, Bran) Pass,[43] in 1426 also provided for protection to merchants coming to Brassó *from* the "Transalpine" (i.e. Transcarpathian) parts and *returning* there subsequently, against customs abuses at Törcsvár.[44] This is a sign of the fact that not only merchants of Brassó went to regions beyond the Carpathians, but Wallachian traders also brought their wares, including oriental spices, to Brassó. Sigismund's successor on the Hungarian throne, Albert of Habsburg, also espoused the cause of "Transalpine" trade of merchants of Brassó and Barcaság in the opening

[40] For the interpretation of the charter see: A Levante-kereskedelem erdélyi útvonala I. Lajos és Zsigmond korában (The Transylvanian Route of Levantine Trade in the Ages of Louis I and Sigismund), *Századok*, 1975, No. 1, p. 48.

[41] Michne (Mihnea), a Tîrgovişte merchant maintained regular business relations with Niklaus Proll of Szeben, supplying chiefly pepper and purchasing knives. When Proll died he had a claim of 281 florins on Mihnea, and a debt of 31,000 knives and 3 quintals pepper (to be paid to the customs officers). However, the widow repudiated this debt and the court of justice of Szeben decided in favour of the widow. Thereupon the Wallachian voivod Radul (Radul cel Mare IV; see later) himself put in a word at Szeben and the seven Saxon quarters in the interest of Mihnea, with reference to the testimony of several Wallachian merchants (including Dragata of Argeş and Kyrka of Tîrgovişte). Documents: Radul's letter to Szeben, Tîrgovişte, April 12, 1500; see: Eu. de Hurmuzaki: *Documente privitoare la Istoria Românilor* (hereafter: *Documente privitoare*), XV, 1, Acte şi scrisori din arhivele oraşelor ardelene (Bistriţa, Braşov, Sibiu) publicate de N. Jorga, Bucureşti, 1911, pp. 152–153; Radul's letter to the seven Saxon quarters, Tîrgovişte, April 12, 1500: *ibid*, pp. 153–154; the Council of Szeben appointed a day for investigating the case, Szeben, April 25, 1500: *ibid*, p. 154. Radul to Szeben, Tîrgovişte, May 31, 1500: it is not fixing of a date which is required but prompt decision of the issue: *ibid.*, pp. 154–155. Unfortunately the final outcome of the lawsuit is unknown.

[42] A part of the pertinent source material see: Levantine Trade and Hungary in the Middle Ages, *Études Historiques Hongroises* 1975, I, pp. 300–303.

[43] (Fr. Zimmermann–) G. Gündisch: *Urkundenbuch zur Geschichte der Deutschen in Siebenbürgen*, IV, Hermannstadt, 1937, pp. 102–103, 365–367.

[44] (Zimmermann–) Gündisch: *Urkundenbuch*, IV, pp. 248–249.

months of 1438 by making Vlad Dracul, the Voivod of Wallachia, promise that *Saxon* merchants would not be harassed in his country, and furthermore would be protected against the Turks.[45] However, a few months later he extended his protection to those arriving from and returning to "partibus Transalpinis": castellans and customs officers of Törcsvár were instructed against extracting unwarranted and excessive payments from Wallachian *(Volachus)* merchants, because as a retaliation traders of Brassó and Barcaság would be treated similarly at Wallachian customs stations.[46] About this time Voivod Vlad Dracul himself turned in the commercial interest of his subjects to the town council of Brassó,[47] in 1441 to János Hunyadi as Voivod of Transylvania, urging repeatedly the cessation of the abuses perpetrated by Törcsvár officials,[48] who, as evidenced by a charter of the Transylvanian Voivods Miklós Újlaki and János Hunyadi from the year 1446, did not refrain from molesting merchants of Brassó similarly by exacting excessive customs duties.[49] The issue continued to remain on the agenda in *both* relations: as Governor of Hungary, in 1452 János Hunyadi again warned the castellans of Törcsvár to treat merchants, "signanter . . . *Volahos*", correctly and refrain from demanding "indebitum tributum";[50] in 1453 János Hunyadi, in 1454, King László V issued similar commands to the castellans of Törcsvár (and neigbouring Királykő [Piatra Craiului]) in order to safeguard the interests of merchants of *Brassó*;[51] in the next year it was again János Hunyadi who issued a charter providing for the protection of merchants on their way from "Transalpine parts" to Transylvania as well as of traders of Brassó travelling to Wallachia.[52]

Hence there can be no doubt that the active trade of Wallachians with Brassó did exist as early as the 1420s and 1430s, but up to the middle of the century the commercial activities of Brassó burghers in Wallachia appear to have been preponderant. This is supported by the leaders of the town having induced in 1443 the Transylvanian Voivods Miklós Újlaki and János Hunyadi to renew their charter

[45] Gündisch: *Urkundenbuch zur Geschichte der Deutschen in Siebenbürgen*, V, Bukarest, 1975, pp. 3–4.

[46] Gündisch: *Urkundenbuch*, V, pp. 8–9.

[47] J. Bogdan: *Documente şi regeste privitoare la relaţiile Ţării Rumîneşti cu Braşovul şi Ungaria in secolul XV şi XVI* (hereafter: *Documente şi regeste*), Bucureşti, 1902, pp. 43, 55–56.; Gündisch: *Urkundenbuch*, V, pp. 9–10.

[48] Bogdan: *Documente şi regeste*, p. 53. Gündisch: *Urkundenbuch*, V, p. 74. Cf. letters of the same year addressed to the Council of Brassó by Miklós Ujlaki and János Hunyadi, Voivods of Transylvania, and by Vlad Dracul, Voivod of Wallachia; see: Bogdan: *Documente şi regeste*, p. 52. Gündisch: *Urkundenbuch*, V, pp. 90–91.

[49] Gündisch: *Urkundenbuch*, V, pp. 164; cf. pp. 107, 146.

[50] Gündisch: *Urkundenbuch*, V, p. 352.

[51] Gündisch: *Urkundenbuch*, V, pp. 405–406, 441–442.

[52] J. Teleki: *Hunyadiak kora Magyarországon, X, Oklevéltár* (The Age of the Hunyadis in Hungary, X, *Documents*), Pest, 1853, pp. 487–488. Gündisch: *Urkundenbuch*, V, pp. 509–510. Further on, cf. with King Matthias's charter of 1467 in which merchants of *Brassó* and Barcaság "in negotiationibus seu mercantiis ad partes transalpinas et ab illic redeuntes" were exempted from the payment of toll at Törcsvár as a reward for their merits in loyalty; see: Hurmuzaki: *Documente privitoare*, XV, 1, 65, and also the charter of the Transylvanian Voivod János Pongrác of Dengeleg from the year 1468 forbidding the castellans of Törcsvár again to fleece "negotiatores . . . cum rebus eorum *de Vlachya* ad Brassoviam et inde iterum ad propria redeuntes"; *ibid*, p. 69.

protecting their Transcarpathian trade; this document included numerous paragraphs referring to their earlier privileges, particularly to the charter issued by the Wallachian Voivod Mircea in Latin and Slavic in the year 1413.[53]

According to this deed customs duty was levied on goods exported over the Törcsvár Pass at the stations *Ručar* (Ruffa Arbor), *Dîmbovița, Tîrgoviște, Tîrgușor* (Novum Forum) and *Brăila,* tariff depending on kind and quantity; in case of further transport or crossing the Danube *("si cum mercimoniis suis transierint ultra Danubium"),* and subsequently upon their return from the region of the Black Sea or from parts beyond the Danube *("venientes de marinis partibus seu Transdanubium")* a thirtieth payment was exacted ("de centum persolvant tria") on their exports and imports, respectively.[54] Obviously, in his charter dated August, 1444, at Tîrgoviște, Voivod Vlad Dracul alluded to this text, confirming the privileges granted by his father Mircea to Brassó and recognized recently ("ultimo modo") by János Hunyadi.[55] His successor, Vladislav II (Vladislav Dan)—helped to power[56] by János Hunyadi against Vlad Dracul who had become untrustworthy after the defeat of Varna—concluded with Brassó a new agreement between 1447 and 1452, providing for mutual adherence to earlier arrangements and free use of the *"route of Prahova"*[57] leading into Wallachia from the Tömös (Timiș) Pass.[58] When, in the dispute over the ownership of Fogaras (Făgăraș) and in the subject of Turkish policy[59] "conflicts and differences were provoked" between Vladislav and Hunyadi[60] and when, in spring of 1456, the reign of Vladislav was toppled with Transylvanian support by his rival, Dracul's son, Vlad Țepeș,[61] in the autumn of the same year the new Voivod of Wallachia ensured commercial freedom in his country to burghers of Brassó in return

[53] Bogdan: *Documente și regeste,* pp. 3–5. (Zimmermann–) Gündisch: *Urkundenbuch,* IV, pp. 425–426.

[54] Gündisch: *Urkundenbuch,* V, pp. 106–107.

[55] Gündisch: *Urkundenbuch,* V, pp. 145–146. In the age of János Hunyadi the route in question also served the military supply of the settlement on the Black Sea coast: Chilia (which came under Hungarian control for a time in the year 1448). In 1453 Vladislav II requested the Council of Brassó to forward "caute et secrete . . . ad curiam et domum nostram in *Tergovistia,* ab hinc tandem . . . caute et occulte ad *Braillam,* ab hinc vero usque castrum *Kilye*" the weapons sent by János Hunyadi for the defence of Chilia, *ibid.* p. 391. In 1454 it was Hunyadi himself who warned the Brassó Council that after the *census* on St. Martin's Day "duo milia sagittas, quindecim arcus, ducenta amenta vulgo ideg et duas *centenas aut masas* ferri . . . pro conservatione civitatis nostrae *Kylia* usque *Brailla* conduci facere debeatis": *ibid.,* p. 446.

[56] For relations of Vladislav with János Hunyadi and the town of Brassó see: Gündisch: *Urkundenbuch,* V, p. 205 (1447); pp. 259–260 (1448); etc.

[57] As far back as the year 1358 the charter of Louis I was the first to grant preference in support of the "transalpine" trade of Brassó merchants, permitting free passage to Wallachia between the rivers *Prahova* and *Bodza* (Buzău); see: Fejér: *Codex,* IX, 2, Budae, 1833, p. 688

[58] Bogdan: *Documente și regeste,* pp. 59–60. Gündisch: *Urkundenbuch,* V, pp. 227–228.

[59] Bogdan: *Documente și regeste,* pp. 60–61. Gündisch: *Urkundenbuch,* V, pp. 336–337. Cf. Teleki: *op. cit.,* X, pp. 322–323, 333–334. Gündisch: *Urkundenbuch,* V, pp. 337–339, 513–514.

[60] Teleki: *op. cit.,* X, p. 487. Gündisch: *Urkundenbuch,* V, p. 510.

[61] Teleki: *op. cit.,* X, pp. 527–528. Gündisch: *Urkundenbuch,* V, pp. 519–520, 530–538; Cf. pp. 542–543.

for right of asylum against the Turks and later, at the end of 1457, on the basis of reciprocity.[62]

It is worth while to compare with the texts of these sources the letter addressed by Vlad Ţepeş to the authorities of Brassó—about two decades later (1476), when he endeavoured to recapture his throne with Transylvanian and Moldavian help (with success for a few months). "Corruption" of old traditions is mentioned and promises are held out to restore the Wallachian privileges of merchants of Brassó and Barcaság in the form "of old times under Voivod Mircea", as enjoyed in the period of "the great Voivod Vlad" (Dracul) and in his own first reign: to trade "*without scale*", "to purchase freely . . . on every market of everything they need", and "to pay justly imposed customs duty, as earlier".[63]

Thus, in the meantime the situation had changed thoroughly. However, in his letter of 1476 Vlad Ţepeş omitted to mention that it was he who had initiated the change, "corrupting" old customs in the Wallachian trade of Brassó merchants, when as far back as his first reign--after consolidation of his power against Dan, a claimant to the throne–[64] he carried out a turn-about of commercial policy. Most probably it was in the year 1458 that he introduced the "*scale*" i.e. obligatory places for depositing wares from Brassó, actually the institution of "*borderland fairs*" endowed with staple rights.[65] In the opening months of 1459 merchants of Brassó and of Barcaság staying in Wallachia were treated with hard violence,[66] and Barcaság was attacked by an armed force.[67]

Regarding restrictions of Transcarpathian trade of the Brassó merchants the successor of Vlad Ţepeş, Radul III (cel Frumos), followed in the footsteps of his

[62] Bogdan: *Documente şi regeste*, p. 62. Gündisch: *Urkundenbuch*, V, pp. 540–541, 581.

[63] October 7, 1476; see: Bogdan: *Documente şi regeste*, pp. 64–66. Soon after (October-November, 1476) the merchants of Brassó were informed that the whole of Wallachia was occupied and the roads were equally clear for them in the directions of *Rucăr, Prahova, Teleajen*, as well as Buzău; *ibid.*, pp. 66–67. Cf. with the letter of István Báthory, Lord Chief Justice and Commander of the Royal Army fighting in Wallachia, dated Nov. 11, 1476, in which he informed the town of Szeben that Basarab (Laiotă) had been driven out of Wallachia, Tîrgovişte was taken and his troops were encamped near to Bucharest; see: Teleki: *op. cit.*, XI, *Documents*, Pest, 1855, pp. 575–576. Hurmuzaki: *Documente privitoare* XV, 1, p. 95. It must be remarked here that as far back as August 4, 1475, in a letter addressed to the town of Szeben from Argeş. Vlad Ţepeş again called himself "Wayvoda, partium Transalpinarum"; *ibid.*, pp. 84–85. In his charter August 15, 1475, King Matthias again regarded him as the Voivod of Wallachia; see: Teleki: *op. cit*, XI, pp. 539–542; in August–September of the year 1475 the town of Szeben was instructed to pay as aid 200 florins to the son of Dracul who actually received this sum; see: Hurmuzaki: *Documente privitoare*, XV, 1, pp. 86–87. For turns in the struggle of Laiotă and Ţepeş for the throne in the year 1476 see: *ibid.*, pp. 86–96.

[64] Teleki: *op. cit.*, X, pp. 582–583. Hurmuzaki: *Documente privitoare*, XV, 1, pp. 48–49. Gündisch: *Urkundenbuch*, V, pp. 555–556, 579–580.

[65] For the introduction of the "scale" and the "borderland fairs" see: Gündisch: Cu privire la relaţii lui Vlad Ţepeş cu Transilvania în anii 1456–1458, *Studii*, 1963, No. 4, pp. 681–696. Manolescu: *op. cit.*, 1965, pp. 55–57.

[66] Information is provided, among others, in the letter of Basarab Dan, the pretender, dated April 5, 1459; see: Bogdan: *Documente şi regeste*, pp. 68–69. Hurmuzaki: *Documente privitoare*, XV, 1, pp. 50–51. Of course Dan made economic concessions to Brassó and waived his claim to the return of Wallachian merchants' goods retained in Brassó; *ibid.*, pp. 53–54 (1460).

[67] Hurmuzaki: *Documente privitoare*, XV, 1, pp. 52, 54, 56 (1459, 1460).

predecessor. This is indicated by a note of the Hungarian King Matthias addressed to Radul in the year 1468: merchants of Brassó "should be allowed to retain their old privileges, customs and rights; their activities and trading during their stay in Wallachia should not fall under local jurisdiction".[68] The king's intervention is unlikely to have had effect. In his letter (from the period between 1462 and 1470) Radul reproached the merchants of Brassó for having failed to settle their considerable debts to Wallachian traders and made full payment of these liabilities a precondition of his permit consenting to their free travelling and trading in his country (as applied for several times).[69] In his charter dated from Bucharest, 1470, besides complaining of similar grievances Radul stipulated as a condition of the permit that ". . . my men should be allowed to move . . . and trade freely in your country. . ." and ". . . should be permitted to go anywhere in the King's country, *even as far as Várad*" (Oradea). "And if somebody leaves his merchandise there [i.e. in Brassó] . . . *upon his return* he should be free to recover his goods and do with them what he can."[70] Although in the autumn of 1473 his successor Basarab II (cel Bătrîn, also known as Laiotă), who appeared at the time only as a pretender, again assured the Brassó burghers that they would be able to communicate and trade freely in Wallachia, and "let bygones be bygones",[71] as soon as he came into power his tone changed, becoming similar to that of Radul. His reply to the petition put in by the town council in 1474 ran as follows: ". . . Your Honours' merchants should sell their wares at my princely seats, at Tîrgovişte and Tîrguşor and Cîmpulung; but they should sell *wholesale* to our people, and *not frequent other market towns.* However, if Your Honours will grant our merchants freedom to buy and sell *everywhere in the country of the King, at Várad and Kolozsvár, at Temesvár and Rozsnyó as well as in Barcaság* [at Oradea and Cluj, at Timişoara and Rişnov as well as in Ţara Bîrsei], we shall let Your Honours' tradesmen buy and sell everywhere in our country."[72]

The tests of the above-quoted charters of 1470 and 1474 make it clear how the situation had changed. In fact, bilateral grievances, resort to force had of course also

[68] Hurmuzaki: *Documente privitoare*, XV, 1, pp. 68–69.

[69] Bogdan: *Documente şi regeste*, pp. 71–72. Our thanks are due to Z. Szász for having translated from Rumanian into Hungarian the text of charters quoted with reference to the work of Bogdan in Note 63 et seq.

[70] Bogdan: *Documente şi regeste*, pp. 71–72. Cf. his letter of the same year from Buzău, according to which "irascamur contra vos" (sc. Brassovienses); because they tolerated espionage against him by Ştefan, Voivod of Moldavia, and also sold weapons to the Moldavians; see: Hurmuzaki: *Documente privitoare*, XV, 1, pp. 75–76; furthermore a letter from the year 1472 when his reign was already threatened by Basarab Laiotă, too; *ibid.*, pp. 78–79.

[71] Bogdan: *Documente şi regeste*, pp. 75–76.

[72] Bogdan: *Documente şi regeste*, pp. 80–82. Here it has to be stated that unlike Bogdan who put the date of the charter at 1474, recent Rumanian historical research has put the date of the document at 1517, while the commercial policy of Basarab Laiotă is denoted as retrograde compared to that of his predecessors; see: Manolescu: *op. cit.*, 1957, p. 124; 1965, pp. 58, 61. Uncertainty derives from the first words of the undated document—"I Voivod Basarab"—which may refer to Basarab Laiotă (1474–1477) or to Neagoe Basarab (1512–1521). It is, however, certain that the essence of the wishes expressed here were also contained by the letter of Radul cel Frumos quoted before (Note 70) and dated 1470 beyond any doubt.

occurred earlier.[73] The new *economic* feature emerged owing to the class of Wallachian merchants having grown stronger in the meantime. Tradesmen coming from "Transalpine" parts were no longer content to forward their wares *to Brassó*, but also strove to penetrate the Transylvanian market, *"right up to Várad"* and furthermore to secure the right to *take back with them* freely their unsold wares from Brassó. On the other hand, they were no longer willing to let Saxon merchants of Transylvania travel *beyond* the Cîmpulung-Tîrgovişte-Tîrguşor line, to the Danube, to Brăila or the coast of the Black Sea; and even along the route thus curtailed they wished to restrict the sale of commodities by Transylvanian merchants to *wholesale deals*, in order to keep the profits accruing from sales in retail to themselves. As a result of the altered *political* power relations the Voivod of Wallachia could be won over to support the claims of Wallachian merchants who paid the Voivod taxes after their income.[74] As Turkish pressure increased and attacks were renewed–the Pasha of Szendrő (Smederevo) made an onslaught against Várad itself just in the year 1474, then invaded the territory up to the river Fehér Körös (Cris)[75]– the political influence and the military strength of the Hungarian King and the Voivod of Transylvania seemed to weaken in the Transcarpathian region, compared to conditions in the age of János Hunyadi.

Let it be interposed here: the commercial aspirations expressed in the above charters sound familiar. Wallachian merchants with the support of the voivod made on *Brassó* demands which were similar to those their predecessors had attempted to realize a century before in their dealings with *Nagyszeben*, without political backing. The charter of Louis I from the year 1382 was intended to frustrate these endeavours, declaring–as it did[76]– that "mercatores extranei" arriving from Wallachia to Szeben, particularly with pepper, saffron and other spices, were *not allowed* to travel *further into Transylvania* but were to market their goods in Szeben, exclusively in *large lots*, and commodities must *not be taken back* to Transalpine parts because they could not be forwarded any further or sold in retail. To baffle similar endeavours, the burghers of Brassó, in 1468, contrived to obtain from King Matthias a charter *providing for*

[73] In addition to the above-mentioned cases see: Gündisch: *Urkundenbuch*, V, pp. 357 (1452), 468 (1454), 539 (1456), 552 (1456–1461). Hurmuzaki: *Documente privitoare*, XV, 1, pp. 54 (1460), 68 (1468), 91–92 (1476); etc. From aspects of our subject, the cases mentioned by King Matthias in his letter addressed to Brassó in 1459, are of particular interest. It says: "nonnullae res ad septem milia flor. auri per certos homines partium *transalpinarum* nuper, dum videlicet ... guerra et turbationes per Waywodam transalpinum [sc. Vlad Ţepeş] suscitatae fuissent, in medio vestri repositae extitissent", and the authorities of Brassó refuse to give them back; furthermore "cum pridem castellani ... comitum Siculorum nostrorum in *Therch* a quibusdam hominibus in falsa et sinistra via proficiscentibus certam quantitatem *piperis* ad valorem sexingentorum flor. auri se extendentem abstulissent, tunc ... [the authorities of Brassó] eosdem castellanos nostros captivassent, nec prius dimisissent, donec ab eisdem huiusmodi quantitatem piperis extorsissent"; see: Hurmuzaki: *Documente privitoare*, XV, 1, pp. 52–53.

[74] In Basarab's above-mentioned letter addressed to Brassó we may read: "... if we permit Your Honour's merchants to buy and sell in our towns, how will our poor and our merchants make money ... how will they be able to pay tax to ourselves"; see: Bogdan: *Documente şi regeste*, p. 81.

[75] B. Hóman and Gy. Szekfü: *Magyar történet* (Hungarian History), 2nd ed., Budapest, 1936, II, p. 507.

[76] See Note 39.

staple right in their dealings with Wallachian and Moldavian merchants,[77] while charters from the year 1482 *prohibited retail sales* by "foreign merchants" in Saxon towns.[78]

At the beginning of the reigns of Wallachian voivods who succeeded Vlad Ţepeş, and Laiotă, the demands of their merchants were mostly moderated—particularly at times when the voivod had come into power with Transylvanian support; however, later—chiefly when a pretender turned to Brassó for help—they were renewed. Thus in his letters written in 1479–80 to the town council and to the Transylvanian voivod Stephen Báthory, Basarab III (cel Tînăr or Ţepeluş) still emphasized the freedom of trade enjoyed by merchants of Brassó in Wallachia;[79] but in 1480-81—when his relations to Stephen Báthory assumed a hostile character—the wishes and grievances of his own merchants were again given dominant emphasis.[80] "... you refuse to let them sell to other Hungarian merchants", he accused the authorities of Brassó; "if you feel so inclined you do not permit them to return with their wares ... but retain their *pepper*" and in doing business "... you cause a loss in pepper with the sieve".[81] For these reasons he threatened to introduce counter-measures which implied the reestablishment of "borderland fairs" initiated in his time by Vlad Ţepeş and the complete debarring of the merchants of Brassó from trading in Wallachia: "... come and take delivery of commodities from our merchants at the border, our merchants will pay customs duty to the Turks and to ourselves, you will do so to the Hungarians."[82] His successor, Vlad III (Călugărul)—who had lived in Transylvania before coming into power[83]—in the first few years of his reign (1482–84) also abolished the restrictions hampering the commercial activities of Brassó burghers in Wallachia[84] and assured them of free trade within his country, also *"beyond*

[77] "... dum et quando ac quotienscunque mercatores aut quicunque alii cuiuscunque conditionis existant homines, qui cum eorum mercantiis et rebus venalibus sive de Transalpinis partibus sive de Moldavia ad ipsam civitatem nostram Brassoviensem pervenerint, illi huismodi eorum mercantias ac res venales in praedicta civitate nostra Brassoviensi deponere et collocare, easdemque ibidem et non alias vendere et cum eisdem commutationes rerum facere possint et valeant..."; see: Teleki: *op. cit.*, XI, pp. 353–354. Cf. the charters of King Matthias from the years 1466, 1470 and 1489 which prohibited the export of raw hides and corn by the Wallachian and Moldavian merchants who came to Transylvanian Saxon towns: *ibid.*, XI, pp. 156–158, 408–409. Hurmuzaki: *Documente privitoare*, XV, 1, pp. 60–61, 75, 130–131.

[78] Teleki: *op. cit.*, XII, pp. 224–225.

[79] Bogdan: *Documente şi regeste*, pp. 88–89, 99–100. Hurmuzaki, *Documente privitoare*, XV, 1, pp. 104, 109.

[80] Teleki: *op. cit.*, XII, pp. 173–174 (1481). Hurmuzaki: *Documente privitoare*, XV, 1, pp. 110, 112, 115 (1481).

[81] Pepper has to be sifted, the sack with the pepper powder has to be weighed and returned to the seller—this can be read in the guild regulations of the merchants of Kassa in 1446; MGSZ, 1898, p. 32. The phrase "you cause a loss in pepper with the sieve" may have referred to violation of such a rule of the trade.

[82] Bogdan: *Documente şi regeste*, pp. 102–103.

[83] Hurmuzaki: *Documente privitoare*, XV, 1, pp. 114 (1481).

[84] "... wherever men of Brassó should come with their commodities, to any marketplace or the Danube or anywhere, whether to sell or to buy, they may trade freely ... be it in whatever goods"; see: Bodgan: *Documente şi regeste*, pp. 116–117.

Tîrguşor";[85] however, in the year 1491 he made angry reproaches on account of the wrongs suffered by his men and threatened to take repressive measures.[86] This may have contributed to King of Hungary, Wladislas II warning at the close of the same year the castellans of Törcsvár against collecting illicit customs duties from Wallachian merchants "de *pipere* et piscibus", because such proceedings would be detrimental to his twentieth revenues and provoke the Voivod of Wallachia into treating Transylvanian merchants similarly.[87] On the score of abuses by the customs officers of Törcsvár, in 1493 Prince Vlad actually had mountain passes closed to arrivals from Brassó.[88] Although the next year an agreement was reached providing for reopening of the passes and the restoration of commercial relations[89], soon similar measures were threatened by way of reprisal for holding up and inflicting losses on Wallachian merchants.[90] In 1497 his son, Radul IV (cel Mare) again had all passes leading into Wallachia closed to merchants of Brassó—at the time on that score that his adversary, the pretender Mihnea, was given refuge in "Transylvanian regions".[91]

The next year, actually the next decade brought new developments. In 1498 Wladislas II pledged Törcsvár for ten years, in 1508 for another twenty years, to Brassó. This was, of course, an advantage for the "Crown Town" (that is how it became possible, for example, that Keilhau, a merchant of Brassó having wide interests in spice imports, should simultaneously be the Castellan of Törcsvár),[92] but suited the Wallachians all the less. When Wladislas II again pledged the castle to Brassó in January, 1508,[93] Radul IV—not long before his death and the accession of Mihnea to

[85] Bogdan: *Documente şi regeste*, p. 117.

[86] "And your men came to Brăila, to Floci [south of Brăila, in the neighbourhood of Feteşti, on the bank of the Danube] and to all parts along the Danube" while "our men were not treated justly in your parts". But . . . "your men are quite in my hand"; see: Bogdan: *Documente şi regeste*, pp. 120-122. Cf. *ibid.*, pp. 122-123, 124-125, 127, 128-129.

[87] Hurmuzaki: *Documente privitoare*, XV, 1, p. 132.

[88] Hurmuzaki: *Documente privitoare*, XV, 1, p. 135.

[89] Hurmuzaki: *Documente privitoare*, XV, 1, pp. 136-137. From the charter we learn that merchants of *Brassó*, too, were, as before, exposed to molestations by the toll collectors of Törcsvár "in conductione . . . rerum mercemonialium . . . ad ipsas partes transalpinas"; *ibid.*, p. 137. A charter of 1494 issued by a sub-voivod of Transylvania again draws attention to the wrongs suffered by *Wallachians*, because the officers of Törcsvár have prohibited, "ne aliquis res Volachorum emere audeant"; see: Hurmuzaki: *Documente privitoare*, XV, 1, p. 140.

[90] Hurmuzaki: *Documente privitoare*, XV, 1, pp. 142-143 (1494-1495). "Sciatis"—Wlad wrote to the authorities of Brassó early in 1495—"quod vias claudimus, ut homines nostri ad vos non transiant [!], et vestri ad nos non veniant. Aut putatis, quod *pannum* aut *ferrum* in aliis locis non possumus invenire? In *Moldova* aut in *Turchia* tantum inveniemus, quantum fiet voluntas nostra"; *ibid.*, p. 143.

[91] Bogdan: *Documente şi regeste*, pp. 130-131. Cf. similar complaint of Vlad Călugărul addressed to the town of Szeben in 1494; see: Hurmuzaki: *Documente privitoare*, XV, 1, p. 141, and the letter of János Barcsai, Wladislas II's envoy in Wallachia, addressed to the town of Szeben in the same year, requesting help to get over the border and instructing the authorities not to allow Mihnea to step on Transylvanian soil; *ibid.*, p. 147.

[92] *Quellen zur Geschichte der Stadt Kronstadt in Siebenbürgen*, I, Rechnungen aus dem Archiv der Stadt Kronstadt, I, p. 140.

[93] Bogdan: *Documente şi regeste*, p. 136.

the throne[94]—in February or March of 1508 had "all the roads closed" to travellers from Brassó: "... *the road of Dîmbovița,* the *road of Prahova* and the *road of Teleajen*".[95] Then, the Brassó authorities—having joined forces with Szeben[96] and Beszterce[97]—induced King Wladislas a few months later to renew their staple rights in their dealings with merchants of the Rumanian principalities.[98]

Thus *political* affairs played a rather important role in the development of trade from the region of the Black Sea over Wallachia to Transylvania. The trade was influenced by struggles for the throne of Wallachia, the fluctuating political relations of voivods with Brassó and Transylvania, increasing dependence on the Turkish Court, and direct conquest of the Pontic shores by the Turks.[99] However, the *economic* nucleus of struggles for participation in this trade really lay in Wallachian merchants having grown in strength during the second half of the fifteenth century to become actually rivals of the Transylvanian Saxons. While the merchants of Brassó continued their efforts to maintain their active role in trade transacted south of the Carpathians, Wallachian merchants not only strove to supersede them in

[94] Radul, who at the end of 1507 concluded "pacem seu treugam perpetuam" with Wladislas II and the seven Saxon quarters (see: Hurmuzaki: *Documente privitoare*, I, pp. 177-178), died at the beginning of April, 1508; *ibid.*, XV, 1, p. 181. His successor Mihnea, who had previously lived in "a region of Transylvania" (see Note 91), hastened to assure the town of Szeben early in June that "nolumus nos esse ingrati de beneficiis, quas [!] in Hungaria accepimus"; *ibid.*, pp. 183–184.

[95] Bogdan: *Documente şi regeste*, pp. 135–136. It must be remarked that Manolescu—who also quotes this charter of Radul in his book (however, without the passage referring to blocking the roads)—puts the date of the document at ten years earlier and connects it with the first pledging of Törcsvár; *op. cit.*, 1965, pp. 51-52.

[96] In his letter addressed to Szeben in the year 1500 Radul complained that many of his merchants sustained heavy losses in that town: "Kyrka perdidit V milia florenorum, Dragota perdidit 1000 et 300 flor., Nicula perdidit 3000 flor., Gergina 600 perdidit flor., Dreyusche perdidit 400 flor."; see: Hurmuzaki: *Documente privitoare*, XV, 1, pp. 153-154. Nevertheless, his differences with *Szeben* were less profound [cf. *ibid.*, p. 164 (1504); p. 180 (1508)], since merchants of Szeben, as mentioned before, usually did not pursue *active* trade in Wallachia.

[97] From Moldavia one route to Transylvania led across Radna Pass and through *Beszterce*; this was the route by which the envoys of Ivan III, Grand Duke of Moscow, returned in 1483 from the court of King Matthias at Buda; see: Hurmuzaki: *Documente privitoare*, XV, 1, p. 120. For relations between Beszterce and Suceava (and other places of Moldavia) see: *ibid.*, p. 158 (1502); p. 169 (1504); p. 174 (1506); pp. 187-188 (1508); see also the charter of Wladislas II, dated July 29, 1508, which regulated thirtieth (tricesima) duty to be paid by Moldavian merchants at Beszterce; *ibid.*, pp. 185-186.

[98] "... mercatores de partibus Moldaviae et aliis locis externis ... pro vetere illarum civitatum nostrarum consuetudine et libertate non possent ultra illas civitates nostras cum mercibus eorum progredi, sed in illis duabus civitatibus nostris, cibinensi videlicet et brassoviensi, veluti locis depositions mercium deberent et tenerentur merces suas deponere ... Quapropter ... mercatores forenses et extraneos cum rebus et mercibus eorum, dum ad loca depositionum pervenerint, ad hoc regnum nostrum Hungariae penetrare non permittatis ..."; see: Hurmuzaki: *Documente privitoare*, XV, 1, p. 185 (June 24, 1508).

[99] In 1475 the Turks occupied the most important Black Sea colony of Genoa, Caffa (Feodosia) on the Crimean Peninsula, in 1484 they took Chilia at the mouth of the Danube and Cetatea Albă (Akkerman) at the Dniester estuary.

"Transalpine parts" but also tried to transport their commodities farther and to make their way into the *Transylvanian* market.

The picture of the distribution of spice imports presented by the twentieth register of Brassó for the year 1503 reflects a certain balancing of these contrary aspirations. The merchants of Brassó had by then been compelled to give up the bulk of Wallachian *spice* trade—only the members of a wholesale company: *societas magna*[100] still carried on active business in *this* branch. Gone were the best days of the trade of Brassó merchants[101] when they frequented briskly the road to Brăila and right to the "Great Sea" without any competition. Now, the preponderant part of spices was brought to the town by Wallachian merchants.[102] On the other hand, the latter failed to realize their intention to break into the Transylvanian market. They were barred persistently from doing business in pepper and other spices in regions *beyond* Brassó; profits from such activities remained a source of income to Saxon patrician merchants who were gradually growing indolent.

These facts are confirmed when attention is turned to the *third* question posed in the introduction.

3

We have to examine the question of what was the *further* route of imported spices; in fact, the quantity of South-Transylvanian pepper imports has been found to have far exceeded local demand and consumption.

In connection with the matter under review sources from as far back as the end of the 14th and the beginning of the 15th centuries have called attention to *Nagyvárad* (Grosswardein, Oradea), since from the Saxon towns of Transylvania it was through Nagyvárad that the main road led both to the capital of the country, Buda, and to the centre of North Hungary, Kassa (Kaschau, Košice).[103]

[100] One part of the customs (vicesima) register of Brassó from the year 1503 begins with the following subtitle: "Sequuntur mercatores magni seu grandi et primo societas magna"; *Quellen zur Geschichte der Stadt Kronstadt in Siebenbürgen*, I, p. 36. From the items following this title it emerges that a group of the merchants of the town Brassó formed a wholesale society *(societas magna)* whose main branches of business were the export of cloth and knives to Wallachia and import of spices from there to Transylvania. However, their yearly imports of pepper amounted only to 98 3/4 quintals: 13.73 per cent of the total pepper import of 719 quintals and 15 1/2 pounds (see Table II). The miscalculation in Note 3 on p. 88 of Dan and Goldenberg's *op. cit.*, stems from the authors regarding the *total* of pepper imports entered in the customs (vicesima) register of Brassó (which they have found to amount to 728 1/2 quintals and 510 1/4 pounds) as the import of the wholesale society of Brassó merchants alone; cf. Notes 12 and 25.

[101] Cf. A. L. Schlözer: *Kritische Sammlungen zur Geschichte der Deutschen in Siebenbürgen.* III, Göttingen, 1797, pp. 678–682.

[102] Here it must be remarked that by the year 1503 it was only in the transit of *oriental goods* that Wallachian merchants came in for such a preponderant share; in exports from Brassó to Wallachia and import of Wallachian produce to Brassó it was only by the middle of the 16th century that they gained ascendancy over Transylvanian merchants; see: Manolescu: *op. cit.*, 1965, pp. 132, 135–136, 152–158.

[103] Cf. e. g. E. Mályusz: *Zsigmondkori oklevéltár* (Documents of the Age of Sigismund), I, Budapest, 1951, pp. 622–623 (1399). K. Mollay (ed.): *Das Ofner Stadtrecht. Eine deutschsprachige Rechtssammlung des 15. Jahrhunderts,* Budapest, 1959, p. 190 (1403–1439).

The outstanding significance of fairs of Várad is illustrated the most graphically by the legal proceedings taken in the 1470s against the Chapter of Várad by numerous Transylvanian and Hungarian towns for the moderation of toll exacted by the Chapter at fairs; the lawsuit ended in the year 1478 with the verdict of King Matthias's Palatine, Mihály Guti Ország, in favour of the towns; after the death of King Matthias, at rehearing by the Chief Justice (representing the King's person) in the year 1492, the verdict of the Palatine was confirmed.[104] The line of litigant towns was opened by the Transylvanians, headed by Nagyszeben and Brassó, to be followed by the Hungarian towns of Buda, Pest, and Kassa. These towns achieved the reduction of the toll imposed on commodities in which long-distance trade was carried on by the above-mentioned routes.

A case in point was *livestock* which was driven to the west in huge numbers from Transylvania or from Moldavia through Transylvania.[105] Compared to the tariff levied by the Chapter—registered in 1476 but presumably valid from the turn of the 14th and 15th centuries—the new tariff, declared by the Palatine's verdict in 1478 and confirmed in 1492, reduced toll on oxen per head and on a pair of ox-hides to half (from 2 denarii to 1 denar).[106]

Another instance was *cloth*, the principal item of import from both Buda and Kassa to Transylvania and of export from Transylvania to Wallachia and Moldavia.[107] Toll on the cloth sold was fixed by the Chapter tariff accurately according to sort and piece; here, too, the Palatinate's regulation brought considerable moderation: without discrimination of various western sorts toll on cloth was exacted not according to quality and quantity but simply by cartload, *1 florin per cart.*[108]

Abolishment of certain features of the collection of toll—which aroused particular concern among merchants—was a still more important achievement than the

[104] A. Kubinyi: A városi rend kialakulásának gazdasági feltételei és a főváros kereskedelme a 15. század végén. (Economic Preconditions of the Rise of the Burghers' Class and the Trade of the Capital at the Close of the 15th Century), in: *Tanulmányok Budapest múltjából* (Studies on the Past of Budapest), XV, Budapest, 1963, p. 189 ff. For antecedents of the right of the Várad Chapter to collect fair tolls see the decree issued by the Chapter of Buda in 1392 legalizing relevant charters of the late 13th century, furthermore King Matthias' charter from the year 1477 in which the pertinent charters from the close of the 13th century, from 1343 and 1412 were rewritten and issued at the request of the towns: see: Teleki: *op. cit.*, XII, pp. 15–21. Zimmermann, Werner and Müller, *Urkundenbuch zur Geschichte der Deutschen in Siebenbürgen*, III, Hermannstadt, 1902, pp. 45–46. For the course of the legal proceedings cf. Hurmuzaki: *Documente privitoare*, XV, 1, pp. 92–93 (1476). Teleki: *op. cit.*, XII, pp. 9–10, 26–28, 53–55, 58–69 (1477–1478).

[105] For livestock export from Moldavia see, for instance, (Zimmermann–) Gündisch: *Urkundenbuch*, IV, pp. 498–499 (1437). Gündisch: *Urkundenbuch*, V, p. 262 (1448), p. 280 (1449), p. 498 (1455). *Quellen zur Geschichte der Stadt Kronstadt in Siebenbürgen*, III, pp. 1–2 (around 1500). Hurmuzaki: *Documente privitoare*, XV, 1, p. 165 (1504); etc.

[106] Teleki: *op. cit.*, XII, p. 69. Kubinyi: *op. cit.*, pp. 197–212.

[107] For cloth exports of merchants of Brassó and Barcaság to Moldavia see, e. g., the charter of the Moldavian voivod Alexandru II from 1449 in which customs tariffs are laid down for cloths from Louvain, Cologne, Bohemia (Silesia) and Buda (Bitvar), as well as for rough cloth; Gündisch: *Urkundenbuch*, V, p. 280. In 1482 Ştefan cel Mare, Prince of Moldavia, had cloth bought for himself in Brassó; see: Hurmuzaki: *Documente privitoare*, XV, 1, p. 118; etc.

[108] Teleki: *op. cit.*, XII, p. 68. Kubinyi: *op. cit.*, pp. 198, 213.

moderation of tariffs. On goods representing high value even in relatively small volume toll collectors of the Chapter changed over from piecemeal tariff to more lucrative *ad valorem* duty—a long since customary treatment of such wares elsewhere,[109] and exacted 1 per cent *ad valorem* duty: "ita videlicet: quod a singulis mercantiis unum florenum auri valentibus, singulum denarium talismodi monetae, cuius centrum denarii unum florenum auri valent", as stated by one of the witnesses in court.[110] Of course *ad valorem* duty was not effective unless it was connected with opening of the consignments. At Buda, for instance, the force and weight of levying duty was weakened at the time considerably by the decree of King Sigismund from the year 1404 stating that from merchants of Transylvania duty should be collected "de curribus totis oneratis et non de singulis ac specialibus rebus".[111] The principle of collecting toll per cartload was in agreement with the following paragraph in the Palatine's verdict: "quod singulas mercantias seu res mercatorum quorumcunque exactores tributorum singillatim examinare vel conspicere *non* habeant";[112] consistent declaration of the prohibition to open cartloads had a similar effect in Várad.

In addition to cloth, what *other* commodities may have been carried by the carts which officers of the Chapter were no longer permitted to open, but—as laid down in the text of the verdict—were authorized to collect on *1 florin* as toll, like on fine-quality cloth? [113] Apart from cloth, in all probability knives: another important article imported by Transylvanian Saxons *from the west* and exported to the east; furthermore evidently commodities which stood nearest to the definition of small volumes representing high values: pepper, spices—particularly important items imported by Transylvanian Saxons *from the east.* This inference is supported by the protest of Transylvanian Saxon towns against 1 per cent *ad valorem* duty at the time of the rehearing of the lawsuit in the year 1492, too "... everybody"—they wrote indignantly—, "who is familiar with the volume and number of goods passing here [Várad] ... can judge how often it happened that with unlawful and excessive malpractice the Chapter collected ten golden florins on carts forwarding merchandise worth one thousand florins. Moreover, there are merchants who transport lots of varying value, sometimes worth more, sometimes less, occasionally three or four thousand florins and even more."[114] There can be hardly any doubt that cartloads

[109] S. Domanovszky: *A harmincadvám eredete* (The Origin of Thirtieth (tricesima) Customs), Budapest, 1916, pp. 38–41. A. Pleidell: *A nyugatra irányuló magyar külkereskedelem a középkorban* (Western Foreign Trade of Hungary in the Middle Ages), Budapest, 1925, p. 18.

[110] Kubinyi: *op. cit.*, pp. 194–195.

[111] Zimmermann, Werner and Müller: *Urkundenbuch*, III, pp. 328–329. Mályusz, *Zsigmondkori oklevéltár*, II, 1, 1956, p. 403.

[112] "... sed de quibuscumque rebus mercimonialibus, quae vehuntur in curribus, secundum exigentiam huiusmodi currus onerati aut curruum oneratorum tributa exigantur"; see: Teleki: *op. cit.*, XII, pp. 68–69.

[113] "... de curru *pannis seu aliis mercantiis* bene onerato exigatur florenus unus. . ." Here the term *aliae mercantiae* cannot refer to fish, corn, salt, wool, hay, crude iron, etc., because the tolls to be paid on carts forwarding such commodities were listed separately in the subsequent passage of the verdict and were fixed well under 1 florin; see: Teleki: *op. cit.*, XII, pp. 68–69.

[114] Kubinyi: *op. cit.*, p. 195.

arriving at the fair of Várad, worth thousand or several thousand florins, often comprised consignments of highly valuable spices.

And should by any chance some doubt still linger on this score it will be dispelled by the information held in store for us by a list of the medieval toll-houses of Bihar County.[115] To be sure, this register is from a few decades later, notably from the year 1520, but it may certainly be applied to conditions around the turn of the century,—all the more so as the investigation as a result of which this list was made up was intended explicitly to put a stop to toll abuses of "long standing".[116]

The source is rendered particularly precious by containing also a list of tariff rates to be paid at various toll-houses of the county. Apparently the highest rates were those collected on so-called *currus ligatus.* Whereas the tariff of unloaded carts (currus non oneratus) was between 1 to 4 denarii, that of loaded carts (currus oneratus) between 2 and 8 denarii, rate payable on currus ligatus—mentioned at 13 tolling-houses—was 4 to 75 denarii. This suggests that carts of this name must have often carried especially valuable commodities. Direct light is thrown on the sort of goods by the four cases where toll on currus ligatus was collected not only in money but also in kind—notably in *pepper*;[117] e.g. at Kölesér (Arpăşel) 12 denarii and pepper in the value of 12 denarii were exacted, at Telegd (Tileagd) 32 denarii and pepper in the value of 25 denarii, at Rév (Vadu Crişului) 40 denarii and pepper in the value of 20 denarii, finally in Várad, at the end of Velence Street, 50 denarii and pepper worth 25 denarii.[118] Understandably, the historian was induced to draw the conclusion: "One cannot help thinking that . . . spices, costly and rare oriental specialities were transported on these carts, *'minuta mercimonia'* including, and perhaps in most cases, pepper, too."[119]

This justified conclusion, along with the paragraph quoted from the verdict of the Várad lawsuit, furnishes help to arrive at an accurate interpretation of the expression *currus ligatus.* "When the cart was loaded with such valuable marchandise"—Iványi continued his reasoning—"it must certainly have been covered with some sort of tilt or leather in order to protect the load from damage by the weather,—so it was a *covered* cart and currus *ligatus* may mean this." However, the word *ligatus* does not mean covered but *tied,* fastened down; obviously, *currus ligatus* was the name of carts with covers tied down strongly and transporting also loads worth several thousand florins not rarely, which, in agreement with the Palatine's decision of 1478, confirmed in 1492, not even the toll-collectors of the Chapter of Várad were allowed to open.

[115] It listed the tolls to be paid not at fairs, but on roads, bridges, and at gates. The Bishop and Chapter of Várad collected toll twice in Várad, at the end of Sipos Street and of Velence Street, respectively; see: B. Iványi: *Bihar és Borsod vármegyék vámhelyei a középkorban* (Toll Stations of Bihar and Borsod Counties in the Middle Ages), MGSZ, 1905, pp. 90–93.

[116] Iványi: *op. cit.,* pp. 81–83. Cf. the 14th-century charter dealing with the toll stations of Bihar County; Zimmermann, Werner and Müller: *Urkundenbuch,* II, p. 3 (1342(, p. 119 (1356), p. 221 (1364).

[117] Cf. ". . . transit and import customs duties, besides in definite amounts of money, were often partly or wholly imposed in certain quantities of pepper"; see: Hey d: *op. cit.,* II, p. 639.

[118] Iványi: *op. cit.,* pp. 93–95, 114–117.

[119] Iványi: *op. cit.,* p. 96.

What is more, from the register inferences may be drawn concerning further details of the journey towards Nagyvárad of Saxon carts loaded with valuable wares and forbidden to be opened. When the geographical position of the toll-houses is considered where *currus ligatus* is mentioned in the list, it is obvious that of the four places where toll was collected in pepper, three—Rév, Telegd and Várad itself—, were situated on the banks of the river Sebes Körös, near the "big highroad" leading from Transylvania to Hungary.[120] Information about a few preceding Transylvanian stations on the highway, this side of Király Pass, is found in earlier documents. Such sources are the decree of Sigismund Losonczi from the year 1424 forbidding the castellans of Sebesvár (Bologa) and the tributaries of Bánffyhunyad (Huedin) to collect toll from merchants of Szeben and other Saxon merchants passing with their carts;[121] King Sigismund's charter from the year 1428 containing similar orders to—among others—the toll collectors of Körösfő (Crişeni) and again those of Bánffyhunyad;[122] furthermore the decree of the governor János Hunyadi, issued in the year 1446, in which Sigismund Losonczi was forbidden to collect toll from Transylvanians at Bánffyhunyad and Sebesvár.[123] Körösfő, Bánffyhunyad, Sebesvár, Rév, Telegd—these were the principal stations of the east–west sector of the *magna via* between Kolozsvár and Nagyvárad;[124] this was the main road of Saxon merchants on their way from Brassó and Szeben over Torda (Thorenburg, Turda)[125] and Kolozsvár (Klausenburg, Cluj)[126] to Várad.

Another route was also frequented, especially by travellers from Szeben: over Arad. As shown by the register of Bihar the fourth toll-house where part of the toll was paid in pepper, Kölesér, lay south of Várad. Along this road running from Arad in a south–north direction *currus ligatus* was recorded at two more places, at Tamáshida (Támaşda) and Remete.[127] About certain stations of the preceding, Szeben-Arad sector of the route information is gained from various charters of protection issued in favour of travellers from Szeben. According to these, Arad was approached either through Déva (and Lippa [Lipova]) along the bank of the river Maros: a charter of King Louis from as far back as 1351 provided for free passage "per Devam" after payment of the usual tribute;[128] or through Hátszeg (Haţeg), Szád (Szádvörösmart, Virişmort, north-east of Lugos [Lugoj] and also through Lippa. King Sigismund's above-mentioned charter from the year 1428 sheds light on the latter route, being

[120] Cf. Iványi: *op. cit.*, p. 100.

[121] (Zimmermann–) Gündisch: *Urkundenbuch*, IV, p. 210.

[122] (Zimmermann–) Gündisch: *Urkundenbuch*, IV, pp. 330–331.

[123] Gündisch: *Urkundenbuch*, V, pp. 171–172.

[124] B. Borcsiczky: *A politikai változások befolyása Magyarország kereskedelmi útjaira a 14–15. században* (The Influence of Political Changes on the Trade Routes of Hungary in the 14th and 15th Centuries), Budapest, 1914, p. 24.

[125] In 1471 King Matthias exempted the burghers of Brassó and the inhabitants of Barcaság from the payment of toll at Torda; see: Teleki: *op. cit.*, XI, pp. 434–436.

[126] For the road sector Torda-Kolozsvár see: Gründisch: *Urkundenbuch*, V, pp. 74–75 (1441), p. 575 (1457).

[127] Iványi: *op. cit.*, pp. 116–117.

[128] Fejér, *Codex diplomaticus Hungariae ecclesiasticus ac civilis*, IX, 2, Budae, 1833, p. 66. Zimmermann, Werner and Müller: *Urkundenbuch*, II, p. 84.

addressed—among others—to the toll collectors of Hátszeg;[129] four years earlier Pipo of Ozora, Count of Temes, instructed the Castellan of Szád not to collect toll from merchants of Szeben and other Saxon towns;[130] and, finally the order of King Sigismund in 1433 to István Rozgonyi, Count of Temes, prohibiting to direct Saxon merchants, particularly those of Szeben, to drive through Morzsina (lying also north-east of Lugos) with the purpose of making them pay tribute by diverting them from their "usual, true, rightful and long-used route" on which they proceed "de ipsis partibus nostris Transsilvanis per oppidum Zaad versus Lippam et de ipsa Lippa ad dictas partes nostras Transsilvanas".[131] From Arad Transylvanians then wound their way through Szeged[132] or Kecskemét to Buda (their exemption from toll at Kecskemét having been assured on several occasions by Sigismund),[133] or, as indicated by their carts with fastened covers, towards Várad through Tamáshida, Remete, or Kölesér.

From Várad the road again branched off in two main directions; westward to Szeghalom—the most western toll station of Bihar County at the time[134]—and through Szolnok in the direction of Pest-Buda;[135] and northward towards Debrecen. After Várad it was along the route from Várad to Debrecen that our *currus ligatus* appeared: at Bihar (Biharea) and Sztár (Esztár) (with 75 and 12 denarii toll, respectively), at Szalárd (Sălard) and Léta (Nagyléta) (with 32 and 4 denarii), and at Hencida (with 12 denarii toll).[136] Finally, after Debrecen they are encountered at Sámson (with 8 denarii tariff); this already points to the northward route of Debrecen-Kassa.[137]

In the meantime the valuable loads changed hands mostly already in Nagyvárad, and to a smaller extent in Debrecen. Light is thrown on this transaction by a source from the period between the above-mentioned lawsuit of Várad and the toll register of Bihar, corresponding in date to the twentieth register of Brassó: by entries of the *Handelsgesellschaft von Kaschau* in the years 1502–1503.

This commercial company, founded by a few members of the merchants' guild of Kassa, the "Bruderschaft der reichen Cromer",[138] had certainly been in existence and active until 1518: according to the balance sheet of that year, investment of 5,000

[129] See Note 122.

[130] (Zimmermann–) Gündisch: *Urkundenbuch*, IV, p. 209.

[131] (Zimmermann–) Gündisch: *Urkundenbuch*, IV, pp. 497–498. Six years earlier István Rozgonyi, then Count of Győr, Fejér and Bakony, issued a letter of protection in favour of Szeben merchants on their way to Vienna; *ibid.*, p. 272.

[132] In 1475 King Matthias instructed the mayor of Szeben to reimburse from the royal revenue Tamás Kádár, burgher of Szeben, for the price of his 98 oxen seized at the King's order by János Szilágyi, magistrate of Szeged, counting 3 florins per head; see: Teleki: *op. cit.*, XI, pp. 542–543.

[133] Zimmermann, Werner and Müller, *Urkundenbuch*, III, pp. 565–566 (1413), pp. 636–637 (1415).

[134] Iványi: *op. cit.*, pp. 89, 101, 119.

[135] Borcsiczky: *op. cit.*, pp. 27–28.

[136] Iványi: *op. cit.*, pp. 95, 100–101, 121–123.

[137] Iványi: *op. cit.*, pp. 101, 125. Borcsiczky: *op. cit.*, pp. 27–28.

[138] MGSZ, 1897, pp. 190–192; 1898, pp. 31–34; 1903, pp. 342–352. Cf. the article by the present author: Szófejtés és gazdaságtörténet. Crom–cromer–kalmár (Etimology and Economic History. Crom–cromer–kalmár) *Magyar Nyelv* (Hungarian Language), 1976, No. 4, pp. 422–429.

florins capital brought 20 per cent profit.[139] The "Handelsregister" which have come down to us from 1502 and 1503 permit insight into the character of its business activities—resembling those of the *societas magna* of Brassó—and their rather simple mechanism.[140]

The starting-point of this mechanism was the purchase by the company in Cracow of textiles, in the first place *cloth*, partly against some exports of wine (from the Cracow wholesale dealers György Thurzó and János Haller).[141] The smaller part of the imported textile wares was then sold by the company on the market of Kassa—the buyers, besides people of Kassa, here, too, included Transylvanians: a merchant of Segesvár (Schässburg, Sighişoara), two of Beszterce–, but the bulk was offered for sale at fairs in the region beyond the river Tisza: in Varsány, at the fair held on the day of St. Demetrius, in Debrecen at that held on the day of St. George, but above all in *Nagyvárad* at fairs on the days of minor- and major Ladislaus, George, Giles, Francis, Emeric, Epiphany, Elisabeth, and Whit Sunday, respectively.

The purchasers were mostly *Transylvanian merchants*, from Brassó, Beszterce, Kolozsvár, Segesvár, Szászrégen (Sächsisch-Reen, Reghin); not a single Wallachian is found among them. "Merchants of Kassa, having bought various kinds of cloth in Poland, Cracow, . . . could not transport their goods to Transylvania, but took them half-way to Nagyvárad, Debrecen. Here they were met by merchants of Brassó, Kolozsvár, etc., who came not empty-handed but loaded with spices, chiefly pepper to be sold to tradesmen of Kassa, who, in their turn, supplied the North-Hungarian regions with these and other articles."[142] What is more, merchants of Brassó who came to Debrecen and Nagyvárad to do business—who sometimes paid wholesale lots of cloth purchased from merchants of Kassa or parts of the lots in *pepper*—can in several cases be identified personally among the pepper importers entered in the twentieth register of Brassó for the year 1503. Such a person was Peter Schwarz who made part-payment with half a quintal of pepper, or Keilhau and Ailda who paid 8 quintals.[143]

[139] L. Kemény: *Kassai Kereskedelmi Társaság 1518-ban* (Commercial Company of Kassa in 1518), MGSZ, 1897, p. 482.

[140] Gy. Kerekes: *A kassai kereskedelmi társaság följegyzései 1502- és 1503-ban* (Records of the Commercial Company of Kassa in the Years 1502 and 1503), MGSZ, 1902, pp. 106–117. Cf. O. R. Halaga: Kaufleute und Handelsgüter der Hansa im Karpatengebiet, *Hansische Geschichtsblätter*, 85, Köln-Graz, 1967, p. 83.

[141] The most important cloth consignments of the two business years were sent by György Thurzó from Cracow in the total value of 8,709 florins; see: Kerekes: *op. cit.*, p. 109.

[142] Kerekes: *op. cit.*, p. 107.

[143] Cloth purchases were settled with 8 quintals of pepper by Johannes Benckner, too, who figures in the twentieth (vicesima) register of Brassó for the year 1503 only as an exporter of cloth and knives, but was most probably also a member of the *societas magna* and, like Peter Schwarz, visited also the fairs of not only Nagyvárad, but also of Debrecen. The following items can be read in the *registrum debitorum* of Brassó for the year 1505: "Item Swarz Peter tenetur 300 flor. zw bezalen, wan her von Debricz kymt . . . Item domino Johanni Benckner dedimus kanth. piperis 6, quos vexit ad nundinas Dobricienses, ut ibidem vendat", in: *Quellen zur Geschichte der Stadt Kronstadt in Siebenbürgen*, I, p. 176; similarly: *ibid.*, p. 180 (1506). According to the *registrum debitorum* of the year 1518 Benckner also visited Buda: "Item domino Johanni Benckner dedimus in monetis pro solutione bombardistarum, quas Budae emerat civitati, flor. 100"; *ibid.*, p. 214.

About the price of pepper here we gain information from a deal made in 1502 when 1 quintal and 17 pounds of pepper changed hands for 58 florins.[144] This pepper price—calculated in 60-pound quintals (kanthners) used in the twentieth register of Brassó—corresponds to 45.19 florins per quintal and, compared to the cloth-price entries in the "Handelsregister" of Kassa,[145] this means that Transylvanian Saxon merchants could buy for the price of 1 quintal pepper (and offer on the Transylvanian market or export to Wallachia) of the most expensive cloths marketed by the Kassa company 1 1/4 piece of cloth from Bruges, 2 1/4–3 piece of cloth from Mecheln, 3 1/2–3 3/4 piece of "Colcister",[146] 4 1/2 piece of cloth from Maastricht; of the cheaper sorts: of Silesian cloths and of "Sorèze" they could actually buy 11–18 piece.[147]

*

With reference to the foregoing the third question posed in the introduction of the present paper may be answered as follows.

The further route—the main branch of the further route—of spice consignments, imported to South-Transylvanian Saxon towns from the region of the Black Sea, led from *Brassó* and *Nagyszeben* to the important town of *Nagyvárad* east of the river Tisza, from there to the centre of North Hungary (Eastern Slovakia), to *Kassa*. Wallachian merchants had no share in the turnover of these sectors of the route; the bulk of the valuable spices was handled by *Transylvanian Saxon* merchants up to Várad, from there by *traders* of *Kassa*.

It may be added that on the evidence of our sources this route, leading through the Wallachian principality to Transylvania and Hungary, provided for undisturbed spice supplies even in the early 16th century; in the years when Venetian galleys found hardly any spices at the eastern supply parts of the Mediterranean, Alexandria and Beirut;[148] in the years which—as a result of the circumnavigation of Africa and the appearance of the Portuguese in East India—brought to Mediterranean spice trade a crisis lasting several decades.[149]

[144] Kerekes: *op. cit.*, p. 116.

[145] Halaga: *op. cit.*, p. 83.

[146] Halaga (*op. cit.*, p. 83) regarded this as cloth from Colchester, England. However, it may be supposed that in the German source *Colcister* (Kerekes: *op. cit.*, p. 116: Kalciszter) was a spelling error instead of Colcischer or Colnischer (of Cologne). Cf. e. g. the form *Colnisch* in the Budai Jogkönyv (Lawbook of Buda), in: *Ofner Stadtrecht*, pp. 197, 201.

[147] The sorts of cloth occurring in the twentieth (vicesima) registers of Brassó are predominantly identical with those of the assortment imported by merchants of Kassa from Cracow and sold in Nagyvárad to buyers from Brassó.

[148] Heyd: *op. cit.*, II, pp. 531–532. Braudel: *op. cit.*, I, pp. 493–494.

[149] V. Magelhães-Godinho: Le repli vénitien et la route du Cap, 1496–1533. In: *Hommage à Lucien Febvre*, Paris, 1953, II. pp. 287 ff. and B. Pullan (ed.): *Crisis and Change in the Venetian Economy in the Sixteenth and Seventeenth Centuries*, London, 1968, Introduction, pp. 3–6.

APPENDIX

to Note 25

On p. 305 of *op. cit.* 1965, Manolescu puts the weight of the quintal used in the customs (vicesima) register of Brassó at 58.929–59.864 kilograms, with reference to Fr. Pall: Relaţiile comerciale dintre braşoveni şi raguzani, *Revista Arhivelor,* Seria nouă, 1, Bucureşti, 1958, p. 98. Pall, on the other hand, started from the assumption that in Transylvania the Hungarian quintal was used and the above-mentioned kilogram equivalents were quoted by him from Hóman: *op. cit.*, p. 118. Cf. Note 22.

But can the *kanthner* of South-Transylvanian customs registers be really regarded as identical with the Hungarian (Buda) quintal *(centner)*? The question is also justified by the fact that in the customs register of Brassó for the year 1503 itself (kept in Latin), three terms are used for quintal: *centenarium* (or *centenarius*), *massa* (or *masa*), and *kanthner* (later, sometimes *kanthuarus* or *cantaro* too). Moreover, whereas *centenarius* refers, for instance, to fish, to copper, and *massa* to wax and sulphur, *kanthner* refers invariably and exclusively to *oriental spices,* and to raisins, cotton, and rice; *op. cit.*, I, pp. 1–3, 5–6, 11–16, 21–22, etc. Similar observations can be made in the Brassó sources of the following decades; *op. cit.*, II, pp. 84, 126, 254–255, 384, 462–463, etc.; III, pp. 1, 92, 137–138, 142, 311, etc., as well as in the source material of Nagyszeben from the years 1494–95 and 1500–1509; *op. cit.*, I, pp. 138, 196, 311, 313–315, 317–318, 320, 322–327, 330–334, 336–337. These facts again suggest that the analogue of the *kanthner* of Brassó and Szeben should be sought not in Hungary but rather south–south-east of Transylvania. And there it is soon found, as *kantar* was a weight unit used for centuries in the Ottoman Empire and also in Wallachia. It is probable that this *kantar*—containing 44 okka (1 okka being 1.276–1.289 kilogram)—weighed 56.144–56.716 kilograms: J. Jäckel: *Neueste europäische Münz-, Mass- und Gewichtskunde,* Wien, 1828, I, 150–151. J. Littrow: *Gedrängter Abriss der Münz-, Mass und Gewichtskunde,* Güns, 1834, 33. A. Ereky: *Mérték-, súly- és pénzisme* (Measures, Weights, and Coinages), Székesfehérvár, 1881, pp. 40, 156, 307, 316.

Use of the *kantar (kanthner)* in South-Transylvanian Saxon towns too for weighing pepper and other spices (and a few oriental commodities) was similar to the use of the Turkish *aspera* (ozpora) in Transylvania. It may have played a part here that valuable pepper was obviously brought to Brassó and Szeben in carefully tied up sacks whose pepper content, indicated by Levantine suppliers in *kantars,* was checked at South-Transylvanian customs stations. For instance, in a customs account of Nagyszeben from the year 1509 it is stated that the weight of imported pepper proved to be "primus saccus kanthner 1 minus libra[m] 1, secundus saccus kanthner 1 minus libra[s] 3"; *op. cit.*, I, p. 327; cf. *ibid.*, pp. 324-325 (1505).

The question arises whether it is possible that the *kanthner* used in Nagyszeben and Brassó for weighing pepper (containing 80 or 60 pounds, respectively) slightly fell behind in weight compared to the *centner* used in Pozsony for weighing pepper, implying a Buda *centner* of 120 pounds in the opinion of Kováts. This is, of course, impossible unless there was a considerable difference in weight between the pounds *(libra).* And this may, indeed, be inferred from the various attributes of the word pound *(libra)* encountered in South-Transylvanian sources: in accounts of Nagyszeben *libra Hungaricalis* (e.g. *op. cit.*, I, p. 9), *libra levis* (p. 327), *libra gravis* (p. 330), in accounts of Brassó also *libra levis* and *libra gravis* (e.g. *op. cit.* I, pp. 214, 216); furthermore *libra gravioris ponderis* (II, pp. 327, 540) and *novi ponderis* (III, p. 452). A "heavy" pound may actually have been double the weight of a "light" pound. (For instance the *libra grossa* of Milan corresponded to 0.75 kilogram, the *libra sottile* to 0.32 kilogram; see: Jäckel: *op. cit.* II, p. 93).

The above-mentioned view is supported by the charter of King Matthias dated February 14, 1489, in which all authorities of Transylvania are instructed (evidently without avail) to use henceforward no other weights than those of the seven Saxon quarters and Brassó, and "una et eadem ulna, unis etiam *centenariis sive massis* necnon *canthar et libris,* aliisque similibus ponderibus negotiari, utique et frui debeant". As may be seen, the text of the charter, too,—which specified the above-mentioned weights twice—made a difference between *centenarius (sive massa)* and *canthar.* Motivation of the instruction is not less interesting, explaining as it does that certain towns and boroughs "inter se adhuc *triplicem et quadruplicem differentiam* [!] in eiuscemodi ulnis et ponderibus haberent"; see: Teleki: *Hunyadiak kora Magyarországon. Oklevéltár,* XII, Pest, 1857, pp. 432–434.

The issue of the kilogram equivalent of the *kanthner*—like the numerous problems of the history of old units of weight and measure—cannot be regarded as closed by the evidence presented. However, it must be remarked that while we put the *kanthner* at 56.144–56.716 kilograms we calculate with lower values than the majority of scholars. Manolescu (*op. cit.*, p. 305) and Pall (*op. cit.*, p. 98)—with reference to Hóman, as mentioned before—have assumed quintals of 58.929–59.864 kilograms, i.e. Hungarian quintals (of Buda) of 120 pounds; as another variant Pall (*op. cit.*, p. 97) also thought 63.695 kilograms (= 100 Turkish pounds; cf. Hóman: *op. cit.*, p. 101) possible. Goldenberg (*op. cit.*, p. 399) regards the weight of the quintal figuring in 16th-century customs accounts of Nagyszeben as 67.2 kilograms, i.e. equivalent to the 120-pound Vienna quintal. Dan and Goldenberg (*op. cit.*, p. 88, Note 3) express the opinion that the *kanthner* used in the customs register of Brassó for the year 1503, consisting of 120 pound of 560–636 grams each, amounted to 67.2–76.32 kilograms. According to A. Schaube (*Handelsgeschichte der romanischen Völker des Mittelmeergebiets bis zum Ende der Kreuzzüge,* München–Berlin, 1906, p. 814) the *cantarius* of Venice (= 150 *librae grossae*) was equivalent to 72 kilograms. Jäckel (*op. cit.*, I, p. 195) even knew about a Turkish *kantar* which weighed 74.84 kg. On the other hand, Schaube put the *Alexandrian* kantar (cantarius forforinus) only at 43.5 kilograms, the *Genuese* at 47.25 kilograms; Lane put the *Alexandrian* (cantara forfori) at 94 Englisch lbs (42.58 kilograms), the *Portuguese* at 112 English lbs (50.74 kilograms); Ashtor put the Alexandrian (kintār fulfulī) at 45 kilograms; Braudel mostly calculated it as "approximately 50 kilograms". For the latter see their works quoted in the Notes.

ADDENDA

THE TRANSYLVANIAN ROUTE OF LEVANTINE TRADE AT THE TURN OF THE 15TH AND 16TH CENTURIES

Page 5, Note 1:

See the preceding paper in this volume.

Page 13, Note 25:

For another estimate of the weight of *kanthner*, used in the South–Transylvanian border towns, see the Comment on Appendix.

Page 16, Note 37:

The recent estimate of the Australian economic historian *C. H. H. Wake* corroborates the opinion of F. C. Lane. Wake put Venice's annual pepper import in the 1490s at 7570 metric quintals, then revised it to about 7000 metric quintals: The Volume of European Spice Imports at the Beginning and End of the 15th Century, The Journal of European Economic History (=JEEH), XV, 3 (1986), p. 634.

Page 17, Note 40:

For the interpretation of the charter issued by King Louis for Nagyszeben in 1382, see: Die Verkehrsroute des Levantehandels nach Siebenbürgen und Ungarn zur Zeit der Könige Ludwig von Anjou und Sigismund von Luxemburg. In: Europäische Stadtgeschichte in Mittelalter und früher Neuzeit. Hg. von W. Mägdefrau, Weimar, 1979, pp. 61–66.

Page 28:

Instead of "The principle... in Várad" (lines 11–15) read as follows: A similar allowance was granted by the Palatine's verdict of 1478 to the Transylvanian and Hungarian merchants at the fair of Várad, as against the excessive claims of the local Chapter: "quod singulas mercantias seu res mercatorum quorumcumque exactores tributorum singillatim examinare vel conspicere non habeant."[112]

Page 33, Note 149:

The discovery of the direct sea route to India as well as the incorporation of the central part of Hungary into the Turkish Empire after the fall of Buda (1541) involved, of course, major changes concerning the routes and sources of spice supply to this country.

The altered conditions and new developments have been discussed by the present author in another paper: Levantine Trade and Hungary in the 16th–17th Centuries. In: Venezia e Ungheria nel contesto del barocco Europeo. Ed. by V. Branca, Firenze, 1979, pp. 71–84. — For our main conclusions see: *The East–Central European Aspect of the Overseas Discoveries and Colonization*, pp. 193–194, in this volume. — Conf. *M. Małowist*, Le commerce du Levant avec l'Europe de l'Est au XVIe siècle. In: Mélanges en l'honneur de Fernand Braudel, Toulouse, 1973, I, pp. 349–357; *C. H. H. Wake*, The Changing Pattern of Europe's Pepper and Spice Imports, ca 1400–1700, JEEH, VIII, 2 (1979), pp. 381, 394–395; *N. Steensgaard*, The Asian Trade Revolution of the 17th Century. The East India Companies and the Decline of the Caravan Route, Chicago, 1974, pp. 154–171.

Pages 34-35, Appendix:

In the Turkish customs registers of the Balkan area there were figuring two kinds of *kantar* (quintâr) in this period. One of them is shown as equal to 40 *okka*, the other as 44 *okka*. Since the *okka* averaged 1.282 kilogram, the *kantar* in question weighed either 51.28 or 56.408 kilograms: *W. Hinz*, Islamische Masse und Gewichte, Leiden, 1955, p. 27; *H. Inalcik*, Bursa and the Commerce of the Levant, Journal of the Economic and Social History of the Orient, III (1960), pp. 137, 147. — In the second case the total yearly pepper import of Brassó (Kronstadt, Braşov) and Nagyszeben (Hermannstadt, Sibiu) in the opening years of the 16th century amounted to 465.366 metric quintals which sum corresponds to the estimate arrived at in the text; in the first case it came to only 423.06 metric quintals. Even in this case, the yearly volume of pepper imported from the direction of the Black Sea through the south-eastern customs stations of Transylvania at the beginning of the 16th century, was more than four times as much as the annual quantity of pepper imported from the direction of the Adriatic through the principal western customs station of Hungary around the middle of the 15th century.

VIII

Zur Geschichte der Handelsbeziehungen zwischen Österreich und Ungarn im 15. und 16. Jahrhundert

Aus dem umfangreichen Problemkreis — dessen spätere Entwicklung in gewissen Aspekten auch die Aufmerksamkeit des hochgeschätzten Jubilars auf sich gezogen hat [1]) — möchten wir diesmal bloß eine einzige Frage anschneiden: Wir wollen Ungarns westlichen Tuchimport [2]) um die Mitte des 15. und um die Mitte des 16. Jahrhunderts einer vergleichenden Untersuchung unterziehen.

Die Auswahl beider Zeitpunkte findet in den Quellengegebenheiten ihre Begründung. Es haben sich nämlich von den wichtigsten Quellen der älteren Geschichte des ungarischen Außenhandels, von den sogenannten Dreißigstzollbüchern [3]), nur sehr wenige bis auf unsere Zeit erhalten. Erhalten haben sich aber glücklicherweise das Dreißigsteinnahmebuch der Stadt Preßburg (Pozsony, Bratislava) aus dem Finanzjahr 1457—58 [4]), einer Stadt, die im westlichen Außenhandel eine hervorragende Rolle gespielt hatte, — und die Einnahmebücher des Hauptdreißigstamtes Preßburg, seiner Filialen und anderer Stellen, insgesamt 19 Dreißigstämter der westlichen Grenzscheide, aus dem Kalenderjahre 1542. Das Dreißigstbuch von Preßburg ist bereits Anfang unseres Jahrhunderts von F. Kováts einer gründlichen statistischen Bearbeitung unterworfen worden [5]);

---

1) Vgl. Hanns Leo Mikoletzky *Die Anfänge der Industrie und der Staatsfinanzen Österreichs im 18. Jahrhundert* in *XIIe Congrès International des Sciences Historiques. Rapports* 4 (Horn—Wien 1965) 191—200.

2) In unseren Ausführungen behalten wir den üblichen Ausdruck „Tuch" bei, obwohl darunter nicht nur Tuche im alten Sinne des Wortes, sondern auch neuere Schafwollstoffarten gemeint sind. — Vgl. Walter Endrei *Középkori angol textil-importunk gyapjuszövetei* [Die Schafwollstoffarten des ungarischen Textilimports aus England im Mittelalter] in *Századok* 104 (1970) 288.

3) Wie der Dreißigst zum Wertzoll des ungarischen Außenhandels geworden war, erörtert Sándor Domanovszky *A harmincadvám eredete* [Die Herkunft des Dreißigstzolls] (Budapest 1916).

4) Von Ende April 1457 bis Ende April 1458.

5) Ferenc Kováts *Nyugatmagyarország áruforgalma a XV. században a pozsonyi harmincadkönyv alapján* [Der Warenverkehr Westungarns im 15. Jahrhundert auf Grund des Preßburger Dreißigsteinnahmebuches] (Budapest 1902).

die Dreißigstbücher aus dem Jahre 1542 sind erst unlängst von G. Ember erschlossen und bearbeitet worden [6]).

Die Geschichtsforschung kann nicht der Aufgabe ausweichen, die von den beiden Quellen (Quellengruppen) gebotenen zahlenmäßigen Daten einer vergleichenden Analyse zu unterwerfen, — selbst dann nicht, wenn die Daten aus dem Jahre 1457—58 sich ausschließlich auf Preßburg beziehen, die aus dem Jahre 1542 hingegen auf eine Reihe von Dreißigstämtern der westlichen Grenze, von Ödenburg (Sopron) über Preßburg bis Skalitz (Szakolca, Skalica), auf Dreißigststellen, die am Außenhandelsverkehr mit sehr verschiedenem Gewicht teilnahmen. Um so weniger kann man dieser Aufgabe ausweichen, als sich zwischen den beiden Quellengruppen nicht nur Ähnlichkeiten, sondern auch unerwartete Unterschiede sehen lassen.

Beschränken wir diesmal unsere Aufmerksamkeit nur auf die Importseite des ungarischen Außenhandels, so läßt sich die wichtigste Ähnlichkeit dadurch bezeichnen, daß im Jahre 1457—58 78,76 Prozent der Preßburger Einfuhr, im Jahre 1542 hingegen 68,67 Prozent der westlichen Einfuhr Webewaren (insbesondere Tuch, daneben auch Leinwand und Kleidungsstücke) ausmachten. Der hervorragende Anteil der Textilien war Mitte des 15. Jahrhunderts — und blieb auch Mitte des 16. Jahrhunderts — das Hauptmerkmal von Ungarns westlicher Einfuhr.

Wir stoßen aber auf einen überraschenden Unterschied, sobald wir nicht die Prozentanteile, sondern die absoluten Ziffern derselben Einfuhr unter die Lupe nehmen. Das Dreißigstbuch der Stadt Preßburg aus dem Jahre 1457—58 führt eine Einfuhr von mehr als 166 000 fl. (Forint) Zollwert an, und innerhalb dessen eine mehr als 15 000 Stück ausmachende Tucheinfuhr von beinahe 100 000 fl. Zollwert, insgesamt eine 130 000 fl. übersteigende Textilieneinfuhr an; die Dreißigstbücher aus dem Jahre 1542 registrieren hingegen bloß eine Einfuhr von 141 000 fl. Zollwert, innerhalb dessen eine ungefähr 11 000 Stück ausmachende Tucheinfuhr im Werte von ungefähr 56 000 fl., insgesamt eine sich auf etwa 97 000 fl. belaufende Textileinfuhr. Mit anderen Worten (bloß den Tuchverkehr hervorkehrend): der Gesamttuchimport der 19 Dreißigststellen der westlichen Grenzscheide (Preßburg miteinbegriffen) blieb im Jahre 1542 wesentlich hinter dem Tuchimport zurück, welcher im Finanzjahr 1457—58 allein von der Stadt Preßburg abgewickelt worden war.

Es entsteht die Frage: Haben wir diesen überraschenden Unterschied im Volumen der westlichen Tucheinfuhr bloß den äußerst günstigen Umständen des Jahres 1457—58 einerseits, und den besonders ungünsti-

---

[6]) Győző Ember *Zur Geschichte des Außenhandels Ungarns im XVI. Jahrhundert* in *Études historiques* 1 (Budapest 1960) 536—587.

gen Umständen des Jahres 1542, den damaligen Kriegsverhältnissen, der „Krisensituation“ [7]) andererseits zuzuschreiben, oder lassen sich hinter den „short term fluctuations“ auch die Spuren von langfristigeren Veränderungen austasten: Merkmale von Veränderungen, die in der Struktur der westlichen Tucheinfuhr Ungarns zwischen Mitte des 15. und Mitte des 16. Jahrhunderts eingetreten waren?

*

Das Dreißigstbuch von Preßburg 1457—58 spiegelt jenen Zustand wider, in dem der wichtigste Landweg des europäischen Tuchhandels vom Westen nach Osten — von den Niederlanden ausgehend über Aachen, Köln, Frankfurt am Main und Nürnberg [8]), und eine wichtige Abzweigung davon: die von Regensburg über Österreich nach Preßburg führende D o n a u l i n i e — die Hauptstraße von Ungarns westlicher Tucheinfuhr war [9]). Dieser Lage entsprach auch die Zusammensetzung des Preßburger Tuchimports: von 15 139 Stück waren 9236 Stück, das heißt 61,4 Prozent, westeuropäischen, bzw. west-mitteleuropäischen (englischen, flandrischen, niederrheinischen, oberdeutschen, sowie italienischen) Ursprungs. Innerhalb dessen erreichten die niederrheinischen Produkte einen hervorragenden Anteil: Allein aus dem Aachener und Kölner Raum wurden 5858 Stück eingeführt, fast aufs Haar so viel wie aus den ost-mitteleuropäischen (böhmisch-mährischen und schlesischen) Sorten insgesamt (5843 Stück) [10]).

Auf dem Donauweg aber, welcher aus den oberdeutschen Städten über Wien und Preßburg nach Ungarn führte, ging der Verkehr bereits Ende der 1450-er Jahre sturzartig zurück und blieb wegen der österreichischen Parteikämpfe und Geldentwertung, später auch infolge der Fehden zwischen Kaiser Friedrich III. und dem ungarischen König Matthias, fast bis zum Jahrhundertende sehr beschränkt. Die Einnahmen des Preßburger Dreißigstamtes, die sich 1456—57 noch auf 8399 fl. und 1457—58 auf

---

[7]) *Erste Tagung des Seminars für Sozial- und Wirtschaftsgeschichte der Philipps-Universität* (Marburg an der Lahn 1967) Diskussionsprotokoll 23—26.

[8]) Vgl. František G r a u s *Die Handelsbeziehungen Böhmens zu Deutschland und Österreich im 14. und zu Beginn des 15. Jahrhunderts* in *Historica* 2 (Praha 1960) 85, 97.

[9]) Ferenc K o v á t s *A magyar arany világtörténeti jelentősége és kereskedelmi összeköttetéseink a nyugattal a középkorban* [Die weltgeschichtliche Bedeutung des ungarischen Goldes und die Handelsbeziehungen Ungarns zum Westen im Mittelalter] in *Történeti Szemle* 11 (Budapest 1922) 136—137; Ambrus P l e i d e l l *A nyugatra irányuló magyar külkereskedelem a középkorban* [Der ungarische Außenhandel nach dem Westen im Mittelalter] (Budapest 1925) 76.

[10]) K o v á t s *Nyugatmagyarország* 106—111.

6854 fl. beliefen, fielen im Finanzjahr 1458—59 bereits auf 3921 fl. zurück, erreichten 1459—60 einen Tiefstand von 479 fl. und machten auch 1460—61 bloß 794 fl. aus [11]). Die Wiener Mauteinnahmen, die im Durchschnitt der Jahre 1455—1459 2436 Pfund ausmachten, erreichten im Durchschnitt der Jahre 1460—1464 bloß 1266 Pfund und sind auch in den 1470—1480-er Jahren im Großen und Ganzen auf demselben Niveau geblieben [12]).

Der Verkehr auf der Donau-Handelsstraße belebte sich erst vom letzten Jahrzehnt des 15. Jahrhunderts an wieder; erst dann wurde sie wieder zu einem der Hauptkanäle der Strömung der westmitteleuropäischen, besonders der süddeutschen Textilien nach Osten. In Linz wurden 1496, 1498 und 1499 jährlich 5000 bis 6000 Stück Tuch auf den Markt geworfen, etwa die Hälfte davon von oberdeutschen, vor allem Nürnberger Kaufleuten —, wahrscheinlich überwiegend für den österreichischen Verbrauch [13]). Die nach Ungarn bestimmten Waren wurden nach Wien und Preßburg weitergeführt. Die Mauteinnahmen von Wien beliefen sich im Jahresdurchschnitt 1495—1499 bereits auf 2402 Pfund, kamen also dem Durchschnitt der Jahrhundertmitte nahe [14]); der Dreißigst von Preßburg wurde 1494—1495 wieder für 5000 fl. (samt dem von Ödenburg), verpachtet [15]), und mehr als drei Viertel der hiesigen Einfuhr machten nach dem Dreißigstbuch 1495—1496 wieder die Textilwaren aus [16]).

In den ersten Jahrzehnten des 16. Jahrhunderts setzte sich der Belebungsprozeß auf dem Donauweg fort: Die Wiener Mauteinnahmen kamen in den 1520er Jahren bereits den 3500 Pfund nahe oder haben sie sogar überstiegen; der Dreißigstertrag von Preßburg wurde um 1523 auf 6000 fl. geschätzt [17]). Dies fiel zeitlich mit dem Aufschwung des Nürnberger Webereigewerbes zwischen 1520 und 1530 zusammen, welcher seinerseits großenteils gerade den günstigen Möglichkeiten auf den ungari-

---

[11]) Ferenc Kováts *Korakapitalisztikus gazdasági válság Magyarországon I. Mátyás király uralkodása alatt* [Eine frühkapitalistische Wirtschaftskrise in Ungarn während der Regierungszeit König Matthias I.] in *Dissertationes in honorem Dr. Eduardi Mahler* (Budapestini 1937) 187.

[12]) Friedrich Engel-Janosi *Zur Geschichte der Wiener Kaufmannschaft von der Mitte des 15. bis zur Mitte des 16. Jahrhunderts* in *Mitteilungen des Vereines für Geschichte der Stadt Wien* 6 (1926) 59.

[13]) Theodor Mayer *Der auswärtige Handel des Herzogtums Österreich im Mittelalter* (Innsbruck 1909) 157—160; Wilhelm Rausch *Handel an der Donau* 1: *Die Geschichte der Linzer Märkte im Mittelalter* (Linz 1969) 205—212.

[14]) Engel-Janosi *Wiener Kaufmannschaft* 59.

[15]) Johann Christian von Engel *Geschichte des ungrischen Reichs und seiner Nebenländer* 1 (Halle 1797) 127.

[16]) Kováts *A magyar arany* 126.

[17]) Engel-Janosi *Wiener Kaufmannschaft* 59; Ludwig v. Schedius *Etwas über den Zustand der ungrischen Finanzen im Anfange des XVI. Jahrhunderts* in *Zeitschrift von und für Ungern zur Beförderung der vaterländischen Geschichte, Erdkunde und Literatur* 3 (Pesth 1803) 101.

schen Märkten zu verdanken war [18]). Diese Möglichkeiten wurden vom oberdeutschen Textilhandel vor allem über Wien ausgenützt, aber — nach den Angaben der Geschäftsbücher des in Österreich eingebürgerten oberdeutschen Handelshauses, der Firma Funck — auch über Wiener-Neustadt. Die über diese letztere Handelsstraße geführten Waren wurden freilich nicht beim Preßburger, sondern beim Ödenburger Dreißigstamt verzollt. Zwischen 1524 und 1538 waren beinahe ein Drittel der Schuldner der Firma Funck Einwohner von Ödenburg und Güns (Kőszeg), so daß sich Wiener-Neustadt als der Hauptvermittler von Textilwaren nach West-Transdanubien erwiesen hat [19]).

Der Vorstoß der oberdeutschen Produkte ist auch für die Zusammensetzung der in den Dreißigstbüchern des Jahres 1542 registrierten Tucheinfuhr — 9608 Stück und 47 Ballen, insgesamt etwa 11 000 Stück — kennzeichnend. Verschwunden ist innerhalb der west- und west-mitteleuropäischen Sorten der überwiegende Anteil der niederrheinischen Produkte, welcher bei der Preßburger Einfuhr vom Jahre 1457—58 noch zu beobachten war. Das Aachener Tuch figuriert nun mit einem einzigen Ballen, und Kölner Tuch kommt gar nicht vor; ihre Plätze werden nun von den oberrheinischen und süddeutschen (vor allem Nürnberger) Waren eingenommen, die mit ihren 2463 Stück und 15 Ballen im Jahre 1542 etwa 26 Prozent der in den Dreißigstbüchern registrierten Einfuhr ausmachten. Auf eine noch wichtigere Veränderung deutet aber die Zunahme des Anteils der ost-mitteleuropäischen Produkte hin. Der Anteil der west- und west-mitteleuropäischen Tuchsorten, welcher 1457—58 noch 61,4 Prozent betrug, erreicht 1542 höchstens 41—42 Prozent; der Anteil der böhmisch-mährischen und schlesischen (vor allem Breslauer) Waren ist hingegen — mit 6396 Stück und 4 Ballen — von 38,6 Prozent auf 58—59 Prozent der Gesamteinfuhr angestiegen [20]).

Der Schwerpunkt des westlichen Tuchimports Ungarns hatte sich also — trotz des Erscheinens wichtiger neuer Produkte der westeuropäischen Textilindustrie [21]) und trotz der beträchtlichen Einfuhr süddeutscher Waren — 1542 bereits auf die mährischen und schlesischen Produkte verschoben [22]).

---

[18]) Ingomar Bog *Wachstumsprobleme der oberdeutschen Wirtschaft 1540—1618* in *Forschungen zur Sozial- und Wirtschaftsgeschichte* 10 (Stuttgart 1968) 72—75.

[19]) Othmar Pickl *Das älteste Geschäftsbuch Österreichs. Die Gewölberegister der Wiener Neustädter Firma Alexius Funck (1516 bis ca. 1538) und verwandtes Material zur Geschichte des steirischen Handels im 15./16. Jahrhundert* (Graz 1966).

[20]) Auf Grund der bisher nicht publizierten Belege der Dreißigstbücher 1542, die uns Győző Ember freundlichst mitgeteilt hat.

[21]) Siehe unten Anm. 36.

[22]) Diese Tatsache wird etwas später auch durch türkische Quellen bestätigt, die den westlichen Import der eroberten Teile Ungarns beleuchten. Über die

Wenn dem Übergewicht der west-, bzw. west-mitteleuropäischen Tucheinfuhr eine vorherrschende Lage der Donau-Einfuhrstraße entsprochen hatte, so mußte das Vordringen der mährischen und schlesischen Tuchsorten — selbst wenn ihre Einfuhr auch über Preßburg ansehnliche Ausmaße angenommen hatte — im ungarischen Textilimport notwendigerweise ein Ansteigen der Bedeutung der Handelsstraßen nördlich der Donau zur Folge haben.

*

Von den Handelsstraßen nördlich der Donau muß zuerst der mährische Weg des näheren betrachtet werden. Die Regulierung und Begünstigung dieser Straße diente in den dreißiger Jahren des 14. Jahrhunderts noch dem Zwecke, für die flandrischen, rheinischen und süddeutschen Kaufleute unter Vermeidung des 1312 wieder geltend gemachten Stapelrechts von Wien [23]) vom West-Nordwesten her, über Böhmen und Mähren, mit Berührung von Prag und Brünn, und weiter nicht über Preßburg, sondern über Neuburg (Holics, Holič), Sassin (Sasvár, Šaštín) und Tyrnau (Nagyszombat, Trnava) mit der ungarischen Hauptstadt eine Verbindung herzustellen [24]). Selbst wenn diese Verbindung zur Zeit der Hussitenkriege unterbunden worden war, wurde sie um so wichtiger zur Zeit der Kämpfe zwischen Friedrich und Matthias, als nicht nur Nürnberg und andere oberdeutsche Städte, sondern auch Salzburg mit Ungarn über Brünn Handel trieben [25]). In den ersten Jahrzehnten des 16. Jahrhunderts hatte zwar die mährische Handelsstraße ihre Funktion als „Umweg" bereits verloren — es wurde ja der unmittelbare Verkehr entlang der Donau wiederhergestellt, was auch durch das Aufhören des

---

türkische Zollstation Vác (Waitzen) wurden vom 22. Juli 1563 bis zum 9. März 1564 insgesamt 3797 Stück Tuch eingeführt, davon 2989 Stück mährisches und schlesisches Produkt; in Buda wurden im Jahre 1571 insgesamt 4220 Stück Tuch von westlicher Herkunft verzollt, darunter 2828 Stück aus Schlesien und Mähren. — Gyula Káldy-Nagy *Statisztikai adatok a török hódoltsági terület nyugat felé irányuló áruforgalmáról 1560—1564-ben* [Statistische Angaben zum westlichen Warenumsatz des unter Türkenherrschaft stehenden Gebietes von Ungarn 1560—1564] in *Történeti Statisztikai Évkönyv 1965—66* (Budapest 1968) 38—39; Lajos Fekete — Gyula Káldy-Nagy *Budai török számadáskönyvek 1550—1580* [Rechnungsbücher türkischer Finanzstellen in Buda 1550—1580] (Budapest 1962) 577.

[23]) *Die Rechte und Freiheiten der Stadt Wien* 1, bearb. v. J. A. Tomaschek (Wien 1877) 88—89.

[24]) Domanovszky *Harmincadvám* 8—10; Pleidell *Külkereskedelem* 36—41.

[25]) Mayer *Der auswärtige Handel* 53, 74, 122, 147; Hans Schenk *Nürnberg und Prag* (*Gießener Abhandlungen zur Agrar- und Wirtschaftsforschung des europäischen Ostens* 46, Wiesbaden 1969) 169—170.

Wiener Stapelrechts befördert wurde [26]) —, sie hat aber ihre Bedeutung im Außenhandel gar nicht verloren. Die Grenze gegen Mähren erreichte gerade zu dieser Zeit einen sehr ansehnlichen Anteil an der ungarischen Ausfuhr, nämlich im Viehexport [27]); es kann aber auch von ihrer Rolle in der Einfuhr, das heißt im Import der böhmisch-mährischen Tuche nicht abgesehen werden, obwohl die aus dem Jahre 1542 erhalten gebliebenen Dreißigstbücher der Ämter der mährischen Handelsstraße, Neuburg, Sassin und Tyrnau, wie auch des ebenfalls zur Tyrnauer Dreißigstgruppe gehörenden Skalitz und des damals schon selbständig gewordenen Wartberg (Szempc, Senec) nur Ausfuhrposten aufweisen; Einfuhr wird in ihnen gar nicht erwähnt [28]).

Es muß aber in Betracht gezogen werden, daß die ungarische Kammer damals die Einnahmen der genannten Dreißigsstellen mit einem Pfandbesitzer namens Alexius Thurzó, einem der reichsten Magnaten des Landes, zu teilen hatte, und daß die erhalten gebliebenen Dreißigstregister Tagebücher der königlichen Dreißigstbeamten sind, die nur die zugunsten der Kammer eingetriebenen Zölle anführen [29]). Eine königliche Verordnung 1545 gibt uns Information darüber, wie in den vorangegangenen Jahren die Teilung der Einnahmen dieser „inscribierten" Dreißigststellen vor sich gegangen war: Aus den Zöllen der Ausfuhr erhielt der König einen Anteil von 50 bis 100 Prozent; die Einfuhrzollgebühren fielen demgegenüber meistens völlig dem Pfandbesitzer zu [30]). In den aus dem Jahre 1542 erhalten gebliebenen Tagebüchern der Tyrnauer Dreißigstgruppe figurieren also aller Wahrscheinlichkeit nach ausschließlich Ausfuhrposten nicht deshalb, weil über diese Zollstellen keine Einfuhr erfolgte, sondern deshalb, weil die Einfuhr in die Tagebücher der königlichen Dreißigstbeamten nicht eingetragen wurde. Die Einfuhrzollgebühren wurden ja völlig von denen des Pfandbesitzers eingetrieben.

*

Eine noch größere Aufmerksamkeit als der mährischen muß der schlesischen Handelsstraße gewidmet werden, die aus nordwestlicher Richtung auf Ungarn zuführte. Im Bereiche des Exports wurde

---

26) Mayer *Der auswärtige Handel* 161—162.

27) Zsigmond Pál Pach *The Role of East-Central Europe in International Trade (16th and 17th centuries)* in *Études historiques* (Budapest 1970) 244—245.

28) Győző Ember *Külkereskedelmünk történetéhez a XVI. században* [Zur Geschichte des ungarischen Außenhandels im 16. Jahrhundert] in *A Magyar Tudományos Akadémia Társadalmi-Történeti Tudományok Osztályának Közleményei* 8 (Budapest 1958) 325, 335.

29) Ebenda 322—323.

30) Ignác Acsády *Magyarország pénzügyei I. Ferdinánd uralkodása alatt 1526—64* [Die Finanzen Ungarns unter der Regierung Ferdinand I.] (Budapest 1888) 133—134.

ihre Bedeutung Ende des 15. und in den ersten Jahrzehnten des 16. Jahrhunderts vor allem durch die Kupferausfuhr der Fugger gesichert [31]); gleichzeitig erfuhr aber auch der Import, hauptsächlich der Importverkehr von Textilwaren, eine Belebung auf diesem sogenannten „oberen Weg" [32]), welcher, von Breslau und Teschen (Český Tešin) kommend, über den Jablunka-Paß führend, bei jenen Zollstellen im Waagtal mündete, die zum Trentschiner Hauptdreißigstamt gehörten und sich 1542 ebenfalls im Pfandbesitz des Alexius Thurzó befanden [33]). Aus diesem Jahre sind uns leider Dreißigstbücher von keiner der beiden Parteien (weder vom Pfandbesitzer, noch von der königlichen Kammer) erhalten geblieben, die die Einnahmen dieser Stellen untereinander teilten. Erhalten haben sich aber die einige Jahre früher, für die damaligen Vize-Pfandbesitzer Nikolaus und Peter Kosztka verfertigten Register einer dieser Zollstellen, des Silleiner (Zsolna, Žilina) Dreißigstamtes; und zwar von 1529 bis 1537 unvollständig, unter ihnen aber das Register vom Jahre 1530 vollständig. Demzufolge sind in diesem Jahr über diese einzige Dreißigststelle wenigstens 1312 Stück und 38 Ballen, insgesamt etwa 2400 Stück, 1531 hingegen, im Verlaufe eines Dreivierteljahrs, wenigstens 663 Stück und 131 Ballen, insgesamt etwa 4500 Stück ausländisches Tuch nach Ungarn eingeführt worden [34]), was die Größenordnung der in den Dreißigstbüchern vom Jahre 1542 nicht figurierenden nordwestlichen Textileinfuhr wenigstens einigermaßen beleuchten kann.

Der steigende Verkehr des „oberen Weges" hing mit den Neuerscheinungen der Textilindustrie und Textilhandels, mit der Erweiterung der Nachfrage nach Wollstoffen mittelmäßiger und billiger Qualität — gegenüber den früheren hochwertigen Tuchsorten — zusammen. Die Produkte der neuen Zweige des niederländischen und englischen Webereigewerbes [35]) waren in Mitteleuropa eingedrungen und erreichten auch die

---

[31]) Gusztáv Wenzel *Okmánytár a Fuggerek magyarországi nagykereskedése és rézvállalatának történetéhez* [Urkunden zur Geschichte des ungarischen Handels- und Kupferunternehmens der Fugger] in *Történelmi Tár* (Budapest 1882) 632—634; Ernst Koch *Das Hütten- und Hammerwerk der Fugger zu Hohenkirchen bei Georgenthal in Thüringen 1495—1549* in *Zeitschrift des Vereins für Thüringische Geschichte und Altertumskunde* 26 (Jena 1926) 308—309.

[32]) Heinrich Wendt *Schlesien und der Orient. Ein geschichtlicher Rückblick* (Breslau 1916) 51—61; Engel-Janosi *Wiener Kaufmannschaft* 48.

[33]) Acsády *Magyarország pénzügyei* 134; Ember *Külkereskedelmünk* 322.

[34]) Pavel Horváth *Príspevok k obchodným stykom Slovenska so Sliezskom a Moravou v prvej polovici 16. stor.* in *Historické štúdie* 11 (Bratislava 1966) 168, 187, 189.

[35]) Henri Pirenne *Une crise industrielle au XVIe siècle. La draperie urbaine et la „nouvelle draperie" en Flandre* in *Bulletin de la Classe des lettres de l'Académie royale de Belgique* 5 (Bruxelles 1905) 490—521; Herbert

ungarischen Märkte [36]). Aber diese Entwicklungstendenzen „modernen Typs" wurden auch von einigen deutschen Städten, sogar ost-mitteleuropäischen Bezirken befolgt: Sie haben nicht nur die westeuropäischen Waren vermittelt, sondern — mit ihnen konkurrierend — auch ihre eigene Textilindustrie entwickelt, insbesondere auf dem Gebiete der Herstellung von billigeren, konkurrenzfähigen, für einen breiteren Absatzmarkt bestimmten Stoffarten [37]). Zur selben Zeit, als Wien und die westungarischen Städte (Preßburg, Ödenburg) sich in diese neue Richtung der Gewerbeentwicklung nicht einschalten konnten und bereits in den letzten Jahrzehnten des 15. und in den ersten des 16. Jahrhunderts Merkmale einer industriellen Stagnation und Reagrarisation aufwiesen [38]), läßt sich gerade in den mittleren und unteren Teilen Schlesiens, besonders in Görlitz, sowie in den nördlichen und südwestlichen Städten Mährens, so auch in Iglau, ein beachtlicher Fortschritt in dieser Richtung beobachten, welcher auch die zeitweiligen Rückfälle zu überwinden imstande war [39]). Die schlesischen und mährischen Wollstoffe mittelmäßiger und billiger Qualität haben — wie aus den Dreißigstbüchern 1542 ersichtlich — auch in der über die Zollstellen der westlichen Grenzscheide abgewickelten Einfuhr einen hervorragenden Platz eingenommen; im Nord- und Nordwestverkehr aber machten sie den weit überwiegenden Teil der Gesamteinfuhr aus: In der Silleiner Einfuhr von etwa 2400 Stück im Jahre 1530 waren 925 Stück mährisches und mehr als 1000 Stück (30 Ballen und 172 Stück) schlesisches (Görlitzer) Tuch, während die westeuropäischen und deutschen Waren nur mit kleineren Posten vertreten waren: das

---

Heaton *The Yorkshire Woollen and Worsted Industries. From the earliest times up to the Industrial Revolution* (Oxford 1920) 68—88; E. L. J. Coornaert *Un centre industriel d'autrefois. La draperie-sayetterie d'Hondschoote XIVe—XVIIIe siècles* (Paris 1930) 10—21, 244—246; D. C. Coleman *An Innovation and its Diffusion: the „New Draperies"* in *The Economic History Review* 2nd Ser. 22 (1969) 419—422.

36) Unter den neueren, billigeren Schafwollgeweben, die von den „echten" Tuchsorten zu den „New Draperies" etwa einen Übergang bildeten, fanden besonders die englischen „Kersey"-(kersie-) Stoffe eine zunehmende Nachfrage auf den ostmitteleuropäischen Märkten im 16. Jahrhundert. 1457—58 wurden nur 3 Stück „Kirsing" in Preßburg verzollt; die Dreißigstbücher von 1542 registrieren hingegen schon 272 Stück, die türkischen Zollabrechnungen von Waitzen 1563—64 (7½ Monate) 520 Stück, die von Ofen 1571 aber 1128 Stück „Karasia"-Gewebe innerhalb der importierten Textilwaren.

37) Wendt Schlesien 31; György Székely *A németalföldi és az angol posztó fajtáinak elterjedése a XIII—XVII. századi Közép-Európában* [Die Verbreitung der niederländischen und englischen Tuchsorten in Mitteleuropa im 13.—17. Jahrhundert] in *Századok* 102 (1968) 12.

38) Mayer *Der auswärtige Handel* 111—112; Engel-Janosi *Wiener Kaufmannschaft* 41—42; Jenő Szücs *Das Städtewesen in Ungarn im 15.—17. Jahrhundert* in *Studia Historica Academiae Scientiarum Hungaricae 53* (Budapest 1963) 117—118, 123—124.

39) Wendt *Schlesien* 15, 61; Horváth *Príspevok* 173—174.

„Lundisch" (Londoner) mit 66 Stück, das Aachener mit 3 Ballen und 15 Stück, das Nürnberger mit 5 Ballen [40]).

Der Importverkehr in Sillein war auch Mitte des Jahrhunderts rege. „Eine äußerst gesuchte, belebte Handelsstraße führt von hier aus ... nach Schlesien und Mähren" — meldeten 1560 die zur Untersuchung gegen die Dreißigstbeamten entsandten Beauftragten über das Silleiner Dreißigstamt. Und sie bezeichneten als wichtigsten Posten der hiesigen Einfuhr auch weiterhin das Tuch [41]).

*

Wir müssen in östlicher Richtung sogar noch weiter gehen; die schlesischen und mährischen Stoffarten mittelmäßiger und billiger Qualität fanden nämlich nicht nur von Nordwesten, sondern auch von Norden her über P o l e n einen Weg zu den ungarischen Märkten, hauptsächlich über die im internationalen Verkehr so wichtige Handelsstraße Breslau—Krakau [42]), und von hier aus über Bochnia, Alt- und Neu-Sandez (Stary-Sącz, Nowy-Sącz), weiter über die Zipser Städte, bzw. Bartfeld (Bártfa, Bardejov) und Eperies (Eperjes, Prešov) nach Kaschau (Kassa, Košice) [43]). Die Hauptausfuhrartikel im Handelsverkehr zwischen Kaschau und Krakau waren das Kupfer der oberungarischen (ostslowakischen) Bergstädte und die Weine der Kaschauer und Tokajer Weingegenden, die Haupteinfuhrartikel hingegen — die Textilwaren [44]). Die Kaschauer Handelsgesellschaft — welche die Webewaren fast ausschließlich von Krakauer Großkaufleuten bezog — hat zwischen 1501 und 1504 außer westeuropäischen (englischen, flandrischen, niederrheinischen) Sorten auch

---

[40]) H o r v á t h *Príspevok* 187—189. — Sillein war freilich nur eine der im Waagtal gelegenen, bzw. zum Hauptdreißigstamt Trentschin gehörenden Stellen, wo die Einfuhr aus Schlesien und Mähren verzollt wurde. 1500—1505 bezeichnete man Trentschin als den Hauptdurchgangsort der Breslauer Waren. Die Trentschiner Kaufleute selbst führten über diese Zollstelle im Jahre 1530, 1532 und 1536 108, 112 bzw. 229 Stück mährisches Tuch ein.

[41]) Sándor T a k á t s *A harmincadosok elleni vizsgálat 1560-ban* [Die Untersuchung gegen die Dreißigstbeamten im Jahre 1560] in *Magyar Gazdaságtörténelmi Szemle* 6 (Budapest 1899) 252.

[42]) Stanisław K u t r z e b a *Handel Krakowa w wiekach śriednich na tle stosunków handlowych Polski* (Kraków 1903) 12—13; W e n d t *Schlesien* 20—21.

[43]) Adorján D i v é k y *Felső-Magyarország kereskedelmi összeköttetése Lengyelországgal főleg a XVI—XVII. században* [Die Handelsverbindungen Oberungarns zu Polen hauptsächlich im 16.—17. Jahrhundert] (Budapest 1905) 21—23; Albert G á r d o n y i *Felső-Magyarország kereskedelmi utjai a középkorban* [Die Handelsstraßen Oberungarns im Mittelalter] in *Közgazdasági Szemle* 32 (Budapest 1908) 19—20.

[44]) K u t r z e b a *Handel Krakowa* 24; Erik F ü g e d i *Kaschau, eine osteuropäische Handelsstadt am Ende des 15. Jahrhunderts* in *Studia Slavica Academiae Scientiarum Hungaricae* 2 (Budapest 1956) 208.

schlesisches (Görlitzer) Tuch in Verschleiß gebracht, bzw. nach den Märkten der Städte Debrezin (Debrecen) und insbesondere Großwardein (Nagyvárad, Oradea Mare) vermittelt [45]).

Der polnisch-ungarische Verkehr führte an solchen Zollstellen — an dem Kaschauer Hauptdreißigstamt und seinen Filialen [46]) — vorbei, auf welche sich die aus dem Jahre 1542 erhaltenen Dreißigstbücher ebenso wenig erstreckten, wie auf die Ämter im Waagtal, die die schlesische Handelsstraße überwachten. Die Zollbücher einer der Kaschauer Gruppe gehörenden Dreißigststelle, nämlich die von Bartfeld, sind aber doch auf uns gekommen, wenngleich mit einer früheren Provenienz: 1504—1507. Sie weisen einen überwiegenden, 79prozentigen Anteil der Textilien auf und innerhalb dessen ein entscheidendes Übergewicht der ost-mitteleuropäischen Tuchsorten: Aus dem 1361 Stück betragenden durchschnittlichen Jahresimport machten die mährischen und schlesischen Produkte mittelmäßiger und billiger Qualität 1336 Stück aus, während die westeuroischen und niederrheinischen Webewaren nur mit verschwindend geringen Posten vertreten waren [47]). Und daß der Import vom Norden her auch in der Mitte des Jahrhunderts bedeutsam geblieben war, läßt sich durch eine Kaschauer Dreißigstrechnung beweisen, welche um kaum anderthalb Jahrzehnte jünger ist als die Dreißigstbücher vom Jahre 1542. Demnach entrichteten 1555 allein die Bürger der Stadt Kaschau einen Zoll von 2672 fl. nach ihrem Import aus Polen, den sie überwiegend eben über Bartfeld abwickelten [48]). Dies ist eine ansehnliche Summe, besonders wenn wir bedenken, daß 1542 der Gesamtimport aller Dreißigststellen der westlichen Grenze nicht mehr als 6761 fl. Zolleinnahmen erbrachte [49]), und wenn wir in Betracht ziehen, daß die Bürger der Stadt Kaschau im Sinne ihrer alten Privilegien nur die Hälfte der Dreißigstgebühren zu entrichten verpflichtet waren [50]). Obwohl die erwähnte Rechnung den

---

45) *A kassai kereskedelmi társaság följegyzései 1502 és 1503* [Akten der Kaschauer Handelsgesellschaft 1502—1503], bearb. v. György Kerekes in *Magyar Gazdaságtörténelmi Szemle* 9 (Budapest 1902) 108; Ondřej R. Halaga *Kaufleute und Handelsgüter der Hanse im Karpatengebiet* in *Hansische Geschichtsblätter* 85 (Köln-Graz 1967) 83.

46) Laut dem Gesetzartikel 34/1498 hatte das Kaschauer Hauptdreißigstamt folgende Filialen: Bartfeld, Leutschau (Lőcse, Levoča), Käsmark (Késmárk, Kežmarok), Lublau (Lubló, Stara Lubovna), Sztropkó (Stropkov) und Homonna (Humenné). Im Jahre 1557—58 funktionierte schon eine Dreißigststelle auch in Eperjes.

47) Erik Fügedi *Magyarország külkereskedelme a XVI. század elején* [Der Außenhandel Ungarns zu Beginn des 16. Jahrhunderts] in *Agrártörténeti Szemle* 11 (Budapest 1969) 7.

48) Lajos Kemény *A kassai harmincad története a XVI. század végéig* [Die Geschichte des Kaschauer Dreißigstamtes bis zum Ende des 16. Jahrhunderts] in *Magyar Gazdaságtörténelmi Szemle* 1 (Budapest 1894) 308.

49) Ember *Külkereskedelmünk* 335.

50) Kemény *A kassai harmincad* 304, 307, 309.

Dreißigstertrag nur nach Einfuhr und Ausfuhr detailliert und uns über die Zusammensetzung des Warenverkehrs keine Auskunft gibt, läßt sich mit Recht voraussetzen, daß die Einfuhrzolleinnahmen vor allem auf den Import von Textilwaren zurückzuführen sind. Etwa zwei Jahrzehnte später berichtet ja auch der Kaschauer Kaufmann Gergely Kalmár in seinem „Regestum" über seine Krakauer Geschäfte, daß er dort überwiegend Tücher — meistens Breslauer Sorte — erworben habe [51]); und auch die Dreißigstbücher der Städte Kaschau, Leutschau, Eperies und Bartfeld aus dem Jahre 1585 — deren Bearbeitung jetzt im Gange ist — beleuchten den vorwiegenden Anteil der Wollstoffe, vor allem der schlesischen Produkte, an der Einfuhr aus Polen [52]).

Der Handelsverkehr zwischen Krakau und Ungarn, der auf eine alte Vergangenheit zurückblickte, ist auch im Verlaufe des 16. Jahrhunderts rege geblieben, seine Warenzusammensetzung hat sich aber einigermaßen verändert. Eine seiner Hauptfunktionen bestand nunmehr darin, nach Ungarn und Siebenbürgen schlesische und mährische Textilien zu vermitteln [53]).

*

In der Periode zwischen der Mitte des 15. und der Mitte des 16. Jahrhunderts sind also im ost-mitteleuropäischen Straßennetz des internationalen Textilhandels und gleichzeitig damit in den Handelsstraßen des ungarischen Tuchimports Verschiebungen eingetreten. Mitte des 15. Jahrhunderts „war Wien der beinahe ausschließliche, privilegierte Ort der Beschaffung der aus Westen importierten Waren nach Ungarn; und neben dem Wiener Markt verschwand sozusagen die Bedeutung der böhmisch-mährischen, schlesischen und polnischen Märkte im westungarischen Warenverkehr" [54]). Bis zur Mitte des 16. Jahrhunderts ließ die vorherrschende Stellung der Wiener Handelsstraße im westlichen Import Ungarns nach, da die Bedeutung (vielleicht auch der mährischen, gewiß aber) der schlesischen und polnischen Handelswege in der Vermittlung des wichtigsten Einfuhrartikels, des Tuches, zunahm.

---

[51]) *Kalmár Gergely deák regestumja kereskedéséről 1574—82* [Die Handelsakten des Gergely Kalmár 1574—82], bearb. v. György Kerekes in *Magyar Gazdaságtörténelmi Szemle* 10 (Budapest 1903) 72—73.

[52]) Rohergebnisse der Untersuchungen von Frau Judith Pákh, die sie mir freundlicherweise mitteilte.

[53]) Jan M. Małecki *Die Wandlungen im Krakauer und polnischen Handel zur Zeit der Türkenkriege des 16. und 17. Jahrhunderts* in *Die wirtschaftlichen Auswirkungen der Türkenkriege*, hg. von Othmar Pickl (Graz 1971) 148—149. — Vgl. Harald Prickler *Das Volumen des westlichen ungarischen Außenhandels vom 16. Jahrhunderts bis 1700*, ebenda 140, 143.

[54]) Kováts *Korakapitalisztikus gazdasági válság* 193.

256

Diese Verschiebung der Handelslinien — die sich auch im Vergleiche der Tucheinfuhr der westlichen Grenze 1542 zur Tucheinfuhr Preßburgs 1457—58 widerspiegelt [55]) — hängt einerseits mit den politischen Geschehnissen, mit den Türkenkriegen und der türkischen Eroberung, zusammen, deren Auswirkungen in dieser Beziehung eine weitere Untersuchung erfordern [56]). Andererseits ist aber dies auf die neuen Entwicklungen im Tuchgewerbe und Tuchhandel, auf die Veränderungen ihrer Warenzusammensetzung zurückzuführen. Der Schwerpunkt des Textilumsatzes hat sich nämlich von den alten hochwertigen Tuchsorten auf die neueren Wollprodukte mittelmäßiger und billiger Qualität verschoben, — auf solche einfachere Stoffarten, deren Herstellung inzwischen auch in einigen, Ungarn verhältnismäßig nahe gelegenen mährischen und schlesischen Bezirken beachtliche Ausmaße angenommen hat.

[55]) Von 1549 an zeichnete sich ein großer Aufschwung im westlichen Außenhandel Ungarns ab, der sich vorwiegend aber auf die Ausfuhr (vor allem auf die Ochsenausfuhr) bezog. — Ignác Acsády *Közgazdasági állapotaink a XVI. és XVII. században* [Die wirtschaftlichen Zustände Ungarns im 16. und 17. Jahrhundert] (Budapest 1889) 48—49; Prickler *Das Volumen* 134—137.

[56]) Pach *The Role of East-Central Europe* 240—241.

ADDENDA

ZUR GESCHICHTE DER HANDELSBEZIEHUNGEN ZWISCHEN ÖSTERREICH UND UNGARN IM 15. UND 16. JAHRHUNDERT

Page 244, Note 3:

For the foundation of the frontier customs system in Hungary, see recently from the present writer: A harmincadvám eredete (The Origins of the "Thirtieth" Duty), Budapest, 1990.

Page 246, Note 8:

For the main overland routes of European cloth trade: *J. A. van Houtte*, Les grands itinéraires du commerce (XIIIe–XVIIIe siècles). In: Trasporti e sviluppo economico. Atti della Quinta Settimana di Studio (Prato, 1973), Firenze, 1986, pp. 90-92.

Page 247, Note 15:

The customs registers of the West–Transdanubian town Sopron (Ödenburg) that have partly survived from the years 1483–1490 indicate that the cloth import of the place (though much smaller in volume) presented a composition largely similar to that of Pozsony (Pressburg/Bratislava) in 1457–1458: *J. Házi*, Sopron szabad királyi város története (A History of the Royal Free Town Sopron), II, 4. Különféle számadások és adójegyzékek (Various Accounts and Tax Registers) 1454–1495, Sopron, 1936, pp. 316–350. — Conf. Note 19.

Page 248, Note 20:

The research findings of *Gy. Ember* have been published in the meantime: Magyarország nyugati külkereskedelme a XVI. század közepén (The Western Trade of Hungary in the Middle of the 16th Century), Budapest, 1988, pp. 75–78.

Page 252, Note 36:

According to the customs registers of Zágráb (Zagreb/Agram) from 1545–1558 kersey accounted for nearly half of the woollen imports. Obviously, this middle quality fabric of English textile industry entered Hungary from the south–western direction, too, Venetian and Ragusan merchants acting as intermediaries: *Zs. Teke*, The Import of Woollen Cloth in Zagreb in the Middle of the 16th Century. In: Economy, Society, Historiography. Dedicated to Zs. P. Pach on his 70th Birthday. Ed. by F. Glatz, Budapest, 1989, pp. 88–

89, 91. — Conf. *L. Stone*, Elizabethan Overseas Trade, The Economic History Review, 2nd Ser., II, 1 (1949), p. 58; *R. Davis*, England and the Mediterranean 1570–1620. In: Essays in the Economic and Social History of Tudor and Stuart England. Ed. by F. J. Fisher, Cambridge, 1961, p. 120; *F. Braudel*, La Méditerranée et le monde méditerranéen à l'époque de Philippe II^2, Paris, 1966, I, pp. 194–195, 292, 550, 559–562.

Page 255, Note 51:

The customs books of Kassa (Kaschau/Košice) from the year 1555 reveal the prevalence of Silesian cloths (those of Görlitz/Zgorzelec and Breslau/Wrocław) among imports, with a customs value of 20 695 florins. The second place belonged to kersies (8808 florins), the third one to fabrics of Nuremberg (6103 florins): *Gy. Granasztói*, The Commerce of Kassa in the 16th Century. In: Economy, Society, Historiography, op. cit. p. 68. — For the increasing flow of Görlitz and Breslau cloths through Cracow towards Kassa and other North Hungarian (Slovakian) towns during the 16th century, also see *M. Wolański*, Schlesiens Stellung im Osthandel vom 15. bis zum 17. Jahrhundert. In: Der Aussenhandel Ostmitteleuropas 1450–1650. Hg. von I. Bog, Köln–Wien, 1971, pp. 128–129.— For cloth and kersey imported from Vienna through Pozsony to Kassa simultaneously: *S. Takáts*, Kassa kereskedői 1557-ben (The Merchants of Kassa in 1557), Magyar Gazdaságtörténelmi Szemle (Hungarian Economic History Review), XIII (1906), pp. 125–127.

Page 255, Note 52:

Meanwhile *Mrs Pákh* has published her treatise: A szövetbehozatal szerepe és struktúrája Bártfa, Eperjes, Kassa és Lőcse külkereskedelmében a 16. század végén (The Role and Structure of Textile Imports in the Foreign Trade of Four North Hungarian Towns in the Late 16th Century). In: Történeti Statisztikai Tanulmányok (Essays in Historical Statistics), IV (1980). — Silesian cloths accounted for 58 to 92 per cent, kersies for 6 to 21 per cent, Moravian fabrics for 3 to 8 per cent of the woollens brought into the above four towns from northern and western directions: pp. 77–78. — Later on the share of Moravian imports (including cloths of Iglau/Jihlava) increased considerably: *R. Fišer*, Dovoz moravského sukna na levocsky trh v první polovině 17. století, Časopis Matice Moravské, LXXXVIII, 1–2 (1969), pp. 39, 48–49.

Page 255, Note 53:

As for the textile imports of Transylvania, relevant data are available from the papers of *Fr. Pap*, written on the basis of the customs books of Kolozsvár (Klausenburg/Cluj) from the years 1599–1637. They evidence a similar shift from expensive western cloths to cheaper products such as kersey, and Silesian and Moravian sorts: Schimbul de mărfuri între Cluj şi Polonia în registrele vamale clujene (1599–1637). In: Acta Musei Napocensis (=AMN), XIV (1977), pp. 380–382; Comerţul Clujului cu oraşele Slovaciei de astăzi. In: AMN, XVI (1979), pp. 238–239, 247; Comerţul Clujului cu Viena. In: AMN, XVIII (1981), pp. 178–180.

IX

The Shifting of International Trade Routes in the 15th–17th Centuries*

The close of the 15th century is one of the great turning-points in the economic history of Europe.

Up to the second half of the 15th century, European economic development had tended — as far as its main trend is concerned — to equalize the differences in the development levels of Western and Eastern Europe, to advance the East European societies that had started later on the road to feudal development. Yet, since about the end of the 15th century, an opposite trend emerged and began to assert itself increasingly. Instead of further diminishing, let alone disappearing, the gap between Western and Eastern Europe grew larger and more pronounced. While the disintegration of the medieval order, the rise of capitalist relations, began and proceeded in several countries of Western Europe — of course at varying rates, in different variants, and even through occasional setbacks — the feudal system survived, and even consolidated in several respects, in the countries of Mid-Eastern Europe, and the rule of late feudalism was prolonged for centuries.

Until quite recently, *international* research in economic history was chiefly concerned with only one facet of this development process: with the economic growth of the countries of Western Europe in the modern times. Since, however, this process coincided in time, and was obviously connected with the overseas discoveries, with colonization, with the establishment of the new routes of world trade, the majority of researchers concentrated their attention on these sources of West-European economic growth, and showed considerably less interest in the *Mid-East-European aspects* of the topic than in the broad set of problems involved in the *overseas colonial relations*. This attitude is reflected also in Volume IV (The Economy of Expanding Europe in the Sixteenth and Seventeenth Centuries) of The Cambridge Economic History of Europe, published in 1967. Although it is stated in the Preface that the principal problem of the economic history of this era is the development of modern world economy, the subject is narrowed down within this scope to the relations and interactions of West European and colonial economies: apart from a few laudable exceptions, the Mid-East-European aspects are largely

* A shortened form of this paper was read at the IVth Congress of the International Economic History Association, Session I/3 (Bloomington, Ind., U.S.A., September 11, 1968).

excluded from the majority of chapters dealing with the factual questions of economic history, thus also from the study of the trends in international trade in the 16th and 17th centuries.

And it also appears from the majority of older and more recent studies on this stirring period of European economic history that the treatment of the rise of modern world economy in the 16th and 17th centuries has been restricted to the relations of Western Europe with the colonial territories, and the negative trend in the development of Eastern Europe has usually been explained by the statement that the latter *failed* to join in this great process of transformation. Applying a certain simplification, we may sum up this explanation as follows: the shifting of the principal trade routes, mainly as a consequence of the great discoveries at the end of the 15th century, the shifting of the centre of expanding international trade from the Mediterranean to the Atlantic, promoted the economic growth of Western Europe, while in the countries of Central and Eastern Europe, which *did not take part* in the discoveries, in colonization and long-distance maritime trade, and did not share in the abundant sources of capital accumulation, these changes entailed economic stagnation, even recession; consequently, these territories were increasingly falling behind in progress as compared to the West European countries where capitalist development had set in.

Needless to say that to disclose the Mid-East-European factors and aspects of the development of modern world economy is a task to be accomplished largely by the researchers of the countries of Mid-Eastern Europe, including the economic historians of Hungary. Yet, we must admit that, until quite recently, we have done but very little to fill this gap, though we have succeeded in defining some main features of the Hungarian economic development in this period, especially in the field of agrarian history. However, as concerns the broader aspects of the topic, we have contented ourselves — apart from one or two attempts *(Wittman)* — with making reference to the above explanation, though in a modified, more subtle form. Yet, if it is true that the history of West European economic growth in this period can hardly be written without paying due attention to the East European relations, it must be equally true that, speaking in a summary manner, the history of the economic backwardness of Mid-Eastern Europe cannot be written without making a thorough study of the economic progress of Western Europe, which was promoted — in particular ways[1] — *both* by East European *and* by overseas colonial relations.

The most comprehensive question of the international economic history of the 16th and 17th centuries can, therefore, be put like this: *what was the*

[1] We should like to emphasize: *in particular ways*. For some simplifying explanations had nearly placed a sign of equality between these two relations, and tried to characterize the conditions in certain East European countries by applying to them the term of colonial dependence.

correlation, the interdependence between the three principal factors of the early development process of world economy, i.e. the West European, the East European and the colonial economies; how did the changes, taking place in this or that relation, affect the whole system of interrelationships?

This fundamental problem can also be formulated in the following way: ***what was the role of Eastern Europe, on the one hand, and of the overseas colonies, on the other, in the capitalist growth of Western Europe***; what were the similarities and differences between the East European countries and the colonies as regards their economic relations with Western Europe; what were the similar and different features in their relative positions within the expanding international trade, within the unfolding interregional division of labour?

But we may give another formulation, too: in what manner did the appearance of overseas colonies, their joining in world trade and world market, affect, through the transmission of West European economic demands and needs, the economic conditions of Eastern Europe; how did these conditions change in the successive phases of the development process of colonization and world economy; finally, what identical and what different features can be detected between the various countries of Eastern Europe in respect to their international economic role and their position in the world market?

1.

This comprehensive and ramifying set of problems — perhaps only a projection of the outlines for a programme of work for the time being — can be approached from several angles, from several aspects.

It might be no mistake to conclude that one possible approach is the study of the ***shifting of the principal routes of international trade in the 15th—17th centuries.***

The more so as the thesis of the shifting of trade routes in works dealing with the economic history of that time is recurring again and again, if only as a brief reference in many cases, presented as though it were a generally known, clearly understood, unequivocally interpreted process. Yet, in the background of this recurring formula there are highly dissimilar interpretations of the shifting of international trade routes, mainly as concerns the valuation of the immediate effects of overseas discoveries, i.e. whether the discovery of the New World and the substitution of the "*Cape-route*" for the traditional route of Eastern spice trade is to be regarded as the starting point of this process.

On the other hand, this almost stereotyped formula also conceals another problem. The emphasizing of the changes in the *routes* of international trade has proved suitable to cover up, to a certain extent, a more deep-rooted process, i.e. the shifting that occurred in the *character*, in the *commodity structure* of international trade. Yet, in our judgment, the latter was the more important, the basic change. In the 15th and 16th centuries — after historical precedents of some hundred years — the weight of international trade in Europe began to shift increasingly from the *expensive "Levant" commodities, luxury articles to the bulky goods for mass consumption;* it was at that time that "modern" international trade, stimulated by the inherent demands of European economy and based on a wider consumer market, began to emerge and to overshadow medieval long-distance trade, satisfying primarily the luxury needs of high-class (and rich burgher) consumers.

In the following the term *modern type* will be applied to international trade which was based on the development of agricultural and industrial commodity production, took its root in, and had a stimulating effect on, the division of labour over wide regions, in contrast to long-distance trade of the *medieval type* (old type), which was *not connected* with the development of commodity production and division of labour in Europe, but fulfilled, in essence, the role of supplying the spices and luxury articles of the East to the markets of Europe.

In the 14th and 15th centuries, prior to "*Carreira da India*", Eastern spices and luxuries were carried to the eastern ports of the Mediterranean through a long chain of Indian-Arabian trade relations. From there they were taken, mainly on Venetian and Genoese vessels, to the towns of North Italy, to *Venice* first of all, one of the greatest emporia of medieval Europe, the principal distribution centre of Levant articles. From Venice the goods were carried to other parts of Europe by land, river, or sea. German merchants took them along the mountain paths of the Alps to the South German towns, from where they were transported, partly on the Danube, to the countries of Mid-Eastern Europe — including Hungary —, partly on the Rhine to Flanders; by sea they reached Marseilles, Barcelona, and other ports of the western Mediterranean; through the Straits of Gibraltar they were taken, again mainly on Venetian and Genoese vessels, to England, the Netherlands and Northern Europe. The *character* and with it the *principal routes* of medieval long-haul trade were determined by the predominance of Levant luxuries. The *main centre* of medieval "world trade" was the *Mediterranean*, and its entire system of routes — by sea, river and land — was connected with the North Italian towns that occupied a central position in the Mediterranean region.

Along with this "rich trade" still retaining its dominant role, there also appeared, as early as the 13th century, the trade in certain agricultural and industrial products of the European economy. Transgressing the limits of local markets, and supplying far-away regions, it represented the rudiments of international trade of the modern type. This development made itself felt also in the Mediterranean area, but it was the establishment of another European trade centre, the *Baltic-North Sea area* that derived most benefit from it. It was from here that commodities for mass consumption — the agricultural produce, grain first of all, of Eastern Europe's adjoining territories — were taken as long-distance exports towards the West and South-West, to the coasts of the Atlantic, mainly to the ports of the Netherlands, to be exchanged for Levant articles brought from the Mediterranean, but also for the manufactured products of Western Europe, for Flemish cloth, first of all. The expanding trade in bulky agricultural mass produce resulted in an increasing use of waterways for long-distance transports; this, in turn, increased the demand for another bulky commodity that was practically untransportable overland. This was timber, the principal raw material of shipbuilding, whose abundant source was also to be found in the Baltic region.

In the 14th and most of the 15th century, maritime trade on the Baltic and the North Sea was characterized by the preponderance of the merchants of the *Hanseatic League*. It has often been said that they played the same role in the Baltic as the Venetians and the Genoese in the Mediterranean. But this holds good only in part. True enough, Hanseatic trade was, to a certain extent, similar to that of the North Italian towns as concerns its organization, methods and radius of action; but the commodity structure of this trade was more "modern", with a much higher proportion of mass products, than that of the Mediterranean trade, whose most important branch, even in face of the increasing trading activity of Venice, Genoa and Ragusa in grain (and wool), continued to be the Levant articles. Rich senators and urban patricians were mainly interested in the latter, while grain trade was distributed among many minor agents *(Aymard)*.

With the development of commodity production, and the expansion of modern-type trade relations, the relative importance of the two international trade centres, the Mediterranean and the Baltic-North Sea area shifted in *favour of the latter*. It was namely the ties of the old-type "rich trade" that connected the Mediterranean with the rest of Europe, while the trade in mass consumption goods remained virtually within the Mediterranean: its grain trade — though already of substantial volume in the 16th century — was able to meet, at most, the needs of the Mediterranean area only, and even that to a dècreasing extent in the second half of the 16th century *(Braudel)*. But it was these very mass consumption goods of primary production that were exported to ever increasing quantities[2] from the Baltic regions to Western Europe: Baltic grain was carried by Atlantic coast shipping during the 16th century not only to the Netherlands, but as far as Spain, and by the end of the century, through the Straits of Gibraltar, even to the Mediterranean itself.

Thus the bulk of international trade began to shift from the Mediterranean to the Atlantic in such a way that Atlantic coast shipping, the principal

[2] In the middle of the 16th century, the long-distance corn trade of the Mediterranean region amounted to some 50 thousand tons per annum; about the same time, yearly 40—60 thousand lasts of grain, i.e. at least the double of the above quantity, were shipped from the Baltic through the Sound towards the Atlantic coasts (Parry, Faber, Rybarski).

carrier of the mass-consumption goods of European economy, was increasingly becoming, owing to modern-type market relations, the main artery of international trade.

Hence, the process of "the shifting of international trade routes" did not begin with, and did not start from, the discovery of the New World or of the direct route to India by the Spaniards and the Portuguese, causing the transfer of the bulk of international trade from the Mediterranean to the Atlantic and the "Cape-route". *The basic factor of the process was the internal growth of European economy, the unfolding of commodity production and division of labour.* As a result, certain areas of Western Europe raised increasing demands for foodstuffs and raw materials, which were supplied from the Baltic regions and the territories of Eastern Europe connected with them by waterways, and carried to the consumers mainly by the Atlantic coast shipping, in exchange for Levant articles and Western European manufactures.

In other words: *the internal growth of Europe's economy led to a transformation of the character, of the commodity structure of international trade. And it was this transformation that led, in turn, to the shifting, and the change of direction, of the routes of international trade.*

2.

Agricultural exports from the Baltic were handled at first mainly by the merchants of the German Hanse who, however, towards the close of the 15th and especially during the 16th century, had to yield more and more ground to the Dutch who had benefited from the changes in the character and the routes of international trade.

The rising trade activity of the Dutch was from the outset closely connected with the spreading of new-type trade relations. The Dutch became specialists in transporting *bulky mass commodities* (grain, timber for shipbuilding, fish, salt), gaining thereby a considerable technical and economic advantage over the Hansards in this field. Moreover, it was the Dutch who first used regularly the direct sea route from the Baltic to the North Sea via the Sound, while the Hansards largely used the old overland route from Lübeck to Hamburg, loading their goods on ships again only there — i.e. at the North Sea — for sea transport farther to the South West, mainly to Bruges in the Southern Netherlands, their most important "*Stapelplatz*" abroad *(Vollbehr)*.

The "discovery" of this *direct sea route* for shipping bulky goods — no matter how short this section is — was an important event in the history of *the shifting of trade routes*. This shift of the Baltic-North Sea trade route, which contributed to the decline of Lübeck and Bruges, and the rise of Antwerp, made itself felt already at the end of the 15th century — another fact showing that the changes in the system of international trade routes did not begin with the discoveries overseas, but *prior* to them, and that they were connected with the internal development of the European economy, with the changes in the character of international trade.

While the Dutch became the experts of shipping bulky goods, the Venetians were, and continued to be, specialists in the "rich trade" whose hegemony in international commerce was tied to the dominating role of medieval-type long-haul trade in spices and Levant articles. Thus, the decline of Venetian trade was not due, or not primarily due, to the opening of a new direct sea route for Eastern spice trade by way of the Cape of Good Hope; we know that in certain periods of the 16th century (as between 1550 and 1570), and even at the beginning of the 17th century, the old Red Sea route of spice trade did not cease to be competitive and at times even flourishing *(Lane)*. The decline of Venetian trade was due mainly to the fact that the character, the commodity structure of international trade had changed at the expense of Eastern spices and luxuries, and in favour of commodities stemming from the internal growth and interregional division of labour of the European economy.

The changes in the character, in the commodity structure of international trade, the resulting shift of the principal trade routes, also involved as a matter of necessity a change in the intermediaries of this trade: the hegemony shifted gradually from the North Italian and the Hanseatic merchants to the Dutch, and, later on, to the English.

When at the *end* of the 16th century, the Dutch — and still with them the Hansards and already the English too — took advantage of the grain crisis in Northern Italy and penetrated through the Straits into the Mediterranean sea trade, importing grain and other goods and exporting Levant luxuries and Mediterranean products, it meant not only the pushing back of Mediterranean merchant shipping (sea-borne trade between the Mediterranean and the Netherlands had been transacted almost exclusively by Venetian and Genoese vessels at the *beginning* of the 16th century), but it meant at the same time the *reversal of the main direction of Atlantic coast traffic.* While earlier it was Mediterranean shipping that expanded northwards, to the Atlantic, now it was Atlantic trade that made headway southwards, into the Mediterranean.

3.

The other facet of the growth and advance of modern-type international trade, resulting from the development of European commodity production and division of labour, is the growing importance in the international trade of the 15th and 16th centuries of *manufactured goods*, chiefly of *cloth*, for the use of wider masses of consumers.

Though cloth, along with the Levant luxuries, had already been earlier an important item of medieval long-haul trade — high-quality cloths of *Flanders* and Northern Italy reached the countries of Mid-Eastern Europe, including Hungary, as early as the 13th and 14th centuries, — they had been available in relatively small quantities, at high prices, and so mainly for the satisfaction of *high-class* (and rich burgher) needs. During the 15th and 16th centuries, international trade in cloth came to be multiplied, supplying wider masses of an expanded market in larger quantities. The "*nouvelle draperie*", and later the "*sayetterie*", both developed in Flanders, differed from earlier cloth production not only in their location — the former being shifted from the towns to the country — but also in that they produced now, in addition to fine, high-priced cloth, *simpler and less expensive sorts*, mainly from Spanish raw wool *(Pirenne, Coornaert)*.

Up to then, *Northern Italy's* textile industry had also used mainly Spanish wool, but this was now increasingly absorbed by Flemish cloth manufacturing. By the middle of the 16th century, about half of all Spanish wool exports was already directed to Flanders; the rest was still taken by Venetian, Genoese and Ragusan vessels to the ports of Northern Italy, and from there to the centres of the textile industry, to Florence and Milan. In the 17th century, practically the entire Spanish wool trade was already flowing to the Netherlands, handled mainly by Dutch merchants. Thus Mediterranean traffic was pushed into the background by Atlantic coast shipping also in the field of wool (and cloth) trade *(Cipolla)*.

During the 15th and most of the 16th century, still large, though decreasing quantities of wool were also exported from England to the Continent, mainly to the Netherlands. Unlike Spanish wool trade, English wool exports were handled mainly by English merchants, at least as far as Calais (which was English up to the middle of the century); it was from here that the shipments were unloaded by Flemish merchants who carried them on their own vessels to Antwerp.

While *English wool* exports diminished, the volume of *English cloth* exports grew more than twofold during the 16th century,[3] largely due to the fact that the "*new drapery*" also started in England, producing simpler, cheaper sorts for mass consumption. While cloth exports to North Germany, Scandinavia and the Baltic ports were mostly of the heavy, hard-wearing type — which, in the first half of the 16th century, were still handled mainly by Hanseatic merchants who at that time still enjoyed privileges in London — the exports to Flanders were primarily "white cloths", taken there for dyeing and dressing, but now mainly by English merchants. Up to the end of the 1560's the company of English exporters *(Merchant Adventurers)* also had its headquarters in Antwerp *(Clapham, Lipson)*.

[3] About 1500 some 50 thousand cloths, a quarter of a century after 75 thousand cloths were exported from London. In the year 1540 the exports already exceeded 100 thousand, in 1550, however, 130 thousand cloths. In 1606 the Merchant Adventurers alone exported from London nearly 100 thousand ("white" and dressed) cloths (Fisher, Friis).

Thus the port of *Antwerp* was the centre of international textile trade for about three quarters of the 16th century. It was from here that Flemish and partly English cloths were exported to various directions: in the southern section of Atlantic coast shipping — together with copper and hardware — to Spain. to Portugal, to be exchanged for wool, Eastern spices and Mediterranean products; over the North Sea and the Baltic Sea to the Scandinavian and Baltic countries, mainly to Poland, in exchange for grain and timber; on continental waterways, of which the Rhine was the most important, to Central and Southern Germany. The horse-drawn Rhine barges returned to the Netherlands with linen, fustian, copper and hardware; the imported Flemish and English cloths were partly sold in the German market itself — whose broadening mass-consumption character also appears from the fact that these textiles became part of the clothing of South German peasantry —, partly passed on to Mid-Eastern Europe, and so also to Hungary, where, according to manorial accounts, surveys and other sources, they also showed a trend of expanding consumption *(van Houtte, Jeannin, Székely).*

The commercial rise of Antwerp[4] in the 16th century indicates the establishment of new arteries of international trade, the growing importance of the traffic of the Atlantic coasts. And this resulted largely from the internal development of Europe's economy, from the emergence of a new-type of international trade from the growth of trade supplying *grain* (and other primary products) from the Baltic regions to Western Europe, and from the expansion of *cloth* trade (and that of other manufactures) going from the Netherlands and England to the rest of Europe - which, in turn, brought about a substantial change in the traditional system of long-haul trade routes.

Hence, the formula "shifting of the routes of international trade" comprises two different processes. It means not only that there was a shift in the routes of medieval long-haul trade — of the traffic of Eastern spices and Levant articles — resulting from the discoveries. What is primarily involved here is that owing to the internal development of European economy, international trade of a modern type, an interregional exchange of mass consumption goods came into existence — a trade whose routes were necessarily different, or, more exactly, did not necessarily coincide with the routes of the old-type long-haul trade.

4.

It is all the more justified to distinguish between the two processes — though later they became closely intertwined — as the shifting of the routes of international trade to the Atlantic coasts was primarily a result of the establishment of modern-type commercial relations; the discoveries, the *opening*

[4] It should be noted, however, that the centre of corn trade from the Baltic to the Netherlands developed in *Amsterdam* as early as the 1530—40's.

of new sea routes, in turn, were originally stimulated *not* by the demands of the *new-type* trade, but rather by those of the old-type long-haul trade: to procure the spices of the East in a direct way and to take possession of the fabulous treasures of the Orient as well.[5]

And what is more: not only the stimuli, the motive forces of the discoveries were of the "old type", but also the newly opened sea routes were used for quite a long time for shipping mainly the articles of medieval long-haul trade: spices from the Far East, and precious metals from Spanish America were mostly carried to Europe by these routes. It was only later, with the development of slave labour on the West Indian settlements, that the products of the plantation economy — luxuries themselves at first — came in for a greater share of this trade; it took a long time before the overseas colonies — first the American, then the Far-Eastern colonies — became the large markets for the industrial products of Western Europe. The *new* sea routes became the routes of *new-type* world trade as late as the agricultural and industrial mass-consumption goods gained decisive importance in determining the character and structure of the overseas traffic, and the colonies became increasingly concerned with a "world-wide division of labour" *(Lenin)*.

But the world market in this modern -- capitalist — sense only emerged after a long process of development, subsequent to the events of the late 15th century: the discovery of the New World and the sailing round Africa. The Portuguese and the Spaniards were the discoverers, and the first beneficiaries, of the new routes of overseas trade: they were the principal suppliers of Far-Eastern spices and American precious metals to Europe during the 16th century.

For *Portugal*, the "Grocer King", the main function of its East Asian organization was, besides colonial plundering, the regular supply of spices from the Malay Archipelago to Goa, its principal settlement in India, and then on the back route of "*Carreira da India*", to Lisbon. Spice shipments from the Portuguese capital reached the Dutch and English ports as early as the first decade of the 16th century, and evoked a severe crisis in Mediterranean spice trade. The Portuguese played an important -- though sometimes fluctuating — role in supplying Europe with Eastern spicery throughout the century. Up to the middle of the century, this supply went through Antwerp first of all, which had become the chief distribution centre of Portuguese spice shipments by then. Thus, the 16-century prosperity of Antwerp was *partially* the result of the opening of the new, direct sea route of Far Eastern trade, although the city's commercial rise was *based*, as we have seen, on its central position in international cloth trade.

[5] In the background of the greed for gold — which drove the Portuguese towards the western coasts of Africa even before 1492 — we can detect, of course, the needs of growing European trade: its shortage of money, and "gold crises" (ENGELS).

Resembling the Portuguese expansion in several respects, the nature of the relations of Spain with her American colonies was determined in the 16th century by a ruthless conquest, by the plundering of treasure, and, from the middle of the 1540's, by the discovery and exploitation of the world's richest silver-mines. This resulted in an influx of silver carried by the ships of New Spain and the Isthmus fleet to Seville, then to Cádiz, in the second half of the 16th century — which was the vital point of the colonial dominion for the Spanish Crown. The importation of agricultural produce from the New World, the beginnings of plantation farming, were incomparably less important:[6] they did not assume larger proportions before the end of the 16th century in Portuguese-dominated Brazil and in the Spanish-Caribbean area. (The latter developments led, in turn, combined with the labour demand of the silver mining, to the growth of African slave-trade.)

Yet, the spectacular hegemony of the Portuguese and the Spaniards over the oceans lacked sufficent technical-economic foundations. *They played a subordinate role in Atlantic coast shipping, which became the main artery of European commerce at that time, while they were taking a prominent part in trans-atlantic trade and in trading on the Indian Ocean.* So the latter was not an organic increment, not a concomitant of the former — as it was with the Dutch and the English later on — but was spanning those immense distances without being supported by pillars, so to speak.

This contradictory situation revealed itself in the inadequacy of their shipping-technical attainments, which was felt decisively, and took a heavy penalty, whenever a rival appeared on the scene *("História trágico-marítima")*. But the more deep-rooted problem was that their expansion over the oceans was void of sufficient economic foundations: it was not a requirement inherent in the development of their commodity production and trade activities.

There are many references in the relevant literature *(Haring, Goris,* etc.) that the Portuguese, in shortage of goods for sale, were not able to fill their cargo space with useful load other than precious metals when "sailing out"; that, owing to the backwardness of Spanish industry, it was not possible to meet from Spanish sources the demands for cloth and other industrial products that were raised increasingly by the Spanish settlements in America at the end of the century; that 9/10 of the exports to the American colonies were of non-Spanish origin already at the time of Philip II, and that the export share of the home industries continued to decrease, and so on. All this illustrates that the colonial expansion of the Portuguese and Spaniards was not supported by standards actually attained in *commodity production.* We should like to complete, however, the pertinent conclusions of the literature by point-

[6] 95.6 per cent of the shipments coming in 1594 from the Spanish Indies to the mother country consisted of precious metals (overwhelmingly silver): the proportion of other goods was insignificant (2.8 per cent cochineal, 1.2 per cent hides, 0.3 per cent indigo). In 1609 the share of precious metals was 84 per cent, of other products 16 per cent (HAMILTON).

ing out another fact, which was of even more considerable consequence in the circumstances discussed, i. e. at the early stage of the unfolding world market in the 16th century. This fact is that not even the development level of Portuguese and Spanish *trade activities* was advanced enough to serve as a firm foundation of their overseas expansion, since the latter started and proceeded *not* by conforming to the *new* requirements of international commerce, not by trading in the mass-consumption products of European economy. While they were flooding Europe with spices and precious metals, the European interregional trade conveying mass-consumption goods from and to their mother countries was not in their hands. In the last decades of the 16th century Spain was already dependent on Dutch trade for her grain and timber imports, on Dutch and English shipping for exporting wool and wine, for importing cloth *(Heaton, Parry)*.

The fact that Portuguese and Spanish expansion was not rooted in the internal development of their economies, in their active participation in international trade of the modern type, was determinant in another respect, too. The abundant profits drawn from doing business in Eastern spicery, and the treasures of the American silver-fleets, could not become factors of the economic growth of the countries of the Iberian Peninsula, could not promote their capitalist transformation, but were trifled away, flowed out through various channels. Consequently, these countries were not able to exert an actual hegemony in the ocean trades, and to preserve their leading position permanently, let alone to control the unfolding world market. It is a characteristic fact that despite the opening of the "*Cape-route*", the traditional routes of Eastern spice trade were used again after some time, and the Venetians were still competing — up to the end of the 16th century — with their rivals who used the direct sea route *(Lane, Braudel)*, so that it was not the penetration of the Portuguese into East India, but only that of the Dutch (and of the English) that dealt a fatal blow to the Levant spice trade of Venice.

The accumulation of capital drawn from the plundering of colonies, from the ocean trade in spices and precious metals, was able to promote economic growth and capitalist transformation, only where it was channeled to an accumulation which was created by international trade of the modern type based on the development of commodity production and division of labour, and where the former served the enlargement and multiplication of the latter.

5.

That is just the point where the main difference appears between Portuguese-Spanish and Dutch maritime expansion and world-trade hegemony.

From the second half of the 15th up to the end of the 16th century, the Dutch were only engaged in *Atlantic coast trade*, ranging from the Sound down to the Straits; this was crowned by their intrusion into the Mediterranean at the close of the 16th century. It was in these trading activities that they gradually gained ascendancy over the Hanse and Venice and were trained for further growth; it was in these activities that they accumulated considerable merchant capital as well as professional skills in both shipbuilding and sailing, and in all dodges of the "*carrying trade*".

Dutch sailors carried, for the most part, not the products of the Northern Netherlands, but those of other regions and countries. But this carrying trade was already international trade of the *modern type*, with increasing participation in Atlantic coast shipping, the *principal route* of European traffic at that time. It meant, on the one hand, the conveyance of the grain, timber and other primary products of the East European territories connected with the Baltic, and, on the other, of the cloth and other commodities of the West European industrial areas at the Atlantic coasts, and, finally, of the agricultural produce (wool, wine, oil, etc.) of the Mediterranean region.

It was *from*, and *in addition to*, this European trade of the modern type that the Dutch started — almost simultaneously with their penetration into the Mediterranean — their expansion over the oceans: both on the Atlantic and on the Indian Ocean.

At the end of the 16th, and early in the 17th century, the Dutch made their way into the Spanish *West Indies* and the territories on the Portuguese-American coasts. Their intrusion was marked by plundering, conquering and by unchallengeable commercial superiority, which led to a rapid decline in the trade between the Spanish colonies and Seville already in the second quarter of the 17th century *(Chaunu, Sluiter)*. From Western Europe they began importing also to these territories industrial goods, mainly cloth and hardware, in exchange for the special products of colonial agriculture: sugar from the developing plantations of Brazil and later of the West Indies — at first a luxury, but shortly a current article in European consumption — as well as tobacco and other colonial produce. They soon had an important share in West African slave-trade directed towards the sugar-plantations as well as in carrying Peruvian silver and Brazilian gold to Europe. Thus, certain elements of modern-type international trade were already present in the trans-atlantic activities of the Dutch — but, up to the middle of the 17th century, these elements were not yet characteristic of the relations of West European economy and the American colonies.

Almost simultaneously with their intrusion into the American coasts, the Dutch performed their "spectacular irruption" into the *Indian Ocean* to overthrow the Portuguese hegemony in spice trade, and, after establishing their Batavia base, to gain control, within two or three decades, over the principal spice-growing islands of the Malay Archipelago. Breaking away from the practice of the Portuguese, they left India on their flank, and established direct contact with the sources of spices; also carried useful load when "sailing out", shipping — besides precious metals and money — also European products to East India *(Glamann)*. This, however, was hardly of any importance as a trade in industrial exports: its volume was considerably less than that of the exports to the Spanish-American colonies. It merely served as a support of, and a supplement to, the colonial methods of import trade.

The appearance of the Dutch on the Indian Ocean *dealt a blow to both Portuguese and Levant (Venetian) spice trade*. The Dutch sailed in the southern part of the ocean, unlike the Portuguese who had taken the northerly course. As a result of this *shift of the sea route*, the Persian Gulf and the Red Sea were shut out of international shipping; this reacted necessarily on Mediterranean spice trade, which drew its supplies mainly on this route. Although the Venetians, the medieval monopolists of the long-haul trade in Eastern spices, continued trading between the Levant, the Aegean and the Adriatic for quite a long time, their accumulated capital and sea power were crumbling more and more. The shift of routes resulting from the rise of modern-type international trade, the emergence of the new — and newest — route of the old-type spice trade, and its control by the Dutch: all these factors combined to reduce the Adriatic Sea to the rank of a "somnolent backwater" by the second half of the 17th century *(Parry)*.

All this goes to show that the rise of the Dutch world-trade was a much more organic, better-founded process than that of the Portuguese and the Spaniards. So it was not by chance that while maritime expansion was not interlinked with the capitalist transformation of feudal economy and medieval society in Spain and Portugal, on the contrary, it contributed — in the last analysis — to their survival, to the interposal of a protracted historical period (much similar to belated feudalism in Eastern Europe), economic development in the Netherlands, and increasing participation in the modern-type trade, made here the conditions ripe — as early as the last decades of the 16th century — for the war of independence that fulfilled the function of a *bourgeois revolution*. And the Dutch, after getting rid of the yoke of feudal order and foreign rule, became, in the period after the revolution, the "model capitalist nation of the 17th century" *(Marx)* and expanded further their international trading activities both in Europe and on the seas.

Most of the 17th century was the era of Dutch hegemony in world trade; the centre of international commerce shifted from Antwerp to *Amsterdam* already in the last decades of the 16th century.

Amsterdam was, above all, the *principal grain market* for Western Europe: the grain prices quoted at its commercial exchange affected the price level in Gdańsk, Hamburg or London, just as in Lisbon, Madrid or even Venice. The bulk of the grain shipments from the Baltic went to Amsterdam; the imported grain covered most of the consumption in the Northern Netherlands, not only of the urban population, but, to a considerable extent, of the peasantry as well. From Amsterdam the grain-carriers proceeded to the Iberian Peninsula and to the Mediterranean.[7] In years of good harvest, Dutch agents purchased large quantities of grain at low prices in Gdańsk and other ports of the Baltic; this grain was amassed in Amsterdam, where, according to a source of 1603, about 700 000 quarters of cereals (above the quantity intended for regular exports) were always kept in the granaries, to be exported at high prices, in case of crop failure, besides the above territories, to France and England, too *(Slicher van Bath, Małowist, Baasch).*

The Dutch played an equally prominent role in trading in Baltic timber (for ship-building first of all) and in the products of the "Grand Fishery"; they also supplied fisheries with salt, casks, food, exploited new fishing grounds, developed new fishing and processing methods and put on the market the final product all along the Atlantic coasts of Western Europe.

The conveyance of the grain and timber of the Baltic, and of the herring of the North Sea was *one* of the foundations of Dutch commercial supremacy.

The *other* was the trading in West European cloth and other manufactures. As the independent cloth industry of the Northern Netherlands developed (Amsterdam, Leyden), Dutch control over international textile trade consolidated even more during the 17th century. Despite growing Dutch-English rivalry, practically the entire volume of cloth exports from the Netherlands was carried to the markets by Dutch merchants; England's increasing cloth export — which formerly had been largely in the hands of the Hansards in the Baltic-North Sea area — was now handled by English and Dutch merchants, but with a greater share of the latter. A significant role was assigned here to Hamburg, which, changing over to Dutch-English relations, became an important gate for the flow of English cloth imports to Mid-Eastern Europe *(Baasch, Lipson).*

The old competitors of the Dutch, the *Hanseatic merchants* still represented considerable power up to the end of the 16th century, and were to be taken into account not only in trading with the regions of the Baltic and North Sea, but also with the Iberian and Mediterranean area. But they were having a *losing battle with the Dutch,* who combined commercial elasticity, professional skill and cheap rates of freight with aggressiveness and growing naval forces. And when the Thirty Years War dealt a heavy blow to the economic life of Germany, the Dutch were left as the unchallenged masters of Atlantic coast trade.

Thus, after a transitory period in the 16th century, roughly by the time Venice lost her position, the decline of the German Hanse was also complete.

[7] The seizures of Dutch shipping in Iberian ports in 1595 and 1598 each involved between 400 and 500 ships. In 1593 most of the ships arriving at Leghorn to bring grain from sources outside the Mediterranean, loaded at Amsterdam (Braudel, Parry).

By the middle of the 17th century the transformation of the entire system of medieval international trade had taken place: there occurred a change in its commodity structure as well as in its main routes and chief intermediaries. The picture was completed by the *decline of overland routes between Northern Italy and Southern Germany* by which transalpine trade, thriving in the 15th and 16th centuries, was transacted and proceeded along the Rhine towards the Netherlands. South German merchants used these routes to bring Flemish cloth and German manufactures (fustian, linen, hardware, norimbergeries) to Italy in exchange for Eastern spices and Mediterranean products *(Schulte, Brulez)*.

But the changes that had taken place in the routes and the sources of the spice trade, and the shift of the main artery of interregional trade to the Atlantic coasts, rendered South German merchants less and less interested in the Italian relations and made them orientate increasingly to the Dutch markets where they could purchase everything they wanted and could sell all their merchandise. In addition, the fact that Dutch *shipping* had also made its way into the Mediterranean, rendered the *overland* trade relations between the Netherlands and Italy, formerly one of the main domains of South German trading activity, largely superfluous. Thus, transalpine traffic and with it the overland trade between the Netherlands and Italy had fallen back considerably by the 17th century by the time when Dutch hegemony in world trade and the leading role of Amsterdam blossomed out fully.

Amsterdam was now the principal market not only for Baltic grain but also for Eastern spices, for American colonial produce as well as for precious metals *(van Dillen, Barbour)*.

All these facts throw light upon the economic foundations and sources of the rise of the Dutch. Dutch trade "adjusted" itself exactly to the *principal trend* of European economic growth — to the trend of growing agricultural and industrial commodity production, of developing interregional division of labour — becoming thereby both the beneficiary and the promoter of this trend. It was from this modern-type European trade that Dutch overseas expansion derived; it was into this accumulation of capital that the big profits drawn from East Indian and American trades were chanelled.

Hereby we came to the turning point in the history of merchant capital. Because we must distinguish between merchant capital accumulated in *medieval-type* long-haul trade, and merchant capital derived from the unfolding *modern-type* international trade. The former, despite its considerable volume, remained, in the last analysis, an outward element, a sort of "decoration", or even a parasite, of European economy. (This was the substance of Venetian capital, and virtually also of the accumulation realized — although in new circumstances — by the Portuguese and Spanish colonial powers). The latter, however, i.e. merchant capital derived fundamentally from modern-type European trade, and multiplied later by "primitive accumulation of capital" feeding on colonial sources, became a motive force in the capitalist transformation of European economy.

Only the appearance of this "modern" type of merchant capital made it possible for merchant capital in general — which, together with loan capital, had been the ancient, "antediluvian form of capital" (Marx) — to begin being transformed into industrial (productive) capital. It was exactly the unfolding of modern-type international trade that indicated and stimulated the processes within the production itself — the growth of agricultural and industrial commodity production, the development of social division of labour - which brought about the conditions for the penetration of money capital into production.

In the 17th century, this further step was taken by the Dutch in part only; its full realization was left to the new competitor, also combining modern-type European trade with colonial expansion: to the English.

6.

In the foregoing we have given an outline of the transformation of international trade, of the changes that affected its structure, routes and intermediaries in the course of two centuries. We now feel that we are justified to draw two conclusions.

One is this: *In the period between the end of the 15th and the middle of the 17th century, the overseas colonies were not yet tied to the West European economy in the sense of a modern world market, that is by a modern-type international trade based on the division of labour; only the rudiments of such relations could be discerned, and only in the case of the American colonies.*

The other conclusion is this: In the period under consideration, it was rather the countries of Mid-Eastern Europe that were linked to the expanding West European economy in a "modern" way, by new-type international trade relations based on the development of commodity production, both as suppliers of mass-consumption foodstuffs and as buyers of mass-consumption manufactures.

After the foregoing, we only have to add a few remarks as to the first conclusion. As we have seen, the new ocean routes were used in the 16th century to import from the colonies to Europe partly *precious metals* — obtained by plundering methods and by exploiting the newly disclosed mines by slave labour —, partly *pepper and other spices*, the main merchandise of medieval long-haul trade. These imports of "traditional" commodity structure — though of multiplied volume — were added to by imports of the new plants and other agricultural produce of the New World such as tobacco, cocoa, dyestuffs, drugs and hides, but the latter were, and remained for a considerable time, of minor significance *(Hamilton, Chaunu)*.

Sugar- cane, the third colonial treasure after precious metals and spices, though established in the *Spanish- and Portuguese-American colonies* as early as the first half of the 16th century, set out on its world-wide commercial career only in the last decades of that century, when it was supplied in volume from the Brazilian plantations tilled by Negro slaves. Most of Europe's sugar consumption, running up in the first half of the 17th century, was covered by shipments from Brazil. Considerably less sugar was still grown on the plantations of the Spanish-Caribbean area at that time. The English and French colonies, established in the West Indies in the first decades of the 17th century, were engaged, besides growing some cotton, indigo etc., mainly in cultivating tobacco in small-scale, farmer-type economies. Yet West Indian tobacco was soon challenged by the production of Virginia, the first North American "*Tobacco Colony*", which, since the demand for tobacco on the European markets was only beginning to grow at that time, resulted in considerable overproduction by the end of the 1630's. This situation was cleverly exploited by the Dutch merchants, who were familiar also with the conditions in Brazil: from the 1640's on they "came and taught growing sugar-cane" to the English and Franch settlers in the West Indies *(Rich, Masefield)*.

And the decisive change took place in a few decades after the middle of the 17th century: the settlers of some islands turned in a generation from tobacco growers into sugar-cane planters, tobacco giving way to sugar, and farmer economy to plantation economy based on slave-labour. The typical "*sugar colonies*" of the Antilles (Jamaica, Barbados, Martinique, etc.) came into being, multiplying sugar exports to Europe and raising at the same time rapidly increasing demands for slave-labour as well as for cloth and other industrial products. Moreover, it was in the smaller West-Indian English colonies that monocultural sugar production advanced to such a degree that considerable food imports (grain, meat, fish) were needed. They were supplied partly from England (Ireland), partly from the North American British colonies *("New England"* and *"Bread Colonies")*. And these North American colonies — which at that time had hardly any export products available for the trans-atlantic trade — re-exported to Europe part of their sugar imports from their commerce with the Antilles to pay for their industrial imports *(Newton, Clapham)*.

This *trans-atlantic trade* between America and Europe (and West Africa), *ever growing since the middle of the 17th century, and increasingly assuming the character of a modern-type trade based on the division of labour*, was initially handled mainly by Dutch merchants. Later on, also supported by Cromwell's discriminating acts, which proved to be a more effective means against the Dutch on the American than on the European waters, this trade was taken over, in respect to their own colonies, by the English. At the end of the 17th century, their West Indian colonies already played a highly important role in their international trade: their share in England's total imports and exports was higher than that of all other British colonies *(Williams)*. The enormous increase in the tonnage of the English merchant fleet during the *period following the English bourgeois revolution* was concentrated mainly in the trade with the American colonies, in addition to European coasting trade. Taken as a whole, the trade with North and South America was expanding so rapidly at that time — exactly because its modern features became dominating —, that there was a substantial increase in English (and French) shipping without Dutch shipping decreasing in absolute terms. We should like to emphasize, however, that all these were already the developments of the period *following* the middle of the 17th century.

While in respect of the *American* colonies the "modern trend" in international trade relations began to take shape from the middle of the 17th century, a comparable change in relation to the colonies in the *Far East* had not yet even begun by then. Here, partly the methods of the first period of colonization continued to be prevailing, partly changes differing in character from those in the American relation had taken place.

As concerns the *imports* from the East Indies, their principal items, both under the Portuguese and in the first half-century of Dutch rule, continued to be the traditional spices. It was not until the beginning of the 18th century that coffee appeared on the market as a product of the plantations of Java, reaching, however, together with tea, a considerable share in the imports of the Dutch East India Company only by the middle of the 18th century *(Glamann)*.

Exports to the Far Eastern colonies continued to be insignificant as for the industrial articles. Goods exported by the Dutch to the East Indies — mainly weapons, metals, linen, norimbergeries — were also dwarfed by the amount of exported precious metals and coins for which they purchased their imports (of course, at prices securing them big profits). And, what is more, the English East India Company also exported, during the 17th century, mainly precious metals in exchange for their spice and dyestuff imports.[8]

The difference from the American relations can be clearly illustrated in the case of textiles, the chief manufactured item of modern-type international trade. While the exportation of West European textiles, mainly *English woollen fabrics*, to the American colonies continued to run up during the second half of the 17th and the first half of the 18th century — English exports in woollen fabrics increased threefold in the 17th century, and were doubled

[8] Precious metals accounted for more than 3/4 of the exports of the English East India Company, while the share of exported goods was hardly 1/4 even at the beginning of the 18th century. The share of commodities in the exports of the Dutch East India Company was even lower (LIPSON, GLAMANN).

again in the 18th, with a considerable share of the American colonies —, hardly any products of the European textile industries reached the Far-Eastern markets in those days. On the contrary, a flow of goods in the opposite direction was seen for a long time to come. Already the Portuguese carried *Indian cotton fabrics* to the Malay islands in exchange for their spice shipments. When the Dutch and English succeeded the Portuguese, this practice was expanded in a way that increasing quantities of textiles, mainly Indian printed cotton fabrics (calicoes), were also imported to Western Europe.[9] The inexpensiveness, attractive colours and patterns of Indian cotton goods soon captured the markets, especially for the less well-to-do consumers, in England, France and elsewhere, irrespective of import prohibitions and other restrictive measures taken to protect the woollen industry. Meanwhile, cotton printing and processing also gained ground in England, to grow dramatically strong from the 70's of the 18th century onward, by which time it began to be equipped with machinery, and to sweep away the spinning and weaving handicrafts in India within a few decades, and turn the Far-Eastern colonies into huge outlets for the English textile industries *(Wadsworth, Sandberg)*.

But all this was already the development of a later period, of the Industrial Revolution. Thus, the new character of international trade in relation to the Far East began to take shape only more than a hundred years later than in relation to some American colonies.

7.

In the first period of the development of modern world economy, it was not yet the overseas colonies, but rather the countries of Mid-Eastern Europe that were joined to the economy of Western Europe in the sense of a modern market, that is by ties of an emerging new-type international trade: by exports of mass-consumption foodstuffs and imports of mass-consumption manufactures. This was our second conclusion, which we are going to demonstrate now more closely by the examples of *Poland* and *Hungary*.

Poland (and Lithuania) played a significant role in the supply of 16-century Western Europe by *exporting* three sorts of important mass produce: *grain* (rye), *cattle* (oxen) and *fur*. Apart from other export products (timber, potash, hemp, etc.), Poland was represented mainly by these commodities in the European system of the emerging new international trade. By the *middle of the 16th century*, these three articles accounted for nearly 90 per cent of

[9] In the second half of the century the share of textiles in the total volume of Dutch imports rose to 36 per cent (1668–70), later to nearly 55 per cent (1698–1700), as contrasted to 14–16 per cent in the first half of the century. Concerning the imports of the English East India Company (more exactly, that portion of the imports which was consumed in England) it was held in 1621 that they included more or less equal amounts of pepper, other spices and indigo (roughly 1/3 each); in 1677, however, the share of pepper and dyestuffs was estimated to be only about 10 per cent, and that of cotton fabrics as high as 66 per cent (Glamann, Lipson).

Poland's exports to the West. While cattle and fur were exported overland, grain was carried on the sea route, mainly via Gdańsk (Danzig). Taken as the average of 1565—85, the share of grain in Poland's sea-borne exports was 66 per cent *(Rybarski, Samsonowicz, Mączak).*

As concerns Hungary's exports to the West, the pattern was even simpler. Apart from *copper*, Hungary had virtually, in the middle of the 16th century, only one important export article to offer to the West (the same, by the way, as one of Poland's export goods): it exported *cattle* (oxen) in considerable quantities. This single commodity, however, also accounted for about 90 per cent of the exports registered in the customs books of the year 1542, which included nearly 5/6 of the total western trade (excluding copper) of the country *(Ember)*.[10]

The pattern of *imports* presents a similar picture. In the middle of the 16th century, *cloth* accounted for 60 per cent of total Polish imports from the West; its share in sea-borne imports was 48 per cent, taken as the average of 1565--85. In Hungary's western imports in 1542 textile goods had a share of 68 per cent, including *cloth* 40 per cent, linen 12 per cent and clothing articles 15 per cent.[11]

What were, under these circumstances, the *trade balances* of Poland and Hungary in their West European relations by the middle of the 16th century?

As regards the sea-borne foreign trade of Poland, the findings of valuable investigations, covering almost one century, are available *(Mączak)*. Even if the main proportions found out by these investigations are likely to be modified with the figures of overland foreign trade taken into account, it remains doubtless that the bulk of Poland's foreign trade with the West was handled by the Baltic ports, mainly via Gdańsk; hence, the trade balance in the West European relations was basically determined by the shipments of the Baltic Sea.[12]

During the 16th century, the aggregate value of the western exports from the Baltic ports was considerably higher than that of their western imports: the large-scale grain exports practically ensured a stable and *favourable* trade balance. Calculated as the average of 1565—85, the annual value of Polish sea-borne exports amounted to about 1 158 000 thalers, the value of imports to 400 000 thalers, i.e. to only 34 per cent of the exports; thus the export surplus — discounting the price difference between ports of entry and exit — was 52 per cent.

[10] Total livestock exports accounted for more than 93 per cent, including a share of 87—88 per cent of cattle. The share of wine and hides was about 2 per cent for each. Grain exports were practically negligible.

[11] Significant import items were hardware, norimbergeries (and groceries), with a share of about 10 per cent for each. Pepper import accounted for 3.5 per cent.

[12] Gdańsk (Danzig) was by far the most important of all Baltic ports: nearly 80 per cent of Poland's sea-borne exports were shipped here. The rest was shipped in the ports of Elbląg (Elbing), Szczecin (Stettin), Ryga (Riga) and Królewiec (Königsberg) (Rybarski, Dorosenko, Jeannin).

For Hungary, we can rely on the statistical analysis of the data drawn from the customs books for the year 1542 *(Ember)*. It appears that in the trade with the West — interpreted with the above limitations — the value of exports was about 323 000, that of imports 141 000 florins, i.e. only 43—44 per cent of the exports, which means that the trade balance in the western relation was highly favourable for Hungary as well.[13]

How did this picture of Polish and Hungarian trade relations with the West, as illustrated by the above figures, take shape by the middle of the 16th century? How does this situation compare with the conditions that prevailed a *century back?*

We do not know of investigations also indicating the quantitative proportions of *Poland's* exports and imports in the 15th century. But it appears from Polish and Soviet studies published during the last one or two decades that Poland's grain exports to Western Europe, and especially to the Netherlands, were not insignificant even before the so-called Thirteen Years' War fought with the Teutonic Knights in the middle of the 15th century, at least in lean years with poor crops *(Lesnikov)*. When, as a result of this war, Poland had again access to the mouth of the Vistula, all tributaries of the river were already used for carrying goods, increasing quantities of grain (and timber), to Gdańsk. On the other hand, during the 15th century a change took place in the structure of Poland's imports, too: besides Levant goods and fine cloths, ever growing quantities of cheaper, lower-quality textiles — products of the developing Flemish "*nouvelle draperie*", as well as Bohemian and Silesian cloths — were imported to the country *(Hoszowski, Małowist)*.

There is again a certain resemblance to *Hungary* also in this respect. It appears from the customs books of Pozsony — the customhouses of the border town Pozsony controlled a substantial proportion of Hungary's trade with the West — that there was also an abrupt rise in Hungary's foreign trade around the middle of the 15th century: its volume grew about fivefold between 1440 and 1457. Western industrial products, textiles first of all, were already imported in considerable amounts. In the fiscal year 1457—58 more than 15 000 pieces of high- and lower-quality West European, Silesian and Bohe-

[13] Polish and Czech researchers put the question: How was the considerable export surplus of Poland's Baltic sea-borne trade balance compensated for? They find the answer partly in the fact that Poland, as well as other Baltic regions, drew funds from the West: Dutch merchants often came to Gdańsk, with ballast in their ships and purchased grain for cash. On the other hand, reference is made to the fact that overland trade going from Western Europe to the East (mainly via Leipzig) had a branch that was in interrelationship with the sea-borne trade of the Baltic. This overland trade, which carried mainly Far Eastern spices and industrial luxuries to Eastern Europe, compensated for part of the deficit of sea-borne trade that existed on behalf of the western partners (Bogucka, Hroch). Hungarian researchers have not yet considered this question — they rather emphasized the dependence of Hungarian foreign trade on South German capital, as opposed to the picture that emerged from the statistical analysis of the customs books of 1542.

mian cloth as well as about 10 000 pieces of fustian and linen imports passed the customs office of Pozsony, textiles representing an aggregate value of more then 117 000 florins (which amounted to nearly 79 per cent of the total imports handled here).

Based on the customs books of Pozsony for the fiscal year 1457—58 — their historico-statistical analysis has been available since the beginning of this century *(Kováts)* — as well as on other documentary evidence (contemporary estimates of Hungary's total customs revenues, lease-contracts, etc.) the Hungarian literature of economic history presents the following picture of the western trade relations of our country by the middle of the 15th century:

The overwhelming majority of imports, about 70—75 per cent, consisted of West European, Silesian, Bohemian textiles; the principal item of exports, about 55—60 per cent, was livestock, chiefly cattle bred in Hungary (or in the regions east of Hungary).[14]

Imports accounted for about 2/3 of our total trade with the West, while the share of exports was only 1/3; to compensate for this *import surplus* of about 50 per cent, gold and silver coins in the value of 200—300 000 florins went abroad every year (which in the period between the decrease in African gold imports and the appearance of American gold, played an important role in meeting the gold coin requirements of European trade).

If we compare this picture of Hungary's foreign trade of the mid-15th century with the situation prevailing about one century later, i.e. with what we have seen in the customs journals of 1542, — disregarding other significant changes — the most conspicuous difference is the *vanishing of the adverse character of the trade balance, and the appearance of a highly active balance.* So it ought to be asked, how it was possible that the balance of Hungary's western foreign trade underwent such a substantial change from the *middle of the 15th to the middle of the 16th century?* This question must be put even if our pertinent literature might have exaggerated to a certain degree the adverse character of the balance in the 15th century, and even if certain objections can be raised to the conclusions drawn from the analysis of the customs journals of 1542.[15]

[14] In these imports the share of hardware (mainly of South German origin) and that of spices was about 10 per cent each, the share of clothing articles was about 5 per cent; as concerns exports, copper accounted for 20—25 per cent, hides and other animal products for about 10 per cent, wine for 5—6 per cent (Paulinyi, Szűcs).

[15] Two objections were raised in particular: it is not true that the customs journals of 1542 comprise almost 5/6 (84 per cent) of Hungary's foreign trade with the West — as has been stated by their analyser — but less than that; some import-duty items are missing at certain customs points not because no import duties were levied there, but rather because the source is incomplete. — We are of the opinion that 1542 (the year following the capture of Buda by the Turks) was in all probability poor in respect to foreign trade (the total volume must have been higher in other years), which, however, must have affected imports and exports alike. On the other hand, we regard it as an actual (and inevitable) incompleteness of the customs journals that there the copper-export items are practically absent (showing only a share of 0.33 per cent of all exports), simply because copper exports were free of duty at that time

Namely all these corrections may only reduce the extent of the change, but cannot by all means eliminate the substantial difference between the states at the middle of the 15th and at the middle of the 16th century.

As far as our present information goes, we only can see the cause of this change in the *large increase in Hungarian cattle exports* that took place in this very period, i.e. between the middle of the 15th and the middle of the 16th century.[16]

Accordingly, Hungary's bilateral participation in international trade of the new type started not at once, but in two successive waves. If the abrupt increase in *textile imports* from the West took place already around the middle of the 15th century, the boom in *cattle exports* to the West may have represented the next wave in the upward trend of Hungarian foreign trade. It would seem, therefore, that the further increase in Hungary's customs revenues during the second half of the 15th century (as appears from contemporary estimates) cannot be merely ascribed to the further growth of industrial imports (as has been concluded by some researchers), but may rather be attributed to the upswing in Hungarian (cattle breeding and) cattle exports. As it appears from the concordant evidence of a number of Hungarian and other sources, it was exactly in these decades that Hungarian cattle exports — after antecedents going farback — began to increase on a large scale, which rising to an annual volume of several ten thousands in the late 15th and in the first decades of the 16th century, played already an outstanding role in the meat supply of Vienna and the South German towns.[17]

The route starting *from* and going *through* Hungary was *one* of the main routes of cattle trade from Eastern to Western Europe. It was namely also partly through Hungary that the livestock of the important breeding areas east of Hungary — Wallachia, Moldavia — were driven to the West. Cattle was first brought to the intermediate markets of Transylvania — Nagyszeben, Brassó, Nagyvárad (Sibiu, Braşov, Oradea) —, then to the annual fairs of the boroughs of the Hungarian Plain (Debrecen, Szeged), and to those of the towns

(PROBSZT). Yet, if copper exports are included, it results exactly in an increase of the export surplus, or compensates at least for the import items that were possibly left out from the customs journals.

[16] Our attention is called to this increase also by the fact that the share of livestock in total exports grew from 55—60 per cent to 93—94 per cent during that time, even if the latter export share was calculated without copper exports. And this was for the most part an actual increase in volume, not a rise in prices, since the "price revolution", including the rise of the price of cattle, began to make itself felt also in Hungary only in the 1550's.

[17] The older and more recent German literature of economic history (SACHS, ABEL) cites numerous facts concerning the cattle exports from Hungary to the South German markets in the second half of the 15th century and after, and the important role they played especially in the supply of Nuremberg. The relevant Hungarian literature abounds even more in data of this nature. For instance, the Council of Nuremberg accounted for the rise in the price of beef in 1518 by the circumstance that one year before there had been a cattle-plague in Hungary "which largely supplies Germany with cattle". In 1526, the city of Augsburg was of the opinion that Hungarian oxen must be purchased first of all, since they give the best meat (THALLÓCZY, TAKÁTS, etc.).

Pest and Buda, where the Hungarian cattle-breeders of the Plain appeared with considerable supplies of livestock. Then the herds of cattle — both of Hungarian and eastern breed — were usually driven to the big market places of the western border zone of Hungary (Szered, Sempte, Galgóc, etc.) to be taken by export merchants to Austria and Moravia (especially to Vienna and Auspitz).[18] From Vienna, it was mostly German merchants who drove them on to Regensburg, Nuremberg, Augsburg, and sometimes even as far as the Rhine-Main area. So this first main route of the East-West cattle trade served primarily the meat supply of the *South German* towns.

The other main route of interregional cattle trade connected the large breeding areas of the Ukranian-Moldavian steppe and the Podolian table-land with the western markets. The principal stations along this route passing through Poland were Lwów, Lublin and Cracow with their bustling annual fairs *(Rybarski, Samsonowicz)*. At Cracow the route forked: one branch led through Moravia and Bohemia — mainly via Pilsen — also to Regensburg and Nuremberg, the other through Silesia in the direction of Leipzig, Buttstädt, Frankfurt am Main and Cologne. The principal driving route was the latter: cattle exports from Poland — whose annual volume was estimated in the first half of the 17th century at 40—60 000 head of cattle *(Horn)* — supplied with meat chiefly the towns of *Central Germany* (north of the Main).[19]

While the towns of South and Central Germany were supplied with meat by Hungarian and Polish cattle exports from the East European regions, the case was different with the big trading centres of the Baltic-North Sea-area. The latter were supplied mainly by cattle exports from Denmark, which also showed a large increase during the 15th and 16th centuries, and amounted to an annual 55—60 000 head of cattle in the period preceding the Thirty Years's War. About 1/4 of this volume was taken up by Hamburg, Lübeck and other towns north of the Elbe; 3/4 were driven across the Elbe to feed Cologne, but especially Amsterdam, the great consumer centre *(Wiese)*. The Amsterdam market alone absorbed some 20—35 000 cattle per year at the end of the 16th and early in the 17th century — taking into account, in addition to internal consumption, also the supply of sailors. (About 2000 head of cattle per year were slaughtered and embarked as salted meat only for the supply of ships bound for the East Indies). *Thus the Netherlands, one of the principal consumers of Polish grain, covered their meat requirements not from Poland or Hungary, but from Denmark.*

[18] In addition to the western and north-western direction, the third route of Hungarian cattle exports led towards the south-east, through Transdanubia to Venice.

[19] Mention should be made here of the *third* important overland route of primary goods-trade from Eastern to Western Europe by which, however, not cattle but fur exports were handled. The furs of the Russian-Lithuanian forest zone were carried on the Mogilev—Wilno—Warsaw—Gniezno—Poznań route mainly towards Leipzig. Also considerable cattle exports were driven from the busy markets of Lublin to the West along the Poznań—Leipzig route (Topolski, Grycz).

8.

Finally, we must put the question: How did Poland's and Hungary's western trade relations develop later on, i.e. in the period between the middle of the 16th and the *middle of the 17th century?*

As concerns *Poland*, we can rely here, too, mainly on the findings of the investigations made on its sea-borne trade *(Mączak)*. Polish grain exports — calculated in thalers and at current prices — grew more than twofold, comparing the annual averages of the years 1565—85 and 1625—46, and increased from 66 to 80 per cent of the total sea-borne exports of Poland. During the same period — calculated in the same manner — cloth imports increased about 3,5-fold, and accounted for 52 per cent of Polish sea-borne imports.

What is of special interest here is not only the fact that the *rate of increase in cloth imports was considerably higher than that in grain exports*, but especially the circumstance that the import and export increases, calculated at current *prices*, concealed great differences in *volume*. While behind the more than twofold increase in the value of grain exports between the years 1565—85 and 1625—46 (in the case of rye, the principal export produce, reckoned for the whole period) there was only an increase in volume of hardly over 10 per cent, but a rise in price of more than 50 per cent — due to the "price revolution" which chiefly affected foodstuffs —, the 3.5-fold rise in value of the cloth imports — reckoned similarly for the entire period — represented almost the same increase in volume.[20]

In such circumstances, the balance of Polish maritime trade *remained active* — except a few years — up to the middle of the 17th century, but already showed a *downward trend:* compared to the 52 per cent average of the years 1565—85, the export surplus dropped to 9 per cent in the period between 1625—46. Then, in the second half of the 17th century, the balance turned adverse; the price revolution being over, the grain prices did no longer provide compensation for quantity, and the stagnant and later *decreasing grain exports* were no longer able to counterbalance the large-scale imports of cloth (and luxuries).[21]

[20] For the evaluation of the Polish grain exports, the following must yet be considered: 1. The data of the years 1565—85 already represent the impact of the "price revolution". — 2. The comparison of the averages of the years 1565—85 and 1625—46 does not express the considerable growth of the exports in the first decades of the 17th century (especially in 1608, and 1618—21), since the 1620—30's show a higher average in respect of prices, but a lower one in respect of volume (and do not show, of course, the peak of grain exports in 1649, the highest in the century). — 3. Rye exports did not develop parallel with wheat exports, mainly because in the first half of the 17th century (especially in 1618—21, 1639—44, 1646—49) the share of wheat in total grain exports increased considerably. — 4. As concerns the production basis of Poland's sea-borne grain exports, a substantial change took place between 1570 and 1620. About 1570, the basis of grain exports was mainly the territory north of Warsaw called "Royal Prussia". By the 1620's the role of the regions south of Warsaw increased, especially that of "Little Poland", whose share in the increase of exports had grown meanwhile to the multiple of the national average (Baasch, Wyczanski, Faber).

[21] Between 1600 and 1649 the average annual quantity of grain carried through the

This adverse change in Polish grain exports around the middle and in the second half of the 17th century can be explained from the angle of production rather than from the market aspect. It happened in several cases already in the 1630's and 1640's that ballast was left in Dutch vessels leaving Gdańsk, as the grain supply of the Gdańsk market was not able to meet the West European demands *(Bogucka)*. The decrease in grain exports can be ascribed mainly to a decrease in the yield ratios, which, in turn, can be traced back to the predominance of the *"folwark"-system utterly exploiting labour services and ruining the peasant economies.*[22]

For the development of *Hungary*'s foreign trade with the West in the period between the mid-16th and the mid-17th centuries, there are unfortunately no research findings available, comparable to the evaluation of the data of Polish maritime trade, or even to the statistical analysis of the Hungarian customs books for the years 1457—58 and 1542. Here we have to rely on some — in fact quite numerous — single data to give an outline of the principal trends.

So much is established fact that the dominant share of manufactured goods, primarily of *cloth*, in total *imports*, which had prevailed, as we have seen, around the middle of the 15th and 16th centuries, did not decrease in the next century either, it even became more pronounced. The majority of the merchants in the towns of "Royal Hungary" were engaged mainly in importing industrial articles from abroad, especially textiles and hardware. It is a characteristic example that the imports of four towns — Kassa, Lőcse, Eperjes, Késmárk (Košice, Levoča, Prešov, Kežmarok) — handled through the trade routes leading from Moravia into the Vág valley, amounted to the value of 20 000 florins in 1610, and of more than 54 000 florins in 1619; within this volume, there were more than 6000 cloths in 1610, and nearly 20 000 cloths in 1619, produced mainly in Oberlausitz, Silesia and Moravia. The merchants of Kassa, on the other hand, purchased in Poland not only Silesian and South German (Wroclaw and Nuremberg) cloths, but also English fabrics ("karasia"= kersey, "londis"); the price-lists of the tailors' guild of Kassa (1627, 1635), quoting prices according to the material used, mention "English coats" and "English skirts".[23] Manorial accounts and lists of payment of the 16th and 17th

---

Sound westwards amounted to 68,500 lasts; between 1650 and 1699 to 55,800 lasts; between 1700 and 1749 to 31,800 lasts (FABER).

[22] In addition to the problems of the *supply*, there emerged factors, which may also have reduced the *demand* in Western Europe for Baltic grain in the second half of the 17th century. From the 1660's onward for about one century, England became a grain-exporting country. Growing potatoes and maize of American origin on a larger scale was started in Europe: at the close of the 17th century, the former already played an important part in the mass-consumption of Ireland, the latter in that of Spain. A demographic stagnation or decline took place in some countries of Western Europe during the century (MASEFIELD, FABER, SLICHER VAN BATH).

[23] An English source — surveying the foreign markets of the various sorts of English cloth — mentions Hungary as early as 1561 as one of the principal buyers of "kersie" woven in Hamsphire (LIPSON). The Polish investigations reveal the gaining ground in the 16th—17th century Poland of the lighter and cheaper sorts of cloth, especially of the "karazja" (kersey)

centuries testify to a rather wide use in Hungary of English cloths (classified according to quality as "londis" or "fájlondis"); lead seals (quality marks) of cloth (inscribed "Honni soit qui mal y pense") have been unearthed in excavations both in the "Royal" and the Turkish-occupied Hungary *(Szücs, Székely, Huszár)*.

As concerns the western *exports* of Hungary, grain exports continued to be insignificant. From the thirties-forties of the 16th century onward, and especially in the first half of the 17th century, the "allodial" economy of the feudal landowners — corresponding to the Polish folwark-system — developed also in the Royal Hungary; but the grain of the Hungarian allodial farms — in lack of adequate river and sea communications — could not reach the West European markets, and was carried even to the neighbouring or near regions (Austria, North Italy) in small quantities only.[24]

Hungary's exports to the West continued to be marked by the *preponderance of cattle export*. While the customs books for the year 1542 registered the exportation of 27—28 000 oxen, it is highly probable that sales abroad increased later in the course of the 16th century. (More than 180 000 oxen were sold at the weekly markets in Vienna from 1549 to 1551; some 55 000 head of cattle arrived there in 1592, and so on.) So the estimated export of annual 40—50 000 oxen to Vienna in the second half of the 16th century seems to be correct *(Makkai)*. The dealers of the South German towns were purchasing Hungarian cattle chiefly at the markets of Vienna, and of Auspitz in Moravia, in addition.

Exportation of cattle proved to be most profitable in the second half of the 16th century. The "price revolution" affected this commodity considerably, and cattle prices rising more steeply abroad than in Hungary, ensured sizeable profits to the Hungarian exporters. No wonder, then, that, besides the peasant and burgher merchants of the cattle-trading centres in Western Hungary (Nagyszombat, Győr, Magyaróvár), several members of the Hungarian aristocracy and lesser nobility threw themselves eagerly into this branch of business, too.

Yet from the turn of the 16th and 17th centuries on, Hungarian cattle exports presented a *much more contradictory picture*. On the one hand, unsold cattle was often driven back from Vienna and Auspitz to Hungary; on the other, many complaints were made about the insufficient supplies of cattle at foreign markets, the decrease of customs revenues and the slackness of trade.

---

made in England (and also in Gdańsk and Silesia), and the proceeding of these fabrics from Poland to other East European regions (TOPOLSKI).

[24] In 1591 a Hungarian big landowner was negotiating with a Venetian factor for selling grain. During the negotiations the Venetian received instruction from home "not to buy more grain, as there are hopes that they can get grain enough on the sea route from Danzig". It appears, Baltic grain shipped on the sea route and carried mainly by the Dutch, was competitive even in Venice compared to Hungarian wheat, which was carried largely overland (PACH).

The latter seems to be corroborated also by the statements of recent German research in economic history. It has been found that, while cattle from Poland, Hungary and Denmark alike were offered for sale at Cologne fairs at the close of the 15th century, the meat requirements of Cologne were met solely by cattle from Denmark one century later *(Abel, Wiese)*.

The periodic lags in Hungarian cattle-deliveries in the first half of the 17th century can be attributed to several factors. The activities of the peasant-burgher cattle-dealers of Western Hungary (Győr, Magyaróvár, Nagyszombat) and of the Great Plain (Kecskemét, Debrecen) encountered more and more difficulties, due partly to the war-time situation at the turn of the century, and later to the aggressive interference of the privileged cattle-trade companies (Landesverlegerische Viehcompagnie: 1622, Kaiserliche Ochsenhandlung: 1651) established upon the initiative of the Vienna Court; partly to the competition and oppressive-restrictive measures of the Hungarian aristocracy and lower nobility, who, while building up their allodial economies much similar to the Polish folwarks, also threw into the scales their manorial rights, feudal prerogatives and duty exemptions against their market rivals *(Pach)*.

But cattle trade proved, in the long run, not so profitable as in the 16th century for the Hungarian big landowners either. The rise in prices slowed down to stop altogether; the disparity between foreign and home prices decreased, and had practically vanished by the middle of the 17th century *(Zimányi)*.

Foreign market relations did not develop favourably anyway for Hungary's cattle exports. In the second half of the 16th century, the South German towns still raised an increasing demand for meat, so that their agents sometimes travelled as far as the region of the North Sea to buy Danish cattle, too. Early in the 17th century they still made repeated efforts for securing the smooth flow of cattle deliveries from Hungary and in the 1620's several towns (Nuremberg, Ulm, etc.) made complaints in turn against the "Landesverlegerische Viehcompagnie" for preventing them from buying directly from Hungarian cattle-dealers in Vienna as they had done it "for countless years" *(Sachs, Takáts)*. But these decades already mark the *end of the heyday of the South German towns*, resulting in the subsequent decrease in number of population, purchasing power and meat consumption.[25]

It was due to such factors that the second half of the 17th century was marked by the impoverishment of the Hungarian peasant-burgher cattle-dealers, the withdrawal from business activity of the big landowners and the *decline of Hungarian cattle exports*. This obviously led also to an adverse trend in the balance of western trade: to a development similar to that in Poland, even if the factors involved were not fully identical in respect to both countries. *Unlike Polish sea-borne grain exports, Hungarian overland cattle exports*

[25] The city of Nuremberg, one of the principal consumers of Hungarian beef, had a population of 20,000 in 1449, 40,000 in 1662, and 25,000 in 1806 (Kulischer).

moved not towards the Atlantic centre of the rising modern-type international trade, but mainly towards the South German towns, which — with the decline of the trans-alpine routes between Northern Italy and South Germany — fell themselves victims to the shift of international trade routes in the 15th—17th centuries.

*

In the foregoing we have made two statements.

In the first period of the rise of modern world economy, the overseas colonies were not yet attached to the economy of Western Europe in the sense of a modern world-market, by a new-type international trade based on the division of labour, but above all as suppliers of the principal commodities of the old-type long-haul trade: of spices, and precious metals obtained through plunder or exploited by slave-labour, — as the sources of the so-called "previous" or "primitive" accumulation of money capital.

In the period between the middle of the 15th and the middle of the 17th century, it was rather the countries of Mid-Eastern Europe that began to be linked to the expanding West-European economy in a "modern" way, by the ties of the unfolding new-type international trade based on the development of commodity production, — as suppliers of mass-consumption foodstuffs and buyers of mass-consumption manufactures.

Let us now, by way of conclusion, add a third remark.

The industries of the advancing countries of Western Europe were stimulated — apart from their expanding home markets — by these very foreign markets of Mid-Eastern Europe, by these very interregional trade relations, to step up their commodity production, to break through the restrictions of the guilds and handicraftsmanship, to establish the various forms of the putting out system and the manufactories. The capitalist industries of Western Europe were raised and grew strong largely on these markets of Mid-Eastern Europe, which enabled them to absorb increasing proportions of the money capital accumulated from international trade and colonial exploitation, to turn it into productive capital, and to produce increasingly, in addition to their home and European markets, also for overseas markets, to meet the needs of manufactured exports to the colonies.

References

Abel, W.: *Geschichte der deutschen Landwirtschaft vom frühen Mittelalter bis zum 19. Jahrhundert.* Stuttgart, 1962.

Aymard, M.: *Venise, Raguse et le commerce du blé pendant la seconde moitié du XVIe siècle.* Paris, 1966.

Baasch, E.: *Hamburg und Holland im 17. und 18 Jahrhundert.* (Hansiche Geschichtsblätter, 1910.)

Baasch, E.: *Holländische Wirtschaftsgeschichte.* Jena, 1927.

Barbour, V.: *Capitalism in Amsterdam in the Seventeenth Century.* Baltimore, 1950.

Bogucka, M.: *Handel bałtycki a bilans handlowy Polski w pierwszej połowie XVII wieku.* (Przegląd Historyczny, 1968.)

Braudel, F.: *La Méditerranée et le monde méditerranéen à l'époque de Phillipe II.* Paris, 1949.

BRAUDEL, F.—ROMANO, R.: *Navires et marchandises à l'entrée du port de Livourne, 1547—1611.* Paris, 1951.

BRULEZ, W.: *L'exportation des Pays-Bas vers l'Italie par voie de terre au milieu du XVIe siècle.* (Annales Économies-Sociétés-Civilisations, 1959.)

CHAUNU, H. et P.: *Seville et l'Atlantique, 1504—1650.* Vol. VIII. 1. Paris, 1959.

CIPOLLA, C. M.: *The Decline of Italy: the Case of a Fully Matured Economy.* (The Economic History Review, 1952.)

CLAPHAM, J.: *A Concise Economic History of Britain from the Earliest Times to 1750.* Cambridge, 1949.

COORNAERT, E.: *Un centre industriel d'autrefois. La draperie-sayetterie d'Hondschoote, XIVe—XVIIIe siècles.* Paris, 1930.

DILLEN, VAN J. G.: *Amsterdam marché mondial des métaux précieux au XVIIe et XVIIIe siècles.* (Revue Historique, 1926.)

DOROSZENKO, W. W.: *Eksport Rygi na Zachód w okresie przynależności do Rzeczypospolitej, 1562—1620.* (Zapiski Historyczne, 1966.)

EMBER, GY.: *Zur Geschichte des Außenhandels Ungarns im XVI. Jahrhundert.* (Etudes Historiques, I. Budapest, 1960.)

ENGELS, F.: *Letter to K. Schmidt.* London, October 27, 1890.

FABER, J. A.: *Het probleem van de dalende graanaanvoer uit de Oostzeelanden in de tweede helft van de zeventiende eeuw.* (A.A.G. Bijdragen, 9. 1963.)

FISHER, F. J.: *Commercial Trends and Policy in Sixteenth Century England.* (The Economic History Review, 1940.)

FRIIS, A.: *Alderman Cockayne's Project and the Cloth Trade.* Copenhagen—London, 1927.

GLAMANN, K.: *Dutch-Asiatic Trade 1620—1740.* Copenhagen — The Hague, 1958.

GORIS, J. A.: *Étude sur les colonies marchandes méridionales (portugais, espagnols, italiens) à Anvers de 1488 à 1567. Contribution à l'histoire des débuts du capitalisme moderne.* Louvain, 1925.

GRYCZ, M.: *Handelsbeziehungen der Stadt Poznań bis Ende des XVII. Jahrhunderts.* (Studia Historiae Oeconomicae, 1967.)

HAMILTON, E. J.: *American Treasure and the Price Revolution in Spain, 1501—1650.* Cambridge, Mass., 1934.

HARING, C. H.: *Trade and Navigation between Spain and the Indies in the time of the Hapsburgs.* Cambridge, Mass., 1918.

HEATON, H.: *Economic History of Europe.*[2] New York—Evanston, 1948.

HORN M.: *Handel wolami na Rusi Czerwonej w pierwszej połowie XVII w.* (Roczniki Dziejów Społecznych i Gospodarczych, 1962.)

HORVÁTH, P.: *Hromadný vývoz dobytka z juhozápadného Slovenska do rakúskych a českých krajín na začiatku 17. storočia.* (Historické Štúdie, 1968.)

HOSZOWSKI, S.: *The Polish Baltic Trade in the 15th—18th Centuries.* (Poland at the XIth International Congress of Historical Sciences in Stockholm. Warszawa, 1960.)

VAN HOUTTE, J. A.: *Anvers aux XVe et XVIe siècles: expansion et apogée.* (Annales Économies-Sociétés-Civilisations, 1961).

HROCH, M.: *Die Rolle des zentraleuropäischen Handels für den Ausgleich der Handelsbilanz zwischen Ost und West.* (Manuskript.)

HUSZÁR, L.: *Merchant's Seals of the 16th and 17th Centuries.* (Folia Archeologica, 1961.)

JEANNIN, P.: *L'activité du port de Koenigsberg dans la seconde moitié du XVIe siècle.* (Bulletin de la Société d'Histoire Moderne, 1958.)

JEANNIN, P.: *Le commerce de Lubeck aux environs de 1580.* (Annales Économies-Sociétés-Civilisation, 1961.)

JEANNIN, P.: *Les relations économiques des villes de la Baltique avec Anvers au XVIe siècle.* (Vierteljahrschrift für Sozial- und Wirtschaftsgeschichte, 1956.)

KOVÁTS, F.: *A magyar arany világtörténeti jelentősége és kereskedelmi összeköttetéseink a nyugattal a középkorban* [The World-historical Significance of Hungarian Gold and Hungary's Trade Relations with the West in the Middle Ages]. (Történeti Szemle, 1922).

KOVÁTS, F.: *Nyugat-Magyarország áruforgalma a XV. században a pozsonyi harmincadkönyv alapján* [West Hungary's Trade in the 15th Century, Based on the Customs Journals of Pozsony]. Budapest, 1902.

KULISCHER, J.: *Allgemeine Wirtschaftsgeschichte des Mittelalters und der Neuzeit.* I—II. München—Berlin, 1928—29.

LANE, F. C.: *The Mediterranean Spice Trade.* (The American Historical Review, 1940.)

LENIN, V.I.: *The Development of Capitalism in Russia.* Chapter VIII/V. (The Significance of the Frontiers. Home or foreign market?)

Лесников, М. П.: *Некоторые вопросы бальтийского-нидерландской торговли хлебом в конце 14—начале 15 века.* (Средние Века, 1955.)
LIPSON, E.: *The Economic History of England.*[4] *Vol. II—III. The Age of Mercantilism.* London, 1947.
MĄCZAK, A.: *Der polnische Getreideexport und das Problem der Handelsbilanz 1565-1655.* (Manustript)
MĄCZAK, A.: *Export of Grain and the Problem of Distribution of National Income in Poland in the Years 1550—1650.* (Acta Poloniae Historica, 1968.)
MAKKAI, L.: *Der ungarische Viehhandel 1550—1650.* (Manuskript.)
MAŁOWIST, M.: *The Economic and Social Development of the Baltic Countries from the 15th to the 17th Centuries.* (The Economic History Review, 1959.)
MAŁOWIST, M.: *Die Problematik der sozial-wirtschaftlichen Ges chichte Polens vom 15. bis zum 17. Jahrhundert.* (La Renaissance et la Réformation en Pologne et en Hongrie 1450—1650. Budapest, 1963.)
MAŁOWIST, M.: *Z zagadnień popytu na produkty krajów nadbaltyckich w Europie zachodniej w XVI wieku.* (Przegląd Historiczny, 1959.)
MARX, C.: *The British Rule in India.*
MARX, C.: *Coming Results of the British Rule in India.*
MARX, C.: *The Capital.* Vol. I. Chapter IV. *(The Transformation of Money into Capital).* Vol. I. Chapter XXIV. *(The so-called Primitive Accumulation).* Vol. III. Chapter XX. *(Contributions to the History of Merchant Capital).*
MASEFIELD, G. B.: *Crops and Livestock.* (The Cambridge Economic History of Europe. Vol. IV. The Economy of Expanding Europe in the Sixteenth and Seventeenth Centuries. Chapter V. Cambridge, 1967.)
NEWTON, A. P.: *The European Nations in the West Indies 1493—1688.* London, 1933.
PACH, Zs. P., *Das Entwicklungsniveau der feudalen Agrarverhältnisse in Ungarn in der zweiten Hälfte des XV. Jahrhunderts.* (Etudes Historiques, I. Budapest, 1960.)
PACH, Zs. P.: *Die Abbiegung der ungarischen Agrarentwicklung vom Westeuropäischen.* (Studia Historica, 1964.)
PARRY, J. H.: *Transport and Trade Routes.* (The Cambridge Economic History of Europe. Vol. IV. Chapter III.)
PAULINYI, O.: *Ipar, kereskedelem* [Industry, Trade]. (Magyar művelődéstörténet. II. Budapest, s.a.)
PIRENNE, H.: *Une crise économique au XVIe siècle. La draperie urbaine et la nouvelle draperie en Flandre.* (Bulletin de la Classe des Lettres de l'Académie Royale de Belgique, 1905.)
PROBSZT, G.: *Königin Maria und die niederungarischen Bergstädte.* (Zeitschrift für Ostforschung, 1966.)
RICH, E. E.: *Colonial Settlement and Its Labour Problems.* (The Cambridge Economic History of Europe. Vol. IV. Chapter VI.)
RYBARSKI, R.: *Handel i polityka handlowa Polski w XVI stuleciu.*[2] Vol. I—II. Warszawa, 1958.
SACHS, C. L.: *Metzgergewerbe und Fleischversorgung der Reichstadt Nürnberg bis zum Ende des 30jährigen Krieges.* Nürnberg, 1922.
SAMSONOWICZ, H.: *Die Jahrmärkte in Polen im 16. Jahrhundert.* (Manuskript.)
SANDBERG, L. G.: *Movements in the Quality of British Cotton Textile Exports 1815—1913.* (The Journal of Economic History, 1968.)
SCHULTE, A.: *Geschichte des mittelalterlichen Handels und Verkehrs zwischen Westdeutschland und Italien.* Leipzig, 1900.
SLICHER VAN BATH, B. H.: *The Agrarian History of Western Europe A. D. 500—1850.* London, 1963.
SLICHER VAN BATH, B. H.: *Die europäischen Agrarverhältnisse im 17. und der ersten Hälfte des 18. Jahrhunderts.* (A.A.G.Bijdragen, 13. 1965.)
SLUITER, E.: *Dutch-Spanish Rivalry in the Caribbean Area 1594—1609.* (The Hispanic American Historical Review, 1948.)
SZÉKELY, GY., *Niederländische und englische Tucharten im Mitteleuropa des 13—17. Jahrhunderts.* (Annales Universitatis Scientiarum Budapestinensis de Rolando Eötvös nominatae, 1966.)
SZŰCS, J.: *Das Städtewesen in Ungarn im 15—17. Jahrhundert.* (La Renaissance et la Réformation en Pologne et en Hongrie 1450—1650. Budapest, 1963.)
TAKÁCS, S.: *A magyar tőzsérek és kereskedők pusztulása* [The Decline of Hungarian Traders and Merchants] (Szegény magyarok. Budapest, s.a.)
THALLÓCZY, L.: *Középkori gazdaságtörténeti adatok Nürnberg levéltáraiból* [Documents of Medieval Economic History in the Archives of Nuremberg]. (Magyar Gazdaságtörténelmi Szemle, 1900.)
TOPOLSKI, J.: *The Role of Gniezno in International Trade.* (Acta Poloniae Historica, 1968.)

VOLLBEHR, F.: *Die Holländer und die deutsche Hanse.* Lübeck, 1930.
WADSWORTH, A. P.—DE L. MANN, J.: *The Cotton Trade and Industrial Lancashire 1600—1780.* Manchester, 1931.
WIESE, H.: *Die Fleischversorgung der nordwesteuropäischen Großstädte vom XV. bis zum XIX. Jahrhundert unter besonderer Berücksichtigung des interterritorialen Rinderhandels.* (Jahrbücher für Nationalökonomie und Statistik, 1966.)
WILLIAMS, E.: *Capitalism and Slavery.* Chapel Hill, N. C. 1944.
WITTMAN, T.: *Az „árforradalom" és a világpiaci kapcsolatok kezdeti mozzanatai (1566—1618).* [The "Price Revolution" and the Beginnings of World Market Relations (1566—1618)]. Budapest, 1957.
WYCZANSKI, A.: *Tentative Estimate of Polish Rye Trade in the Sixteenth Century.* (Acta Poloniae Historica, 1961.)
ZIMÁNYI V.: *Quelques aspects de la regression économique et sociale du XVIIe siècle.* (Manuscrit.)

ADDENDA

THE SHIFTING OF INTERNATIONAL TRADE ROUTES IN THE 15th–17th CENTURIES

Page 287:

In this paper by *Mid–Eastern Europe* the same area is understood that has been termed, in the more usual manner, *East–Central Europe* in other writings of the volume.

Page 288:

In Volume V of The Cambridge Economic History of Europe (The Economic Organization of Early Modern Europe), published in 1977, East–Central European relations turn up more frequently. This reflects the rising interest in the topic and the more lively contacts between Western and Eastern European historians from about 1960 onwards.

Page 290:

For a closer inspection of the routes of medieval–type long–haul trade, see the papers on Levantine trade in this volume.

Page 291:

As for commercial and financial techniques, the trade of the German Hanse lagged well behind that of the North Italian towns, but its character and commody structure was more modern, with an overwhelming share of prime necessities and mass products; conf. *M. Postan,* The Trade of Medieval Europe: the North, and *R. S. Lopez,* The Trade of Medieval Europe: the South. In: The Cambridge Economic History (=CEHE), II, Trade and Industry in the Middle Ages. Ed. by M. Postan and E. E. Rich, Cambridge, 1952, pp. 119–120; 291. — For cloth and cotton trade in the Mediterranean: *E. Ashtor,* Levant Trade in the Later Middle Ages, Princeton, 1983, pp. 203, 268, 357, 462; 174–179, 318–323.

Page 291, Note2:

Sicily, the chief granary of the western Mediterranean exported, on an annual average, about 10 000 tons of grain between 1532 and 1578, mostly to Spain, but also in varying quantities to several towns of South Europe and North Africa; conf. *F. Braudel,* Le Méditerranée et le monde méditerranéen à l'époque de Philippe II², Paris, 1966, I, pp. 517, 520, 525–526; *F. Mauro* and *G. Parker,* Spain. In: An Introduction to the Sources of European Economic History 1500–1800. Ed. by C. Wilson and G. Parker, London, 1980, pp. 41–42.

Pages 294-295:

While English wool exports diminished, the volume of English cloth exports grew more than twofold during the 16th century. The peak was attained in 1565 when over 134 000 cloths were exported from London alone. In that year textiles accounted for 78 per cent of all English exports; the share of wool, once high, went down to 6,3 per cent. However, at this time the growth of cloth exports still had but little to do with the "new draperies" proper (at this point the text calls for some correction), but was largely due to an increasing trade in broadcloth and kersey. English broadcloth was mainly produced in the West Country and shipped to Antwerp, for the most part by the regulated company of London exporters, the Merchant Adventurers. Kersey was a lighter and less expensive woollen, mostly produced in Yorkshire (hence "northern kersies"). This fabric was much in demand on North German and East-Central European markets, less affluent than those of the Netherlands. Therefore, its share in English exports was growing from the mid-1560s when the Merchant Adventurers moved their headquarters from Antwerp to Northern Netherlands (and finally to Hamburg). Thus, kersey may be regarded as a middling sort between traditional broadcloths and new draperies (in the strict sense of the term). The latter did already exist in Elizabethan England, but began to flourish only in the first part of the 17th century. — For the whole subject see: *F. J. Fisher*, Commercial Trends and Policy in Sixteenth–Century England, The Economic History Review (=EHR), X, 2 (1940), pp. 96–97; *L. Stone*, Elizabethan Overseas Trade, EHR, 2nd Ser., II, 1 (1949), pp. 37–40, 45, 50, 58; *F. J. Fisher*, London's Export Trade in the Early Seventeenth Century, EHR, 2nd Ser., III, 2 (1950), pp. 152–154. — Recent study on Antwerp, as the most important centre of international textile trade for much of the 16th century: *A. K. L. Thijs*, Les textiles au marché anversois au XVIe siècle. In: Textiles of the Low Countries in European Economic History. Proceedings of the Xth International Economic History Congress. Ed. by E. Aerts, Leuven, 1990, pp. 76–86.

Page 295, Note 4:

Early in the 16th century Antwerp also emerged as an important port for Baltic grain shipments, Amsterdam not yet dominating the whole grain market in the Netherlands. Moreover, the Scheldt–city tried all through the first half of the century to fortify its position as a centre of the transit trade in grain and to extend its contacts with Gdańsk and the Baltic, but could not prevent Amsterdam from finally becoming the foremost granary of the West European coastal areas: *H. Van der Wee*, The Growth of the Antwerp Market and the European Economy (14th–16th Centuries), The Hague, 1963, II, pp. 120–122, 157–158, 217–218, 225. — Conf. *A. E. Christensen*, Dutch Trade to the Baltic about 1600, Copenhagen–The Hague, 1941, pp. 34, 190, 371, 402–403.

Page 300:

For the shift of the centre of world trade from Antwerp to Amsterdam, see the statistical comparison of the import and export activities of both international markets around the mid–16th century and in 1667–1668, respectively: *M. Morineau*, Contribution à l'histoire économique des Provinces–Unies. In: Dutch Capitalism § World Capitalism. Ed. by M. Aymard, Cambridge–Paris, 1982, pp. 295–302. — "Amsterdam is not a simple reproduction of Antwerp. ... She innovates": p. 303. — Conf. *P. Jeannin*, The Sea–Borne and the Overland Trade Routes of Northern Europe in the 16th and 17th Centuries, The Journal of European Economic History, XI, 1 (1982), p. 50.

Pages 300-301:

It has been written in the text perhaps exaggeratedly that Baltic grain covered "most" of the consumption in the Northern Netherlands. However, it remains certain that the grain shipped to Amsterdam fed up to half the population of the maritime provinces in any year of the 17th century, and it was the existence of the grain trade — the mother trade *(moedercommercie)*, as it was called — that served as a necessary condition for Dutch economic specialization in both town and country: *J. De Vries*, The Dutch Rural Economy in the Golden Age, 1500–1750, New Haven, 1974, pp. 169–173. — For another foundation of Dutch supremacy in the trade of mass-consumption goods, the North Sea herring fishery *(groote visscherij)*: *A. R. Michell*, The European Fisheries in Early Modern History. In: CEHE, V. Ed. by E. E. Rich and C. H. Wilson, Cambridge, 1977, pp. 148–153, 172–185; *Christensen*, op. cit. 371, 465.

Page 302:

For the decline of the overland trade, flowing between Northern Italy and Southern Germany through Venice, also see: *D. Sella*, Crisis and Transformation in Venetian Trade. In: Crisis and Change in the Venetian Economy in the 16th and 17th Centuries. Ed. by B. Pullan, London, 1968, pp. 94, 97. — A partly differing view has been formed by *W. Brulez*, Les transports routiers entre les Pays–Bas et l'Italie aux XVIe et XVIIe siècles. In: Trasporti e sviluppo economico secoli XIII–XVIII. Atti della Quinta Settimana di Studio (Prato, 1973), Firenze, 1986, pp. 257, 259, 262. — Another irreparable loss for Venice was the decline of her cloth production by the same time. In the last three decades of the 17th century annual output dipped from 5000 to 2000 cloths — a far cry from the 25 000 cloths, produced yearly at the close of the previous century. The failure was mainly due to the growing export of Dutch and English stuffs — lighter and cheaper fabrics — towards the Levantine markets: *D. Sella*, The Rise and Fall of the Venetian Woollen Industry: In: Crisis and Change, op. cit. pp. 108–109, 119–120; *G. Felloni*, Italy. In: An Introduction to the Sources, op. cit. pp. 12–15, 35.

Page 305, Note 8:

Recent research has found out that the share of commodities in the exports of the Dutch East India Company had been less insignificant. However, it should be noted, firstly, that the exported European goods were mainly intended for either the maintenance of the apparatus of the Dutch Company overseas or for sale to the Europeans living abroad; only a very few of these articles entered the Asian markets proper. Secondly, no doubt bullion and coin formed the main part — two thirds of the value — of the cargo in each outgoing Dutch ship, even in the first half of the 18th century. Thirdly, the constant importation of Asian products caused a permanent drain of gold and silver from Europe towards Asia, where large amounts of precious metals were continuously taken out of the circulation and, in fact, hoarded: *I. Schöffer–F. S. Gaastra*, The Import of Bullion and Coin into Asia by the Dutch East India Company in the 17th and 18th Centuries. In: Dutch Capitalism, op. cit. pp. 221–224, 231–232; *A. Attman*, Dutch Enterprise in the World Bullion Trade 1550–1800, Göteborg, 1983, pp. 95–103.

Page 307-310:

The customs books that have survived from the year 1542 shed light on Hungary's western trade only in a narrow sense of that direction, as they do not cover the transports controlled by the north–western and south–western customs stations. For the problems of registrations in the customs books in question (including the very low share of wine and the virtual non–appearance of copper) as well as for a more detailed presentation of Hungarian and Polish trade balances, see the paper *The Role of East–Central Europe in International Trade (16th and 17th Centuries)* in this volume. — The first passage in Note 14 (concerning the mid–15th century Hungary) calls for a correction as follows: In the imports the share of hardware (mainly of South German and Styrian origin) and that of "norimbergeries" (sundries) was about 8–10 per cent each, spices accounted for about 5 per cent. — A more precise formulation of the last passage in Note 16 is this: The Price Revolution began to make itself felt also in Hungary in the early 16th century, but it swept on only from the 1550's. Conf. *Št. Kazimír*, Adalék a XVI. és XVII. századbeli árak és bérek fejlődéséhez (A Contribution to the Development of Prices and Wages in the 16th and 17th Centuries), Történelmi Szemle (Historical Review), XIX, 1–2 (1976), pp. 167--210.

Page 313:

The decline of west–bound Polish grain exports can be explained both from the angle of production and from the market aspect (instead of the formula: "from the angle of production rather than from the market aspect"). As for the market side, it should be noted that in seventeenth–century Western Europe much of industry shifted from town to country. The rural industries were based on the peasant craftsman who divided his labour between agricultural and industrial activities. He might be employed at a lower wage, since he himself produced part of his food and was not protected by guild regulations from wage cut. These developments also combined to reduce the food demand on western markets, and brought about — along with other factors (Note 22) — a fall in grain prices that went back more than those of other goods. — For the decrease in supply of and demand for Polish grain also see: *W. Rusiński*, The Role of Polish Territories in the European Trade in the 17th and 18th Centuries. In: Studia Historiae Oeconomicae, III, Poznań, 1969, pp. 115–119; *E. Harder–Gersdorff*, Lübeck, Danzig und Riga. Ein Beitrag zur Frage der Handelskonjunktur im Ostseeraum am Ende des 17. Jahrhunderts. In: Hansische Geschichtsblätter, 96. Jg. Köln–Wien, 1978, pp. 110–112, 121–122. — As a consequence, from the middle of the 17th century onwards the Baltic sea–borne trade began to reshape, with timber, other "naval stores" and Swedish iron prevailing in western exports: *S. E. Åström*, From Cloth to Iron. The Anglo–Baltic Trade in the late 17th Century, I, Helsinki, 1963, pp. 29–32, 41–44; *Ch. A. Piirimäe*, O vliianii bal'tiiskoi torgovli na process genezisa kapitalizma v Zapadnoi Evrope (konec XVI–XVII v.). In: Problemy genezisa kapitalizma. Red. S. D. Skaskin, Moscow, 1970, pp. 13–19, 50–56; *J. A. Faber*, Structural Changes in the European Economy During the 18th Century as Reflected in the Baltic Trade. In: From Dunkirk to Danzig. Shipping and Trade in the North Sea and the Baltic, 1350–1850. Ed. by W. G. Heeres *et al.*, Hilversum, 1988, pp. 88–92. (The latter writer left the decrease in Polish grain supply out of consideration).

X

THE ROLE OF EAST-CENTRAL EUROPE IN INTERNATIONAL TRADE

(16TH AND 17TH CENTURIES)

The issue raised in the title would seem to suggest the following answer: the role of East-Central-European countries[1] in international trade diminished in the 16th and 17th centuries. For it was these centuries that witnessed the enormous expansion of international commerce, the shifting of trade routes from the Mediterranean basin to the coasts of the Atlantic, to regions ever more distant from East-Central Europe. These centuries saw new continents join in the developing modern world economy, continents of vast dimensions which offered an immeasurable wealth of natural treasures.

There can be no doubt that the shifting of international trade routes and the emergence of a new long-distance transport centre on the Atlantic coasts had, in the final analysis, an adverse effect on the Eastern part of Europe, contributing as they did to the retardation of development, to the delay of capitalist transformation and to the interposal of a protracted era of belated feudalism, regardless of whether or not the change was due primarily to the opening of new ocean routes, to the circumnavigation of Africa and the discovery of America, regardless, moreover, of how far the routes of medieval long-haul (Levant) trade had earlier affected the countries of East-Central Europe.[2]

Historically however, this adverse effect on East-Central Europe, these causal relationships did not assert themselves so directly or so explicitly as interpreted by numerous authors who have drawn the conclusion that in consequence of the above-mentioned changes the role of East-Central Europe in international trade was relegated to the background; being barred or remote from the main stream of international commerce, the towns themselves and in general the attained level of bourgeois development declined; consequently there occurred an increasing lag of progress in these territories compared to conditions in Western Europe.[3]

[1] In this paper by East-Central Europe the following countries are understood: Poland, Bohemia, Hungary and Croatia.

[2] For the first question see Zs. P. Pach, The Shifting of International Trade Routes in the 15—17 Centuries, *Acta Historica Acad. Sci. Hung.*, 1968, tom. 14, no. *3—4*, pp 287—321. The second question is to form the subject of a separate study in connection with the historiographic problem mentioned in Note 3.

[3] To the best of our knowledge G. Berzeviczy was the first to state this opinion in the pertaining Hungarian literature, in his works on international trade between Asia and Europe (1808) and on northern trade (1814). Their Hungarian translation: J. Gaál, *Berzeviczy Gergely élete és művei* (The Life and Works of Gergely Berzeviczy), Budapest 1902, pp 288—290, 306, 307. — In German historiography this interpretation was drawn up at the same time by K. D. Hüllmann, *Geschichte des byzantinischen Handels bis zum Ende der Kreuzzüge*, Frankfurt 1808, and A. H. L. Heeren, *Versuch einer Entwicklung der Folgen der Kreuzzüge für Europa*, Göttingen 1808. — Conf. F. Bastian, Die Legende vom Donauhandel im Frühmittelalter, *Vierteljahrschrift für Sozial- und Wirtschaftsgeschichte*, XXII. Bd. 1929, pp 292—296.

In the light of closer inspection these conclusions appear to be simplifications calling for correction. The results of recent research evidence that the role of East-Central Europe in international trade actually became more important and increased in the period under review. It was the character and the peculiar traits of this growth on the one hand, and the new elements in the development of modern world trade as it embarked on a new stage of the process on the other, that subsequently made conditions ripe for, and ushered in, approximately by the middle of the 17th century, the unfavourable turning-point and negative trend in the international commercial-economic role of East-Central Europe, perhaps, it may be added, also in her historical destiny.

In the present paper a few important events of the above indicated process of development are to be outlined in brief.

I

The study of international trade in this age, indeed, from as far back as from the 15th century, is being rendered fascinatingly difficult not only by the immense field involved, but also, and chiefly, by its extraordinary intricacy, by the very fact that we are all the time faced with two different types of long-distance trade governed by dissimilar principles, namely international trade of the *medieval* and of the *modern* type respectively, yet interwoven and intertwined in historical reality.

Here we have to clear the meaning of the terms applied. In the present work the term "modern" refers to the type of international commercial relations which originated from the economic growth of Europe, from the advancement of commodity production, from progress in the social division of labour, and which provided increasing quantities of mass-consumption goods (and industrial raw materials) to steadily widening buyers' markets, contrary to the "medieval type" (old type) of long-haul trade, which, in essence, did not imply an exchange of goods produced by the European economy, but mostly dealt in oriental spices and luxury articles, supplying Levant commodities to European markets in order to satisfy the luxury demands of the upper-class (and rich burgher) consumers.

The three most important features of the development process forming the subject of the present paper may be described by the use of the above terms (definitions) as follows:

1. International trade of the modern type — which sprang from the inner growth of European economy and gained ever new impetus from its inevitable, inherent demands — developed in the 15th and 16th centuries, after antecedents going far back into the past — gradually overtook long-haul trade of the medieval type, to achieve steadily rising prosperity, to outstrip and supersede medieval commercial activity (or to transform it according to the modern pattern[4].)

[4] The change in the meaning of the term "colonial goods" is typical of the latter. At the beginning it meant chiefly spices, and luxuries; later it came to refer to sugar, tea, etc. which gradually became the elements of mass consumption. For the medieval meaning of colonial goods (Kolonialwaren) see E. E. Rich, Preface, *The Cambridge Economic History of Europe*, Vol. IV, *The Economy of Expanding Europe in the Sixteenth and Seventeenth Centuries*, Cambridge 1967, p. 13.

2. The development of modern-type trade, the change in commodity structure on international markets in favour of mass-consumption goods, induced a shift of the principal trade routes and their direction: the routes used for the interregional delivery of mass-consumption goods necessarily differed from those of the old-type long-haul trade. The Mediterranean basin lost in commercial significance compared to the zone of the Baltic and the North Sea; while Atlantic coast shipping — from the Sound to Gibraltar -- having to satisfy the strongly increasing needs of the new-type market relations — was becoming the main artery of international traffic.

3. The change in the character, in the commodity structure of international trade and the consequent shift of the principal trade routes also involved as a matter of necessity a change in the intermediaries of this trade: from the North Italian (Venetian, Genoese) and North German (Hanseatic) merchants commercial hegemony gradually passed into the hands of the Dutch, and later to the English. From the outset the rising trade activity of the Dutch was closely connected with the establishment of the new-type trade relations: as intermediaries they carried to the West the grain and other primary products of Eastern European regions adjacent to the Baltic, bringing in exchange cloth and other manufactured goods from the industrial regions of Western Europe situated along the Atlantic coast.[5]

4. Of course, in the development of international trade in the 15th—17th centuries, the three features briefly outlined in the foregoing refer only to *one* principal process and its *European aspect*. The *other* principal process, which passed *beyond Europe*, began with the discovery and use of the new ocean routes from the turn of the 15th century, after the discovery of America and the opening of a direct sea route to India.

Though in the further course of events the two processes came into close interaction and were in many respects intertwined, it is justified to distinguish between them, all the more so as the growing preponderance of Atlantic coast traffic and the rise of Dutch trade resulted primarily from the expansion of the new-type trade relations; the discoveries, the incentive to set out to find new ocean routes, in turn, originally came not from the claims created by the expansion of the modern-type commerce, but from those of the old-type medieval long-distance trade which stimulated the quest in the endeavour to acquire its chief articles, oriental spices, by a direct route, and to take possession of the fabulous treasures of India.

It must be added here that in the 16th century and during some decades of the 17th the imports brought from the East and the West Indies by the new ocean routes to Europe may be said to have retained their old-type commodity structure: from the Far-East it was spices in the first place, from Spanish America precious metals which were shipped to Europe.

It is worth while to mention in this connection a few revealing facts. Precious metals, predominantly silver, accounted for 95.62 per cent of the value of shipments which arrived in 1594 from the Spanish Indies to Spain, other kinds of goods amounting to no more than a mere fraction of the total. In 1609 the share of precious metals was still 84 per cent, that of other products

[5] For fuller details and analysis of these events see our paper cited in Note 2, particularly pp 289—303.

only 16 per cent.[6] Of the shipments carried by the Dutch East India Company in the years between 1619 and 1621 to the United Provinces 74 per cent consisted of pepper and other spices, and hardly more than a quarter was made up of other colonial articles.[7] At the same time (1621) the imports of the English East India Company (to put it more accurately: the part of imports to be consumed in England) were estimated to comprise pepper and other spices up to two thirds of the total.[8]

Let us now turn our attention to East-Central Europe and the kinds of goods supplied to West European markets during the same period by two countries of this region, by Poland and Hungary.

Poland (and Lithuania) played a significant role in the supply of 16th century Western Europe by the export of three sorts of goods, notably grain (rye), cattle (oxen), and fur. These three articles amounted to nearly 90 per cent of the country's exports to western markets by overland- and maritime routes. Most of the cattle and fur exports were forwarded overland, while the bulk of the grain was shipped from Baltic ports. In the years between 1565 and 1585, on the average, grain alone accounted for 66 per cent of Polish seaborne exports, the rest consisting of raw materials (timber, potash, hemp).[9]

In the middle of the 16th century Hungarian exports to the West were marked by the preponderance of two important mass products: cattle (oxen) and copper were supplied in considerable quantities. According to records from the year 1542, which present an enlightening picture of Hungarian foreign trade with western countries, but do not comprise the copper exports, 90 per cent or so of the registered transactions referred to cattle exports.[10] About two decades later nearly 90 per cent of exports to the West from Hungarian territory occupied by the Turks derived similarly from the supply of cattle.[11]

All this indicates that in the 16th century and in the first decades of the 17th the American and East Asian colonies provided to Western Europe for the most part precious metals and spices, that is the characteristic items of *old-*

[6] The share of other goods in 1594: cochineal, 2.82 per cent; hides, 1.16 per cent; indigo, 0.29 per cent. — E. J. Hamilton, *American Treasure and the Price Revolution in Spain, 1501 - 1650,* Cambridge, Mass. 1934, pp 33, 34.

[7] About 10 per cent was made up of drugs and dyestuffs, 16 per cent of various textiles, while the share of pepper supplies alone amounted to 56 per cent. — K. Glamann, *Dutch-Asiatic Trade 1620—1740,* Copenhagen-The Hague 1958, p. 13.

[8] One third consisted of indigo and other dyestuffs. — With reference to Th. Mun, *A Discourse of Trade from England unto the East Indies (1621)* in E. Lipson, *The Economic History of England,*[4] Vol. II, *The Age of Mercantilism,* London 1947, p. 288.

[9] Timber had a 5 per cent, flax and hemp a 12 per cent, tar and potash a 14 per cent share in sea-borne exports. — A. Mączak, Eksport zbożowy i problemy polskiego bilansu w XVI–XVII w, *Pamiętnik X powszechnego zjazdu historików polskich w Lublinie,* Warszawa 1968, p. 183. — H. Samsonowicz, Die Jahrmärkte in Polen im 16. Jahrhundert, *Erste Tagung des Seminars für Sozial- und Wirtschaftsgeschichte der Philipps-Universität zu Marburg an der Lahn,* 1967.

[10] Gy. Ember, Zur Geschichte des Außenhandels Ungarns im XVI. Jahrhundert, *Etudes historiques,* Budapest 1960, Vol. I, pp 549—550. The commodity structure of Hungary's foreign trade and the share of copper export, etc. are dealt with in Chapter II of the present paper.

[11] Gy. Káldy-Nagy, Statisztikai adatok a török hódoltsági terület nyugat felé irányuló áruforgalmáról 1560—1564-ben, *Történeti Statisztikai Évkönyv 1965—66* (Statistical Data of Western Trade in Turkish-occupied Territory in the Years 1560—1564. Historico-Statistical Year-Book), Budapest 1968, p. 32.

type long-haul trade, whereas in the same period countries of East-Central Europe supplied to West European markets grain and meat in the first place, that is the most important *agricultural* mass-consumption articles of the *new*-type international commerce, as well as industrial raw materials produced by agriculture and mining. This may be pointed out as the fourth essential feature of the studied developments.

5. Let us now take a look at the commodities sent *from* Western Europe to the countries of East-Central Europe. In the middle of the 16th century textiles (woollen cloths) accounted for 60 per cent of West European exports to Poland; taken as the average of 1565—85, their share in sea-borne Polish imports was 48 per cent. After textiles salt occupied the second place in maritime trade, hardware in overland transports.[12] As regards Hungary, in many respects the picture is again similar. Over 68 per cent of imports from the West registered in the relevant records of 1542 was made up of textiles, including cloths (40 per cent), garments (15 per cent), and linen (12 per cent). Here, too, hardware, with a share of approximately 9 per cent, came after textiles.[13]

Thus, during the 16th century it was textiles in the first place that were supplied to the countries of East-Central Europe: various woollen fabrics from England and the Netherlands, from districts along the Lower Rhine and from Southern Germany, furthermore Bohemian, Moravian and Silesian stuffs, and also hardware, that is to say the most important *industrial* commodities of the unfolding new-type international trade.

In the course of the 16th century the American colonies, that is Spanish America and Brazil, under Portuguese rule, also developed an increasing demand for the industrial products of Western Europe, as testified by documentary evidence presented in studies dealing with commerce between the New World and Europe.[14] However, widening of the range of manufactured goods exported from Western Europe to America and the establishment of modern-type relations in trans-Atlantic trade were accelerated only after the Dutch had penetrated into the Caribbean area and in particular after the English and French had founded their colonies in the West Indian Archipelago.[15]

As concerns, however, the export of West European industrial products, particularly textiles, to Far Eastern colonies, such activities were insignificant in the 16th century and failed to show noteworthy growth even during the 17th. It is generally stated in the pertaining literature that the Portuguese, when "sailing out", were virtually unable to fill their cargo space with useful loads apart from precious metals and copper wares, for lack of goods to be offered

[12] See Note 9 and B. Zientara, Eisenproduktion und Eisenhandel in Polen im 16. und 17. Jahrhundert, *Tagung zu Marburg*, 1967.

[13] See Note 10.

[14] From older literature C. H. Haring, *Trade and Navigation between Spain and the Indies in the Time of the Hapsburgs*, Cambridge, Mass. 1918, pp 9, 62- 64, 117, 118, 133- 137, 185--187, 204, 211- 213. — Lately extensive material (with an exaggerated emphasis on trade cycles) has been made available in H. et P. Chaunu, *Séville et l'Atlantique 1504 1650*, Vol. VIII. 1. *Les structures. Structures géographiques*, Paris 1959; F. Mauro, *Le Portugal et l'Atlantique au XVIIe siècle*, Paris 1960.

[15] See the preceding note and Note 3 of Chapter III in which we return to the subject.

for sale.[16] Though Dutch exports to East India were more varied — embracing fire-arms, metals, linen, wine and norimbergeries — their value nevertheless amounted to no more than a few per cent of their outgoing shipments, being practically dwarfed by the quantities of precious metals and coins which the Dutch gave in exchange for their import goods, purchased, of course, at prices securing a rich profit.[17]

As a matter of fact the Asian trade of the Dutch underwent a considerable transformation in the second half of the 17th century. However, the change of commodity structure affected *imports* from East India to the Netherlands rather than *exports* from Europe to the Far East. What, then, did this change imply? In imports the share of oriental textile fabrics rose to 36 per cent by 1668—70, to increase to nearly 55 per cent in the years 1698—1700, far surpassing the 14 to 16 per cent of the first half of the century. Hence, by the close of the 17th century textiles became essential items on the list of Dutch imports from Asia, rising in commodity structure to the leading position formerly occupied by pepper, the spice which enjoyed the liveliest demand.[18]

In many respects a similar start and like developments are noticeable in the Asian trade of the English. The English East India Company, too, exported mainly precious metals (bullion), incurring thereby violent attacks and rousing a long drawn-out heated parliamentary and literary debate between the "bullionists" and the "antibullionists".[19] The Act of Parliament put into force in 1663 nevertheless approved of the export of bullion, so that in the second half of the 17th century, like in the first, precious metals still accounted for the best part of the total value of the Company's exports, their share varying between 70 and 90 per cent during the whole time of the 17th century as well as in the opening decades of the 18th.[20]

From the very outset the English endeavoured to export cloths — *woollen* fabrics (kersey, etc.) — to the Far East too, but they soon found that such articles proved to be "dead weight" in those regions, and the exported pieces were eaten by moths and ants.[21] Moreover, on the routes of the English East India Company a flow of goods in the opposite direction was soon started and increased: the Company itself began to import textiles, notably *cotton* fabrics (calico, etc.) to Western Europe. Owing to their inexpensiveness, their attractive colours and patterns, Indian printed cotton fabrics captured an extensive market in a short time, particularly among consumers of modest means in England, France, and elsewhere, notwithstanding a renewed harsh censure of the Company's commercial activities, import prohibitions and restrictive

[16] See, e. g., J. H. Parry, Transport and Trade Routes, *The Cambridge Economic History of Europe*, Vol. IV, p. 165. — J. A. Goris, *Étude sur les colonies marchandes méridionales (Portugais, Espagnols, Italians) à Anvers de 1488 à 1567. Contribution à l'histoire des débuts du capitalisme moderne*, Louvain 1925, pp 239—243. — Copper goods and trinkets were carried by the Portuguese chiefly to their West African colonies.

[17] Glamann, *op. cit.*, pp 40—48.

[18] *Ibid*, pp 13—15, 20—22, 134—139, 265.

[19] Detailed information about the controversy — which lent strong impetus to the development of English literature on economic science — is to be found in Lipson, *op. cit.*, Vol. II, pp 277—303.

[20] K. N. Chaudhuri, Treasure and Trade Balances: the East India Company's Export Trade, *The Economic History Review*, 2nd Series, Vol. XXI, No. *3* (1968), pp 482—484.

[21] Lipson, *op. cit.*, Vol. II, pp 277, 278, 286.

measures intended to protect the woollen industry. It is characteristic of the turn of events that in 1677 the share of spices and dyestuffs was estimated to be only about 10 per cent, and that of cotton fabrics as high as 66 per cent in the imports of the English East India Company (more exactly, in the part of imports made available for consumption in England).[22]

All this goes to show that in the 16th and 17th centuries the East Asian colonies were no buyers' markets for textile goods (woollen fabrics) from Western Europe, on the contrary: it was rather from these colonies that textiles (cotton fabrics) were taken to West European markets, — in contrast to some countries of East-Central Europe (for instance Poland and Hungary) which absorbed during the same period considerable quantities of textile articles from England, the Netherlands, the Rhineland (and other regions). This statement may be said to summarize the fifth characteristic feature of the process of development under consideration.

Thus, in respect of imports and exports alike, we found that while trade between Western Europe and the American colonies as well as between Western Europe and the East Asian colonies — though pursued by the use of the newly discovered ocean routes — was marked during the era in question by the preponderance of an old-type commodity structure, reminding of the medieval long-haul commerce, relations between Western Europe and East-Central Europe actually proved to be the carriers of the developing modern-type trade relations. The import requirements of Western Europe in agricultural produce and staple foodstuffs were for the greater part covered by the countries of East-Central Europe, and it was the latter which absorbed a considerable part of West European exports in the most important industrial products for mass consumption.

The statement put forward in the introduction of the present paper rests on this very basis: compared to earlier conditions, the role of East-Central Europe in international trade positively increased instead of losing ground in the period under review.

II

The role and position of East-Central Europe in the rising international commerce of modern type, which we have endeavoured to illustrate by citing a few characteristic facts from the foreign trade of Poland and of Hungary in the 16th century, resulted from the events which shaped the history of the 15th-17th centuries.

This role, evident from the middle of the 15th, assumed a definitely developed form during the 16th century; by the mid-17th century it had reached its zenith and was on the wane.[1]

[22] Silks (raw and woven) and saltpetre accounted for another 13 per cent respectively. — Lipson, *op. cit.*, Vol. II, p. 288, with reference to *The East India Trade, a most Profitable Trade to the Kingdom (1677)*.

[1] Certain features of this position in international trade (export of agrarian products, import of manufactured goods) became traditional and even ingrained in subsequent centuries, but under the essentially changed conditions of the whole system of international trade. — See Chapter III of the present paper.

The principal stages of this process are to be presented in the following with reference to the case of Hungary.

1

As concerns Hungary the *first stage* of the process can be distinguished — partly also from the quantitative angle — in the middle of the 15th century. This has been made possible chiefly by the survival of the customs books of Pozsony (Bratislava) for the fiscal year of 1457—58, and the careful historico-statistical analysis of this valuable source.[2] The custom-house managed by the customs officers of the border town Pozsony controlled a substantial part of Hungary's trade with the West.[3]

What are the most obvious conclusions to be drawn from the data found in the customs books of Pozsony? Among the goods imported from the West, textiles, cloths first of all, were predominating both in value and quantity. During the fiscal year of 1457—58 over 15 000 pieces of cloth, nearly 10 000 pieces of fustian and linen, and a not inconsiderable number of ready-made garments passed through the customs office of Pozsony into Hungary. These textiles represented an aggregate value of more than 130 000 florins, which amounted to 78.76 per cent of the total imports handled here.[4]

The commodity structure of the cloth imports is equally noteworthy. The kinds of imported cloths widely varied in quality; according to the customs tariffs there were eight- to ninefold differences in the prices: beside the most

[2] F. Kováts, *Nyugatmagyarország áruforgalma a XV. században a pozsonyi harmincadkönyv alapján* (West Hungary's Trade in the 15th Century, Based on the Customs Journals of Pozsony), Budapest 1902. — It is an important question of source-criticism how far the customs journals of Pozsony may be used as a mirror of foreign trade, since they are taken to "summarize the elements of domestic and foreign trade" *(Op. cit.*, p. 8.). This has raised the apparently justified doubt whether the work of "F. Kováts was suitable for comparison", that is, for comparison with later sources of Hungary's trade with the West. (Gy. Ember, Magyarország XVI. századi külkereskedelmének történetéhez (Contribution to the History of Hungarian Foreign Trade in the 16th Century), *Századok*, 1961, No. *1*, p. 44.) Investigation of the question — detailed treatment of which is outside the scope of the present paper — has led to the conclusion that of the imports registered in the customs books of Pozsony maximum 4 per cent was of Hungarian origin, of the exports maximum 0.8 per cent remained within the borders of the country. Therefore the customs journals for the fiscal year 1457—58 may be used as a reliable basis for estimating foreign trade — with due regard to the fact that they only contain records of the commodities which passed through Pozsony. — The data from 1457—58 to be quoted below are based on *op. cit.*, pp 21, 76—81, 86—88, 94, 106—111, 116—119, 122—129, 131, 139, 184—185, 190—192, 194—197, if no other source is indicated.

[3] In the mid-15th century the customs stations of Buda and Oroszvár were leased by the town of Pozsony, too. At these places westbound trade was much smaller: in the fiscal year of 1456—57 the customs revenue was 1756 florins in Buda, 2633 florins at Oroszvár, but in Pozsony it amounted to 8398 florins (Kováts, *op. cit.*, p. 5.). — The inhabitants of Pozsony paid only half of the customs duty; in case of full payment the customs revenue of Pozsony alone would have amounted to 11 326 florins. — For the other customs stations where merchandise bound for the West passed in the middle of the 15th century see Note 14.

[4] The customs value of imported goods totalled 166 564 florins, including 99 544 florins for 15 139 pieces of cloth. 6499 pieces of various kinds of linen were imported, 3188 pieces of fustian, furthermore 72 140 hats and 15 128 pairs of hose. — At the time a part of the fine cloth probably travelled through the country, to be forwarded in a south-eastern direction. (See Note 25 later.)

expensive, high-quality cloths the proportion of goods of middling- and modest (cheaper) quality was steadily increasing. Moreover, cloth imports displayed a remarkable variety of provenance, for they included products from not only nearby countries, such as Bohemia and Moravia, Northern Italy and South Germany, but also from more distant regions, from England, the Netherlands and from the Lower Rhineland, in much larger lots than earlier.[5]

Classification by quality and origin is usually interpreted summarily by appraising cloths from Italy and Western Europe as first-rate, those from the Lower Rhineland and South Germany as second-rate, while Bohemian, Moravian and Silesian goods are ranked as third-rate.[6] These categories, however, call for some modification, owing to the results of recent investigations which have elucidated the names of certain cloths. With due regard to these modifications, in the total imports that passed through the customs office of Pozsony in the fiscal year 1457—58, the share of West European cloths proved to have been higher, than the figures to be found in earlier estimates. It has furthermore been revealed that English and Dutch consignments also contained supplies of cloths of lower quality.[7]

These facts may be explained by the development at this time in Flanders of the *nouvelle draperie* which differed from old-type clothmaking not only in the site of its workshops — which had been removed from the towns to rural districts (*draperie rurale*) — but also by producing, in addition to costly, high-quality fabrics, plainer, lighter, and cheaper kinds of cloth for an ever widening buyers' market.[8]

Although the actual "new drapery" was introduced in England only about a century later by Flemish immigrants, cheaper woollen fabrics (worsted, kersey, etc.) appeared here, too, in the course of the 15th century; they were soon set apart from "real" cloth on account of their width and quality, to be later ranged into the category of new drapery products.[9] Bohemian, Moravian and Silesian, even a few Polish and Hungarian towns, moreover, not only dealt in woollen cloths of West European and of German make, but at the same time, competing with the foreign products, they developed their own textile indus-

[5] Earlier occurrences have been dealt with by Gy. Székely, A németalföldi és az angol posztó fajtáinak elterjedése a XIII—XVII. századi Közép-Európában (Various Kinds of Flemish and English Cloths in Thirteenth-Seventeenth Century Central Europe), *Századok*, 1968, No. *1—2*, pp 4—11.

[6] First in Kováts, *op. cit.*, p. 102, and since then in general.

[7] Of the woollen fabrics falling under moderate tariff (half a florin) *kirsing*, *vorstat* and *dornisch* referred not to German, but to English (kersey, worsted) and Flemish (Dorn = Doornijk = Tournai) cloths. Cloth of Maastricht (also with ½ florin customs duty) belonged to merchandise of mediocre quality as well. Light Arras cloth imported in large lots (1165 pieces) with only ¼ florin customs duty was one of the inexpensive stuffs in wide demand. — Conf. Székely, *op. cit.*, pp 8, 21, 30. — W. Endrei, Középkori angol textilimportunk gyapjúszövetei (Hungary's Medieval Imports of English Woollen Fabrics), *Századok*, 1970. (In press).

[8] H. Pirenne, Une crise industrielle au XVIe siècle. La draperie urbaine et la "nouvelle draperie" en Flandre, *Bulletin de la Classe des lettres de l'Académie royale de Belgique*, Bruxelles 1905, No. *5*, pp 490—521. — E. Coornaert, *Un centre industriel d'autrefois. La draperie-sayetterie d'Hondschoote, XIVe—XVIIIe siècles*, Paris 1930, pp 10—21, 244—246.

[9] H. Heaton, *Economic History of Europe.*[2] New York-Evanston 1948, pp 232, 233. (partly with reference to the author's paper: *The Yorkshire Woollen and Worsted Industries*, 1920). — J. Clapham, *A Concise Economic History of Britain from the Earliest Times to 1750*, Cambridge 1949, pp 164—167, 241—246.

tries despite the far from inconsiderable difficulties which had to be surmounted. They went in for the cheaper kinds of cloth of which they could produce competitive qualities or for fabrics intended to satisfy the requirements of certain strata of consumers, for instance of the peasantry.[10]

This new tendency in the development of the Flemish and English textile industries, shortly followed also by Central Europe, was stimulated by the new requirements of expanding domestic and foreign markets: the rising demand for cheaper kinds of cloth for mass consumption besides the luxury fabrics for the high-born and the rich. On the testimony of the documentary evidence to be found in the customs books of Pozsony for the fiscal year 1457—58, this applied also to Hungary in a certain degree. It was in fact the increase of textile imports by leaps and bounds, the considerable growth in the quantity of cloths brought from Western and West-Central European countries, and within the total of imports the ever more considerable share of cheaper fabrics destined for mass consumption which indicate the "first wave", the first stage of Hungary's participation in the developing modern-type international trade about the middle of the 15th century.[11]

The discussion of other items recorded as imports in the customs books of Pozsony for 1457—58 being outside the scope of the present paper[12], we now turn to the issue whether or not exports in any commodity equalled in the same period the spectacular growth of textile imports.

An affirmative answer to this question holds good only relatively, although more than half of all exports consisted of one commodity, notably of livestock. The total volume of exports registered in the customs books of Pozsony remained far behind that of imports; thus, whereas textile goods, amounting to 78.76 per cent of imports, represented, as mentioned before, a customs value of over 130 000 florins (with cloth accounting for close on 100 000

[10] Székely, *op. cit.*, p. 12.

[11] The question may be raised whether or not the "first wave" was connected with the middle of the 15th century, simply because it is the customs books of 1457—58 which have survived; cloth imports may have been of similar volume earlier. The source material of Pozsony argues against such an assumption. The town of Pozsony had leased the customhouses of Pozsony, Buda and Oroszvár from the year 1440 and records of final settlement have come down to us, though the customs journals have been lost. These records reveal that from 1440 to 1457 the yearly customs revenue increased to approximately fivefold; Pozsony's revenue alone rose still higher. Therefore F. Kováts was justified in stating that it was in the mid-15th century that Hungary's foreign trade with the West rapidly expanded (*op. cit.*, p. VI, pp 5, 7, 8). — This is indicated also by the finding that simultaneously with the increase of imports and larger supplies of various kinds of cloth the prices of textiles gradually sank on the Pozsony market in the years between 1440 and 1460. (*Op. cit.*, pp 21, 22.)

[12] The second item on the list of imports — of much smaller volume than textiles but nevertheless important and illustrative — was hardware (predominantly knives) with a share of over 12 per cent. In the fiscal year 1457—58 as many as 1 617 282 knives passed through the customs office of Pozsony with the customs value of 18 239 florins. Part of these consignments may also be assumed to have travelled through the country to some south-eastern destination. — The typical articles of medieval long-distance trade, pepper and other spices, were, in turn, imported only in the value of 4 344 florins, which accounted for not more than 2.6 per cent of the total import registered at Pozsony in 1457—58. Obviously this did not cover the demand of Hungary: spices (along with expensive Italian cloths) were imported also from the south-west as well as from the south-east (together with oriental textile fabrics). — See Note 25.

florins), the total customs value of live-stock providing 54.63 per cent of all exports failed to reach the sum of 11 000 florins. On the other hand — and this point deserves special mention — within the group of live-stock none of the involved species gained preponderance: cattle and sheep exports amounted to approximately equal values, while the share of horse exports was smaller.[13]

On closer inspection attention is roused first of all by exports of cattle (oxen), especially in view of later events. In the fiscal year of 1457—58, 1466 oxen were driven across the border through Pozsony, in the value of 4153 florins, amounting to 21 per cent of the total value of exports.

When it comes to estimating these figures, which appear to be rather small in the light of evidence from the 16th century, it should not be forgotten that the information derived from the customs books of Pozsony for 1457—58 refers only to the droves that passed through the customs area of Pozsony and by no means to the whole of live-stock exports from Hungary to the West in that year. In this connection it should be borne in mind that exports to the west, whether taken in the wider or narrower sense of the term, could pass the border at several other custom-houses whose contemporary customs books and official records have not come down to posterity, and it certainly cannot be regarded as impossible that larger droves of cattle than those registered in Pozsony passed through the customs at other places as early as the mid-15th century.[14]

Therefore all that can be said with full assurance is that cattle exports to the West — the demonstrable beginnings of which go back to several preceding centuries[15] — already were considerable by the middle of the 15th cen-

[13] The 1466 oxen exported represented 4153 florins, the 6144 sheep and lambs 4218 florins, the 430 horses 2436 florins, in customs value. If exports of animal products (ox-hide, honey, wax) are added to live-stock exports the total share rises to 61 per cent, but the customs value still hardly exceeds 12 000 florins. Most of the other exported articles are also agrarian products. Live-stock export is followed by wine export with a 23.21 per cent (4592 florins), and fish exports with a 10.82 per cent (2141 florins) share. Grain exports were practically negligible. — The customs value of the exported goods totalled 19 783 florins.

[14] In a wider sense, Hungary's north-western and south-western exports, on which customs duty was paid at the customs office of Trencsén (and its outstations) and at Slavonian custom-houses, also count as western trade. From the aspect of strictly western trade, in addition to the customs office of Pozsony, its outstations have also to be taken into consideration — the one at Oroszvár was certainly active at the time, leased, as has been mentioned before, by the town of Pozsony — as well as the customs office of Sopron. (A list of these "old" customs offices was laid down a few decades later in Act 1498 : 34.) — Conf. Gy. Ember, Külkereskedelmünk történetéhez a XVI. században (Contribution to the History of Hungary's Foreign Trade in the 16th Century), *A Magyar Tudományos Akadémia Társadalmi—Történeti Tudományok Osztályának Közleményei* (Publications of the Section of Social and Historical Sciences of the Hungarian Academy of Sciences), Vol. **VIII** (1958), No. *4*, pp 312, 313. — Besides these old frontier customs stations, custom-houses established later in the interior of the country (Buda, Székesfehérvár, Pataj) have also to be taken into account. (In Act 1498 : 34 they are mentioned as customs stations to be closed down.) — It is possible that they had been put into operation to collect customs duty on the increasing droves of cattle exports. — Conf. A. Kubinyi, Budai kereskedők udvari szállításai a Jagelló-korban. (Supplies by Merchants of Buda to the Court in the Jagello Age), *Budapest Régiségei.* Vol. **XIX,** Budapest 1959, p. 105. — The custom-house of Buda was doubtlessly active in the mid-fifteenth century: it was leased by the town of Pozsony together with the stations in Pozsony and Oroszvár. (See Note 3.)

[15] L. Endlicher, *Rerum Hungaricarum Monumenta Arpadiana,* Sankt Gallen 1849, p. 492. (Customs-tariff of Győr for the year 1255). — F. Knauz, *Monumenta Ecclesiae Strigoniensis,* Vol. II, Strigonii 1882, p. 240. (Customs-tariff of Esztergom for the year

tury.[16] However, in the light of the documentary proof furnished by the customs books of Pozsony, a town which played an outstanding role at the time in Hungary's transactions with the West, cattle exports had not yet become a basic commodity of Hungarian western foreign trade, or a factor as important as were textile imports in being linked to the new-type international trade.

As regards copper, the other principal export commodity of 16th century Hungary, the situation is not quite similar. Though it is an incontrovertible fact that copper mining in the Besztercebánya (Banská Bystrica) district and the export of its production began to flourish only in the closing years of the 15th century, after the Fugger-Thurzó Company had started to operate in Hungarian mining, there can be no doubt that the extremely small volume of copper exports figuring in the customs books of Pozsony for 1457—58 — accounting for altogether 3.6 per cent of the total of exports — is far from representing the share contributed by North-Hungarian (Slovak) copper in the course of the 15th century to exports to the West before they reached their height.[17]

In exports through Pozsony the share of copper was small because none of the consignments forwarded to the three most important foreign markets of Hungarian copper, namely to Venice, Flanders, and Southern Germany, left the country by strictly western routes. Lots with Venice as their destination were sent in a south-western direction, partly by way of Pettau (Ptuj), partly through Buda, Slavonia and Dalmatia to be shipped at Zengg (Senj). Goods for Flanders were first dispatched north to Cracow, from where they travelled along the old important overland route of long-distance traffic to Western Europe, or they were taken still further north, on the Vistula, to Gdańsk, to reach the Flemish market by the Baltic-North Sea maritime line, the importance of which in the unfolding modern-type international trade was strongly increasing. In the Netherlands Hungarian copper served to cover the raw material requirement of the brass industry in the Lower Rhine region (between the rivers Rhine and Maas). Even the copper exported from Hungary to Southern Germany did not get to Nuremberg, the other centre of copper and brass industry, usually by the direct western route: a "détour" touching Cracow and leading through Breslau (Wrocław) was given preference.[18]

1288). G. Korn, *Breslauer Urkundenbuch*, Vol. I, No. 122. (Customs-tariff of Breslau [Wrocław] for the year 1327). — Conf. F. Lütge, Der Handel Nürnbergs nach dem Osten im 15—16 Jahrhundert, *Beiträge zur Wirtschaftsgeschichte Nürnbergs*. Vol. I, Nürnberg 1967, p. 370.

[16] Conf. Th. Mayer, *Der auswärtige Handel des Herzogtums Österreich im Mittelalter*, Innsbruck 1909, pp 100, 101. — W. Abel, *Geschichte der deutschen Landwirtschaft*, Stuttgart 1962, pp 114—116. — F. Lütge, *Strukturwandlungen im ostdeutschen und osteuropäischen Fernhandel des 14—16 Jahrhunderts*, München 1964, pp 28, 29.

[17] In the customs books of Pozsony copper exports of only 393 cwts are registered in the value of 717 florins. However, it is an important fact that "red" copper was handled here — though of second-rate quality but fit for industrial use — and not crude ("black") copper. (Kováts, *op. cit.*, pp 191, 195, 196, 200.)

[18] O. Paulinyi, *A középkori magyar réztermelés gazdasági jelentősége*, Különnyomat a Károlyi Árpád Emlékkönyvből (Economic Significance of Hungary's Medieval Copper Production, Reprint from the Árpád Károlyi Memorial Volume), Budapest 1933, pp 6—8, 15—16. — H. Wendt, *Schlesien und der Orient*, Breslau 1916, pp 61, 62. — O. R. Halaga, Kaufleute und Handelsgüter der Hanse im Karpatengebiet, *Hansische Geschichtsblätter*, Vol. 85, Köln-Graz 1967, pp 66—70, 74—76.

This practice may be attributed chiefly to the fact that Hungarian copper, except some "red" copper, was unfit for immediate industrial processing, being so-called black (or crude) copper which contained, among others, a considerable amount of silver; before the Thurzó-Fugger period Hungarian metallurgy was incapable of refining this crude product, of isolating the silver and the pure copper required by the industry.[19] The contemporary modern method of refinement consisted of dissociating the silver and the copper by smelting with lead.[20] However, the sources of lead nearest to the copper mines of Northern Hungary were situated on the northern slopes of the Carpathians: in the neighbourhood of Cracow (Olkusz, Trzebinia). The above-described technology of refining copper was established in that region, in all probability, as early as the turn of the 14th and 15th centuries, with the cooperation of South German merchant-capitalists who held interests in precious metal- and copper production. From this time coppersmiths of Nuremberg could obtain pure copper from Cracow.[21]

From the middle of the 15th century nearer sources of raw material assumed a growing importance in supplying the South German copper industry, namely the mines of the Mansfeld area in Central Germany. The produced copper was refined in the foundries of Thuringia or in the outskirts of Nuremberg.[22]

Only sporadic data are available concerning the volume of Hungarian copper production and exports in the times preceding the Thurzó-Fugger period. On the whole, the conclusions which assigned to copper the second place in the exports of 15th century Hungary and estimated its share at $\frac{1}{4}$ to $\frac{1}{5}$ of the total value of exports to the West in the wide sense of the term, can hardly be regarded as exaggerated.[23]

[19] Black copper — produced from the mined copper ore by roasting — contained also baser metals as well as often considerable amounts of precious metals, chiefly silver. "Red" copper and "fine" copper which still contained silver were obtained at further stages of refining, then silver and pure copper were isolated from fine copper. — Paulinyi, *op. cit.*, pp 5, 8—10.; E. Molnár, *A magyar társadalom története az Árpád-kortól Mohácsig* (The Social History of Hungary from the Arpadian Era to the Battle of Mohács), Budapest 1949, p. 171. —Since Hungarian metallurgy was still unable to perform the above-mentioned procedures up to the close of the 15th century, only red copper could be supplied for industrial use, in much smaller quantities than crude copper. Therefore it is understandable that second-rate red copper, fit for industrial use, *was exported* through Pozsony in 1457—58, presumably to Nuremberg, for the export of the registered lots of copper was transacted by the biggest commercial firm of Pozsony, Albert Gailsam and Co., well known for its relations to Nuremberg. (Conf. Note 17 above.)

[20] For the "*Saigern*" method see J. N. Nef, Mining and Metallurgy in Medieval Civilisation. *The Cambridge Economic History of Europe*. Vol. II. *Trade and Industry in the Middle Ages*, Cambridge 1952, pp 479, 480 — For the introduction of the method known from the time of Late Antiquity as an "innovation" and dates of its earlier use in medieval metallurgy see next Note, *op. cit.*, p. 648.

[21] W. v. Stromer, Nürnberger Unternehmer im Karpatenraum. Ein oberdeutsches Buntmetall-Oligopol 1396—1412, *Kwartalnik Historii Kultury Materialnej*. R. **XVI** (1968), nr. *4*, pp 641—661.

[22] W. Möllenberg, *Die Eroberung des Weltmarkts durch das mansfeldische Kupfer. Studien zur Geschichte des Thüringer Saigerhandels im XVI. Jahrhundert*, Gotha 1911, pp. 4—11. — E. Paterna, *Da stunden die Bergkleute auff. Die Herausbildung von Formen kapitalistischer Produktionsverhältnisse und der Klassenkampf der Bergarbeiter im mansfeldischen Kupferschieferbergbau von der Mitte des 15. Jahrhunderts bis zum deutschen Bauernkrieg 1525*, Berlin 1960, Vol. I, pp. 25—38.

[23] O. Paulinyi, Ipar, Kereskedelem (Industry, Trade), *Magyar Művelődéstörténet*. Vol. II, Budapest s. a., pp 171, 172.

In spite of certain recent statements on the subject, we do not think that the general picture presented in the Hungarian literature on economic history dealing with the approximate structure of Hungarian foreign trade with the West in the middle and the second half of the 15th century calls for more than minor modifications. This picture is based, of course, not only on data found in the customs books of Pozsony for the fiscal year 1457—58 but also on records of copper export as well as on other sources (including contemporary estimates of customs revenues and lease-contracts).[24]

The bulk of imports, about 75 per cent, consisted of textiles, mainly cloth, from West European and West-Central European countries. The other, much smaller, items were hardware, mostly of South German and Austrian (Styrian) provenance, "norimbergeries" and sundries totalling 15 to 20 per cent, and, finally the typical articles of medieval long-distance commerce, spices, which accounted for approximately 5 per cent.

In exports, of considerably smaller volume, the value of the principal item, live-stock (cattle, sheep, horses) ran up to approximately 55 per cent; added to this, the share of crude copper amounted to 20 to 25 per cent, while wine, fish, and animal products (hides, etc.) yielded respectively roughly 5 to 10 per cent of the total.

Imports accounted for about $^2/_3$ of Hungary's total trade with the West, while the share of exports was only $^1/_3$; hence, the country's trade balance in the western relation was extremely adverse. To compensate for this import surplus, gold coins and silver in the value of 200—400 000 florins went abroad every year[25] (which, in the period before the appearance of American precious

[24] *Ibid.*, pp 169, 170. — The picture outlined here has been accepted by Hungarian historiography ever since, with slight alterations; see, e. g. J. Szücs, Das Städtewesen in Ungarn im 15—17. Jahrhundert. La Renaissance et la Reformation en Pologne et en Hongrie. 1450—1650, *Studia Historica Acad. Sci. Hung.* **53,** Budapest 1963, p. 108. — Lately E. Fügedi has claimed the necessity of significant corrections in the "traditional" picture of Hungarian medieval trade in his paper, Magyarország külkereskedelme a 16. század elején (Hungary's Foreign Trade in the Early 16th Century), in *Agrártörténeti Szemle,* 1969. No. *1—2,* pp 1—17. — For our remarks see Note 25.

[25] Fügedi's correction reduces the deficit to approximately 100 to 150 000 florins (for the most part in southern and eastern trade). Though his paper is entitled "Hungary's Foreign Trade in the *Early 16th Century*" we have to state our view here because on the ground of his conclusions Fügedi wishes to correct the "traditional" picture outlined above.

(a) When dealing with Hungary's western trade relations the author relies on no other source than "the exemplary work of F. Kováts" based on the customs journals of Pozsony for the fiscal year 1457—58. In fact, regarding the structure of imports and exports respectively he mostly uses the percentual values of trade registered in the customs books of Pozsony for the fiscal year 1457—58. What is more: he starts from the "traditional" proportion of $^1/_3$: $^2/_3$ regarding the relative share of exports and imports in the western direction.

How is it possible then to arrive at a widely different balance of foreign trade? It lies outside the scope of the present work to go into a thorough analysis of Fügedi's comments, only one delicate point is to be raised here.

The author accepts the $^1/_3$: $^2/_3$ ratio of export and import trade with the West as the "actual ratio" on the evidence of the customs books of Pozsony. Since he knows very well that only a small fraction of copper exports were registered in the customs books of Pozsony, he adds copper exports (calculated on the basis of production in the years 1504—1507, so that he combines the copper export figures of the Thurzó—Fugger period with those of 1457—58).

metals, played a noteworthy role in meeting the gold coin requirements of European trade).[26]

In 15th century East-Central Europe Hungary did not stand alone with her ever more lively foreign trade, her initial steps to join in modern-type international commerce on the one hand, and her adverse trade balance, with a concomitant heavy flow of her precious metals and coins to the West, on the other. Notwithstanding the differences found in export items, the picture presented by Bohemia is similar by and large. In the decades following

---

However, the 33.3 per cent: 66.7 per cent ratio of western trade is not that seen — from the truly exemplary statistical analysis of F. Kováts — in the customs books of Pozsony (where the total turnover is made up of only 10.62 per cent export and 89.38 per cent import). These figures derive from the calculations of O. Paulinyi who also started from the customs books of Pozsony, but took into consideration other facts as well. One of the most important of these facts is copper export, the share of which in export commodity structure he put not at 3.6 per cent as found in the customs books of Pozsony, but at 20 to 25 per cent (though estimating the size of copper exports not by the figures of the Thurzó—Fugger Company, but by production in the preceding period). That is how Paulinyi came to draw up a balance according to which imports amounted "only" to twice, and not to eightfold, the value of imports.

Thus, Fügedi doubles copper exports, giving their value as 143 860 florins the second time. This is the principal source of the remarkable improvement of the balance by 100 to 150 000 florins.

Of course, it is possible that around the middle of the 15th century the debit balance of Hungary's trade with the West amounted only to 200 000 or 300 000 florins and not to 400 000 florins (as asserted by Szücs, *op. cit.*, p. 108). In any case Fügedi's paper is unlikely to offer any contribution to a more accurate approach from the angle of quantity.

Further, it may be regarded not only as possible, but almost as certain that the deficit of the balance of western trade was much smaller in the early 16th century than it had been in the middle of the 15th. This statement, however, cannot be made with reference to the customs books of Pozsony for the fiscal year of 1457—58, but has to be based on the analysis of subsequent developments which are to be dealt with in Chapter II, 2 of the present paper.

(b) Though Fügedi's paper is not acceptable as regards Hungary's foreign trade with the *West*, it may be appreciated all the more for the truly revealing information it contains concerning northern and eastern relations. As regards Hungary's foreign trade with the *North*, statistical analysis of the entries found in the customs books of Bártfa (Bardejov) for the years 1504—1507 bears witness to considerable import of textiles (predominantly Bohemian, Moravian and Silesian cloths of medium- and cheaper quality), and to still more significant wine export (to Poland). The evidence derived from the customs books of Nagyszeben (Sibiu) for the year 1500 and of Brassó (Braşov) for the year 1503 in *eastern* relations inform us about the re-export of West European and South German cloths and of Styrian cutlery, as well as about the import of spices and oriental textile fabrics. (Conf. Notes 4 and 12.) — For analysis of partly identical source material see S. Goldenberg, Der Südhandel in den Zollrechnungen von Sibiu (Hermannstadt) im 16. Jahrhundert, *Revue des études sud-est européennes* Tome **II** (1964), No. *3—4*, pp 385—421. — Finally, the author has drawn a noteworthy conclusion concerning the significant volume of Hungary's *southern* trade with the Turks before the Battle of Mohács (even if its numerical appraisal — putting its share to 20 per cent of the total of Hungarian foreign trade — is held to be an over-statement).

[26] F. Kováts, A magyar arany világtörténeti jelentősége és kereskedelmi összeköttetéseink a nyugattal a középkorban (The World-historical Significance of Hungarian Gold and Hungary's Trade Relations with the West in the Middle Ages), *Történeti Szemle*, 1922, p. 130. — O. Paulinyi, Magyarország aranytermelése a XV. század végén és a XVI. század elején (Hungary's Gold Production in the Late 15th and Early 16th centuries), *A Klebelsberg Kunó Magyar Történetkutató Intézet Évkönyve*, Budapest 1936, pp 79—81. — Stromer, *op. cit.*, pp 647, 649. — Halaga, *op. cit.*, p. 84. — Conf. R. de Roover, La balance commerciale entre les Pays Bas et l'Italie au quinzième siècle, *Revue belge de philologie et d'histoire*, Vol. **37** (1959), pp 374—376.

the Battle of Lipany (1434) exports increased in agricultural produce, even in products of handicraft industry, (particularly in cloth, which found a ready market in Hungary, too). Yet trade with the West rested on the import of consumers' goods and the export of silver: deficit was balanced by the export of precious metals.[27]

Hungary and Bohemia, whose gold and silver had attracted western merchants for a long time, actually joined in the new-type international trade, but in part they still retained its old-type forms, too; as the two precious-metal reservoirs of medieval Europe both countries held the interest of foreign merchants.

Although Poland lacked precious metals, her foreign trade showed a similar advance in western relations about the middle of the 15th century: along the overland routes of cattle and fur exports running across the country[28] and especially on the Baltic when, as a result of the so-called Thirteen Years' War fought against the Teutonic Knights, Poland regained access to the mouth of the Vistula[29]. This livelier trade with the West produced a similarly unfavourable balance in most years of the century, at least in shipments by the Baltic route which was assuming outstanding significance in the modern-type trade. Sea-borne exports to Western Europe also increased, in grain and particularly in timber, a raw material in strong demand by Dutch, English, and even Portuguese shipyards, but their value fell far behind that of the steadily growing imports the bulk of which was made up, here too, of cloth (Flemish and English fabrics) and salt from Brittany.[30]

It was the needs of West European economic development which induced Hungary and the other East-Central European countries to join in the unfolding modern-type international trade and started the rise of their trade with the West. In certain regions of Western and West-Central Europe industrial production (spinning and weaving handicrafts in particular, furthermore metal industries) reached the first steps towards capitalism, in various forms of the putting out system, when, besides meeting domestic requirements, it became necessary to acquire foreign selling markets, to find areas for continuous exports. Moreover, these regions began to develop a continuous demand for imports of certain quantities of foodstuffs and raw materials. These new elements — the need of exports in the first place — created new motives which induced West European trade to approach the countries of East-Central Europe.

[27] J. Janáček, Der böhmische Außenhandel in der Hälfte des 15. Jahrhunderts. *Historica*, Vol. **IV** (1962), Praha, pp 49, 58. — H. Schenk, Die Beziehungen zwischen Nürnberg und Prag, 1450—1500, *Tagung zu Marburg*, 1967.

[28] H. Samsonowicz, Handel Lublina na przełomie XV i XVI w, *Przegląd Historiczny*, Tom **XIX**, Zeszyt *4*, 1968, pp 612, 613.

[29] M. Małowist, Die Problematik der sozial-wirtschaftlichen Geschichte Polens vom 15. bis zum 17. Jahrhundert, *La Renaissance et la Réformation en Pologne et en Hongrie 1450—1650*, Budapest 1963, p. 17.

[30] A. Mączak—H. Samsonowicz, La zone Baltique; l'un des éléments du marché européen. *Acta Poloniae Historica*, **XI** (1965) Warsaw, pp 77, 78, 82. — The debit balance of the trade passing through the most important Baltic port, Gdańsk, grew worse during the first half of the 15th century, deficit increasing from 1 : 2.2 to 1 : 3.5, culminating at the middle of the century, to diminish gradually from 1 : 3 to 1 : 1.4 in the years between 1460 and 1475 (*Ibid.*, p. 83.). For the latter tendency and further improvement see Note 44 of Chapter II, 2.

This incipient contact with western modern trade, however, indicates the advance of the countries of East-Central Europe as well. Business became feasible because the internal development of these countries reached a level which afforded a basis for such activities: in addition to luxuries for the ruling classes, new features appeared in the market demand; there arose new requirements for plain consumers' goods, for industrial products. On the other hand, a more advanced stage of agriculture and mining made it possible to export certain primary products. Joining in the new-type international trade could come about only because the demands and endeavours of western trade found the countries of East-Central Europe not in a backward state, stagnating on the level of feudal natural economy, but with broadening relations of market economy, and in historical circumstances where the principal trend of European economic development was progressing towards a levelling of the stage of West- and East European development and towards getting over the backwardness of the East European societies which had stepped on the road of feudalism at a later date.[31]

In this first period of joining in the modern-type international commerce the balance of foreign trade necessarily showed an adverse character in the East-Central European countries, since the new developments had been elicited and launched by the dynamism of West European economic growth and its active need of foreign markets. In addition, the fact that the western trade relations of certain East-Central European countries (Hungary and Bohemia) were partly still marked by earlier, "old-type" features, by the unaltered attraction of their precious metals, their gold and silver coins, for western merchants, also contributed to rendering the trade balance unfavourable.

The question to be raised here is whether the countries of East-Central Europe found means to correct their adverse foreign trade balance in the further course of events, whether they were able to answer the "challenge" of western imports with adequate exports. To view the topic from a wider perspective: whether, like Western Europe, they were able to increase and develop their commodity productions to the first steps towards capitalism, while availing themselves of the possibilities afforded by joining the modern-type international trade.

2

The above outlined picture of Hungary's foreign trade with the West may be compared with the situation prevailing about one century later; with reference to the case of Hungary, the *second stage* of the process in the course of which East-Central Europe came to participate in the evolving modern-type international trade is seen in the mid-16th century. This has been made possible chiefly by the customs journals of the year 1542 that have survived and been studied thoroughly.[1] This source is all the more valuable

[31] Zs. P. Pach, Das Entwicklungsniveau der feudalen Agrarverhältnisse in Ungarn in der zweiten Hälfte des XV. Jahrhunderts, *Studia Historica Acad. Sci. Hung.*, Vol. 46, Budapest 1960, pp 44—45.

[1] Gy. Ember, Külkereskedelmünk történetéhez a XVI. században (Contribution to the History of Hungary's Foreign Trade in the 16th Century). *A Magyar Tudományos Akadémia Társadalmi—Történeti Tudományok Osztályának Közleményei* **VIII** (1958), No. *4*, pp 309—348;

as the journals refer not only to the customs office of Pozsony (Bratislava) (as do the books of 1457—58), but to several customs offices on the western border; therefore, theoretically, they throw a light on the entire, strictly interpreted, westbound foreign trade of Hungary.[2]

On the testimony of the journals of 1542, the overwhelming share and volume of textile goods continued to be the most characteristic feature of Hungary's imports from the West. In the year 1542 cloth of approximately 56 000 florins value, linen of over 17 000 florins, and clothing articles of about 21 000 florins value passed through the customs houses of the western border into the country so that the aggregate customs value of textiles, amounting to over 97 000 florins, accounted for 68.67 per cent of the total of imports. Even though these figures — numerically as well as percentually — fell behind those registered in the customs books of Pozsony for 1457—58 (a point to be dealt with later), the remarkably large share of textile goods remained the principal characteristic of imports from the West.[3]

The other items of import, falling far behind textiles, are also very similar to those purchased in the 15th century. Hardware, chiefly knives, accounted for 9 per cent of imports, norimbergeries and sundries for 7.26 per cent, spices (pepper in the first place) for 3.84 per cent (to say nothing here of goods with a still smaller share).

Thus no essential modification can be observed in the structure of imports compared to the mid-15th century pattern. The situation is, however, quite different in exports. In the customs books of Pozsony for 1457—58, live-stock exports already showed a majority, yet, both in share and value they remained far behind the principal import article, cloth; moreover, the item of livestock comprised exports of several species of animals. Compared to these records, the journals of 1542 reveal a substantial change. Whereas the customs value of textile articles, accounting for 68.67 per cent of imports, was under 100 000 florins, the value of live-stock exports exceeded 300 000 florins and accounted for 93.42 per cent of all the exports registered in the customs journals. Within live-stock exports the absolute preponderance of one species of animal is manifest, for the export of oxen alone represented

---

Magyarország XVI. századi külkereskedelmének történetéhez (Contribution to the History of Hungarian Foreign Trade in the 16th Century), *Századok*, 1961, No. *1*, pp 1—46. — The data quoted in the present paper from the customs journals for the year 1542 have been borrowed from these two studies or calculated from the figures they contain.

[2] The customs journals from the year 1542 refer to 19 custom-houses: to that of Pozsony and its outstations north and south of the Danube (of the latter to that of Sopron and another four stations), furthermore to the custom-house of Óvár; of Nagyszombat (Trnava) and its outstations, as well as to that of Szempc (Senec).

[3] In the cloth imports of approximately 10 500 pieces, West European (English, Flemish, Lower Rhenish) cloths, but chiefly Silesian and South German fabrics are encountered. Cloth of Breslau (Wrocław), and of Nuremberg occupied the first place in the total volume and value, respectively. (Verbal communication of Gy. Ember.) — I. Bog informs us about still larger cloth export from Nuremberg to Hungary (*Erste Tagung des Seminars für Sozial- und Wirtschaftsgeschichte der Philipps-Universität zu Marburg an der Lahn*, 1967, Diskussionsprotokoll, pp 24, 25). — On South German textile fabrics passing through Wiener Neustadt between 1524 and 1538 see O. Pickl, *Das älteste Geschäftsbuch Österreichs. Die Gewölberegister der Wiener Neustädter Firma Alexius Funck, 1516- ca. 1538, und verwandtes Material zur Geschichte des steyrischen Handels im 15—16. Jahrhundert*, Graz 1966.

a value of 275 000 florins, a share of over 85 per cent, numerically 27 529 animals.[4]

Beside this overwhelming preponderance of live-stock, notably cattle (oxen) exports, other items of agrarian products were practically dwarfed; wine, fish, and hides, which accounted respectively for 5 to 10 per cent of mid-15th century exports to the West hardly had a total share of 6 per cent in the exports registered in the customs journals of 1542, let alone grain export which had been and still was of almost negligible volume.

Truly astonishing here is the small share of wine. In mid-15th century exports to the West, wine accounted for about 5 to 10 per cent of the total value, in the customs books of Pozsony actually for 23.21 per cent; wine exports through Pozsony in the customs value of 4592 florins were handled chiefly by Moravian merchants in exchange for their supplies of cloth.[5] The customs journals of 1542, on the other hand, show wine exports to have had a share of altogether 1.91 per cent, amounting only to 6200 florins customs value, though prices had risen in the meantime. To make the issue still more questionable it must be added that not only wine exports from Pozsony and its environs passed through the customs offices figuring in the customs journals of 1542, but also consignments from the Sopron—Ruszt wine-lands, whether the carriers used the "lower route" leading through Pozsony, or, less often, the "upper route" running from Sopron through Lower Austria to towns of Bohemia, Moravia and Silesia.[6]

In connection with this issue it should be taken into consideration that the establishing of taverns by landlords was becoming a widespread practice in the meantime, the principal form of selling wine being based on exploiting the "forced" rural market. However, this consumption could hardly have reduced the volume of exports which had to comply with certain qualitative requirements.[7] A more acceptable explanation is that part of the actually delivered exports of wine were not entered in the customs journals because they were duty-free. Ruszt, which belonged to the royal estate

[4] The majority of oxen exports (15 513 head) passed through Szempc where there had been no custom-station in the 15th century. Considerable exports (8678 head of oxen) passed through Nagyszombat which was an insignificant branch station of the customs office of Trencsén (Trenčín) in the 15th century. (Conf. Act 1498 : 34; Ember, *op. cit.*, 1958, pp 312, 315). Although such important new customs stations had been established in the meantime to handle exports of oxen to the West, 1994 head of oxen – over half a thousand more than in 1457—58 — were driven west in 1542 after having been passed by the customs office of Pozsony.

Compared to exports of oxen in the value of 275 290 florins and the total of cattle exports amounting to 282 777 florins, exports of horses for 13 671 florins and of sheep for 4614 florins were insignificant. Stagnation of sheep export (more precisely, its decline since prices had risen in the meantime) also indicated a noteworthy change compared to the commodity structure of exports in 1457—58.

[5] F. Kováts, *Nyugatmagyarország áruforgalma a XV. században a pozsonyi harmincadkönyv alapján* (West Hungary's Trade in the 15th Century, Based on the Customs Journals of Pozsony), Budapest 1902, pp 185, 192, 207.

[6] H. Prickler, Zur Geschichte des burgenländisch-westungarischen Weinhandels in die Oberländer Böhmen, Mähren, Schlesien und Polen, *Zeitschrift für Ostforschung*, **14.** Jg. (1965) Heft *4*, pp 736—738.

[7] Zs. P. Pach, Die ungarische Agrarentwicklung im 16—17. Jahrhundert. Abbiegung vom westeuropäischen Entwicklungsgang. *Studia Historica Acad. Sci. Hung.*, Vol. **54.**, Budapest 1964, pp 18—20.

of Óvár from 1519, enjoyed permanent exemption from customs duty; Sopron, Kőszeg, and a few other villages, having suffered heavy damage during the campaigns of 1529 and 1532, were exempted from duty for a certain period of time.[8] It should furthermore be taken into account that foreign trade in wine must have been badly limited in 1542 by the vicissitudes of war.[9]

The next point to be examined is the trade in copper which, with an approximately 20 to 25 per cent share in the commodity structure of mid-15th century exports, was second to live-stock alone. Obviously, its importance may be assumed to have increased during the period of the Thurzó-Fugger Company's activity. This must have been the situation still in 1542, too, for it was only a few years later (in 1546) that the House of Fugger withdrew from Hungarian (Slovak) copper mining. Yet, the share of copper exports registered in the journals of 1542 was remarkably small, amounting only to 0.33 per cent.

This figure, even more striking than the diminished ratio of wine exports, may be ascribed to two circumstances. First, a certain quota of copper exports may have been free of duty, for different reasons. This issue calls for further studies and analyses.[10] Secondly, as in the 15th so also in the 16th century, and consequently in 1542, the major part of exported copper did not leave the country on any of the strictly western routes, but passed at south-western, north-western and northern customs offices whose journals have been lost. This assertion is confirmed by incontrovertible documentary evidence concerning the routes used by the Thurzó-Fugger Company for their copper exports.[11]

In the late 15th and early 16th centuries, this big company exported large quantities of copper by the traditional south-western route, with the essential difference that a copper refinery (*Saigerhütte*) was set up near the Carinthian town Villach, at Fuggerau, from where it supplied to Venice copper not in its crude form (containing also silver), but in a refined form fit for industrial use. However, from the opening decade of the 16th century copper export to Italy gradually lost ground to exports to the Netherlands, notably to Antwerp; a traditional outlet of Hungarian copper for some time, Antwerp became the principal buyers' market in the Fugger period (right up to the 1560s). Whereas around 1500 over 32 per cent of the Com-

[8] Prickler, *op. cit.*, Heft *2*, p. 299; Heft *3*, pp 500-501; Heft *4*, pp 731, 732.

[9] Numerical details about wine exports from Sopron are available from some twenty-five years later. From May, 1566, to March, 1567, 11 673 *akó*s of wine were sold in other countries, chiefly in Bohemia, see I. Házi, Az 1566. évi soproni borkereskedelem (Wine Trade of Sopron in the Year 1566), *Soproni Szemle*, 1959, pp 151—157, 288. Since in Sopron the *akó* was of 72.5 liters volume, this quantity exceeded the wine exports which passed through Pozsony in 1457—58 by approximately 70 per cent. (9185 *akó*s; 1 Pozsony *akó* = 54.1527 l. — Kováts, *op. cit.*, pp 185, 194.)

From the above cited evidence it clearly emerges that about the middle of the 16th century West Hungary's wine export considerably exceeded the value registered in the customs journals of 1542.

[10] Conf. G. Probszt, Königin Maria und die niederungarischen Bergstädte, *Zeitschrif für Ostforschung*, **15**. Jg. (1966) Heft *4*.; Ember, *op. cit.* (1961), p. 5.

[11] The latest account of the trade routes used by the Fuggers for their copper exports comes from J. Vlachovič, Slovak Copper Boom on World Markets of the 16th and the First Quarter of the 17th Centuries. *Studia Historica Slovaca*. I, Bratislava, 1963, pp 68, 69 — with numerous references.

pany's copper exports went to Venice and Triest, and only 24 per cent to Antwerp, a few years later Italy was the destination of not more than 13 per cent, and the Netherlands of nearly 50 per cent. In the 1510s and 20s this ratio underwent a further modification in favour of western exports.[12]

At this time the route of Hungarian copper to western markets did not lead directly westward, but first turned north-west or north. It followed the valley of the river Vág, touching Rózsahegy (Ružomberok) and Zsolna (Žilina), passing, consequently, through the area of the Trencsén (Trenčín) customs office, to leave the country by the mountain pass of Jablonka in the direction of Wrocław. From here (through Leipzig) the copper was taken to the other, Thuringian refinery of the Fuggers (to Hohenkirchen near Georgenthal), or on the Oder to Szczecin (Stettin), or via Poznań and Toruń, on the Vistula, to Gdańsk. Another route of the Hungarian copper exports, the most important one, led to Cracow, then on the Vistula similarly to Gdańsk, from where the goods were shipped by the Baltic-North Sea route to Antwerp.[13]

One cannot help wondering why no considerable quantities of Hungarian copper were taken to Southern Germany, particularly by the direct western (Danube) route, in the first half of the 16th century, that is in the Fugger period.[14] At the time Nuremberg was a flourishing centre of copper industry; moreover, the Fugger Company was in a position to supply not only crude (and second-rate) copper, but also the refined product fit for industrial use, even directly from Besztercebánya (Banská Bystrica), for a refinery had been put into operation in the meantime here, too.[15]

The truth is that Nuremberg, even though the bulk of the raw material requirements of its copper industry was covered at this time by the Mansfeld district of Central Germany,[16] was actually interested also in Hungarian

[12] H. van der Wee, *The Growth of the Antwerp Market and the European Economy (fourteenth-sixteenth centuries)*, The Hague 1963, I, Statistics, p. 523. Hungarian Copper Trade. Average Yearly Copper Exports of the Fuggers, 1497—1538. -- Other exports of copper were forwarded to Nuremberg, Leipzig, Hamburg, Frankfurt on the Main, and Lüneburg, in all probability with the Netherlands as the final destination of a considerable part of these consignments, too. (*Ibid.*, p. 522.)

[13] Besides the work mentioned in Note 11 and its sources, see P. Jeannin, Le cuivre, les Fugger et la Hanse, *Annales, Économies-Sociétés-Civilisation.* 1955, No. 2, pp 229—236; O. R. Halaga, Kaufleute und Handelsgüter der Hanse im Karpatengebiet, *Hansische Geschichtsblätter*, **85.** Jg (1967), pp 69, 70.

[14] Statements published in the Fugger literature agree with the evidence found in the Hungarian customs journals of 1542. The route leading to South Germany via Pozsony and Vienna was seldom used by the Company; Hungarian copper more often arrived at Nuremberg and other German towns from Cracow, Breslau (Wrocław) or Hohenkirchen. -- M. Jansen, *Jakob Fugger der Reiche*, Leipzig 1910, pp 140, 143; Vlachovič, *op. cit.*, p. 69; van der Wee, *op. cit.*, I, p. 522.

[15] At Mostyenic, near Zólyomlipcse (Moštenica, Slovenská L'upča) — as stated already by O. Paulinyi, *A középkori magyar réztermelés gazdasági jelentősége* (Economic Significance of Hungary's Medieval Copper Production). Reprint from the Árpád Károlyi Memorial Volume. Budapest 1933, p. 9.

[16] In the 1530s about 24 000 cwts of pure copper was marketed every year by the refineries of Thuringia; of this quantity approximately 10 000 cwts went to Nuremberg. In addition to copper from Mansfeld, Bohemian (Kutná Hora, Kuttenberg) and from time to time Tyrolean copper also played a certain part in the raw material supply of Nuremberg. — On this subject see W. Möllenberg, *Die Eroberung des Weltmarkts durch das manfeldische Kupfer. Studien zur Geschichte des Thüringer Saigerhandels im XVI. Jahrhundert*, Gotha, 1911, pp 48, 49; R. Klier, Nürnberg und Kuttenberg, *Mitteilungen des Vereins für Geschichte der Stadt Nürnberg*, **48.** Bd. 1958, p. 76.

copper and made attempts in this direction as well.[17] In turn, the Fuggers, though they supplied some quantities of copper from Hohenkirchen to South Germany, too, were much more interested in the main international market of copper, an industrial raw material which could be utilized in numerous ways.[18] As has been shown, from the first decade of the 16th century they reduced their activities on the North-Italian copper market, too, and turned to the centre of the modern-type international traffic on the Atlantic coast, notably to Antwerp which, during two thirds of the 16th century, occupied a central position in international copper — as well as textile — trade.[19] Big quantities of copper and copper articles were forwarded from Antwerp, among other places to Spain (Seville) and Portugal (Lisbon), to be sent from there to overseas colonies in the form of coins, utensils, and, last but not least, as rings and bracelets for a highly lucrative "barter" with the natives.[20]

As a result of large investments and the use of the best techniques known to the age, copper mining and metallurgy made progress and prospered at Besztercebánya in the Thurzó—Fugger period: between 1494 and 1546 the average yearly copper production of the Company amounted to about 24 000 cwts.[21] If only 80 per cent of the total production is taken to have been exported[22] and calculation is based on 7 Rhenish florins per cwt, regarded

[17] For the attempts of Nuremberg in 1525, when the Fuggers were temporarily barred from activity, see F. Lütge, Der Handel Nürnbergs nach dem Osten im 15—16. Jahrhundert, *Beiträge zur Wirtschaftsgeschichte Nürnbergs*, I. Bd., Nürnberg 1967, pp 356—360; for the copper deliveries from Hohenkirchen to Nuremberg, E. Koch, Das Hütten- und Hammerwerk der Fugger zu Hohenkirchen bei Georgenthal in Thüringen 1494—1549, *Zeitschrift des Vereins für thüringische Geschichte und Altertumskunde*, Neue Folge, **XXVII**, Bd., Jena 1927, pp 118, 119.

[18] Apart from articles of everyday use (vessels, etc.) — usually made of brass (alloy of copper with zinc) — copper was an important raw material of war industry (gun-founding), of building- and shipbuilding industries, as well as of coinage; for use in colonial trade see Note 20.

[19] P. Jeannin, Les relations économiques des villes de la Baltique avec Anvers au XVIe siècle, *Vierteljahrschrift für Sozial- und Wirtschaftsgeschichte*, **43.** Bd. 1956, p. 205; J. A. van Houtte, Anvers au XVe et XVIe siècle: expansion et apogée, *Annales, Économies-Sociétés-Civilisations*, 1961, No. *2*, p. 256. — Conf. Zs. P. Pach, The Shifting of International Trade Routes in the 15th—17th Centuries, *Acta Historica Acad. Sci. Hung.* (1968) tom. **14**, *no.* 3—4. p. 295.

[20] J. A. Goris, *Études sur les colonies marchandes mériodionales (Portugais, Espagnols, Italiens) à Anvers de 1488 à 1567. Contribution à l'histoire des débuts du capitalisme moderne*, Louvain 1925, pp 239—243. — C. H. Haring, *Trade and Navigation between Spain and the Indies in the time of the Hapsburgs*, Cambridge, Mass. 1918, p. 156. — Lütge, *op. cit.*, p. 355.

[21] The numerical data of the Fugger Company's copper- (and silver) production have been grouped lately by Vlachovič, *op. cit.*, p. 70. — The figures for the period from 1494 to 1546 as well as the yearly average of approximately 24 000 (23 899) cwts calculated from these data refer to the amount of refined copper gained at one *Saigerhütte* at home and two abroad of the Company. — Conf. the estimate of Paulinyi who put the average yearly copper production in the period from 1504 to 1507 at about 28 000 cwts, including approximately 19 000 cwts of first-rate and 9000 cwts of second-rate copper. — *Op. cit.*, p. 9 and *Magyar Művelődéstörténet*, Budapest s. a. Vol. II, p. 192. — See also E. Molnár, *A magyar társadalom története az Árpádkortól Mohácsig* (The Social History of Hungary from the Arpadian Era to the Battle of Mohács), Budapest 1949, p. 177.).

[22] The smallest volume of exports has been considered. For instance the figures of Vlachovič (*op. cit.*, p. 71) suggest that in the years between 1510 and 1519 about 83 per cent of the production was exported to Antwerp alone (more than half of it via Gdańsk). The statistics of van der Wee (*op. cit.*, vol. I, p. 523) also show a higher ratio of exports, naturally with due regard to the fact that the consignments were entered there in Antwerp

as an exceedingly low price in the middle of the century, Hungarian copper represented an item amounting to over 100 000 Hungarian florins on the list of exports. Hence, it undoubtedly occupied the second place, coming directly after cattle, in the commodity structure of Hungary's exports to the West in the years around the customs journals of 1542.[23]

Let us revert here for a moment to the customs journals of 1542, containing records of only a mere fraction of these large-scale copper exports, in order to find out what the balance of western foreign trade looked like without copper exports. It actually displays essential differences compared to the mid-15th century picture. According to the data registered in the customs journals, exports to the west amounted to about 323 000, imports from the west to about 142 000 florins, that is to say imports came to no more than 43–44 per cent of exports.[24] Hence, even without copper, western trade showed a highly active balance, contrary to the very adverse balance (despite copper exports) observed in the middle of the 15th century. An amazing turn-about, indeed. The question inevitably arises how it was possible that the balance of Hungary's western foreign trade underwent such a far-reaching change from the middle of the 15th to the middle of the 16th century. This question has to be posed even if numerical conclusions regarding the adverse character of the balance in the 15th century may have been exaggerated in some degree,[25] and even if the data obtained by the study of the customs journals of 1542 are incomplete and liable to rouse certain objections.[26] All apposite cor-

---

cwts (equivalent to 47.0156 kg.; op. cit. p. 78), whereas the above quoted figures of production refer to mine cwts (= 1.135 Vienna cwt = 63.56 kg). — 1 Rhenish florin = 0.8 Hungarian florin. (Conf. Vlachovič, *op. cit.*, pp 73, 77, 78.) — The result of our calculations of the value of copper export may therefore be denoted as minimal. – E. Fügedi – starting from the production figures laid down by Paulinyi – puts the yearly amount of copper exports at 143 860 florins in the early 16th century. (Magyarország külkereskedelme a XVI. század elején (Hungary's Foreign Trade in the Early 16th Century), *Agrártörténeti Szemle*, 1969. No. *1—2*. p. 9.)

[23] Even when they left the country by a northward route, copper exports have to be regarded in a wider sense as western trade, for the bulk was finally carried to buyers' markets of Western Europe. On the other hand, the part of wine export carried northward — which, as pointed out before (II, 1. Note 25), was of considerable volume as early as the opening decade of the 16th century — cannot be treated as western trade, because the great majority of these consignments of wine were sold on Polish markets.

[24] The customs value of Hungary's strictly western trade amounted to 465 282 florins on the evidence of the customs journals of 1542, imports accounting for 30.46 per cent in the value of 141 732 florins, exports for 69.48 per cent in the value of 323 272 florins. (A tiny fraction, 0.06 per cent of total trade, came from "mixed" items defying distribution.) — Ember, *op. cit.*, 1961, p. 11.

[25] See Chapter II, 1, Note 25.

[26] Three objections may be raised. — (a) Contrary to the author's statement (Ember, *op. cit.*, 1961, p. 6), [the entries to be found in the customs journals of 1542 do not embrace almost 84 per cent of the total of Hungary's western foreign trade in the wider sense of the word; they comprise a smaller part. — (b) They do not cover even the whole of strictly western trade, because at certain custom-houses only exports were registered, and no imports. The reason of this is not that these custom-houses did not collect customs duty because the merchants arriving from other countries had already paid duty at a customs station lying nearer to the border (Ember, *op. cit.*, 1958, p. 323) but that the source is incomplete. — (c) The surviving customs journals, unfortunately from 1542, refer to a war year following the capture of Buda Castle by the Turks, hence a year which "cannot be regarded as characteristic of the period" and much rather reflects "extraordinary conditions". — Conf. J. Szűcs, Das Städtewesen in Ungarn im 15—17 Jahrhundert. La Renaissance et la Réformation en Pologne et en Hongrie, 1450– 1650, *Studia Historica*

rections may only reduce the extent of the change, but they cannot by any means eliminate the essential difference between mid-15th century and mid-16th century conditions.

The cause of this change should be ascribed to the joint effect of two factors, namely the limited possibilities of imports from, and growing possibilities of exports to, the West.

The first factor is closely connected with political events, with the capture of Buda by the Turks and the Turkish occupation. This is all too clearly illustrated by a comparison between the import figures of 1457—58 and 1542. As has been cited before, imports of a customs value of 166 000 florins, including cloth imports of over 15 000 pieces in the value of nearly 100 000 florins, with a total of over 130 000 florins for textile imports, are registered in the customs books of Pozsony. In the customs books of 1542, on the other hand, records refer only to imports of 141 000 florins customs value, including cloth imports of about 10 500 pieces in the value of about 56 000 florins, while the total value of textiles is approximately 97 000 florins.

The fact that the total imports passing through the western customhouses in 1542 — even without the import data of certain customs stations[27] — fell far behind the imports handled at Pozsony alone in 1457—58, emphasizes the change too strongly. It should be borne in mind that 1542, the year following the fall of Buda and the time of attempts to recapture it, cannot have favoured foreign trade and import activities. In the 1550s years western trade, imports and exports alike, certainly did assume larger proportions. Yet it is beyond doubt that the Ottoman conquest and the occupation of Central Hungary by the Turks confined the market of western products in the country and permanently limited the expansion of import trade.[28]

Acad. Sci. Hung., Vol. **53.** Budapest, 1963, p. 131; furthermore I. Bog, J. Janáček and O. Pickl's contribution at the conference on economic history held in Marburg in 1967. *Diskussionsprotokoll*, Marburg 1968, pp 23 -26.

The first objection — even without more ground than the facts stated in connection with copper exports — is justified as regards western trade in a wider sense. At the same time it is clear that taking copper export into account brings a considerable surplus of exports.

The second objection, the possible incompleteness of the journals cannot be ruled out even in connection with strictly western trade. However, it must be remarked here that such gaps have been encountered not only in records of imports, but also in those of exports — as shown by wine export from West Hungary.

As concerns the third objection it is evident that 1542 was an unfavourable year for foreign trade: the "extraordinary conditions" prevailing in 1542 doubtlessly reduced the total volume of trade. That these adverse conditions affected both import and export is proved by documentary evidence: both in earlier years (before 1526) and later, already in the 1550s and '60s, exports of oxen are known to have been much larger than those registered in the customs journals of the year 1542. Therefore the year 1542, if not in respect of total volume of foreign trade, but in the proportions of the balance of trade may after all have been on the whole typical of the "period", of course of the period *following* the fall of Buda and dismemberment of the country into three parts (less so of the period preceding 1541). — To these points we shall come back later.

[27] See Note 26.

[28] The occupation of the capital by the Turks in itself entailed such consequences, for Buda and Pest were the most important markets and distribution centres of merchandise imported from the West before the conquest. — A. Kubinyi, Budai kereskedők udvari szállításai a Jagelló-korban (Supplies by Merchants of Buda to the Court in the Jagello Age). *Budapest régiségei*. Vol. **XIX.** Budapest 1959, pp 109—110.

Of course, this does not imply that henceforth only so-called Royal Hungary (and Transylvania) counted as markets of western import articles, of textiles and hardware, of various kinds of cloth. Such commodities continued to reach the part of the country which was under Turkish rule but contrived to maintain active trade relations.[29] However, sales were hampered and restricted by the ravages of the wars and the vicissitudes of the occupation,[30] and after a certain consolidation of conditions under the newly established rule also by the circumstance that in several respects occupied territories were integrated into the economic domain of the Ottoman Empire. Hungary's trade with the Turks had not been insignificant before the Battle of Mohács, and oriental textile imports (silks, woollen fabrics, etc.) passed through the Transylvanian customs stations Brassó (Braşov) and Nagyszeben (Sibiu) as well as through the then still functioning southern customs offices of Nándorfehérvár (Beograd) and Temesvár (Timişoara).[31] After the fall of Buda, when the country was torn into three parts, the supply of goods from the Balkan provinces of the Turkish Empire was unavoidably multiplied. In the 1570s the value of cloth imported from the West to Buda was surpassed in a steadily increasing degree by that of textile articles arriving from the Balkan areas under Turkish rule.[32]

[29] Goods imported from the West reached Turkish-occupied parts of Hungary not only from a strictly western direction, but also from the south-west, passing through the Slavonian custom-houses (Murska Sobota, Nedelica, Varaždin) which were under the management of the Treasury of Lower Austria; therefore their customs journals are not available. The commodity structure of these imports of smaller volume was similar: by these routes, too, merchants brought in cloths (the kinds figuring in the customs journals of 1542), as well as articles of clothing (chiefly hats) and hardware (knives). — L. Ruzsás, Városi fejlődés a Dunántúlon a XVI--XVII. században (Urban Development in Transdanubia in the Sixteenth and Seventeenth Centuries), *Szigetvári Emlékkönyv 1566—1966*, Budapest 1966, pp 210, 211.

[30] This is clearly illustrated by the turn of events connected with the Hungarian import of Nuremberg cloth, an important item on the import list (conf. Note 3). The prosperity experienced by the textile industry of Nuremberg between 1520 and 1530 was due mainly to favourable sales on Hungarian markets. However, when Hungary was torn by war and paralyzed by occupation, cloth production sank rapidly at Nuremberg. This applies not only to the years of the large campaigns, for the volume of production remained permanently small: in 1568 cloth production amounted only to 18 per cent of the output of the 1520s. — I. Bog's contribution at the conference of economic history in Marburg. *Diskussionsprotokoll*, pp 24, 25.

[31] S. Goldenberg, Der Südhandel in den Zollrechnungen von Sibiu (Hermannstadt) im 16. Jahrhundert, *Revue des études sud-est européennes*, Tome II, No. *3--4*, 1964, p. 390; Fügedi, *op. cit.*, pp 4, 8.

[32] The customs duty collected in 1571 at Buda on clothing imported from the West and from territories of the Turkish Empire respectively was in a proportion as is 80 to 140. In 1573 the customs duty collected on the goods imported from these two directions showed a proportion of 40 : 150; in 1580 the ratio was 5 : 150. The enormous shift which took place in a few years can be interpreted only as a consequence of Turkish restrictive measures explaining why stocks of western merchandise were completely exhausted at Buda and Pest, while Balkan clothes were worn almost exclusively. — L. Fekete — Gy. Káldy Nagy, *Budai török számadáskönyvek 1550—1580* (Turkish Account Books of Buda 1550--1580), Budapest 1962, pp 577, 578.

Another line of Turkish economic policy, displaying a similar tendency, becomes noticeable in the same period by the settlement of Turkish-Balkan burghers, following the garrison troops, in Transdanubian towns and boroughs of occupied Hungary. These new settlers also increased the demand for textile imports from the Balkans. — Ruzsás, *op. cit.*, pp 213—216.

The second factor of the change in trade balance stems from the large increase of exports, notably cattle export, in the period from the middle of the 15th to the middle of the 16th century. In this respect, too, comparison of the entries of 1457—58 and those of 1542 furnishes revealing information, particularly when the compared data are interpreted properly. According to the customs books of Pozsony, during the year they cover, 1466 oxen were driven across the border in the customs value of 4153 florins, which amounted to 21 per cent of the exports passing through Pozsony. However, from the journals of 1542 we learn about the export of 27 529 oxen to the West, whose customs value, 275 290 florins, represented 85.15 per cent of the registered exports.[33] The huge difference between the two respective groups of data has to be denoted as characteristic even if we are fully aware of the facts that the customs books for 1457—58 inform us only about the droves of oxen passing at the customs office of Pozsony (and it is admitted that larger exports of cattle than those registered at Pozsony may have been dealt with at other customs stations as far back as the mid-15th century);[34] on the other hand, the customs journals of 1542 comprise the records of all the custom stations of the strictly speaking western routes, referring, though, to a poor year as regards trade activities.

Thus, Hungary's bilateral participation in international trade of the new type started not parallel, but in two successive waves. If the abrupt rise in textile imports from the West took place already around the middle of the 15th century, the boom in cattle exports to the West may have represented the next wave in the upward trend of Hungarian foreign trade. Export of live-stock was in fact considerable about the middle of the 15th century, but on the strength of the concordant evidence of a number of Hungarian and

---

In the second half of the 16th century imports of "Turkish goods" (*res turcales*) — chiefly of silks and cloths — increased not only in Turkish-occupied territory but also in the Principality of Transylvania and in Rumanian principalities under Turkish supremacy. Simultaneously re-export of West-European cloth from Transylvania to Wallachia and Moldavia was strongly reduced compared to the early 16th century (see Chapter II, 1, Note 25), since western textiles were scarce in Transylvanian towns as well. — Goldenberg, *op. cit.*, p. 397.

The origin of "Turkish goods" was exceedingly varied coming as they mainly did from Asian and Balkan regions of the Ottoman Empire. Moreover, from the closing decades of the 16th century — when after the French — British (and Dutch) trade also penetrated into the eastern basin of the Mediterranean and the English Levant Company began to export cloths to this region, English products (and their imitations) appeared among lots of "Turkish goods". — F. Braudel, *La Méditerranée et le monde méditerranéen à l'époque de Philippe II*,[2] Paris 1966, Vol. I. pp 563—565.

[33] In 1457-58 2.83 florins of customs value was counted per ox, in 1542 10 florins. Customs value per piece of cloth amounted to 6.57 florins in 1457—58, to 5.33 florins in 1542. It is common knowledge that the calculation of customs value itself is far from being void of problems, that changes of customs value cannot be regarded as identical with changes in prices, that the term "a piece of cloth" referred to pieces of widely varying length, etc. (conf. Kováts, *op. cit.*, pp 22, 189; Ember, *op. cit.*, 1958, p. 327; Endrei, *op. cit.*). The over 3.5 fold increase of customs value per ox between 1457—58 and 1542, and its reduction to about 0.8 per piece of cloth during the same period may nevertheless be denoted as significant. Two facts can certainly be deduced from these figures. First, at the latter date cattle export from Hungary to the West was closely affected by the beginnings of the price revolution, by the rise of agrarian prices; secondly, in the period between the two points of time the share of inexpensive fabrics destined to cover the needs of the wider masses increased in cloth imports from the West.

[34] See Chapter II, 1, Note 14.

other sources, the date of the real upswing, the "second wave", may be put to the closing years of the 15th century and the opening decades of the 16th.[35] Mention should be made at this point of the case of Nuremberg, one of the principal comsumers of Hungarian beef in the 16th century. During the greater part of the 15th century this city imported live-stock chiefly from Poland, and as late as 1482 it turned to the merchants of Poznań to arrange for imports of cattle. In 1518, however, by the same city Hungary was already declared to be the country which "largely supplies Germany with cattle".[36] Let us add here an evidently exaggerated but nevertheless characteristic statement made at Austro-Hungarian talks in 1525: five cattle fairs were held every year in the frontier towns of Austria and "from time immemorial 8, 10, 16, even 20 thousand oxen have been driven from Hungary each year to all of these markets".[37]

[35] The route starting *from*, and going *through*, Hungary was *one* of the main routes of cattle trade from Eastern to Western Europe.

The growth of Hungary's cattle exports may be ascribed to an upswing in cattle breeding on the Hungarian Plain. (Zs. P. Pach, Das Entwicklungsniveau der feudalen Agrarverhältnisse in Ungarn in der zweiten Hälfte des XV. Jahrhunderts, *Studia Historica Acad. Sci. Hung.*, Vol. **46.**, Budapest 1960, pp 31 - 33). In addition, from the important breeding areas east of Hungary — from Wallachia and Moldavia — part of the live-stock to be exported to the West was also driven through (Transylvania and) Hungary.

Customs registers of South Transylvanian custom-houses of the early 16th century (Nagyszeben = Sibiu and Brassó = Braşov) also furnish evidence of cattle import, but it was chiefly at the more northerly custom-house of Beszterce (Bistriţa) that large droves of oxen passed from Moldavia into Transylvania. — Goldenberg, *op. cit.*, p. 395; Fügedi, *op. cit.*, pp **4**, 9.

In the later course of the 16th century, Turkish economic policy — the realization of which in Hungary has been shown above from several angles — was concentrated in the Rumanian principalities under Ottoman supremacy on preventing the export of agrarian products, also of cattle, to the West, so as to divert them through monopolistic channels for the supply of Constantinople. These measures were partly successful; on the proof of the customs registers of Nagyszeben, agrarian exports from Wallachia to Transylvania practically ceased in the second half of the 16th century. The monopolistic endeavours of the Porte also affected the foreign trade of Moldavia, but in a lesser degree. In the middle and second half of the 16th century droves of many thousand head of cattle were moved from Moldavia to Venice (partly via the southern regions of Turkish-occupied Hungary), or driven to Transylvania (Beszterce) and from there to the big cattle fairs of the Hungarian Plain, but chiefly to Poland, first and foremost to Lwów (Lvov), the starting-point of the *other* main route of interregional cattle trade. — For details see Goldenberg, *op. cit.*, p. 420. — H. Samsonowicz, Handel Lublina na przełomie XV i XVI w, *Przegląd Historyczny*, Tom **XIX**, Zeszyt *4*, (1968) p. 612. — J. Nistor, *Die auswärtigen Handelsbeziehungen der Moldau im XIV, XV und XVI. Jahrhundert*, Gotha 1911, pp 9, 81 etc. — M. Dan—S. Goldenberg, Le commerce balkano—levantin de la Transylvanie au cours de la seconde moitié du XVIe siècle et au début du XVIIe siècle, *Revue des études sud-est européennes*. Tome **V**, (1967) No. *1—2*, pp 87—117. — L. Lehr, Comerţul Ţării Româneşti şi Moldovei în a două jumătate a secolului XVI şi prima jumătate a secolului XVII, *Studii şi materiale de istorie medie*, Vol. **IV**, Bucureşti 1960, pp 242 - 288.

[36] Lütge, *op. cit.*, pp 369, 371. — The data referring to the year 1518 have been published in Hungarian literature, too, by L. Thallóczy, Középkori gazdaságtörténeti adatok Nürnberg levéltáraiból (Documents of Medieval Economic History in the Archives of Nuremberg), *Magyar Gazdaságtörténelmi Szemle*, 1900, p. 79. — In 1526 the other principal consumer, the city of Augsburg, definitely discriminated between Polish and Hungarian beef in favour of the latter. — S. Takáts, *Szegény magyarok* (Miserable Hungary), Budapest s. a., p. 135.

[37] S. Takáts, Osztrák határvásárok a 16. század első évtizedében (Fairs at Austrian Frontier Towns in the First Decade of the Sixteenth Century), *Magyar Gazdaságtörténelmi Szemle*, 1906, p. 128.

Such and similar sources support not only the conclusion that the boom in Hungarian cattle export and the swing-over of the adverse western trade balance to an active one took place in the decades directly preceding 1526,[38] but also the statement that the year of the customs journals, 1542, was a poor year in exports and imports alike, when, notwithstanding its considerable volume, cattle export remained far below the earlier achieved level. In subsequent years cattle exports again increased, rising much higher than did textile imports, for, strangely enough, instead of being restricted under Turkish rule, cattle breeding on the Great Plain and the export of oxen were rather promoted[39] — as a contradictory phenomenon of "development due to destruction."[40] From the late 1540s and the early 1550s there are available records bearing testimony to cattle export having risen over twice the 1542 volume, and such single data have been confirmed by statistical evidence referring to the early 1560s, as will be shown later.

In contrast to the other principal item of Hungarian exports, to copper, in the case of cattle the definite preponderance of the South German market is indisputable. Most of the herds of cattle were driven to Regensburg, Augsburg, Ulm, and especially Nuremberg, some of them even as far as the Rhine-Main district. To these regions the route ran straight westward, through Vienna,[41] or in a north-western direction, through Moravia, preferably

[38] A. Kubinyi arrives at a similar conclusion by approach from another angle. (*Op. cit.*, p. 102.) — On the strength of rough calculations based on the rentage stipulated in late 15th century leases of custom stations and on the budget of 1523, in 1494—95 33.3 per cent of western trade taken in a wider sense (certainly including deliveries via south-western routes) passed through Slavonian custom-houses; by 1523 the figure sank to 15.4 per cent. On the other hand, in 1494—95 only 36.4 per cent, but in 1523 61.5 per cent passed through the custom-houses of Buda and Székesfehérvár. Since, according to the author's reasoning, the latter custom stations were set up chiefly to handle exports (of cattle — conf. Chapter II, 1, Note 14), the rapid growth of their share indicates the upward trend of cattle exports as a result of which the balance of Hungarian foreign trade swung over and became active in the years between 1494—95 and 1523.

In this connection we wish to add that besides the strictly western cattle exports (which went to South German towns in the first place), trade in a south-western direction (passing through Slavonian custom-houses on the route to Venice) also throve in the decades before the Battle of Mohács. This was, moreover, the time when the first permits (*appaldos*) were issued providing for the duty-free passage of droves with Venice as their destination, reducing the revenues of custom stations on the Slavonian border. — See K. Tagányi, Marhakivitelünk Velencébe 1514-ben (Hungary's Cattle Exports to Venice in 1514), *Magyar Gazdaságtörténelmi Szemle*, 1899, p. 144. — T. Kardos, Velencei vonatkozású gazdaságtörténeti adatok a Jagelló-korból. 1502—1518 (Facts of Economic History Referring to Venice in the Jagello Era. 1502—1518), *Századok*, 1951, pp 435, 437, 442; Takáts, *op. cit.*, pp 151- 154.

For the later course of trade passing through Slavonian custom-houses see Notes 29, 43 and Note 43, Chapter II, 3.

[39] Until quite recently western literature did not take notice of this fact known in Hungarian economic history from the researches of S. Takáts. — See the correct arguments of Gy. Káldy-Nagy (later op. cit., p. 46.) against conclusions drawn by B. H. Slicher van Bath, W. Abel, and F. Lütge to the effect that the considerable rise of meat prices in Western Europe after 1550 was due partly to cattle supplies from Hungary (and South Eastern Europe in general) having diminished as a result of the Turkish occupation. It was only in his last work that Lütge (*op. cit.*, p. 374) modified this statement, to some degree, after having studied the latest works of Hungarian economic historiography.

[40] Conf. Pach, *op. cit.* (1964), pp 15—16.

[41] The cattle fairs held in the frontier towns of Austria became less important after 1526, while the weekly markets of Vienna grew more animated. It nevertheless happened

through Hustopeče,[42] after having passed the West Hungarian customs stations whose journals of 1542 have survived.[43] Hence the overwhelmingly high share of cattle in the exports registered in the journals.

Thus, under the impact of special forces Hungary's western foreign trade balance underwent a substantial change between 1458 and 1542: its adverse character vanished and by the latter date it became highly active. This change was brought about by specific factors, but, it must also be added, it was not a unique event in East-Central Europe. Similar developments occurred in Poland, to put it more accurately: in the Baltic Sea trade which basically determined the western trade balance of Poland and was of eminent importance for the unfolding of the modern-type international commerce. The balance, after having exhibited an adverse character during the greater part of the 15th century, began to improve in the 1480s and 90s,[44] to become highly active and remain stable throughout the 16th century, as a result of the large-scale grain export to the Atlantic coast in the first place.[45] The boom in grain export, this immensely significant "new wave" of foreign trade, almost coincided with the strong increase of Hungarian cattle export[46] and

---

even at the end of the 16th century that 5—6000 oxen were driven to these fairs (at Bruck, Ebenfurt, etc.) from Hungary. — See Note 37.

[42] Notwithstanding the increasingly bustling weekly markets of Vienna, business was still transacted on a large scale at the weekly fairs of Auspitz (Hustopeče) in Moravia (*Wochenmarkt mit ungarischen Ochsen*), particularly because the town was favourably situated to German merchants who drove the animals on. — S. Takáts, Az auspitzi (pusztapécsi) magyar marhavásárok régi kiváltságlevelei (Old Charters of Hungarian Cattle Fairs at Auspitz (Hustopeče), *Magyar Gazdaságtörténelmi Szemle*, 1905, p. 228. — Conf. P. Horváth, Príspevok k obchodným stykom Slovenska so Sliezskom a Moravou v 1. polovici 16. stor. *Historické Štúdie* XI (1960) Bratislava, p. 180. – M. Bělohlavek, Die Rolle Pilsens im Transitviehhandel des 16. Jahrhunderts, *Tagung zu Marburg*, 1967.

[43] The preponderance of the South German market and the western routes leading to South Germany in cattle exports around 1542 by no means implies that the North Italian market (Venice) and south-western routes in the latter direction may be disregarded. South-west-bound cattle exports passed through Slavonian custom-houses whose journals of the year 1542 have perished. The volume of nearly contemporary exports are, however, known: in the year 1544, 9326 head of cattle were driven from the Hungarian Plain over the southern zone of Transdanubia to the West. — Ruzsás, *op. cit.*, p. 207.

Thus the mid-16th century cattle exports travelling along the south-western routes — directly to Styria, Carinthia, the Krain, from there to North Italy (but partly also to Vienna) — were not insignificant, as they accounted for over $^1/_3$ of the total western exports in the year 1542.

[44] A. Mączak—H. Samsonowicz, La zone Baltique; l'un des éléments du marché européen. *Acta Poloniae Historica*, XI (1965) Warsaw, pp. 79, 82. — The adverse balance of the trade transacted through Gdańsk, the most important Baltic port, reduced between 1460 and 1475 from 1 : 3 to 1 : 1. 4, turned active by 1492 with 1 : 0. 8. — H. Samsonowicz, *Untersuchungen über das Danziger Bürgerkapital in der zweiten Hälfte des 15. Jahrhunderts*, Weimar 1969, pp 33—34.

[45] A. E. Christensen, *Dutch Trade to the Baltic about 1600*, Copenhagen-The Hague 1941, pp 42—48. – S. Hoszowski, The Polish-Baltic Trade in the 15th—18th centuries, *Poland at the 11th International Congress of Historical Sciences in Stockholm*, Warsaw 1960, p. 121. – A. Wyczański, Tentative Estimate of Polish Rye Trade in the 16th Century, *Acta Poloniae Historica*, IV (1961) Warsaw, pp 125—130. – A. Mączak, Export of Grain and the Problem of Distribution of the National Income in Poland in the years 1550—1650, *Acta Poloniae Historica*, XVIII (1968) Warsaw, pp. 91—95.

[46] Cattle export also played an important role in 16th century Polish foreign trade: the other main route of interregional cattle trade — which connected the huge breeding areas of the Ukrainian – Moldavian steppe and the Podolian table-land with the western buyers' markets — started from or led through Poland. — Conf. Note 35, and Chapter I, Note 9.

exerted a similar but still more potent influence on the trade balance, particularly from the 1550s, when the "price revolution" produced the steepest rise in the prices of agrarian products.[47] On the average of the years from 1565 to 1585, Polish sea-borne exports amounted to 1 158 000 thalers, sea-borne imports, in turn, to 400 000 thalers or so, which represented only 34 per cent of total exports; therefore the export surplus came to 52 per cent, after the deduction of price differences between import and export harbours.[48]

The questions raised by the initial, 15th century stage of the developing modern-type international trade have thus been answered in a positive sense by the second, 16th century, period of the process. Foreign trade recovered both in Poland and Hungary and even became very active: both could answer the "challenge" of western imports with increasing exports.

The answer is positive, but by no means unequivocal. Not only the character of foreign trade relations — import of industrial products against exports of foodstuffs and raw materials — call attention to the contradictions of the answer, but also the special features of production relations in the branches serving as the basis of exports, especially in those forming the basis of exports to the coasts of the Atlantic. Mention should be made in this connection of the domination of Hungarian copper production by foreign capital, and of the preponderance of *folwark* economy in Poland's grain production, both facts being unfavourable as to inte nal development of capitalism in these countries.

In the case of Hungary the contradictions inherent in foreign trade were aggravated by grave political developments: Turkish rule had a hand in limiting textile imports from the West while promoting westbound cattle export. Lastly, unlike Polish sea-borne grain trade, Hungarian cattle exports, transacted overland, were not taken to the Dutch centre of the rising modern-type international traffic, but for the most part to South German, and North-Italian, towns which still prospered in the middle of the 16th century. But the next century brought to them a stage of stagnation and decline at a time when the Northern Netherlands, having fought their bourgeois revolution and achieved independence, were in their heyday.

3

Finally, a brief survey is to be given of the development of Hungary's foreign trade with the West from the middle of the 16th century, that is, in the *third stage* of the investigated process.

As regards the western trade relations of Hungary in the period between the mid-16th and the mid-17th centuries, unfortunately we lack sources comparable to the customs books of 1457—58 and of 1542, as well as comprehensive statistical works resting on the analysis of research findings. Here we have only the support of customs records of more limited significance, referring

[47] S. Hoszowski, The Revolution of Prices in Poland in the 16th and 17th centuries, *Acta Poloniae Historica*, II (1959) Warsaw, pp. 10—13.

[48] A. Mączak, Eksport zbożowy i problemy polskiego bilansu w XVI—XVII w., *Pamiętnik X powszechnego zjazdu historików polskich w Lublinie*, Warszawa 1968, p. 183.

to narrower areas[1], and have to rely on incomplete series of data in our present attempt to outline the main trends of this stage of development.

It is an established fact that the share of textile import in the total of imports, conspicuous in 1457—58 as well as in 1542, continued to dominate. This remained a characteristic feature of the commodity structure of imports from the West in the territory under Turkish rule, too, notwithstanding the restrictive factors, notably war-time vicissitudes and the growing volume of eastern textile supplies.[2] Imports of textile articles from the West (cloth, clothing, linen) passing in seven and a half months through the Turkish custom station of Vác, with the customs value of around 28 000 florins, accounted for 81.24 per cent of total imports handled here. Approximately 6000 pieces of cloth were imported here within a year.[3] A few years later, in 1571, 4220 pieces of cloth passed through the Turkish custom-house of Buda, at both places chiefly cloths from Silesia (Wrocław), Moravia (Jihlava, Kisniz), South Germany (Nuremberg), and from England.[4]

As for "Royal Hungary", the majority of the burgher merchants in the towns were engaged mainly in importing textiles and hardware. The textile imports of Royal Hungary, far exceeding those of the Turkish-occupied territory, were of considerable volume also in the opening decades of the 17th century. It is a characteristic example that merchants of four towns

[1] A fair basis of comparison to the customs books of 1542 is afforded by the Turkish journals of customs duties paid on trade passing through Vác in 1563—64 and their expert analysis by Gy. Káldy-Nagy in Statisztikai adatok a török hódoltsági terület nyugat felé irányuló áruforgalmáról 1560—1564 (Statistical Data of Western Trade in Turkish-occupied Territory from 1560 to 1564), *Történeti Statisztikai Évkönyv 1965—66* (Historico-Statistical Year-Book), Budapest 1968, pp 27—29. — The journals give a wide picture of export from the Turkish-occupied part of Hungary to the West, a less complete one of imports from the West, because the bulk of the latter arrived to Buda and not to Vác. (*Op. cit.*, p. 46.) — An important source-book which also contains the Turkish customs journals of Buda provides information about imports that reached Buda in subsequent decades: L. Fekete—Gy. Káldy-Nagy, *Budai török számadáskönyvek 1550—1580* (Turkish Account Books of Buda 1550—1580), Budapest 1962 (see particularly pp 560—586). — From "Royal Hungary" we know about the survival of 16th—17th century journals of customs offices which controlled foreign trade in the northern direction (Lőcse, Eperjes, Bártfa); therefore these journals promise only indirect information about strictly western trade. Their analysis is in progress.

[2] See Chapter II, 2, Notes 30—32.

[3] Káldi-Nagy, *op. cit.*, pp 38, 39.

[4] Fekete—Káldi-Nagy, *op. cit.*, p. 577. — It must be remarked here that only 885 pieces of western cloth were passed by the Turkish custom station of Buda in 1573; presumably the reduction was due to the restrictive measures of the Turks. (Conf. Chapter II, 2, Note 32.)

Western cloths reached Turkish-occupied Hungarian territory, notably the eastern zone of Transdanubia, through custom-houses on the Slavonian border, too. (See Chapter II, 2, Note 29.) Here the falling off of imports and the diminution of customs revenue before the year 1566 were caused by the overbearing attitude of the authorities of Szigetvár which frightened away foreign merchants; later various campaigns, particularly the ravages of the Fifteen Years' War around the turn of the century, led to the decline of the Transdanubian boroughs and to the shrinking of buyers' markets. — L. Rúzsás, Városi fejlődés a Dunántúlon a XVI—XVII században (Urban Development in Transdanubia in the Sixteenth and Seventeenth Centuries), *Szigetvári Emlékkönyv 1566—1966* (Memorial Volume of Szigetvár, 1566—1966), Budapest 1966, pp 210, 211, 226—230.

of North Hungary — Kassa, Lőcse, Eperjes, Késmárk (Košice, Levoča, Prešov, Kežmarok) — while using the north-western trade route leading from Moravia along the Vág valley,thus passing through the customs stations of Trencsén (Trenčín), imported goods in the value of 20000 florins in 1610, over 54 000 florins in 1619, including more than 6200 pieces of cloth in 1610 and nearly 20 000 pieces in 1619, the bulk of which came from Silesia and Moravia.[5] In this connection it is noteworthy that the merchants of Kassa, as well as of towns in the Szepes district (Eperjes and Bártfa, Bardejov), as a rule preferred to transact foreign trade with their northern neighbour, Poland, exporting considerable quantities of wine and importing cloth and other articles, chiefly from Cracow.[6]

According to the customs books of Bártfa for the years 1504—1507, the commodity structure of these cloth imports brought from the north in the early 16th century was marked by the almost exclusive predominance of Bohemian, Moravian and Silesian fabrics — 1336 pieces out of the yearly 1361.[7] On the other-hand, other sources reveal that at about the same time (1501—1504) the merchants of Kassa sold in their town as well as sent to regions beyond the river Tisza and on Transylvanian markets not only textiles from the afore-mentioned countries, but also cloths from Western Europe (England, the Netherlands, the Lower Rhineland) and, of course, from South

[5] T. K., Lőcse, Késmárk, Eperjes és Kassa vámmentes árubehozatala 1610-ben (Duty-free Imports of Levoča, Kežmarok, Prešov and Košice in 1610), *Magyar Gazdaságtörténelmi Szemle*, 1899, p. 284. - T. S., Posztóbehozatal Morvaországból 1619-ben (Cloth Import from Moravia in 1619), *Magyar Gazdaságtörténelmi Szemle*, 1899, p. 195. — Conf. J. Szücs, Das Städtewesen in Ungarn im 15—17. Jahrhundert, *La Renaissance et la Réformation en Pologne et en Hongrie 1450—1650*, Budapest 1963, p. 132.

[6] L. Kemény, A kassai harmincad története a XVI. század végéig (History of the Customs Office of Kassa to the End of the 16th Century), *Magyar Gazdaságtörténelmi Szemle*, 1894, pp 308, 309; S. Domanovszky, *A szepesi városok árumegállító joga* (Staple-right of Towns in the Szepes District), Budapest 1922, pp 5, 6, 28; E. Fügedi, Kaschau, eine osteuropäische Handelsstadt am Ende des 15. Jahrhunderts, *Studia Slavica Acad. Sci. Hung.* II (1956) Budapest, pp 207, 208.

Wine export to Poland — which was not insignificant as early as the first decade of the 16th century (see Chapter II, 1, Note 25) — relied on the wine-production of the north-eastern vine-lands of Hungary. In the second half of the 16th century it assumed steadily increasing proportions, to rise in 1610 to 12 684, in 1611 to 17 206, "big casks". — A. Divéky, *Felső-Magyarország kereskedelmi összeköttetése Lengyelországgal, főleg a XVI—XVII. században* (Commercial Relations of North Hungary and Poland, with Special Reference to the Sixteenth and Seventeenth Centuries), Budapest 1905, pp 62—70. - S. Takáts, Borkivitelünk Lengyelországba 1610-ben és 1611-ben (Hungary's Wine Export to Poland in 1610 and 1611), *Magyar Gazdaságtörténelmi Szemle*, 1899, pp 88, 89. — Since a "big cask" was of 339 liter capacity, wine exports from the Tokaj wine-growing district of Hungary and from the vine-lands in the upper reaches of the river Tisza amounted at this time to nearly tenfold of the wine exported from Sopron in the year 1566. (Conf. Chapter II, 2, Note 9.)

For a tentative comparative estimation of *northern* wine exports and *western* cattle exports see I. N. Kiss, Nagybirtokok árutermelése és külkereskedelme a XVII. századi Magyarországon (Commodity Production and Foreign Trade of the Large Estates in Seventeenth Century Hungary), *A Magyar Mezőgazdasági Múzeum közleményei 1967—1968*, Budapest 1968, p. 153. — Conf. G. Komoróczy, *Borkivitelünk Észak felé. Fejezet a magyar kereskedelem történetéből* (Hungary's Wine Export Northward. A Chapter in the History of Hungarian Trade), Kassa 1944, pp 249—253.

[7] E. Fügedi, Magyarország külkereskedelme a 16. század elején (Hungary's Foreign Trade in the Early 16th Century), *Agrártörténeti Szemle*, 1969. No. *1—2*, p. 7.

Germany.[8] There is no reliable evidence to throw light on the route by which these cloths of Western Europe reached Kassa, but it seems highly probable that they came via Cracow.[9] However, the fact that in the second half of the century merchants of Kassa purchased in Poland Silesian and South German (Wrocław and Nuremberg) cloths as well as English fabrics has been confirmed by documentary evidence. English products can be identified in the list of goods imported from Cracow by the Kassa merchant Gergely Kalmár (1574—82) under the name of *londis* and of *karasia*,[10] the latter word having certainly been used as the Hungarian version of the English term kersey (*kersie*).[11]

As mentioned before, kersey was an important, relatively cheap stuff for mass consumption, put on the market by English woollen cloth makers following the modern trend, which in the course of time came to be ranged into the category of new draperies. In the early 17th century every effort of the English East India Company failed to create a market for this article in the Far East colonies[12], though it had found a market on the European Continent as far back as in the 15th century and enjoyed a lively and increasing demand in the second half of the 16th century under the names of *karazja, karasia, karazsia* on East-Central European markets: in Silesia, Poland, and Hungary.[13] The customs books of 1542 bear witness to the import of 272 pieces; but 520 pieces are found to have been registered in the customs journals of Vác for the years 1563—64, and 1128 pieces in the Turkish customs journals of Buda for 1571.[14] Hence, the English merchant who in his survey of the foreign markets of various kinds of English cloth in 1561 mentioned Hungary as one of the

[8] O. R. Halaga, Kaufleute und Handelsgüter der Hanse im Karpatengebiet, *Hansische Geschichtsblätter*, **85.** Jg. 1967, pp 71, 83. — Conf. Fr. Kavka, Český a slovenský obchod s textilními výrobky v rumunských zemích (do pol. 17 stol.), *Sborník historický*, **V.** Praha 1957, pp 138—142. — The name "Colchester" can hardly be supposed to have stood for English cloth; evidently "Colcischer" = Kölscher = Kölner (from Cologne) was misread in this form. — Conf. Gy. Székely, A németalföldi és az angol posztó fajtáinak elterjedése a XIII—XVII. századi Közép-Európában (Flemish and English Cloths in 13th—17th Century Central Europe), *Századok*, 1968, No. *1—2.* p. 16.

[9] In these years the largest consignment of cloths, in the value of 8709 florins, was sent by János Thurzó from Cracow to Kassa. — Halaga, *op. cit.*, p. 83.

[10] Gy. Kerekes, Kalmár Gergely deák regestumja kereskedéséről 1574—82 (Register of Gergely Kalmár on his business transactions 1574—82), *Magyar Gazdaságtörténelmi Szemle*, 1903, p. 72.

[11] *Zs. P. Pach*, The Shifting of International Trade Routes in the 15th—17th Centuries, *Acta Historica Acad. Sci. Hung.*, 1968, tom. 14, no. *3—4,* p. 313. — Conf. *W. Endrei*, Középkori angol textilimportunk gyapjúszövetei (Hungary's Medieval Imports of English Woollen Fabrics), *Századok*, 1970.

[12] E. Lipson, *The Economic History of England*,[4] Vol. II, *The Age of Mercantilism*, London 1947, pp 277, 278, 286.

[13] M. Małowist, *Studia z dziejów rzemiosła w okresie krzyzysu feudalizmu w Zachodniej Europie w XIV i XV wieku*, Warszawa 1954, pp 219—243. — J. Topolski, The Role of Gniezno in International Trade, *Acta Poloniae Historica* **XVIII** (1968) Warsaw, pp 196—200. — The manufacture of *karazja* after the English pattern was introduced in Gdańsk and in Silesia *(karazja górska)*, too.

[14] 1542: verbal communication of Gy. Ember. — 1563—64: Káldy-Nagy, *op. cit.*, p. 38. — 1571: Fekete—Káldy-Nagy, *op. cit.*, p. 577 (in 1573 import of this kind of cloth also sank at Buda as low as 283 pieces). — Besides Italian (*purgamal* = Bergamo) and South-German *(nurisleniensis = nurimbergiensis)* fabrics *karasia* also formed part of south-western imports: Ruzsás, *op. cit.*, p. 211. — Further evidence from 1591: *Magyar Gazdaságtörténelmi Szemle*, 1899. p. 35; 1610: *Ibid.*, p. 284; 1627, 1633: *Ibid.*, 1901, pp. 37—39; 1635: *Ibid.*, pp. 471, 472, 482.

principal buyers of kersey woven in Hampshire, and of "northerns", was a well informed man.[15]

Beside kersey other traditional kinds of English cloth ("real cloth") also found favour in contemporary Hungary. These were sometimes summarily referred to as "English": according to the price-lists of their guild, in the years 1627 and 1635 the tailors of Kassa made "English coats" and "English skirts".[16] The word *londis* (from London) — which may be supposed to have also been used as a collective term for English cloths — is encountered still more frequently in Hungarian sources from the 16th and 17th centuries, in manorial accounts, in lists of payments, and in family records. London cloth was brought to Hungary not only in varied colours but also in pieces of varying quality; this is evident from the names of different sorts of *londis*, as *fájlondis* and *közlondis*, indicating the social standing of those who bought them (or to whom they were given as part of their emoluments).[17] Lead seals and quality marks of cloth (inscribed "Honni soit qui mal y pense"), unearthed at excavations both in the "Royal" and the Turkish-occupied Hungary and found to date mostly from the 16th century testify alike to the use of various kinds of English cloth in these regions.[18]

Until the late 1560s English cloth and kersey were forwarded to East-Central Europe mainly from Antwerp, the centre of international textile trade, partly as Dutch shipments over the Baltic to Gdańsk, partly by continental waterways and overland routes via South German towns, Wrocław or Cracow.[19] Thus consignments could reach Hungary from the west, the north-west or the north.[20] From the late 16th century, however, German North Sea ports, especially Hamburg, which had contrived to establish strong Dutch-British commercial relations, became one of the principal gates through which English textile fabrics were brought to the Continent.[21] Presumably this influenced also the route of Hungarian textile imports, affecting even the quantity of supplies going to or through the markets of Germany labouring under the adverse circumstances created by the Thirty Years' War.[22]

[15] Lipson, *op. cit.*, Vol. II, pp. 188, 477. — The term "northern" obviously refers to Yorkshire which was a centre of the manufacture of kersey and worsted.

[16] *Magyar Gazdaságtörténelmi Szemle*, 1901, pp 37, 38; pp 471, 472, 482.

[17] On these issues see Székely, *op. cit.*, pp 27 29.

[18] L. Huszár, Merchant's Seals of the 16th and 17th Centuries, *Folia Archaeologica*, **XIII** (1961) Budapest, pp 187—197.

[19] Topolski, *op. cit.*, pp 196, 197. - M. Grycz, Handelsbeziehungen der Stadt Poznań bis Ende des XVII. Jahrhunderts, *Studia Historiae Oeconomicae*, **2**. Poznań 1968, p. 53. - Pach, *op. cit.*, pp. 294, 295.

[20] Import from the Mediterranean region cannot be ruled out either. Lipson, *op. cit.*, Vol. II, p. 344. — Conf. Chapter II, 2, Note 32 and Székely, *op. cit.*, p. 31.

[21] E. Baasch, Hamburg und Holland im 17. und 18. Jahrhundert, *Hansische Geschichtsblätter*, **XVI.** Bd. Jg. 1910, H. *1*, pp 55, 56. — R. Ehrenberg, *Hamburg und England im Zeitalter der Königin Elisabeth*, Jena, 1896. pp 310 -313. Lipson, *op. cit.*, Vol. II, pp 201, 204, 209, 211, 228, 239, 268.

[22] For the increase of England's cloth exports to the Continent in the course of the 16th century, difficulties of export trade in the first half of the 17th century see F. J. Fisher, Commercial Trends and Policy in Sixteenth Century England, *The Economic History Review*, Vol. **X** (1940), No. *2*, pp. 99, 100. – London's Export Trade in the Early Seventeenth Century, *The Economic History Review*, 2nd. Ser, Vol. III (1950), No. *2*, pp 153, 154. - J. D. Gould, The Trade Depression of the Early 1620s, *The Economic History Review*, 2nd Ser., Vol. **VII** (1954), No. *1*, pp 81—90. - A. Friis, *Alderman Cockayne's Project and the Cloth Trade*, Copenhagen 1927, passim.

The next issue to be investigated is how Hungarian western export developed in the meantime. Grain exports continued to be insignificant. From the thirties-forties of the 16th century, and particularly in the first half of the 17th century, the *"allodial"* economy of the feudal-landowners — corresponding to the Polish *folwark*-system — has been extended also in "Royal Hungary".[23] However, for lack of adequate river- and sea communications[24], the grain of the Hungarian allodial farms — unlike that of Poland — could not reach the West European markets in the period of the "price revolution" which precipitated a steep rise in the prices of agrarian products; and when the boom was over by the mid-17th century, it was carried only in small quantities even to neighbouring or near regions (Austria, North Italy).[25] Hungary's exports to the West continued to be marked by the preponderance of cattle export (oxen) and the considerable share of copper.[26]

Whereas the customs books for the year 1542 — a far from prosperous year for foreign trade — registered the exportation of not more than 27 529 oxen via western routes, the number of droves soon rose to the level attained before the disastrous Battle of Mohács and doubtlessly exceeded it later in the

[23] Zs. P. Pach, Die ungarische Agrarentwicklung im 16—17. Jahrhundert. Abbiegung vom westeuropäischen Entwicklungsgang, *Studia Historica Acad. Sci. Hung.* **54**, Budapest 1964, pp 24—30, 45—49.

[24] The following incident sheds a revealing light on the limitation of Hungarian grain export for lack of adequate river- and sea communications. In 1591 — at the time of the Italian wheat crisis — the agent of a Hungarian big landowner was negotiating with a Venetian factor for the sale of grain. During the talks the Venetian received instructions from his employers not to buy any more wheat until further notice as there were hopes of getting enough grain by sea from Danzig (Gdańsk) with the permission of the Queen of England. — P. Jedlicska, *Eredeti részletek gróf Pálffy-család okmánytárához 1401—1658* (Original Details Contributing to the Family Archives of the Counts Pálffy), Budapest 1910, p. 420. — Apparently, sea-borne Baltic (Polish) grain, shipped mainly by the Dutch, could compete even in Venice with Hungarian wheat which was transported mostly overland. — Conf. M. Aymard, *Venise, Raguse et le commerce du blé pendant la seconde moitié du XVIe siècle*, Paris, p. 1966, pp 155—157, 161—163.

[25] In the 1620s and 30s Hungarian big landowners occasionally exported considerable quantities of grain to Vienna and Wiener Neustadt at a high profit; by the middle of the century the imports of Austrian landowners to Hungary sometimes surpassed in volume the modest grain sales effected by the Hungarian big estates of the western frontier zone. — Jedlicska, *op. cit.*, pp 105, 153. — S. Takáts, A dunai hajózás a XVI. és XVII. században (Navigations on the Danube in the Sixteenth and Seventeenth Centuries), *Magyar Gazdaságtörténelmi Szemle*, 1900, pp 257—266. — J. Belitzky, *A magyar gabonakivitel története 1860-ig* (Hungarian Grain Export until the Year 1860), Budapest 1932, pp 27—29. — J. Tholt, *A sárvári uradalom majorgazdálkodása a XVII. század első felében* (Allodial Farming on Sárvár Estate in the First Half of the Seventeenth Century), Budapest 1934, pp 62, 66.

For mid-17th century exports of grain to Italy by the Zrínyis and other landlords of the south-western region (through Italian merchants) see *Magyar Gazdaságtörténelmi Szemle*, 1904, pp 70, 71.

[26] As pointed out several times, wine export was an important item in Hungary's foreign trade in northern relations (Poland; see Note 6 of the present Chapter), but it also remained noteworthy in western direction.

Of the two western districts of vine-land, that in the outskirts of Pozsony (Bratislava) exported its wine chiefly to Moravia, that surrounding Sopron mainly to Silesia. In the middle of the 17th century (1650—1657) an average 5 to 10 000 *akós* of wine were forwarded from the vine-lands of Sopron via Vienna, 83 per cent of which went to Silesian towns. — H. Prickler, Zur Geschichte des burgenländisch-westungarischen Weinhandels in die Oberländer Böhmen, Mähren, Schlesien und Polen, *Zeitschrift für Ostforschung*, **14.** Jg. (1965) H. 3, pp 512—515. — In volume these exports fell short of the exports of Sopron in the year 1566. (Conf. Chapter II, 2, Note 9.)

second half of the century. There is available evidence to confirm that within a period of three years, from 1549 to 1551, nearly 188 000 oxen, in the ten years between 1548 and 1558 roughly 550 000 head of cattle, were sold at the Vienna weekly markets; of the latter only some 46 000 were purchased by the butchers of Vienna, the rest went to Augsburg, Nuremberg and other German towns.[27]

These figures agree with the results of the historico-statistical analysis of the customs revenues recorded by the Turks in their books at Vác: in 1563—64 live-stock accounted for 96.82 per cent, oxen for 88.61 per cent, of total exports of the value of 341 350 florins which passed in seven and a half months westward through the custom station of Vác. In the months in question this implied 30 248 head of cattle, calculated for the year 47—48 000 animals; in the preceding years (1560—61 and 1561—62) the yearly average may be supposed to have been still higher, near on 60 000 animals.[28] Western cattle exports continued on — or rather above — this level until the close of the century (at least until the beginning of extensive military operations during the Fifteen Years' War). In 1580, 75 000 head of cattle passed through the customs at Vác, in 1588 more than 84 000 oxen were driven across the bridge of Érsekújvár (Nové Zámky), in the summer months of 1592 some 55 000 were sold at the weekly markets of Vienna.[29]

Even in the light of international comparison this level proves to have been very considerable. Along the other main route of cattle exports from East-Central Europe, leading through Poland, about 40 000 head of cattle were driven yearly to western buyers' markets (chiefly to Central Germany). The cattle exports of Denmark, absorbed by Hamburg and other North German towns, but chiefly by Amsterdam, rose to 55 to 60 000 head in the best years before the Thirty Years' War.[30]

[27] S. Takáts, *Szegény magyarok* (Miserable Hungary), Budapest s. a., p. 135; *Emlékezzünk eleinkről* (Our Elders' Memory), Budapest s. a., p. 334.

[28] Káldy-Nagy, *op. cit.*, pp 32, 46.

At Vác the route of the herds of cattle forked. The principal line led to the cattle fairs of Érsekújvár (Játó-puszta), Szered, Sempte, Galgóc (Nové Zámky, Sered, Šintava, Hlohovec), to cross the border at one of the custom-houses north of the Danube. The greater part of the droves of oxen exported in 1542, counting 15 513 head, passed at the custom station of Szempc (Senec). — S. Takáts, *Rajzok a török világból* (Sketches of Hungary under Turkish Rule), Budapest 1917, Vol. III, p. 16. — Gy. Ember, Külkereskedelmünk történetéhez a XVI. században, (Contribution to the History of Hungary's Foreign Trade in the 16th Century), *A Magyar Tudományos Akadémia Társadalmi-Történeti Tudományok Osztályának Közleményei*, Vol. **VIII**, (1958) No. *4*, p. 337.

The other route ran south of the Danube, to the market of Győr and from there in the direction of the custom-house of Óvár. In 1542 the traffic on this line was insignificant; it grew all the more lively in the last third of the sixteenth century. From the letter of a Turkish customs official at Vác from the year 1581 we learn that since 1569 cattle exports touching Győr increased from 15 000 to 30 to 40 000 head; therefore the amount of the customs duty collected by the customs office of Óvár — subordinated to the Treasury of Lower Austria — was much larger than that paid down at Szempc. The increase of traffic on the Győr—Óvár route was most probably connected with the fall of Szigetvár (1566), as a result of which cattle exports which used to pass through Slavonian custom stations (conf. Chapter II, 2, Note 43) were for a time driven via Győr. — Takáts, *Szegény magyarok*, pp 135, 147, 151, 153. — Ruzsás, *op. cit.*, p. 219.

[29] Káldy-Nagy, *op. cit.*, p. 47. — *Magyar Gazdaságtörténelmi Szemle*, 1897, pp 194, 195. — Takáts, *Szegény magyarok*, p. 156.

[30] A. Mączak, Export of Grain and the Problem of Distribution of the National Income in Poland in the Years 1550–1650, *Acta Poloniae Historica*, **XVIII** (1968) Warsaw, pp 89,

Exportation of cattle proved to be extremely lucrative in the second half of the 16th century. This agrarian commodity was also strongly affected by the "price revolution" and cattle prices having soared much higher abroad (in Vienna and in South German towns, that is on accessible and ready markets of Hungarian exports) than at home,[31] Hungarian exporters pocketed large profits. No wonder that besides the peasant and burgher merchants of the cattle-trading centres in Western Hungary (Nagyszombat, Győr, Magyaróvár), and the cattle-breeders and dealers of some boroughs of the Great Plain (Kecskemét, Debrecen), several members of the Hungarian aristocracy and lesser nobility also threw themselves eagerly into this branch of business.[32]

However, from the turn of the 16th and 17th centuries, Hungarian cattle exports presented a much more contradictory picture. First of all, stocks were decimated and trade was hampered by the Fifteen Years' War.[33] Large droves were nevertheless exported at that time, for at Stomfa (Stupava) on the north-western frontier alone, a station of the customs office of Pozsony, more than 7000 oxen passed in the year 1602.[34] But later unsold cattle was often driven back to Hungary from Vienna and Hustopeče; on the other hand, many complaints were made about insufficient supplies of cattle at foreign markets, the decrease of customs revenues and the slackness of trade.[35] The latter seems to be corroborated also by the statements of recent German research in economic history. It has been found that at the close of the 15th century cattle from Poland, Hungary and Denmark alike were offered for sale at Cologne fairs, whereas one century later the meat requirements of Cologne were met solely by Danish supplies.[36] In fact, Danish cattle exports which — as mentioned before — supplied the new centres of international trade on the Atlantic coast in the first place, also found their way to German markets south of Cologne.[37]

The periodic lags in Hungarian cattle deliveries in the first half of the 17th century can be attributed to several factors. The activities of the peasant-burgher cattle dealers of Western Hungary and of the Great Plain came up against more and more difficulties, due partly to the war-time situation at the turn of the century and later to the aggressive interference of the privileged cattle-trade companies (Landesverlegerische Viehcompagnie, 1622; Kaiserliche

90. — M. Horn, Handel wołami na Rusi Czerwonej w pierwszej połowie XVII w., *Roczniki Dziejów Spolecznych i Gospodarczych* **XXIV** (1962) Poznań, p. 86. — H. Wiese, Die Fleischversorgung der nordwesteuropäischen Großstädte vom XV. bis XIX. Jahrhundert unter besonderer Berücksichtigung des interterritorialen Rinderhandels, *Jahrbücher für Nationalökonomie und Statistik*, Band **179**, Heft *2*, Stuttgart 1966, p. 128.

[31] V. Zimányi, *Quelques aspects de la régression économique et sociale du XVIIe siècle.* (Manuscript)

[32] Pach, *op. cit.*, 1964, pp 20—22.

[33] Takáts, *Szegény magyarok*, p. 159. — Pach, *op. cit.*, 1964, pp 53—54. — Ruzsás, *op. cit.*, p. 228.

[34] In 1608, however, at Stomfa exports fell to about 2000. — P. Horváth, Hromadný vývoz dobytka z juhozápadného Slovenska do rakúskych a českých krajín na začiatku 17. storočia, *Historické Stúdie*, **XIII** (1968) Bratislava, p. 115

[35] Takáts, *Szegény magyarok*, p. 142 (1629), p. 176 (1639); *Magyar Gazdaságtörténelmi Szemle*, 1900, p. 172 (1615); 1903, p. 4 (1627—28); 1899, p. 89 (1631).

[36] W. Abel, *Geschichte der deutschen Landwirtschaft vom frühen Mittelalter bis zum 19. Jahrhundert*, Stuttgart 1962, pp 115, 160.

[37] Abel, *op. cit.*, pp 159, 160.

Ochsenhandlung, 1651),[38] but partly also to the competition and oppressive-restrictive measures of the Hungarian aristocracy and lesser nobility who, while building up their *allodial* economies, closely similar in system to the Polish *folwarks*, also threw into the scales their manorial rights, feudal prerogatives and exemptions from duty to get the better of their market rivals.[39]

However, even for the aristocracy in the long run cattle trade ceased to be as profitable as it had been in the 16th century. The rise in prices slowed down, to stop altogether after another brief boom in the 1620s. The disparity between foreign and home prices diminished and practically vanished by the middle of the 17th century.[40]

Foreign market relations did not develop favourably anyway for Hungary's cattle exports. In the second half of the 16th century the South German towns still raised an increasing demand for meat, so that their agents sometimes travelled as far as the region of the North Sea to buy Danish cattle, too.[41] Early in the 17th century they still made repeated efforts to secure a smooth and even flow of cattle deliveries from Hungary, and in the 1620s several towns (Nuremberg, Augsburg, Ulm, etc.) protested in turn against the activities of the "Landesverlegerische Viehcompagnie" which prevented them from purchasing directly from Hungarian cattle-dealers in Vienna as they had done for "countless years".[42] But these decades already mark the end of the heyday of the South German towns, followed before long by a decrease in the number of population, in purchasing power and meat consumption.[43] The Hungarian cattle, however, could not be driven to more distant markets; Hungary's main export product did not find its way to the West-European centres of modern-type international trade.[44]

[38] Takáts, *Szegény magyarok*, pp 163, 202.

[39] Pach, *op. cit.*, 1964, p. 51, — This fact emerges from several data quoted by Takáts, too, though he attributed all responsibility for "the decline of Hungarian traders and merchants" to Vienna alone. For the falling off of cattle-trade in the boroughs of Turkish-occupied Transdanubia see Ruzsás, *op. cit.*, p. 230.

[40] Zimányi, cited manuscript.

[41] Wiese, *op. cit.*, p. 136.

[42] C. L. Sachs, *Metzgergewerbe und Fleichversorgung der Reichstadt Nürnberg bis zum Ende des 30jährigen Krieges*, Nürnberg 1922, pp 107, 222. - F. Lütge, Der Handel Nürnbergs nach dem Osten im 15—16. Jahrhundert, *Beiträge zur Wirtschaftsgeschichte Nürnbergs*, Nürnberg 1967. Vol. I, p. 375. — Takáts, *Szegény magyarok*, p. 167.

[43] The city of Nuremberg, one of the principal consumers of Hungarian beef, had a population of 20 200 in 1449, 40 300 in 1662, 29 200 in 1806. -- J. Kulischer, *Allgemeine Wirtschaftsgeschichte des Mittelalters und der Neuzeit*, München—Berlin 1929, Vol. II, p. 252.

[44] In the late 16th and early 17th centuries Frankfurt on the Main may be regarded as the most distant market of Hungary's cattle exports *to the West*. — A. Dietz, *Frankfurter Handelsgeschichte*, Frankfurt a. M., 1910—1925. Vol. II, pp 110, 235; Vol. IV, pp 14, 47, 113.

In the 17th century Venice still remained the principal market of Hungary's *south-western* cattle export. Owing to the fall of Szigetvár, exports were diverted from the previously used line and herds of cattle were driven along the Győr—Magyaróvár route (see Note 28). However, in the decades following the Fifteen Years' War south-western traffic increased and grew much livelier than it had ever been in the 16th century. As early as 1610, Légrád on the river Drava was mentioned as one of the centres of cattle-trade with Venice; according to the report of Daniel Rauch, chief customs official of Slavonia, from the year 1633, 40 000 head of cattle passed here yearly, to be driven along roads never leaving the Zrínyi estates, to the port of Buccari (Bakar) where they were shipped to Venice. These records refer to the famous cattle exports of the Zrínyis which caused a serious conflict

It was due to such factors that in the second half of the 17th century the Hungarian peasant-burgher cattle dealers were impoverished, the big landowners abandoned business activity, and Hungarian cattle exports declined.

Hungary's other export commodity, copper, reached foreign countries in a different way. After the Fuggers had withdrawn from Hungarian (Slovak) copper production, in the middle of the 16th century the copper mines of the Besztercebánya (Banská Bystrica) district came under the management of the Treasury, but the monopoly of marketing and exportation of copper remained in the hands of German (Augsburg) capitalists who, keeping strictly within the sphere of commerce, rather depressed than advanced production. First it was the Fuggers themselves, later the firms Manlich, then Link, Welser, and subsequently Paller-Weiss who exploited the monopoly of sales ensuring enormous profits: on the basis of contracts with the Treasury they acquired the bulk of the copper produced by the mines struggling to cope with innumerable difficulties, at prices which, though showing an upward tendency, were still far below those paid on the world market. From the amounts due for the copper they paid only some contribution to overhead

with the Treasury of Vienna and often roused debates in the diets of feudal Hungary. (Conf. Acts 1630 : 23, 1635 : 43, 1638 : 54, etc.)

Therefore, the remarkably small amount of customs duty collected by the Slavonian customs authorities in the year 1630 gives no ground for concluding that south-western export had lost importance. The route used by the Zrínyis for moving their cattle exports, not infrequently with armed escort, did not pass any custom-house. What is more, landlords much inferior to the Zrínyis in position, generally followed at the time a similar practice, exporting their products "*sub specie propriae allodiaturae*" without paying any customs duty, as described with praiseworthy accuracy by Daniel Rauch in his later records (1655).

By the cattle-trade of the Zrínyis Hungarian live-stock gained direct access to the Venetian market, notwithstanding exports from the Rumanian principalities and Transylvania through Turkish-occupied territory and Zara (Zadar), and exports passing through the Austrian hereditary provinces (Styria, Carinthia, Krain, Görz), leased by the Treasury of Styria to Italian "*appaldatores*". Within the framework of the "*appaldo*" (and with the "free cattle licences" granted to Italian merchants) not infrequently 10 to 12 000 head of cattle were exported in a year, often without any payment of customs duty.

In the 1650s and '60s the extensive cattle export of the Zrínyis came up against the ever more vigorous measures of the Court of Vienna; retaliation for the Wesselényi conspiracy, the execution of Peter Zrínyi and the confiscation of his properties (1670—71) put an end to it. The investigators of farming on the confiscated estates of the Zrínyi family under the management of the Treasury have been able to detect hardly any trace of cattle-trade in the 1670s, for the latter (like the bulk of 16th and 17th century cattle export) did not rest on allodial production, and exports to Venice have already reverted to the "traditional" pattern: *appaldo* and the routes leading through the hereditary provinces of Austria.

However, in the later course of events these routes were also doomed to decline. Western exports tapered off when the golden age of the South German towns was over; south-western ones with the eclipse of Venice. — For the above comments see *Magyar Gazdaságtörténelmi Szemle*, 1898, pp 577—589. — Takáts, *Szegény magyarok*, pp 173, 174. — Gy. Ember, Magyarország XVI. századi külkereskedelmének történetéhez (Contribution to the History of Hungarian Foreign Trade in the 16th Century), *Századok*, 1961, p. 6. — Pach, *op. cit.*, 1964, p. 44. — Ruzsás, *op. cit.*, p. 219. — N. Kiss, *op. cit.*, p. 140. — L. Lehr, Comerţul Ţării Româneşti şi Moldovei în a două jumătate a secolului XVI şi prima jumătate a secolului XVII, *Studii şi materiale de istorie medie*, Vol. IV, Bucuresti 1960, 256—258. — C. M. Cipolla, The Decline of Italy: the Case of a Fully Matured Economy, *The Economic History Review*, 2nd Ser., Vol. V (1952), No. 1, pp 178—185. — H. Kellenbenz, *Le déclin de Venise, Aspetti e causa della decadenza economica veneziana nel secolo XVII*, Venezia—Roma 1961, p. 142.

charges and kept the rest as amortization of their loans to the Court. Thus around the middle of the century they got yearly 12—23 000, in the closing decades a yearly average of 12 000 cwts of refined copper for exportation.[45] In the 1550s and 1560s the principal route for carrying exports remained the same as that used in the Fugger period, leading through Gdańsk — or Szczecin — over the Sound to Antwerp.[46]

The decline of Antwerp — which along with other reasons caused a crisis on the international copper market in the 1570s — induced exporters of Hungarian copper to look for new clients and to revive relations with former markets. In the 1580s and 90s Viennese firms connected with South German merchants, about the turn of the century particularly Lazarus Henckel (with interests in Hungarian cloth import and cattle export, too), endeavoured to increase copper exports also to Nuremberg — via Vienna — and renewed exports to Venice where hardly any sales had been made after the first decade of the 16th century.[47] Under these new conditions, too, the principal route of Hungary's copper exports led north-north-west, but instead of the Vistula-Gdańsk or Oder-Szczecin direction it followed the Elbe-Hamburg line. From this North Sea port copper consignments, avoiding passage over the Sound, were shipped to the new centre of international trade of modern type, Amsterdam, or straight to the coast of the Iberian Peninsula.[48] Thus, from the turn of the 16th and 17th centuries Hamburg and Amsterdam took the place of Antwerp also in copper trade. Hamburg, which had become one of the gates through which English cloth flowed to East-Central Europe, acquired a key position in the sale of Hungarian copper at markets on the Atlantic coast, too. At the same time the hegemony of Amsterdam in world trade was fed and upheld from East-Central Europe not only by Baltic grain and timber, but also by copper from the Carpathians.

But Hungarian copper exportation did not benefit for a long time from the new international copper boom ushered in about the turn of the century by

[45] Gy. Szekfü, *Magyar Történet*[2] (Hungarian History), Budapest 1935, Vol. III, pp 131—133, 586—587 (with references to earlier literature). — J. Vlachovič, Slovak Copper Boom on World Markets of the 16th and the First Quarter of the 17th Centuries, *Studia Historica Slovaca*, I (1963) Bratislava, pp 72—77, 79, 81, 87 (with references to recent literature). — Second-rate "*Preisser*" and "*Libet*" copper (conf. Chapter II, 1, Note 19 and Chapter II, 2, Note 21) were also monopolized for periods of varying length. At other times Besztercebánya was free to sell these products. In the middle of the century their yearly yield was about 1000 cwts.

[46] Vlachovič *op. cit.*, p. 78. — H. Srbik, *Der staatliche Exporthandel Österreich von Leopold I. bis Maria Theresia*, Wien—Leipzig 1907, pp 137, 138.

[47] J. A. van Houtte, Anvers aux XVe et XVIe siècles: expansion et apogée, *Annales, Économies — Sociétés — Civilisations*, 1961, No. 2, p. 278. — H. van der Wee, *The Growth of the Antwerp Market and the European Economy (fourteenth—sixteenth centuries)*, The Hague 1963, Vol. II, Interpretation, pp 250—254. — J. Kallbrunner, Lazarus Henckel von Donnersmark, *Vierteljahrschrift für Sozial- und Wirtschaftsgeschichte*, **XXIV**. Bd., H. *2*., 1931, pp 151—155. — J. Kallbrunner, Hans Steinberger. Ein Beitrag zur Geschichte der Montanwirtschaft im Zeitalter Kaiser Rudolf's II, *Vierteljahrschrift für Sozial- und Wirtschaftsgeschichte*, **XXVII**. Bd. H. *1*, 1934, pp 17—19. — G. Probszt, Der Neusohler "Kupferkauf", *Vierteljahrschrift für Sozial- und Wirtschaftsgeschichte*, **XL**. Bd., H. *4*, 1953, pp 292—324.

[48] Srbik, *op. cit.*, pp 40, 41, 53, 139, 140. — Vlachovič, *op. cit.*, pp 85, 86, 90. — H. Kellenbenz, *Unternehmerkräfte im Hamburger Portugal- und Spanienhandel, 1590—1625*, Hamburg 1954, pp 83, 170, 202, 278. — V. Barbour, *Capitalism in Amsterdam in the Seventeenth Century*, Baltimore 1950, pp 75, 93, 105, 111, 118, 128.

the increased issue of copper coins in Spain and the resulting rise in the price of copper.[49] In the 1620s many thousand cwts of Hungarian copper were already piled up in the warehouses of Amsterdam and Hamburg.[50] It was not the demand which diminished but supplies multiplied; Swedish copper which had been unable to compete with Hungarian copper in the 16th century,[51] now appeared in steadily increasing quantities on West-, North-, and Central European markets, at Amsterdam in the first place. In fact, the income derived from copper exports provided one of the financial resources of Sweden's Great Power politics. Under Gustavus Adolphus the Swedish government spared no effort to spur on the increase of production, the exploitation of new mines, and the activities of exporters, the military successes achieved by the king in the Thirty Years' War having made the way clear for expansion.[52] In 1628 his chancellor, Oxenstierna, approached the ruling prince of Transylvania, Gábor Bethlen, who for a time had held Besztercebánya, too, during his campaigns against the Habsburgs, as a partner of equal economic strength, with the offer to establish a joint monopoly of the international copper market.[53] However, the actual situation presented an entirely different picture at this juncture: Sweden's copper production had risen to nearly fourfold of the yield of the Besztercebánya mines.[54] In the second quarter of the 17th century Swedish copper production continued to increase, to culminate in the year 1650 in an output of over 3000 metric tons, which corresponded to 50 000 cwts as counted in the unit measurement used at Besztercebánya.[55] In addition to the Swedish supplies of overpowering volume, other new competitors appeared on the international market, notably Japanese[56] and Chilean copper.[57]

Under such conditions Hungarian copper mining and exportation were unable to regain their former prosperity. In the second half of the 17th century the yearly production of the Besztercebánya mines was down to 3—4000 cwts, amounting hardly to the double together with the output of the copper mines of Szomolnok (Smolník).[58] It still served as a considerable security of loans raised by the Treasury; Hungarian copper (particularly when forwarded via

[49] E. J. Hamilton, *American Treasure and the Price Revolution in Spain, 1501–1650,* Cambridge Mass. 1934. — H. Heaton, *Economic History of Europe,*[2] New-York–Evanston 1948, p. 267.

[50] Vlachovič, *op. cit.*, p. 94.

[51] W. Möllenberg, *Die Eroberung des Weltmarkts durch das mansfeldische Kupfer. Studien zur Geschichte des Thüringer Saigerhandels im XVI. Jahrhundert,* Gotha 1911, 49, 87. — P. Jeannin, Les relations économiques des villes de la Baltique avec Anvers au XVIe siècle, *Vierteljahrschrift für Sozial- und Wirtschaftsgeschichte,* XLIII. Bd. H. *3.* 1956, p. 205.

[52] E. F. Heckscher, *An Economic History of Sweden,* Cambridge, Mass. 1954, pp 72, 85—88.

[53] S. Szilágyi, Oklevelek Bethlen Gábor és Gusztáv Adolf összeköttetéseinek történetéhez (Documents Concerning the History of the Connection between Gábor Bethlen and Gustavus Adolphus), *Történelmi Tár,* 1882. pp 241, 242. — Conf. A. Várkonyi's paper in this volume.

[54] Vlachovič, *op. cit.*, p. 95.

[55] Heckscher, *op. cit.*, p. 87. — Conf. Chapter II, 2, Note 22.

[56] K. Glamann, The Dutch East India Company's Trade in Japanese Copper, 1645—1736, *The Scandinavian Economic History Review,* I, Copenhagen 1953.

[57] C. H. Haring, *Trade and Navigation between Spain and the Indies in the Time of the Hapsburgs,* Cambridge, Mass. 1918, p. 156.

[58] Srbik, *op. cit.*, pp 52, 53, 126, 128, 429. — S. Takáts, Két világkereskedelmi cikkünk a XVIII. században (Two Hungarian Articles of International Trade in the Eighteenth Century), *Magyar Gazdaságtörténelmi Szemle,* 1903, p. 103.

Hamburg-Amsterdam), was still good business for foreign concerns, for the Dutch and British companies who occupied the former position of the South Germans from the end of the 17th century;[59] but on the international copper market it could only play a subordinate role.[60]

In fact, copper was the only Hungarian mass product for export which — while enriching foreign concerns and failing to become a source of accumulation of capital at home — found its way in the 16th century to markets on the Atlantic coast in considerable quantities. Yet even this product was unable to consolidate its position so as to keep it during the second half of the 17th century at the West European centres of international trade of modern type. The then modern organization and techniques introduced and established by the Thurzó-Fugger Company in its time had long become things of the past, and the copper export of the rising Swedish economy proved to be an invincible competitor.

At present we are still unable to draw up a comprehensive picture of the quantitative changes which took place during the 17th century in the balance of Hungarian foreign trade with the West. Nevertheless it is justified to infer that the decline in the export of the two most important Hungarian export articles to the West, cattle and copper, resulted in an unfavourable change, even in case of the stagnation or reduction of textile imports.[61] It may be taken for certain that the highly active balance of the 16th century showed a downward trend or possibly turned passive by the middle and second part of the 17th century. This course of events in Hungary should be regarded again not as a single, isolated case, but as a characteristic trend of East-Central European development which has been demonstrated quantitatively in connection with Poland. Until the mid-17th century the balance of Polish Baltic Sea-trade remained active, except in a few years, but displayed a noticeably downward tendency: the average export surplus of 52 per cent in the years between 1565 and 1585 sank to 9 per cent in the period of 1625—46.[62] Then, in the second half of the 17th century, the balance turned adverse; the price revolution — which had produced a much steeper rise in grain than in textile prices — was over, and the stagnant, later decreasing grain exports were no longer able to counterbalance the large-scale imports of cloth (and luxuries).[63]

[59] See the preceding note.

[60] In 1690 one of the most eminent experts in metallurgy of the age, E. Odhelius (Odelstierna), was commissioned by Charles XI to make a thorough study of metal production and trade all over Europe on the spot. In his report, which is certainly the most comprehensive source on the mining and trade of metals in late seventeenth-century Europe, Odhelius also pointed out the difficulties of Swedish copper production but nevertheless came to the conclusion, "though copper is mined at many places in and outside Europe, the yield is dwarfed by the abundance of Swedish copper". -- Heckscher, *op. cit.*, pp 87, 293.

[61] Conf. Note 22.

[62] A. Mączak, Eksport zbożowy i problemy polskiego bilansu w XVI—XVII. w., *Pamiętnik X powszechnego zjazdu historików polskich w Lublinie*, Warszawa 1968, p. 183. -- M. Bogucka, Handel bałtycki a bilans handlowy Polski w pierwszej połowie XVII wieku, *Przegląd Historiczny*, Tom **LIX**, *2* (1968) Warszawa, pp 245—250.

[63] S. Hoszowski, The Polish Baltic Trade in the 15th—18th Centuries, *Poland at the 11th International Congress of Historical Sciences in Stockholm*, Warsaw 1960, pp 125, 144, 145. -- A. Mączak--H. Samsonowicz, La zone Baltique; l'un des éléments du marché européen, *Acta Poloniae Historica*, **XI** (1965) Warsaw, pp 80, 81, 85.

III

Thus, neither Hungarian nor Polish economy was able to benefit in the long run from the favourable opportunities afforded by the period under review, that is to use their opportunities for the permanent promotion and capitalist transformation of their commodity production in the prevailing specific historical conditions which gave the countries of East-Central Europe a chance to play a role of increasing importance in international trade.

These specific conditions were due mainly to three factors.

1. In the period from the end of the 15th century to the middle of the 17th the overseas colonies were not yet attached to the economy of Western Europe in the sense of a modern world market, that is by a new-type international trade based on mass-consumption goods. From the Far East it was chiefly the favoured articles of the old-type long-haul trade, spices, which were brought to Europe; from America it was precious metals, obtained first through plunder then by exploiting the newly disclosed mines by slave labour. The influx of American treasure resulted, in turn, in the depreciation of money and, along with other factors, led to the "price revolution" which brought a sudden, steep rise in prices.

2. In this first period of the emergence of the modern international economy the countries of East-Central Europe were in fact the ones to join the expanding economy of Western Europe in a "modern" way, by the ties of the rising new-type international trade based on the advancement of commodity production and division of labour — as suppliers of mass-consumption foodstuffs and of industrial raw materials, furthermore as buyers of manufactured products for mass consumption.

3. This role of East-Central Europe in international trade (exporting foodstuffs and importing industrial products) limited and hindered industrial-urban growth in the countries involved, where the level was anyway below that of Western Europe in this respect from the beginning of the period. This role contributed to the intracontinental industrial-agrarian division of labour and to increasing the differences in the level of development between Western and Eastern Europe, but without implying from the outset unequivocally the economic subordination, the dependence or exploitation of East-Central Europe. On the contrary: it could have become a source of the accumulation of capital in these countries. In fact, the "price revolution" sent up the prices of agrarian products much higher than those of industrial articles; a gap was thereby created between the relative prices of industrial and agricultural products, which in its turn ensured favourable "terms of trade" and an active trade balance to the countries of East-Central Europe in their western relations.

However, by the middle of the 17th century the situation thoroughly changed from all three aspects.

1. Whereas colonial trade with the Far East still showed no sign of any modern-type transformation,[1] in relations with America significant changes had ensued or were beginning to become apparent.

[1] For developments in the Far East see Chapter I, Notes 18 and 22.

The influx of precious metals from the Spanish West Indies, which had grown more and more plentiful until the year 1595, began to display a tendency to diminish between 1601 and 1630, to sink at a rapid rate from 1631 to 1660.[2] The formerly principal feature of economic relations with the American colonies noticeably dwindled by the middle of the 17th century.

Simultaneously with the shrinking of precious metal shipments, the flow of sugar-cane, the other colonial treasure of America, to Western Europe, assumed steadily increasing volume. Sugar started on its world-wide commercial career as early as in the last decades of the 16th century from the Portuguese-American colonies, from the Brazilian plantations tilled by Negro slaves. However, large-scale exports to Europe — when this luxury became a widely used consumers' commodity — date only from the middle of the 17th century, after the foundation of their Caribbean "Sugar Colonies" by the English and the French.[3]

The development of the West Indian sugar colonies lent an impetus to European exports to America, too, because they raised a rapidly increasing demand for slave labour as well as for textile fabrics and other industrial products. Moreover, their specialized monocultural sugar production advanced to such a degree that considerable grain (and other food) imports were needed. They were supplied partly by the North American British "Bread Colonies". These North American colonies — which at the time had hardly any export products available for trans-Atlantic trade — re-exported to Europe part of their sugar imports from their commerce with the Antilles, to pay for their industrial imports.[4]

This trans-Atlantic trade between America and Europe (and West Africa), steadily growing since the middle of the 17th century and increasingly assuming the character of a modern-type trade based on the division of labour, was at first handled mainly by Dutch merchants. Later on this trade was taken over by the English, where their own colonies were concerned. Exportation of English woollen fabrics — having encountered difficulties in the first half of the century — increased in the period following the Civil War, due to seizing the possibilities offered by colonial markets, too, so that, calculated for the whole of the 17th century, exports rose to approximately threefold.[5] About this time trade with America — mainly because its modern traits were becoming dominant — expanded so rapidly that the cargo volume of

[2] Imports of precious metals amounted to over 35 million pesos in the years from 1591 to 1595, to nearly 25 million in the years between 1626 and 1630, to not more than 17 million in the period 1631—1635, but to less than 3.4 million pesos in the years 1656 to 1660. — E. J. Hamilton, *American Treasure and the Price Revolution in Spain, 1501—1650*, Cambridge Mass. 1934, pp 34—36.

[3] In addition to the works cited in Chapter I, Note 14, see E. E. Rich, Colonial Settlement and its Labour Problems, *The Cambridge Economic History of Europe*, Vol. IV. *The Economy of Expanding Europe in the Sixteenth and Seventeenth Centuries*, Cambridge 1967, pp 338—350. — G. B. Masefield, Crops and Livestock, *Ibid.*, pp 289—295.

[4] A. P. Newton, *The European Nations in the West Indies, 1493—1688*,[2] New York 1967, pp 196—199, 279—285. — J. Clapham, *A Concise Economic History of Britain from the Earliest Times to 1750*, Cambridge 1949, pp 238, 281, 285, 291.

[5] E. Lipson, *The Economic History of England*,[4] Vol. II. *The Age of Mercantilism*, London 1947, p. 189. — Conf. J. Kulischer, *Allgemeine Wirtschaftsgeschichte des Mittelalters und der Neuzeit*, München—Berlin 1929, Vol. II, p. 167.

the British merchant fleet was enormously increased without any decline of Dutch shipping in absolute terms.[6]

Thus, by the time the features marking the first stage in economic relations with the American colonies began to recede, the new character of these relationships, connected with the international division of labour, became apparent. Modern world economy stepped in a new, second stage of rise, when the trans-Atlantic routes became the routes of modern-type international trade.

In this second period of the development of modern world economy the role of East-Central European countries, their relative significance in international trade diminished in the eyes of West European economy, for the time was over when commercial relations with East-Central Europe were the principal bearer of the evolving modern-type trade relations.[7]

2. In the first period of the development of modern world economy the "challenge" of western imports and the favourable situation for agricultural exports under the influence of the price revolution stimulated the countries of East-Central Europe to increase agricultural market production. *Peasant* farming was encouraged as well, but the formerly insignificant commercial activities and commodity production of the *landlords* was promoted more forcibly, with two alternative trends of development, namely the use of hired labour, implying the initial steps towards a bourgeois *"new nobility"*, or of forced labour, involving a feudal, *"Gutsherr"*-type solution.[8] These steps made it possible to increase agrarian exports to the West considerably and to satisfy the growing demand for agricultural products amidst the prosperity which marked the 16th century, at a time when the struggle between peasant and landlord commodity production was still going on and landlord production still implied two alternative lines of development.

By the early 17th century, however, the fight ended with the victory of the *"Gutsherr"* trend relying on the use of forced serf labour. To base agrarian commodity production chiefly on the peasantry or a "new nobility" would have called for changes giving the whole of national economy a bourgeois character: for a simultaneous initiation of capitalist development of industrial

[6] Lipson, *op. cit.*, Vol. III, p. 139. — J. H. Parry, Transport and Trade Routes, *The Cambridge Economic History of Europe*, Vol. IV, pp. 206, 207.

[7] The import requirements of Western Europe in staple foodstuffs were still covered chiefly by the East-Central European countries, for the influence of American grain imports made itself felt only much later. However, the role of the East-Central European countries in international trade was reduced in this respect too from the middle of the 17th century, owing partly to the internal limits of production of agricultural exports, partly to factors which curtailed the demand for agrarian imports in Western Europe.

From the 1660s England became a grain-exporting country for about one century. Growing potatoes and maize of American origin on a large scale was started in Europe; at the close of the 17th century, the former already played an important part in the mass-consumption of Ireland, the latter in that of Spain. A demographic stagnation or decline took place in some countries of Western Europe during the century.

For these circumstances see Clapham, *op. cit.*, pp 283, 284. — Lipson, *op. cit.*, Vol. II, pp 448—464. — Masefield, *op. cit.*, pp 276—278, 299. — K. F. Helleiner, The Population of Europe from the Black Death to the Eve of the Vital Revolution, *The Cambridge Economic History of Europe*, Vol. IV, pp 50—55.

[8] For the types and trends of agrarian development see Zs. P. Pach, Die ungarische Agrarentwicklung im 16—17. Jahrhundert. Abbiegung vom westeuropäischen Entwicklungsgang, *Studia Historica Acad. Sci. Hung.*, Vol. 54., Budapest 1964, pp 9, 10, 31—34.

commodity production. This could not happen, because the lag of industrial-urban development which was manifest even in the second half of the 15th century grew worse during the 16th century. The role played by the countries of East-Central Europe in international trade, the ties that came to link them to the new type of trade also worked against progress in this respect: import of industrial products, which restricted the domestic possibilities of industrial growth, and agrarian export which favoured the economic activities of the landlords by enabling them to produce market commodities without having to invest capital, by exploiting unpaid serf labour; and also to push ahead in the export business to the detriment of burgher-peasant dealers.

However, the very fact that the feudal landlord trend became dominant in agrarian development soon brought to the surface its own grave, inherent contradictions. By the middle and second half of the 17th century it came up against self-created objective obstacles which restricted commodity production and exportation. This was shown by the unfavourable turn in Polish grain exports which may be explained by the conditions and methods prevailing in production rather than by market conditions. As early as in the 1630s and 40s it occurred not infrequently that Dutch vessels sailed out of Gdańsk harbour with ballast in the cargo space because grain supplies available on the Gdańsk market did not suffice to cover West European demands.[9] Later, between 1650 and 1699 the average yearly volume of grain forwarded to the West over the Sound sank to 55 800 lasts, as opposed to the yearly average of 68 500 between 1600 and 1649, and in the period from 1700 to 1749 it fell to a mere 31 800 lasts.[10] The diminution of grain exports was due mainly to a decrease in the yield ratios, which, in turn, may be ascribed to the domination of commodity production by landlords exploiting forced labour to the utmost, ruining the peasant tenures by the stablization of the *folwark* system.[11] The profound inner contradictions of commodity production by feudal landlords with forced work were manifested by its crippling effect on peasant tenures, its own source of labour and of instruments of labour. The feudal preponderance was also partly responsible for the decline of Hungary's cattle exports, though their principal basis had been and remained cattle-breeding at boroughs and villages, and not on landlord-managed estates; here it revealed itself in the landlords' interference with the activities of peasant-burgher cattle-traders, in the competition and oppressive-restrictive measures of the feudal nobility.[12]

Thus, the shrinking of the commercial role of the East-Central European countries in the West European economy, its loss of significance on the world

[9] M. Bogucka, Handel bałtycki a bilans handlowy Polski w pierwszej połowie XVII wieku, *Przegląd Historiczny*, Tom **LIX**, (1968) *2* Warszawa, p. 252.

[10] J. A. Faber, Het probleem van de dalende graanaanvoer uit de Oostzeelanden in de tweede helft van de zeventiende eeuw. *A. A. G. Bijdragen*, **9**. Wageningen 1963, p. 12.

[11] J. Topolski, La régression économique en Pologne du XVIe siècle, *Acta Poloniae Historica*, **VII** (1962) Warsaw, pp 46—49. — W. Szczygielski, Die ökonomische Aktivität des polnischen Adels im 16—18. Jahrhundert, *Studia Historiae Oeconomicae*, Vol. 2, 1967, pp 85—87.

For the factors which also reduced the demand in Western Europe for Baltic grain in the second half of the seventeenth century see Note 7.

[12] See Chapter II, 3, Note 39.

market by the middle of the 17th century resulted not only from the rapid growth and changed character of trans-Atlantic commerce and the rise of the new routes of modern-type international trade, but also from the fact that about the same time East-Central European commodity production, instead of advancing, fell into a state of stagnation and decay.[13]

3. Finally, the "price revolution" came to an end by the middle of the 17th century.[14] The boom ceased, and so did the gap between relative prices of industrial and agrarian products. The stagnation or decline affected agricultural commodities in the first place, so that their prices dropped low in relation to those of manufactured goods.

The western trade of East-Central Europe — import of industrial, export of agrarian products — was no longer marked by favourable proportions in the exchange of goods and by possibilities conducing to the accumulation of capital. On the contrary: it already meant unfavourable "terms of trade", diversion of value, and exploitation, illustrating the validity of the law that "... the favoured country recovers more labour in exchange for less labour."[15] Intracontinental division of labour in Europe became traditional and even ingrained in subsequent centuries, but henceforth unequivocally to the disadvantage of the countries of East-Central Europe: in their relations to Western Europe, which had entered on the stage of industrial growth and capitalist transformation, they were on the whole reduced to the rank of an agrarian zone in an economically subordinate, dependent, and inferior position.

*

It was on these grounds that we stated in the introduction of the present paper: compared to the earlier situation, the role of East-Central Europe actually increased in the period under consideration. It was the character

[13] This setback, this stagnation in the *export capacity* of the East-Central European countries in their supplies to the West can be demonstrated directly and numerically (by the drop in Polish grain exports, Hungarian cattle- and copper exports). Moreover, it may be added here — though sufficient quantitative evidence is not available for the present — that sooner or later a similar tendency necessarily asserted itself in their *demand for imports* from the West, too. In fact, the predominance of the feudal-landlord trend crossed and hindered urban-bourgeois development as well as the bourgeois development of the peasantry, thus delaying the emergence of social strata representing modern-type consumption and narrowing the basis of modern-type national and international trade.

[14] For the latest summing up of the problems of "price revolution" and the period that followed, with plenty of references, see F. P. Braudel—F. Spooner, Prices in Europe from 1450 to 1750, *The Cambridge Economic History of Europe*, Vol. IV, from p. 378. particularly pp 421, 464, 467, 481. — Concerning grain prices conf.: B. H. Slicher van Bath, Die europäischen Agrarverhältnisse im 17. und der ersten Hälfte des 18. Jahrhunderts, *A. A. G.Bijdragen* **13**, Wageningen 1965, p. 144. — For prices in Poland see S. Hoszowski, The Revolution of Prices in Poland in the 16th and 17th Centuries, *Acta Poloniae Historica*, **II** (1959) Warsaw, from p. 7, particularly pp 10– 13. — Conf. M. Małowist, Die Problematik der sozial-wirtschaftlichen Geschichte Polens vom 15. bis zum 17. Jahrhundert, *La Renaissance et la Réformation en Pologne et en Hongrie, 1450–1650*, Budapest 1963, pp 20, 25. — For changes of prices in Hungary, see V. Zimányi, *Quelques aspects de la régression économique et sociale du XVIIe siècle*, (Manuscript.)

[15] K. Marx, *Capital, A Critique of Political Economy*, Vol. III, Moscow 1962, p. 233.

and the peculiar traits of this growth on the one hand, and the new elements in the development of modern world trade as it embarked on a new stage of the process on the other, which subsequently made conditions ripe for, and ushered in, approximately by the middle of the 17th century, the unfavourable turning-point and negative trend in the international economic-commercial role of East-Central Europe, what is more, in her historical destiny for several centuries.

ADDENDA

THE ROLE OF EAST–CENTRAL EUROPE IN INTERNATIONAL TRADE (16TH AND 17TH CENTURIES)

Page 217:

For the second question raised in Note 2 and for the problem of the East European routes of medieval long–haul trade, referred to in Note 3, see the paper *Levantine Trade and Hungary in the Middle Ages (Theses, Controversies, Arguments)* in this volume.

Pages 225-234:

For a more detailed discussion of the quality and composition of western cloth imports to Hungary in 1457–1458 and 1542, respectively, see the paper *Zur Geschichte der Handelsbeziehungen zwischen Österreich und Ungarn im 15. und 16. Jahrhundert* in this volume.

Page 226, Note 1:

There are two estimates, rather different, of the customs value of pepper imports ($166\frac{2}{3}$ centners = about 98 metric quintals) registered in the customs book of Pozsony (Pressburg, Bratislava) for the fiscal year 1457–1458. One of them comes to 2834 golden florins, the other mounts up to 5004 golden florins: *Kováts*, op. cit. pp. 79–8l. — Reckoning with the first figure, we get to 4344 florins as an aggregate customs value of imported pepper and other spices (as indicated in the text); in the second case the sum runs up to 6515 florins. — Instead of "The discussion of other items" (page 226, line 18) read "The detailed examination of other items"; instead of "one commodity" (line 23) read "one commodity–group"; instead of "estimating these figures" (page 227, line 10) read "interpreting these figures".

Page 229, Notes 19-22:

The American scholar, whose study on metallurgy has been referred to, is *J. U. Nef.* — The Slovak medievalist *P. Ratkoš* tried to demonstrate that the *Saigern*–technique of raw copper refining (that is separation of silver and pure copper by smelting with addition of lead) had already been in use in Slovakia (Northern Hungary) before the Thurzó–Fugger Company started to operate in the mining district of Besztercebánya (Neusohl, Banská Bystrica) in 1494–1495: Das Kupferwesen in der Slowakei vor der Entstehung der Thurzó–Fuggerschen Handelsgesellschaft. In: Der Aussenhandel Ostmitteleuropas 1450–1650. Hg. von I. Bog, Köln–Wien, 1971, pp. 584–599. — However, the arguments brought forward by Ratkoš are not convincing, since he did not consider the successive phases of copper refinement: black or raw (crude) copper — fine or rich copper (*Reichkupfer*) — pure copper (*Garkupfer*); therefore, he failed to distinguish the *Saigerhütten* from the less developed types of copper smelteries which were not yet capable of the final operation of copper refining. See our remarks in: Precious Metals in the Age of Expansion. Papers of the XIVth International Congress of the Historical Sciences (San Francisco, 1975). Ed. by H. Kellenbenz, Stuttgart, 1981, pp. 300–302. — In the environs of Nuremberg the *Saigern*–technique was already known in the beginning of the 15th century at least, but the general spread of the method in this area and, shortly thereafter, in the Mansfeld district took only place between the 1460s and 1480s: *E. Westermann*, Die Bedeutung des Thüringer Saigerhandels für den mitteleuropäischen Handel an der Wende vom 15. zum 16. Jahrhundert. In: Jahrbuch für die Geschichte Mittel– und Ostdeutschlands, XXI, Berlin, 1972, pp. 81–89; *L. Suhling*, Der Saigerhüttenprocess. Die Technologie des Kupfersaigerns, Stuttgart, 1976, pp. 56–75.

Page 230, Notes 24-25:

As for the trade balance of late–medieval Hungary, *E. Fügedi* presented his considerations once more: Der Aussenhandel Ungarns am Anfang des 16. Jahrhunderts. In: Der Aussenhandel Ostmitteleuropas, op. cit. pp. 56–85. — Since his reasoning has not changed, our objections have not expired:

1) The ratio of 33.3 per cent for exports/66.7 per cent for imports is not that seen in the customs book of Pozsony from 1457–1458; here the total of western trade consisted of only 10.62 per cent exports and 89.38 per cent imports.

2) The 1/3:2/3 ratio (as calculated by O. Paulinyi) already included copper exports; therefore it is not permissible to take copper into account once again.

3) Sources from the middle of the 15th century and those from the early 16th may not be treated indiscriminately, since in the meantime significant changes had occurred in Hungary's western trade (as explained in the text pp. 234, 242–243).

O. Paulinyi also propounded his view again. Bringing forward partly new evidence, he completed and confirmed his former statements: around the middle of the 15th century the deficit of Hungary's trade balance amounted to about 200 000 florins in relation to Western and Central Europe and to some 100 000 florins in that to Italy. To compensate the import surplus in these two relations, about 300 000 golden florins went abroad annually, that is almost three quarters of the country's annual gold production, calculated by Paulinyi at 1500 kgs for the same period: Nemesfémtermelésünk és országos gazdaságunk általános alakulása (The Production of Precious Metals and the Development of National Economy in Hungary) 1000–1526, Századok, 1972, no. 3, pp. 561–602. — The prominent medievalist *E. Mályusz* regarded Paulinyi's figures as exaggerated and counted the yearly gold production of the country to have been only about 800 kgs in those days: Das ungarische Goldgulden in Mitteleuropa zu Beginn des 15. Jahrhunderts. In: Études Historiques Hongroises 1985, Budapest, 1985, II, pp. 32–33. — However, his reasoning is vulnerable, for he set out from the estimates of the revenues drawn by the Hungarian King from gold mining (the so–called *urbura* which, in principle, took the tenth part of the gold produced); whereas Paulinyi studied the accounts rendered by the Royal Chambers of Mines.

Another point has been touched upon by *Gy. Ember*. Considering that some eighty years later, in 1542, the aggregate trade balance of the country's western border customs stations already was highly active (see p. 239 in our text), but the balance of the Pozsony station itself remained adverse even at that time, he put the question whether or not it was possible to suppose that the situation had been similar as early as 1457–1458: Aktív vagy passzív? Külkereskedelmünk a XV. században (Surplus or deficit? Hungary's Foreign Trade in the 15th Century), História, V (1983), no. 4, pp. 55–56. — Well, it is certainly not impossible that larger droves of cattle than those registered in Pozsony passed through the western border at other places already in 1457–1458 (see p. 227). Yet it is sure that the real boom of the Hungarian cattle export — the predominant surplus factor of the aggregate trade balance in 1542 — only dated from the latter part of the 15th century. The customs station of Nagyszombat (Tyrnau, Trnava) — which controlled nearly a third (30.85 per cent) of the westbound cattle export in 1542 — had been but an insignificant outstation of the Trencsén (Trentschin, Trenčin) customs office even at the end of the 15th century; moreover, the customs station of Szempc (Wartberg, Senec) — through which more than the half (55.21 per cent) of the cattle droves left the country in 1542 — had not yet existed in those days (as attested by Act 34 of the Diet 1498 which listed the customs stations and outstations of the country; see p. 235, note 4).

All in all: we do not think that the picture outlined in the text of the structure of Hungary's western trade, with a debit balance of 200 000 to 300 000 florins around the middle of the 15th century, calls for more than minor modifications. Eventually, it should be borne in mind that exactly the Hungarian gold and silver which acquitted the deficit of the country's trade balance in the western relation stimulated the western merchants, more than anything up to the Late Middle Ages, to trade with this country.

Page 232, Note 27:

For the adverse trade balance of and the outflow of silver from medieval Bohemia, also see *F. Graus*, Die Handelsbeziehungen Böhmens zu Deutschland und Österreich im 14. und zu Beginn des 15. Jahrhunderts. In: Historica, vol. II, Praha, 1960, pp. 106–110.

Page 237, Notes 14-16:

Recent research into copper production and trade of the Mansfeld district: *E. Westermann*, Das Eislebener Garkupfer und seine Bedeutung für den europäischen Kupfermarkt 1460–1560, Köln–Wien, 1971. — As for the international copper markets, the results of Westermann are largely concordant with the sketch outlined in our text (pp. 228–229, 237–238). Sorts of Tyrolean copper were sold in South Germany, and also on South-European markets; "Eislebener" (that is Mansfeld) copper was partly worked up in the brass industry of the Lower Rhine region (Aachen, first of all), partly sold in Nuremberg and North Germany; Hungarian copper was exported to Venice in diminishing quantities, to Antwerp (later on to Hamburg and Amsterdam) in increasing amounts, and from here partly shipped to the Iberian Peninsula. — It is worth adding that around the middle of the 16th century copper consignments from Besztercebánya were also delivered to Turkish traders (Hungarian merchants acting as intermediaries), in exchange mainly for "Turkish articles" (which still included oriental spices): Debrecen története (A History of the Town Debrecen in Hungary), I. Ed. by I. Szendrey, Debrecen, 1984, p. 373. — To be sure, mining in the central Balkan regions, rather significant in the Late Middle Ages, already was on the decline at this time: *S. Ćirković*, The Production of Gold, Silver and Copper in the Central Parts of the Balkans from the 13th to the 16th Century. In: Precious Metals, op. cit. pp. 54, 57, 60; conf. the century-old basic work by *C. Jireček*, Die Handelsstrassen und Bergwerke von Serbien und Bosnien während des Mittelalters, Prag, 1879, pp. 41–58.

Pages 240-241:

It is beyond doubt that the occupation of Central Hungary by the Turks after 1541 and the recurrent Turkish wars restricted western import trade. All the same, a rather significant purchasing power turned up on Hungarian markets in the second half of the 16th century, due to the boom of cattle exports and the rise in prices of agricultural products. This is why English kersies as well as Moravian and Silesian cloths of middling quality were much in demand in those days, similarly to Poland; see pp. 247–250.

Page 242, Note 33:

The over 3.5–fold rise in customs value per head of cattle between 1457–1458 and 1542 is certainly exaggerated. 2.83 florins, as a customs value for 1457–1458, corresponded to the contemporary average market price of cattle in Pozsony. (*Kováts*, op. cit. pp. 188–190.) In 1542, in turn, the official customs valuation at 10 florins far exceeded the actual price which was not more than 4–6 florins per head in those days. (For the method of customs valuation, see *Gy. Ember*, Magyarország nyugati külkereskedelme a XVI. század közepén (Hungary's Western Trade in the Middle of the 16th Century), Budapest, 1988, pp. 566–567; for the actual cattle prices, *S. Takáts*, Szegény magyarok (Miserable Hungary), Budapest, s.a. pp. 132–133, 144–147.) Taking the actual cattle prices into account, we ought to reduce the export surplus considerably; but adding the copper and wine exports (hardly registered in the customs books of 1542), we can state beyond doubt that the western trade balance of Hungary was highly active at that time. — *H. Prickler* believed that the balance had become still more favourable later on (80 per cent exports: 20 per cent imports) and estimated the annual cattle export at 150 000–200 000 head (including transit droves from Moldavia) for the peak period 1575–1588: Das Volumen des westlichen ungarischen Aussenhandels vom 16. Jahrhundert bis 1700. In: Die wirtschaftlichen Auswirkungen der Türkenkriege. Hg. von O. Pickl, Graz, 1971, pp. 137, 140, 143. — However, his figures are excessive: the actual increase in cattle exports was not proportional to the increase in customs revenues (which served as starting point for his calculations), since the customs duty to be levied on cattle has been raised several times between 1542 and 1620 (as it is apparent even from his paper: p. 133).

Page 252, Note 28:

Between 1577 and 1583 the annual average of the export directed to Venice by the company of the Pettau (Ptuj) merchant Lucas Bazin, a Venetian by birth, amounted to 17225 oxen. However, merely a tiny fraction (hardly 2 per cent) left the country through the Slavonian customs stations, the overwhelming majority being driven out on the Győr (Raab)–Óvár (Ungarisch–Altenburg) route: *O. Pickl*, Die Auswirkungen der Türkenkriege auf den Handel zwischen Ungarn und Italien im 16. Jahrhundert. In: Die wirtschaftlichen Auswirkungen der Türkenkriege, op. cit. pp. 104–105.

Page 253, Note 30:

In the decade of 1610–1620 Danish exports reached its absolute peak at a level of 40 000–45 000 oxen from the Kingdom and 5000–7000 from Slesvig: *E. L. Petersen*, Production and Trade in Oxen 1453–1750: Denmark. In: Internationaler Ochsenhandel (1350–1750). Akten des 6th International Economic History Congress (Edinburgh, 1978). Hg. von E. Westermann, Stuttgart, 1979, p. 145.

Page 258, Notes 61-63:

The unfavourable changing in the balance of trade by the middle and second part of the 17th century is evident for both Hungary and Poland, but the degree of change has not yet been elucidated. It is possible that the export surplus diminished in large measure, but the balance did not turn adverse. As for Poland, "the Baltic corn trade reached its peak in the first part of the 17th century, whereas cattle exports displayed a sustained growth, from some ten thousand head in the 16th century up to 80 000 in the 18th. Accordingly, oxen trade had an increasing effect on Poland's trade balance": *J. Baszanowski*, Ochsenzuchtgebiete und Ochsenausfuhr aus Polen vom 16. bis 18. Jahrhundert. In: Internationaler Ochsenhandel, op. cit. p. 134. — In Hungary cattle trade played a decisive role in exports throughout the whole period, for grain exports (to Austria) grew to considerable size as late as the middle of the 18th century: *F. Eckhart*, A bécsi udvar gazdasági politikája Magyarországon Mária Terézia korában (The Economic Policy of the Vienna Court in Hungary in the Time of Maria Theresa), Budapest, 1922, pp. 190, 318.

Page 263, Note 13:

As for the downward tendency in the capacity of the East–Central European countries to absorb western manufactures, the developments of English woollen trade are highly instructive. After the successful sixteenth–century break–through in East–Central Europe, London exporters in the first part of the 17th century already regarded these markets as saturated by English products. The export of woollen fabrics coming under the term of "shortcloths" — of which about three–quarters were shipped from London to Northern Sea and Baltic ports and from there for a great part to East–Central European markets – took a downward trend as early as 1614, i.e. already prior to the outbreak of the Thirty Years' War. A Hamburg factor of the big London export company, the Merchant Adventurers, noticed one of the causes with sharp eyes. In 1623 he reported on the conditions of the North German peasant who, although paying less monetary rent than his English counterparts, is "tied to great slavery, to bring in his landlords' corn, and, in fine, to do him all the servile work that is to be done"; peasants living in such miserable circumstances could hardly be expected to buy imported English woollens. — Cited by *R. H. Tawney*, Business and Politics under James I. Lionel Cranfield as Merchant and Minister, London, 1958, pp. 44–45. — For the discription of this turn of events (which gave the London wholesale merchants a strong impulse to look for new export markets, partly through the Mediterranean in the Levant, partly through the Iberian ports in the American colonies), see from the present writer: East–Central Europe and World Trade at the Down of Modern Times, Acta Historica Acad. Sci. Hung., XXVII, 3–4 (1981), esp. pp. 300–309.

XI

THE EAST-CENTRAL EUROPEAN ASPECT OF THE OVERSEAS DISCOVERIES AND COLONIZATION

1.

The subject to be discussed in the A1 session of the Leuven Congress: *The European discovery of the world and its economic effects on preindustrial society (1500–1800)* can be approached form three main aspects:

a) The direct effects of the European expansion on the "discovered" extra-European regions themselves, that is on the newly *colonized territories* in America, Africa and the Far East (including their intercolonial relations to each other).

b) The effects or reactions of the overseas discoveries on the colonizing European "motherlands" (home countries), that is on the development of economy and society in *Western Europe.*

c) The effects or interferences of the overseas expansion on the preindustrial economy and society in the *Eastern European* — especially East-Central European — countries, which did not take part in the discoveries and colonial ventures, but felt their transmissions and consequences sooner or later.

These three sorts of effects became related to one another and mutually influenced each other in the historical process of the formation of the *early modern world economy.*

Consequently, the inherent issue of the subject under discussion can be put like this: what was the correlation and interaction between the three main factors or components of the early modern world economy — that is the West European, the East European and the overseas (colonial) economies? How did the changes, taking place in this or that relation, affect the whole system of interdependencies?

This basic problem can also be formulated in the following way: what was the role of the newly discovered overseas territories on the one hand, and that of the Eastern area of Europe on the other, in the economic growth of the Western part of the Old World? What were the similarities and differences between the East European countries and the overseas colonies as regards their economic relations with Western Europe? What were the common and divergent features of their position in the framework of the unfolding international division of labour?

From the East-European angle, we may add a third formulation, too: in what manner did the discoveries, the appearence of the overseas colonies, their joining in world trade and world market affect the economic needs and demands of Western Europe towards the Eastern European area? How did these demands and transmissions change in the successive phases of colonization and emergence of modern world economy?

On the successive phases of the process, i.e. the periodization of the space of time under discussion (1500–1800), a few more words need to be said in advance.

Apart from some historical *antecedents* prior to 1500, which are to be touched upon briefly, there is a significant turning-point or dividing line within the given space of time, namely somewhere around the middle of the 17th century. Thus, we can distinguish the *first* period of the economic effects of the discoveries (in other words: the first phase of the nascent modern world economy) from the *second* period of the process roughly about the mid-17th century.

2.

From among the historical *antecedents* we do not cite here the earlier expeditions of European discoverers, but the earlier beginnings of the so-called economic shift from the Mediterranean to the Atlantic, so often attributed by historians to nothing else but the overseas discoveries. Our concern is whether or not the crossing of the Atlantic and the "Carreira da India" is to be regarded as the starting point of this economic shift.

As a matter of fact, as early as the 14th–15th centuries the weight of international trade in Europe began to shift increasingly from the luxuries to the necessities, from the precious Levantine wares and other high-priced articles to the bulky goods for mass-consumption. It was that time that a "*modern-type*" international trade emerged, and stimulated by the internal growth of the European economy and based on a widening consumer market, it began to overshadow the "*medieval-type*" long-haul trade, which had met primarily the luxury demands of high-class (and rich burgher) consumers.

With the development of market production and long-distance trade in commodities of prime necessity, the relative importance of the two central regions of European commerce, the Mediterranean and the Baltic Sea area, began to shift in the favour of the latter. For it was above all the ties of the medieval-type "rich trade" that connected the Mediterranean with the rest of Europe, while its trade in mass-consumption goods remained virtually within the basin itself. On the other hand, it was from the Baltic region that everyday consumer goods (grain first of all) and industrial raw materials (timber, copper etc.) were exported in increasing quantities to Western Europe, along the coasts of the Atlantic. Thus the weight of international trade began to shift from the Mediterranean to the Atlantic in such a way that Atlantic coast shipping, the principal carrier of the bulky goods of European production, was increasingly becoming the main artery of the modern-type long-distance commerce.

Hence, the economic shift from the Mediterranean to the Atlantic did not begin with the discovery of the New World and the "Cape-route" by the Spaniards and the Portuguese, respectively. The primary motive of this transfer was in the internal growth of the European economy, in the rise of market production and division of labour. As a result, several regions of Western Europe with a growing industry, Netherlands first of all, raised increasing additional demand for agricultural produce and raw materials which were supplied largely from the Baltic region and the East European territories connected with it by waterways. These commodities, in turn, were carried to the Western consumers mainly by the Atlantic coast shipping, from the Sound to the Straits (and, later on, even through the Straits into the Mediterranean basin).

Then, of course, the process of shifting was greatly promoted and quickened by the overseas discoveries and the commercial expansion across the Atlantic and around Africa.[1]

3.

It is all the more justified to distinguish between the two components of the process — though later they became closely intertwined — as the start of the economic shift to the Atlantic was due to the growing trade in bulky goods for common consumption or for industrial use; the discoveries, the opening up of the new sea-routes, however, were originally stimulated not by the demands of such a "modern-type" trade, but rather by those of the "medieval-type" long-haul commerce: to obtain the valuable eastern spices in a direct way and to get hold of the fabulous treasures of the Orient.

Moreover, not only the stimuli of the discoveries were of the "old type", but also the newly opened sea-routes were used for quite a long time for shipping mainly the traditional wares of "rich trade": spicery and precious metals. As a matter of fact, in the first period of the economic effects of the discoveries (in other words: in the first phase of the rise of modern world economy) the overseas colonies were attached to their Western European motherlands by a medieval-type long-distance commerce rather than in terms of a modern world market. In the 16th century Far Eastern Portuguese colonies supplied Europe

1 For a more detailed discussion see from the present author: *The Shifting of International Trade Routes in the 15th–17th Centuries, Acta Historica Academiae Scientiarum Hungaricae* (= AHA), XIV, 1968, pp. 287–321.

primarily with spices, through Lisbon and Antwerp.[2] In the first part of the 17th century English and Dutch colonial imports, which had taken over from the Portuguese, presented almost the same commodity structure. Around three-quarters of what the Dutch East India Company landed in Amsterdam[3] and two-thirds of what was imported by the English East India Company to the home country was still pepper and other spices between 1619 and 1621.[4] From Spanish America, in turn, it was mainly bullion (largely silver) that was carried by the New Spain and Isthmus fleet to Seville and Cádiz; its share in the total value of Spanish imports was more than 95% in 1594 and still as high as 84% in 1609.[5]

At the same time, from the late 15th century up to the early 17th, it was rather the countries of Eastern Europe — more precisely: of *East-Central Europe* — that began to be linked to the expanding Western European economy in a "modern" way, by the ties of an evolving new-type international trade, namely as suppliers of mass-consumption foodstuffs (agricultural products) and raw materials as well as buyers of manufactured consumer goods, first of all textiles. This obviously appears from the contemporary foreign trade data of two East-Central European countries, Poland and Hungary.

Poland provided Western European consumers mainly with grain (primarily rye) and also cattle and furs (the latter were transit goods from Russia). In the middle of the 16th century these three commodities amounted to about 90% of her exports to the West. Cattle and furs went overland, but rye and wheat were shipped on the Baltic-North Sea route to Atlantic ports, overwhelmingly Amsterdam.[6] Of Poland's sea-borne exports cereals alone came to an average of 66% of

2 V. Magelhães-Godinho, *L'économie de l'empire portugais aux XVe et XVIe siècles*, Paris, 1969.

3 Of Dutch imports drugs and dyestuffs accounted for about 10%, various textiles for a further 16% in 1619–1621, while pepper imports alone amounted to 56%, together with other spices to 74%: K. Glamann, *Dutch-Asiatic Trade 1620–1740*, Copenhagen–The Hague, 1958, p. 13.

4 In 1621, according to the contemporary economist Thomas Mun, one-third of the English Company's imports consisted of indigo and additional dyestuffs, all other of spicery: E. Lipson, *The Economic History of England*[4], Vol. II, *The Age of Mercantilism*, London, 1947, p. 288.

5 The share of other imported goods was insignificant; for 1594: cochineal 2,82%; hides, 1,16%; indigo, 0,29%; others, 0,11%: E. J. Hamilton, *American Treasure and the Price Revolution in Spain 1501–1650*, Cambridge, Mass., 1934, pp. 33–34.

6 R. Rybarski, *Handel i polityka handlowa Polski w XVI stuleciu*[2], Warszawa, 1958, Vol. I, pp. 162-170, 195–197, 245–248; Vol. II, pp. 5–14; H. Samsonowicz, *Les foires en Pologne au XVe et XVIe siècle sur la toile de fond de la situation économique en Europe*. In: *Der Aussenhandel Ostmitteleuropas 1450—1650*. Hg. von I. Bog, Köln–Wien, 1971, pp. 255–258; A. Attman, *The Russian and Polish Markets in International Trade 1500–1650*, Göteborg, 1973, pp. 39–40, 48–50, 53–55.

the total over the years 1565–1585. The rest comprised of timber, tar, hemp and other raw materials especially required by the ship building industry.[7]

Hungary's three main export items to the West also were foodstuffs and raw materials: cattle, wine and copper. In the customs journals from 1542 which embrace a great part of Hungary's western trade, but do not include the copper consignements, cattle accounted for nearly 90% of the registered export value.[8] Some two decades later cattle (oxen) also amounted to almost 90% of the exports which went westward from the Turkish-occupied Hungarian Plain.[9] While the herds of cattle were driven mostly to the South German towns (via Vienna or Moravia) and to Venice (via Laibach/Ljubljana), the Hungarian wine was exported mainly to Silesia and, in increasing quantities, to Poland, satisfying the demands of Polish noblemen who get rich by the profitable grain trade directed to the Atlantic coasts.[10] The North Hungarian (Slovakian) copper, in turn, reached the Atlantic littoral on its own way, especially after the Fugger-Thurzó Company had started to operate in copper mining of Neusohl (Besztercebánya/Banská Bystrica).[11] Whereas around 1500 over 32% of the Company's copper export went (mainly through Villach) to Venice and Triest, and only 24% to Antwerp (via Danzig/Gdansk and Stettin/Szczecin), in the 1530s Northern Italy was the destination of not more than 12–15%, and the Netherlands of nearly 50%.[12] From Antwerp copper and copper articles were carried among other places to Seville and Lisbon, to be sent from there to overseas colonies, also in the

7 Timber amounted to 5%, flax and hemp 12%, tar and potash 14%: A. Mączak, *Eksport zbozowy i problemy polskiego bilansu w XVI–XVII w.* In: *Pamietnik X powszechnego zjazdu historyków polskich w Lublinie*, Warszawa, 1968, p. 183. — Danzig/Gdansk played the leading role in Poland's Baltic trade, with a predominant share of grain export. In other Baltic ports the proportion of raw materials was higher; of Riga's exports not less than 60% consisted of flax and hemp in the 1590s: V. V. Dorosenko, *Eksport Rygi na zachód w okresie przynaleznosci do Rzeczypospolitej 1562–1620*, *Zapiski Historyczne*, 1966, p. 7.

8 Gy. Ember, *Zur Geschichte des Aussenhandels Ungarns im XVI. Jahrhundert.* In: *Études historiques*, Budapest, 1960, Vol. I, pp. 549–550.

9 Gy. Káldy-Nagy, *Statistische Angaben über den Warenverkehr des türkischen Eroberungsgebietes in Ungarn mit dem Westen in den Jahren 1560–1654.* In: *Annales Universitatis Budapestinensis, Sectio Historica*, XI, Budapest, 1970, pp. 275, 289, 291.

10 F. Lerner, *Die Bedeutung des internationalen Ochsenhandels für die Fleischversorgung deutscher Städte im Spätmittelalter und der frühen Neuzeit.* In: *Internationaler Ochsenhandel 1350—1750.* Hg. von E. Westermann, Stuttgart, 1979, p. 210; Gy. Komoróczy, *Borkivitelünk észak felé* [Wine Export from Hungary to the North], Kassa, 1944, pp. 245–253; H. Prickler, *Zur Geschichte des burgenländisch-westungarischen Weinhandels in die Oberländer Böhmen, Mähren, Schlesien und Polen*, *Zeitschrift für Ostforschung*, 1965, pp. 500-501, 731–738.

11 O. Paulinyi, *A középkori magyar réztermelés gazdasági jelentősége* [The Economic Significance of the Hungarian Copper Production in the Middle Ages], Budapest, 1933, pp. 4–8; J. Vlachovič, *Slovak Copper Boom on World Markets in the 16th and First Quarter of the 17th Centuries*, *Studia Historica Slovaca*, I, Bratislava, 1963, pp. 70–73, 77–78.

12 H. Van der Wee, *The Growth of the Antwerp Market and the European Economy (14th—16th Centuries)*, The Hague, 1963, Vol. I, p. 523.

form of coins, and even of rings and trinkets for lucrative "barter" with the natives.[13]

While exporting mass-consumption foodstuffs and raw materials to the West, the *East-Central European countries* imported mainly manufactured consumer goods from that direction. In the middle of the 16th century textiles accounted for 60% of the total western imports to Poland, and for 48% of her sea-borne imports, taken as the average of 1565–1585. After woollen cloths salt occupied the second place in maritime trade towards Poland, but hardware in overland commerce.[14] As regards Hungary, the picture is again similar to a considerable degree. About 68% of the western imports registered in the customs journals from 1542 was made up of textiles, including cloths (40%), clothing articles (15%), linen (12%). Here, too, hardware, with a share of some 9%, came after textile goods.[15]

The composition of cloth imports is not less relevant. The gaining ground of middle quality and cheaper sorts is noticeable, among others that of the kersey (named *karazja, karasia* in East-Central Europe), a lower-priced fabric of the English woollen industry, which met the demands of wider strata of consumers on the Polish and Hungarian markets.[16] A survey of the various destinations of English woollen export from 1561 listed Hungary as a remarkable market for "Hampshire kersies and northerns".[17] The North German factor of the famous London businessman Lionel Cranfield reported to his employer around the turn of century that "it is generally seen ... that, when corn is well sold at Danzig, then all sorts of cloth and kersies sell away in Poland".[18] From his letters information on the Hungarian market can be obtained, too. He did his main trade in northern kersey largely with German, in particular Nuremberg merchants, from whom it turned up in Hungary "where kersies are most vented".[19] On the other hand, the English fabric also reached Hungary from the South,

13 J. A. Goris, *Études sur les colonies marchandes méridionales (Portugais, Espagnols, Italiens) à Anvers de 1488 à 1567*, Louvain, 1925, pp. 239–243.

14 See Notes 6-7, and also B. Zientara, *Eisenproduktion und Eisenhandel in Polen im 16. und 17. Jahrhundert*. In: *Der Aussenhandel Ostmitteleuropas 1450–1650*, op. cit., pp. 279–281.

15 See Notes 8–9, and also from the present author: *Zur Geschichte der Handelsbeziehungen zwischen Österreich und Ungarn im 15. und 16. Jahrhundert*. In: *Mitteilungen des Österreichischen Staatsarchivs*, XXV, 1972, pp. 244-256.

16 Rybarski, op. cit., Vol. I, pp. 164–165; Vol. II, pp. 24, 35, 110, 134, 157–204, 303; Káldy-Nagy, op. cit., pp. 281–282; E. Vass, *Türkische Beiträge zur Handelsgeschichte der Stadt Vác (Waitzen) aus dem 16. Jahrhundert, Acta Orientalia Academiae Scientiarum Hungaricae*, XXIV, 1971, p. 12; W. Endrei, *Az angol karasia Magyarországon* [The English Kersey in Hungary], *Századok* [Centuries], 1974, pp. 785–800.

17 Lipson, op. cit., Vol. II, p. 188. — A centre for kersey production was in Yorkshire; hence "northern kersies": E. M. Carus-Wilson, *The Woollen Industry*. In: *The Cambridge Economic History of Europe* (= CEHE), Vol. II, *Trade and Industry in the Middle Ages*. Edited by M. Postan and E. E. Rich, Cambridge, 1952, pp. 418–419.

18 B. E. Supple, *Commercial Crisis and Change in England 1600–1642*², Cambridge, 1964, p. 29.

19 R. H. Tawney, *Business and Politics under James I. Lionel Cranfield als Merchant and Minister*, London, 1958, pp. 41, 57—58, 60.

due to the mediation of Venice, and later to the cargoes of the English Levant Company, unloaded in Adriatic ports.[20] — All in all: the western imports of the East-Central European countries in the 16th century were marked by the predominance of textiles (with an increasing proportion of lower-priced sorts) and the significant share of iron-wares, that is by the supply of manufactured consumer goods characteristic of the modern-type international trade.

In the course of the 16th century the *American colonies*, Spanish-America and Portuguese-Brazil, also developed some buyer's market for West European manufactures.[21] However, widening of the range of industrial exports to the New World and rising of modern-type relations in the transatlantic trade were accelerated only during the subsequent century, namely after the Dutch had penetrated into the Caribbean and, in particular, after the English and French had established their settlements in the West Indies.

As concerns the *Far Eastern colonies*, in turn, the industrial export from Western Europe was insignificant in the 16th century and failed to show noteworthy growth even during the 17th. The Portuguese, when "sailing out", were virtually unable to fill their cargo space with useful load other than precious metals and copper, for lack of goods to be offered for sale.[22] Though Dutch exports to East India were more varied (comprising of fire-arms, metals, linen, wine and norimbergeries), their invoice value nevertheless amounted to not more than a few per cent of their outgoing shipments, being practically dwarfed by the bullion and specie which they gave in exchange for their imports, overwhelmingly pepper and spices.[23] And though the English made attempts from the very outset at exporting cloths and kerseys to the Far East, too, they soon had to realize that such articles were "dead commodities" there, lying unsold and "eaten up with moths and white ants."[24] Thus, in exchange for colonial imports the English East India Company, too, exported mainly precious metals and

20 R. Davis, *England and the Mediterranean 1570–1620*. In: *Essays in the Economic and Social History of Tudor and Stuart England*. Edited by F. J. Fisher, Cambridge, 1961, p. 120; Zs. Teke, *The Import of Woollen Cloth in Zagreb in the Middle of the 16th Century*. In: *Economy, Society, Historiography*. Dedicated to Zs. P. Pach on his 70th Birthday. Edited by F. Glatz, Budapest, 1989, pp. 83–91.

21 C. H. Haring, *Trade and Navigation between Spain and the Indies in the Time of the Hapsburgs*, Cambridge, Mass., 1918, pp. 62–64, 133–136, 211–213; H. et P. Chaunu, *Séville et l'Atlantique 1504–1650*, Vol. VIII, 1, Paris, 1959.

22 J. H. Parry, *Transport and Trade Routes*. In: CEHE, Vol. IV, *The Economy of Expanding Europe in the 16th and 17th Centuries*. Edited by E. E. Rich and C. H. Wilson, Cambridge, 1967, p. 165.

23 Glamann, op. cit., pp. 40–48.

24 Lipson, op. cit., Vol. II, pp. 277–278, 286. — Cf. "English cloth will not sell [in India]; it was only bought at first by great men to cover their elephants and make saddles for their horses. But for garments they use none in these parts": cited by F. J. Fisher, *London's Export Trade in the Early 17th Century*, *The Economic History Review* (= EHR), 2nd Ser., III, 2, 1950, p. 157.

specie, their share varying between 70 and 90% of the total export value throughout the 17th century as well as in the early 18th.[25]

All this goes to show that in the *first phase* of the economic effects of the discoveries and colonization it was not yet the overseas colonies, but rather the East-Central European countries that were tied to the economy of Western Europe in terms of a modern world market. In other words: in the *first period* of the nascent world economy it was not yet the *inter*continental trade between the West European motherlands and their colonies, but rather the *intra*continental trade between the western and eastern (east-central) regions of Europe that realized modern-type relations in the long-distance commerce. The advancing industrial areas in Western Europe were stimulated — besides interior motives — by the market chances in East-Central Europe to step up commodity production, to outdo guild-based craftsmanship and to establish the initial forms of manufactories.

4.

In the 16th century the West European markets offered not only growing demand for the East-Central European agricultural products and raw materials, but also favourable terms of trade, due to the so-called Price Revolution. This remarkable phenomenon of the first period of the emergent world economy was connected with both the overseas discoveries and the new-type developments in intra-European trade.

From the middle of the 1540s on, with the influx of American treasure to the Old World, the enlarged supply of bullion resulted in a depreciation of money and a rise in prices.[26] However, the price-advance had started in several areas of Western Europe a few decades earlier, since German and Portuguese-African ("West-Sudanese") silver and gold had already increased the amount of precious metals in circulation.[27] On the other hand, the shifting in the commodity structure of international trade from luxuries to necessities, has been followed by a shift in the price structure, too. It was primarily mass-consumption foodstuffs and raw materials that went up in price; luxuries and manufactures were lagging behind in this respect.[28]

25 K. N. Chaudhuri, *Treasure and Trade Balances: the East India Company's Export Trade*, EHR, 2nd Ser., XXI, 3, 1968, pp. 482–484.

26 E. J. Hamilton, *The History of Prices before 1750*. In: *XIe Congrès International des Sciences Historiques*, Stockholm, 1960, Vol. I, pp. 144–164.

27 *Precious Metals in the Age of Expansion.* Papers of the XIVth International Congress of Historical Sciences (San Francisco, 1975). With Final Remarks by H. Kellenbenz, Stuttgart, 1981, pp. 307–328.

28 F. Braudel–F. Spooner, *Prices in Europe from 1450 to 1750*. In: CEHE, Vol. IV, pp. 378, 421, 464–467; P. H. Ramsey (ed.), *The Price Revolution in 16th-Century England*, London, 1971; W. Abel, *Agrarkrisen und Agrarkonjunktur. Eine Geschichte der Land- und Ernährungswirtschaft Mitteleuropas seit dem hohen Mittelalter²*, Hamburg–Berlin, 1966, pp. 113–120, 145, 152, 175.

The price revolution, or rather "agrarian price" or "price structure revolution" was not limited to Western Europe; through the expanding network of intracontinental trade relations it affected all European countries involved in the nascent modern world economy. It also reached East-Central Europe, and resulted in a rise of agricultural prices on the domestic markets, too.[29]

The agrarian boom (also prevailing in Hungary, despite the Turkish occupation of the middle area of the country) appealed to several groups of noble landowners in East-Central Europe to involve themselves in commerce — where possible, in the export business, where not, in the domestic trade. In order to increase the quantity of marketable produce, they returned from money rents to rents in kind in many places and expanded their seigniorial demesnes (*Gutswirtschaft, Vorwerk, folwark, allodium*). At first they used paid labour, too, but from the late 16th century on unpaid servile labour became overwhelming in the rural economy. It was thus that the immediate advantage of high agricultural prices and favourable terms of trade turned into a historical disadvantage in the long run for the East-Central European countries, the strenghtening of servile bonds being the result."[30]

The re-appearance of serfdom ("*zweite Leibeigenschaft*", *Erbuntertänigkeit, poddaństwo, perpetua rusticitas*) was not long to bring to the surface its own inherent contradictions. By the middle of the 17th century the system encountered the barriers it itself had set to production and trade by the deterioration of peasant holdings. This was shown, among others, in the decline of west-bound Polish grain exports, explicable partly from the production, partly from the market side. In the 1630–40s it already occurred more than once that Dutch vessels left Gdansk with ballast in their cargo space since grain supply in the port did not suffice to meet West European demands.[31] On the other hand, from the 1660s on England became a grain-exporting country and remained so for nearly a century. "Grain was exported largely to Holland, and at one time it was thought that England would supplant the Baltic lands as the granary of the Dutch."[32] English corn was also carried to the Iberian Peninsula, previously another regular market for Baltic grain. In addition, the cultivation of maize

29 S. Hoszowski, *The Revolution of Prices in Poland in the 16th and 17th Centuries, Acta Poloniae Historica* (= APH), II, 1959, pp. 7–12; St. Kazimír, *Nacrt vyvoja cien obilnín na Slovensku v 16. a 17. stor.* In: *Agrikultura*, 9, Bratislava, 1970; V. Zimányi, *Mouvements des prix hongrois et l'évolution européenne (XVIe–XVIIIe siècles)*, AHA, XIX, 1973, pp. 305–333.

30 For a more detailed discussion see from the present author: *Die ungarische Agrarentwicklung im 16.–17. Jahrhundert. Abbiegung vom westeuropäischen Entwicklungsgang*. Budapest, 1964. — For Poland: M. Małowist, *Die Problematik der sozial-wirtschaftlichen Geschichte Polens vom 15. bis zum 17. Jahrhundert*. In: *La Renaissance et la Réformation en Pologne et en Hongrie 1450—1650*, Budapest, 1963; J. Topolski, *La régression économique en Pologne du XVIe au XVIIIe siècle*, APH, VII, 1962, pp. 46–49.

31 M. Bogucka, *Handel baltycki a bilans handlowy Polski w pierwszej polowie XVII wieku, Przegląd Historyczny*, LIX, 1968, pp. 248–251.

32 Lipson, op. cit., Vol. II, pp. 459–460; T. S. Ashton, *Economic Fluctuations in England 1700–1800*, Oxford, 1959, p. 183.

and potatoes — both of American origin — came into use in Europe: the latter in Ireland, the former (along with rice) in Italy and Iberia had become important in mass consumption by the late 17th century.[33] As a consequence of these changes in supply and demand, the quantity of grain shipped westward through the Sound sank from the annual average of 68,500 lasts in the years 1600–1649 to the average of 55,800 lasts between 1650 and 1699, and merely to 31,800 lasts in 1700-1749.[34]

A parallel tendency can be observed in the case of Hungarian overland cattle exports that were based overwhelmingly on livestock breeding of the Hungarian Plain, the outskirts of "peasant towns". However, big landowners and lesser alike, while expanding their "allodial" agriculture similar to the Polish folwark-management, joined in the cattle trade as well, making use of their nobiliary prerogatives against the peasant-burgher cattle-dealers. At the same time the main foreign consumers of Hungarian livestock, the South German towns and Venice, felt increasingly the difficulties deriving from the commercial shift from the Mediterranean to the Atlantic. These circumstances combined to the subsequent decline of Hungary's westward cattle trade, whose annual volume had been at the least 60–80,000 heads in the 1560–1580s (some researchers estimate 100,000 or even more). After troubles and fluctuations in the first part of the 17th century, and a steep fall in the second (which ruined a lot of peasant-burgher cattle-dealers), only about 56,000 heads were exported yearly even in the 1730s, and it was as late as the 1760s that the annual average regained that of two centuries before.[35]

As concerns the other main Hungarian export — and indeed the one which had found its way to the Atlantic coast markets (Antwerp, later Hamburg and Amsterdam) — even this product was not able to keep its position in the West European centre of modern-type international trade during the 17th century. In the days of the Fugger-Thurzó Company (1494–1546), the average yearly copper production of Neusohl had

33 G. B. Masefield, *Crops and Livestock*. In: CEHE, Vol. IV, pp. 276–278, 299–301; B. H. Slicher van Bath, *Agriculture in the Vital Revolution*. In: CEHE, Vol. V, *The Economic Organization of Early Modern Europe*. Edited by E. E. Rich and C. H. Wilson, Cambridge, 1977, pp. 78–79.

34 J. A. Faber, *Het probleem van de dalende graanaanvoer uit de Oostzeelanden in de tweede helft van de zeventiende eeuw*. In: *A. A. G. Bijdragen*, Vol. 9, Wageningen, 1963, p. 12. — Cf. W. S. Unger, *Trade through the Sound in the 17th and 18th Centuries*, EHR, 2nd ser., XII, 2, 1959, p. 213.

35 L. Makkai, *Der ungarische Viehhandel 1550–1650*. In: *Der Aussenhandel Ostmitteleuropas 1450–1650*, op. cit., p. 492; H. Prickler, *Das Volumen des westlichen ungarischen Aussenhandels vom 16. Jahrhundert bis 1700*. In: *Die wirtschaftlichen Auswirkungen der Türkenkriege*. Hg. von O. Pickl, Graz, 1971, p. 140; *Magyarország ki-és beviteli forgalma az 1733–1743. évben* [Hungary's Export and Import Trade in the Years 1733–1743], *Magyar Gazdaságtörténelmi Szemle (= MGSz)* [Hungarian Economic History Review], 1894, pp. 100–101, 362–363; 1895, pp. 65-73; 1897, pp. 358–359; F. Eckhart, *A bécsi udvar gazdasági politikája Magyarországon Mária Terézia korában* [The Economic Policy of the Vienna Court in Hungary in the Time of Maria Theresa], Budapest, 1922, p. 218.

amounted to about 24,000 cwts (at the least four-fifths of this produce having been exported), and in the second part of the 16th century to 12–23,000 cwts. In the early 1610s, however, it came only to 8–10,000, and about 1650 merely to 3-4000 cwts.[36] By that time Sweden's copper production, far below the Hungarian figure in the previous century, ran up to some 50,000 cwts in 1650. Thus, further on Hungarian copper could only play a subordinate role on the world market where, in addition to the Swedish produce, new competition appeared in the form of Japanese and Chilean copper.[37]

Along with the set-back in market production and west-bound export of foodstuffs and raw materials, a similar trend was manifested in the decreasing capacity of the East-Central European region to absorb western industrial imports. Previously, at the time of the 16th-century Price Revolution, a significant purchasing power had turned up in this region, due to the boom in grain and cattle exports on favourable terms of trade. Consequently, there were good markets in Poland and Hungary for imported cloth and kersey, arriving from both the north-western and south-western direction. However, the Price Revolution slowed down already from the early 17th century on, and after intense fluctuations that differed by countries and commodities, it stopped generally by the middle of the century. The boom ceased and so did the favourable terms of trade for agricultural produce. At the time of a general fall in prices, agricultural prices went back more than those of other goods practically everywhere. From the movement of prices related to each other we can state that the depression in the 17th century was, above all, an agrarian slump and caused grave problems to countries engaged mainly in agricultural exports.[38] Consequently, the purchasing power for imported woollen fabrics on the Polish and Hungarian markets decreased. It was the peasantry whose purchasing power was most affected by the depression, all the more as it coincided with the stabilization of the "second serfdom".

This turn of events was soon reflected in the figures of the English woollen trade, too. English broadcloth and kersey exports, after the rapid rise in the first and second parts of the 16th century, respectively, began to decrease from the early 17th century on.[39] The decline was especially marked in the North

36 Vlachovič, op. cit., 70, 72–79, 81–87; H. Srbik, *Der staatliche Exporthandel Österreichs von Leopold I. bis Maria Theresia*, Wien–Leipzig, 1907, pp. 38, 43, 52–53, 126–128, 429.

37 E. F. Heckscher, *An Economic History of Sweden*, Cambridge, Mass., 1954, pp. 72, 85—88; K. Glamann, *The Dutch East India Company's Trade in Japanese Copper 1645–1736*, *The Scandinavian Economic History Review*, I, 1953; Haring, op. cit., 156.

38 P. Chaunu, *Le renversement de la tendance majeure des prix et des activités au XVIIe siècle*. In: *Studi in onore di A. Fanfani*, Milano, 1962, Vol. IV, pp. 219–255; B. H. Slicher van Bath, *Die europäischen Agrarverhältnisse im 17. und in der ersten Hälfte des 18. Jahrhunderts*. In: *A. A. G. Bijdragen*, 13, Wageningen, 1965, p. 144; Abel, op. cit., p. 152.

39 F. J. Fisher, *Commercial Trends and Policy in 16th-Century England*, EHR, X, 2, 1940, pp. 96–97; Idem, *London's Export Trade in the Early 17th Century*, EHR, 2nd Ser., III, 2, 1950, pp. 152–155.

German and Baltic ports: from 73,421 cloths in 1606 to 25,270 in 1640; and exactly these ports were the main intermediaries towards the East-Central European consumer. During the same time kersey, that had been so popular on East-Central European markets in the days of the agrarian boom, virtually disappeared as an export item: the 12,039 northern kerseys of 1606 can be contrasted to a mere 175 sent to North German ports in 1640.[40] The same holds true of the Adriatic ports, the other route of supply for the Hungarian consumer. In 1598 the Levant Company exported 18,031 kerseys to the Mediterranean, but in 1621 merely 2 300 kerseys and ceased exporting this fabric altogether after 1629.[41]

The unfavourable change in East-Central European market conditions from the beginning of the 17th century, induced the London wholesale merchants to look for new commercial routes and outlets. Hence also the initial attempts (mentioned above) by the English East India Company to export cloths and kersies to the Far East, failures though they had been. More successful were the endeavours to export lighter and cheaper mixed stuffs — the so-called new draperies — to Southern Europe and even further afield. Indeed, the rise of "new draperies" can be considered as the reaction of English textile industry to the narrowing demand for "old draperies" in East-Central Europe, in particular: an innovation that adapted to the needs and climate of the newly opened markets in the South. "The Spanish market was made especially attractive by internal inflation and colonial purchases." In 1609 almost 46%, in 1640 about 65% of the new light fabrics were exported from London to Spanish and Mediterranean ports, and from the former to the American colonies, too. In the 1660s nearly two-thirds of the English textile exports were in new draperies, and by the end of the century the figure had reached almost three-quarters of the total.[42]

All this goes to show that *intra*continental commerce between West and East-Central Europe, which had grown vigorously both westwards and eastwards in the 16th century, slackened and receded in the course of the 17th century. Its share diminished in the expanding world trade.

5.

For, on the contrary, *inter*continental commerce between Western Europe and the overseas colonies produced a significant growth, and even a steep rise in some respects, during the 17th century.

40 Supple, op. cit., pp. 259–262.

41 L. Stone, *Elizabethan Overseas Trade*, EHR, 2nd Ser., II, 1, 1949, p. 58; Davis, op. cit., pp. 118–122.

42 C. H. Wilson, *Cloth Production and International Competition in the 17th Century*, EHR, 2nd Ser., XIII, 2, 1960, pp. 210–211; D. C. Coleman, *An Innovation and its Diffusion: the "New Draperies"*, EHR, 2nd Ser., XXII, 3, 1969, p. 422; Fisher, op. cit. [1950], pp. 154–155, 158; Supple, op. cit. p. 153.

As concerns the *Far Eastern* relation of colonial trade, the new developments affected imports from East India rather than exports to the Far East. As stated above, bullion and specie were still the substantial elements of both Dutch and English exports in the latter part of the 17th century, European commodities having a dull market in Asia.[43] Their import trade, in turn, underwent a considerable transformation. Of the shipments carried by the Dutch East India Company to Amsterdam in 1619–1621, only 16% consisted of oriental textile fabrics. By 1668–1670, however, the share of textile goods rose to more than 36%, and by 1698–1700 to nearly 55%, indisputably taking over the lead from pepper in the commodity structure of imports. In addition, it was at the same time that tea and coffee first appeared in quantities worth mentioning among Dutch imports (together making up 4,24%). In the first part of the 18th century they also became significant import items.[44]

Similar developments are noticeable in English-Asiatic trade. As aforesaid, in 1621 the imports of the English East India Company were estimated to comprise of pepper and other spices up to two-thirds, of indigo and other dyestuffs up to one-third of the total. In 1677, however, the share of spices and dyestuffs was estimated to be only about 10%, and that of cotton fabrics as high as 66%.[45] The import of Indian calicoes, hardly mentioned before, went up to an annual average of 240,000 pieces by 1663–1669, and to that of 861,000 by 1699–1701, two-thirds of the latter quantity being re-exported to continental Europe.[46] Indian printed cotton fabrics, attractively coloured and patterned and low in price, quickly gained a mass market in England, France and elsewhere, irrespective of restrictive measures taken to protect the woollen industries. Moreover, the growing European demand for these commodities resulted in the establishing of the cotton industry in England — an industry which later became the mainstay of the Industrial Revolution.[47]

As regards, in turn, the *American* relation, the new developments substantially transformed both import and export trade in the 17th century.

The influx of precious metals from the Spanish Indies, which kept increasing up to 1595, took a downward trend from 1601 to 1630 and ebbed down abruptly from 1631 to 1660. There was a concomitant decline in the whole commerce between Seville and the Spanish colonies, also due to the Dutch intrusion into the

43 See Notes 21, 23, and M. A. P. Meilinck-Roelofsz, *Aspects of Dutch Colonial Development in Asia in the 17th Century*. In: *Britain and the Netherlands in Europe and Asia*, London, 1968, p. 66.

44 Glamann, op. cit. [1958], pp. 13–15, 18, 20–22, 134–139, 165, 183, 212.

45 A further 13–13% consisted of silks (raw and finished) and saltpetre: Lipson, op. cit., Vol. II, p. 288, with reference to "The East India Trade a most Profitable Trade to the Kingdom" [1677].

46 R. Davis, *English Foreign Trade 1660–1700*, EHR, 2nd Ser., VII, 2, 1954, pp. 153–165. — The share of spice trade had fallen back to 3% by 1699–1701: ibid., pp. 163—166.

47 J. Kulischer, *Allgemeine Wirtschaftsgeschichte des Mittelalters und der Neuzeit*, München–Berlin, 1929, Vol. II, pp. 169–171; A. P. Wadsworth–J. de L. Mann, *The Cotton Trade and Industrial Lancashire 1600–1780*, Manchester, 1931.

American coasts at the turn from the 16th to 17th century.[48] But the recession in transatlantic trade in the second quarter of the 17th century proved to be temporary, since along with the dwindling of the bullion flow, and especially after 1660, the influx of other American treasures, such as sugar and tobacco, grew heavily. These new currents of trade derived increasingly from the newly established English and French settlements in the West Indies and North America.

American sugar began its career in long-haul trade from the Portuguese-Brazilian plantations in the late 16th century; whereas the English and French colonies, founded in the Antilles in the early 17th century, started mainly with cultivating tobacco on a small-farming scale. But West-Indian tobacco was soon challenged by that of Virginia, the first "Tobacco Colony" in North America. The competition induced the English and French settlers in the Caribbean to change over from tobacco to sugar-cane, from farmer-type economy to plantation, based on slave-labour.[49] From that time on the English and French "Sugar Colonies" multiplied sugar supply for Europe, evoking a drop in prices and changing sugar from a luxury into consumer goods for broader strata. Although Dutch merchants had been mainly engaged in this trade at the beginning, it was the English who, in respect of their own colonies, later gained the ascendancy, also supported by Cromwell's discriminative acts which proved to be more effective against the Dutch on American than on European waters.[50] Sugar imports from the West Indies to London, insignificant in the first part of the century, reached the annual average of 148,000 cwts in 1663–1669, and 371,000 cwts in 1699–1701. Similarly, tobacco shipments from Virginia and Maryland to London rose from 4 500 cwts in the 1630s to about 100,000 cwts by the end of the century, a third of the imported sugar and two-thirds of the tobacco being re-exported to continental Europe. "The *new type* of English trade expansion, dependent on the creation of English settlements and trading centres outside Europe, made its way by the cheapness of supply drawn from them, creating *new mass markets*."[51]

At the same time the Sugar Colonies also encouraged West European and West African exports to America, as they raised increasing demands for textiles, other manufactures and slave labour. Moreover, the minor English settlements in the West Indies were the first to specialize in sugar-cane cultivation to such a degree as to demand considerable grain imports, too; these were partly met from England and Ireland, partly from the North American "Bread Colonies", established in the last third of the 17th century. These North American colonies, in turn, which at the time

48 Hamilton, op. cit. [1934], pp. 34–36; E. Sluiter, *Dutch-Spanish Rivalry in the Caribbean Area 1594–1609, The Hispanic American Historical Review*, 1948; H. et P. Chaunu, op. cit., Vol. VI, 1, Paris, 1956, pp. 338–340, 474.

49 E. E. Rich, *Colonial Settlement and its Labour Problems*. In: CEHE, Vol. IV, pp. 338–350; Masefield, op. cit., pp. 289–295.

50 L. A. Harper, *The English Navigation Laws*, New York, 1939, pp. 242–245; J. H. Parry, op. cit., pp. 206–207.

51 Davis, op. cit. [1954], pp. 152—153, 165.

had hardly any produce of their own for transatlantic trade, re-exported part of their West Indian sugar imports in exchange for European manufactures.[52] Thus, industrial exports from Western Europe, chiefly from England, to America assumed growing dimensions. In the 1660s the share of European ports in the export value of English miscellaneous manufactures amounted to more than 61%, that of American and other colonial markets hardly to 39%; by the end of the century, however, the proportion became the reverse: 39% to European ports contrasted with 61% to American and other colonial ports. "Thus in the 17th century the English brass-, copper-, iron-ware, silk and linen, hat-making and tailouring, glass- and earthen-ware and paper, cordage and leather industries and others, were being fostered by their protected *market across the Atlantic.*"[53]

All in all: by the time when *intra*continental trade between Western and East-Central Europe subsided, the dynamic increase and substantial transformation of the *inter*continental trade already began to attach the American colonies to the West European economy with the ties of modern-type commercial relations. While in the first period West-European industries had been raised to a considerable degree on East-Central European markets, in the *second period* of the nascent modern world economy — in other words: in the *second phase* of the economic effects of the overseas discoveries and colonization — it was chiefly the American colonies which provided the main external market stimulus for the West European industrial growth.

By this time the transatlantic lines — and as for imports, the Cape-route, too — became the routes of a modern-type international commerce, carrying industrial and agricultural products increasingly for the common consumer. At the beginning of the 17th century, apart from trading with East India, England transacted almost all of her foreign trade with Europe. At the end of the century, however, nearly a third of English imports came from her colonies and about 30% of her exports were made up of American and Far Eastern goods (mainly tobacco, sugar and cotton fabrics); to the colonies went more than 15% of all English exports. "English trade as a whole now depended to a great extent upon the *extra-European* world."[54] Thus, the newer economic effects of the discoveries and colonization called forth the disappearance of the former historical situation wherein *intra-European* east-west trade had primarily realized the modern type of international commerce. In the second period of the rise of modern world economy East-Central Europe lost of its commercial significance.

52 A. P. Newton, *The European Nations in the West Indies 1493–1688*[2], New York, 1967, pp. 196–199, 279–285.

53 The values for the 1660s: £ 136,000 and £ 86,000; for 1699–1701: £ 161,000 and £ 259,000: Davis, op. cit. [1954], p. 154.

54 Davis, op. cit. [1954], pp. 150, 162.

6.

Finally, during the 17th century East-Central Europe saw the end of a historical period also from the point of view of the "old-type" international commerce, namely the spice trade. The change is clearly noticeable in the case of the Hungarian capital Buda, a frequented market for eastern spices in both the 15th and 16th centuries.

Medieval Buda received spices and other "Levant articles" mainly from Venice, through the famous *Venezianerstrasse*. It was from Vienna that oriental goods went to Western Hungary's trade centre and chief customs station Pressburg (Pozsony/Bratislava) and from there on to Buda. According to the customs journals of Pressburg 166$^{2}/_{3}$ centners of pepper — roughly 98 metric quintals — valued at about 5 000 gold florins, were imported in the fiscal year 1457–1458.[55] In the early 16th century this supply route became uncertain, due to the temporary setback in Venice's Levantine trade, but it recovered before long. According to the customs journals of 1542 the western pepper import amounted to some 163 centners again, at a value of about 4900 florins.[56]

After the middle of the 16th century, however, a new and plentiful route of spice imports opened up towards Buda, as a consequence of its incorporation into the Turkish Empire. According to the Turkish customs journals of Buda, in the fiscal year 1571–1572 roughly 320 metric quintals, in 1573–1574 about 550 metric quintals of pepper were brought to Buda from Turkish territory, mainly from Constantinople, through Belgrade.[57] These data give evidence of considerable pepper imports from the Mediterranean in the 1570s, and confirm the assertion that the appearance of the Portuguese in India did not bring with it the final decline of the Levantine spice trade. After the crisis in the early 16th century, this trade bloomed again on the traditional routes of the Levant and did not cease to be competitive with the "Atlantic" pepper, in spite of all the obstacles raised by the Portuguese.[58] What is more, the above data

55 F. Kováts, *Nyugat-Magyarország áruforgalma a XV. században a pozsonyi harmincadkönyv alapján* [The Trade of Western Hungary in the 15th Century on the Basis of the Customs Book of Pressburg], Budapest, 1902, pp. 78–81. — It should be noted that there also was another important supply route of eastern spices to medieval Hungary, going from the Black Sea coasts through Wallachia to Transylvania. According to the customs books of Hermannstadt (Nagyszeben/Sibiu) and Kronstadt (Brassó/Brasov) from the years 1500 and 1503, respectively, more than 460 metric quintals of pepper were imported to Transylvania. But this considerable amount of pepper contributed to the supply of Buda only in a small degree, being transported mainly to Wardein (Várad/Oradea) and Kaschau (Kassa/Kosice); see from the present author: *Le commerce du Levant et la Hongrie au Moyen Age*, *Annales ESC*, XXXI, 1976, pp. 1176–1194.

56 Gy. Ember, *Magyarország nyugati külkereskedelme a XVI. század közepén* [The Western Trade of Hungary in the Middle of the 16th Century], Budapest, 1988, pp. 93, 148.

57 Worked out on the basis of: L. Fekete–Gy. Káldy-Nagy, *Budai török számadáskönyvek* [Turkish Account Books of Buda], *1550–1580*, Budapest, 1962, pp. 13–276.

58 First demonstrated by F. C. Lane, *Venetian Shipping during the Commercial Revolution*, *American Historical Review*, XXXVIII, 1933, pp. 219–239, and *The Mediterranean Spice Trade: Further Evidence of its Revival in the 16th Century*, ibid., XLV, 1940, pp. 581—590.

reveal that not only Venice benefited from the 16th-century revival of the Mediterranean spice trade, but large quantities of eastern spices reached the European market through Constantinople as well.

In 1591 the Transylvanian Prince's ambassador to the Sublime Porte depicted Constantinople as still a lively market of "spiceries", and even a quarter century later the importation of spices from the Turkish Empire to Hungary and on, to Vienna (!) was talked of as an old practice which must be renewed now, when the "long war" with the Turks (1593–1606) was over and the first trade agreement with the Porte has been signed (1615). The old practice was described as taking Hungarian merchants to Vienna where they would buy merchandise necessary for the Turks, and carry it to Turkish territories; there, in turn, they would purchase "Turkish articles": silk, cotton, drugs and *spices from Constantinople*, to bring them back to Vienna.[59]

But the situation changed radically during the course of the next decades. Exactly fifty years later, in 1665, when the time came for the signing of the second trade agreement between the Habsburg and the Turkish Emperors, the winds were already blowing another way. Typical here is the activity of the first *Wiener Orientalische Handelskompanie*, established for Vienna-Constantinople trade. In the first *export* shipment of the Company, which left Vienna in July 1667, among other things we find 35 quintals of pepper, 9 quintals of indigo, further saffron and nutmegflowers. In the next spring another 18 quintals of pepper, 4 quintals of indigo, 3 quintals of ginger, and in February 1672 another 20 quintals of pepper, 10 quintals of ginger and 5 quintals of cloves began the journey *from Vienna to Constantinople*! On the other hand, the cargoes *imported* by the Company from Constantinople to Vienna included the usual "Turkish articles", but *no spices*.[60]

The picture is fairly convincing. During the first part of the 17th century a radical turnabout has occurred in the international spice trade. From the middle of the century onwards, eastern spices were no longer imported from Constantinople to Hungary and on, to Vienna, but rather from Vienna through Hungary to Constantinople! This is a clear indication of the fact that by that time the traditional caravan routes of the Levantine spice trade have truly and definitely declined; the Dutch and the English world sea-trade has achieved a monopoly. From then on, the Dutch and the English supplied the "Atlantic" pepper to the entire European market, and indeed — directly or indirectly — to the Levantine market.[61]

59 *Történelmi Tár* [Historical Collection], Budapest, 1881, pp. 173–180, 693–694; S. Takáts, *A dunai hajózás a XVI. és XVII. században* [The Danube Shipping in the 16th and 17th Centuries], MGSz, 1900, pp. 172–176, 194–197, 202–203.

60 For a detailed discussion see from the present author: *Levantine Trade and Hungary in the 16th–17th Centuries*. In: *Venezia e Ungheria nel contesto del barocco europeo*, Firenze, 1979, pp. 72-81.

61 Cf. H. Wätjen, *Die Niederländer im Mittelmeergebiet zur Zeit ihrer höchsten Machtstellung*, Berlin 1909, p. 337; H. Kretschmayr, *Geschichte von Venedig*, Vol. III, Stuttgart, 1934, p. 367; R. Mantran, *Instanbul dans la second moitié du XVIIe siècle*, Paris, 1962, pp. 577–580.

ADDENDA

THE EAST–CENTRAL EUROPEAN ASPECT OF THE OVERSEAS DISCOVERIES AND COLONIZATION

Page 181, Note 2:

The reference is to be completed: *V. Magelhães–Godinho,* L'économie de l'empire portugais aux XVe et XVIe siècles, Paris, 1969, pp. 550–551, 830–831.

Page 183, Note 13:

The opening of trade with West Africa and the Indies brought in its wake an unprecedented demand for copper and copper wares. From the later 15th century to the middle of the 16th, the Portuguese government — which had a nominal monopoly of the Guinea trade — annually imported about 10 000 quintals (580 752 kg) of copper, for a great part through Fugger agents. Some of the metal stayed in Portugal itself to be minted into coins or used domestically; after 1500 some of it departed with the *Carreira da India* where it took its place with silver as an indispensable lubricant of the spice trade; a large portion of it was destined for West Africa: *Magelhães–Godinho,* op. cit. pp. 374–375. — In the Guinea trade rings, bracelets, necklaces and, especially, basins of copper and brass were a standard currency for purchasing slaves, gold and ivory. In many parts of West Africa copper played much the same role that gold played in Europe: it was the *metalle de luxe,* used primarily for objects of prestige, ornamentation and ritual. In large measure it was scarcity that determined the role of copper in that region. While gold and iron were plentiful, there were only two deposits of copper ore in sub–Saharan West Africa, and even they were of brief exploitation: *E. W. Herbert,* The West African Copper Trade in the 15th and 16th Centuries. In: Precious Metals in the Age of Expansion. Papers of the XIVth International Congress of the Historical Sciences (San Francisco, 1975). Ed. by H. Kellenbenz, Stuttgart, 1981, pp. 119–130.

Page 185, Notes 26-27:

The influx of American treasure also involved an unfavourable change in the position of Central and East–Central Europe in world economy. In the later Middle Ages several countries of that area — Saxony, Bohemia, the Tyrol, Silesia and Hungary — had assumed a position of dominance in supplying all Europe with precious metals. Between 1460 and 1530 the annual output of silver in Central and East–Central Europe increased more than fivefold; it probably reached a maximum during the decade 1526–1535, with an annual quantity of about 85 000 kgs. However, the discovery of the extraordinarily rich argentiferous ores in Spanish America, and particularly the opening about 1546 of the famous mines of Potosí in Peru (Bolivia), dealt a heavy blow to European silver mining. Thenceforth American silver — more than 60 per cent of which went the way of Seville — took over the lead. During the decade 1551–1560 its annual output amounted to about 135000 kgs, in 1581–1590 to nearly 270 000 kgs, in 1591–1600 to some 300 000 kgs; the peak was reached between 1601 and 1610, with over 380 000 kgs. By that time a sharp decline had become apparent in most silver mining plants of Central and East-Central Europe. On the eve of the Thirty Years' War the annual silver production in that area was perhaps less than a third as great as it had been in the 1520s and 1530s: *J. U. Nef*, Silver Production in Central Europe 1450–1618, Journal of Political Economy, XLIX (1941), pp. 575–576, 584–589; *Á. Szászdi*, Preliminary Estimate of Gold and Silver Production in America 1501–1610. In: Precious Metals, op. cit. pp. 152, 165–167.

In gold production it was Hungary that took the first place in Europe prior to the discovery of America; her annual output — 1500 kgs at least — was preceded only by West Africa at the end of the 15th century. During the next century, in turn, American gold gained ground increasingly. The production of gold in Spanish America came to an annual average of over 1000 kgs during the decade of 1511–1520, to 2700 kgs in 1531–1540, and to nearly 3900 kgs in 1541–1550; it reached a maximum, with 6350 kgs yearly, between 1581 and 1590. Compared with the latter figures, the European production proved to be modest (Hungarian output in the 16th century failed to attain its former level), and even Africa's contribution was moderate. — To be sure, the inflow of precious metals from Spanish America took a downward trend in the early 17th century, and was rapidly declining between 1631 and 1660; but from the last decade of the century onwards the gold of Portuguese America (Brazil) set out on its international career, hereby accomplishing the radical change in gold supply of the European markets. — For both silver and gold production see: *F. Braudel*, La Méditerranée et le monde méditerranéen à l'époque de Philippe II², Paris, 1966, I, pp. 422–440; *Magelhães–Godinho*, op. cit. pp. 270–271; *P. J. Bakewell*, Silver Mining and Society in Colonial Mexico: Zacatecas, 1546–1700, Cambridge, 1971; *F. Mauro*, Le Brésil du XVᵉ à la fin du XVIIIᵉ siècle, Paris, 1977, pp. 148–149; *O. Paulinyi*, The Crown Monopoly of the Refining Metallurgy of Precious Metals in Hungary and Transylvania, 1325–1700. In: Precious Metals, op. cit. pp. 29, 37–39; *Szászdi*, op. cit. pp. 151, 157–158, 167. — In addition, the classic work of *A. Soetbeer* is still indispensable: Edelmetall–Produktion und Werthverhältnis zwischen Gold und Silber seit der Entdeckung Amerika's bis zur Gegenwart, Gotha, 1879, especially pp. 23–27, 31, 49, 107–109.

Page 187, Note 35:

Instead of "p. 218" read "p. 318" in the bottom-line.

Page 188, Note 37:

Sweden's annual copper production was below 3000 metric quintals until the 1570s, with a rise to about 6000 metric quintals by 1590. After a small downward movement, a mostly continuous rise can be seen by the middle of the 17th century, to over 30 000 metric quintals (which corresponded to 50 000 cwts as counted in the unit of measure used in Neusohl): *K. Kumlien*, Staat, Kupfererzeugung und Kupferausfuhr in Schweden. In: Schwerpunkte der Kupferproduktion und des Kupferhandels in Europa, 1500–1650. Hg. von H. Kellenbenz, Köln–Wien, 1977, pp. 241–242. — For Japan's copper export: *K. Glamann*, Japanese Copper on the European Market in the 17th Century. In: Schwerpunkte, op. cit. pp. 280–289; *A. Kobata*, Production and Trade in Gold, Silver and Copper in Japan, 1450–1750. In: Precious Metals, op. cit. pp. 274–275. — For the beginnings of Chilean copper export to Europe: *Szászdi*, op. cit. pp. 151, 170.

XII

BUSINESS MENTALITY AND HUNGARIAN NATIONAL CHARACTER*

1

The development and spread of business mentality in modern times has been one of the major subjects of economic history. Scholars have approached the problem in a number of ways: a historiographic review would require a paper of its own. Here, we must rest content with a brief indication of three possible approaches. One is to examine what has been called the "capitalistic spirit", on the assumption that the growth of modern capitalism is attributable primarily to intellectual factors. Max Weber and Werner Sombart propounded such notions, obviously intending to provide an alternative to Karl Marx's interpretation of capitalism. These explanations initiated heated debates even between the two above scholars in the first decades of the century. Weber, as it is well known, deduced the "spirit of capitalism" from the Protestant ethic, more particularly from Calvinist Puritan morals, whereas Sombart believed that it had had its origin rather in the ideas of Judaism, in the traditional business sense of the Jewry.[1]

Others considered the growth of the spirit of capitalism a process far too complex to be attributable to a single major source. They emphasized the multi-facetedness of the determining factors of what is called the "entrepreneurial psychology" , and referred to the various social attitudes and value judgements characterizing businessmen and entrepreneurs, which differed from nation to nation in early modern Europe. This approach, exemplified lately in the chapter by Barry Supple in Volume V of *The Cambridge Economic History of Europe*,[2] has already linked entrepreneurship with the social and socio-psychological characteristics of various nations or, one might say, with the differences in their "national characters".

The social status of trade and entrepreneurship, the degree of prestige they enjoyed, or the lack of it, mostly depended on and was proportionate to the degree to which the nobility, the traditional European ruling class, participated in business life. This is precisely what makes possible a third, narrower approach to the subject,

* Lecture delivered at the opening session of the Eighth International Economic History Congress (Budapest, August 16, 1982).

[1] See esp.: M. Weber: Die protestantische Ethik und der Geist der Kapitalismus (1905), in: *Gesammelte Aufsätze zur Religionssoziologie,* I, Tübingen 1920; W. Sombart: *Die Juden und das Wirtschaftsleben,* München–Leipzig 1911, and: *Der Bourgeois. Zur Geistesgeschichte des modernen Wirtschaftsmenschen,* München 1913. *Cf.* chiefly: R. H. Tawney: *Religion and the Rise of Capitalism,* London 1926; H. Sée: Dans quelle mesure Puritains et Juifs ont-ils contribué aux progrès de capitalisme moderne, *Revue Historique,* 155 (1927), pp. 57–68.

[2] B. Supple: The Nature of Enterprise, in: E. E. Rich and C. H. Wilson (eds.): *The Cambridge Economic History of Europe, V, The Economic Organization of Early Modern Europe,* Cambridge 1977, esp. pp. 402–407, 447–461.

which regards the economic behaviour of the land-owning class in the various countries as the starting point. "Why did the poorer section of the French provincial nobility not respond to the repeated invitations of the government in the seventeenth and eighteenth centuries to imitate the example of their English, Dutch, and Italian counterparts, by becoming a *noblesse commerçante?*" — asked Albert Goodwin at the Twelfth International Congress of Historians (Vienna, 1965),[3] now in a manner that struck "right at the heart" of the national character.

Let us now also set out from asking a similar question, when attempting to analyse the relation of the Hungarian national character to business-mindedness and entrepreneurship. The approach could well be justified by the fact that for a long time many have described the Hungarian character by projecting certain features of the nobility on to the whole of the nation. The Hungarian nobility, in turn, had become known all over Europe, from the eighteenth century on, as the antipole of the *noblesse commerçante,* as the standard bearers of a feudal mentality which considered trade and industry to be beneath their dignity.

2

The economic attitude of the noble classes towards commerce and enterprise showed obvious differences even in the countries on the Atlantic coast of Europe in early modern times. Spain represented one extreme: their nobility (the *hidalgos*) felt a profound aversion towards any kind of a bourgeois manner of life. England, where entrepreneurial activity was least hindered by legal or mental obstacles, and part of the nobility forged close links with the urban middle classes, occupied the opposite end of the international spectrum.[4] The company of the well-to-do London cloth exporters, the *Merchant Adventurers*—as we know from 17th century English authors such as Wheeler, Petty or Chamberlayne—engaged apprentices who were "for the most part gentlemen's sons" and, contrary to the continent, "it became the normal practice in England for the younger sons of the gentry and sometimes of the nobility" to be bred to trade, "without prejudice of their gentility". Apprenticeship in trade "was the usual upbringing for the younger sons of the gentry" and it was commerce which made it possible for "several good families to rise from modest beginnings", as well as for "many a declining gentry of the kingdom to recover their strength".[5] The wealthier merchants were partly the sons of landowners' families themselves and, anyhow, they had received similar education and moved in the same society; and "in England, unlike in France, it was generally accepted that they could not be socially distinguished from the other group".[6] In his book *Le parfait*

[3] A. Goodwin: The Social Structure and Economic and Political Attitudes of the French Nobility in the Eighteenth Century, in: *XII. Congrès International des Sciences Historiques,* Rapports I, Wien 1965, p. 361.

[4] *Cf.*: A. Goodwin: General Problems and the Diversity of European Nobilities in the Modern Period, in: *XII. Congrès International des Sciences Historiques,* Rapports I, pp. 345–348; F. Braudel: *La Méditerranée et le monde méditerranéen à l'époque de Philippe II,* Seconde édition, Paris 1966, II, p. 59; B. Supple: *op. cit.,* pp. 450–451; W. Sombart: *op. cit.* (1913), pp. 172–193, 266–281.

[5] Quoted by E. Lipson: *The Economic History of England, II. The Age of Mercantilism,* Fourth Edition, London 1947, pp. 191–192.

[6] R. H. Tawney: The Rise of the Gentry, 1558—1640, *The Economic History Review,* XI, 1941, 4. — *Cf.* in England "it was often impossible to distinguish between landowners' and financial interests"; there were no strong barriers between the gentry and the urban middle classes; younger sons of the gentry adopted professions in the town administration and in commerce, whereas rich merchants and other urban notabilities bought estates and joined the gentry: G. M. Trevelyan: *English Social History,* 3rd Edition, New York–Toronto–London 1946, pp. 83–84, 163–165.

négociant (1675) the Frenchman Jacques Savary set the following example for his fellow countrymen: "In England, commerce is regarded so respectable that even noblemen of the highest ranks trade in wool and livestock".[7] It was this very "secret": a practical attitude towards economy and commerce which another Frenchman, Pierre Coste wanted to teach to the French nobility at the end of the 17th century by translating the English philosopher John Locke's pedagogical work.[8]

A largely similar order of social values asserted itself in the Netherlands. There—as a third French writer quoted as an example to his compatriots in the final phase of the *ancien régime*—"... the profession of commerce is esteemed ... The merchant there is honoured and regarded as a member of a class which is the strongest pillar of the United Provinces. The road to honours and the highest dignity in the state is open to him. He can marry into the patrician families which are in the possession of the most distinguished offices of the Republic and which do not consider being in business themselves or training their children for such a career below them ... but in France, Spain, Portugal ... there persists a barbarous prejudice against this profession..."[9]

As it is known, this prejudice was even embodied in the law in France: a whole series of edicts—the most important in 1560—was issued during the 16th century expressly forbidding the *gentilshommes* to engage in commerce under pain of *dérogeance*, that is forfeiting their noble status and privileges (particularly their immunity from taxes).[10] *Vivre noblement*—living nobly, i.e. living on their rents and annuities *(vivre de ses rentes)*[11]—was the privilege and also the obligation of nobility, and engaging in commerce, rural work or in common trades was considered incompatible with this. Dispensation from the *dérogeance* could only be granted by the sovereign.[12] True enough, the principle of incompatibility was not always observed, and kings, from the reign of Charles IX on, gave individual or local licences now and then, mostly to noblemen and ennobled persons *(anoblis)* living in busy seaports or market towns, such as Marseilles, Bordeaux and Lyon. But the royal licenses were restricted to sea or wholesale trading and definitely excluded retail trade, shopkeeping and innkeeping.[13] Even the royal ordinance of 1629 *(Code*

[7] Quoted by H. Hauser: *Les débuts du capitalisme français*, Paris 1931, p. 277. — Around 1630, however, the British economist Thomas Mun (who wrote his book *England's Treasure by Forraigne Trade* at about that time) was of the opinion that the social appreciation of commerce in England and the participation of nobility "in this noble vocation" were unsatisfactory as compared with "other countries". The relevant text was published by L. Stone: *Social Change and Revolution in England, 1540—1640*, London 1965, pp. 128–129. — Mun must have had in mind the example of Holland.

[8] The first French translation of John Locke's *Thoughts on Education* was published in 1695 by P. Coste under the title *De l'education des enfants:* R. H. Tawney: *op. cit.*, p. 1.

[9] Quoted by H. Heaton: *Economic History of Europe*, Revised Edition, New York–Evanston 1948, p. 223.

[10] G. Zeller: Une notion de caractère historico-social: la dérogeance, *Cahiers Internationaux de Sociologie*, 21, 1965. pp. 43–45.

[11] "Nobles et ecclésiastiques doivent vivre de leurs rentes et revenues, et non de leur peine et travail", as it was declared in a collection of official formulas published in 1627. Quoted by G. Zeller: *op. cit.*, p. 54. — For the different opinions concerning *vivre noblement* see G. Huppert: *Les Bourgeois Gentilshommes*, Chicago–London 1977, pp. 73, 84–102.

[12] M. Bloch: *La société féodale*, Paris 1939, pp. 72–73; R. Mandrou: *Introduction à la France moderne, 1540–1640. Essai de psychologie historique*, Paris 1961, pp. 143–158; P. Chaunu, R. Gascon: *Histoire économique et sociale de la France, 1450–1660*, in: F. Braudel, E. Labrousse (eds): I, *1, L'état et la ville*, Paris 1977, pp. 208–214, 365–368.

[13] G. Zeller: *op. cit.*, pp. 47–49; G. Huppert: *op. cit.*, pp. 30, 190. — Royal and ducal *ordonnances* remained from as early as the 15th century, which forbade noblemen to participate in commerce, although the expression *dérogeance* was not yet in use. However, even these early texts laid a particular

Michau), prompted by Richelieu, allowed one single general exception for the *gentilshommes*: to take part in sea trade ventures as partners without becoming unworthy of nobility; apart from that, participation in commercial or financial transactions, "either personally or through others", was still forbidden.[14] As a matter of fact, Savary's above-mentioned *Le parfait négociant* (1675) was something like an apology for the occupation of merchants or, more exactly: wholesale merchants (it is to be noted that in the age of King Louis XIV, *négociant* meant just wholesale merchant, as opposed to the much lower *marchand* or even *boutiquier*).[15] All the same, even as late as 1678, de La Roque, the author of the famous *Traité de la noblesse*, expressed a notion deeply rooted in public opinion when he wrote: "Frenchmen regard it as not only unworthy, but straight out sinful when a nobleman takes to business, since they do not consider that genteel enough. People who choose such occupations become cowardly, and exchange the shadow of laurels for that of the shops *(celui des boutiques)*".[16] Although the gap between the principle and the practice became ever more perceptible, the major part of the nobility obviously did not break with this prejudice (and could not, either, because of the lack of capital and business experience), not even when Richelieu, Colbert and their successors already encouraged them to participate in overseas trade without injury to their nobiliary privileges.[17]

No significant change occurred until the 18th century, when an increasing number of French noblemen became involved in maritime trade and other big business ventures. Contrasting both with the less prosperous provincial gentry which bogged down in its former way of life and mentality, and the absolutist government which, in the last phase of its existence and under the slogan of *rien innover*, tended towards the maintenance of the traditional restrictions,[18] an economically mobile *noblesse d'affaire* emerged which—as Fernand Braudel points out—became rather like their Dutch and English counterparts in many respects: they developed an interest in sweeping away the obstacles that stood in the way of capitalist evolution, among them the vestiges of *dérogeance*, on the eve of the Great Revolution.[19] In the

---

emphasis upon the prohibition against retail trading and innkeeping. An ordinance of 1435 declared that tax had to be paid "by those noblemen who sell by retail or sell wine and spirits... because it does not suit noblemen to be innkeepers (*taverniers*)". In 1456, the Duke of Brittany confirmed the privileges of those nobles "who engaged in wholesale trading in several articles without selling first hand and by retail". The latter, as well as those who kept taverns or inns (*tavernes ou hostelleries*) or traded in livestock, were to lose their privileges and could recover them only by changing their way of life. At about the same time, in Troyes, the old market town of Champagne it was left to the choice of the nobles whether they wished to live *noblement ou marchandement*: G. Zeller: *op. cit.*, pp. 41, 46, 49.

[14] The relevant paragraphs 452 and 198 of *Code Michau* and a similar measure of the royal decree of 1669 have been published by G. Zeller: *op. cit.*, pp. 57–58; *cf.* R. Gascon: *op. cit.*, p. 365.

[15] G. Zeller: *op. cit.*, pp. 59–60, 63.

[16] Quoted by R. Gascon: *op. cit.*, p. 365 and G. Zeller: *op. cit.*, p. 62. — De La Roque also recorded that in London and in other towns of England several less well-to-do nobles kept inns without any social disadvantage: G. Zeller: *op. cit.*, p. 71.

[17] W. Sombart: *op. cit.* 1913, pp. 178–181; A. Goodwin: *op. cit.* (The Social Structure...), pp. 361–363; B. Supple: *op. cit.*, pp. 448, 456; B. Behrens: Government and Society, in: *The Cambridge Economic History of Europe*, V, p. 571.

[18] G. Zeller: *op. cit.*, pp. 68–69. — In his *Esprit des lois* (1748) even Montesquieu took a stand *for* the tradition of *dérogeance* and *against* the trading of nobility and the English practise. His reasoning was clear: "Il est contre l'esprit du commerce que la noblesse le fasse dans la monarchie... Il est contre l'esprit de la monarchie que la noblesse y fasse le commerce. L'usage qui a permis en Angleterre le commerce à la noblesse est une des choses qui ont le plus contribué à affaiblir le gouvernement monarchique": quoted by G. Zeller: *op. cit.*, p. 67; *cf.* A. Goodwin: *op. cit.*, p. 362.

[19] F. Braudel: Civilisation matérielle, Économie et Capitalisme. XVe—XVIIIe siècle, 2. *Les Jeux de l'Échange*, Paris 1979, pp. 424–425. — *Cf.* G. Richard: *Noblesse d'affaires au XVIIIe siècle*, Paris 1974;

middle of the century, Abbé Coyer's book (*La noblesse commerçante,* 1756) in which he insisted on the termination of "the strange and obsolete law of *dérogeance*", still gave rise to heated debates.[20] However, most of the presentations *(cahiers)* which had been prepared for the *États Généraux* of 1789 demanded the abolition of "this barbarous prejudice".[21]

3

Dérogeance had already vanished in France when it was still in full flower in Hungary. Although the Hungarian nobility was not forbidden to engage in commerce and trade by law, the very same spirit pervaded the views and practices of its majority even as late as the end of the 18th century. "The decorum of nobility is to be preserved" and "a gentleman who takes up trade ought to forfeit his privileges" —Károly Koppi, professor of world history at the University of Pest around 1790, argued, even though he watched the developments of the French Revolution with sympathy.[22]

The die-hard conservatism of the Hungarian nobility was in those days attacked not only by ill-disposed German pamphleteers, e.g. Leopold Hoffmann in Vienna in 1790,[23] but also by Hungarian writers, poets, economists who, prompted by patriotic feelings and a positive approach to reforms, pointed out some striking anomalies in the existing conditions. In his essay published in German in 1784, Count János Szapáry joined issue precisely with those, who harangued ceaselessly that "trading was incompatible with Hungarian laws and their forefathers had lived happily without trading". He refuted both positions: Hungarian noblemen of yore did trade (they had supplied Poland and Silesia with wine as well as Austria and Styria with corn), Greeks and Jews had stepped in their place only later; and it was possible to develop commerce under the existing laws without injury to nobility.[24] Another noted Hungarian economist of the time, Baron Miklós Skerlecz (who was the author of the most important documents propounded by the Commission of Commerce established by the Diet of 1790–91), although accepting the opinion that the Hungarian constitution was "of a military character and therefore incompatible with trade", recommended legislation in order to make "wholesale trading" a gentlemanly activity. He also suggested (obviously with a knowledge of the relevant

G. Chaussinand-Nogaret: Aux origines de la Révolution: noblesse et bourgeoisie, *Annales E. S. C.*, 1975, 2–3, pp. 265–278. According to the latter author the *Traité* by de La Roque (contrary to public belief) did not belong any more to the standard reading of the nobility on the eve of the Revolution: *op. cit.*, p. 277. — See also: G. Huppert: *op. cit.*, pp. 176–177.

[20] H. Lévy-Brühl: La noblesse de France et le commerce à la fin de l'Ancien Régime, *Revue d'Histoire moderne,* 1933, pp. 220–227.

[21] G. Zeller: *op. cit.*, p. 73.

[22] S. Eckhardt: *A francia forradalom eszméi Magyarországon* (The ideas of the French Revolution in Hungary), Budapest 1924, pp. 35, 147, 158, 167; A. Horváth: *Koppi Károly*, Szeged 1940, pp. 34–36. Quoted by K. Benda: *A magyar jakobinus mozgalom iratai* (Documents of the Hungarian Jacobin movement). Budapest 1957, Introduction, p. XXXIV.

[23] L. Hoffmann: *Ninive. Fortgesetzte Fragmente über die dermaligen politischen Angelegenheiten in Ungarn,* Wien, 1790; see S. Eckhardt: *op. cit.*, pp. 35–38; S. Eckhardt: A magyarság külföldi arcképe (The Hungarian image abroad, in: Gy. Szekfű (ed.): *Mi a magyar?* (What makes a Hungarian?), Budapest 1939, pp. 105–106.

[24] Count J. Szapáry: *Der unthätige Reichtum Ungarns wie zu gebrauchen*, Nürnberg 1784, p. 12. Hungarian translation: J. Székely: *Magyarország meddő gazdagságának hogy lehetne hasznát venni* (How to make use of Hungary's unproductive wealth,) Budapest 1878, pp. 12–13.

French literature and probably also of Abbé Coyer's book) a wording of the relevant article in §145 of his work *Projectum legum motivatum* as follows: "Engaging in any kind of retail business is an honest trade; but the exploitation of mineral wealth and, in particular, wholesale foreign trade or the establishment of factories are such noble vocations that they detract nothing from the status of a gentleman or an aristocrat".[25] The prejudice that "being a merchant ... or artisan is a low occupation in the esteem of Hungarians" must be discarded at last, urged the poet Ferenc Verseghy (later a Hungarian Jacobin), in a pamphlet addressed to the Hungarian Diet in 1790. Noblemen and those in particular "who do not have estates big enough to enable them to live like noblemen" should be encouraged to commercial or industrial activities, even by guaranteeing them "special privileges".[26] "The path of honour is free to the daring; commerce and the workshops of noble trades are open; and is it not more respectable for impoverished gentlemen to become citizens of means, than to stay what they are: noble vagabond outlaws"—the young writer József Kármán burst out and agitated passionately in 1794.[27] The experience of Western nations gave the same warning, Szapáry, Verseghy and other authors argued, among them the first Hungarian bibliographer, István Sándor who, meditating on *"Nobility and Commerce"* (1796), attributed England's economic progress precisely to the fact that "of all the countries where nobility and, therefore, ancient pride: *Ahnenstolz* was prevailing, England was the first to throw away the shackles of prejudice. The English nobility was the first to reject the notion that trading was shameful".[28] The polyhistor physician, József Sándorfi also invited Hungarians in his treatise in 1808 to follow the English example and to learn trades and commerce because, as long as Hungarian noblemen "do not become more interested in commerce, they would remain of little worth, little wealth ... and little experience and foreigners would continue to grow rich at their expense".[29] The pseudonymous writer of an article in the periodical *Nemzeti Gazda* (The National Husbandman) also referred to England in 1814: "Where is a greater private person, a greater nobleman, a greater count or a greater duke than an English merchant of that sort—although he is a merchant". "... the Hungarian does not take a view of commerce as he should ... We are disgusted with what comes along with our national occupation: agriculture."[30]

Such advice and proposals had but little effect. The great awakener of the Hungarian reform movement Count István Széchenyi bitterly asked his fellow aristo-

[25] P. Berényi: *Skerlecz Miklós báró művei* (The works of Baron Miklós Skerlecz), Budapest 1914, pp. 309, 446.

[26] F. Verseghy's anonymous pamphlet in verse in the spring of 1790: A Magyar Hazának anyai szózatja az ország napjára készülő magyarokhoz (The motherly invocation of the Hungarian land to the Hungarians preparing for the National Diet), Quoted by K. Benda, *op. cit.*, p. 175; *cf.* Introduction, p. XXXIII.

[27] J. Kármán: *A nemzet csinosodása* (The improvement of the nation) (1794), Budapest 1981, p. 14.

[28] I. Sándor: A nemességről s kereskedésről (On nobility and commerce), in: *Sokféle* (Miscellanea) IV, Győr 1796, pp. 12–13.

[29] J. Sándorfi: A magyar nemességnek szóló jovallásom (My suggestion to the Hungarian nobility), in: *Sokféle,* IX, Vienna 1808, p. 121.—József Sándorfi, a physician from the town Nagyvárad was a friend of István Sándor, editor of the periodical *Sokféle*. It is possible that this article was also written by the latter.

[30] Filosilvester: Kitől lehet a hazában jutalmasabban vásárolni bécsi portékát,—a magyar kereskedőtől-é, vagy a némettől,—vagy az örménytől,—vagy a zsidótól?—és miért egyiktől inkább, mint a másiktól? (From whom can we buy Viennese goods at more reasonable prices in this country: from the Hungarian merchant or the German or the Armenian or the Jew?—and why more from the one than from the other?), in: *Nemzeti Gazda* (The National Husbandman), XII, 22 March 1814, pp. 183–186.

crats sixteen years later in 1830: "Does our work, as far as trading is concerned, deserve mention? Did we do anything to increase the number of our products or to improve and popularize them? Did we try to seek commercial relations, particularly with other nations? Would not all products dry up in our own places, if the Jew did not call on us for them?" It is no wonder, therefore, that "on the whole, there is no trade or any such buying and selling which could be called trade deservedly, and what still exists, stands on feeble legs".[31] The aversion for trade persisted among the majority of the landed gentry as well. "Many landowners view this trading activity and toil with disdain and consider themselves born to nobler tasks", Széchenyi said in 1830.[32] Another prominent Hungarian reformer Baron Miklós Wesselényi outlined a similar picture the following year: "... the magnates and the lesser nobility... many of them consider the burghers and their occupations beneath their dignity and status, with a certain bloated arrogance ... Trade is regarded as a menial job by some people ... the merchant is not worthy of our friendship or our conversation for many of us. The depressing consequence of such prejudices is that even the little trading one finds in our country is in the hands of foreigners".[33]

And the gentlemanly contempt for trade, the *dérogeance* spirit of the Hungarian nobility has soon become known as a Hungarian national characteristic and a specific feature of the Hungarian mentality.

When, in the late 1830s Mihály Horváth wrote the first Hungarian history of industry and trade in two volumes, he considered that "trading did not play such a major role in Hungarian history as to have a considerable impact on the nation's history" and attributed the "meagreness of Hungarian trading" (in addition to political vicissitudes and natural obstacles) largely to "such inner causes" as "were rooted ... in the nation itself"; therefore, "the nation's very mentality and spiritual make-up of the people were also the sources of several failures".[34]

And when some years later, Jácint Rónay wrote the first Hungarian work on characterology (published in 1847 under the title *Jellemisme*) it was clear that he already considered the lack of business-mindedness and a contempt for trading as organic components of the Hungarian national character. He found a vivid parallel not in modern French but in ancient Roman history: "Roman patricians were forbidden to trade, to practice manufacture by the *Lex Claudia*; there is no such clear law in Hungary, yet the *Lex Claudia* asserted itself as a custom, and custom is law in this country, the land of prescriptions". It was always more important to the Hungarians "to become gentlemen. This word rings well everywhere in the world

[31] Count I. Széchenyi: *Hitel* (Credit), Pest 1830, pp. 139–140, 110.

[32] *Op. cit.*, p. 140; *cf.* p. 177. — "Practical knowledge is so sparsely scattered on the vast fields of imagination (among Hungarians) like ships on the billows of the wide ocean; there is hardly any diligence or economic, industrial or commercial cleverness; so much so that certainly even the Turks outwit us in respect of our industrial and commercial spirit, although at least not in that of our agricultural knowledge." "The lesser nobility is increasing in number. Their thoughtless pride does not let them engage in industry and commerce and they think it to be beneath their dignity to strive for wealth honestly, by cleverness and knowledge." "...in the strict sense of the word there is still no vigorous tradesmen's, craftmen's and merchants' class in our country so far, and there will not be either, as long as the law does not protect both their persons and their possessions in the strongest way and the public does not appreciate them better than now": Count I. Széchenyi: *Világ, vagyis felvilágosító töredékek némi hiba s előítélet eligazítására* (Light or enlightening fragments to correct some errors and prejudices), Pest 1831, pp. 68, 72.

[33] Baron M. Wesselényi: *Balítéletekről* (On prejudices) (written in 1831), Bucharest 1833, pp. 75–76.

[34] M. Horváth: Az ipar és kereskedés története Magyarországban a három utolsó század alatt (The history of industry and trade in Hungary in the last three centuries), (1840), in: *Horváth M. kisebb történelmi munkái* (M. Horváth's minor historical works), III, Pest 1868, p. 28; *cf.* p. 154.

but particularly so in Hungary." Commerce remained alien to the mentality of the "proud Hungarians".[35]

But "really, what is that national mentality, that peculiarity? Does it come into this world fully-fledged...? Or does it flow slowly and grow, progress and develop quietly?" — one may ask in Széchenyi's words.[36]

And was it true at all that trade and commerce had always been alien to the Hungarian nobility because of their pride and conceit?

Earlier Hungarian history, particularly the economic history of the 16th and 17th centuries proves the diametrical opposite.

4

"Hungarian noblemen" according to an official military report dated 1550 "engage in trading, employ merchants as assistants and trade in cattle, cloths, food, copper and all sorts of other commodities. That is the practice all over Hungary indeed."[37] According to an official report of the Pozsony Treasury (the fiscal authority) in 1563 "most of the magnates and gentlemen trade in cattle, hides, cloth, horses, plum and others, and they all would like to be exempt from customs duty".[38] A Hungarian nobleman, György Hédervåry exposed his intentions at the beginning of the 1540s: "The desire of my heart is ... to buy a ship capable of holding a thousand measures of barley and wheat. I shall then take barley, flour and other victuals with me", in order to sell them for good profit.[39] At the end of the 1560s, another aristocrat György Báthori of Ecsed declared that, because of the destruction of his properties by the Turks, "there was nothing else left for him but to supply his own needs by constant working" and, therefore, he requested the king to grant him permission for duty-free wine export to Poland as "there were markets

[35] J. Rónay: *Jellemisme, vagy az angol, francia, magyar, német, olasz, orosz, spanyol nemzet, nő, férfiú és életkorok jellemzése lélektani szempontból* (Characterology or the characterization of the English, French, Hungarian, German, Italian, Russian and Spanish nations, women, men and age-groups from a psychological viewpoint), Győr 1847, pp. 108, 74–75.

[36] I. Széchenyi: *op. cit.*, (1830), p. 31.

[37] "Die hungarischen Herrn die treiben Kaufmannschaft, nehmen auch Kaufleut zu Handgesellen, mit Vieh, Tuch, Blei, Kupferwerk und aller anderer Handtierung, schreiben Mautbrief, dass man frei passieren soll lassen... So doch der Brauch im ganzen Land Hungern ist": quoted from the May 1550 report of the Captain-General of Royal Hungary's mining district by S. Takáts: *Szegény magyarok* (Poor Hungarians), Budapest 1927, p. 143. — General reference can be made here to Sándor Takáts's articles and books published successively from the late 1890s to the end of the 1920s; it is mostly his merit that Hungarian cattle trading in the 16th and 17th centuries was described. It is to be mentioned too that the first steps in this field had been taken by Ignác Acsády who, on the basis of numerous data, had already established earlier that during the period in question "distinguished magnates also participated actively in the Hungarian cattle export" and "a good many noblemen were also engaged in cattle trading" and that "the nobility also greatly participated in wine trading": *Közgazdasági állapotaink a XVI. és XVII. században* (Our economic conditions in the 16th and 17th centuries), Budapest 1889, pp. 62–63, 69–70; *cf.* note 91 below.

[38] "...magnates plerique et nobiles negotiationes instituunt bobus, cutibus, panno, equis, prunis etc. voluntque exempti esse vectigalibus, unde exortas ante scimus et exoriri nunc quoque videmus magnas contentiones cum officialibus fisci..." The report of the Treasury mentioned later again: "Jam magnates et nobiles lucri cupiditate adeo in quaestum sunt effusi, ut tenuioribus negotiandi materiam praeripiant": V. Fraknói (ed.): *Magyar Országgyűlési Emlékek* (Documents of the Hungarian Diets), IV, Budapest 1876, pp. 515–516.

[39] "Est mihi animus..., ut emam unam navem, quae mille metretas ordei et tritici ferre potest. Ordeum, farinam et alia victualia mecum ducam": *A Hédervåry-család oklevéltára* (The Hédervåry family archives), II, Budapest 1922, p. 122.

to be held and he wished to send his wine there".[40] "Our noble lords" the noted Protestant preacher, Péter Bornemisza, wrote not much later "hoard wine, wheat, meat, and other food in plenty until there is a dearth, in order to sell at quadrupled prices".[41] One could quote much in the same vein about Hungarian noblemen and magnates of the 16th century. Far from looking down on trade or considering it beneath their dignity, they engaged in it as the most natural thing in the world and made it their daily practice.

Just as in case of the German *Gutsherren* and *Ritter*[42] east of the Elbe or the Polish *pans* and members of the *szlachta*[43] and also the English gentry[44]—not to mention some groups of the French *gentilshommes*,[45] though bound by *dérogeance* —the Hungarian landowners were also driven to trade in agricultural produce and to market production by the major incentive of the general European phenomenon of the 16th century: the economic boom, known, since Georg Wiebe, as the price

40 "...cum ex tanta depredatione bonorum eius, quam passus est, nihil aliud supersit illi, quam continuis laboribus necessitatibus eius prospicere, Maiestati V. S.... humillime supplicat, quatenus dignetur clementer suis litteris annuere, quod salvum sit illi vina in Poloniam educere, cum brevi ibidem nundinae sint celebrandae, ad quas dicta vina mittere vellet..." Quoted from the report of the Szepes Treasury in April 1559 by Gy. Komoróczy: *Borkivitelünk észak felé. Fejezet a magyar kereskedelem történetéből* (Our wine export to the North. A chapter from the history of Hungarian trading), Kassa 1944, p. 297. — "At that time, in the sixties, the number of applications generally increased... which mentioned the devastation by the Turks as the reason for the necessity of making money by export trade. That the actual reason was different... is well demonstrated by the fact that the majority of the landowners who were granted permissions did not live in the usual target area of the Turkish raids." (*Op. cit.*, p. 59). — György Báthori sent wine to Poland in the subsequent years as well and set up a whole commercial network. (*Op. cit.*, pp. 125, 321.)

41 *Bornemisza Péter válogatott írásai* (P. Bornemisza's selected writings), 1553–1584. Collected by I. Nemeskürty, Budapest 1955, p. 229. The passage is from 1574; *cf.* also pp. 164–165 (1584).

42 The orientation of East German landowners towards economy and the development of *Gutsherrschaft* in Brandenburg-Prussia, Pomerania and Mecklenburg has been dealt with by an ever-increasing literature since G. F. Knapp turned his attention to the phenomenon in 1887, worked out the conceptions of *Grundherrschaft* and *Gutsherrschaft* and located their historical dividing line by the River Elbe: *Die Bauernbefreiung und der Ursprung der Landarbeiter in den älteren Teilen Preussens,* Zweite Auflage, München–Leipzig 1927, pp. 1–66. — A critical survey of the earlier literature was offered and reference was made to the influence of the rise in agrarian prices by F. L. Carsten: The Origins of the Junkers, *The English Historical Review,* 62/243, 1947, pp. 145–178.

43 From the similarly extensive Polish literature pertaining to the subject, we mention only J. Rutkowski's basic study: La genèse du régime de la corvée dans l'Europe Centrale depuis la fin du Moyen Age, in: *La Pologne au VIe Congrès International des Sciences Historiques,* Varsovie 1930; and from among the more recent ones: M. Małowist: Le commerce de la Baltique et le problème des luttes sociales en Pologne aux XVe et XVIe siècles, in: *La Pologne au Xe Congrès International des Sciences Historiques,* Varsovie 1955; and W. Rusiński: Hauptprobleme der Fronwirtschaft im 16. bis 18. Jahrhundert in Polen und den Nachbarländern, in: *Première Conference Internationale d'Histoire Économique,* Paris–La Haye 1960, pp. 415–423. — They referred to the "general rise" in the grain prices in the European market and the increasing West European demand for Polish grain as from the end of the 15th century.

44 From British literature we mention in the first place R. H. Tawney's works: *The Agrarian Problem in the Sixteenth Century,* London 1912, Torchbook Edition, New York–Evanston–London 1967, esp. pp. 177, ff., and *op. cit.*, (*The Rise of the Gentry*) mainly pp. 11–16; and F. L. Carsten: *op. cit.*, pp. 168–170. — *Cf.* note 48 below.

45 In the middle of the 16th century, the "dear life" (*la vie chère*) also compelled several members of the nobility in France who lived on fixed peasant services (rents) and particularly the poorer noblemen in the countryside (*hoberaux*) to look for other sources of income: to try commerce, as well as demesne farming, to take land and tithe on lease and to apply, therefore, for exemption from *dérogeance*. However, the *cahier* presented in 1560 was refused by Charles IX. The edict of Orléans (as it has been mentioned before) maintained the prohibition and it was to be repeated by further *ordonnances*: G. Zeller: *op. cit.*, pp. 43–45, 50; see the passages for which note 10 above and note 65 below have been given. — *Cf.* H. Hauser (ed.): *La vie chère au XVIe siècle: la réponse de Jean Bodin à M. de Malestroict (1568),* Paris 1932.

revolution.[46] As a matter of fact, severe misfortunes befell Hungary just at that time. The country had been torn into three parts after 1541, as a result of the Osmanli Turkish conquest—Royal Hungary, ruled by the Austrian branch of the Habsburg dynasty, the Transylvanian principality which was semi-dependent from the Turkish Empire and the territory under Turkish rule—and suffered great human and material losses in the course of the almost continuous Turkish wars. For all that, the country had already been linked to all-European trade and the nascent modern world economy by so many strands that it could not isolate herself from the effects.[47] The Western European price revolution reached Hungary, too, from about 1500 and from the middle of the 16th century with full momentum. And what is particularly worth noting is that the price revolution—as recent research has shown—was principally an *agrarian* price revolution:[48] the prices of agricultural products (and raw materials) increased at a considerably higher rate than the prices of industrial commodities (and the wages) in Hungary, as well as in England and in continental Western Europe.[49] Whereas in the early 16th century the price of one ox

[46] G. Wiebe: *Zur Geschichte der Preisrevolution des XVI. und XVII. Jahrhunderts,* Leipzig 1895. — Previous literature was comprehensively interpreted and completed by P. Simiand: *Recherches anciennes et nouvelles sur le mouvement général des prix du XVIᵉ au XIXᵉ siècle,* Paris 1932. — Basic research concerning the influx of precious metals from America has been carried out and a modern explanation of the "quantitative monetary theory" first represented by Jean Bodin as a reason for the *vie chère* has been given by E. J. Hamilton: *American Treasure and the Price Revolution in Spain, 1501–1650,* Cambridge (Mass.) 1934; and in a summary form: The History of Prices before 1750, in: *XIᵉ Congrès International des Sciences Historiques,* Göteborg–Stockholm–Uppsala 1960, Rapports I, pp. 144–164.

[47] Zs. P. Pach: The Role of East-Central Europe in International Trade (16th and 17th Centuries), in: *Études Historiques Hongroises 1970,* Budapest 1970, pp. 217–264; I. Wallerstein: *The Modern World-System, Capitalist Agriculture and the Origins of the European World-Economy in the Sixteenth Century,* New York 1974, esp. pp. 67–129.

[48] Participants of the heated debate which lasted for about two decades in recent British (and American) literature concerning the Tawney-thesis (the rise of the English gentry and its market-oriented husbandry during the century preceding the Civil War: see notes 6 and 44 above and the relevant paragraphs) still ignored or almost ignored the *agrarian* character of the price revolution. Tawney himself argued that, as an effect of the price rise and inflation, the expenditures of landowners had increased, whereas their incomes from the traditional money rents had lost their value. Since "agrarian society was under strain", a considerable part of the English gentry had actually got out of these straitened circumstances in such a way as some section of the French nobility attempted to do in the same period (see note 45): transformation of the rent system in their estates, demesne farming, stockbreeding or grain production for the market or trading enterprise: *op. cit.*, pp. 7–14. — H. R. Trevor-Roper, who criticized Tawney the sharpest, wanted to substitute the thesis of the decline of the *mere* gentry (i. e. the gentry of the countryside, dealing only with agriculture) for the thesis of the rise of the gentry and set out from the wrong view that "there had been an agrarian crisis in the 16th century": The Gentry, 1540–1640, *The Economic History Review, Supplement I,* 1953, pp. 1–55. — The result of recent research that the price revolution pushed up mostly the prices of agricultural products reinforces, of course, Tawney's thesis as opposed to his critics who, after all, agreed with him in the opinion (which happens to be of crucial importance in respect of the present considerations) that several members of the gentry—and of the nobility as well—turned to trade during the century preceding the English Revolution. For a short summary of the debate see L. Stone: *The Causes of the English Revolution, 1529–1642,* London 1972, pp. 26–43.

[49] Recent discussions of West and Central European developments of the price revolution and the subsequent period of the decline of prices: F. B. Braudel—F. Spooner: Prices in Europe from 1450 to 1750, in: E. E. Rich and C. H. Wilson (eds): *The Cambridge Economic History of Europe, IV, The Economy of Expanding Europe in the Sixteenth and Seventeenth Centuries,* Cambridge 1967, pp. 378 ff., esp. pp. 421, 464, 467, 481; B. H. Slicher van Bath: *The Agrarian History of Western Europe 500–1850 A. D.,* London 1963, pp. 197–198, 206–212; P. H. Ramsey (ed.): *The Price Revolution in Sixteenth-Century England,* with an Introduction by the editor, London 1971; W. Abel: *Agrarkrisen und Agrarkonjunktur. Eine Geschichte der Land- und Ernährungswirtschaft Mitteleuropas seit dem hohen Mittelalter,* Zweite Auflage, Hamburg–Berlin 1966, pp. 13, 113–120, 145, 152, 175.—The price revolution in the countries of East-Central Europe: S. Hoszowski: The Revolution of Prices in Poland in the 16th and 17th Centuries, *Acta Poloniae Historica,* 2, 1959, pp. 7–12, and: Central Europe and the Sixteenth- and Seventeenth-Century Price Revolution, in: P. Burke (ed.): *Economy and Society in Early Modern Europe,*

had bought about one middle-quality Moravian cloth on the Hungarian market, by the end of the century it had bought three.[50] Therefore, if the Hungarian landowners had little incentive to trade in agricultural products earlier, up to the late 15th century (they left it to peasants and burghers, and made them pay money rents and local tolls),[51] in the 16th century they responded to the rising agricultural prices (which were forced up also by the significant demand for food and fodder for the armies during the Turkish wars) by changing their economic behaviour. They turned towards the market themselves,[52] and no anti-mercantile national character or class-pride held them back from doing so.[53] This was true even of the highest nobility. Members of prominent families, the holders of leading political and military offices, captains of castles who distinguished themselves in the fight against the Turks, almost to a man were busy trading in cattle, wine and grain.[54] Tamás Nádasdy, the Palatine of the 1550s, regularly bought livestock to be driven to Austria and he was one of the most assiduous husbandmen of Royal Hungary: he established about a dozen seigniorial demesnes on his estates in Transdanubia (at Sárvár, Léka and Kapuvár) and had them cultivated by paid—i.e. not only servile—labour in order to produce as much grain for sale as possible. While he pondered over the security of Transylvania and the chances of uniting the torn country, "Friar George", a man of the cloth and politician of vision also sent considerable herds of oxen on their way to the West; and Sebestyén Thököly laid the foundation of the fortunes of his rising

New York–London 1972, pp. 85–103; Št. Kazimír: Način vývoja čien obilnín na Slovensku v 16. a 17. stor., in: *Agrikultura, Zbornik Pol'nohospodárskeho Múzea v Nitre,* 9, Bratislava 1970, and: Adalék a XVI. és XVII. századbeli árak és bérek fejlődéséhez (To the development of prices and wages in the 16th and 17th centuries), *Történelmi Szemle* (Historical Review), 19, (1976), 1–2, pp. 167–210; V. Zimányi: Mouvements des prix hongrois et l'évolution européenne (XVIe–XVIIIe siècles), *Acta Historica Academiae Scientiarum Hungaricae,* 19 (1973), pp. 305–333.

50 V. Zimányi's calculation, quoted by courtesy of the author.

51 Zs. P. Pach: The development of Feudal Rent in Hungary in the Fifteenth Century, *The Economic History Review,* 2nd Ser., XIX/1 (1966), pp. 1–14.

52 Data referring to the participation of Hungarian noble landowners in the trade of agricultural produce became rather frequent from the end of the 15th century: see note 71 below. — In 1525, the party of the lesser nobility reproached the Lord Chief Justice Ambrus Sárkány as follows: "You have been trading in wine and cattle and harassing the poor while we have been defending the border fortresses": V. Fraknói: *Magyarország a mohácsi vész előtt a pápai követek jelentései alapján* (Hungary before the Mohács Disaster as shown in the reports of the Papal nuncios), Budapest 1884, p. 147. — Hereby new light is thrown upon the argumentation of C. Pfahler, a scholar of the old Hungarian legal system of agrarian relations who worked in the early 19th century. He alleged that the labour duties of the serfs "initium sumebant, quo tempore (i. e. around 1514, in his opinion) agricultura magis efflorescente *operamque ideo cultoris magis remunerante* lucri cupido dominos incessit, ut quemadmodum in Germania domini terrarum fecerunt, magna latifundia sibi reservarent, opere colonorum suorum excolenda": *Jus Georgicum regni Hungariae et partium eidem adnexarum,* Keszthely 1820, p. C.

53 No significant impact (either encouraging or discouraging) of religious convictions can be proven in the development of the trading activity of Hungarian landowners. All of them aspired to the tithes of the Church in order to increase their income in grain and wine which could be taken to market (*cf.* contemporary endeavours in France; note 45 above). In their own estates they had the right to take the tithe on lease (Ac: 1548:61), later, however, admitting the prior claim of the Treasury around the border fortresses (Act 1563:68 etc). Protestant preachers often lashed out against the mercantile eagerness of noble landowners; such quotations from Péter Bornemisza are given above too. — Th. Mayer had mentioned it as a counter-argument to M. Weber's thesis (see note 1 above and the relevant text) that the economic endeavours of the Calvinist nobility in Hungary were in no way different from those of the Catholics: *Deutsche Wirtschaftsgeschichte der Neuzeit,* Leipzig 1928, p. 27.

54 Commercial activities and market production by 16th century Hungarian landowners were dealt with more thoroughly by the present author in the monograph: *Nyugat-európai és magyarországi agrárfejlődés a XV–XVII. században* (Agrarian development in Western Europe and in Hungary from the 15th to the 17th century), Budapest 1963, pp. 139 ff. German version: *Die ungarische Agrarentwicklung im 16.–17. Jahrhundert. Abbiegung vom westeuropäischen Entwicklungsgang,* Budapest 1964, pp. 12, ff. All the data for which no notes are given in this paper, have been taken from there: pp. 168 ff, pp. 97 ff.

family by cattle trading at about the same time. István Dobó, the heroic defender of Eger castle in 1552, carried on cattle trading in the middle of the century in partnership with other noble lords, Ferenc Zay and Sebestyén Bornemisza and supplied grains in the 1570s to the market of the important mining town, Selmecbánya. The family of Miklós Zrínyi, who fell in the defence of Szigetvár (1566), took over the control of cattle-driving to Venice in the latter part of the century. The wholesale grain exporter to and importer from Austria and the biggest purveyor of the royal army around that time was the same Miklós Pálffy, who made his military fame particularly by recapturing Győr castle (1598). István Illésházy, who was to have a prominent role in Bocskay's uprising against the Habsburgs (1604—1606), traded extensively in grain and cattle from his domain at Szentgyörgy-Bazin in North-West Hungary and he was well known not only as an ardent wine-grower and husbandman but also as an astute vintner.[55] The list could be continued with the trading and farming Thurzós, Serédis, Balassas, Révays etc. The participation of Hungarian magnates in the wine trade was also considerable. Among those who exported wine to its main market, Poland, in the latter part of the 16th century, we can find the names of the Homonnays, the Mágócsys, Simon Forgács and Zsigmond Rákóczi.[56] Nor did the middle and lesser nobility despise profitable business: in the numerous acts of the Diets concerning commerce we can read both about "the mightier and the lesser" and about "magnates and gentlemen".[57]

It is no exaggeration, therefore, to draw a parallel in this respect between sixteenth century enterprising market-minded Hungarian landowners, who employed paid labour, too, and showed certain capitalist features, and their contemporaries in England, the "commercial nobility" and the "rising gentry". The quotations from the Hungarian sources ring very similar to the contemporary English statement (1577): "Widely respected landowners ... themselves become livestock dealers, butchers, leather-merchants, sheep breeders, timber-merchants *et denique quid non*?"[58]

[55] "Ferenc Zay's career is very interesting. He was a soldier, a diplomatist, a merchant, a husbandman and a writer in one person": L. Thallóczy: *Csömöri báró Zay Ferenc 1505–1570* (Baron Ferenc Zay of Csömör, 1505–1570), Budapest 1885, p. 3. — Son of the defender of Eger, "Ferenc Dobó was the best husbandman and the first of all merchants of his own age": S. Takáts: *Régi magyar kapitányok és generálisok* (Old Hungarian captains and generals), second, enlarged edition, Budapest, n. d., p. 384. — Miklós Pálffy traded not only in grain from his demesne farms or rents in kind, but also in grain obtained by taking the tithes on lease or by buying it from the peasants of villages and market-towns. He did not sell the produce on the spot, on his estates but, by his domainal officials and agents, he had them sent to market himself (partly to Vienna where he had business connections with military provisionment commissaries Grafenauer and, later, Pichler). Moreover, according to actual demand, he also negotiated grain-import from Austrian landowners to Hungary (e.g. to supply the garrison at Komárom), "by which he entered the purely commercial field, too". Other landowners from North-Western Hungary (Counties Pozsony and Nyitra) also participated in the grain trade in a similar way: e.g. in 1570, commissariat officer Jeromos Pech bought a major quantity from Gáspár Tardy in Vienna for the starving garrisons of Transdanubian fortresses. About these see J. Belitzky: *A magyar gabonakivitel története 1860-ig* (The history of Hungarian grain exports until 1860), Budapest 1932, pp. 23–27. — Further data are given by G. Wenzel: *A Fuggerek jelentősége Magyarország történelmében* (The importance of Fuggers in Hungarian history), Budapest 1882, pp. 54–62; P. Jedlicska: *Kiskárpáti emlékek Vöröskőtől Szomolányig* (Lower Carpathian relics from Vöröskő to Szomolány), Budapest 1882, p. 25, and esp.: *Adatok erdődi Pálffy Miklós, a győri hősnek életrajza- és korához* (Data to the life and age of Miklós Pálffy of Erdőd, the hero of Győr), Eger 1897, pp. 6, 107, 128, 145, 155, 164, 184, 208–209, 221, 232, 234–235, 248, 615, 644–645, 654, 669, 672–673. — See also Á. Károlyi: *Illésházy István hűtlenségi pöre* (The impeachment of István Illésházy), Budapest 1883, pp. 20–22.

[56] I. Acsády: *op. cit.*, pp. 70–72; Gy. Komoróczy: *op. cit.*, pp. 51, 60–61, 72–73, 96–97, 302.

[57] Acts 1498:35 and 1500:41–42, and later Acts 1543:26, 1548:55, 1553:18, 1557:16, 1558:44 etc.

[58] Quoted by H. R. Trevor-Roper, *op. cit.*, p. 7. — Francis Bacon wrote about a nobleman he knew personally that "he was a great merchant of cattle and grain and a great lead- and ironmonger and he also

The enterprising Hungarian noblemen of the 16th century, however, preserved features of a feudal landlord, too. For just as they were not deterred from the market and from trading by prejudice or ingrained habits, they felt no scruples either about exercising their feudal powers in their new sphere of activity. They increased the labour dues of their serfs, too, and collected rents from them in kind again in order to increase their stocks of grain and wine.[59] A significant quantity of the collected, "seized" and purchased wine they sold in the "forced market" of their own estates. Whereas the French nobles, as mentioned above, were definitely forbidden to keep inns of their own, in the 16th century it came to be one of the most important and long-lasting sources of income for the Hungarian landowners to sell wine and to keep inns in their manors *(popinatio, educillatio)*.[60] They also used their class privileges on the market against their peasant-burgher competitors: they did not only secure exemption from local tolls within the country but in many cases from paying "the thirtieth", the export duty as well, at least "in respect of the livestock bred on their own manorial estates". Then they declared the cattle they bought to have been bred in their own herds, so as to be able to export them duty-free.[61] Similar methods were applied in wine-export.[62]

It was precisely during the peak period of the price revolution and cattle exports to the West (to Vienna, the South German towns and Venice) that the "burghers of the Hungarian free and mining towns" submitted a petition to the Diet of 1574 that "trading in hides, horses, oxen and other similar goods should not be allowed to the lords and the gentlemen". The Estates of the Realm, of course, "considered that this could not be granted", and they even incorporated in law their own principle of the time "that magnates as well as noblemen should be free to trade in any merchandise".[63]

The same practice prevailed in contemporary Poland as well. "The Polish nobles ... threw themselves into commerce" and, "retaining their immunities, they deprive the Treasury of the customs duties they would have to pay", wrote a French diplomat who saw the River Vistula almost at the same time, in 1573 (in connection with the short-lived reign in Poland of King Henry III of France).[64]

What he saw in Poland could well be striking for the French traveller because it was practically contrary to contemporary developments in France. Sure enough, the depreciation of the monetary rents payable by the peasants and the agrarian price revolution drew the attention of certain groups of the French nobility, too, to agricultural production and commerce of their own. Thirteen years earlier, in 1560, the nobility of Touraine had requested the king, "to permit the noblemen who were reduced to poverty by the severity of customary law and the devastation of war to practise commerce or other trades without being declared undeserving of their noble

---

traded in other goods": *ibid.* — "The English gentry... were not held back by any rule like *dérogeance* from increasing their incomes from any sources, yet, unlike in the Netherlands, they never lost their country roots": R. H. Tawney: *op. cit.*, 1941, p. 3.

59 See note 54.

60 The financial authority (the Szepes Treasury) stated in 1570 that the keeping of manorial inns "is widely spread in the country and is regarded as a regular income": *Magyar Gazdaságtörténelmi Szemle* (Hungarian Economic History Review) 1896, p. 70.

61 Acts 1567:36, 1569:17, 1574:25, 1596:56, 1597:35 etc.

62 "Powerful magnates... but others too... seize and buy up the wine of their serfs beyond that obtained from their own vineyards and thereby they export and sell enormous quantities of wine without paying any customs duty...": quoted from a report of the Szepes Treasury to the Pozsony Treasury in 1599 by Gy. Komoróczy: *op. cit.*, p. 293.

63 Act 1574:37, *cf.* Act 1563:57.

64 Quoted by G. Zeller: *op. cit.*, pp. 71–72.

status and deprived of their privileges". But the government refused to give permission in the following laconic answer: "The King, for good reasons and considerations, does not agree". Practically this very same standpoint was repeated by the royal decrees of 1579 and 1606 as well; and the edict sent out on the occasion of the famous *États Généraux* of 1614 also took a stand by the upholding of the prohibition that noblemen were not to be allowed to participate in trade.[65]

5

But let us return to the "Hungarian magnates and nobles" who, at about the same time, were confirmed by the Act of the Diet in their right "to trade freely in any merchandise".

And they did trade indeed, not only at the peak of the 16th century price revolution but also during the first part of the 17th, when the market was already rendered uncertain by violent fluctuations of agricultural prices. A number of aristocrats, holders of high offices continued to busy themselves with cattle and produce trading.[66] The Princes of Transylvania Gábor Bethlen and György Rákóczi I were among them, as well as the president of the Treasury of Royal Hungary Pál Pálffy and his brother István, the Palatine Miklós Eszterházy, the Archbishop of Esztergom Péter Pázmány or the Bán (governor) of Croatia, György Zrínyi, and later his sons: the poet and general Miklós Zrínyi and his brother Péter, etc. The Treasury often paid the purveyors of the army partly by land-grants: family estates of considerable sizes were established this way. Landowners continued trading in wine, too: Zsigmond Prépostváry, Miklós Jakabfalvy and later Ferenc Wesselényi and István Vitnyédi appeared among the exporters of wine.[67] Besides the magnates, lesser nobles frequently acted as merchants and cattle-dealers in this period as well.[68]

A report from the middle of the 17th century (1655), handed in to the Treasury by a senior clerk of the Slavonian (South-West Hungarian) customs office, Daniel Rauch offered a comprehensive picture of the trading by magnates and lesser nobles of the time. The officer stressed that "the members of nobility ... all engaged in trade"; but left no doubt that such business had become increasingly dominated by feudal methods, privileges and arbitrary regulations, more than before. "The magnates and gentlemen having taken to trading, ... as soon as they saw a gain in anything, they took it over for themselves; they deprived common people and merchants of all the opportunities." And the "noble lords" pretended that the grain, wine, cattle and other products obtained in any way was *"pro propria allodiatura"*: originated from their own seigniorial demesnes, and sold them duty-free within the country as well as abroad.[69]

Thus, the noblemen of seventeenth century Hungary carried on their trading activities without changing their feudal manners or mixing with the burghers in towns. In this respect, they clearly differed from their English counterparts:[70] they

65 *Op. cit.*, pp. 43–44.

66 Regarding all these, reference is to be made to the monograph by the present author mentioned in note 54: pp. 200 ff. and 41 ff., respectively; (as for the sources: pp. 257 ff. and 119 ff., respectively).

67 *Történelmi Tár* (Historical Collection), 1871, p. 147; 1899, p. 139; S. Szilágyi: *Erdély és az északkeleti háború. Levelek és okiratok* (Transylvania and the North-Eastern War. Letters and documents), Budapest I, 1890, pp. 492–493; *cf.* Gy. Komoróczy: *op. cit.*, pp. 126–127, 321.

68 *Cf.* Acts 1618:30, 1622:48, 1625:36, 1630:17, 1635:70–71, 1638:49, 1658:83 etc.

69 *Magyar Gazdaságtörténelmi Szemle,* 1898, pp. 577–589.

70 In the century preceding the English Revolution, Tawney wrote with some exaggeration but certainly bringing out the main tendency of development, "those social categories which used to be applied

remained feudal lords even on the market, asserting their prerogatives and extending them. Exemption from customs duty soon became a similar nobiliary privilege as immunity from taxes: it was not the trading nobles who were obliged to pay customs duties, but rather the trading burghers who tried to gain nobility precisely in order to avoid duties; this retrograde tendency in trade was pointed out by the author of the above report.[71]

Contemporary sources reveal similar tendencies in production too. The employment of paid labour on seigniorial demesnes came rare and unpaid services prevailed and became overwhelming. In the first part of the 17th century, the landlords frequently imposed them *"ad libitum"*, at will on their serfs, who, by then, were bound to the soil not only legally but in practice as well. The agrarian system of late feudalism, termed the "second serfdom", unfolded and became consolidated in Hungary, in many respects similarly to developments in Poland and the East German principalities.[72]

All this coincided in time with the end of the agricultural boom and the price revolution. The rocketing of prices lost impetus already from the early 17th century or, rather, was replaced by sharp fluctuations, depending on the particular country and the types of commodities. The price revolution was over partly by the 1620s and '30s and completely by around 1650. And if the rise in prices used to affect mainly agricultural produce, the depression took a similarly agrarian pattern: the price of grain decreased much more almost everywhere than that of other products.[73]

And, sure enough—and this can hardly be regarded as a mere coincidence—by this time there did appear the figure of the Hungarian nobleman who gave up trading, and withdrew completely from commercial activities. It came to pass, back in 1615, that the Hungarian Treasury turned to a former wholesale dealer, János Bornemisza for information about the prospects of Oriental trade through the Turkish Empire. The nobleman answered: "I cannot comment on the present situa-

---

to distinguish between the landowners' and the merchants' classes and have remained conceptions retaining their legal importance in France and on German soil, have lost their once precise meaning in Britain. ...The landowner who lived on the profits and rents of his estate producing for the market and the merchant or the banker who was also a landowner at the same time, did not represent two, but only one class... In respect of the sources of their incomes both of them were *bourgeois*": *op. cit.* 1941, p. 18.

71 *Magyar Gazdaságtörténelmi Szemle,* 1898, p. 581. — Exemption from (internal) customs duty, unlike immunity from taxes, had not been a privilege of the nobility originally; merchants of burgher and peasant origin had achieved local or national exemption from customs duty; burghers and peasants: they were the main representatives of trading in the 14th and 15th centuries. It was as late as about the end of the 15th century that noblemen began to take a share in trading themselves; first only to get equal advantages as the burghers of the royal free towns (Acts 1498:35, 1500:41–42), as a sign of their emerging participation in the commercial activities and their developing interests in the market. However, by the 17th century, exemption from customs duty became a feudal privilege, too, a privilege that trading "gentlemen and noblemen" used against their competitors of burgher and peasant origin. — "Exemption from the thirtieth (in foreign trade) was not mentioned in the privileges which were granted to towns at about the turn of the 16th and 17th centuries": D. Oszetszky: *A hazai polgárság társadalmi problémái a rendiség felbomlásakor* (Social problems of the town burghers in Hungary during the decline of feudalism), Budapest 1935, p. 31.

72 See the literature given under notes 42, 43 and 54.

73 See the literature referred to under notes 46 and 49. — "Although still there is a lot to be done in the field of research into the reciprocal relations of prices, on the whole it is clear that the 17th century and the first half of the 18th century are characterized by a general decline in prices" and that in this period "the grain prices fell deeper nearly everywhere than the prices of other goods... On the basis of the movement of prices as related to one another it may be stated certainly that the 17th century depression was first of all a grain depression from the economic point of view, and it caused grave difficulties mainly to the typical grain-producing countries, which difficulties were aggravated by the dependence of these countries on the international market": B. H. Slicher van Bath: Die europäischen Agrarverhältnisse im 17. und in der ersten Hälfte des 18. Jahrhunderts, in: *A. A. G. Bijdragen, 13,* Wageningen 1965, p. 144.

tion, having devoted my life just to my small land".[74] It occurred in 1642 that a Hungarian magnate, István Héderváry, a descendant of the same György Héderváry, who exactly one hundred years earlier (as will be remembered) had wanted to buy a ship to further his trading, portrayed himself in a letter addressed to one of his relatives, thus: "... you reproach me not for my wedding, nor for my great expenses; for my poor father also considered keeping his own table decent as satisfaction enough; neither can I live otherwise, since I am my father's son".[75] And only a few decades later, at the very beginning of the 18th century, a Transylvanian magnate, Miklós Bethlen related in his autobiography that when he had practised "honest trade" during the 1670s and '80s in wine, cattle and wheat, "my ill-wishers besmeared me that the merchant blood shows in me, that my mother was the daughter of one" (i.e. of a merchant).[76] And when he drew up a large-scale plan for the establishment of a Transylvanian trading company and referred to the example provided by West European nations, he received the following opinion from a committee consisting of mainly magnates and noblemen and delegated by the 1703 Transylvanian Diet (convened in Gyulafehérvár): "The English, Dutch and the German are both apt and professional in trade by their nature. However, we, especially those who could invest money in trade, are not only ignorant of commerce (as no one in our families has ever dealt with commerce [?!]) but we do not even know what trade consists in."[77]

And how characteristic it was of the changes of times! Trading—which, in the 16th century, had still been a natural way of life for lots of Hungarian magnates and noblemen—became, by the end of the 17th, such an unfamiliar activity for the majority that they blackened those who continued to pursue it and regarded themselves as people entirely devoid of any mercantile sense and expertise.

As above, we had defined the general European phenomena of the 16th century, that is the price revolution and agrarian boom as the major incentives driving the Hungarian landowners (or, at least, significant groups of them) to trade and market production. Now, perhaps, we are not mistaken if we explain the withdrawal of the bulk of the Hungarian landowning class from trade and market precisely by the close of the price revolution and agrarian boom—these similarly general European phenomena—on the one hand, and by the emergence of the "second serfdom" and the prevalence and the unlimited exploitation of unpaid servile labour—these East-Central European phenomena—on the other. The system of the "second serfdom", which restricted the mobility and the market production of the peasantry (the rural population) and hindered the urban development and the formation of the bourgeoisie, also impeded the modernization of the class of landowners. The mentality of the Hungarian nobility also became more inflexible in the wake of this: feudal manners became unambiguous, capitalist features wore off and trading turned into

[74] *Magyar Gazdaságtörténelmi Szemle,* 1900, p. 112.

[75] *A Héderváry-család oklevéltára,* II, p. 260.

[76] *Gr. Bethlen Miklós önéletírása* (The autobiography of Count Miklós Bethlen). Published by L. Szalay, I, Pest 1858, pp. 172–173. — In a former part of his autobiography Miklós Bethlen wrote that his grandfather on the mother's side, Miklós Váradi had been a merchant who had moved from Várad to Kolozsvár and "had been an agent for Gábor Bethlen and had managed several trading affairs for him because *even the prince traded in wax, honey, cattle* in Vienna, Venice and Breslau": *op. cit.*, pp. 145–147. — For Miklós Bethlen's economic and trading activities in the 1670s see also *op. cit.*, pp. 379–380.

[77] Quoted by I. Lukinich: Egy erdélyi kereskedelmi társaság terve 1703-ból (The project of a Transylvanian trading company from 1703), *Századok* (Centuries), 1914, pp. 475–476. — Miklós Bethlen wrote about this opinion that the members of the committee themselves „extranea magna commercia captum suum superare fatebantur": *Gr. Bethlen Miklós önéletírása* II, Pest 1860, p. 292.

an activity bearing the mark of *dérogeance*.[78] In the course of the 17th century, the Pálffys, Thurzós, Homonnays, Thökölys, Mágócsys and other prominent and affluent families dealt less and less with cattle trading; they participated in livestock and wine export only occasionally and, by the end of the century, they retired from business completely.[79] "At the end of the 17th century, the owners of vast domains appeared mainly as growers and primary sellers. By the turn of the century, it became very rare to find a landowner who ... would have got involved in risky trading in grain, either grown on his own estates or purchased elsewhere."[80]

[78] S. Takáts sketched out the 16th century Hungarian trade by the magnates and the lesser nobility but he disregarded the feudal features of this commerce. Similarly, he was the first who described "the decline of Hungarian cattle traders and merchants" from the middle of the 17th century. As the sole reason for the decline he pointed out the economic policy of the Habsburgs and the "biassed and greedy measures" taken by the government authorities in Vienna against Hungarian merchants. The thus ruined Hungarian cattle traders "were replaced by foreigners and the number of Greek, Armenian, Serbian and Bulgarian merchants continuously increased" at the end of the 17th and the beginning of the 18th century: *Szegény magyarok* (Poor Hungarians), *op. cit.*, pp. 237–238, 247. — In his general study J. Berlász already emphasized the latter point: he explained the "decline of Hungarian cattle dealers belonging to the lesser nobility" by the fact that, from the middle of the 17th century, "the Greek, Jewish, Armenian and Serbian merchants, infiltrating Hungary from the Turkish Empire and obtaining privileges from magnates and princes, supplanted both Hungarian and German merchants to a great extent": Ipar és kereskedelem (Industry and trade), in: S. Domanovszky (ed.) *Magyar művelődéstörténet* (Hungarian cultural history), Budapest, n. d., III, p. 212. — Gy. Komoróczy, however, connected the commercial change with a kind of mental change at the beginning of the 18th century: "after Rákóczi's war of independence, the way of life of the nobility seemed to change all of a sudden. The noblemen who had traded so far sank into enervated indifference... The souls were seized by a psychosis of aversion to enterprise and of expectance... As if the loss of the war of independence had brought about a moral introversion among the people, an attitude which trading would not fit into...": *op. cit.*, pp. 127–128. — J. Belitzky also came to the conclusion that "by that time (after 1711 or 1715) the grain trade had already fallen out of the hands of the landowners completely. They were to be simply producers and, disregarding some exceptional cases, did not deal with resale. This was a natural consequence of the fact that the higher nobility became a court nobility": *op. cit.*, p. 45.

Although we do not deny the impact of these factors (to different degrees and in different ways, of course), we think the main reason is to be found in what has been propounded in the text. (Adding that the system of the "second serfdom" impeded the development of inner market and the growth of domestic demand for agricultural products.) Therefore, we consider G. Tolnai's view as the nearest to ours (despite his misunderstanding of the real tendency in the payment of customs duties): "The decree of 1608 (which ceded the issue of the serfs' migration to the jurisdiction of every single county) gave the right to use servile labour at will into the hands of the nobility... The same decree was to disaccustom the lesser noblemen to work, to earning their living by trade and, thereby, it was to become natural for them that, in possession of their privileges, they were to live on the labour of their serfs... Cattle trading (which, among all branches of export trade, yielded the greatest income) was in the hands of Hungarian cattle dealers completely in the 16th century. It was the same with the wine trade; but, together with cattle trading, it also came to be managed by foreigners instead of the indolent Hungarian noblemen of the 17th century. These developments were not accidental, but necessarily connected with the circumstances, (the legal system codified by) Werbőczi and the decrees of 1608. Werbőczi's work largely contributed to the decline of the mercantile attitude of Hungarians, since, according to the *Tripartitum*, the exemption from customs duty of the privileged noblemen was suspended when they carried (their produce) for trading purposes [?!] Thus, inevitably, trading slowly became such an occupation for the noblemen which was incompatible with their nobiliary privileges": *Régi magyar főurak. Életforma és műveltség az újkorban* (Old Hungarian magnates. Way of life and culture in early modern times), Budapest 1939, pp. 110–111. — *Cf.* B. Hóman, Gy. Szekfű: *Magyar történet* (Hungarian history), 2nd edition, Budapest 1935, III, pp. 548–549.

[79] J. Berlász: *op. cit.*, p. 214.

[80] J. Belitzky: *op. cit.*, p. 16. — By the last decades of the 17th century, changes occurred in the mechanism of military purveyance and provisionment of the army. As compared to the supply provided by the great landowners (which, in turn, was partly based on their purchase, a practice which could be observed particularly in the case of Miklós Pálffy — see note 55 above), the purchasing and supplying activities of such commercial companies as the Viennese *Orientalische Kompagnie* and such army purveyor enterprises as that of Samuel Oppenheimer in Vienna came to the foreground and were privileged by the emperor. The practice of what is called the "portion-system" was also introduced (meaning the direct provi-

Among the circumstances of the period following the expulsion of the Turks and Ferenc Rákóczi II's war of independence, when there were favourable conditions for the acquisition of large estates and for resettlement as well, i.e. from the 1710s to the 1730s, some of the "great acquirers" (such as Sándor Károlyi or Antal Grassalkovich) still showed some economic agility and entrepreneurial ability reminiscent of the former market-minded noblemen of the age of the agrarian boom and the price revolution, but these features vanished in about one or two generations' time.[81] A type of *"absentee"* landlord came into being, living far from his domains, spending money excessively, upkeeping a luxurious residence in Vienna, concerned about his estates only to get as much money as possible.[82] And if he did not detach himself from economic activity completely and sent instructions from the distance, urging more frequent and profitable sales (as did the new owners of Rákóczi's confiscated estates in Regéc and Sárospatak: Duke Leopold Trauthson and his son Wilhelm), he was to experience a great deal of "tardiness in trading" on the part of his bailiffs. (Two hundred years later this was to be explained by the historiographers of the estates as nothing else but a consequence of an "unbusinesslike attitude", due to the "special mental character" of Hungarians.)[83] Even if the

sioning in kind of the military forces): *op. cit.*, pp 28–30; S. Takáts: Dunai hajózás a XVI. és XVII. században (Shipping on the Danube in the 16th and 17th centuries), *Magyar Gazdaságtörténelmi Szemle*, 1900, pp. 265–273; K. Fajkmajer: *Zur Geschichte der ersten orientalischen Kompagnie*, Wien 1909, pp. 654–658; F. Szakály: Oppenheimer Sámuel működése különös tekintettel magyarországi kihatásaira (Samuel Oppenheimer's activity with special regard to its effects in Hungary), in: S. Scheiber (ed.): *Magyar-zsidó oklevéltár* (Hungarian-Jewish Archives), XVI, Budapest 1971, pp. 36–38, 48–53, 58–62.

81 S. Takáts: *Szalai Barkóczy Krisztina, 1671–1724* (Krisztina Szalai Barkóczy, 1671–1724), (wife of Sándor Károlyi), Budapest 1910, pp. 71, 180, 189–193, 231–248; I. Wellmann: *A gödöllői Grassalkovich-uradalom gazdálkodása, különös tekintettel az 1770–1815 esztendőkre* (Husbandry on the Gödöllő Estates of the Grassalkovich family, with particular regard to the years 1770–1815), Budapest 1933, pp. 7–28; W. Endrei–L. Makkai: Az első főúri textilmanufaktúrák Magyarországon (The first textile manufactories of magnates in Hungary), *Történelmi Szemle* (Historical Review), 3, 1970, pp. 330–332, 337–340.

82 Around 1790, Baron Miklós Skerlecz imputed it partly to them that the assets of the Hungarian commercial balance were reduced to nothing through their luxury in Vienna: Berényi: *op. cit.*, pp. 113–114; *cf.* F. Eckhart: *A bécsi udvar gazdasági politikája Mária Terézia korában* (The economic policy of the Viennese Court in the time of Maria Theresa), Budapest 1922, p. 167 and Gy. Ember: A barokk rendi társadalom (Feudal society in the baroque period), in: S. Domanovszky (ed.): *Magyar művelődéstörténet* (Hungarian cultural history), Budapest, n. d., IV, p. 145.

83 E. Jármay–I. Bakács: *A regéczi uradalom gazdálkodása a XVIII. században* (Husbandry on the Regécz estates in the 18th century), Budapest 1930; J. Ravasz: *A sárospataki uradalom gazdálkodása a XVIII. században* (Husbandry on the Sárospatak estates in the 18th century), Budapest 1938. — "Duke Leopold Trauthson lived in Vienna permanently and the money and the wine he needed were sent to him there every year. His heir, Duke Wilhelm Trauthson came to the estates for a short stay only once, in 1726": E. Jármay–I. Bakács: *op. cit.*, p. 23. — "At first the duke received the money through the Oppenheimer Bank; like the German and Austrian magnates of the age, he was also a client of the Oppenheimer Bank in Vienna. (*Cf.* note 80 above.) Later he got it remitted by way of the Tokaj salt-office, the Szepes or Zólyom treasuries or the Szomolnok copper mine... The other part of the net income was the surplus. This often amounted to 10–15–17,000 forints... but the surplus was left to its fate, whereas the estates would have needed so much investment, improvement and modernization according to the demands of the age": *op. cit.*, p. 71. (On the Sárospatak estates, the surplus was smaller but it usually amounted to a few thousand forints there, too, even disregarding the arrears: J. Ravasz: *op. cit.*, p. 102.) — For "tardiness in trading", "special mental character" and "indifference to business" (referring to Gyula Szekfű, *cf.* note 104 below): pp. 49 and 72. — For the economic instructions of the duke: pp. 13–14, 101–102, as well as pp. 14, 37, 39. — In 1723, for instance, he wrote to the bailiffs that he disliked vintners going to the estates because, realizing the low local prices of wine, they conformed to those. In order to avoid it, he would have found it advantageous that the bailiffs should buy a suitable number of oxen, should have waggons made by the coach-builders of the estates and got the wine transported to the Galgóc market. This would have been the only way to sell the vintage for a good price and not just waiting all the time as the personnel liked to do: Gy. Komoróczy: *op. cit.*, p. 173. — The

aristocratic landlords stayed at home for shorter or longer periods in their newly built luxurious domestic residences—so did the builders of the most splendid ones: the Dukes Eszterházy[84] who were also the richest—it came to be actually characteristic of the management of the large estates in Hungary during the 18th century that the surplus of wine or other produce (the quantity of which greatly depended on the geographical situation, the market conditions, the development of the demesne farming, the labour system of the domain and other factors) was usually not taken to the market,[85] but the Greek, Armenian or Jewish buyer was waited for on the spot instead.[86] Even inn-keeping and selling wine to the peasants was gradually discontinued by the management of the estates (although this well-paying but, obviously, *dérogeance*-like form of trading activity was based on the landlords' privileges): by the end of the century numerous manorial inns were taken on lease by the Jews settling in the villages. There were other kinds of trading activity, too, which had to be covered in and around the large estates the management of which had drawn back from commerce. This is why several big landowners permitted and promoted the settlement of Jewish merchants on their estates and protected them by the force of their seigniorial rights (like the Eszterházys did in

instructions were carried out neither in Regéc (Jármay, *op. cit.*, p. 49) nor on the Sárospatak domain where "the serfs did not have to provide long-distance transport (which was such an arduous labour duty on certain estates)... mainly because hardly any produce was to be taken to far-away markets (the Polish vintners carried away the wine from the spot)": J. Ravasz: *op. cit.*, p. 27; *cf.* 72, 91.

[84] G. Tolnai: *op. cit.*, pp. 132–138, 153–158; *cf.* I. Wellmann: *op. cit.*, p. 12.

[85] "The noblemen engaged in trading so far... seem to have got tired of the organizing and enterprising activities... of their predecessors and all at once they abandoned active trading and waited for the merchants to come to their estates and tried to attract them there by artful means." "...a sort of weak-heartedness came upon the people and almost compelled them to wait for the arriving merchants with arms folded." Apart from his comments, Komoróczy's establishment of the facts (*op. cit.*, pp. 127, 173 etc.) at which he arrived through the general examination of the wine export to Poland, and the results of the monographs by Jármay and Bakács, as well by Ravasz concerning the selling of wine to mainly Polish vintners on the Regéc and Sárospatak estates (note 83) are practically confirmed in respect of trading in other agricultural produce by those monographs (mostly published within the framework of the series edited by S. Domanovszky) which examined the management of other estates in certain periods of the 18th century: Cs. Csapody: *Az Eszterházyak alsólendvai uradalmának gazdálkodása a XVIII. század első felében* (Management of the Alsólendva estates of the Eszterházys in the first part of the 18th century), Budapest 1933; E. Gerendás: *Az esztergomi főkáptalan garamszentbenedeki birtokterülete a XVIII. század második felében* (The Garamszentbenedek estates of the Esztergom Cathedral chapter in the second part of the 18th century), Budapest 1934; L. Bojt: *A fejérvári őrkanonokság (custodiatus) birtokainak története a XVII. század végétől 1833-ig* (The history of the estates of the Fehérvár custodian canonry from the end of the 17th century to 1833), Budapest 1935; I. Wellmann: *op. cit.*; Zs. P. Pach: *Az Orczy-birtokok gazdálkodása a XVIII. század második felében* (The management of the estates of the Orczys in the second part of the 18th century), MS, 1943. — On the basis of these it may be established that the development of demesne farming based on servile labour and the increasingly *commodity producing* character of certain large estates in the 18th century did not bring about an increase in their *mercantile* character and commercial activities in general. The produce was usually sold to the consumers or the merchants on the spot and was not transported to more frequented markets by the personnel of the estates or employed agents.

[86] F. Eckhart: Kereskedelmünk közvetítői a XVIII. században (Agents of our commerce in the 18th century), *Századok*, 1918, pp. 356 ff.; L. Schäfer: *A görögök vezető szerepe Magyarországon a korai kapitalizmus kialakulásában* (The leading role of the Greeks in the emergence of early capitalism in Hungary), Budapest 1930; L. Zoltai: *Debrecen város százados küzdelme a görög kereskedőkkel* (The century-long struggle of the town of Debrecen against Greek merchants), Debrecen 1935; Ö. Füves: *Görögök a Duna-Tisza közén* (Greeks between the rivers Danube and Tisza), in: *Antik Tanulmányok* (Ancient Studies), 1966. 1, pp. 92–98; K. Schünemann: Die Armenier in der Bevölkerungspolitik Maria Theresias, in: *A gr. Klebelsberg Kúnó Magyar Történetkutató Intézet Évkönyve* (Yearbook of the Count Kúnó Klebelsberg Historical Research Institute), III, Budapest 1933, pp. 212–242.

Kismarton, the Pálffys in Pozsonyváralja and Stomfa, the Batthyánys in Rohonc, the Zichys in Óbuda and the Károlyis in Nagykároly).[87]

On the other hand, there was the Hungarian country gentleman who lived mainly on the serfs' services in rents and labour on his medium-sized or small estate, engaged at most in the local county affairs and entangled possessory legal actions, besides going to weddings and huntings and offering hospitality to neighbours and county notabilities. This type of nobleman became the characteristic figure of the majority of the Hungarian ruling class in the 18th century, unaware of the market conditions and not even interested in them, looking down on commerce, regarding trade as an occupation unworthy of gentlemen or Hungarians.[88] The conservative poet, Baron Lőrinc Orczy championed precisely this lack of business-mindedness as the criterion and the specific feature of the Hungarian character, when other voices began to be heard in the 1780s:

> Heated debates rage among us,
> Does shameless trade befit the Magyars?
> For it may indeed corrupt our morals,
> Say, where do you think it might lead us?
>
> In counties Zemplén, Szabolcs, Ung and Bereg
> Much money, food and wine fill all the cellars.
> Need we more? Should our lives be disconcerted?
> So that more money might stuff all our purses?[89]

And in the 1830s and '40s—as mentioned earlier—the view that trading is alien to the Hungarian mentality, that the lack of business-mindedness derives from the character of the nation, was expressed even by historians and other scholars; as a

[87] Taking the manorial still-room on lease was frequently the first step towards obtaining the inn in the same way: E. Jármay: *op. cit.*, p. 48; Cs. Csapody: *op. cit.*, p. 45; J. Ravasz: *op. cit.*, pp. 72, 90. Taking the domainal inn on lease as well as peddling and hawking often led to trading in grain, wine or wool on a major scale. In this connection see: I. Virág: *A zsidók jogállása Magyarországon 1657–1780* (The legal status of Jews in Hungary, 1657–1780), Budapest 1935, esp. pp. 24–47; A. Sas: Kis Lázár tündöklése és bukása. Egy zsidó üzletember élettörténete és sorsa Mária Terézia korában (The rise and fall of Lázár Kis. The life and fate of a Jewish businessman in the time of Maria Theresa), *Századunk* (Our century), 1934, 1, pp. 1–13. — *Cf.* S. Takáts: *op. cit.*, p. 36; E. Gerendás: *op. cit.*, p. 130; F. Eckhart: *A bécsi udvar gazdaságpolitikája Magyarországon 1780–1815* (Economic policy of the Viennese court in Hungary, 1780–1815), Budapest 1958, pp. 164–165, 337–338. — "Later, too, (after 1790) the settlement of Jewish merchants in order to improve trade was promoted by the big landowners and government authorities could not interfere with it." Endeavours and measures aimed at the limitation of the immigration and settlement of Jews "could not be carried out against the interests of the large estates, because the new tradesmen were necessary for them to manage the sale of their products": *op. cit.*, pp. 340–341.

[88] For the types of landowners in 18th-century Hungary *cf.* I. Wellmann: *A magyar mezőgazdaság a XVIII. században* (Hungarian agriculture in the 18th century), Budapest 1979, pp. 96–99. — The owners of minor estates in Transylvania "had modest incomes but they cut back their expenses even more, despised the very idea of selling or buying, enterprising or speculation, did not make efforts to increase their incomes and disdained money as a means of deceit. They maintained their gentlemanly households like this, with limited needs but, just because of this, without being in distress and therefore they had the reputation of being good husbandmen": *op. cit.*, p. 97, based on the *Memoirs of Sándor Mezőkövesdi Újfalvy*, Kolozsvár 1941, pp. 168–182. — The poet Ferenc Kazinczy described his maternal grandfather, Bossányi, the landowner in Bihar as a man who did not care much of his property, and held his stud, his herds of cattle and sheep for pleasure and not for profit and his shepherds gave account to him at will: *Pályám emlékezete* (Memories of my career), Budapest 1879, p. 6.

[89] Baron L. Orczy: Tokajban való érkezés télen (Arrival at Tokaj in winter), in: *Két nagyságos elmének költeményes szüleményei* (Poetical writings of two noble wits) (Poems by Lőrinc Orczy and Ábrahám Barcsay), Pozsony 1789, pp. 184–186.

matter of fact, not approvingly but critically.[90] Since the relevant historical sources had not yet been discovered then, this characterization was projected back to earlier times as well. That is why the historian Mihály Horváth wrote, in the belief that the way of thinking in the 16th and 17th centuries had been the same as in his own time; "The common opinion (of those days), at least that of the noble classes, ... biassed by prejudice, ... cherished the most absurd ideas concerning commerce."[91]

6

It is beyond the scope of this paper to follow the later course of such ideas about the anti-mercantile disposition and attitude of the Hungarian national character and their survival almost to this day. We can only touch upon some peculiar features of Hungarian economic and social development in the 19th and 20th centuries, which provided new ground for the maintenance, and even the reinforcement of such stereotypes.

Sure enough, the forerunners and the advocates of the national reform movement participated with hard words in the "heated debates" mentioned by Lőrincz Orczy and opposed the indolence of the nobles who looked down on trading. (Some of their statements have been quoted above.)

And indeed, the grain boom of the Napoleonic wars and the wool boom of the 1820s and 1830s (which was connected with the West European industrial revolution) offered economic incentives for the Hungarian big landowners again to develop their market production and to rationalize the management of their estates.[92]

Moreover, during the Hungarian *Vormärz,* i.e. in the decades preceding the 1848 revolution, certain groups of the nobility with medium-sized and smaller estates, too, were stimulated to adopt bourgeois habits and to turn towards the market. This

[90] This view soon appeared in geographical and ethnographical literature as well. "No inclination for venture runs in the blood" of the Hungarians, "they are averse to any kind of commercial transaction": J. v. Csaplovics: *Gemälde von Ungern,* Pesth 1829, II. pp. 7–8, 20. — *Cf.* J. G. Elsner: *Ungarn durchreiset, beurtheilet und beschrieben,* Leipzig 1840, I, p. 305; J. Erdélyi, E. Fényes (ed.): *Nemzeti iparunk* (Our national industry), Pest 1843, p. 141.

[91] M. Horváth: *op. cit.*, p. 59. — The second unaltered edition of M. Horváth's work on the history of industry and trade came out in 1868 (see note 34 above). Some twenty years later, however, I. Acsády (in his work quoted above in note 37) already pointed out that "all sections of the ruling class were in trade then (in the 16th century), whenever they had the opportunity, and according to all indications a nobleman's being in trade at that time was not regarded as discreditable or incompatible with his social position": *op. cit.*, p. 69. Nevertheless, Acsády's statement became neither common nor professional knowledge.

[92] B. Iványi Grünwald's introduction to the critical edition of Count I. Széchenyi's *Hitel* (Credit), Budapest 1930, esp. pp. 8–38; Gy. Mérei: *Mezőgazdaság és agrártársadalom Magyarországon 1790–1848* (Agriculture and agrarian society in Hungary 1790–1848), Budapest 1948, p. 42 ff.; Zs. P. Pach: A tőkés termelés feltételei a magyar mezőgazdaságban 1848-ban (The conditions of capitalist production in the Hungarian agriculture in 1848), *Társadalmi Szemle* (Social Review), 1948, 2, pp. 109–123; I. Szántó: *A parasztság kisajátítása és mozgalmai a gróf Festetichek keszthelyi ágának birtokain 1711–1850* (Peasant movements and expropriation on the Keszthely-branch Festetich estates 1711–1850), Budapest 1954, pp. 111–114, 134–146. — The development of commodity production on large estates went together with the increasing role and activity of chiefly Jewish merchants buying up and marketing the products of the estates. "During the French wars the new merchants trading in grain and wool raised considerable capital. A number of them made a fortune of several hundred thousand forints. Their riches can be taken as the first trading capital in Hungary which was invested in industrial enterprises in the subsequent decades": F. Eckhart, *op. cit.*, 1958, p. 341. — For the military purveyances, the purchases by the treasury, the firms trading in land produce see Belitzky, *op. cit.*, pp. 93–104, 113, 131–132, 140.

is why it became possible for the middle nobility to act as the leading class of the 1848—49 bourgeois revolution which terminated serfdom in Hungary.[93]

However, after the failure of the revolution and war of independence and then after the Austro-Hungarian Compromise *(Ausgleich)* of 1867 this process was partly impeded, and could advance only in the peculiar forms and within the limits determined by previous historical developments ("second serfdom" and anti-mercantile nobility).

One of the peculiarities of the development of capitalism in Hungary in the latter part of the 19th century can be observed in the ways and means of capitalization on the large estates. The new great agrarian boom in Europe (between 1850 and 1870), the termination of the internal Austro-Hungarian customs frontier, the growth of Austrian and Czech manufacturing industry offered favourable conditions for Hungarian agriculture in respect of markets and prices again. Under the influence of the new prosperity, numerous Hungarian big landowners really took steps to adopt capitalist patterns and to modernize *production*;[94] yet, in contrast with their predecessors in the 16th and 17th centuries but continuing the 18th century traditions, they themselves refrained from participation in *commerce,* and left the occupation of selling their produce (doing which they kept regarding as beneath their dignity) to mainly Jewish merchants.[95]

93 Louis Kossuth expected the members of the middle nobility to take on bourgeois habits and form, together with urban elements, a national "middle estate" similar to Western middle classes, for "without a self-dependent, constitutional middle class our nation will not survive": *Pesti Hírlap* (Pest daily), 234, 1843, March 20. — *Cf.* note 6 and 70 above. — The thesis of the middle-class function of the Hungarian lesser nobility or that of the representation of the bourgeoisie by nobles was formulated by József Révai (1932): Marx és a magyar forradalom (Marx and the Hungarian Revolution), in: *Marxizmus, népiesség, magyarság* (Marxism, populism, Hungarian identity), Budapest 1949, p. 111 ff.

94 K. Galgóczy: *Magyarország, a Szerbvajdaság s Temesi-bánság mezőgazdasági statisticája* (Agricultural statistics of Hungary, the Serbian Voivodeship and the Temes Banat), Pest 1855, pp. 366–400; I. Nagy: *A mezőgazdaság Magyarországon az abszolutizmus korában 1849–1867* (Agriculture in Hungary in the age of absolutism 1849–1867), Budapest 1944, pp. 84–92, 99–104; Zs. P. Pach: A magyarországi és oroszországi porosz utas agrárfejlődés egyező és eltérő vonásairól a XIX. század második felében (On the similar and divergent features of the Prussian type agrarian development in Hungary and Russia in the second half of the nineteenth century), *Közgazdasági Szemle* (Economic Review), 1958, 1, pp. 56–78; Gy. Bodrog: A tőkés gazdálkodás kialakulása az előszállási uradalomban (The formation of capitalist economy in the domain of Előszállás), *Agrártörténeti Szemle* (Agrarian History Review), 1966, 4, pp. 524–543; M. Szuhay: A szántóföldi termelés fejlődése a magyar mezőgazdaságban 1867–1914 (The development of agricultural production in Hungary 1867–1914), *Agrártörténeti Szemle,* 1971, 1–2, pp. 38–63; J. Oláh: *Az akasztói-vésztői uradalmak gazdálkodása a XIX–XX. század fordulóján* (The economy of the Akasztó-Vésztő domains at the turn of the nineteenth to twentieth century), Budapest 1975, esp. p. 21, pp. 143–156; T. Tóth: *Nagybirtoktól a nagyüzemig. A mernyei uradalom gazdálkodása a jobbágyfelszabadítástól az első világháborúig* (From large estate to large scale farming. The economy of the Mernye domain from the abolition of serfdom up to World War I), Budapest 1977, esp. pp. 165–172, 241–242, 317–336. — *Cf.* note 96.

95 This had already been noticed perspicaciously by János Makkai whose characterization is to the point in spite of some historical inaccuracy: in the 18th and 19th centuries "two things were considered "gentlemanlike" by our big landowners and lesser nobility alike: husbandry on their own estates and public service amidst circumstances and ideals changed... That is why even immediately before World War I the ideal magnate or medium landowner was expected to produce as much as possible but not to take pains to sell his corn and animals himself. ...Bringing up animals for breeding, driving nice bulls and horses to fairs were acts of distinction, but marketing cattle and horse was disliked and yielded to the Jews and the gipsies. Traders in livestock had become despised persons, held in contempt. They were called "copers" *(kupec).* Several anecdotes were told about the coper, and the dishonourable features which a Hungarian nobleman would have unwillingly admitted to be his own were imputed to this character. — Similarly, it was beneath the dignity of the Hungarian landlords to sell the corn they grew. They waited for the agent to come to the spot instead of looking for world market themselves. They did not associate in time... Only production but not marketing was regarded as gentlemanlike": *Urambátyám országa. Középosztályunk illemrendszerének és társadalmi viselkedésének szociográfiája* ("My dear

Another peculiarity of Hungarian capitalist development was that these very agricultural produce wholesale merchants or, rather, their second generation—with the participation of foreign capital, too—were to become the founders of a number of banking institutions and manufacturing enterprises in Hungary in the period following the Austro-Hungarian Compromise. Aristocrats and higher ranks of the lesser nobility also received a share of the profits of these capitalist enterprises, but usually not through actual participation in the venture, organization or management, but rather through nominal positions held in boards of directors or supervisory bodies. Both a parallel and a counterpart of this connection was the phenomenon that capitalist entrepreneurs appeared on the large estates with their activities covering not merely trading in produce but, here and there, also production: as capitalist leaseholders they paid rents to the landowners thus giving their share in the profit.[96]

It was this very situation which the movement of agricultural co-operatives and the activity of the Association of Hungarian Husbandmen (both of which had been started by Count Sándor Károlyi) attempted to change from the 1890s on. Although it was to be called an "agrarian" tendency both by contemporaries and in later literature, thereby contrasting it with the prevailing trend of economic policy called "mercantile", the aim of the movement was exactly to develop mercantile aspirations in the owners of large estates in Hungary, to put an end to their anti-commerce attitude, to help them to sell their produce themselves and to become independent entrepreneurs and businessmen instead of the fairly profitable but subordinate participation in the industrial and banking enterprises or the simple practice of relying on the rents paid by the leaseholders. Under the leadership of the great landowners, the agrarian movement wished to bring into activity wider circles of the "Christian gentlemen's society of husbandmen", those medium estate-owners who — because of the agrarian slump which followed the boom in the late 19th century[97]—kept going downhill financially in great numbers.

---

fellow" country. Sociography of the etiquette and social behaviour of the Hungarian middle class), Budapest, n. d. (traceable from the text: 1941), pp. 225–226. *Cf.* H. Ditz: *A magyar mezőgazdaság* (Hungarian agriculture). Translated from German by G. Halász, Pest 1869, pp. 185–186 and I. Nagy, *op. cit.*, pp. 93–94. — In the 16th century the cattle dealer was called "broker" *(tőzsér)*, without any pejorative shade of its meaning.

96 For the development of the capitalist banking system and manufacturing industry in Hungary see I. T. Berend–Gy. Ránki: *A magyar gazdaság száz éve* (A hundred years' Hungarian economy), Budapest 1972, p. 24 ff. — For industrial bourgeoisie (at first in the milling industry) risen from traders in land produce; landowners in capitalist enterprises see V. Sándor: *Nagyipari fejlődés Magyarországon 1867–1900* (The development of large scale industry in Hungary 1867–1900), Budapest 1954, pp. 68–74, 85–87, 242–245, 372, 569; I. T. Berend–Gy. Ránki: *Magyarország gyáripara az imperializmus első világháború előtti időszakában, 1900–1914* (Manufacturing industry in Hungary before World War I, 1900–1914), Budapest 1955, pp. 134, 142, 164–171. — For the capitalist lease system see Gy. Szabad: *A tatai és gesztesi Eszterházy-uradalom áttérése a robotrendszerről a tőkés gazdálkodásra* (The transition on the Eszterházy estates of Tata and Gesztes from serf system to capitalist husbandry), Budapest 1957, pp. 404–420; J. Puskás: A tőkés nagybérlet a XIX. század végi Magyarországon (The capitalist lease system in the late nineteenth century Hungary), *Történelmi Szemle*, 1–2, 1957, pp. 90–103; L. Für: *A csákvári uradalom a tőkés gazdálkodás útján 1870–1914* (The Csákvár estates on the way to capitalist husbandry 1870–1914), Budapest 1969, pp. 283–328; J. Pintér: Föld- és regálebérletek a vallásalapítványi uradalmak ceglédi gazdasági kerületében a XIX. század utolsó harmadában (Lease of land and manorial rights in the Cegléd economic district of the domains of ecclesiastical foundations towards the end of the nineteenth century), *Agrártörténeti Szemle*, 1973, 3–4; *cf.* P. Sándor below, *op. cit.*, pp. 336–404.

97 From the abundant contemporary literature: Gy. Rácz: *A magyar földbirtokosság anyagi pusztulása* (The financial collapse of the Hungarian landowning class), Budapest 1906. — *Cf.* P. Sándor: *A XIX. század végi agrárválság Magyarországon* (The agrarian crisis of the late nineteenth century in Hungary), Budapest 1958, esp. pp. 148–156.

For a third feature of the emergence of capitalism in Hungary was the very fact that the development of bourgeois mentality among the middle and lesser noblemen (which, as mentioned above, had started in the decades preceding the 1848 revolution) came to a standstill and their majority was unable to join in the stream of economic transformation. These noble families, who lost unpaid labour as a consequence of the abolition of serfdom and lacked capital and business experience, sank into poverty and debts—especially during the agrarian crisis at the end of the century. Their sons moved to the cities *en masse* but seldom engaged in commerce or business. They flooded the soon overdeveloped *public service*, took positions in the state, county and municipal administration, from the highest to the clerk level, for there they could remain "gentlemen", according to their traditional order of values, and were not degraded to the state of common citizens.[98]

The period after the 1867 Compromise saw the re-emergence, "second flowering" as it were, of the *dérogeance* concept of the nobility in the gentry-world of Hungary. It was even more conspicuous and glaring—being even more anachronistic—than it had been earlier in the feudal world. It was precisely in the late 19th and early 20th centuries that the figure of the Hungarian gentleman making merry with tears in his eyes to sobbing gipsy violins and of the card-playing, duelling hussar officer became known and notorious and was so frequently seen by foreigners as the embodiment of the Hungarian national character.[99]

Contemporary and later Hungarian fiction offered many realistic descriptions of the decline of the middle and lesser nobility and of its transformation into what is called the "gentry" in Hungary; apparently with a meaning of the word different from the original English term. Hungarian novels from the *Egy régi udvarház utolsó gazdája* (Last owner of an old mansion-house) by Pál Gyulai to the brilliant works of Kálmán Mikszáth and Zsigmond Móricz provided faithful reports on a gentry mentality, which regarded the preservation of even the appearance of a gentlemanly way of life as of paramount value; the true Hungarian behaviour being to keep aloof from capitalism and business with feudal pride, or with a conviction that success in these fields was, at any rate, unattainable.

And one may ask the question: why could Mór Jókai, so distant from this realistic view, the faithful portrayal of the gentry, become the most popular and most widely read novelist of the Hungarian public at the time (many of his novels were published in translations). The answer—or at least part of it—is likely to be found in a paradox: The "great story-teller" created and described a type which was almost non-existent in Hungarian reality: his brilliant engineers, husbandmen, merchants, entrepreneurs and bankers offered fascinating compensation for the bourgeois development of the nobility which did not actually take place and for the national dreams that were not fulfilled. The successful heroes of Jókai's novels outwitted not only blind caprices of nature and human wickedness, but overcame also the failures and awkward realities of Hungarian history.[100]

[98] At about the turn of the century they, in particular, were called "gentry" — with an obvious difference from the original meaning of the English word. — *Cf.* P. Hanák: Vázlatok a századelő magyar társadalmáról (Sketches of the early twentieth century Hungarian society), in: *Magyarország a monarchiában* (Hungary in the Austro-Hungarian Monarchy), Budapest 1975, pp. 357–374.

[99] *Cf.* S. Eckhardt: A magyarság külföldi arcképe (Hungarian image abroad), in: *Mi a magyar?* (What makes a Hungarian?),pp. 118, 127.

[100] *Cf.* D. Keresztúry: A magyar önismeret útja (The course of Hungarian self-knowledge), in: *Mi a magyar?* pp. 161–162; D. Kerecsényi: *Magyar irodalom* (Hungarian literature), *op. cit.*, p. 337; I. Dékány: *A magyarság lelki arca. Magyar néplélektani rajzok* (Hungarian mentality. Ethnopsychological sketches of the Hungarians), Budapest 1942, p. 212.

7

Following fiction belatedly, historians also began to describe the course of the declining gentry, the contradictions of which were even more explicit after the First World War.

The people who resettled into the remaining one third of historic Hungary from territories lost after the Peace Treaty of Trianon, a considerable portion of whom were precisely the descendants of impoverished noble families, further increased the numbers of those who expected *civil service positions* or military commissions from the state to enable them to carry on their "gentlemanly" way of life.

This social stratum which preferred to call itself the "gentle middle class" or the "historic middle class", having filled its ranks with elements of other social origin, carried on the gentry conventions, the traditional lack of business mentality and aversion to commerce. "...in order to conceal their own weak-heartedness and indolence, they successfully propagated the absurd nonsense that it was a gentlemanly job to work as a clerk in the revenue office, while being an entrepreneur or a merchant was unsuitable for Hungarians"—as a member of the class put it in a self-critical tone.[101] At the same time, some sections of this middle class were about to penetrate the field of business with the help of the counter-revolutionary state power on the band-waggon of extreme right-wing, anti-Semitic political movements, to take the despised—but also deeply desired—positions in the economy out of the hands of the bourgeoisie, a significant part of which were Jews.[102]

A stereotype of the Hungarian national character — sometimes not devoid of a certain self-complacency, yet still mainly with a critical edge, and the demand for change—became crystallized in this socio-political atmosphere. The most prominent Hungarian historian of the interwar period, Gyula Szekfű wrote about the "anti-commercial and anti-capitalist talents of the Hungarian race" already in 1920 in his widely acclaimed work *Három nemzedék* (Three generations),[103] and stated two years later that "such facts of economic history... that Hungarians do not work as merchants and cannot be accustomed to do so are well known to everybody and have even become platitudes recently". And in this latter study of his, entitled *A magyar bortermelő lelki alkata* (The mental constitution of the Hungarian wine-grower), he himself claimed to have proved "how much the principle of trading and production for profit disagreed with the Hungarian nature", that "Hungarian agriculturists were lacking in practical business acumen" and that, "concerning our

[101] G. Paikert: *Ahogyan egy magyar a magyart látja* (Hungarians as seen by a Hungarian), Budapest 1942, p. 11.

[102] *Cf.* Gy. Ránki: Gondolatok az ellenforradalmi rendszer társadalmi bázisának kérdéséhez az 1920-as évek elején (Thoughts on the question of the social basis of the counter-revolutionary regime in the early 1920s), *Történelmi Szemle,* 1962, 3–4, pp. 353–368; M. Lackó: Vázlat a szélsőjobboldali mozgalmak társadalmi hátteréről Magyarországon az 1930-as években (An outline of the social background of the extreme right movements in Hungary in the 1930s), *Történelmi Szemle,* 1962, 3–4, pp. 449–467.

[103] Gy. Szekfű: *Három nemzedék. Egy hanyatló kor története* (Three generations. The history of a declining era), Budapest 1920, p. 291. — "...it is well known that a Hungarian did not stoop to trade in feudal Hungary. He yielded it to the aliens: Jews, Macedonians, Greeks, Armenians, Serbs": *op. cit.*, p. 72. — The notable contemporary critic of *Three Generations* Elemér Mályusz agreed with Szekfű in this: "The members of lesser nobility had no inclination to trade by which they could have earned their living... Széchenyi recommended industry and trade to them. It was in vain, as we know": A reformkor. nemzedéke (The generation of the reform era), *Századok,* 1923–24, pp. 42–43. See also: by the same author: A helytörténeti kutatás feladatai (Tasks of research into local history), *Századok*, 1923–24, p. 551: "...the land remained the only source of property and prosperity for the Hungarian nobility, since industry and trade were alien to a nobleman's nature..."

racial make-up, we became unquestionably convinced that it is almost the opposite of what the German expresses by the term: '*wirtschaftlich*' and it is as far from what we call commercial talent and flexibility as heaven is from earth and fire from water". It was in the same year (1922) that a renowned colleague of the former, Ferenc Eckhart published his significant monograph *A bécsi udvar gazdasági politikája Mária Terézia korában* (The economic policy of the Viennese Court in the time of Maria Theresa), in which he gave voice to a similar opinion. "...Hungarian mentality was not at all conducive to the development of capitalism... The Hungarians of the 18th century would have had to be good organizers and good merchants to turn the economic development of our country into the same direction as in the Western states..., they would have had to take care of the economic questions and even the rich should not have been ashamed to deal with them and to discard all the principles of living in a seigniorial manner... All these bourgeois characteristics were quite far from the mental habit of Hungarians, *nobility and peasantry alike*... Undoubtedly, the Hungarians may be listed among those peoples which have the least inclination to develop in a capitalist direction."[104]

Other historians and social scientists of the age also described the Hungarian national character in terms of this pattern. Disregarding the evidence of earlier periods (in particular, the not at all anti-mercantile inclinations of 16th and 17th century nobility), they applied the term "*unwirtschaftlich*" not only to the Hungarian gentry, but also to embrace the whole nation, the "Hungarian race", throughout its entire history.

The works on "national characterology" which became fashionable especially during the late 1930s, reflected partly anti-Semitic tendencies but, for the most part, contrasted the sober equanimity, the "comfortable sluggishness", the "inherited national inertia"[105] of the Hungarian people with the Fascist German racial myth in particular, and these works on characterology considered the aversion of the Hungarian character to commerce as tantamount to evidence, and differed, at most, in the matter of *terminus a quo*. "There is no doubt that the Hungarian mind, from its very beginnings, was disinclined to what we now call the bourgeois way of life... The Hungarian ideal has remained, almost to this day, the politically interested,

[104] Gy. Szekfű: *A magyar bortermelő lelki alkata. Gazdaságtörténelmi tanulmány* (The mental character of the Hungarian wine grower. A study of economic history), Budapest 1922 (= Faji sajátságaink a gazdaságtörténet világánál (Our racial characteristics in the light of economic history), *Minerva I*, 1922), pp. 24–25, 46–47, 64, 81–82. — F. Eckhart: *A bécsi udvar gazdasági politikája Magyarországon Mária Terézia korában* (The economic policy of the Viennese Court in Hungary in the time of Maria Theresa), Budapest 1922, pp. 273–274. — *Cf.* "The Hungarians had neither inclination nor talent for trading; in fact, the animosity against this branch of economy can still be observed in the descendants of the late nobles and serfs as well": Schäfer, *op. cit.*, (*Közgazdasági Szemle*, 1930, 1–2), p. 17. — The agrarian historian Gerendás rejected this conception — together with theories that the Hungarians are deficient in and disinclined for trading, nevertheless he himself admitted that "the land was the only property of the Hungarian nobility, and of the serfs as well, because of the aversion they felt to industrial and commercial professions": *op. cit.*, p. 8. — Wellmann, examining the 18th century agrarian conditions of the Gödöllő estates, found that "the Hungarian peasant adhered to the soil best... To work for others as a cotter, to be an artisan or a dealer did not suit him. The German peasants on the other hand, made the least effort to get hold of more land, they were much more inclined to follow trades, to become grocers, to run taverns etc. The Slovaks stand somewhere between the two (the numerical proportion of the Slavs among the traders is inflated by Serbian (mostly Greek) shop- and innkeepers): *op. cit.*, 1933, p. 38. — The same author wrote about the "economic indifferentism of the Hungarian peasant" too, and referring to Szekfű and Eckhart took the "indisposition of the Hungarian race for profiteering" as a well-known fact: p. 84, 101; for example, there were no Hungarians to be found among the trading elements of the Gödöllő estates "because they had always preferred land to speculation, and were too proud to kow-tow to others": p. 167.

[105] M. Babits: A magyar jellemről (On the Hungarian character), in: *Mi a magyar?* pp. 59, 65, 86.

militant noble gentleman"—a Hungarian philosopher of history, Tibor Joó wrote in 1937.[106] "We were also traders in our own way... Yet buying and selling had never been our province. We left that to the Greeks, Armenians and Jews"—the ethnographer Károly Viski expressed in 1939,[107] in accordance with the other noted authors in a volume of essays *Mi a magyar*? (What makes a Hungarian?), edited by Gyula Szekfű.[108] "Commerce was carried on only by despised immigrants who stood outside feudal society: Armenians, Greeks and Jews. Noblemen did not lower themselves to such occupations. Their legal successor, the Hungarian middle class, has inherited this attitude and has a certain aversion to careers in business right to this day" and "remnants of the scorn and hate which feudal society had felt for commerce... can be found in general public opinion even today"—was the judgement of another ethnographer, János Kósa in the early 1940s.[109]

And what is particularly worthy of attention is that this self-identification, this auto-stereotyping fell on good soil not only amongst the "historic middle class" and conservative public opinion but also among progressive intellectuals and politicians. "The Hungarian people", the humanist poet and scholar Mihály Babits wrote in 1939, "like, at cornhusking time to tell the story of the prince, who set out to try his luck; yet they themselves are not keen to try their luck... Hungarians are both lazier and more clever: they sail the seven seas only in imagination". "This personality type does not get ahead in the world, since he does not really want to."[110]

And a last quotation: "Whatever they say about the Hungarian trading this way or that way in the past and that... Armenians, Jews, Germans crowded him out later on can only be patriotic exaggeration and cannot, in essence, be true." The truth is that: "We do not like trading and have always despised bothering with money and goods, the coming and going, the bargaining and lies." "And this is true

[106] T. Joó: A magyar nemzeti szellem (The Hungarian national mentality), *Magyarságtudomány* (Hungarology), 1937, Vol. 3, p. 31. — While Paikert, *op. cit.*, p. 7, (*cf.* pp. 10–11): "...the Hungarians being resourceful artisans and merchants in the Middle Ages according to the historical evidence, later, mainly because of the enormous losses in human life during the Turkish occupation of Hungary in the 16th and 17th centuries, were too much reduced in number to produce tradesmen too, besides soldiers, husbandmen, public servants and politicians. That is why the Hungarians practically did not deal with economic, industrial, commercial questions right up to the end of the last century". — *Cf.* F. Eckhart, *op. cit.*, pp. 274–275: "...the Hungarian mentality could have gradually been changed only by an economic policy supervised with the utmost benevolence and promotion for the part of the reigning dynasty..., re-educating it either by endearment or enforcement... What actually happened was just to the contrary... Knowing the Hungarian way of thinking the inveteracy or stiffening of the feudal approach to economic questions can be regarded as the natural consequence of an economic policy directed against the country".

[107] K. Viski: A magyar jelleg a néprajz tükrében (The Hungarian type in the light of ethnography), in: *Mi a magyar?* p. 374.

[108] *Cf.* "The image of 'gentlemanlike' way of living which was considered typically Hungarian by the national self-consciousness of the millenial Hungarians took shape in gentry circles having a leading part in the political and social representation of the nation. And although trading, industry and the so-called open professions were not felt worthy of this ideal social image, achievements in these fields were recorded to the credit of the Hungarian civilisation too": D. Keresztúry: A magyar önismeret útja (The way of Hungarian self-knowledge), in: *Mi a magyar?* p. 162.

[109] J. Kósa: Magyar rendiség és osztálytársadalom (Hungarian estate system and class society), *Magyarságtudomány*, 1942, Vol. 1, No. 3, p. 370. — *Cf.* "There were many thousands of people (and still there are) who felt commercial or factory office work degrading because it goes ill with "gentlemanlike social standing"; while a touch of noble tradition, they thought, is still to be found in their own stables": I. Dékány: *op. cit.*, p. 214.

[110] Babits: *op. cit.*, p. 67. — The psychologist I. Boda regarded it as a "typical characteristic sign of the Hungarians" that "they attach value to neither material goods and successful getting on in life nor economical adaptation to it which are largely appreciated by other people": *A magyar személyiség nevelése* (Fosterage of Hungarian personality), Budapest, n. d. (1942), pp. 150–151.

not only of Hungarians of noble birth but also of peasant Hungarians. This is why it is so difficult to guide Hungarians to careers in business, no matter how much all the ministers implore them, or how much all the university professors prompt them to it. For, to be sure, a good number of these counsellors... would not like to become traders either. Neither would I, so why should I blame them?" — professed the radical peasant democrat, Péter Veres in the early 1940s.[111]

8

And let us add that even the great turn of Hungarian history, i. e. the year 1945 did not put an end to such stereotypes and the social views and attitudes behind them.

During the first period of socialist development, in a strongly centralized, planned economy, trading and enterprise, a commercial mentality and business sense were not, and could not be, management requirements; indeed, a lack of them appeared more desirable. In the framework of the plan instruction system the central economic leadership did not need merchants or businessmen in the nationalized firms but, apart from engineers and technicians, "clerks" were called for in the economy, men who were to follow the detailed plan instructions with the maximum possible exactness. In short: *public servants* were needed again.

The change began only during the last fifteen years, when we began to better understand the significance of commercial and monetary considerations, the relevance of market regulators to a socialist planned economy, and particularly in the most recent years, when "enterprise" and "entrepreneurial spirit" practically became the key words of our economic thinking.

These circumstances make it timely for us once again, as in the Reform Era and in the 1930s, to turn to our "national characterology" and to attempt to probe, with today's means and methods, how business-mentality squared or contrasted with national character in Hungary's history, and in particular her economic history.

The working-hypothesis arrived at in the course of this enquiry (which is intended, of course, to be a beginning only) can be outlined as follows:

We reject the notion of a timeless national character, of a present *donnée* since time immemorial, and lasting for ever.

Yet, we do not deny that the specific features of the economic and social development of various nations brought about certain specific characteristics in their national make-up, some of which do have an influence on economic behaviour. And we recognize that some attitudes, thus also those of economic relevance, at times become so permanently fixed that they survive the socio-economic conditions that have given them rise. They may survive from the feudal past even to the socialist present and arise again and again in our days, too, under completely different conditions and in a different conceptual context, like the question formulated with patriarchal naivity by the poet Lőrinc Orczy some two hundred years ago:

"Does shameless trade befit the Magyars?
For it may indeed corrupt our morals..."

[111] P. Veres: *Mit ér az ember, ha magyar?* (What is a Hungarian worth), Budapest, n. d. (1941), pp. 31-32, 38–39, 123. — "The Hungarians are either good workers or real gentlemen. The members of our nobility did not work, were not in trade but at war, engaged in politics, ate, drank, were pipe smokers and slumbered a lot. Our peasants having grown rich recently are very much the same... we are no first-class merchants or clerks, but we do not overestimate these professions either": *op. cit.*, pp. 124–125.

The question of today will be answered by tomorrow. Let us hope that the answer will be to the benefit of both business mentality and Hungarian national character.

ADDENDA

BUSINESS MENTALITY AND HUNGARIAN NATIONAL CHARACTER

Page 144, Note 70:

The Hungarian aristocrats of the 17th century were mostly averse to mixing with burghers.As for the middle and lesser nobility, the story is more complex. From the territories occupied by the Turks after the fall of Buda (1541), many disseized noblemen took to flight to Royal Hungary under Habsburg rule and settled there mainly in the free-towns. These nobles, who managed to preserve much of their privileged status even when living in town, exerted an attracting and assimilating influence on the upper circles of the urban population, the merchant patricians. The well-to-do burghers made efforts to get patents of nobility for themselves, too, craving for social prestige and progressively adopting the life-style and habits of the nobles. Inter-marriages also occurred, in spite of controversies. A good many urban merchants preferred to invest their capital in arable land and vineyards; sooner or later they even left off trading to live the life of the born noblemen. — On these developments, closely related to the formation of the Hungarian "national character" (irrespective of ethnic origin), a special paper has been prepared by the present writer: Embourgeoisement or Ennoblissement in Early Modern Hungary? (In press)

Page 150, Note 87, and Page 155, Note 102:

For the historical literature, both older and recent, dealing with the role of Jews in Hungary's economic life, see the bibliographical survey compiled lately by *Gy. Zeke* in Appendix to *L. Gonda,* A zsidóság Magyarországon (The Jews in Hungary) 1526–1945, Budapest, 1992, pp. 330–389.

Page 154, Note 100:

Some realistic descriptions of the historical path of the Hungarian gentry by prominent novelists: *P. Gyulai,* Egy régi udvarház utolsó gazdája (Last Owner of an Old Mansion-House), Pest, 1867; *K. Mikszáth,* A Noszty-fiú esete Tóth Marival (The Young Noszty's Story with M.T.), Budapest, 1908; *Zs. Móricz,* Uri muri (Gentlemen's Spree), Budapest, 1928; etc. — The romantic "counterpoint" in *M. Jókai*'s novels: Fekete gyémántok (Black Diamonds), Pest, 1870; Az aranyember (The Golden Man), Pest, 1872; etc. — The fascinating books of Jókai were popular with practically all strata of the Hungarian public. Confronted with his successful heroes, the frustrated descendants of the former nobility might have reasoned that *they*, too, could achieve the same, should they truly wished to or should they prefer that way of life. The efficient newcomers of the bourgeoisie, in turn, might have thought that it was *them* who realized the ambitions of the nation that others were merely dreaming of.

Page 156, Note 105:

In the interwar Europe the problem of national character came into the limelight mainly in those countries that had lived through several failures and detours in their modern history. Those nations that were more successfully progressing along the lines of modernization did not much bother about self–defining; in fact, the English– and Frenchmen often viewed themselves ironically. The Germans, in turn, published a number of meditations about national character, especially after the defeat in the World War I (E. Kahler, H. Kaiserling, L. Ziegler, E. Spranger and others).

The impact of German thinkers is perceptible in the work of the Hungarian philosopher *L. Prohászka*, entitled Vándor és bujdosó (Wanderer and Refugee). The author regarded the type of "refugee" as dominant for the Hungarian character, with an inclination to seclusion and with a restriction to mere self–defence and a modest but stable subsistence. The Germans, on the contrary, were more of a "wanderer", restless and agile, with ever reviving aims and efforts. When these two attitudes met in history — Prohászka argued — the German mentality made the Hungarian one a bit more open and active; yet the effect had always been thwarted by inherent instinct of the "refugee". This characterization was not at all distant from the image of *Unwirtschaftlichkeit*, outlined by Gy. Szekfű, but by the time it was published (1932–1936) the advance of German fascism gave rise to quite different connotations. They reflected the feeling of impending danger, on the one hand, and the eager desire of the extreme right for the Hitlerite pattern, on the other. — Prohászka's work and its interpretations have been discussed by *M. Lackó*, Korszellem és tudomány (Time–Spirit and Scholarship), Budapest, 1988, pp. 168–186.

Page 157, Note 109:

Let us cite here a passage of what the Hungarian Governor Miklós Horthy had told Adolf Hitler at their meeting at Klessheim on April 16, 1943: "Hungary has generally got many difficulties with the Jews, since there live 200 thousand more of them in Hungary, which is a small country, than in Germany... Hungary herself is to blame for this situation, for the Hungarians have held for thousand years that it was not becoming for a nobleman to deal with money and had their business and finance done by Armenians, Greeks and, eventually, by Jews. This is why the Jews have played such a great role in Hungary. There aren't even enough Hungarian economists to replace them": Hitler hatvannyolc tárgyalása (Sixty–eight Negotiations of Hitler), 1939–1944. Ed. by *Gy. Ránki*, Budapest, 1983, pp. 82–83.

INDEX

For Product Safety Concerns and Information please contact our EU representative GPSR@taylorandfrancis.com Taylor & Francis Verlag GmbH, Kaufingerstraße 24, 80331 München, Germany

Batch number: 10725917

Printed by Printforce, the Netherlands